THE HIGH SIERRA

Peaks, Passes, and Trails

Second Edition

R. J. SECOR

THE
MOUNTAINEERS

 Published by
The Mountaineers
1001 SW Klickitat Way, Suite 201
Seattle, WA 98134

First edition 1992, second edition 1999

Published simultaneously in Great Britain by Cordee, 3a DeMontfort Street, Leicester, England, LE1 7HD

Manufactured in the United States of America

Edited by Uma Kukathas
Maps by Marge Mueller
Sketches by Dee Molenaar
All photographs by R. J. Secor, unless otherwise noted
Cover and book design by Ani Rucki
Book layout by Margarite Hargrave
Cover photograph: *Mt. Whitney, California, Iceberg Lake at sunrise* © James Martin

Library of Congress Cataloging-in-Publication Data
Secor, R. J.
  The High Sierra : peaks, passes, and trails / R. J. Secor.   2nd ed.
    p.   cm.
  Includes bibliographical references and index.
  ISBN 0-89886-625-1
    1. Mountaineering—Sierra Nevada (Calif. and Nev.)—Guidebooks. 2. Trails—Sierra Nevada (Calif. and Nev.)—Guidebooks. 3. Sierra Nevada (Calif. and Nev.)—Guidebooks. I. Title.
GV199.42.S55S43   1999
796.52'2'097944—dc21   98–53701
                                                         CIP

Contents

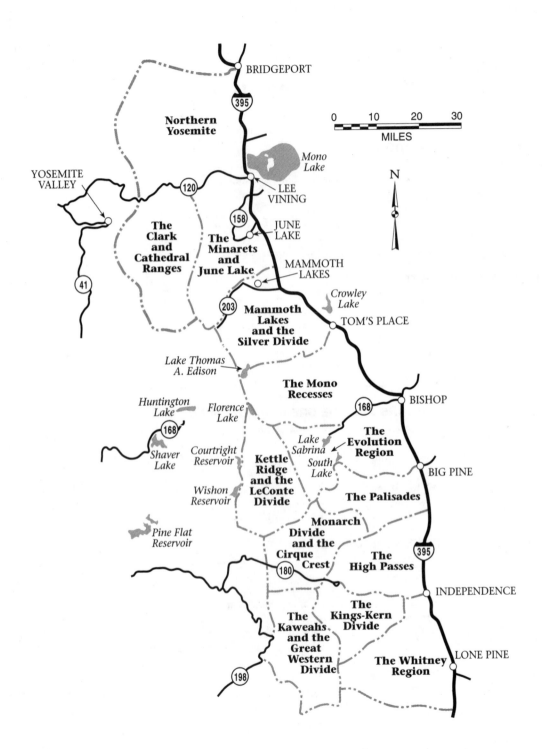

CHAPTER 6. MONARCH DIVIDE AND THE CIRQUE CREST

CHAPTER 7. KETTLE RIDGE AND THE LECONTE DIVIDE

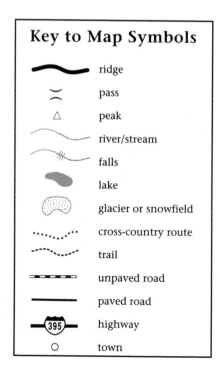

Key to Map Symbols

ridge	
pass	
peak	
river/stream	
falls	
lake	
glacier or snowfield	
cross-country route	
trail	
unpaved road	
paved road	
395 highway	
○ town	

CHAPTER 13. THE CLARK AND CATHEDRAL RANGES

CHAPTER 14. NORTHERN YOSEMITE

North Cotter and Mount Clarence King. Photo by R. J. Secor.

Acknowledgments

SECOND EDITION

I am very grateful for the input, advice, and genuinely constructive criticism I received from the following people: Todd Swain, Richard J. Schreiber, Greg Vernon, Sam Roberts, Alan Swanson, Chris Keith, David Babich, Larry Tidball, Dan Richter, Bill Oliver, Jon Inskeep, Charles M. Wylder, David C. Hardy, Peter Green, Chris Libby, H. Adams Carter, Alois Smrz, Bruce Watts, David Nettle, Harry A. Marinakis, David Hammerbeck, David Harden, Peter Cummings, Daniel Roitman, Bob Wyka, Matthias Selke, David Evans, Bob Sumner, Franklin Lowenthal, Bernard Gilbertson, Stacy Ringelspaugh, Paul E. Graff, Asher Waxman, Matt Pinelli, Craig Peer, Ron Jones, Patty Kline, Mark Spencer, Tom Sexton, Bruce Bindner, Doug Jones, Tony Watkin, Claude Fiddler, Dieter Goetze, Jerry Tinling, Rick Sanger, Tina Stough, Nancy Pallister, Eve Laeger, Bob Kanne, Barbara Cohen, Gerry Cox, Ellen Holden, Jon Stark, Rose Watabe, Judy Martsolf, Nikyra Calcagno, Robert SP Parker, Michael Olwyer, Gary Colliver, Beth Epstein, Galen Rowell, John Rawlings, Norman Boles, John Fischer, Richard Leversee, Rick Chval, Aaron Schuman, Steve Eckert, Jim Ramaker, Pat Ibbetson, David Harris, Rich Calliger, Peter Maxwell, Craig Clarence, John Bees, Mark Wallace, Jim Curl, Paul Richens, Steve Roper, Cameron Burns, Jim Watters, E. C. Joe, Chris Jones, Irene Bearsdley, Rick Evans, Tom Blum, Debbie Bird, Ralph Moore, Shirley Crowley, Bart O'Brien, Alec Isabeau, John Moynier, Nile Sorenson, Don Peterson, and Alan Bartlett.

I also wish to thank the publishing staff of The Mountaineers Books, under the direction of Art Freeman, for supporting this project. Uma Kukathas served as the book's editor, and the production details were coordinated by Cindy Bohn, Christine Ummel, and Ani Rucki.

FIRST EDITION

I had the pleasure of meeting and working with many people in the creation of this work. And it would not be complete without the assistance I received from them.

Primary recognition should go to the authors of the first guidebooks to the High Sierra: Walter A. Starr, Jr., Hervey Voge, Andy Smatko, and Steve Roper. Walter A. Starr, Jr., had nearly completed his *Guide to the John Muir Trail and the High Sierra Region* before his untimely death in The Minarets in 1933. During the course of my research I located a copy of his climbing notes and rediscovered some of his routes that had been overlooked. In the early 1950s, Hervey Voge accepted the job of collating the work of twenty-three authors to create the first *Climber's Guide to the High Sierra*. The 1954 and 1965 editions of this work were logically oriented and extremely accurate, and many climbers considered it to be the only authoritative book describing the approaches and routes in the range. It is regrettable that Hervey Voge died in 1990, before the publication of this book. The 1972 edition of Voge's work, titled *Mountaineer's Guide to the High Sierra* and edited by Andy Smatko, included descriptions of many previously overlooked peaks. The first modern climber's guide, written by Steve Roper in 1976, included technical rock climbing descriptions of routes done in Tuolumne Meadows and the High Sierra during the 1960s and early 1970s. Steve Roper graciously allowed me to review the notes he collected to update his own, and this book is much stronger because of his assistance. In the following introduction I have used, with permission, numerous ideas, as well as some of the phraseology, from two of Steve Roper's books, *The Climber's Guide to the High Sierra* and *Timberline Country: The Sierra High Route*, both published by the Sierra Club.

I am also grateful for the assistance I received from the staff of several institutions. These include the Pasadena Public Library, the Milliken Library of the California Institute of Technology, the Honnold Library of the Claremont Colleges, Sequoia and Kings Canyon National Parks, and the United States Geological Survey's Ice and Climate Project at the University of Puget Sound in Tacoma, Washington. David Hirst of the Ice and

Climate Project sent me the aerial photographs of the glaciers of the High Sierra at record speed, and I am especially grateful for the attention he gave to this work.

Alan Bartlett patiently answered my questions on the remote rock walls of northern Yosemite, and John Moynier pointed out to me some previously overlooked peaks and pinnacles in the Rock Creek area. John Fischer, formerly of the Palisade School of Mountaineering, deserves special recognition for filling in the gaps in my knowledge about the Palisades. John reviewed the first draft of that chapter, and provided me with information on cross-country and climbing routes that had somehow escaped my attention. He is the outstanding authority on this region of the High Sierra.

But most of the credit should go to those individuals who provided me with small bits of information that eventually added up to the bulk of this book. Some of these people are close friends whom I have known for years; others I met only briefly when our paths crossed in the High Sierra; and some I have never met. But they all took the time to give me their route descriptions and answer my questions. It breaks my heart to reduce this to an alphabetical list: Bob Ayers, Mike Baca, How Bailey, Scott Bailey, Bob Bandy, Allan Bard, Ron Bartell, Dick Beach, Rick Beatty, Don Borad, Bill Bradley, Graham Breakwell, Tom Brogan, Lloyd Brown, Harry Brumer, Cameron Burns, Jim Butler, Pat Butler, Fred Camphausen, Miguel Carmona, Jim Cervenka, Pat Christie, Gerry Cox, Fred Crostic, Peter Cummings, Glen Dawson, Diana Dee, Jeff Dozier, Tom Duryea, Dave Dykeman, Bob Emerick, the late Arkel Erb, Jim Erb, Tim Forsell, Andy Fried, Howard Gates, Rich Gnagy, Nancy Gordon, Vi Grasso, Arold Green, Gary Guenther, Todd Handy, David Harden, Bob Hartunian, the late Carl Heller, John Hellman, Rich Henke, Larry Hoak, Fred Hoeptner, Ellen Holden, Delores Holladay, Gerry Holleman, Pat Holleman, Stan Horn, Marty Hornick, George Hubbard, Ron Hudson, Bill Hunt, Sigrid Hutto, Robin Ingraham, Jr., Jon Inskeep, Rick Jali, Mike Jelf, Horton Johnson, Ron Jones, Walton Kabler, Jerry Keating, Chris Keith, Bruce Knudtson, Bill Krause, Barbara Lilley, Bob Lindgren, Mike Loughman, Larry Machleder, Gordon MacLeod, Barbara Magnuson, Roy Magnuson, Mark Maier, Owen Maloy, Igor Mamedalin, Doug Mantle, Harry Marinakis, Gene Mauk, David Mazel, Rob Roy McDonald, the late John Mendenhall, the late Ruth Mendenhall, Rene MeVay, Frank Meyers, Mary Sue Miller, Kathy Moore, Jim Murphy, Tom Naves, Ti Neff, Edward Nunez, Bart O'Brien, Bill Oliver, Donna O'Shaughnessy, the late Bruce Parker, Dave Petzold, Don Pies, Allan Pietrasanta, Steve Porcella, Phil Rabichow, Tom Randall, Cuno Ranschau, Barbara Reber, John Reed, John Ripley, Jim Roberts, Bob Rockwell, Steve Rogero, Casey Rohn, Maggie Rohn, the late Norm Rohn, Galen Rowell, LeRoy Russ, Bill T. Russell, Theresa Rutherford, Jim Shirley, Don Slager, Ursula Slager, Alois Smrz, Robert Somoano, Chuck Stein, Maria Steinberg, Reiner Stenzel, Tina Stough, Bill Stronge, Scott Sullivan, Steve Thaw, Bill Thomas, Larry Tidball, George Toby, Ed Treacy, Maris Valkass, Dale Van Dalsem, Dave Vandervoet, Greg Vernon, Roy Ward, Ron Webber, John Wedberg, Vieve Weldon, the late Fred Wing, Diana Worman, Pete Yamagata, Nozomu Yamanaka, and Chuck Yeager.

And I am grateful to the publishing staff of The Mountaineers, under the direction of Donna DeShazo, not only for supporting this project, but also for working with me in creating the final copy of this work. Rick May served as this book's editor, and the production details were coordinated by Marge Mueller and Lynne Fischer.

Chapter 1

Introduction

The High Sierra, which I have defined as the region between the southern boundary of Sequoia National Park and the northern boundary of Yosemite National Park, is the best place in the world for the practice of mountains. By the practice of mountains, I am referring to hiking, cross-country rambling, peak bagging, rock climbing, ice climbing, and ski touring. The region is part of the highest mountain range in the contiguous United States, the Sierra Nevada, yet the enviable California climate almost guarantees excellent weather for an extended mountain journey. The High Sierra has an excellent system of trails, and cross-country travel is relatively easy among the alpine meadows, lakes, and talus slopes near timberline. This alpine region has a natural beauty that is unequaled, and the streams and lakes make this area a fishing paradise. It is an unspoiled wilderness, and it is possible to start a hike in the desert of the eastern Sierra and finish the trip among the lush redwood groves on the western slope. Cross-country skiers can find a stable snowpack during most of the winter, and will enjoy outstanding backcountry skiing over perfect corn snow during the spring. The mountains, crags, and domes of the High Sierra are an inspiration to climbers, who will find sound rock among these arêtes, faces, and chimneys.

All who wander the area will take away treasured memories. Here are some of mine: the distant sound of a roaring stream as I descended a trail into the Middle Fork of the Kings River; the mechanical movements of my axe, hammer, and crampons as I climbed an ice gully in the autumn; skiing velvet snow across a high plateau during the spring; looking out over the range while giving an upper belay at the end of a difficult pitch over rough yet solid alpine granite; climbing a peak and discovering that the summit register predates the twentieth century; and enjoying hundreds of timberline camps, with the sky filled with more starlight than air.

One of my goals in life is to go around the world three times and visit every mountain range twice. But whenever I have wandered other mountains, I have been homesick for the High Sierra. I am a hopeless romantic, and therefore my opinions cannot be regarded as objective. But how can I be objective while discussing the mountains that I love?

HISTORY

The first people to explore the High Sierra were the Native Americans. The Paiutes from the Owens Valley and the Mono Indians from the Mono Lake region crossed the range to trade with the tribes in the Central Valley: the western Mono, Miwok, and Yokut tribes. The Indians typically crossed the Sierra crest at Mono Pass (north), Mammoth Pass, Mono Pass (south), Taboose Pass, and Kearsarge Pass. These crossings of the range were usually done by men and women in small parties during summer and fall. Trading was usually conducted outside of the mountains in the home grounds of the host tribe.

It should be stressed that the Indians used many other routes and passes aside from those listed above, which were the main routes used by heavily laden parties. The objective of most Native American parties was to cross the High Sierra easily and quickly with heavy loads of goods.

11

Signs of Indian life have been found throughout the range, in the most remote canyons and atop the highest peaks. I believe that it can be safely said that Native Americans had visited all major and most minor river drainages, crossed all of the major passes, and may have climbed a few of the High Sierra's peaks.

The first systematic, scientific exploration of the High Sierra itself (as opposed to simply finding a way across the mountains) took place from 1863 to 1864. The California Geological Survey, under the direction of Josiah Dwight Whitney, visited Yosemite Valley, and then moved north. In 1863 Whitney, Charles Hoffman, and William Brewer made the first ascent of Mount Hoffman—the first recorded ascent in the High Sierra.

The year 1864 was the banner year in the early exploration of the High Sierra. The Whitney Survey headed for the South Fork of the Kings River and visited the rival of Yosemite, Kings Canyon. On July 2, Hoffman and Brewer climbed a high peak that could be seen to the east of their camp along Roaring River. This peak was subsequently named Mount Brewer by other members of the survey, but the two climbers were astounded by the view of higher peaks to the east and southeast. This discovery excited Clarence King in particular, who along with Richard Cotter volunteered to explore this area.

Cotter and King spent five days crossing the Kings-Kern Divide, traversing the headwaters of the Kern River, and climbing Mount Tyndall. From the summit of Mount Tyndall, King swept the horizon with his level and discovered the highest peak in the Sierra Nevada, Mount Whitney, named in honor of the leader of the California Geological Survey. After returning to their camp along the Roaring River, King temporarily left the survey on one of his many attempts to climb Mount Whitney.

The next major explorers of the High Sierra were the shepherds. There were many large flocks of sheep in California's Central Valley in the 1850s. The land was cheap, and the mild climate combined with ample pasturage led many owners of these flocks to great riches, especially during the Civil War. Farmers proceeded to buy up the land in the Central Valley in the late 1860s, and the shepherds were forced to move into the meadowlands in the foothills of the Coast Range and the western Sierra Nevada. These were the American shepherds, who had first claim on the most favorable pasturage available. Shepherds who were recruited from Europe—French, Basque, Spanish, Portuguese, Italian—had to search for less desirable forage that was far up in the High Sierra. These shepherds were amazingly industrious, and probably led their sheep to every high mountain meadow then in existence. Sheep grazed in one of the most remote areas of the High Sierra, Goddard Creek, prior to 1879.

This was in the days before there was control over public lands, and the damage caused by the sheep was overwhelming. Before they were overgrazed, High Sierra meadows had shoulder-high grass; this is a rare sight today. The shepherds brought in far too many sheep, which they took to the highest meadows as soon as the snow had melted. The meadows were wet at this time, and the grass had not yet reached its full height as it would later in the summer. Hooves trampled the wet ground, exposing the grass roots, and the animals finished off the meadow quickly because the grass was short. The flock moved on to the next meadow, and the process was repeated. The hot, dry Sierra summer soon dried out the ground, and the grass roots died, leaving bare, dusty patches, which were taken over by weeds, brush, and eventually trees. The worst cases had such severe water and wind erosion that other plants could not take root, and the meadows became sand flats within five years. Also, domestic sheep introduced diseases against which the native bighorn sheep had no immunity, and the bighorn herds were soon decimated.

The most famous shepherd was John Muir. It could be said that his experience as a shepherd led to his becoming America's foremost conservationist of the late nineteenth and early twentieth centuries. In 1869 he guided 2,000 sheep to Tuolumne Meadows. Muir was shocked by the damage caused by the sheep, as they ate and trampled out wide scars through the high grass and flowers of the meadows. He called the sheep "hoofed locusts," and wrote, "To let sheep trample so divinely fine a place seems barbarous!"

It was only a matter of time before the shepherds were forced out of business either by elimination of their forage or by governmental protection of public lands. The latter began in the 1890s with the creation of Yosemite National Park, Sequoia National Park, and the Sierra Forest Preserve. The government gradually assumed control over the land, but the damage had been done. Some meadows disappeared forever under cover of forests; others now consist of open spaces marked by sand, dust, and weeds. They haven't recovered to this day.

Shepherds have been almost universally detested in the literature of the American West. Although the shepherds of the High Sierra used the mountains with no concern for the future, it must be remembered that they explored the farthest reaches of the range, establishing trails and cross-country routes along the way, and provided hospitality and route information to the mountaineers from the cities (including John Muir, once a shepherd himself) who started to visit the High Sierra in the latter part of the nineteenth century.

After his brief tenure as a shepherd, John Muir worked for a time at a sawmill in Yosemite Valley (logging was another destroyer of the Sierra Nevada, but the loggers confined their activities to the western slopes, rather than the more remote High Sierra). The purpose of his journeys had more to do with biological and geological discoveries than geographical surveys of watersheds and the heights of peaks. It is known that he climbed Cathedral Peak, Mount Ritter, and Mount Whitney, and may have made the first ascent of Mount Humphreys or Mount Darwin. But instead of creating a "macro-record" of his journeys, he made a "micro-record" of the things he saw in nature, and was the first to recognize the important role that glaciers played in the creation of the High Sierra landscape.

Mountaineers from the city, interested in mountain exploration and conquest for its own sake, began to visit the High Sierra in the 1890s. One of these individuals was Theodore Solomons, who first had the idea of a trail along the Sierra crest (now known as the John Muir Trail) in 1884 at the age of fourteen. In 1892, accompanied only by a mule, he set out on his first expedition, exploring Tuolumne Meadows, the Lyell Fork of the Tuolumne River, and the forks of the San Joaquin River. He returned to the mountains in 1894 with Leigh Bierce, son of newspaperman Ambrose Bierce, and continued south from the southernmost point of his 1892 journey, ascending Mono Creek and Bear Creek and climbing Seven Gables. Solomons returned to the Bear Creek region again in 1895 in the company of Ernest Bonner. They moved to the South Fork of the San Joaquin River, where they left their pack animals with a shepherd. Shouldering heavy packs, they ascended Evolution Creek, named after the prominent evolutionists by Solomons, who also named the great peaks at its head. They climbed Mount Wallace, attempted Mount Darwin, and then retraced their steps to the South Fork of the San Joaquin River. From its head they climbed Mount Goddard and then proceeded down the Enchanted Gorge (one of the most remote parts of the High Sierra even today) to the Middle Fork of the Kings River. They descended to Tehipite Valley before crossing the Monarch Divide via Granite Pass and dropping down to Kings Canyon.

While Solomons and Bonner were exploring the Middle Fork of the Kings River, Bolton Brown climbed out of Kings Canyon and crossed the Monarch Divide on the first of his three expeditions to the Kings River area. From Simpson Meadow, Brown climbed Mount Woodworth and sketched the Palisades. He then ascended Cartridge Creek and climbed Mount Ruskin from Cartridge Pass. From the summit, Brown saw and named Split Mountain to the east and Arrow Peak to the south. The latter peak was an irresistible siren for him, and he climbed its northeast spur.

In the summer of 1896, Brown and his bride, Lucy, explored the Bubbs Creek drainage and the upper Kern River area. The newlyweds crossed the Kings-Kern Divide in pouring rain via a sheep route over Harrison Pass. After a miserable bivouac, they trekked across the upper Kern River basin to climb Mount Williamson. (This was the first time that any reliable witnesses had visited this region since the journey of Clarence King in 1864.) A few days later, they climbed Mount Ericsson atop the Kings-Kern Divide. On the same day, Brown continued on alone to the summit of Mount Stanford, which he named after his university, where he was a professor of fine arts. Later during the same summer, Brown made a solo ascent of Mount Clarence King from Paradise Valley. This was the most difficult rock climb done in North America in the nineteenth century. The climb was accomplished solo, by means of artificial chockstones (in this case, a knot in the end of a rope) and a final lasso of the summit block. The Browns returned to the Kings River area again in 1899, this time accompanied by their two-year-old daughter, Eleanor. They explored the beautiful Rae Lakes area east of Mount Clarence King, and Eleanor discovered the delicious taste of trout.

But the greatest explorer of the High Sierra during the late nineteenth and early twentieth centuries was Joseph "Little Joe" LeConte. In all, he made forty-four extended trips to the High Sierra from 1892 to 1930. His scientifically drawn maps, the first to portray the High Sierra accurately, made a significant contribution to further exploration of the range. In 1898, he and Clarence Cory traveled from Yosemite to Kings Canyon. They followed Solomons's route south from Yosemite and climbed Red Slate Mountain and Mount Goddard, with LeConte setting up his plane table and transit on each summit to measure other Sierra peaks. They were unable to find a route for their animals across the Goddard Divide, but after consulting a nearby shepherd they found a route across the barrier now known as the LeConte Divide, and eventually arrived in Kings Canyon. But LeConte had viewed the distant Palisades during this trip, and he decided to explore them over the next few years.

In 1902, LeConte, his wife, Helen Marion Gompertz LeConte, and Curtis Lindley crossed the Monarch Divide from Kings Canyon and ascended the Middle Fork of the Kings River and Cartridge Creek—Bolton Brown's route of 1895. From the lake at the head of the creek, which LeConte named Marion Lake, they crossed what is now known as Frozen Lake Pass and ascended Split Mountain. Their supplies were almost exhausted, however, and only Lindley and LeConte were able to make a short side trip to the north to Observation Peak to scout out the approaches to the Palisades. LeConte returned the following year, and with James Hutchinson, James Moffitt, and Robert Pike, he again went north from Marion Lake, skirting the eastern slopes of Observation Peak, descended to Palisade Creek, and made camp along Glacier Creek. They climbed to the Sierra crest the next day, and looked down onto the Palisade Glacier, the largest in the range. Turning towards the greatest prize of all, North Palisade, they found their way blocked by a huge gap—The U Notch. Disappointed, they turned in the opposite direction and climbed Mount Sill, a peak that LeConte had spotted and named seven years earlier. The next day, July 25, 1903, the men hiked to the base of the southwest face of North Palisade and climbed the prominent chute leading to The U Notch. The upper part of the chute was blocked by cliffs, but upon descending the chute, LeConte spotted a ledge. This led to easier climbing, and LeConte and his friends soon found themselves atop North Palisade, an enviable first ascent. "LeConte's Ledge," the key to the LeConte Route in the North Palisades, has been sought by climbers ever since.

George Davis of the United States Geological Survey (USGS) was responsible for overseeing the production of detailed, 2-miles-to-the-inch, 30-minute maps of the High Sierra in the early 1900s. The last of these was published in 1912, and the unknown territory that once characterized the High Sierra had been charted. Soon exploration gave way to to the sport of mountaineering.

James Hutchinson was the most prominent mountaineer in the High Sierra in the early twentieth century, making first ascents of Matterhorn Peak, Mount Mills, Mount Abbot, Mount Humphreys, Red and White Mountain, Triple Divide Peak (south), Mount Sill, and the Black Kaweah, in addition to the first ascent of North Palisade. Perhaps the most obscure but virtually omnipresent climber during this period was Charles Michael, the assistant postmaster of Yosemite Valley. A complete record of his climbs has never been found, but he reveled in solo climbs of class 3 and 4 routes, including Michael Minaret, Devil's Crag No. 1, the second ascent of North Palisade, and Michael's Pinnacle in the Kaweahs. Walter A. Starr, Jr., was a young man who loved the High Sierra passionately, climbing forty-two peaks and covering at least 2,000 miles of trails and cross-country routes while researching his *Guide to the John Muir Trail and the High Sierra Region*, published posthumously in 1934. (Starr had died from a fall while attempting a solo ascent of Michael Minaret the year before.)

The mountaineer who lived in the ages of both the pioneers and the rock climbers was the legendary Norman Clyde. He made the first of his first ascents in 1914, and from 1920 to 1946 he came to totally dominate climbing in the High Sierra. It can safely be said that he made at least 1,000 ascents of peaks in the range, and of these approximately 120 were either first ascents of unclimbed peaks or new routes on previously climbed mountains. Clyde was a scholar of the classics, and he would spend hours reading Homer in classical Greek at a timberline campsite, with occasional glances toward the surface of a lake to see if the trout were rising. He was famous for his huge packs, which seldom weighed less than ninety pounds. These packs contained numerous cast iron pots, books in foreign languages ("They last longer that way," he once explained), guns, skis, a small anvil to repair hobnailed boots, ski boots, hiking boots, tennis shoes for rock climbing, camp slippers, five cameras, two fishing rods, reels, plus other essential impedimenta that were necessary to live in the mountains for months on end. Clyde was an eccentric, and many people believed that his equipment was strange (perhaps because he carried no stove, fuel, or water purification system), but as his old friend Smoke Blanchard once pointed out, "Norman was not just visiting the mountains or passing through the peaks. He lived there."

It is a matter of great debate among alpine historians of the High Sierra as to when ropes were first *properly* used to safeguard a party making a difficult ascent. Clarence King and Richard Cotter used ropes while crossing the Kings-Kern Divide in 1864, as did George Anderson on Half Dome in 1875, and Bolton Brown during his first ascent of Mount Clarence King in 1896. Glen Dawson, Jules Eichorn, and John Olmstead used a rope on the second ascent of Michael's Chimney on Devils Crag No. 1 on July 23, 1930, but Dawson wasn't sure if they used it correctly. I believe that the first proper roped climb in the High Sierra occurred on September 7, 1930, when John Mendenhall and Max Van Patten climbed the northeast face of Laurel Mountain. Mendenhall wrote in the 1931 *Sierra Club Bulletin*: "My companion and I were roped, moved one at a time, and employed the belays." The proper use of the rope in rock climbing became common after 1931. That year, Robert L. M. Underhill visited the High Sierra from the East Coast and taught proper rope management to members of the Sierra Club during its annual "High Trip." After this outing, a grand tour of the High Sierra was arranged, and Underhill and other prominent climbers made ascents of the north face of Temple Crag, Thunderbolt Peak, and the east face of Mount Whitney. Rock Climbing Sections of the Sierra Club were soon organized in the San Francisco and Los Angeles areas. Climbers such as Jules Eichorn, Oliver Kehrlein, Glen Dawson, David Brower, Raffi Bedayn, Richard Leonard, Bestor Robinson, and Hervey Voge, as well as many others, made difficult ascents in the High Sierra in the 1930s, at a standard never dreamed of by LeConte or Hutchinson, in relative safety.

The Sierra Club was founded in 1892, but the first annual outing of the club took place in 1901 at Tuolumne Meadows. This annual event came to be known as the "High Trip" and it reached its height in the 1930s. The trip was six weeks long, divided into three two-week segments, and participants (as many as 200) would travel from one end of the Sierra to the other. Packers would relay food and equipment between camps on layover days, while the members of the party would either take in the mountain scene in the valley ("The Meadoweers") or frantically leave the valley and climb peaks ("The Polemonium Club"). A commissary staff ("The Management") fed everyone, using sheepherder stoves. After dinner the group would gather around a large campfire to hear lectures by renowned men of science, performances by talented musicians, or tales of adventure by mountaineers. It is common for mountain travelers of today to look down on this method of travel that was enjoyed so long ago. The Sierra Club High Trips should not be despised. The pity is that they will never return to those days of glory.

After World War II, rock climbers who had learned their craft on the big walls of Yosemite Valley turned their attention to the more remote walls of the High Sierra backcountry. The main character behind these endeavors was Warren Harding, and his ascents of the southwest face of Mount Conness and the east face of Keeler Needle were far ahead of their time. There was a resurgence of interest in some of the fine alpine climbs available in the High Sierra in the late 1960s and early 1970s. The leaders of these efforts were Galen Rowell and expatriate Briton Chris Jones, who discovered classic lines on the west face of Mount Russell, the south face of Lone Pine Peak, and on Charlotte Dome.

In 1974, *Ascent*, the Sierra Club mountaineering journal, stopped publishing the traditional climbing notes on new routes, due to a feeling on the part of its editors that "the Sierra is too close to losing its remaining mystery and its remaining promise." It appears that this action occurred too soon, for although all of the major and most of the minor peaks of the High Sierra had been climbed, there were still countless fine climbs waiting to be discovered. Some of the discoverers were Alan Bartlett, Bart O'Brien, Steve Porcella, Vern Clevenger, Peter Cummings, Alan Roberts, Mike Strassman, Cameron Burns, Craig Peer, Eddie Joe, Richard Leversee, Mike Graber, Herb Laeger, Eve Laeger, David Wilson, Greg Vernon, Claude Fiddler, Alan Swanson, Robert SP Parker, Don Palmer, Todd Vogel, Bruce Bindner, David Harden, and David Nettle. Even if exploratory rock climbing continues at its present rate, I believe that the mystery the range has to offer will not be exhausted for another hundred years.

Are there any unclimbed peaks left in the High Sierra? In 1938 Richard Leonard published a list of peaks for which no records then existed, as an appendix to *Mountain Records of the Sierra Nevada*. There are now records of ascent for all of these peaks—*except for one*. I will not climb this mountain, nor will I reveal its location, living with the idea that there will always be one last unclimbed peak in the High Sierra.

SAFETY

Mountains are extraordinarily dangerous places. Worldwide, more people are killed in the mountains by accident than are shot on purpose. But the High Sierra is a rather benevolent place in comparison with the other great ranges of the world. There are no human-eating animals, killer storms are rare, the rock is relatively solid, and the glaciers are well behaved. The High Sierra is a gentle wilderness. But there are still some things that even experienced hikers and climbers should be aware of when traveling here.

Stream Crossings. A remarkable number of people have drowned while crossing streams in the High Sierra. The force of water should never be underestimated. Water moving at 5 miles per hour (or 7 feet per second) exerts 103 pounds of pressure on 1.2 square feet of the surface of the human body. Also, a person's weight advantage is negated by the buoyant effect of the water.

It is perhaps unnecessary to say that the best way to cross a stream is on a bridge or a log. Lacking these, try to cross the stream in the morning, preferably upstream from a confluence, where the stream is wide and shallow. Some people wear old tennis shoes or sandals to protect their feet during a crossing. Next best is to remove socks and wear only boots in the water.

Some believe that the safe way to cross a swift and deep stream is by using ropes. But this is a dangerous practice. If someone attempts a crossing while being belayed and stumbles, the belayer will be unable to pull the victim upstream. If the victim is lucky, the current will push him or her back to the bank where the belayer is located. More likely, the rope will snag on a rock on the streambed, and the victim has only one direction to go: down, underwater. Others may say that the solution is to have two belayers, one on each side of the stream. This is even more dangerous, because if the victim stumbles, the ropes will assume a V shape, and each side

will keep the victim from being pulled ashore. Neither belayer will have the strength to pull the victim to safety, and again the victim has only one direction to go: down, underwater. *Never* use ropes to cross a stream.

Lightning. Being struck by lightning is a very real hazard in the High Sierra. It goes without saying that you should flee from summits or ridges when thunder is heard in the distance. Lightning can also occur when there aren't any distant signs of an electrical storm approaching. I climbed a peak once during a cloudy day when there weren't any signs of electrical activity. That is, until I reached the summit, when a spark of electricity shot from the summit register to my hand. I didn't sign the register on that peak!

If a party is caught high on a peak during a thunderstorm, the best tactic is to move off the ridge as far as possible and to squat on packs, coiled ropes, foam pads, or other insulators. Don't take shelter under talus, in a rock crevice, or in a cave. Electrical currents go through these places; it is better to keep as low as possible on the surface. Metal climbing hardware will conduct electricity, so it is wise to remove it from your body. Those who experience an electrical storm will witness tremendous flashes of light with thunder louder than the roar of 16-inch guns, painful hail storms, and the air buzzing and cackling overhead. A few have been really lucky to survive after witnessing Saint Elmo's fire glowing off rocks, equipment, and themselves.

Hypothermia. The most dangerous part of a solo trip in the High Sierra is that you may have hypothermia and not know it. Death by exposure usually begins when a tired and hungry hiker pushes his or her limits during cold, wet, and windy weather. The victim will have trouble keeping warm, become weak, cranky, and start to shiver uncontrollably. When the shivering stops, death is imminent. Anybody who starts to exhibit these symptoms should get into a tent or other windproof shelter, remove wet clothes, and slide into a sleeping bag. Consumption of hot drinks and high-energy foods usually speeds recovery. If the victim is or has been shivering uncontrollably, it may be necessary to provide extra heat by having someone strip off his or her clothes and climb into the sleeping bag with the victim. For more information, read *Mountaineering: The Freedom of the Hills*, 6th Edition (Seattle: The Mountaineers Books, 1997).

Rockfall. Natural rockfall is rather rare in the High Sierra. Ordinarily it happens in chutes during strong rain showers, or in snow or ice couloirs with the melting and freezing of ice. The most common type of rockfall is that produced by members of a climbing party. This is best avoided by not knocking off any loose rocks. Other tactics include spreading the party out horizontally or keeping everyone close together so that the impact of a falling rock is minimized. Shout out "ROCK!" when a missile is dislodged, and take cover when you hear this signal.

The typical Sierra peak is composed of "a pile of bricks." This means that the rock is heavily fractured. The rock itself is solid, but the big rocks that make up the peak seem to have been stacked by the Great Architect. Many of these huge blocks are loose even though they appear to be solid. A common accident in the High Sierra occurs when a climber pulls him- or herself up onto one of these blocks, upsetting its balance. The rock falls, taking the climber with it. You should expect talus to be loose, no matter what its size, or where it is located.

Avalanches. The High Sierra has a well-deserved reputation for having a low avalanche danger. This just means that it is low, not nonexistent. It is a good idea to be well informed about potential dangers and learn how to prepare for emergencies. For more information on avalanche safety, see Tony Daffern's *Avalanche Safety for Skiers and Climbers,* 2nd Edition (Seattle: The Mountaineers Books, 1992).

Altitude Sickness. The thin air at high altitudes does strange things to people. The most common illness is known as Acute Mountain Sickness. Symptoms include headache, lack of appetite, nausea, and poor or no sleep. This illness can usually be prevented by gaining altitude slowly. Those susceptible should take a day to gain each 1,000 feet of altitude (this refers to the sleeping altitude). Those with the illness should take the day off, rest, relax, and drink a lot of fluids.

A more dangerous form of altitude illness is High Altitude Pulmonary Edema. This can cause death quickly. Symptoms include shortness of breath, weakness, a high pulse, vomiting, and a cough with frothy, then bloody sputum. The most telltale clue is a gurgling or bubbling sound from the chest, which can be heard by most people without the aid of a stethoscope. If anyone exhibits these symptoms, get him or her down to a lower elevation *immediately,* regardless of inconvenience,

the time of day or night, or the weather. Rescuers should be notified immediately, and a helicopter with oxygen should be dispatched.

Fortunately this illness is rather rare, but it has been observed in the High Sierra. I once met a man displaying all of the symptoms at 10,850 feet. He had taken 4 days to reach that altitude from the trailhead at 7,300 feet.

Weather. Winter typically comes to the High Sierra in mid-November, after the snowfall of a major autumn storm fails to melt. This storm has occurred as early as mid-October and as late as mid-January.

Generally speaking, air temperatures during the winter in the High Sierra are relatively mild (at least when compared to those of the other great mountain ranges in the contiguous United States). The average minimum overnight temperature is approximately 15°F; daytime highs are near freezing in the shade; the air is much warmer in the sunlight.

Although the winter temperatures in the High Sierra are relatively mild, nature usually makes up for this by the amount of snowfall. The May 1915 *Monthly Weather Review* reads: "California, usually thought of as a land of fruit, sunshine, and flowers, also has within its borders the region of greatest snowfall in the United States." Other regions have since been found to receive greater snowfall, but the point remains valid: The High Sierra can receive a phenomenal amount of snow. In the winter of 1969, the town of Mammoth Lakes was buried under snow. I remember opening the door of a ski lodge, taking two steps down the front steps, and then *climbing up* twenty-five steps to see the roof barely visible above the snow.

Winter weather is typically influenced by the low-pressure system in the Gulf of Alaska, the Pacific High, and a high-pressure system of varying strength usually found over the middle of the North American continent. During fall and winter, the Pacific High gradually moves south (in August, the northern edge of the Pacific High is at 40 degrees north latitude, the approximate latitude of Cape Mendocino; in November, its northern edge is at 32 degrees north latitude, a latitude that is south of San Diego). Storms from the Gulf of Alaska or the Aleutian Islands (low-pressure areas) move southeast, are blocked by the Pacific High, and may move east over the Sierra Nevada, depending on the strength and

Skiing across South Lake. Photo by R. J. Secor.

location of the high pressure system over North America. This is the situation in a nutshell.

But there are some variables. An Alaskan storm may move directly southeast, and bring cold temperatures (perhaps 10 to 20° F) and some snow to the northern part of the High Sierra. Skiers hope that these storms first move south, then get stalled over the Pacific Ocean for a while before moving onshore. These storms are warmed by the ocean, pick up more moisture, then bring relatively warm temperatures (perhaps 20 to 30° F) and dump a lot of snow in the High Sierra. However, if there is a strong high-pressure area over the Great Basin, this can divert some storms to the Pacific Northwest. A

strong high-pressure system over the Great Basin can also force air outward from its center. This may take the form of a strong, cold wind blowing out of the east, which is readily felt atop the Sierra crest. (In Southern California, this is known as a Santa Ana wind, which usually feels much warmer because of the low elevation along the coast.)

So, signs of good weather in winter may include a wind out of the east, crisp, cold air, and unlimited visibility. An old joke is that the wind changes direction so that it can go back and bring more snow. Does a wind out of the west mean that a storm is on its way? Maybe. Mountains create their own wind patterns, so wind direction by itself may not mean much; but if there are gusty winds coming from many directions, it could be a sign of approaching storm activity. It is colder at night, so cold air should flow (i.e., wind should blow) downhill at night. A west-facing valley with the wind blowing uphill (out of the west) at night may be a sign of an approaching storm. It could be hazy, perhaps due to a storm pushing air pollution forward into the High Sierra from the Central Valley. High cirrus clouds (especially those with mares' tails) may mean that the weather will change in a few days. Rings around the sun and/or moon could indicate that a storm is due within 24 hours (if the storm arrives in less than 24 hours, then it will likely be short-lived; if the storm arrives later, then it may last awhile). Low, dark clouds usually mean that a storm is imminent.

But most of the winter is quite pleasant and the sun seems to shine every day, all day long. It is interesting to note that professional skiers at Mammoth Mountain are routinely used as subjects in experiments investigating the cause and prevention of skin cancer.

Avalanche forecasts for the Eastern Sierra are available on the Internet from the Cyberspace Snow and Avalanche Center (http://www.csac.org/Bulletins/Calif/current.html).

Spring typically lasts from late April until June. But a winter-type storm (out of the Gulf of Alaska or the Aleutians) is still possible at this time of year. The northern edge of the Pacific High is at 37 degrees north latitude in May, the approximate latitude of Santa Cruz on the California coast and Taboose Pass in the High Sierra. One type of spring storm starts east of Japan and crosses the Pacific Ocean, gaining strength along the way before making a landfall on the West Coast. If there is a weak high-pressure system over the Great Basin, this storm will likely cross over into the High Sierra, dropping a lot of snow, sometimes even more than the total winter snowfall. Experienced ski mountaineers have learned to study weather maps of the entire northern Pacific Ocean before embarking on a trans-Sierra ski tour. In some years there have been as many as five storms lined up along the 37th parallel across the Pacific. It is foolhardy to enter the High Sierra under these conditions.

Please don't think that I am not recommending spring as a time to visit the High Sierra. When the weather is good, it is an excellent time for properly equipped and experienced skiers and mountaineers. The corn snow can be perfect for skiing in April and May, and climbers will find beautiful snow slopes up the peaks rather than miles of talus. In the morning, the snow will be frozen, making upward travel relatively easy. In the early afternoon, the bottom drops out of the snow, just in time for glissades or downhill skiing. The snow-covered mountains give the High Sierra an alpine flavor, and I know some individuals who consider spring to be the only time to visit the High Sierra.

Throughout the winter and spring, you may see snow surveyors making their rounds in the High Sierra. These are men and women who are paid to ski cross-country in the wilderness. They visit snow courses in the backcountry, and measure the depth and density of the snow. The California Department of Water Resources uses this data to predict accurately the amount of runoff that farmers and local water departments can expect during the spring and summer, when the snowpack melts. The High Sierra may be considered a vast reservoir that delivers water for the economic benefit and well-being of the citizens of California. Were it not for the Sierra Nevada, California would just be another desert.

Further Reading: *Atlantic Monthly.* January 1995, pp. 45–58.

The Department of Water Resources makes runoff forecasts in April and May, and this information is published in the local media and on the Internet on the California Snow Page (http://snow.water.ca.gov). This is useful information for the hiker, as it indicates how much snow and how much high water can be expected during a visit to the mountains. These forecasts are expressed in a percentage of normal, based on a fifty-year average. For example, I once hiked for a week in the High Sierra in the middle of June when the snowpack was 43 percent of normal. An ice axe wasn't necessary to cross a particular pass I had to go over, and I never got my feet wet, even when fording a major river. A few years later I repeated the same hike at the same time of year but the snowpack was 205 percent of normal. I had great difficulty crossing the same pass due to a huge cornice, and the river was in flood stage. Generally speaking, you can expect passes that cross the Sierra crest to be more or less snow-free by July 1 in normal (i.e., 100 percent) snow years. During that 205-percent-of-normal snow year, some passes did not become passable to ordinary mortals until mid-August.

Summer in the High Sierra lasts from the end of June through the middle of September. (By the way, mosquitoes are usually present only in early summer.) It is usually quite pleasant, with daily shade temperatures ranging from 50 to 70° F and night temperatures between 30 and 45° F. Temperatures in the sun are much higher due to the high altitude, low humidity, and lack of dust. Protection against glare and sunburn is usually needed. Afternoon showers may be experienced, and the refrain that "it never rains at night in the Sierra" seems to have some validity.

The northern edge of the Pacific High is at 40 degrees north latitude in August, the approximate latitude of Cape Mendocino and Lassen Peak. This effectively blocks any storm from moving in from the Gulf of Alaska or Japan to California. The big weather concern during the summer is the possibility of tropical storms that may bring moist, unstable air into California or the Great Basin from the west coast of Mexico. Such storms are not localized phenomena but rather can cover the entire range with rain (or snow and hail at higher elevations). Signs of these storms include clouds moving out of the southwest and toward the northeast, relatively high humidity, and the presence of thick clouds that cover almost the entire sky at night. Rain at night is an almost sure sign that a major tropical storm has arrived. Tropical storm Norman made a landfall in September 1978 near Los Angeles and brought with it much grief to those in the High Sierra at that time.

A more typical weather phenomenon is the afternoon thunderstorm cycle. After several days of perfectly clear weather, some scattered clouds may appear in the afternoon but disappear by sundown. During the next few days the clouds appear earlier and earlier and grow in size, but still disappear before the end of the day. After about 5 days of this, cumulus "fair-weather" clouds appear in the late morning. By midafternoon these clouds join into thunderheads, which shoot upward far into the sky. The sun disappears behind these clouds and the temperature drops. Thunder rumbles in the distance, and then the clouds drop their loads of rain, hail, and snow amidst flashes of lightning, terrific crashes of thunder, and winds that seem to come from all directions. The precipitation gradually lightens (indicating that the life of the thunderstorm is about to end), and soon the sun reappears. Tents and rain gear are soon dry-

ing, and everyone wonders what all of the fuss was about. Afternoon thunderstorms may continue for a few more days before the cycle is completed.

Autumn in the High Sierra typically lasts from the middle of September to the first major winter storm, which usually happens in mid-November. In many ways fall is the best season to be in the High Sierra. Mosquitoes are completely absent, the nights are crisp and cold, and it seems as if the traveler has the mountains all to him- or herself. Storms during this season can deposit several inches of snow, but the usual Indian-summer weather soon returns and what snow is left quickly disappears. Everyone traveling in the High Sierra during this season should carry warm clothing and a stormproof tent. Travelers should also make certain their camps are positioned so that a convenient escape route leads them to safety, rather than into higher elevations, should the first major winter storm occur.

A meteorological landmark of the High Sierra is the Sierra Wave. This beautiful, long, lenticular cloud may run along the Sierra crest for over 200 miles. It is formed when high, strong winds out of the west hit the western slope of the High Sierra. This forces the moving air upward, where it cools, condenses, and forms a cloud. The wind descends on the east side of the range, where it warms, expands, and becomes clear air. The appearance of a Sierra Wave means only one thing for certain: There are high winds aloft. There may be rain or snow in the wave, or it may simply be overcast. The Sierra Wave can appear in any season, and it can also appear in the absence of other storm signs; this usually indicates that it is only a localized phenomenon. (In this case, you can find better weather by simply moving away from the Sierra crest). But when it appears along with other storm signs, it is another piece of data to consider when you are deciding whether to stay put, move camp to ensure that a high pass does not separate the party from safety, or to go home and watch television.

Rescue. Requests for assistance should be directed to the rangers in the national parks or to the county sheriff outside the parks.

In the final analysis, safety is in the character of the individual rather than in the use of equipment or knowledge of specialized techniques. The judgment of a party can make all the difference between a pleasurable journey and a preventable tragedy.

Sierra Wave. Photo by R. J. Secor.

CONSERVATION

Astronomers at the Lick Observatory atop Mount Hamilton in the Coast Range at one time were able to point their telescope towards the Sierra Nevada and photograph the peaks and passes. This was an interesting diversion for them at sunset, before they began their nightly explorations of the heavens. It is rare today for the astronomers to see the High Sierra from Mount Hamilton due to the pervasive air pollution in the Central Valley.

California is the most populated state in the country. The effects of having too many people in one place, including traffic congestion and air and water pollution,

are apparent. It might seem that most of these city problems would be absent in the wilderness of the High Sierra, but California's large population is having its effect in the mountains as well. All of us, i.e., *you* and *I*, must make the extra effort to leave the mountains unspoiled for the enjoyment of future generations. We must leave no traces of our passing through the mountains, and have as little effect on the terrain as possible.

Go Light. This means traveling as lightly as possible, in terms of the weight on your back or that of your pack animal, and to go light on the terrain. This is a matter of learning to be at home in the wilderness with a few pieces of equipment, rather than carrying and living in an elaborate camp. It is possible to get along with less than you think—in travel, as in life, often "less is more." You will be more comfortable, less tired, and will make the effort to take care of the mountains.

This also applies to those who travel with horses, mules, or burros. Too much equipment translates into more animals that must be rounded up in the morning, fed, groomed, loaded, guided during the day's travel, unloaded, picketed or hobbled, and so on. Too many animals can translate into even more animals to carry their feed!

Low-Profile Camping. Keep your group small, no more than fifteen people on a trail and no more than eight hikers on a trailless, cross-country route. Camp at least 100 feet away from a trail, preferably in an area that is screened from the trail by the terrain or vegetation. Colorful equipment may have caught your eye in the store, but it can be visually offensive in the wilderness. Keep the "improvements" to your camp to a minimum. Trenches around tents and hip holes lead to erosion. And pack out all refuse. Unless each and every one of us starts to show some class, camping in the High Sierra wilderness will be no different from camping at a roadside campground.

Also, you should select "hard" campsites. Meadows, lakeshores, and streamsides cannot take the wear and tear of camping. These soils are moist and soft, and will rapidly disappear from the effects of too many campers, just as meadows disappeared in the nineteenth century from too many sheep. Campsites should be placed at least 200 feet away from any water source, but even this is not enough distance in popular areas.

Fires. Large campfires are passé. At timberline, down wood is being burnt up faster than it is produced. The beautiful snags left standing after lightning strikes are part of the unique scenery of the High Sierra, but even these are being torn apart in the search for more wood. In some places these trees have disappeared completely. Many hikers don't know that they were ever there. Wood at timberline is a finite resource, and it must be used sparingly in the few locales where fires are allowed.

Instead of using a wood fire, cook on a stove. Cooking is much easier, usually faster, and the weight penalty is negligible. If a fire *must* be built, keep it *small*. The best fireplace is the one used throughout rural areas of developing countries: three rocks, approximately the size of grapefruits, arranged to form a triangle with 6-inch sides.

The fire is kept small and easy to control for cooking, with a minimal waste of wood. When camp is broken, let the coals burn down and out, pulverize the ashes to a fine powder, cover the hearth with clean sand, and return the stones to their places of origin. Scatter the surplus wood. The fireplace should be completely gone when you leave.

But do consider using a stove, which can have as much personality as a campfire. Besides, the best way to get to know the night is to crawl into your sleeping bag for complete warmth and watch the heavens circle brightly overhead.

The redundant phrase "wood campfires" appears throughout this book. California state law considers any type of outdoor fire, whether it comes from a wood fire, camp stove or a lantern, to be a campfire. Where wood campfires are prohibited, cooking on a white gas, butane, propane, or kerosene stove is allowed, assuming that wildfire restrictions are not in effect.

Ducks and Blazes. These markers appear regularly along High Sierra routes. Ducks are also known as cairns; a duck is a small cairn erected by well-meaning hikers to show the correct route. The problem with ducks is that they seldom actually show the easiest route. They also have a tendency to direct all cross-country hikers onto the same path. This leads to the creation of a use trail, which usually scars the land above timberline. There are many use trails in the High Sierra (and some are even described in this book) but we must do everything we can to prevent more from being created. I believe that anyone who leaves the trail and sets out cross-country should be capable of finding the correct route on his or her own without the assistance of ducks. Don't build ducks, and destroy all ducks encountered.

Similarly, a party hiking cross-country should spread out when crossing a meadow. It is tempting to "stay on the trail" and follow the leader's footsteps. But this leads to the creation of a rut across the meadow, which soon becomes a permanent scar. It is better and often easier to go around a meadow. If this is impossible, the party should spread out and each individual should make his or her own path, one that at least stands a chance of healing. And don't cut switchbacks while hiking on established trails.

Blazes are scars that have been made on trees to mark the route of a trail or cross-country route. Blazes reached an art form in the late nineteenth century in Yosemite, when the new national park was being patrolled by the cavalry. Common blazes seen in Yosemite are the "T" (for trail) blazes in northern Yosemite and the pointed "Obelisk" blazes in the southern part of the park. Today's hikers should admire these blazes, but not create any new ones.

Historical Artifacts. The National Park Service (NPS) policy defines any object made by humans that is more than fifty years old as a historical artifact. Any such subjects found in the park are the property of the NPS. Typical items are arrowheads, mortar holes, sheepherder stoves, cavalry relics, animal traps, and even the garbage dumps established by the Sierra Club High Trips! It is illegal to remove these artifacts from national parks. Any artifacts found should be left where they are, and their location reported to the NPS.

Fixed Anchors. All climbers must practice safe, ecologically responsible mountaineering in the wilderness of the High Sierra. Safety is the primary concern in climbing, and this may require the placement of fixed anchors. I urge climbers to use restraint and discretion in establishing fixed anchors. These aids should be placed unobtrusively, in locations that will not be visible to other wilderness users. Climbers should remove old fixed anchors and replace them with new, camouflaged material. Removable fixed anchors, such as runners and chockstones, work extremely well in the high country of the Sierra Nevada. Pitons and bolts should only be placed as a last resort, when all other alternatives have been exhausted.

Wilderness Permits. The United States Forest Service (USFS) and the NPS maintain control over the lands under their jurisdictions by issuing permits. Wilderness permits have two purposes: to enable the authorities to educate wilderness users on minimum impact camping techniques and to limit the number of hikers entering the wilderness via the most popular trails ("quota trails") during the most popular season. This "quota period" lasts from the end of June to mid-September in most locations. During this time, permits for these trails can be obtained by making reservations far in advance, but in some places a small number of first-come, first-served permits are saved to be issued each day. The trick to gaining entry into the wilderness during the quota period is to be flexible about your dates of travel and to be willing to use trailheads and trails other than your first choices. Hikers who visit the High Sierra at times other

than during the quota period should have no problem obtaining wilderness permits.

Every trail that starts from a trailhead is identified as either a quota or non-quota trail. A *reserved* wilderness permit is not required for an overnight hike on a non-quota trail, but a wilderness permit is; this can be obtained in person for free at a ranger station.

It must be stressed that all parties must have a wilderness permit in their possession for an overnight hike in a wilderness area, regardless of the time of year. An exception is that Sequoia National Forest does not require a wilderness permit for entry into the Monarch Wilderness while the Sierra National Forest does! Another exception is the Mount Whitney Zone, where wilderness permits are required for both day hikes and overnight hikes. Those without permits will be cited by the rangers who regularly patrol the wilderness; violators receive a verbal order from the issuing officer to leave the wilderness or backcountry immediately as well as an order to appear in court.

Addresses of the ranger stations that issue permits are given in Appendix B. Contact them for the most up-to-date information regarding quotas and advance reservations. A request for a wilderness permit must include the date; places of entry and exit from the wilderness; method of travel (on foot, ski, or horseback); number of people in the group; and number of pack animals that will be taken.

Sequoia and Kings Canyon National Parks require that every member of a party be present to hear the ranger read wilderness regulations aloud when the permit is issued. Neither Yosemite National Park nor USFS ranger stations currently require that the entire party be present to issue a permit. Whoever obtains the permit must inform the other members of the party of the wilderness regulations.

BEARS AND WATER

These two "new" conservation problems have become topics of great discussion among travelers and land managers in the High Sierra and deserve their own special section.

Bears

Grizzly bears are extinct in California, except on the state flag. Black bears (which actually may be black, brown, blue, or cinnamon) are present throughout the

High Sierra ritual: the bear bags. Photo by R. J. Secor.

High Sierra; I once watched one cross an 11,000-foot, snow-covered pass. But there are two types of black bears: wild and domesticated. Wild bears have learned that humans are a source of danger, fleeing when people approach. Domesticated bears have learned that people are a source for food. They don't eat people, but instead dine on campers' food. Domesticated bears have learned not to be afraid of humans, and they prowl through campgrounds and popular wilderness campsites searching for human food. If you encounter a bear, teach it to be afraid of people. Immediately and repeatedly yell, bang pots, clap hands, and throw small rocks, sticks, and pinecones at it. All party members should stand together to try to intimidate the bear. However, don't surround it, but give it a wide, obvious escape route. Of course, beware of a mother with cubs—always maintain a safe distance. Never attempt to retrieve food or gear from a bear; wait until the animal has dropped the item and left the area. A wild bear will probably run away after one small yell but a domesticated bear will continue to loiter in the area, waiting for the opportunity to approach again. You may have to get up repeatedly during the night to scare it away from your campsite.

Bears prefer human food because it is easier to rip open a knapsack than to dig through logs for ants or eat massive amounts of currants and acorns. It only takes one taste of human food for a bear to become addicted. Bears are attracted to anything with an odor, so soap, toothpaste, sunscreen, toothbrushes, cosmetics, and garbage must also be securely stored. Packs should be left on the ground with all pockets, zippers, and flaps open so that a bear doesn't tear it open to find nothing to eat. Federal law requires proper food storage, and violators will be cited with a fine and an order to appear in court. Here are the three approved methods of food storage:

Bear Boxes. Sequoia and Kings Canyon National Parks have placed these metal boxes at popular wilderness campsites. Yosemite National Park does not have any bear boxes in the wilderness but boxes are available at popular trailheads. The Park requires that no food be stored in automobiles. (Some bears break into cars whether or not they smell or see food; they've learned to associate cars with food, just as they associate knapsacks with food.) A bear box is the only bear-proof storage available, but these are not perfect. They are not at every potential campsite but instead only at the most popular spots. I have occasionally encountered a full box. Bear boxes tend to concentrate human impact in one site. Unfortunately, some thoughtless hikers use the boxes for abandoned garbage and surplus food. And unattended caches cannot be left in food boxes for more than 24 hours.

Bear Cannisters. These are plastic barrels with ingenious flush lids that can be opened or closed using a coin. These are immorally expensive, but they can be rented from sporting good stores and from national park concessionaires. Current models weigh almost three pounds and take up a lot of space in a knapsack. But they give the hiker the freedom to store food anywhere. Aside from the expense, weight, and bulk problems, cannisters are also only bear-resistant—not bear-proof. A few hikers have returned to the sites where their cannisters were left to find them missing. It is easy to conclude that a lost cannister was stolen by another hiker, but I suspect that a bear may have rolled it away to attempt a break-in at a more secluded location. Bear cannisters should be covered with rocks in a location away from open packs and other gear.

Bear Bags. Bags containing food can be hung from a tree using the counterbalance method. This is far from being bear-proof and cannot really be considered bear-resistant. In some places (east of Kearsarge Pass, for example) this method is considered improper food storage and those using bear bags will be cited. At best, the use of bear bags is a delaying tactic because a bear will eventually get the food. However, if you do use this method, find a tree with a live, slightly down-sloping branch that extends 10 feet from the trunk and is at least 20 feet above the ground. The end of the branch must be at least an inch thick so that it will support the weight of the food, but not a bear cub. Weight a cord with a rock or stick to make sure it will have enough momentum and toss one end over the branch and back down to the ground. Divide the food into two separate stuff sacks weighing no more than ten pounds each. Tie the rope to one sack, and hoist it to the branch. Tie the other sack on the cord as high as possible, and also tie a loop of cord to this sack to aid in retrieval. Use a long stick to push the second sack upward until it is level with the first sack. The sacks of food should be at least 12 feet above the ground. The food is retrieved by using a long stick to hook the loop of cord on the second sack. Pull the stick and sack down slowly to avoid tangles, untie the second sack, and lower the first sack down to the ground.

Other Countermeasures. Other food storage methods—hanging food from cables or poles, burying it under rocks on talus slopes, hanging it off high boulders, or homemade PVC pipe bear cannisters—don't work. The most dangerous practice is to sleep with food. Remember, wild bears are afraid of people, but a domesticated bear will knock you aside just to sink its teeth in your energy bars. One night at Vidette Meadow the bear box was full so a hiker slept with his food. You guessed it: The bear got his food and the hiker had his ear sewed back on 2 days later in a Fresno hospital.

Regardless of the food-storage method, the best way to avoid encountering a bear is to camp where you are not likely to meet a domesticated bear. Domesticated bears prowl through popular campsites; camp elsewhere. Wild bears flee from smoke but domesticated bears may be attracted to a camper's fire, associating it with human food; don't have a wood campfire. If you *cook* food (rather than eating instant, add-hot-water food) have an early dinner and then hike 1 or 2 miles and camp. And use dark, muted colors for your bear bags to avoid advertising your food. As mentioned at the beginning of this section, bears are present throughout the High Sierra, but these tactics may lessen the probability of encountering a bear in search of a hiker's food.

Water

The other "new" phenomenon is anxiety over *Giardia lamblia* in the lakes and streams of the High Sierra. This is an intestinal parasite that causes giardiasis, which brings with it the possibility of diarrhea, flatulence, foul-smelling stools, nausea, abdominal cramps, and excessive fatigue. These symptoms last about a week and the incubation period is from one to four weeks. But most infected individuals have no symptoms at all. All mountain travelers should be aware of giardiasis, but I believe that the alarm about this infestation has been exaggerated.

The USGS took water samples at several sites in the High Sierra in 1984. The highest concentration of giardia cysts was found at Long Lake along the Bishop Pass Trail: 14 cysts per 100 gallons. The most heavily used trail is the Mount Whitney Trail and most sample sites along Lone Pine Creek reported 0 cysts per 100 gallons. Lone Pine Creek at Trail Camp had 5 cysts per 100 gallons, and 1 cyst per 100 gallons was found in Lone Pine Creek at Whitney Portal.

You will probably not get giardiasis by drinking surface water in the High Sierra. If you do get giardiasis, you probably won't have any symptoms. If you have symptoms, they will probably go away in 7 to 10 days without treatment. Only a very few cases of giardiasis do have serious symptoms. These include malabsorption, weight loss, severe stomach pain. People who experience these symptoms need aggressive medical treatment.

Although *Giardia* has received most of the attention, there may be other things in the surface water in the High Sierra to take precautions against. Water can be purified by boiling, using filters, or adding iodine-based chemical purifiers to it. Heating water to 190° F (at 12,000 feet water boils at 190° F) will kill *Giardia* cysts instantly, but boiling for ten minutes is recommended, as other organisms might be present. Iodine crystals in a saturated water solution is inexpensive, convenient, and is effective against most bacteria and viruses.

Remember, many hikers may be asymptomatic carriers of *Giardia*. Protect water quality in the High Sierra by burying human waste in organic topsoil at least 6 inches deep and at least 100 feet from water sources. Pack out toilet paper. Finding organic topsoil near timberline may be difficult; try under trees where needles are decomposing. The Mount Whitney area has very high use with very little organic topsoil and the USFS recommends that hikers pack out their own human waste in this area.

HOW TO USE THIS BOOK

Each of the thirteen chapters that follow describes a particular section of the High Sierra region. The division used is based very generally upon the drainage patterns of each area. Each chapter includes a brief overview; a list of maps related to the chapter; a grid showing the location of each 7.5-minute map; and descriptions of roads, trails, established cross-country routes, and routes on the peaks.

Sketch maps, drawings, and photographs are also provided to enable the reader to get a better sense of the terrain. These show features, routes, and place names that may not be on the USGS maps. However, the maps in this book should not be used as substitutes for the USGS maps.

A list of each area's land managers, and how they can be contacted, is provided in Appendix B at the end of the book. Hikers will need to contact these land managers to obtain the wilderness permits required to visit these areas.

Special mention should be made of what I call "Wrinkles." It is a rare mountain traveler who is interested in only one single destination during a journey in the mountains. The Wrinkles sections show the reader alternative routes or how various places can be linked together in ways that may not be apparent during home study.

You may notice that no mention of campsites has been made in this guide. This is because the great increase in the numbers of mountain travelers over the last generation has resulted in tremendous human impact on the High Sierra's popular campsites. Besides, in this age of high-tech camping equipment and lightweight stoves, you can camp almost anywhere in relative comfort.

Maps. This book has been written with the assumption that the reader will be using it along with detailed topographic maps of the area he or she is visiting. After all, the purpose of this book is to provide the wilderness traveler with information not provided by a map, and to correct map information that is in error.

The USGS has produced extremely detailed 1:24,000 scale (1 inch = 2,000 feet; the *7.5-minute series*) maps of the entire Sierra Nevada, and these maps have been used as the basis for this book. These maps have replaced the older 1:62,500 scale (1 inch = approximately 1 mile; the *15-minute series*) maps that were published by the USGS. The problem with these newer, large-scale maps is that they are actually *too* detailed. In the past, you could enjoy an extended trip into the mountains and carry only four maps. With the 7.5-minute maps it may be necessary to carry sixteen maps to cover the same area. Several maps may be needed to identify a distant landmark, and it is inconvenient to orient oneself on a map in combination with other maps. Many hikers prefer to use the 15-minute maps.

Another problem has to do with feet and meters. The older maps showed elevations exclusively in feet. Some of the new maps show elevations in meters, but an adjacent map may show the elevations in feet! These maps would be more useful if every map showed elevations in either meters or feet.

Fortunately, the map situation has been resolved by the private sector. Wilderness Press (2440 Bancroft Way, Berkeley, California 94704; 800-443-7227) has published its own corrected and updated 15-minute maps: Devils Postpile, Hetch Hetchy Reservoir, Merced Peak, Mineral King, Mt. Abbot, Mt. Goddard, Mt. Pinchot, Mt. Whitney, Triple Divide Peak, Tuolumne Meadows, and Yosemite. Map Link (30 S. La Patera Lane, Suite 5, Santa Barbara, CA 93117; 800-627-7766) also publishes its own 15-minute maps, printed from the original USGS plates, but these maps have not been updated and corrected: Big Pine, Blackcap Mtn., Devils Postpile, Giant Forest, Hetch Hetchy Reservoir, Kaiser Peak, Kern Peak, Marion Peak, Matterhorn Peak, Merced Peak, Mineral King, Mono Craters, Mount Whitney, Mt. Abbot, Mt. Goddard, Mt. Morrison, Mt. Pinchot, Mt. Tom, Tehipite Dome, Tower Peak, Triple Divide Peak, Tuolumne Meadows, and Yosemite.

But my favorite set of maps of the High Sierra are those published by Tom Harrison Cartography (2 Falmouth Cove, San Rafael, CA 94901-4465; 800-265-9090). His 1:63,360, six-color, shaded-relief topographic trail maps of the Mount Whitney High Country, Kings Canyon High Country, Mono Divide High Country, Mammoth High Country, and Yosemite High Country present the High Sierra in beautiful, three-dimensional detail. Harrison also publishes a John Muir Trail Map-Pack, showing the route of the trail on thirteen reasonably sized sheets of paper.

Another useful set of maps are those published by the USFS: A Guide to the Golden Trout Wilderness/South Sierra Wilderness (1:63,360); A Guide to the John Muir Wilderness and the Sequoia–Kings Canyon Wilderness (1:63,360); A Guide to the Ansel Adams Wilderness (1:63,360); and A Guide to the Hoover Wilderness (1:63,360). All have a scale of 1 inch to exactly 1 mile. These maps are true bargains and cover such a large area that it seems as if they were made for home study on winter evenings. They are available from USFS ranger stations and NPS visitor centers.

Smaller-scale maps that also may be useful are the USGS special series maps of Sequoia and Kings Canyon National Parks and of Yosemite National Park. The scale of these maps is 1:125,000 (1 inch = 2 miles). Another alternative is the 1:100,000 scale (1 centimeter = 1 kilometer) USGS *30 x 60–minute series*. The Three Rivers, Mt. Whitney, Bishop, Benton Range, Shaver Lake, Yosemite Valley, and Bridgeport maps cover the territory of this book. These maps help you to get the "big picture" on a reasonably sized piece of paper, but they are not quite as detailed as those maps mentioned above.

The USFS also publishes recreation maps of the national forests, showing roads, trails, campgrounds, and other human-made and natural landmarks, but no topographic detail. These, combined with local road maps issued by automobile clubs, may be useful for finding remote trailheads.

Place Names. Many of the place names used in this book may not appear on the USGS maps of the High Sierra. Some of these names have been in use for years by hikers, climbers, fishermen, rangers, and packers, but have not yet been officially recognized by the Board of Geographic Names. Forty-five of the names used in this book are my own creations. These are generally named after a nearby feature, or after someone who has made a significant contribution to the exploration of the Sierra Nevada. I have taken the liberty of naming a few places after my friends. Place names that are my own creation include: Alpine Pass, Bard Pass, Bilko Pass, Bolton Brown's Shoulder, Blackcap Pass, Carter Col, Cinder Col, Clinch Pass, Confusion Pass, Conness Pass, Courte-Echelle, Cox Col, Dancing Bear Pass, Davis Lake Pass, Deadhorse Pass, Dykeman Pass, Fleming Pass, Goddard Creek Pass, Grasshopper Pass, Gunsight Pass, Haeckel Col, Keating Pass, Lane Pass, Lilley Pass, Lobe Pass, MacLeod Pass, Mantle Pass, McDonald Pass, McGee Lakes Pass, Merriam Pass, Midway Pass, Mount Mendenhall, Old Bones Pass, Packsaddle Pass, Pete's Col, Post Corral Pass, Pterodactyl Pass, The Right Pass, Rockwell Pass, Rohn Pass, Royce Pass, Ruskie Pass, Russell Pass, Seven Gables Pass, Sluggo Pass, Solomons Pass, Ski Mountaineers Pass, Steelhead Pass, Stough Pass, Treasure Col, Two Passes, Ursula Pass, Valor Pass, Wallace Col, and Wilts Col.

At first glance it may appear that I have gone crazy in naming the features of the High Sierra. But this list is not excessive when you consider that more than 2,100 places are described in this book; also, I only named seventeen of the places after my friends. (My creation of place names in the first edition of this work created considerable comment among reviewers, government bureaucrats, and in a few cases, even among humans.)

Some may say that naming physical features implies that humans have mastery over the land. My reply to this is that, from a guidebook author's point of view, a place without a name isn't a place.

Route Descriptions. I once tried to follow a route description that someone gave me for a remote High Sierra peak. The description said to look for an upside-down "W." I finally gave up and climbed past an "M." What I'm trying to say here is that no matter how good the route description, the hiker's or climber's routefinding ability is the essential ingredient for a safe and successful trip.

The information in this book has come from my personal experience, input from friends, articles and notes that have appeared in semipopular magazines, mountaineering journals, and the newsletters of many small but serious outdoor clubs—and, in four cases, rumor, gossip, hearsay, and speculation. The record of exploration in the High Sierra is incomplete, and I am certain that many places worthy of inclusion in this book have been inadvertently omitted.

Roads are usually described from the point of view of driving up into the mountains. Mileage logs are provided, telling the reader when to turn left or right to a tenth of a mile from a prominent starting point along the road.

Trails are usually described the same way. The mileage (with elevations in feet) in parentheses is from the previously identified point to the nearest quarter of a mile. The mileages in this book may differ from the signs at trailheads or along the trail. These signs are frequently inaccurate, and I have given my best estimate of the distance covered by a trail for a reader to follow instead. If a trail seemed to me to be X number of miles, then that is the distance that I recorded, regardless of what a sign said.

A note on the use of fractions and decimals: Decimals are used to a tenth of a mile when the distance can be accurately determined (e.g., by using an odometer or measuring a straight line on a map). Fractions have been used to a quarter of a mile when the distance has been estimated by hiking.

Cross-country routes are described in the direction in which they are normally traveled.

The headings for each cross-country and peak route may be confusing; examples with explanations are given below.

Disappointment Peak (4242 m; 13,917 ft). This place is named on the map, and its elevations from the new 7.5-minute map and old 15-minute map, respectively, are listed.

Please note that when two elevations are given, they are the *new* and *old* elevations, and not the English/metric equivalents.

"*Whitney-Russell Pass*" *(3980 m+; 13,040 ft+; 0.4 miles NE of Mount Whitney; UTM 898493).* The quotation marks indicate that this place is not named on the map. The old and new elevations are listed; the plus sign indicates that its exact elevation is not on the map. In this case the summit elevation is not exactly 4000 meters or 13,120 feet (which would be the next contour line on the map), but is higher than 3980 meters or 13,040 feet (which is the last contour line found). The location is then given relative to a place named on the map.

Universal Transverse Mercator (UTM) grid coordinates are sometimes listed to help locate ambiguous places. The grid is defined on some maps by the fine black lines that are drawn on the map itself. On other maps, the grid is identified by the fine blue tick marks that are spaced 1 kilometer apart in the margins of the map. As far as this book is concerned, only the two larger (in size of typeface, not numeration) numbers are used. These numbers indicate the easterly and northerly coordinates to the nearest kilometer. A location is identified by a six-digit number. The first three digits indicate the easterly coordinate to the nearest 100 meters and the last three digits are the northerly coordinate. In this case, Whitney-Russell Pass is located 800 meters east of the line marked "89" and 300 meters north of the line marked "49" on the Mount Whitney 7.5- and 15-minute maps.

UTM numbers were determined the old-fashioned way, i.e., with a map, compass, and a pencil (not with a Global Positioning System receiver) and based on the North American Datum of 1927. Future editions of USGS maps may be based on the North American Datum of 1983. The correction for this is to add approximately 85 meters to the easterly coordinate and 10 meters to the northerly coordinate. Check the map legend to see which datum was used to create the map.

Perhaps the most speculative information is the first-ascent party listed for routes on the peaks. The earliest recorded ascent is given credit as the first—when this information can be determined. The party listed may not actually have been the first to climb that peak or route, but were the first to *publish* their ascent of the peak or route. (Almost everybody now knows that the Vikings were the first Europeans to visit North America. But Co-

lumbus gets all the credit because he was the first to publish his discovery.)

First-ascent information is included at the start of the route description for a route on a peak because it contains facts that may be of use to the savvy mountaineer. A first ascent done in June or July would probably have a description of snow or ice cover, which may be absent in August or September. A first ascent of a route done in the 1930s probably has shorter pitches than one done in later decades. Listing the names of the first-ascent party also helps to identify the correct route; this is especially true on crowded faces, such as the west face of Mount Russell. The main purpose of including first-ascent information is to make the book more useful, not to glorify these individuals. And an ascent during the months of December, January, February, March, or April is given credit here as a "winter ascent."

Routes on peaks are usually named by their direction from the summit (e.g., southwest slope or north face). In some cases routes have earned new names through popular usage (e.g., the Swiss Arête on Mount Sill) or they have been renamed by a guidebook author who worships heroes (e.g., the LeConte Route on North Palisade). Route directions (e.g., turn left) are stated from the point of view of facing the summit. If these may be ambiguous, a compass direction is also given, e.g., traverse right (south). I may specify if a traverse is slight (i.e., slightly more vertical than horizontal), diagonal (equal amounts of vertical and horizontal), or horizontal (level).

Many route descriptions are not overly detailed, and a statement that reads, "Follow the south ridge to the summit," should not be taken too literally. The best route will likely involve a climber taking a number of variations on both sides of the ridge, rather than stubbornly staying directly on the crest of the ridge in difficult places.

RATING SYSTEM

The Yosemite Decimal System has been used to rate the difficulty of the terrain described in this book. This system is complex and illogical, and can be confusing to beginners and experts alike. On a more positive note, it seems to have been accepted nationwide by rock climbers and mountaineers, so there should be some basis of understanding among the readers of this book. It also applies to all terrain, from horizontal ground to beyond-the-vertical rock.

Class 1 is walking. Mount Whitney via the trail or the south slope of Mount Kaweah fall into this category.

Class 2 is defined here as difficult cross-country travel. In the High Sierra this is usually talus hopping, which requires the occasional use of hands for balance. Hikers who are not used to class 2 terrain will soon become tired, especially if carrying a heavy pack. Talus can be unstable, and the danger of class 2 terrain is that hikers may stumble among these blocks. It is also possible for a boulder to dislodge and roll over a hiker. Split Mountain (via the north ridge) is an example of class 2.

Class 3 is where the climbing begins. Hands and feet are used not just for balance, but to *hang on to* the rock. Steep or large talus can be rated as class 3. Class 3 is more common on steep faces or along ridges and arêtes. Novices may feel uncomfortable, but the holds are large and easy to locate. A rope should be available to give a belay to anyone who requests it. My favorite description of class 3 is by Steve Roper in the 1976 edition of *The Climber's Guide to the High Sierra*: "Imagine climbing a steep, narrow staircase outside of a tall building without benefit of a railing: scary but easy." The east face of Middle Palisade and Mount Mills via the east couloir are examples of class 3.

Class 4 is on steep rock with smaller holds and a lot of exposure. ("Exposure" is a euphemism for the amount of air beneath your feet.) Ropes and belays should come into continuous use, because a fall will probably be fatal. Taking Steve Roper's analogy one step further, class 4 can be loosely compared to climbing a ladder on the side of a tall building. The handholds and footholds are there, but if you let go, that's the end. Mount Humphreys via the southwest slope and northwest face is class 4.

Class 5 is steep and difficult rock climbing involving the use of protection placed between the leader and the belayer. I differentiate class 4 from class 5 by the hand- and footholds. Class 5 requires obscure holds such as edging, smearing, laybacks, mantles, stemming, underclings, hand jams, toe jams, chimneying, and evangelical hammerlocks used to make upward progress. Types of protection include *runners* (loops of nylon webbing placed around flakes, blocks, and natural chockstones); *chocks* (placed in cracks); *pitons* (hammered into cracks); and *bolts*, which are drilled into solid rock.

Class 5 spans a wide range of difficulty, and so has been divided into several categories. A rating of 5.0 is the easiest class 5 climbing, and 5.14c is the most difficult rating currently known (the scale does not have an upper limit). Mathematically oriented minds would assume that 5.14 is easier than 5.2, but this is not the case. The upper ranges of class 5 have been further divided into four subcategories: a, b, c, and d. An R or X rating refers to the quality and quantity of protection opportunities available: R means run out, with few opportunities; X means no protection.

Aid climbing, where the climber quite literally hangs from the equipment that has been placed on the rock, was once known as class 6, but this is now rated from A0 to A5. A0 is hanging from the rope; this may be a pendulum, a tension traverse, or a rappel. An A1 placement is very simple and will hold a small truck; an A5 placement may be a nest of pitons or stacked nuts that barely supports the climber's weight.

Some technical climbs have been classified into grades, identified as Roman numerals from I to VI. The grade indicates the overall difficulty of the route, i.e., the length, commitment, exposure, continuity, and other factors that give the climber an indication of the seriousness of the route. Generally speaking, a grade I climb takes a couple of hours, consisting of one or two technical pitches, and a low level of commitment. Grade II: 2 to 4 hours and up to four pitches, with a relatively simple escape or retreat route available. Grade III: 4 to 7 hours and up to eight pitches, and escape or retreat will involve technical difficulties. Grade IV: 7 to 10 hours and up to twelve pitches, and retreat is as difficult as completing the route; the hardest pitch is never less than 5.7. Grade V: a full day and perhaps part of the next day to climb up to eighteen pitches; the hardest pitch is never less than 5.8. A Grade VI climb is a big wall, with more than fifteen pitches and taking more than 2 days to complete lots of difficult free and aid climbing. Grades have fallen out of style recently, but they have been continued here because of their usefulness.

Snow and ice climbs are comparatively rare in the High Sierra during the height of summer. Ice axes probably won't be needed after the first of July during a normal snow year, and crampons are seldom really essential. Unless, of course, the climber wants to climb snow or ice. Snow and ice climbs have been rated according to Jeff Lowe's modified Scottish snow and ice rating system that has become accepted by climbers in North

America. The first part of the rating is identified as AI (Alpine Ice) or WI (Water Ice). In the late spring and early summer, AI climbs will consist of frozen névé snow. In the High Sierra, the WI rating arrives in the autumn when the ice will be brick hard, and the ice will get harder until a substantial snowfall in the middle of the winter starts a new cycle. In addition, snow and ice climbs are described in terms of angle and length. Be forewarned: the bergschrund has not been included in the rating; a vertical 'schrund may be there or it may have collapsed into a series of interconnecting ramps, making it easy to overcome. Otherwise almost every snow and ice climb would be rated WI5.

A snow or ice rating of 1 would typically consist of up to 50° snow or 35° ice; the equivalant of class 3 rock. A rating of 2: up to 60° snow or 40° ice; class 4. A rating of 3: up to 80° snow or 75° ice; 5.0 to 5.7. A rating of 4: vertical snow or 85° ice; 5.8 to 5.9. A rating of 5: overhanging cornices or 90° ice; 5.10.

The class number of a climb in this book may mean nothing. It is likely that someone will follow a class 2 route and discover it to be class 3 in reality. Or a class 3 climb may turn out to include a lot of class 4 pitches. Class 4 may include moves up to 5.6 in the real world. And class 4 may turn out to be class 3, class 3 may turn out to be class 2, and so on.

The Yosemite Decimal System has its roots in the Sierra Club classification system first created in 1936. This divided climbs into six classes, class 1 being easy and class 6 severe. A 1936 class 1 would be class 1 or 2 today. A 1936 class 2 would be class 3 today. A 1936 class 3 would be class 4 today. A 1936 class 4 covers everything from class 4 to 5.6 today. A 1936 class 5 would be in the 5.6 to 5.7 range today. No class 6 climbs were identified in 1936.

To confuse matters further, the Sierra Club classification system was changed in 1938. A 1938 class 1 would be class 1 today. A 1938 class 2 would be class 2 to 3 today. A 1938 class 3 would be class 3 to 4 today. A 1938 class 4 would be class 4 to 5.4 today. A 1938 class 5 would be from 5.4 to 5.6 today. In 1938, aid climbing was identified as class 6.

As rock climbing became more popular, the 1938 Sierra Club system was modified further into the Yosemite Decimal System, created in 1952 at Tahquitz Rock in Southern California. This divided class 5 from 5.0 to 5.9 at that time. More difficult climbs became 5.10, 5.11, and so on in the following years. Inevitably, grade inflation occurred at all levels of the Yosemite Decimal System (to paraphrase Yosemite climber Jim Bridwell) due to innocence, ignorance, and insecurity. And this is the bane of the guidebook author. How can one write a current, up-to-date route description without adding (and implicitly approving of) grade inflation?

Also, many routes were climbed before this rating system first came into existence. And some routes that were first climbed fifty years ago are awaiting their second ascent. Combine these factors with the changes in the rating system and grade inflation and we now have rampant confusion.

Having written all of this, I am sure that someone will attempt a class 4 route, only to find it to be 5.6 at his or her favorite bouldering area, and use this incident to vilify me in the alpine media. It is rewarding to know that my work has brought so much happiness to the world.

Readers should put their own judgments ahead of this book. If a route turns out to be more difficult than this book indicates, the user should recognize that it may have been incorrectly classified in the first place (or that the user may be off route). And a relatively low rating for a climb should never keep a climber from backing off from a climb in the interest of safety.

PEAKS AND REGISTERS

Previous guidebooks to the High Sierra have covered some peaks that are not in this book, and vice versa. These other authors were either extremely diligent, and included every closed contour circle no matter how insignificant the peak, or they applied specific criteria to a peak (altitude, routes, etc.) before including it.

I have included a peak in this book when I thought it was worthy of mention. This may sound rather arbitrary, but in the final analysis it is the same criteria that other guidebook authors have used.

Almost all of the peaks in the High Sierra (and a few of the passes) have summit registers. These may be either a few scraps of paper inserted into a pair of nesting tin cans, or the elaborate cast-aluminum boxes with bound blank books that were placed by the Sierra Club many years ago. I never cease to be amazed by these registers. A register may have been placed fifty years ago and be no more than one-third full. It is not uncommon to have three generations of the same family sign the same book. I have seen the simple entries made by Bolton Brown, Norman Clyde, Walter A. Starr, Jr., Nobel laureates, and Pulitzer Prize winners in the registers on a few peaks as well as grandiose entries made by some who draw pictures, write poems, insult the entries of other climbers, curse guidebook authors, and so on.

Peak baggers usually place a code after their names in a register. For example, a number inside a mountain indicates that this is the nth Sierra peak that he or she has climbed. An entry that reads "2X" or "3X" means that this is his or her second or third ascent of that peak. "SPS" means that the climber is a member of the Sierra Peaks Section of the Angeles Chapter of the Sierra Club. "PCS" refers to the Peak Climbing Section, Loma Prieta Chapter, Sierra Club. "RCS" is the Rock Climbing Section of many chapters of the Sierra Club. "NAS" is the Northern Alpine Section, Mother Lode Chapter, Sierra Club. "Yeti" is the mascot of the Vagmarken Mountaineering Club. "SMS" is the Ski Mountaineers Section of the Angeles Chapter of the Sierra Club, while "SMSRT" stands for the Sierra Madre Search and Rescue Team. "OPG" is the Occasional Peaks Gang of the China Lake Mountain Rescue Group or "CLMRG." "SAC" refers to the Stanford Alpine Club. "CMC" can refer to the Colorado Mountain Club, the Chicago Mountaineering Club, or the California Mountaineering Club. "CCC" represents the California Conservation Corps. "AMC" is the Appalachian Mountain Club. "AAC" is the American Alpine Club. "PCOBS" represents the Pacific Crest Outward Bound School. "QBE" stands for Quest Beyond Eagle, an adventure program operated by the Boy Scouts of America. "USMC" and/or "MWTC" is the United States Marine Corps Mountain Warfare Training Center. Contrary to popular belief, "SCMA" does not mean Sierra Club My A**, but rather identifies the Southern California Mountaineers Association. "MGS" stands for the Mountaineering Guide Service, and "PSOM" is the Palisade School of Mountaineering; these entries are frequently seen in the Palisades. And a few pseudonyms frequently appear: "The Lone Ranger," "Abu Jose Bani Sanchez," and the almost ubiq-

uitous "Norman Claude." (Thus far, fourteen people have told me that they are "Norman Claude.")

It has been a long-standing policy of the Sierra Club to remove summit registers when full and place them in the Sierra Club archives kept in the Bancroft Library at the University of California, Berkeley. My personal view is that summit registers should be kept on the summits forever. Registers may have been placed by the Sierra Club, but they don't belong to the Sierra Club; they belong to the peaks. Some of these registers will be stolen by thoughtless souvenir hunters or destroyed by lightning, but that is part of the game. My proposed policy won't work on Mount Whitney, Mount Dana, and other popular peaks, but it worked quite well on some of the "lesser peaks," such as Mount Stanford or the Devil's Crags. At least until somebody removed the registers from these peaks for "safekeeping."

It is worth remembering that the first summit register in the High Sierra was placed by William Brewer and James Gardiner on top of Mount Brewer on July 4, 1864. It remained there until 1895 when it was removed from the summit and placed in the headquarters of the Sierra Club in San Francisco for safekeeping. In 1906 the headquarters of the Sierra Club was destroyed in the San Francisco earthquake and fire.

A NOTE ABOUT SAFETY

Safety is an important concern in all outdoor activities. No guidebook can alert you to every hazard or anticipate the limitations of every reader. Therefore, the descriptions of roads, trails, routes, and natural features in this book are not representations that a particular place or excursion will be safe for your party. When you follow any of the routes described in this book, you assume responsibility for your own safety. Under normal conditions, such excursions require the usual attention to traffic, road and trail conditions, weather, terrain, the capabilities of your party, and other factors. Keeping informed on current conditions and exercising common sense are the keys to a safe, enjoyable outing.

–The Mountaineers

Chapter 2

The Whitney Region

For the purposes of this book, the Whitney region includes the Sierra crest from Shepherd Pass to Cottonwood Pass; it is bounded on the west by the Kern River. This area contains some of the highest peaks in California, as well as deep, glaciated canyons, cirques, hanging valleys, sharp ridges, and high passes, which are all the more dramatic in contrast to the views of the desert to the east.

HISTORY

As soon as Clarence King discovered Mount Whitney from the summit of Mount Tyndall in 1864, the race was on to be the first to climb it. When he and Richard Cotter returned to the California Geological Survey's camp along Roaring River, King begged the field leader, William Brewer, for permission to make another attempt. Realizing that this would be a first-rate opportunity to fill in more blanks on the map, Brewer gave his consent, plus $100 and an escort of two soldiers. King and the soldiers left Visalia and followed the Hockett Trail up the South Fork of the Kaweah River. They crossed the Great Western Divide, descended to the Kern River, and followed a canyon north of what King called "Sheep Rock" (Mount Langley). This route put him too far to the east (the most difficult side of Mount Whitney), and he was forced to retreat.

King returned to the eastern Sierra in 1871 and immediately set out for a prominent peak, assuming that it was Mount Whitney. He and Paul Pinson reached the summit during a storm that obscured the view of surrounding peaks, but they felt confident that they were on the top summit of Mount Whitney. King soon returned to civilization and spread the word that the high-

est mountain in the United States had been conquered.

As it turned out, King had not made it to the summit of Mount Whitney after all. He and Pinson had climbed Mount Langley, and this error was discovered in late July of 1873. King, on the east coast at the time, immediately headed west and on September 19, 1873 he finally stood on the summit. Unfortunately, two parties had preceded him, both consisting of individuals from the Owens Valley. Mount Whitney was first climbed on August 18, 1873 by the "Fishermen": John Lucas, Charles Begole, and Albert H. Johnson. The second ascent was made on August 20, 1873 by William Crapo and Abe Leyda. There was a modest proposal to rename the mountain "Fishermen's Peak," but the name first proposed by William Brewer nine years before remained.

The highest mountain in the United States became the site for many scientific experiments. The first was in 1881, when Samuel P. Langley used the summit for solar heat observations. For the next twenty years the summit was a military reservation, under the control of the U.S. Army Signal Corps, the weather service of the age. A stock trail was constructed to the summit in 1904, and in 1909 a shelter was constructed on the summit by the Smithsonian Institution for use by its astronomers.

The other peaks in the region were eventually climbed. Mount Russell, only 1 mile north of Mount Whitney, became one of the last 14,000-foot peaks to be climbed in California, in 1926.

One of the first roped rock climbs to be done in the High Sierra was the east face of Mount Whitney, in 1931. The other faces of the Whitney massif soon saw roped ascents, and the age of rock climbing had begun.

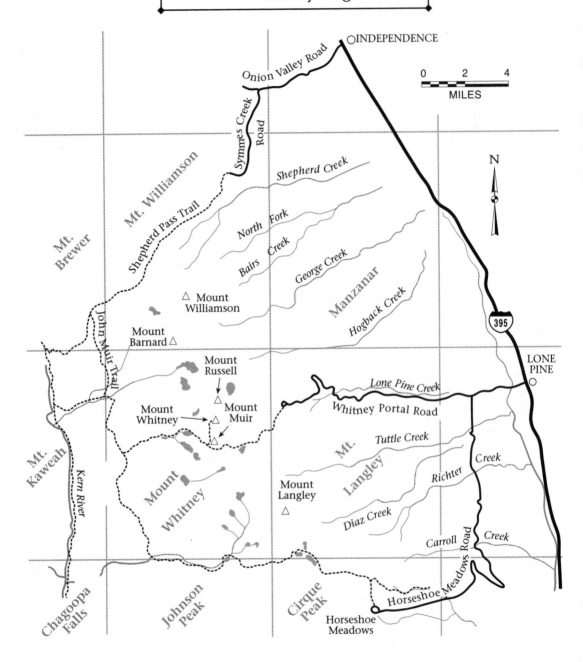

The Whitney Region

INDEPENDENCE

Onion Valley Road

Symmes Creek Road

Shepherd Creek

North Fork

Bairs Creek

George Creek

Hogback Creek

Manzanar

0 2 4
MILES

N

395

LONE PINE

Mt. Williamson

Shepherd Pass Trail

Mt. Brewer

△ Mount Williamson

Mount Barnard △

Mount Russell
△

△ Mount Muir

Mount Whitney → △

John Muir Trail

Mt. Kaweah

Kern River

Mount Whitney

Lone Pine Creek

Whitney Portal Road

Tuttle Creek

Mt. Langley

Richter

Creek

Mount Langley
△

Diaz Creek

Carroll

Creek

Horseshoe Meadows Road

Chagoopa Falls

Johnson Peak

Cirque Peak

Horseshoe Meadows

MAPS

USGS. *7.5-minute series:* Cirque Peak, Johnson Peak, Chagoopa Falls, Mt. Langley, Mount Whitney, Mt. Kaweah, Manzanar, Mt. Williamson, Mt. Brewer. *National park maps:* Sequoia and Kings Canyon National Parks and Vicinity (1:125,000). *30 x 60–minute series:* Mount Whitney, Three Rivers.

USFS. A Guide to the Golden Trout Wilderness/ South Sierra Wilderness (1:63,360); A Guide to the John Muir Wilderness and the Sequoia–Kings Canyon Wilderness (1:63,360).

Tom Harrison Cartography. Mount Whitney High Country.

Map Link 15-minute series. Kern Peak, Mount Whitney.

Wilderness Press 15-minute series. Mount Whitney.

ROADS

Horseshoe Meadows Road

Horseshoe Meadows Road leads to the Cottonwood Pass and New Army Pass trailheads. Head west from Lone Pine along Whitney Portal Road for 3.2 miles. The Horseshoe Meadows Road goes south, passes Granite View Drive after 2.0 miles, and comes to a gate (locked in winter) 4.7 miles later. The road then starts to climb via a few huge switchbacks and comes to the trailhead for the Cottonwood Lakes/New Army Pass Trail after another 13.0 miles. It continues another 0.3 mile to Horseshoe Meadows, with its campgrounds, and the trailhead for Cottonwood Pass, marked with a sign reading "Golden Trout Trailhead."

Granite View Drive

Granite View Drive serves as the approach to the Tuttle Creek Trailhead. Drive west up Whitney Portal Road 3.2 miles from Lone Pine to Horseshoe Meadows Road. Drive south on Horseshoe Meadows Road, past the road leading to Tuttle Creek Campground, to Granite View Drive, 2.0 miles south of the Horseshoe Meadows–Whitney Portal junction. Turn right (west) on the dirt road. After 2.3 miles the road forks; go right, and continue another 2.0 miles to a sandy parking area on a flat that overlooks Tuttle Creek. High-clearance, four-wheel-drive vehicles can continue another 0.5 mile, but the road is steep with loose sand.

Whitney Portal Road

Whitney Portal Road leads from Lone Pine to the Meysan Lake and Mount Whitney Trailheads. Drive west up the road from Lone Pine, passing Horseshoe Meadows Road after 3.2 miles, and continue up the steep grade to Whitney Portal. At 11.3 miles from Lone Pine the road passes the Meysan Lake Trailhead, then the Mount Whitney Trailhead at 12.1 miles. The road ends in a loop 0.2 mile beyond the Mount Whitney Trailhead.

George Creek Road

The only thing harder than hiking up rugged George Creek is driving the last 0.5 mile to the trailhead. This road begins 5.3 miles south of Independence on Highway 395, or 10.3 miles north of Lone Pine on the same highway. Head west on the dirt road, pass a gate (leave it as you found it, i.e., either open or closed), and follow the road as it gradually turns south. Drive past Manzanar Cemetery to a fork 2.5 miles from the highway. Turn right, and continue driving toward the mountains remaining on the main road for 5.0 miles to a junction. The road to Bairs Creek goes right, but George Creek is straight ahead; most people park somewhere along the next 0.5 mile instead of driving all the way to the trailhead which is another 1.3 miles. The last 0.5 mile of the road is the worst; only high-clearance, four-wheel-drive vehicles are suitable.

Symmes Creek Road

Symmes Creek Road leads to the Shepherd Pass Trailhead. Drive west from Independence on Onion Valley Road for 4.5 miles to Foothill Road. Turn left (south) onto the dirt road, and turn right at a fork after 1.3 miles. Continue another 1.6 miles to a corral. This is the stock trailhead; hikers should continue driving to the next fork, 0.4 mile farther. Turn right (west) and drive another 0.5 mile to another fork. Go right, and continue another 0.9 mile to the Shepherd Pass Trailhead for hikers.

TRAILS

Cottonwood Pass Trail and the Pacific Crest Trail   21½ miles

A quota trail. This trail leads from the end of Horseshoe Meadows Road (0 mi; 9,920 ft+) to the summit of

Cottonwood Pass (3½ mi; 11,120 ft+). Wood campfires are prohibited east of Cottonwood Pass. The Cottonwood Pass Trail continues downhill to the southwest, through Big Whitney Meadow, where it eventually meets the Siberian Pass Trail (5 mi; 9,720 ft). One branch of the Pacific Crest Trail heads south and east from Cottonwood Pass to Trail Pass, and, ultimately, to Mexico.

From Cottonwood Pass, the Pacific Crest Trail passes Chicken Spring Lake (½ mi; 11,242 ft), where wood campfires are prohibited. It traverses the southern slopes of Cirque Peak before climbing (to 11,440 ft+) and then descending to a junction (5 mi; 11,215 ft). The New Army Pass Trail is 1 mile north. Continuing westward, the Pacific Crest Trail descends to meet the Siberian Pass Trail (½ mi; 11,139 ft) and it continues descending to meet the end of the New Army Pass Trail (4¼ mi; 9,959 ft). The Pacific Crest Trail continues down Rock Creek where it crosses to the north side of the creek (½ mi; 9,520 ft+). The trail then climbs to the saddle northeast of Mount Guyot (to 10,892 ft+), goes through Guyot Flat, and descends to lower Crabtree Meadow (5½ mi; 10,329 ft). The Pacific Crest Trail heads north from lower Crabtree Meadow to a junction with the John Muir Trail (½ mi; 10,695 ft+). Bears are active throughout this area.

From lower Crabtree Meadow, a shortcut trail gradually climbs to the northeast on the north side of Whitney Creek to meet the John Muir Trail west of Crabtree Ranger Station (1¼ mi; 10,630 ft+).

Cottonwood Lakes Trail and New Army Pass Trail   16 miles

A quota trail. This is the shortest and most direct trail leading from Horseshoe Meadows to New Army Pass. From the trailhead along Horseshoe Meadows Road (0 mi; 10,040 ft+), the trail makes an almost level traverse to Cottonwood Creek past Golden Trout Camp and up the creek to Cottonwood Lakes basin (4 mi; 11,041 ft). Many use trails have appeared among the Cottonwood Lakes, leading fishermen to their favorite spots. Wood campfires are prohibited in Cottonwood Lakes basin, and special fishing regulations have also been established. Bears prowl through this area.

The trail to New Army Pass leads to the west, passes Long Lake and High Lake, and after a short, steep climb, pops out onto the plateau marking the western side of

New Army Pass (4 mi; 11,880 ft+). Wood campfires are prohibited above 10,800 feet west of New Army Pass. The trail descends the western slope to a junction which leads south for one mile to meet the Pacific Crest Trail (3½ mi; 10,920 ft+). The New Army Pass Trail goes north and crosses one of the tributaries of Rock Creek (1 mi; 10,761 ft+). One trail goes northeast from here, leading to the Soldier Lakes southwest of The Major General. Wood campfires are prohibited at lower Soldier Lake. Bears prowl through this area. The New Army Pass Trail continues down Rock Creek to a junction with the Pacific Crest Trail (3½ mi; 9,959 ft).

Mention should be made of two other, older trails leading to Cottonwood Lakes. One trail leaves Horseshoe Meadows Road near the old pack station and ascends Little Cottonwood Creek before descending to Golden Trout Camp after 4 miles. The other trail, which leaves Horseshoe Meadows Road below the new trailhead and climbs up Cottonwood Creek to Golden Trout Camp, is ¼ mile longer than the current New Army Pass Trail, and it involves an extra 500 feet of gain.

At one time there was a trail over Army Pass (0.4 mi NE of New Army Pass), but it has been abandoned. The northeastern aspect of the Army Pass Trail left it packed with snow all summer long after heavy winters, and rockfall was a continuous hazard. Even though the New Army Pass Trail involves an extra 700 feet of gain, it is a much better route.

Meysan Lake Trail   3½ miles

A quota trail. The trailhead for the Meysan Lake Trail is located 11.3 miles from Lone Pine along Whitney Portal Road (0 mi; 7,874 ft+). Walk past the lower Whitney Portal Campground, through the summer-home area, following the signs directing hikers to the correct trail, which starts its climb up the north side of Meysan Creek. The official trail ends just below Meysan Lake (3½ mi; 11,155 ft), but there are many use trails around the lake, and cross-country travel is easy in the upper part of this basin.

This trail is heavily used, and wood fires are prohibited in the entire Meysan Creek drainage.

Mount Whitney Trail   8½ miles

A quota trail. The quota season for this trail has been increased from May 22 to October 15; a Mount Whitney Zone stamp is needed to day hike this trail, and

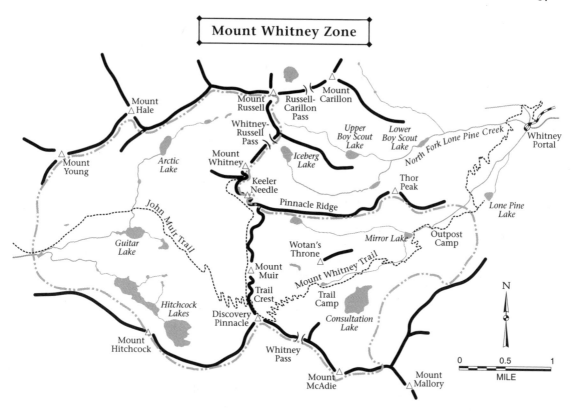

Mount Whitney Zone

campers will also need a wilderness permit in addition to the special zone stamp. This is one of the most heavily used trails in the High Sierra. Wood campfires and pack and saddle stock are prohibited along the trail. Camping is prohibited at Mirror Lake and along Trailside Meadow. Bears are active on the lower portion of the Mount Whitney Trail.

The trail starts at the lower end of the road loop at the end of Whitney Portal Road (0 mi; 8,268 ft+). It gradually climbs the north slope of the canyon and crosses the North Fork of Lone Pine Creek (¾ mi; 8,727 ft+). The trail then climbs and crosses to the south side of Lone Pine Creek and eventually meets the Lone Pine Lake Trail (1½ mi; 9,974 ft+). The Mount Whitney Trail continues to Bighorn Park (also known as "Ibex Park," "Whitney Outpost," and "Outpost Camp"; 1 mi; 10,782 ft+). The trail crosses to the north side of the creek and climbs to Mirror Lake (½ mi; 10,630 ft+), where camping is prohibited. The trail continues to Trailside Meadow (1 mi; 11,352 ft+; no camping) and climbs to Trail Camp (1 mi; 12,039 ft+), which is the last water. Many hikers take their minds off the tedium of climbing to Trail Crest (2 mi; 13,648 ft+) by counting the number of switchbacks encountered. The Mount Whitney Trail then descends slightly to meet the John Muir Trail (½ mi; 13,451 ft+). It is another 2 miles along the John Muir Trail to the summit of Mount Whitney.

Further Reading: Walt Wheelock and Wynne Benti. *Climbing Mount Whitney.* Bishop, Calif.: Spotted Dog Press, 1997, pp. 31–32.

The John Muir Trail 17½ miles

The John Muir Trail goes south from its junction with the Shepherd Pass Trail along Tyndall Creek (0 mi; 10,827 ft+) and makes a gradual ascent to the Bighorn Plateau, where there are wonderful views in all directions. Wood campfires are prohibited at Tyndall Creek. Bears prowl through this area. After meeting the High

Sierra Trail along Wallace Creek (4½ mi; 10,403 ft), the John Muir Trail makes a steep ascent to the south, crosses Sandy Meadow, and meets the Pacific Crest Trail. It then turns east, descending to Whitney Creek and the Crabtree Ranger Station (4½ mi; 10,630 ft). After continuing up the south side of the creek and then crossing it, the trail reaches Timberline Lake (1 mi; 11,089 ft+), where camping is prohibited. Bears prowl through this area. This is the western boundary for the Mount Whitney Zone, and a special zone stamp on the wilderness permit is needed to continue. The trail then passes the north shore of Guitar Lake (1 mi; 11,417 ft+) before climbing to the southeast to meet the Mount Whitney Trail (3 mi; 13,451 ft). The John Muir Trail turns north and eventually arrives at the summit of Mount Whitney (2 mi; 14,491 ft). There is a hut on the summit, but it should not be used as a shelter during a thunderstorm as it does not offer protection from lightning.

The High Sierra Trail   3¼ miles

The High Sierra Trail actually begins near Giant Forest at Crescent Meadow, but description in this chapter is of the portion beginning 1 mile north of Junction Meadow along the Kern River.

From the Kern River (0 mi; 8,793 ft+), the High Sierra Trail adopts a moderate grade and ascends the Wallace Creek drainage to meet the John Muir Trail just north of where it crosses Wallace Creek (3¼ mi; 10,403 ft). Wood campfires are prohibited above 10,800 feet along Wallace Creek. Bears prowl through this area.

Shepherd Pass Trail   13 miles

A quota trail. The Shepherd Pass Trail has a well-deserved reputation for being long, steep, and difficult. In the middle part of the trail, which is east of the Sierra crest, there is 500 feet of loss (or gain, depending on direction). On a more positive note, this trail offers the most direct access to the upper Kern River basin. There are two trailheads for the Shepherd Pass Trail, one for hikers and another for stock (see the description of Symmes Creek Road). Those hiking the stock trail will travel an extra 1¼ miles.

From the hikers' trailhead (0 mi; 6,299 ft+), the trail crosses Symmes Creek four times before beginning its long, steep climb across Symmes Creek Saddle and then descending to Shepherd Creek at Anvil Camp (6 mi; 10,302 ft+). Wood campfires are prohibited at Anvil Camp. The trail crosses the creek again at The Pothole (1 mi; 10,827 ft+); an abandoned trail leads over Junction Pass from here. The Shepherd Pass Trail continues through moraines, and sometimes snowfields, to Shepherd Pass (2 mi; 12,008 ft+). The trail then descends the Tyndall Creek drainage to join the John Muir Trail just south of where the John Muir Trail crosses Tyndall Creek (4 mi; 10,827 ft+), where wood campfires are prohibited.

The Shepherd Pass Trail passes through the California Bighorn Sheep Zoological Area, east of the Sierra crest. Dogs are prohibited in this area.

CROSS-COUNTRY ROUTES

"Diaz Pass"   4040 m+; 13,280 ft+;
0.4 mi SE of Mount Langley

Class 2. This is an old shepherds' route that ascends Diaz Creek from the floor of Owens Valley to cross the Sierra crest just south of Mount Langley. The New Army Pass Trail is much easier!

Tuttle Creek and "Tuttle Pass"
3900 m+; 12,880 ft+

A non-quota trail. This route serves as the approach to the north side of Mount Langley, the eastern approach to Mount Corcoran, southeastern approach to Mount LeConte, and the southern approaches to Peak 3985m (12,960 ft+) and Lone Pine Peak.

From the end of Granite View Drive go up the canyon on a trail to the abandoned stone house constructed as a Hindu ashram in the 1930s. Climb onto the ridge directly above the house; pass a metal shed and then a wickiup before arriving at a faint use trail. The trail forks almost immediately; the left fork is for uphill travel, while the sandy right fork is used to descend. This use trail avoids most of the brush and remains on the north side of the stream until 9,600 feet, where it crosses the creek and disappears. Climb onto a rib on the south side of the canyon, and stay on top of it while hiking up the Tuttle Creek drainage.

Tuttle Pass is a class 2, talus-infested pass crossing the Sierra crest between Mount Corcoran and Mount

Langley. It extends between Tuttle Creek and Rock Creek. It is for adventurous hikers only.

Arc Pass   3920 m+; 12,880 ft+

Class 2–3. This is a convenient route between the Mount Whitney Trail and the upper reaches of Rock Creek. Follow the eastern shore of Consultation Lake and make a gradual ascending traverse to the low point of the pass, east of Mount McAdie. A direct ascent from Consultation Lake to the pass involves much loose rock over steep terrain; it is better to approach the pass from the east. The south side of the pass is easy, as long as you circle Sky Blue Lake on its eastern side. Wood campfires are prohibited above 10,800 feet in Miter Basin, the upper part of Rock Creek. A Mount Whitney Zone stamp on your wilderness permit is needed to cross this pass from south to north.

Crabtree Pass   3820 m+; 12,560 ft+

Class 2. This pass has also been called "Miter Pass." Crabtree Pass is the low point of the ridge between Mount McAdie and Mount Newcomb. It provides access between Crabtree Lakes and upper Rock Creek. A good use trail leads from upper Crabtree Meadow to the Crabtree Lakes. From the highest lake in the basin, ascend a short, steep section of talus to the pass. Descend to Lake 3697m (12,125 ft), and head southwest from this lake before turning east to the inlet of Sky Blue Lake.

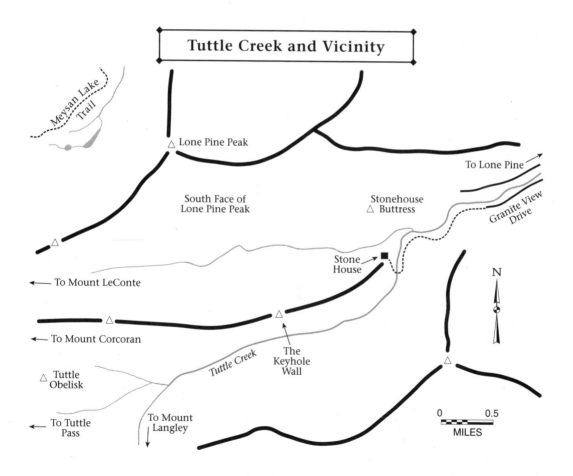

Tuttle Creek and Vicinity

Meysan Lake Trail

△ Lone Pine Peak

To Lone Pine

South Face of Lone Pine Peak

Stonehouse △ Buttress

Granite View Drive

△

Stone House ■

← To Mount LeConte

N

← To Mount Corcoran

△

△

Tuttle Creek

The Keyhole Wall

△ Tuttle Obelisk

△

← To Tuttle Pass

To Mount Langley

0   0.5
MILES

Pass Sky Blue Lake on its east side. Descend Rock Creek on its west bank to a use trail that passes through Miter Basin and leads down to the New Army Pass Trail.

Whitney Pass   4040 m+; 13,280 ft+

Class 1–2. At one time the Mount Whitney Trail crossed Whitney Pass, but this portion of the trail has been abandoned for a long time. This pass is included here only for the record. Discovery Pass is the preferred route.

"Discovery Pass"   4160 m+; 13,400 ft+; 0.1 mi
ESE of Discovery Pinnacle

Class 2. Strictly speaking, this is not a pass. It crosses the southeast ridge of Discovery Pinnacle. It is the easiest, most direct route between the Mount Whitney Trail and the Crabtree Creek drainage and has also been used to climb Mount Hitchcock. From the highest switchback of the Mount Whitney Trail, simply leave the trail and cross the Sierra crest southeast of Discovery Pinnacle. The southeast slopes of the "pass" are sandy, and it is easy to descend to Crabtree Lakes. A Mount Whitney Zone stamp on your wilderness permit is needed to reach the Mount Whitney Trail.

"Pinnacle Pass"   3720 m+; 12,160 ft+;
UTM 863482

Class 3. This pass gives access to the North Fork of Lone Pine Creek from the Mount Whitney Trail. From Mirror Lake, hike up a wide canyon to the northwest, near the base of the cliffs to the north. After ¾ mile, ledges lead up and right (east) to the pass, located immediately to the east of Pinnacle Pass Needle, which is visible from Mirror Lake. The first part of the descent is class 3 on ledges and leads eastward. The lower portion descends diagonally to the west.

From Iceberg Lake to Mirror Lake, climb talus at the first place where the boulders rise prominently against the north face of Pinnacle Ridge. From the top of the talus, climb up the ledges that lead to the pass. A Mount Whitney Zone stamp on your wilderness permit is needed to cross Pinnacle Ridge from north to south.

North Fork of Lone Pine Creek

Class 2. A quota trail (a cross-country route, in reality), and the quota period has been extended from May 22 to October 15. This is the approach for the routes on Mount Whitney's east face. The popularity of this route has resulted in multiple-use trails all along this canyon, and the forest service has placed route markers to mitigate damage. Wood campfires are prohibited in the entire North Fork of Lone Pine Creek drainage. This cross-country route starts approximately 1 mile up the Mount Whitney Trail, where the trail crosses the North Fork of Lone Pine Creek. Leave the trail and hike up the south side of the stream for approximately ½ mile to a point where the canyon walls narrow. Cross to the north bank of the stream near a Matterhorn-shaped rock. Climb up the steep slope above this rock for about 100 feet to the Ebersbacher Ledges. Head east on the ledges until it is possible to turn west on another ledge and continue hiking upstream. The route remains on the north side of the creek to the outlet of Lower Boy Scout Lake. Cross to the south side of the creek and climb up a talus slope to the southwest. The stream forks near Clyde Meadow; cross to the north side of the creek and hike to the outlet of Upper Boy Scout Lake. Cross the outlet and climb the steep, tiring talus slope that is due south from the outlet of the lake. Turn right (west) at the top of this slope, and hike for about ½ mile to the cliff just below Iceberg Lake. This cliff is often wet and/or icy, and it is best to continue west a little farther and climb a cruddy chute to Iceberg Lake.

Further Reading: Walt Wheelock and Wynne Benti. *Climbing Mount Whitney.* Bishop, Calif.: Spotted Dog Press, 1997, pp. 42–43.

"Whitney-Russell Pass"   3980 m+; 13,040 ft+;
0.4 mi NE of Mount Whitney; UTM 898493

This pass is also known as "Whitney Col." It is *not* the low point between Mount Whitney and Mount Russell, but rather the notch immediately northwest of Iceberg Lake. (The low point between Mount Russell and Mount Whitney can be crossed, but it is class 3 on its east side and requires some creative routefinding. Whitney-Russell Pass is the preferred route.)

Class 2 slopes lead from Iceberg Lake to the pass. The western slopes of the pass are gentle, with the exception of some talus. From Arctic Lake, it is easy cross-country hiking to reach the John Muir Trail at Guitar Lake. A Mount Whitney Zone stamp on your wilderness permit is needed to cross this pass.

When crossing the pass from west to east, remember to head for the southern, higher notch, and not the lower, northern notch.

"Russell-Carillon Pass" 4040 m+; 13,280 ft+; 0.5 mi E of Mount Russell

Class 2–3. This pass is also known as "Russell Col." This route provides a direct route between the North Fork of Lone Pine Creek and the Wallace Creek drainage by way of Tulainyo Lake. From Clyde Meadow, ascend sandy slopes to the northwest to the saddle between Mount Russell and Mount Carillon. The north side of the pass is steep, and the best route is to the right (east). It is best to approach Wallace Lake from the south, rather than from the southeast.

Rockwell Variation: This avoids ascending tedious scree slopes. Pass Upper Boy Scout Lake on its right (north) side, and continue up the valley to the steep southeast face of Mount Russell. Turn right (north) and ascend the highest couloir. This leads to the plateau that is south of Russell-Carillon Pass. This route is class 2 up to the pass. But the easiest descent of Russell-Carillon Pass on its east side is via the scree slope down to Clyde Meadow.

"Cleaver Col" 3960 m+; 12,960 ft+; 0.25 mi NE of Mount Carillon

Class 3. This is a steep, difficult, cross-country route connecting the lower portion of the North Fork of Lone Pine Creek with Tulainyo Lake. Leave the North Fork where a stream descends from the northwest at approximately 10,000 feet, and follow the stream uphill. In the upper part of this drainage move to the left (west) and climb up to the pass. It is best to circle around Tulainyo Lake on its south side.

Wallace Creek

At one time a trail led from the John Muir Trail to Wallace Lake, but it has not been maintained for many years. This is now considered a cross-country route, although portions of the trail are still visible.

Leave the John Muir Trail just north of Wallace Creek, where the High Sierra Trail comes in from the west. Hike up to the north side of Wallace Creek to approximately 10,800 feet and cross Wallace Creek to its south side. (This is at UTM 792514; a landmark for this crossing is Waterfall Meadow just downstream from where the creek draining Wales Lake enters Wallace Creek.) Wood campfires are prohibited above 10,800 feet in Wallace Creek. After crossing Wallace Creek, cross the tributary leading from Wales Lake, and continue hiking up the south side of Wallace Creek to the outlet of Wallace Lake.

The easiest approach to Wales Lake is to first head south from the inlet of Wallace Lake and then head southwest to the eastern shore of Wales Lake.

Vacation Pass 3860 m+; 12,640 ft+

Class 2–3. This pass crosses the Sierra crest and extends from George Creek to Wallace Creek. The easiest crossing is ½ mile north of the low point.

George Creek

A non-quota trail. George Creek is a difficult cross-country route. It is used as the eastern approach to climb Mount Williamson, Trojan Peak, and Mount Barnard. This area is open only from April 15 to May 15 and from December 15 to January 1, due to Bighorn Sheep Zoological Area restrictions. Any enthusiastic Sierra mountaineer should climb up George Creek at least once. It is one of the classic bushwhacks of the High Sierra.

From the end of George Creek Road, hike up the north bank of the stream for about ¼ mile to where a cliff bars further progress. Cross to the south side of George Creek on a small logjam. Continue up the south side of the stream for another ¼ mile, then cross to the north side of the stream on a big, broken log, just below some small waterfalls. Hike up the north side of the creek for about ½ mile to where a stream enters George Creek from the right (northwest); you will see a small, sharp, little ridge between two streams. Hike over the ridge (30 feet of gain) and follow the main course of George Creek about 200 yards, and cross to the south side on a log. The route continues up the south bank of the creek to approximately 8,800 feet, where a stream enters George Creek from the left (southwest). (This is the departure point for Vacation Pass.) Cross to the north side of George Creek and hike up to approximately 9,800 feet, where the creek forks. Those headed for Trojan Peak and Mount Barnard should head left (southwest) from here; if Mount Williamson is the objective, go right (northwest). The upper reaches of

MOUNT WHITNEY

MOUNT YOUNG

MOUNT HALE

Whitney-Russell
Pass

This is NOT
Whitney-Russell Pass

Iceberg
Lake

Upper Boy
Scout Lake

Whitney-Russell Pass from the east. Photo by Austin Post, No. 72R2-195, USGS Ice and Climate Project, GeoData Center, University of Alaska, Fairbanks.

George Creek are free of brush, and it is easy to pick out a route.

"Tyndall Col"   3980 m+; 12,960 ft+

Class 2. This pass crosses the Sierra crest between Mount Tyndall and Mount Versteeg, and it leads from the upper reaches of Wright Creek to the lakes of Williamson Bowl. Williamson Bowl is closed from December 15 to July 15 due to Bighorn Sheep Zoological Area restrictions. Wood campfires are prohibited above 10,800 feet in the Wright Creek drainage.

"Rockwell Pass"   3660 m; 12,000 ft+; 1.7 mi SW of Mount Tyndall; UTM 780564

Class 2. This pass has been named here in honor of Bob Rockwell. It leads between the upper reaches of Tyndall Creek and Wright Creek. Wood campfires are prohibited above 10,800 feet in the Wright Creek drainage.

PEAKS

Cirque Peak   12,900 ft; 12,900 ft

First winter ascent February 14, 1971 by Barbara Lilley and party. This peak has a fine view from the summit. It is class 1 from either the New Army Pass Trail or the Pacific Crest Trail. It is also class 1 from Cirque Lake; climb to the saddle south of the peak, then up the ridge to the summit.

Mount Langley   4274 m; 14,042 ft

This is the southernmost 14,000-foot peak in the High Sierra. Clarence King and Paul Pinson climbed it in 1871 believing that they were making the first ascent of Mount Whitney. They found a cairn with an arrow on the summit.

Further Reading: Stephen F. Porcella and Cameron M. Burns. *Climbing California's Fourteeners.* Seattle: The Mountaineers Books, 1998, pp. 32–42.

South Slopes. First ascent 1864 by William Bellows. First winter ascent January 4, 1929 by Orland Bartholomew. Class 1 from the New Army Pass Trail.

Further Reading: Stephen F. Porcella and Cameron M. Burns. *Hiking and Climbing: California's Fourteeners.* Evergreen, Colo.: Chockstone Press, 1996, pp. 16–19.

West Face. Class 2. Climb a wide chute from the Rock Creek drainage. This chute ends approximately ¼ mile north of The Major General. From the top of this chute, climb an easy ridge to the northeast that leads to the summit plateau.

North Face. Class 3. First ascent August 1937 by Howard S. Gates and Nelson P. Nies. Climb a chimney with a chockstone at its head. Leave the chimney in its upper reaches via a ledge, and traverse to the east to a ridge. Follow the ridge to the summit.

Northeast Chute. Class 2–3. From Tuttle Creek, approach this chute east of Point 3620m (11,940 ft) and climb it to the crest of the east ridge of Mount Langley.

East Slope. Class 2. Follow Diaz Creek to its head and ascend the eastern slopes to the summit of Mount Langley.

Southeast Face of Southeast Peak. III, class 5. First ascent April 1977 by Fred Beckey and Will Crjenko. This route has been reported as having eight leads of moderate to serious rock climbing. It ends atop Peak 3878m (12,722 ft), which has been called "Mount Wooly Back."

Southeast Slope. Class 2. First ascent August 15, 1992 by Dan Richter, Asher Waxman, Devra Wasserman, Erik Siering, and John Dodds. Approach this slope from the first bowl to the north of Army Pass. Class 2 talus leads to the southern plateau of Mount Langley.

The Major General   3780 m+; 12,400 ft+

Class 2. First ascent August 1937 by Chester Versteeg and Elizabeth Versteeg. This point is southwest of Mount Langley, and the approach to the class 2 summit block is class 1 from Soldier Lakes or Mount Langley. It is hardly worth the effort.

Mount Guyot   3749 m; 12,300 ft

Class 1. First ascent 1881 by William Wallace. The preferred route of ascent is from the Pacific Crest Trail, which crosses the saddle northeast of the peak. Even though there is a bench mark at the far southwest end of the summit ridge, the high point (and the summit register) is in the middle of the summit ridge.

Joe Devel Peak   4062 m; 13,325 ft

Southwest Slopes. Class 1. First ascent September 1875 by members of the Wheeler Survey. This is a sand climb.

Northeast Ridge from Mount Pickering. Class 2. This

traverse starts on the east side of the ridge from Mount Pickering and ends by following a loose ledge on the western side ridge leading to Joe Devel Peak.

Mount Pickering   4107 m; 13,485 ft

First ascent July 1936 by Chester Versteeg, Tyler Van Degrift, and Oliver Kehrlein.

North Ridge from Mount Newcomb. Class 3. Keep to the west side of the ridge.

West Slope. Class 2 from the upper reaches of Perrin Creek.

Southwest Ridge from Joe Devel Peak. Class 2. Begin this traverse on the west slope of Joe Devel Peak and finish on the east side of the ridge.

South Slopes. Class 2. These consist of talus and sand. An excellent descent route heads southeast from the summit of Mount Pickering to a sandy chute that leads to Erin Lake.

Southeast Ridge. Class 2. First ascent August 27, 1994 by Jim Adler, Kathy Price, Peter Rosmarin, Eric Lesser, and Annemarie Schober. Ascend the stream that drains Erin Lake from Rock Creek. Before arriving at Erin Lake, turn right (north) and ascend slabs and talus to the broad southeast ridge. Follow the ridge to the summit, but traverse slightly towards a saddle after crossing a plateau at about 3900 meters (12,800 feet).

Southeast Slopes. Class 2 from Primrose Lake.

East Slope. Class 2. From Sky Blue Lake hike to the highest small lake to the west, then climb to the saddle east of Mount Pickering. Climb the slope to the summit.

The Miter   3880 m+; 12,770 ft

Southeast Face. Class 3–4. First ascent July 18, 1938 by Sam Fink. From Iridescent Lake or Sky Blue Lake, scramble to the notch immediately south of The Miter's twin summits. Climb over flakes to a large platform, then traverse right (northeast) across small cracks on the exposed slabs to a shallow chute that heads left (northwest) to the top of an arête. Follow the arête to the buttress of the south summit. Work up ledges and chimneys on the southeast face of the buttress to the south summit. The traverse to the higher north summit is easy class 3, with the low point of the notch between the two summits being reached by crawling to the right (east) of a large boulder.

The northwest chute of the north summit has been reported as being class 3.

North Ridge. II, 5.9. First ascent September 1979 by Claude Fiddler and Vern Clevenger.

Mount Corcoran   4180 m+; 13,760 ft+; UTM 882442

There has been considerable discussion as to which of the four summits of this peak is the actual high point. The true summit is immediately south of the prominent notch between Mount Corcoran and Mount LeConte. Mount Corcoran has also been called "Comb Ridge."

North Notch from the West. Class 2–3. First ascent 1933 by Howard S. Gates. From Iridescent Lake, climb the chute leading to the notch north of Mount Corcoran. This chute divides twice near the top; take the right branch both times. The north notch is reached after passing under a huge chockstone. Traverse south 150 feet on ledges west of the crest and then climb a chute that leads to the summit area. There is much loose rock on this route.

North Notch from the East. Class 2–3. First ascent 1958 by Carl Heller. From 11,200 feet on the south fork of Tuttle Creek, climb slabs leading to a canyon to the northwest. Stay high and well to the north to avoid talus, and move into the northernmost of two basins at the head of the canyon. Climb the broad chute leading to the notch between Mount LeConte and Mount Corcoran. Just below the crest, turn to the south (left) and climb a short pitch with a small chockstone to the top of the crest. Traverse south 150 feet on ledges on the west side of the crest, then climb a chute leading to the summit.

Traverse from Mount LeConte. Class 3. A traverse from Mount LeConte to Mount Corcoran has been done, but it requires skilled routefinding. Descend the Northwest Chute of Mount LeConte to a ledge that is 50 feet above the top of the Waterfall Pitch. Traverse south 50 feet on this ledge into the next chute. Descend about 150 feet in this chute, then traverse south on ledges, descending slightly and crossing two ribs to the chute leading to the notch between Mount LeConte and Mount Corcoran.

A common mistake made on this traverse is staying too high after leaving the top of the Waterfall Pitch. This could lead a peak bagger into big air!

Northeast Face. IV, 5.10, A2. This route starts in a crack system to the right of the buttress.

Sharktooth, Southeast Face. II, 5.7. First ascent May 2,

Russell-Carillon Pass from the east. Photo by Austin Post, No. 72R2-195, USGS Ice and Climate Project, GeoData Center, University of Alaska, Fairbanks.

1972 by Hooman Aprin and Fred Beckey. Sharktooth is the sharp peak (Peak 4160m+) south of the high point of Mount Corcoran. This climb has been described as having a number of class 4 and class 5 leads. The route begins at the base of Mount Corcoran and climbs a giant dihedral on Sharktooth itself.

There is also a 5.5 route on the right side of the upper southeast face of Sharktooth.

South Face. IV, 5.10a. First ascent July 4, 1998 by Bart O'Brien and David Harden. This route is on the south face of Peak 4151 m, the southernmost summit of Mount Corcoran. The route starts by climbing a 5.8 chimney

Mount LeConte and Mount Corcoran from the northwest. Photo by R. J. Secor.

at the far, right-hand edge of the south face. Overcome a 5.9 roof at the top of the chimney, where some ledges lead north. Instead of following the ledges, continue straight up a difficult face to a right-facing open book and some blocky ledges to a 5.10a finger crack, ending at a ledge. Traverse up and right to the base of two parallel cracks. Jam up the right crack for about 70 feet until it is possible to move left into the left crack and pull over a difficult ceiling (5.10a). A short stretch of strenuous climbing leads to easier going and an extensive south-facing ledge system (5.10) ending at the base of an ominous, flared, off-width dihedral. Avoid this dihedral by traversing to the left 200 feet and up 40 feet to a flat, exposed ledge. Drop down from the ledge and then face climb to the right and then up large blocks to a small,

steep left-facing inside corner (5.8). Face climb up and right and then make a hand traverse to the left to a thin 5.10a left-facing inside corner that leads up and left to a chimney. Climb the chimney (5.9) and then go up and left (5.7) before climbing up and right to the third ledge. A 5.8 hand crack in a left-facing inside corner ends on a ledge, followed by a couple hundred feet of class 3 and 4 climbing to the summit.

South Ridge. Class 4. This is a traverse of the four main summits of Mount Corcoran. Peak 4151m was first climbed July 20, 1938, from Tuttle Pass by Sam Fink. The complete traverse of the four summits was done by Galen Rowell in August 1970. The two southern summits are class 2 from Tuttle Pass. Sharktooth is class 4 on its west side. From the saddle south of

Sharktooth, descend about 300 feet on the west side of the crest, then traverse north across class 4 rock to the chute leading to the summit area.

Mount LeConte   4246 m; 13,960 ft+; UTM 880446

There is a large plateau between Mount LeConte and Mount Mallory. It can be reached from upper Meysan Lake by climbing a loose, narrow chute that leads to a point on the plateau between these two peaks, or by traversing southwest from Mount Mallory. A large cairn has been built on top of the plateau at the base of the north face of Mount LeConte. This landmark serves as the starting point for four of the routes described here.

Northwest Chute. Class 3. First ascent June 1935 by Norman Clyde. This route has been referred to as the "Northwest Ridge," which is not exactly correct. From the plateau between Mount LeConte and Mount Mallory, follow the ridge to the base of the cliffs of Mount LeConte. Descend 100 feet in elevation on the west side of the cliffs and climb the chute on the northwest side of Mount LeConte. A 15-foot class 3 pitch is soon encountered. In early season it may be covered

with running water and/or verglas, and it is commonly referred to as the Waterfall Pitch. Continue scrambling up the chute to the summit.

Northwest Ridge. Class 4. First ascent August 1994 by Bob Sumner. From the cairn at the base of the north face, traverse to the right on ledges, crossing the crest of the northwest ridge to where the ledges end, dropping only 10 to 20 feet. Climb up for 15 feet (class 3), and then drop down onto another ledge. A short (12-foot) class 4 down climb leads to another ledge, followed by another short class 3 down climb. These lead to a ledge that leads into the upper Northwest Chute, above the level of the Waterfall Pitch.

North Face. I, 5.3. First ascent August 29, 1971 by Carl Heller and Bill Stronge. This route follows cracks directly above the large cairn at the base of the north face of Mount LeConte.

Northeast Face. Class 4. First ascent September 7, 1952 by Steve Wilkie, Barbara Lilley, Wes Cowan, George Wallerstein, and June Kilbourne. From the cairn at the base of the north face, traverse east along an easy but exposed ledge for 400 feet to an area of vertical cracks

Mount LeConte and Mount Corcoran from the west.

and small ledges; this is the first break in the otherwise smooth face. Approximately 200 feet of exposed class 4 leads to the summit.

East Arête. Class 3. First ascent June 12, 1937 by Gary Leech, Smoke Blanchard, and Hubert North. Go to the left and up from the area of small cracks and ledges of the Northeast Face route and across a rib to a chute. Leave the chute near the summit, then finish the climb via the East Arête. This route is less exposed than the Northeast Face.

Southwest Ridge. II, 5.6. First ascent August 1970 by Galen Rowell. From the notch north of Mount Corcoran, follow the ridge to the summit of Mount LeConte.

Further Reading: John Moynier and Claude Fiddler. Sierra Classics. Evergreen, Colo.: Chockstone Press, 1993, pp. 26–27.

Traverse from Mount Corcoran. Class 3. First ascent July 15, 1973 by a party led by Ed Treacy. From the notch north of Mount Corcoran, descend the chute on the west side of the crest for approximately 250 feet. Traverse across the west side of Mount LeConte, ascending slightly and crossing two ridges, to a large couloir. Ascend the couloir about 150 feet to a ledge leading left

Mount Corcoran and Mount LeConte from the east. Photo by R. J. Secor.

Sharktooth

MOUNT CORCORAN

North
Notch

MOUNT LeCONTE

Mount LeConte, North Face. Photo by R. J. Secor.

(north). This ledge ends after 50 feet at a point above the Waterfall Pitch of the Northwest Chute route. Scramble another 300 to 400 feet from there to the summit.

West Couloir. Class 3. First ascent July 17, 1936 by Oliver Kehrlein, Tyler Van Degrift, and Chester Versteeg. A large couloir descends the west side of Mount LeConte to a point just north of Iridescent Lake. Ascend the couloir to the ledge that leads left (north) to a point above the level of the Waterfall Pitch of the Northwest Chute route.

Peak 3925m   12,880 ft+;
1.5 mi SSW of Lone Pine Peak

Southwest Slopes. Class 2. First ascent September 24, 1967 by Ed Lane and Alice Lewis.

West Ridge. Class 4. First ascent August 1970 by Galen Rowell. There is a lot of loose rock on this ridge.

"Tuttle Obelisk"   UTM 905440

This is the striking white tower near the head of the south fork of Tuttle Creek.

Rowell-Jones Route. III, 5.9. First ascent April 1970 by Chris Jones and Galen Rowell. This route begins in a dihedral directly beneath the summit on the obelisk's south side. The first pitch is a 5.9 crack; it is followed by four more pitches of 5.5–5.7. The final pitch dead-ends against the summit block; a hand traverse to the right leads to a ledge that provides access to the top.

School's Out. III, 5.9. First ascent June 1979 by Brent Norum and Alan Bartlett. This route starts a few hundred feet to the right of the Rowell-Jones Route. Climb a right-slanting ramp 200 feet to the base of a large corner. Two pitches up the corner lead to a huge ledge. Climb to the right up a curving crack to the final pitch of the Rowell-Jones Route.

"The Keyhole Wall"   UTM 920445

This nice cliff has also been called "The Keystone," after the formation in the middle of the face with two facing dihedrals that lead up to an overhang at its apex. It is southeast of Point 3233m (10,067 ft).

Saumnambulist. II, 5.8+. First ascent 1980 by Dick Saum, Herb Laeger, and Eve Laeger. This route climbs the left side of The Keyhole Wall. The first pitch consists

Bushmaster

Master
Key

The
Keystone

Clean
Willy's
Escape

Saumnambulist

Yellow Face

Pass Key

The
Locksmith
Route

of a fine 5.7 hand crack that breaks a small roof. The crux is not the roof but some face moves later near the end of the climb. The climb ends on a ledge that leads left to a large inside corner, where rappels lead to the ground.

Master Key. II, 5.8. First ascent July 1984 by Greg Vernon, Herb Laeger, and Jim Murray. This three-pitch route climbs cracks that are about 200 feet left of The Locksmith Route. The route begins with 5.8 moves up a fist crack, followed by 5.7 climbing up cracks to a large water groove. Continue climbing the groove; the crux is passing some vegetation on the second pitch. The climb ends with an easy class 5 third pitch in the groove that leads to some brushy ledges. Traverse right along the ledges and rappel The Locksmith Route.

Bushmaster. II, 5.9. First ascent July 1984 by Greg Vernon, Herb Laeger, and Jim Murray. This route is immediately right of the Master Key route. Begin by climbing the 5.8 fist crack of Master Key. From the top of this crack, go up and right. Thin face and crack climbing leads past a bush (5.9). Belay from an off-width chimney, then continue up the chimney for another pitch. The third pitch goes up the chimney before moving right and up the face, with excellent holds to a series of brushy ledges. Walk right along the ledges and rappel The Locksmith Route.

The Locksmith Route. III, 5.9. First ascent May 18, 1975 by Fred Beckey and Jack Roberts. This route has finger jams, cracks, and face-climbing problems. It climbs the left side of The Keystone. The first two pitches are in a white, right-facing open book. The second pitch ends on a ledge with a tree, which is beyond the left side of the open book. The third pitch goes up and right and over some buckets to an off-width chimney, which ends on a brushy ledge with trees. Move to the right a short distance, beyond a dead tree, and rappel the route with two 165-foot rappels. The first rappel ends near the very bottom of the off-width chimney, at the upper left-hand corner of The Keystone. One more rappel leads straight down to the ground.

The Keystone. III, 5.8. First ascent March 1970 by Galen Rowell and Chris Jones. Climb the left-facing dihedral on the right side of The Keystone to its top. The route ends via an off-width chimney on the brushy ledges that mark the top of The Locksmith Route. Move left along the brushy ledges and rappel The Locksmith Route.

Clean Willy's Escape. III, 5.9. First ascent June 1976

by Alan Roberts and Alan Bartlett. This classic route follows the prominent crack-and-chimney system that makes up the right side of The Keystone. Climb the right-facing dihedral (5.8), then a crack that leads out onto the face. Ascend this crack (5.8), followed by some difficult face moves (5.9) beneath an overhang. This leads to a chimney (5.8) that ends on a large brushy ledge with broken rock above. Go left along this ledge and rappel The Locksmith Route.

Pass Key. II, 5.7. First ascent January 15, 1976 by Fred Beckey and Jack Roberts. Climb a short open book, which is 100 yards east of The Locksmith Route, and ascend a continuous crack-and-chimney system to the top of the cliff.

Yellow Face. II, 5.8. First ascent July 16, 1983 by Rich Smith, Eve Laeger, and Herb Laeger. This route is on the far right side of The Keyhole Wall. A yellow face can be seen to the right of a right-facing inside corner. A crack-and-chimney system leads up to this face (5.4). Four pitches on the Yellow Face itself (5.6, 5.8, 5.7, and 5.4, respectively) lead to the top. Climb down a few feet on the left to a tree. Rappel with two ropes from the tree to a large gully. Another long rappel leads to the ground after some down climbing.

Hangin' Out. III, 5.10. First ascent 1980 by Eve Laeger and Herb Laeger. This route climbs the crack near the edge of the east face of The Keyhole Wall (the wall itself faces south). This route is four pitches long, and the first pitch is the crux.

Peak 3985m 12,960 ft+ and 13,016 ft;
1.2 mi SW of Lone Pine Peak

This peak had two different elevations on some editions of the Lone Pine 15-minute map.

East Ridge. Class 2–3 from Lone Pine Peak.

Kearney Route. V, 5.9, A2. First ascent May 1976 by Shari Nelson, Jay Foster, and Alan Kearney. This route ascends a large chimney system just to the right of center on the south face. The climb finishes through a crack system slightly left of the chimney at its end. One bolt was placed during the 2½ days of the first ascent.

Zig-Zag Dihedral. IV, 5.9. First ascent July 22, 1995 by Bruce Bindner and Pat Brennan. This exposed route is between the South Face route and the Kearney chimney system. It starts by ascending 400 to 500 feet of class

The Keyhole Wall. Photo by R. J. Secor.

3 ledges that are to the right of the gully leading to the Red Baron Tower. Ascend the ledges up and right to an easy class 5 left-facing open book that leads to some ledges. The serious climbing begins by ascending Zig-Zag Dihedral, a right-facing open book (5.9, off-width and layback) followed by a class 4 ledge that leads up and left. Next, climb another 5.9 layback, off-width dihedral followed by a chimney and ledge that leads up left to some ledges. The fourth pitch ascends the sustained 5.9, 3- to 5-inch Crescent Crack, followed by 5.9 face climbing that leads up, then left, then up again past a detached flake. Climb a chimney with a chockstone that leads to a 5.9 face, followed by a right-facing open book. Climb the open book (5.8), then a chimney to a large ledge (the South Face route comes in from the left at this ledge). About 200 feet of 5.4 leads up and right to a big ledge, where the Kearney Route comes in from the right. A 5.6 crack and face then lead up and right to a loose class 4 chimney. Climb the chimney to a ledge and then ascend 5.7 cracks that are to the right of the chimney. Approximately 200 feet of class 3 and 4 leads up and right, followed by 400 feet of specimen class 2 to the top of the face. Protection to 5 inches is needed.

Red Baron Tower. III, 5.7, A2 or 5.10a. First ascent May 19, 1972 by Fred Beckey and Barry Hagen. First free ascent August 1996 by Bruce Bindner and Pat Brennan. This route is to the right of the South Face route, and ends atop a flat platform. Two aid pitches lead to interesting free climbing along a buttress to the platform.

South Face. V, 5.8, A2. First ascent May 1970 by Chris Jones, Joe Faint, and Galen Rowell. This route begins by climbing a ramp that leads to the left from the center of the south face. From the ramp, there are two short aid sections on this otherwise free climb. At one point it is necessary to traverse to avoid an area of rotten rock. You come to a pillar just below the final summit wall. Rappel to the right to a ledge. The climb finishes by ascending the right side of the face. The first ascent took 1½ days.

West Ridge. Class 4. First ascent 1988 by Marty Hornick. There is a lot of loose rock on this ridge.

Lone Pine Peak   3945 m; 12,944 ft

This is an impressive peak when viewed from Lone Pine. The north ridge is a striking sight to the mountain-eer, and rock climbers are intrigued by the mile-wide, 3,000-foot-high big wall on the peak's south face.

From Meysan Creek. Class 2. First ascent July 1947 by Murray Bruch and Fred Johnson. First winter ascent January 17, 1971 by Bob Boyles, Roy Keenan, and Frank Snively. Climb a chute filled with sand, scree, and talus on the northwest slope of the peak; the left side of this chute is mostly composed of talus, and this is the preferred route of ascent. Walk northeast across the summit plateau to the summit.

North Ridge. III, 5.4. First ascent September 1952 by Art Lembeck and Ray Van Aken. This is an interesting, lengthy, and not too difficult route.

Hike up the Meysan Lake Trail to just below Little Meysan Lake, leaving the trail at the 9,400-foot level. Cross Meysan Creek, then climb up and left along a series of ledges and boulders until the crest of the north ridge is reached. Follow the ridge upward, pass through a small notch on the crest, and drop to the left (east) for 100 feet to a gully at the base of the First Tower. Climb the gully for 75 feet and move right to the top of the ridge. Follow the crest of the ridge to an overhanging headwall, which is passed (5.2) via a small gully on the left. This is soon followed by another headwall, which is climbed via an open book (5.4) on the left. Climb cracks and small ledges to the top of the First Tower. Cross over to the south side of the tower and follow a contouring ledge system to some sandy ledges that overlook a deep chute at the base of the Second Tower. This is followed by another class 4 ledge system to an area of polished rock. Climb a gully (5.2) that rises to the right. From the top of the gully, go left and up (5.4). A 300-foot class 3 traverse follows, and leads to a steep chute at the base of the summit headwall. Climb the headwall to a notch on the ridge crest. From this notch, a ledge system contours across the north side of the headwall past the bottom of a large chute (loose rock!) to a small buttress. Climb the buttress (class 3), which forms the right side of the loose chute, and after about 400 feet move left into the chute. Follow the chute up over rock and sandy class 3 ledges and boulders to the summit. *Variation:* First ascent July 12, 1986 by Dick Beach and Bob Good. Instead of approaching the north ridge via the Meysan Lake Trail, leave Whitney Portal Road at an elevation of 6,200 feet (where it begins the steep climb to Whitney Portal). Follow the ridge up from the base in

Mount LeConte, Mount Corcoran, and Vicinity

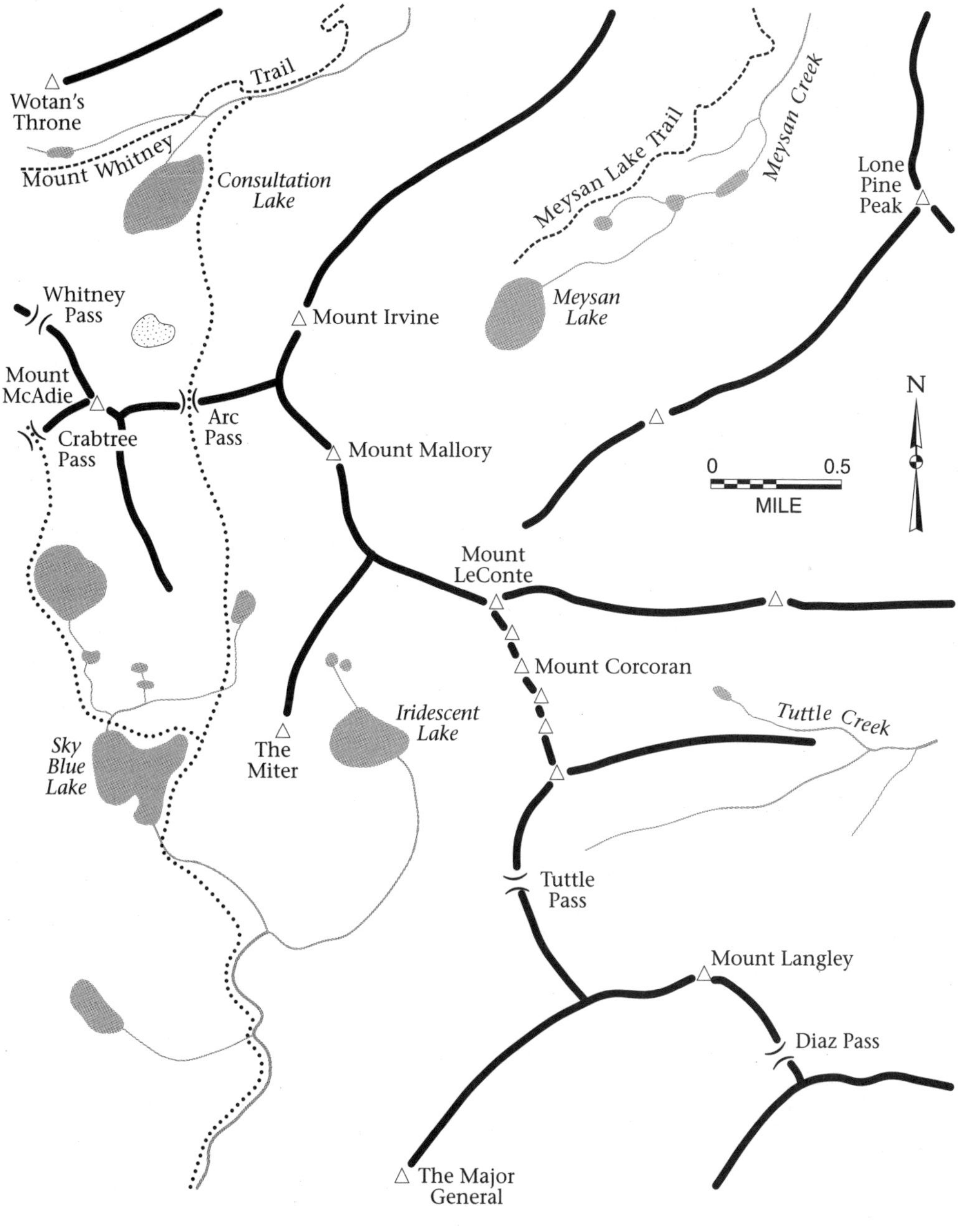

Wotan's
Throne

Trail

Mount Whitney

Consultation
Lake

Meysan Lake Trail

Meysan Creek

Lone
Pine
Peak

Whitney
Pass

△ Mount Irvine

Meysan
Lake

Mount
McAdie

Arc
Pass

Crabtree
Pass

△ Mount Mallory

N

0   0.5

MILE

Mount
LeConte

△ Mount Corcoran

Sky
Blue
Lake

The
Miter

Iridescent
Lake

Tuttle Creek

Tuttle
Pass

Mount Langley

Diaz Pass

△ The Major
General

the Owens Valley, staying to the east side of the ridge near the top. At a large, ball-shaped boulder, cross to the west side of the ridge at a notch to a system of ledges. Class 3 steps lead down to a ledge with a lone pine tree. Another 1,000 feet of scrambling lead to the small notch near the base of the First Tower, where the real climbing begins. This variation involves over 7,000 feet of gain. Incredibly, it was climbed in 1 day on the first ascent. *Variation:* Class 4. First ascent June 23, 1973 by Bill Stronge, Al Greene, Bill Sweatt, and Scott Charlton. Climb toward the north ridge from the Meysan Lake Trail approach. Before reaching the ridge, however, turn right and go around a brushy slope to an arête leading to the notch in the ridge at the base of the summit headwall.

Further Reading: *Rock & Ice.* No. 56 (July–August 1993), p. 128; John Moynier and Claude Fiddler. *Sierra Classics.* Evergreen, Colo.: Chockstone Press, 1993, pp. 33–35.

Bastille Buttress. V, 5.8, A3. First ascent April 1969 by Fred Beckey, Joe Brown, and Chuck Haas. This 2,000-foot buttress is in the Inyo Creek drainage, and it ends at an elevation of 10,500 feet on the north ridge of Lone Pine Peak. This is a deceiving, complex, and difficult route with an arduous approach. The best approach begins along the Meysan Lake Trail. Leave the trail at the 8,400-foot level, cross Meysan Creek, and contour around the lower north ridge of Lone Pine Peak to Inyo Creek.

Begin by scrambling up a gully on the right side of the buttress, then go up and left to a ledge that is 50 feet above the toe of the buttress. The first roped pitch goes up a crack past a small tree to a larger belay tree, and is followed by a short, easy pitch to a big ledge. Climb the face, which is to the left of a left-facing open book, to belay from a flake beneath a roof. Pass the roof on the right, where easy face climbing leads to a belay beneath a large black knob. Climb up and right to a crack, which leads up and left, then face climb up and right to a crack that leads to a small ledge. Another poorly protected pitch then ascends a crack up and right to a belay from the face beneath another large black knob. A bat-hook-and-bolt ladder section follows, and then a lonely 175-foot crack (A1) on the prow of the buttress ends at the bottom of a deep, strenuous chimney. From the top of the chimney, the crux consists of two flared, overhanging pitches of aid and free climbing, which go up and left before

moving right to an exposed outside corner. Continue up this edge to some overhanging flakes, which are bypassed on the left with a tension traverse and friction. Climb straight up before traversing left to a bolt on a sharp outside corner, and climb straight up again to the bottom of a chimney. From the top of this chimney, face climb up and left (passing several bolts and a shallow trough) to a belay tree. This is followed by a class 4 tunnel that ends atop a large ledge. Go to the left side of the ledge. An aid move off a bolt leads to some free climbing. Move up and left, passing several more bolts, to another large ledge. Class 3 leads to the last roped pitch: a crack that leads to the crest of the north ridge of Lone Pine Peak.

The gully to the north of the buttress may be followed for descent, or the north ridge of Lone Pine Peak may be descended back to the Meysan Lake Trail.

Further Reading: *Summit.* April 1972, pp. 2–5; *Summit.* November–December 1983, pp. 12–13.

Northeast Face. Class 4, A0. First ascent July 1952 by Warren Harding. Hike up Inyo Creek to the headwall immediately beneath the summit of Lone Pine Peak. Climb onto the headwall until about 400 feet below the summit. Rappel 200 feet to the next chute south, and ascend this chute to the summit.

Northeast Ridge. IV, 5.7. First ascent July 10–11, 1982 by Phil Warrender and Gary Valle. First winter ascent March 9–10, 1994 by Alois Smrz and Rich Henke. This is the first major ridge to the left of the north ridge of Lone Pine Peak. The ridge is well over 3 miles long and more than 6,900 feet high, with many short to long technical pitches. Follow the crest of the ridge from the Owens Valley, then bypass the First Tower mostly on its north side (5.7) and bypass the Second Tower on its south side (5.5). After fourteen pitches, leave the crest beneath the final headwall, then traverse right several hundred yards to a gully that leads to the summit plateau.

East Ridge. First ascent in the early 1980s by Dave Krueger.

Further Reading: John Moynier and Claude Fiddler. *Sierra Classics.* Evergreen, Colo.: Chockstone Press, 1993, p. 34.

Three Arrows. III, 5.9, A2. First ascent April 1976 by Randy Grandstaff, Hooman Aprin, and Fred Beckey. This route climbs to a sharp rock crest on the east side of Lone Pine Peak. The summit of this formation, as seen from Lone Pine, looks like a collection of arrows. The

Lone Pine Peak from the east. Photo by R. J. Secor.

route involves first climbing a southeast-facing trough/dihedral, then a deep, difficult chimney. There are two short aid sections, and three bolts were placed on the first ascent.

Southeast Slopes. Class 2. First ascent 1925 by Norman Clyde. Go northwest from the Tuttle Creek trailhead, cross the creek, and climb to the saddle behind Point 2480m+ (8,080 ft+; UTM 933462). Pass through the saddle and climb up a gully that leads northwest and then west up to the eastern edge of the huge plateau south of the summit of Lone Pine Peak.

Southeast Slopes, Descent Route. Class 2. Head east along the summit plateau towards a large rocky knob. Skirt this on its left (north) side and descend towards the sharp East Ridge of Lone Pine Peak to a gully. Descend the gully between the East Ridge on the left and a steep area on the right (looking down). When below the level of the steep area, make a sharp turn to the right and continue down the gully until an obvious hill with a saddle to its left becomes visible. Cross the saddle and descend steep gullies and slopes down to Tuttle Creek.

Autumn Ledges. III, 5.8. First ascent October 4, 1997 by Jon Stark, Craig Morris, and Larry Cote. This route ascends the left side of the prominent orange face of the Club Alpin Français Route, marked by a deep, left-facing corner system above a series of ledges. Climb the right fork of the Winter Route to the bottom of the ledges. A pitch of 5.4 leads to a ledge with a symmetrical fir tree. Go directly up from the Fir Tree Ledge on a 5.7 face with flaring cracks to a small ledge. Climb to another small ledge 75 feet above. Move to the left from this ledge and climb to the end of a series of flaring cracks, followed by a 5.8 face move to the main ledge system. Climb the ledges to the bottom of the left-facing corners. Eight more pitches up these corners, with knobs, pockets, and perfect hand cracks lead to the top. The route ends approximately 200 yards from the descent route down the eastern slope.

Lone Pine Peak, South Face. Photo by R. J. Secor.

Club Alpin Français Route. IV, 5.9, A1. First ascent July 13, 1973 by Henri Agresti and Tom Birtley. The east side of the south face of Lone Pine Peak features some brush-covered ledges. This route scrambles up to the left of these ledges to a huge ledge visible from below. From the huge ledge, follow the ridge above the left corner of the ledge and descend from a small notch to the next chute to the left. Climb the chute for 300 feet, and then ascend the ridge to the right of the chute for the remaining fourteen pitches to the summit plateau. The first overhang is turned by its left chimney (5.7), the second and third overhangs are bypassed to the left (A1 both times), and the fourth overhang is avoided by traversing right (5.6) and then up a chimney (5.9).

Dynamo-Hum. IV, 5.10+. First ascent November 1978 by Dick Swindon and Jack Roberts. This is the huge right-facing dihedral to the left of the Club Alpin Français Route on the proper south face of Lone Pine Creek. Climb the dihedral for three 5.10 pitches and turn the roof atop the dihedral to the left. Follow the upper crack system for four pitches. Above these cracks, follow a line of small, right-facing cracks to the top.

Czech Pillar. IV, 5.9. First ascent June 27, 1998 by Miguel Carmona and Alois Smrz. Ascend the drainage to the right of the Winter Route to the base of the orange face marking the start of the Club Alpin Français and Autumn Ledges Routes. Follow the gully to the left, passing the right-facing dihedral of Dynamo-Hum, to a notch. From the notch, climb three pitches (to 5.7) up a pedestal below a right-facing inside corner. At the base of the corner, pass underneath a block (5.6), then climb a steep, strenuous pitch up the corner (5.9). Continue up the corner, climbing under a large flake. At the top, move to the right along a sloping ledge to a belay stance. Move 20 feet to the right to reach a crack system on a steep orange wall. Follow the crack system to the top.

Winter Route. IV, 5.7. First ascent March 1970 by Chris Jones and Galen Rowell. Climb the prominent chute that ascends diagonally from right to left across the south face of Lone Pine Peak. After 1,000 vertical feet, take the left fork and climb a narrow gully with slabs, ending at a notch. Rappel (or down climb) 60 feet down the other side of the notch to a ledge. Continue to the top via the last six pitches of the Direct South Face.

Summer Ridge Route. V, 5.9. First ascent September 1994 by Bruce Bindner and Patrick Brennan. This route starts by ascending the Winter Route for one and a half pitches and then follows the gully on the left side of the serrated ridge. Continue up, eventually climbing on both sides of the ridge, following the easiest way. After seventeen pitches, rejoin the Winter Route at the notch, rappel down the other side, and then follow the last six pitches of the Direct South Face to the top.

Land of Little Rain. V, 5.10c. First ascent June 22–24, 1996 by Miguel Carmona, Jim Mathews, and Alois Smrz. This route ascends the steep, smooth wall in the middle of the south face of Lone Pine Peak. There are three distinct horizontal ledges that run across the lowest part of this wall. Stay on the south side of the canyon from the stone house, keeping at the same level (more or less) as the house, to the base of the wall. Contour toward the creek and find a large, flat boulder at the creek's edge (last water). From the boulder, scramble up a wide slope and go diagonal left to a gully that continues up and left, passing through a large cave, to the first ledge. Go left and up to the second ledge. Follow the second ledge to the far right to a smooth gully. Climb this gully (5.7, fixed pin), and traverse up and left to the third ledge. Cross this ledge system diagonally from right to left to the base of a left-facing, curved, open book. After 1,400 vertical feet of gain from the creek, the real climbing begins.

Easy class 5 climbing leads to the steep, intimidating crack in the open book. Some wide stemming maneuvers (5.10b) lead to the first roof. Traverse horizontally left under this roof and then follow a faint rib up past two bolts to a belay stance (5.9) below the second roof. Climb the left edge of the roof, and then go slightly to the right to meet a hand crack leading to a large ledge (5.9). Move to the left end of the ledge and climb a spectacular, but shallow, 5.10c thin crack/dihedral, followed by a traverse up and right to a large roof; climb up and right to the right edge of the roof that leads to a two-bolt belay stance. The next pitch continues straight up past two bolts and then moves up and left to another two-bolt belay stance beneath three distinct ribs (5.10b). Climb the ribs (5.7), then head up and right to the base of a broken, left-facing dihedral (5.7). The next three pitches go up and left through a sea of pockets (5.4 to 5.7, poorly protected, but easy) to a large ledge (good bivouac site). Follow the prominent left-leaning crack, then face climb (5.7) to an obvious notch on the ridge above, which is the Summer Ridge. Continue up the ridge for five exposed pitches (up to 5.7) to the notch of the Winter Route. Either rappel or down climb the notch (60 feet) to a sandy ledge. Follow the ledge left to a class 4 chimney and gully. From the top of the gully a 5.7 face leads up and left to a broken buttress. Two pitches on the buttress lead to a notch, followed by 300 feet of class 4 to the summit plateau.

Direct South Face. V, 5.7, A0 or 5.9. First ascent May 1970 by Eric Bjornstad and Fred Beckey. First winter ascent March 13–14, 1993 by Alois Smrz and Peter Green. Most of this route is moderate class 5 (5.4 to 5.5), with three leads of 5.7 and a simple tension traverse which goes free at 5.9. It is a great test piece for the recreational climber who wants to apply his or her crag skills on a wilderness big wall. There are many bivouac ledges, and in early season, snow may be available for water.

The route begins about 1 mile upstream from the stone house of Tuttle Creek at the 9,200-foot level. Climb a large, 1,000-foot-long chute, which leads up and right to end behind a prominent tower. (This chute is behind a small ridge on the west side of the tower.) From the top of this chute, climb a large right-facing dihedral for five pitches (class 4 to 5.7). The route now overlooks a prominent gully, and it stays to the right of this gully for four more pitches until the route goes left across the top of the gully. Climb a left-facing dihedral, and from its top go left to the edge of a broad chute. Class 3 and 4 climbing leads up and left for 500 feet to a smaller gully with a hole at its top. Pass through the eye of the needle to some sandy ledges. Walk right along the ledges for approximately 200 feet to the base of a steep chimney, which leads up to a gully. Start climbing again to the left of this chimney by going up slightly left to a crack, and then belay from some boulders. Continue up the crack, and tension traverse right (the only aid on the route; it goes free at 5.9) to a gully. Climb the ugly right side of the gully and its bad chimney (5.5) for two more pitches and move to the right along a sharp ridge that overlooks a big drop-off. The last pitch starts with a traverse across the face to the right before going up to a crack. *Variation:* 5.7. First ascent February 1984 by Miguel Carmona and Alois Smrz. This variation is preferable if there is a lot of snow on the route. The eye of the needle can be bypassed by climbing straight up from the broad chute. This involves class 3 and 4 climbing that bypasses the huge roofs on their left sides before moving to the right to a sandy ledge (the Winter Route comes in from the right here). Walk up and left for 150 feet to the base of a steep chimney, which leads up to a gully that ends on a ledge. This is followed by a 5.7 rock face (with some laybacks). Then climb up and left to a broken buttress. Two pitches on the buttress (5.6 and 5.8 respectively) lead to a notch, followed by 300 feet of class 4 that end atop the summit plateau. *Variation:* First ascent September 26, 1992 by Peter Green and Alois Smrz. The tension traverse that leads to the ugly, bad gully and chimney can be avoided by means of a hand-jam crack (5.8) that goes up and slightly left from the start of the traverse.

Further Reading: *Summit.* April 1972, pp. 2–5; *Summit.* November–December 1983, pp. 12–13.

South Gully. Class 4. Descended May 1970 by Galen Rowell, Joe Faint, and Chris Jones. There is a break in the cliffs at the western end of the south face of Lone Pine Peak. This has been used as a descent route from the south face, but it is better to descend the east slopes of Lone Pine Peak.

Stonehouse Buttress   2660 m; 8,720 ft+;
1.7 mi ESE of Lone Pine Peak; UTM 931461

This crag is the large formation across Tuttle Creek from the stone house. Warning: The rock on Stonehouse Buttress is loose!

Jeanne Neale Route. IV, 5.8, A2. First ascent March 4, 1972 by Dan Hurd and David Boyd. The name of this route commemorates an unfortunate fall by a young woman on another nearby route during an early attempt. Begin climbing the southeast face of the buttress just left of an obvious, large, triangular flake. Climb a jam crack, which leads to a small flake, then traverse down and right from a bolt, and then climb a crack left of an overhang and dogleg to the right. This first pitch ends at the bottom of a flared, overhanging chimney visible from below. Climb the chimney, using some aid at its top, and belay in slings from a bolt left of the overhang. Mixed climbing goes left and up to a small ledge with a bush. A bolt protects a move to another ledge. Climb to the right to the only comfortable belay on the climb. Traverse right and climb a dihedral with two mixed pitches, and turn the overhang on its left side. Climb the left of two cracks to a dead tree. One more pitch leads to the unroping spot, and a few hundred feet of scrambling leads to the summit of Stonehouse Buttress. The first-ascent party used many big pitons on this climb: four 2-inch, three 2½-inch, two 3-inch, and one 4-inch bong.

Chimney Route. IV, 5.8. First ascent January 1970 by Joe Faint and Galen Rowell. This route starts several hundred feet to the left of the Jeanne Neale Route in a prominent, narrow chimney that curves to the right. After passing some chockstones in the upper part of the chimney, move left onto a steep, crackless face and climb chickenheads to the summit of the buttress.

Rots of Rock. IV, 5.9, A2. First ascent April 1987 by Sam Roberts and Mark Bowling. This route is to the right of Milky Way Chimney. Begin by cimbing a moderate (5.7) crack to an alcove. Move left from the alcove and climb a mixed pitch up a thin, overhanging crack, and continue over lower-angled broken rock. This is followed by a steep, knobby wall (5.8) and up a groove of decomposing rock. The groove is followed by a chimney and then several easy pitches to the summit.

Milky Way Chimney. IV, 5.10+. First ascent April 29, 1973 by Jack Roberts, Hooman Aprin, and Fred Beckey. First free ascent May 10, 1980 by Herb Laeger, Eve Laeger, and Mike Jaffe. This is the main left chimney on Stonehouse Buttress. Follow the Chimney Route for two and a half pitches, to the bottom of the narrow chimney. Climb a crack that leads up and left into the main left chimney. Leave the chimney on the left side, then ascend the corner of the buttress.

STONEHOUSE BUTTRESS

Milky Way
Chimney

Chimney
Route

Stonehouse Buttress. Photo by R. J. Secor.

Mount Mallory   4220 m; 13,850 ft

East Slopes. Class 2. Climb an obvious chute that is south of the east ridge of Mount Mallory. This chute leads to the plateau southeast of the peak. *Variation:* Class 2. The plateau can be reached from Tuttle Creek by climbing to the saddle between Mount LeConte and Peak 3925m (12,880 ft+). This is more difficult than the approach from Meysan Lake.

West Slope. Class 2. From the basin south of Arc Pass, climb a chute that leads to the plateau southeast of the peak. A landmark for this chute is a prominent peak on the western edge of the plateau. The chute ends to the north of this prominent peak.

From Arc Pass. Class 2. First ascent July 18, 1936 by Oliver Kehrlein, Chester Versteeg, and Tyler Van Degrift. Climb a broad chute from Arc Pass to the ridge between Mount Mallory and Mount Irvine. Head southeast from the ridge and traverse around the upper part of Mount Mallory's east ridge to the plateau southeast of the summit.

Traverse from Mount Irvine. Class 2. First ascent June 1925 by Norman Clyde. From Mount Irvine, traverse around the upper reaches of the east ridge of Mount Mallory, then hike up the plateau to the summit. *Variation:* Class 3. The ridge between Mount Irvine and Mount Mallory can also be followed. But it is first necessary to descend the east slope of Mount Irvine before climbing to the saddle between the two peaks. The ascent of the ridge leading to Mount Mallory involves squeezing through a tight chimney and a passage through a keyhole.

Mount Irvine   4200 m+; 13,770 ft

From Arc Pass. Class 1. First ascent June 1925 by Norman Clyde. Climb the broad chute leading to the ridge between Mount Irvine and Mount Mallory. Cross

Mount Mallory and Mount Irvine from the east. Photo by R. J. Secor.

the ridge and descend slightly on its east side. Climb to the summit via the easy southeast slope.

West Face. Class 2–3. First ascent 1957 by Charles House. Ascend the fourth chute south of Consultation Lake. Be forewarned: As a descent route, this chute is impossible to find from the summit of Mount Irvine.

North Slopes. Class 1. First ascent May 20, 1995 by Tom Sexton and Bob Rockwell. Leave the Mount Whitney Trail at Bighorn Park and head south onto the big slope leading up to the northeast ridge of Mount Irvine. Go to the left at the top of the slope and climb a loose chute ending on top of the ridge. Follow the northeast ridge to the summit.

East Buttress. V, 5.9. First ascent September 5, 1971 by Bill Stronge and Arold Green. This seventeen-pitch route starts in a dark chimney just to the right of the toe of the buttress. Bypass the towers on the buttress on their right sides until confronted by a wall after ten or eleven pitches. Down-climb or rappel 40 feet to a bowling-pin blade of rock and a ledge on the right. Climb the crack at the left corner of the ledge. This crack consists of 30 feet of 5.9, followed by a 20-foot rising traverse across the face to the right (5.8+). The next two pitches also feature several 5.9 sections followed by a pitch through big blocks that ends on the left side of the buttress with a bivouac spot nearby. Above the bivy, 60 feet of 5.8 crack climbing followed by left trending, loose face climbing leads to a notch in the buttress and easier climbing over blocks and short traverses, passing between small towers. The final tower is climbed on its right side. Several hundred feet of class 4 is followed by a scramble to the distant summit.

East Couloir. Class 4. First ascent 1969 by John

Mendenhall and Bill Dixon. This couloir is to the south of the East Buttress.

East Chute. Class 2. Climb the chute north of the east ridge of Mount Mallory from Meysan Lake.

Traverse from Mount Mallory. Class 2. Descend the east ridge of Mount Mallory until it is possible to descend to the north into the bowl that is east of Mount Irvine. Then ascend the southeast slope to the summit. *Variation:* Class 3. The ridge between Mount Irvine and Mount Mallory can also be followed. Good class 3 rock leads down the northwest ridge of Mount Mallory, squeezing through a tight chimney and passing through a keyhole to the saddle beneath Mount Irvine. Descend into the bowl east of Mount Irvine before climbing the southeast slope to the summit.

Mount McAdie   4206 m; 13,680 ft+
The north peak is the high point.

From Arc Pass. Class 3. First ascent 1922 by Norman Clyde. Ascend the obvious chute leading to the middle peak from Arc Pass. Just before reaching the summit of the middle peak, traverse right (north) through or around a tunnel formed by a leaning slab. Climb up and then down in one of the two class 3 chimneys to a ledge that overlooks the breathtaking notch between the north and middle peaks. Descend the exposed class 3 northwest face of the middle peak for approximately 100 feet, to a point just below the notch. Climb up to the notch, over a rock outcrop, and climb out of the notch (class 3) by traversing upward around the southwest shoulder of the north peak for 50 feet to a horizontal ledge. Traverse across the ledge for 150 feet to the west side of the north peak. Scramble directly up to the summit from here.

Further Reading: John Moynier and Claude Fiddler. *Sierra Classics.* Evergreen, Colo.: Chockstone Press, 1993, pp. 28–29.

West Face. Class 4. First ascent July 1954 by Jim Koontz, Hervey Voge, Norv LeVene, Claire Millikan, Mike Loughman, Ro Lenel, and Bent Graust. This route has much loose rock. It climbs the rock rib north of the chute that leads to the notch between the middle and north peaks, and ends atop the north peak.

Northeast Face. III, class 5. First ascent July 1978 by Mike Daugherty, Jeff Lee, and Woody Stark. From Consultation Lake, traverse from the east (class 4) into a recess below a bowl on the northeast face. Climb class 3

and 4 rock to the bowl. Exit the bowl to the left and climb directly up for two and a half pitches. After gaining the east buttress, climb to the summit on the north side of the east buttress.

Middle Peak. Class 2. First ascent June 1928 by Norman Clyde. This is a simple scramble from Arc Pass.

South Peak. Class 2. First ascent June 12, 1936 by Oliver Kehrlein, Chester Versteeg, and Tyler Van Degrift. Climb a chute on the southeast side of the peak to the summit.

The middle and south peaks of Mount McAdie are connected by a class 3 ridge.

Mount Newcomb   4091 m; 13,410 ft
Southwest Slopes. Class 2. First ascent August 1936 by Max Eckenburg and Bob Rumohr. This is a simple ascent from the upper reaches of Perrin Creek.

Southwest Ridge. Class 3. First ascent August 18, 1956 by George O. Hale. This is the ridge between Mount Newcomb and Mount Chamberlin. The saddle between the two peaks can be reached from the upper Crabtree Lake via class 2 ledges. When traversing between these two peaks, the knife edge crest of the ridge can be bypassed by dropping down the southern side of the ridge to a sandy ledge system at the 12,400-foot level.

Northeast Ridge. Class 3. Either follow the ridge from Crabtree Pass or ascend directly to the ridge from the uppermost lake in the Crabtree Creek drainage.

South Ridge from Mount Pickering. Class 3. Stay on the west side of the ridge when descending from Mount Pickering.

Mount Chamberlin   4014 m; 13,169 ft
East Ridge from Mount Newcomb. Class 3. Descended August 18, 1956 by George O. Hale. The saddle between Mount Chamberlin and Mount Newcomb can be reached via class 2 ledges from the upper Crabtree Lake. The knife edge ridge crest can be avoided by descending to a sandy ledge system at the 12,400-foot level on the southern side of the ridge.

Eastern Pillar of the North Face. V, 5.11a. First ascent September 1992 by Julie Brugger and Andy de Klerk. This route ascends the dihedral and thin crack system for thirteen pitches. The start is marked by a cairn, with a left-leaning flake above. Climb the right side of the flake, passing over some difficult (to 5.10c) roofs to the large slab that crosses the bottom third of the face. Go up and left across the slab to a right-facing open book. Climb the book (5.10b), pass some loose flakes, and then climb the double dogleg cracks (5.10c) to a ledge that is right of another right-facing dihedral. Go to the right and ascend a crack that turns into a right-facing inside corner for four pitches (to 5.11a). Two more pitches (5.9 and 5.8 respectively) lead to class 3 ledges that lead up and right to the top.

Further Reading: John Moynier and Claude Fiddler. *Sierra Classics*. Evergreen, Colo.: Chockstone Press, 1993, p. 32.

North Face. V, 5.10a, A2 or 5.10d. First ascent August 1983 by Claude Fiddler and Bob Harrington. This route climbs the left-facing dihedral system on the north face of the peak, immediately left of the deep chimney that marks the North Pillar. A crack system (to 5.9) leads up and left for three pitches to the large slab atop the bottom third of the face. Go up and left across the slab (class 4) to a left-facing open book that gradually forms a small, blocky roof (5.9). This is followed by a 5.10a off-width dogleg crack that leads to the big left-facing dihedral in the center of the north face. Climb the dihedral for two pitches (to 5.10d), ending at a ledge after a 5.9 chimney. A 5.8 right-facing dihedral leads up and then right to a set of double cracks. Aid climbing leads up a left-facing open book, followed by a pair of roofs, and another pitch of easy aid to a class 4 section that ends atop the route. Carry large protection. *Variation: Hot Damn!* V, 5.10d. First ascent August 26, 1995 by Pat Brennan and Bruce Bindner. This free variation leaves the Fiddler/Harrington route at the ledge above the big left-facing dihedral in the center of the north face. It starts by climbing the face that is left of the right-facing dihedral. Steep, sustained 5.10d run out face climbing leads up and goes to the right to a small left-facing open book. Continue up the book (5.10b) and then go slightly left up a 5.9 hand crack. Go up a crack and over a roof (5.7) followed by

Mount McAdie from the northeast. Photo by R. J. Secor.

Eastern Pillar

North Face

North Pillar

Mount Chamberlin, North Face. Photo by R. J. Secor.

class 4 to a ledge. The last pitch ascends a 5.7 crack. This is followed by a class 4 chimney to the top. Tiny to 5-inch protection is needed.

Further Reading: John Moynier and Claude Fiddler. *Sierra Classics.* Evergreen, Colo.: Chockstone Press, 1993, pp. 30–33.

North Pillar. V, 5.10. First ascent July 1979 by Galen Rowell and Mike Farrell. This route climbs the single vertical system of cracks that leads directly to the top of the pillar that is about 200 yards to the right of the North Face route. The first-ascent party took 8 hours to climb the thirteen pitches.

South and West Slopes. Class 1–2. The difficulty depends on whether you encounter sand or talus.

"Crabtree Crags"   3946 m; 12,960 ft+;
1.1 mi WNW of Mount Chamberlin

This name refers to the rock faces, arêtes, and buttresses that rise above the Crabtree Lakes to the west of Mount Chamberlin.

Harden-O'Brien Route. III, class 5. First ascent July 1991 by Bart O'Brien and David Harden. This route ascends the wall rising above the largest Crabtree Lake; this wall is located at UTM 822443. The left side of this wall features two wide cracks. Several hundred feet down and to the right of these cracks is a Yosemite-like crack system. Climb this crack system (from fingers to fists in size) to a prominent overhang about 200 feet above the ground. Bypass the overhang on its left side, and continue up loose orange rock to a belay in a chimney at an inside corner. Four more pitches lead directly up to the top.

Mount Hitchcock   4019 m; 13,184 ft

From Discovery Pass. Class 2. This traverse is unique in that it starts at a higher elevation than the peak itself. It has been called a "boulder whack," but some climbers believe that this is preferable to hiking up the sandy slopes south and west of the peak.

Southeast Saddle. Class 2. Descended June 20, 1989 by Tina Stough. Climb loose scree from the upper Hitchcock Lake.

Southwest Slopes. Class 1. Ascend these seemingly interminable sandy slopes from the upper Crabtree Lake.

West Slopes. Class 1. First ascent 1881 by Frederick Wales. From the vicinity of Crabtree Meadow, ascend the west shoulder of the peak and cross the plateau to the summit. These sandy slopes are usually descended by those who reach the summit via Discovery Pass. *Variation:* Class 3. First ascent June 20, 1989 by Tina Stough. Leave the John Muir Trail near Timberline Lake and swing around the lower west shoulder of Mount Hitchcock and climb through a rock band to the sandy west slope.

Northeast Face. Class 4. First ascent 1970 by Vern Clevenger. Climb one of the chutes on this face.

Discovery Pinnacle   4192 m; 13,680 ft

Class 2. First ascent September 19, 1873 by Clarence King and Frank Knowles. This is a simple ascent from Trail Crest or via the south slopes from Crabtree Creek.

Thor Peak   3751 m; 12,300 ft

The southeast face of this peak is a spectacular sight from the Mount Whitney Trail near Bighorn Park.

West Arête. Class 2. Descended September 7, 1936 by

Thor Peak, South Face. Photo by R. J. Secor.

Robert K. Brinton, Glen Dawson, and William Rice. This ridge can be reached from either Pinnacle Pass or direct from Mirror Lake. Approach the summit from the northwest slope. The northwest slope can also be approached directly from Upper Boy Scout Lake.

Southwest Slope. Class 2. First ascent by Norman Clyde. From Mirror Lake, climb ledges north to the sloping, sandy plateau southwest of the summit. Cross a notch south of the summit, traverse to the northeast side, and climb up to the summit.

Mirror Point, West Side. Class 1. Mirror Point is the small, detached pinnacle at the far left side of Thor Peak's southeast face.

Mirror Point, Southeast Face. Class 5. First ascent September 6, 1936 by William Rice and Robert K. Brinton. Climb the talus slope northeast of Mirror Lake to an apron. Climb around the apron to its left, then ascend a series of cracks above. The crux is an overhanging 20-foot crack. The route then gradually works to the left (south).

The Shnahz. I, 5.5. First ascent July 9, 1978 by Scott Anderson and Bob Margulis. This route ascends the southwest buttress of Thor Peak. Begin by climbing a ramp to the right of the buttress. This ramp then angles left and leads to a flake near a black watermark. Climb the crack (5.5) and go up and right to the top of the towers on the crest of the buttress. Climb the left and right sides of the buttress for three more pitches of class 3–4 to the summit.

South Crack. III, 5.9. First ascent July 1962 by Tom Condon and Ron Dickenson. Follow the Mount Whitney Trail above Bighorn Park to the top of the switchbacks. Climb a combination of brush and talus up and to the right. Ascend the crack that separates Mirror Point from Thor Peak. After two pitches, traverse right across a system of ledges. There is a series of cracks above, to the right of the left-hand skyline. Climb the second crack from the left (5.9) to the top of the cliff.

Satan's Delight. Class 5. First ascent September 4, 1937 by Howard Koster, Arthur Johnson, and James N. Smith. From the ledge system of the South Crack route, continue traversing on the ledges to a crack that leads to Pink Perch, a high, red-colored ledge. Descend a crack eastward for approximately 100 feet. A delicate move leads to a vertical crack a few feet out on the face. Climb two pitches up the crack to a shelf behind a gendarme. Go right and make another delicate move for 15 feet where the difficulties ease; this pitch ends after 70 feet.

Climb some fine, high-angle blocks, then traverse left high above Pink Perch. Climb a series of ledges to a recess under the blocks that mark the top of the cliff. This climb ends about 100 feet east of the southeast point of Thor Peak.

Pink Perch. Class 4. Descended September 3, 1940 by Carl Jensen, Howard Koster, Wayland Gilbert, and Elsie Strand. This climb ends atop Pink Perch. Follow the South Crack and Satan's Delight approach routes to the top of the slope of talus and brush. A wide ledge runs across the southeast face of Thor Peak. Follow this ledge for about two-thirds of its length, then climb the steep, narrow gully leading diagonally left across the face to Pink Perch.

Odin's Wrath. III-IV, 5.10d. First ascent September 1996 by Pat Brennan and Eric Tipton. Start by climbing a 5.7 pitch to intersect the gully leading to Pink Perch. The route continues above the gully by climbing right-facing corners. The fifth pitch features a classic 5.10 hand crack, followed by a move to the left on a horizontal break. The seventh pitch, the crux, involves face climbing past two bolts above a crack, followed by three more pitches.

Truncated Buttress. II, 5.7, A1. First ascent May 7, 1972 by William Putnam, Tom Cosgrove, and Fred Beckey. This route begins a few hundred feet northeast of the Pink Perch route. It starts at the highest pine tree and climbs a series of jam cracks (with one aid pitch) to the left of a prominent, broken, steep ridge.

Principal Dihedral. III, 5.8, A2. First ascent May 1973 by Fred Beckey, Leland Davis, and Mike McGoey. This route is approximately 200 feet northeast of the Truncated Buttress route in a prominent, long, shallow dihedral. Climb the dihedral for several pitches to where a blank slab is overcome by means of bat hooks. Later, the crux involves jamming a headwall on its left side.

Rainbow Bridge. III, 5.10. First ascent May 1979 by Allan Pietrasanta and Alan Bartlett. This route begins just to the right of the Principal Dihedral route in a long, right-facing dihedral. Two pitches lead to a point just below the top of the dihedral. Go left on a hand traverse to a ledge. A brushy crack leads to another ledge. Go left and up past two bolts to a crack. Three easier pitches lead to the east shoulder of Thor Peak.

Loki. IV, 5.10, A2. First ascent October 1980 by Alan Roberts, Kim Walker, and Alan Bartlett. This route ascends the first major crack system to the right of the Rainbow Bridge route. Five pitches of free climbing lead to a huge ledge. Climb a prominent left-leaning crack. Three more pitches of easier climbing lead to the end of the climb.

The Stemwinder. I, 5.4. First ascent September 7, 1936 by William Rice, Robert K. Brinton, and Glen Dawson. Most of this spectacular route is class 3, with two long technical moves (or two very short technical pitches). Climb to the highest trees that are to the right of the Loki route on the southeast face. Traverse left on a ledge to the base of a short, vertical chimney. Ascend the 15-foot chimney (5.4), and follow a ledge back to the right. Climb cracks and ledges to a large, pale red pinnacle standing out from the main face. From the notch between the pinnacle and the face, traverse right for 20 feet (class 4) to a gully, which slopes up to the left. A broad ledge to the left leads to the top of the climb.

Northeast Slopes. Class 2. Leave the Mount Whitney Trail just below the junction with the Lone Pine Lake Trail. Climb brush and talus to the summit of Thor Peak.

Warm Leatherette. II, 5.10d. First ascent 1984 by Scott Ayers and Bill Leventhal. This route climbs the north buttress of Thor Peak from a point above Clyde Meadow on the North Fork of Lone Pine Creek.

Wotan's Throne   3880 m+; 12,720 ft+

South Face. Class 3. From Trail Camp along the Mount Whitney Trail ascend easy ledges to some broken blocks in the middle of the south face.

Northwest Arête. Class 2. First ascent 1933 by Norman Clyde.

East Chimney. Class 2. First ascent July 10, 1937 by Chester Versteeg. There are three chimneys on the upper part of the southeast face of the peak. Climb the far right-hand chimney to the summit.

Pinnacle Ridge   3980 m+; 13,040 ft+

Traverse. Class 4. First ascent July 10, 1935 by John Mendenhall and Nelson Nies.

So Many Aiguilles, So Little Time. III, 5.10+. First ascent early 1980s by Scott Ayers and Mike Strassman. This route climbs cracks in the center of the south face for six pitches.

"Pinnacle Pass Needle"   3760 m+; 12,320 ft+

Northwest Corner. Class 4. First ascent September 7, 1936 by Robert K. Brinton, Glen Dawson, and William Rice. Climb a crack on the side of the needle facing

Mount Whitney and traverse an arête leading to the summit.

"Trail Camp Crag"

An obvious crack passing through two roofs can be seen to the north of Trail Camp. This two-pitch route is I, 5.8, and was first climbed in June 1994 by Ken Kenaga and Patrick Brennan.

"Trail Crest Tower"   4180 m+; 13,680 ft+;
0.3 mi S of Mount Muir; UTM 845467

This is the first prominent tower south of Mount Muir. The south face route is just left of the southeast corner of the tower. It stays about 10 feet left of this outside corner for its entire length. This three-pitch climb was first climbed by Pete Mack and Pat Brennan in July 1993. The crux was the middle pitch, II, 5.9.

Mount Muir   4271 m; 14,015 ft

From the John Muir Trail. Class 3. First ascent 1919 by LeRoy Jeffers. The summit is about 200 feet above the trail. Leave the trail at an elevation of 13,780 feet; Mount Hitchcock bears 225 degrees magnetic, Mount Hale bears 309 degrees magnetic, and the "neck" of Guitar Lake bears 274 degrees magnetic; UTM 844472. Climb a shallow chute of loose talus and head toward the ridge on the right, where talus blends with the rocks of the summit pinnacle. Move left and climb a chimney to its head. Traverse left across a sloping ledge, then climb a crack to the small summit.

Further Reading: Stephen F. Porcella and Cameron M. Burns. *Hiking and Climbing: California's Fourteeners.* Evergreen, Colo.: Chockstone Press, 1996, pp. 20–22.

East Buttress. Class 4. First ascent July 11, 1935 by Nelson P. Nies and John Mendenhall. This is a splendid route. The buttress is obvious from Trail Camp on the Mount Whitney Trail. From the toe of the buttress, climb to the right of the crest. Approximately halfway up the buttress, move left into a well-fractured chute that leads back to the right, between two gendarmes. Climb large blocks to a notch just beneath the summit. Stay slightly to the left, and climb a steep trough to the summit. *Variation:* First ascent September 1, 1935 by Arthur Johnson and William Rice. Climb the crest of the east buttress to where the difficulties increase. Traverse left, down a ledge and into a chimney on the southeast face

MOUNT MUIR

S'brutal Tower

Variation

East
Buttress

Mount Muir from the southeast. Photo by R. J. Secor

of the buttress. Climb the chimney to the crest of the buttress; a 60-foot squeeze chimney is encountered at the top of the chimney. From the crest of the buttress, climb up and right under a gendarme to the well-fractured chute of the East Buttress route.

East Buttress Direct. III, 5.9. First ascent 1980 by Claude Fiddler and Nancy Fiddler. Stay directly on the prow of the buttress.

Further Reading: Stephen F. Porcella and Cameron M. Burns. *Climbing California's Fourteeners.* Seattle: The Mountaineers Books, 1998, pp. 44–53.

"S'brutal Tower"   4240 m+; 13,920 ft+;
UTM 845475

This is the second tower north of Mount Muir. It is class 1 from the John Muir Trail.

East Prow. III, 5.9. First ascent early 1980s by Scott Ayers and Mike Strassman. The first three pitches of this climb stay to the left of the prow. The remaining five pitches remain on top of the prow.

"Aiguille Junior"   4240 m+; 13,920 ft+;
UTM 845477

This is the next tower north of S'brutal Tower. It is an easy boulder hop from the John Muir Trail.

Breathless. III, 5.10a. First ascent early 1980s by Scott Ayers and Mike Strassman. This route climbs the right-hand east buttress for eight pitches. Finish the climb by traversing to the left edge of the tower high on the buttress.

"Aiguille du Paquoir"   4260 m+; 14,000 ft+;
UTM 845478

This is the next tower north from Aiguille Junior. It is a simple climb from the John Muir Trail.

East Face. IV, 5.9. First ascent early 1980s by Scott Ayers and Mike Strassman. Ascend corners for eleven pitches to the summit.

"Aiguille Extra"   4280 m+; 14,000 ft+;
UTM 846479

Class 1 from the John Muir Trail.

East Buttress. V, 5.10, A2. First ascent July 2–3, 1978 by Werner Landry and Kenny Cook. Gain the toe of the buttress by approaching it from the right. Climb the crest of the buttress (5.6) to a good crack to the right of the base of a chimney. Ascend the crack (5.9) to a ledge.

Climb a thin crack and use aid to traverse into an off-width crack (A2, 5.9). Go up left through a slot (5.7) beneath some ledges. Some class 3 climbing leads to a large ledge, and then 5.7 climbing tends to the right and ends on another ledge. Class 3 to the left leads to a large ledge at the base of a headwall. Leave the ledge via a hand jam (5.10) next to a large block. A layback is followed by a traverse to the right for 30 feet. The traverse ends with a vertical hand jam, which leads to a good belay ledge atop some large blocks. A corner to the right has some aid moves up an overhang. Easy class 5 climbing leads to the summit.

East Face. IV, 5.8, A3 or 5.10a. First ascent June 1971 by Bill Sumner and Mike Heath. First free ascent August 1993 by Ken Kenaga and Pat Brennan. This route follows the prominent dihedral on the east face. It begins with aid (or 5.10) climbing to leave a small platform that is 40 feet above the talus. Follow cracks to the base of the dihedral. Climb the dihedral to a hanging belay beneath an overhang. Pass this on the right and follow the dihedral for three pitches to a step just below the summit. Broken rock and chimneys lead to the summit.

"Third Needle"   4300 m+; 14,080 ft+;
UTM 847481

This peak is easily identified from the east because Pinnacle Ridge abuts its east buttress. It is a simple climb from the John Muir Trail.

East Buttress. Class 5, A1. First ascent September 5, 1948 by John Mendenhall, Ruby Wacker, and John Altseimer. Climb the south side of the buttress, starting from where Pinnacle Ridge ends against Third Needle. After 400 feet of class 4, traverse left and climb a chimney using aid. Then move right into a rotten, bottomless chimney. Climb over the buttress to its north side via a crack. A "thank-God" ledge leads to the notch north of the summit.

Hall of the Yeti King. III, 5.7. First ascent September 12, 1982 by Greg Vernon and George Pfalsy. Climb class 3 up and to the left from the saddle at the western end of Pinnacle Ridge. Instead of climbing the easy gully of the East Face, Right Side route, climb the chute to the right of the gully. Climb this chute for four pitches to the base of a chimney. Climb the chimney for two pitches, and leave it via a ledge. This is followed by an easy pitch that leads back into the chimney. Climb the right wall of the chimney for two more pitches. This route ends a few hundred feet south of the high point of Third Needle.

East Face, Right Side. Class 5. First ascent September 3, 1939 by John Mendenhall and Ruth Mendenhall. From the saddle at the western end of Pinnacle Ridge, climb class 3 up and to the left into an easy gully. Climb the gully about halfway up, to where it is blocked by an overhang. Bypass this on the right side via a short class 5 traverse. Many class 4 pitches then lead to the notch south of the summit.

East Face, Left Side. III, 5.3. First ascent August 1966 by Mike Heath. Follow the East Face, Right Side route to the overhang. Bypass the overhang on the left side and climb a thin buttress, which leads to a narrow, chockstone-filled chimney. Go up and left to a broad ledge that crosses the upper part of the east face. Continue left to a prominent, curving chimney. This leads to the small pinnacle south of the summit.

South Face. III, 5.10c. First ascent June 1994 by Ken Kenaga and Patrick Brennan. Approach this route by climbing one pitch up the East Buttress route, and then class 3 leads left onto the south face. Ascend a right-facing orange corner in the middle of the face for five pitches.

"Crooks Peak"   4320 m+; 14,080 ft+; UTM 846483

This is the second needle south of Mount Whitney. It was formerly known as "Day Needle," but it has been officially named after Hilda Crooks, who hiked up Mount Whitney every year from from her mid-60s to her early 90s. She rode in a helicopter to the summit of her eponymous mountain in 1995. There are no problems encountered while climbing this peak from the John Muir Trail.

East Buttress, Right Side. IV, 5.8. First ascent July 1977 by Ed Conner and John Vawter. Climb the couloir between Crooks Peak and Keeler Needle (loose rock!) for about 300 feet to a point about 30 feet below and left of a prominent roof. Traverse up and left to the crest of the buttress. Follow the buttress to the summit.

East Buttress, Left Side. IV, 5.10. First ascent September 14–15, 1963 by Fred Beckey and Rick Reese. This route begins at the bottom of the couloir between Crooks Peak and Third Needle. Climb the couloir a short distance and move to the right over easy rock to where the chimney narrows to the left of the buttress.

Climb the chimney (5.8) for two pitches and go to the right onto the crest of the buttress. Face climb to the right and climb up a 5.7 crack to a belay stance on a pillar. Continue up and right, climbing the left side of a 5.7 flake to an alcove. Face climb to the left out of the alcove (5.7) and go up three class 4 pitches, gradually moving to the right to the edge of the face, ending at the base of a big pillar. Climb an inside corner (5.9) on the left side of the pillar; the start of this pitch is marked by a fixed bong. Go up and left across some sandy ledges and climb a left-facing inside corner (5.7) to a ledge beyond some loose blocks. Go straight up over a 5.10 roof, followed by an exposed traverse to the right (5.9) to the base of an off-width chimney. Climb the chimney (5.10) ending on a tiny ledge to the right. Another 5.10 pitch leads past a small pillar and a roof to the top. *Variation:* IV, 5.10b. First ascent 1991 by Steve Porcella and Cameron Burns. Instead of climbing the off-width chimney, follow left-leaning cracks that lead to knobby face climbing.

Keeler Needle   4340 m+; 14,240 ft+

This is the first needle south of Mount Whitney. It is an easy climb from the John Muir Trail.

East Face, Right Side. V, 5.9, A2. First ascent 1973 by John Weiland and Jeff Lowe. This route starts on the right side of the east face and climbs six pitches all free except for the last 30 feet, which lead to a large, red dihedral. From the top of the dihedral, work left on ledges to the center of the face below a headwall. The headwall requires steep aid climbing up several different cracks. The aid climbing ends at a ledge, where another pitch up a steep crack leads up the right side of the prow below The Ledge of the Harding Route. Follow the Harding Route to the summit.

The Crimson Wall. V, 5.12-. First ascent August 1991 by Mike Carville, Kevin Brown, and Kevin Steele. This route goes straight up the center of the east face of Keeler Needle. It begins at the very center of the base of the wall and the first pitch ends at a belay just under a 3-foot roof. This is followed by corner systems, blank faces, cracks, and dikes. The seventh pitch features an arching corner (5.11), followed by a huge flake (5.10). The ninth pitch is the crux: a steep, sustained layback in an inside corner. The next pitch joins the Harding Route, following it to the top over the next four pitches.

Harding Route. V, 5.10b. First ascent July 1960 by Warren Harding, Glen Denny, Rob McKnight, and

Desert Frank (a hitchhiker who went a lot farther than he ever expected). First winter ascent March 1972 by Warren Harding, Galen Rowell, and Tim Auger. First free ascent August 21, 1976 by Galen Rowell, Chris Vandiver, and Gordon Wiltsie. This climb begins on the left side of the east face and climbs a prominent crack system. Begin from the base of the couloir between Day Needle and Keeler Needle. Face climbing on a slab with cracks leads up and slightly to the right. The second pitch is hard, with a tough move over a strenuous overhang (5.10). Continue climbing cracks and dihedrals up to the right, where an off-width crack (5.9) leads up to a series of broken ledges. Two class 4 pitches lead to the top of the broken ledges. More face climbing follows (with a 5.8 move in a crack), up to the base of a red dihedral. Climb the dihedral (5.9) to a ledge. This is followed by a trough, with a 5.8 move to the right and up to a sloping ledge. The crux is a 5.10b off-width crack that leads to a belay from a chockstone in the chimney. The chimney becomes easier and then jogs left to another belay from a chockstone. Climb an obvious flake and crack that goes up and to the right (5.7, with some loose rock) to some big ledges. Improbable (yes, it *will* go) 5.7 climbing continues up and to the right, over a face and flakes to The Ledge on the very prow of the east buttress. Another pitch leads to a 5.7 traverse that leads left under a roof, followed by an easy crack. Climb blocks on the arête (or on either side of it) to the summit.

Further Reading: *Summit.* May 1972, pp. 18–25; Galen Rowell. *High and Wild.* San Francisco: Lexicos, 1983, pp. 29–35; *American Alpine Journal.* 1972, pp. 276–81. *Rock & Ice.* No. 41, pp. 46–49; John Moynier and Claude Fiddler. *Sierra Classics.* Evergreen, Colo.: Chockstone Press, 1993, pp. 36–38.

Mount Whitney   4417 m; 14,494 ft

West Slope. Class 2. First ascent August 18, 1873 by The Fishermen: Charles Begole, Albert Johnson, and John Lucas. First winter ascent January 10, 1929 by Orland Bartholomew during his three-month solo ski traverse of the High Sierra. Climb any of the talus chutes to the summit.

Northwest Rib. 5.7. First ascent July 27, 1988 by Galen Rowell. Climb the arête that rises above the outlet of Arctic Lake.

North Slope. Class 2–3. Climb the left side of the north slope, just under the northeast ridge. Ascend some shallow chutes leading to a 50-foot-high wall of broken blocks. Pass through these blocks and climb directly to the summit.

Northeast Ridge. III, 5.10 with a rappel. First ascent July 26, 1982 by Galen Rowell, Claude Fiddler, and Vern Clevenger. This route begins just south of Whitney-Russell Pass. Follow the ridge to the top of the Mountaineer's Route. At one point it is necessary to make a short rappel over an overhang and into a notch.

Cardiovascular Seizure. III, 5.10. First ascent September 1973 by Vern Clevenger and Keith Bell. There is a pillar leaning against the farthest northern portion of the east face, just south of Whitney-Russell Pass. This route begins a short distance north of a chimney on this pillar. Seven difficult pitches lead to the top of the northeast ridge. Either continue up the ridge and descend the Mountaineer's Route or descend a very loose chute south of the climb's finish.

The Rotten Chimney. III, 5.8. First ascent 1973 by Vern Clevenger, Mark Moore, and Julie X. This climbs the chimney on the pillar of Cardiovascular Seizure. Five pitches of difficult crud climbing lead to the top of the northeast ridge.

Mountaineer's Route. Class 3. First ascent October 21, 1873 by John Muir. This is the deep couloir that separates the northeast ridge from the east buttress of Mount Whitney. There is some loose talus in the couloir, and early in the season it usually has hard, frozen snow or ice, even in the late afternoon. This can complicate matters for those using this as a descent route after climbing one of the routes on the main east face of Mount Whitney. It may be better to descend the north slope and return to Iceberg Lake via Whitney-Russell Pass, rather than descending steep snow or ice in rock-climbing shoes.

From Iceberg Lake ascend the north side of the couloir to the notch north of the summit of Mount Whitney. From the notch, descend slightly toward the west, and then climb a wide chute via ledges and ribs to the summit plateau. Those using this as a descent route should note that you leave the summit plateau approximately 75 yards northwest of the outhouse. *Variation:* Many parties continue traversing west from the notch for a distance of approximately 300 yards before turning left and climbing a gentle slope to the summit.

East Buttress. III, 5.6. First ascent September 5, 1937 by Bob Brinton, Glen Dawson, Richard Jones, Howard

Koster, and Muir Dawson. First winter ascent March 22, 1955 by Dave Sowles, Bob Brooke, Tom McCormack and Gil Roberts. (The first-ascent party called this route the "Sunshine-Peewee Route.") Scramble to the notch between the First Tower and the Second Tower on the East Face route. Rope up here, and climb the east face of the Second Tower until you are about 15 feet below its top. Go right along the north side of the tower to a small ledge and crack which lead to the notch behind the Second Tower. The pitch above the notch on the crest of the buttress requires finesse. Follow the buttress up-

ward to the Peewee, a gigantic detached block which, upon closer inspection, could be compared to the Sword of Damocles. Pass the Peewee on its right side. Scramble over blocks (either directly upward or to the right) to the summit. Two weeks after the first ascent, the second-ascent party took 3½ hours to reach the summit from Iceberg Lake; this time is rarely equaled today. *Variation:* 5.7. First ascent May 26, 1974 by Tim Ryan and John Mendenhall. Instead of climbing the crest of the buttress, traverse to the right and slightly up from the notch behind the Second Tower. An almost vertical 5.7 pitch

Mount Whitney, East Face. Photo by Austin Post, No. 72R2-195, USGS Ice and Climate Project, GeoData Center, University of Alaska, Fairbanks.

is encountered after several rope lengths. *Bard Variation:* 5.7. First ascent by Allan Bard. Continue up and left from the Peewee to a short, right-facing corner. Climb the corner (5.7) to ledges on the crest of the buttress. Climb up and left away from a left-facing corner above the ledges. This leads to the blocks and ledges immediately beneath the summit.

Further Reading: Allan Bard. *East Buttress of Mount Whitney.* Bishop, Calif.: Shooting Star Guides, 1991 (a route card); John Moynier and Claude Fiddler. *Sierra Classics.* Evergreen, Colo.: Chockstone Press, 1993, pp. 39, 41–43.

Peewee's Big Adventure. III, 5.9. First ascent 1986 by Joel Richnak and Mike Carville. This route could be considered the direct east buttress. Start climbing about 100 feet to the right of the notch between the First Tower and the Second Tower, but to the left of the prow of the east buttress. Go up and to the right on flakes (5.8) to the notch behind the Second Tower. Ascend the prow of the east buttress to the Peewee. Climb up the crack on the left side of the Peewee, and then go over blocks and ledges to the summit.

East Face. III, 5.4. First ascent August 16, 1931 by Robert Underhill, Glen Dawson, Jules Eichorn, and Norman Clyde. First winter ascent December 30, 1963 by Roy Coats, Bud Couch, David Peterson, Mike Sweeney, and Russ McLean. From the notch behind the First Tower, traverse across the south face of the Second Tower. This is the Tower Traverse (5.3; first ascent August 17, 1934 by Jules Eichorn and Marjory Bridge). This involves ascending an upward-sloping ledge to a shelf that traverses horizontally to a tight chimney. Move left from the top of this chimney and climb the Washboard, a series of class 3 ledges covered with scree. The Washboard ends at a large alcove with a wall on its southern side. Climb the wall on its left side. Traverse across the southern side of this wall along some ledges to an inside corner. Move up and left, then go around a block to the Fresh Air Traverse. This is a long step-across with wild exposure, but relatively easy (5.4). Move 20 feet to the left and climb a smooth face to a broken chimney, which gradually goes back to the right. These two pitches end at the Grand Staircase, a series of steep shelves. Ascend the shelves to the wall at the top of the Grand Staircase. Exit this staircase via a tight chimney/wide crack on the left, in a right-facing open book. Scramble up and right over blocks to the summit. The first-ascent party took an incredible 3¼ hours to finish the climb from the First Tower. Most parties seem to take 6 hours or more to do the route these days. *Variation:* This was the route of the first-ascent party: Instead of taking the Tower Traverse, climb the East Buttress route to the notch behind the Second Tower. Descend a loose chute that leads left (south) to the top of the chimney at the end of the Tower Traverse and the start of the Washboard. *McKusky Variation:* 5.6. First ascent July 20, 1996 by Patrick McKusky, Tony Padilla, and Jeremy Georgelos. The tight chimney at the end of the Tower Traverse can be bypassed by making a short, horizontal traverse to the left from the foot of the chimney, and then climbing a thin crack to the base of the Washboard. *Variation: Shaky-Leg Crack.* 5.7. First ascent June 9, 1936 by Morgan Harris, James N. Smith, and Neil Ruge. There is a large block with a ledge at its top directly above the start of the Fresh Air Traverse. Climb the north inside corner of this block to the large block's ledge, then to a flaring crack followed by a comfortable ledge. Move left and up to the Grand Staircase. This variation is not as exposed as the Fresh Air Traverse, but is much more strenuous. *Variation: Direct Crack.* 5.8. First ascent July 4, 1953 by John Mendenhall. This is a short, strenuous crack about 40 feet south of the inside corner encountered before the Fresh Air Traverse. (It is right [north] from the Shaky-Leg Crack.) *Van Aken Variation:* Instead of climbing the tight chimney at the top of the Grand Staircase, traverse to the right and go around an outside corner to a class 4 ledge that leads upward to easier rock after a few feet. It is class 3 from there to the summit. *Ortenburger Variation:* After climbing the tight chimney at the top of the Grand Staircase, go up and slightly left over blocks to the edge of the plateau, and approach the summit from the south. (Escape Route: If a party backs off from the East Face route, it can probably escape by reversing the Tower Traverse.) Another option is to climb the cruddy chute (class 3) that leads up and right from the end of the Tower Traverse, near the bottom of the Washboard. This leads up to the notch behind the Second Tower of the East Buttress route. It is possible to reach the Mountaineer's Route from here via a long rappel (i.e., two 150-foot ropes). Some parties have done this with two short rappels from the small ledge and crack on the north side of the Second Tower of the East Buttress route.

Further Reading: Allen Steck and Steve Roper. *Fifty*

Classic Climbs of North America. San Francisco: Sierra Club Books, 1979, pp. 276–81; *Summit.* May–June 1982, pp. 26–29; Allan Bard. *East Face of Mount Whitney.* Bishop, Calif.: Shooting Star Guides, 1991 (a route card); John Moynier and Claude Fiddler. *Sierra Classics.* Evergreen, Colo.: Chockstone Press, 1993, pp. 40–41, 43.

The Great Book. IV, 5.9. First ascent August 1974 by Gary Colliver and Chris Vandiver. This route starts to the left of the base of the First Tower, on its southern side. Seven pitches of 5.8 and 5.9 and 300 feet of class 3 lead to the top of the Washboard. Climb the large open book that rises above the Washboard. Use the crack on the right. Two pitches of 5.8 and two pitches of 5.9 end 400 feet below the summit. Scramble over blocks and ledges to the summit.

The Hairline. V, 5.10, A3. First ascent August 2–6, 1987 by Bruce Bindner and Alex Schmauss. This route is between The Great Book and the Direct East Face. Climb a 5.10 face with cracks that don't quite reach the ground. (The first part of this is protected with bolts.) The second pitch starts by ascending a right-facing open book, followed by a right-trending roof that leads up to a ledge. Move to the left side of the ledge and climb a 5.11 crack to a smaller ledge; continue climbing up the loose Orange Bulge using bolts (A3). The fourth pitch ascends bolts to an expanding flake, where a hook move to the right (A2) leads to a right-facing open book. Continue up the book, lassooing a horn along the way, where a 5.9 stem to the left leads to a belay on a slab. Aid climbing then leads up and over roof, followed by some 5.7 to a chimney with a chockstone. A 5.7 off-width crack leads up to the Red Dihedrals. The ninth pitch ascends a pedestal (5.9) keeping left (but not too far left) of the large flake that is visible from the ground, and ends just below the East Face route. Class 3 leads across the East Face route, and the tenth pitch starts with easy class 5 over a roof, and ends with a 5.8 face followed by an A4 crack. This pitch ends on a large ledge that is to the right of a big roof. Climb a thin, expanding crack (A3), and then a 5.9 off-width crack. A 5.7 chimney then leads up to class 4, which leads to the summit. The first-ascent party reported that about 30 percent of the route was aid, and that 44 holes were drilled. Twenty-five pitons should be carried, along with bat hooks, sky hooks, and cams to 5 inches.

Direct East Face. V, 5.9, A3 or 5.10d. First ascent July 6, 1959 by Denis Rutovitz and Andrzel Ehrenfeucht. First free ascent September 1992 by Bruce Bindner and Patrick Brennan. First winter ascent February 1985 by Galen Rowell, Ron Kauk, and Michael Graber. This route follows the enormous crack on the true east face of Mount Whitney. The climb starts 40 feet to the right of some black watermarks on the apron at the bottom of the crack. Climb broken outside corners up and right for 60 feet to some class 4 ledges. These ledges lead left to a slanting crack (5.8), followed by a belay. Climb the chimney above it (5.3) to a large terrace. Go up and right from the terrace to a broken gully, which gradually turns into a narrow crack behind a large flake (5.5), and then move left to a belay behind another flake. Climb up and to the right over cracks and edges; this 5.7 pitch is sustained and poorly protected and ends at a small belay ledge. Climb a jam crack before moving left onto the face and continuing to another small ledge (5.3). This is followed by a 5.7 jam crack and a belay at the base of a chimney. This chimney features a chockstone, and gradually narrows into an off-width crack (5.8; large chocks required) to a belay stance (the perfect bivouac cave is 20 feet below and to the left of this stance). Continue climbing the short, wet crack (5.8) to a large, black, damp cave. Aid climbing leads up and right from the cave; an awkward aid move around the nose of an overhang leads to easy rock (or this pitch goes free at 5.10d). A short 5.7 pitch up a large crack is followed by another short pitch (5.5) up blocks and faces on the left to a large ledge. Go right from this ledge up more blocks and faces (5.5) to the final chimney. This chimney can be avoided by climbing up and left and traversing to the right (5.3). Class 3 then leads to the Fresh Air Traverse of the regular East Face route. *Variation:* The first-ascent party climbed 300 feet up and to the left from the bottom of the face to an open book that leads to the large terrace.

Left Wing Extremist. V, 5.11a. First ascent June 1991 by Galen Rowell and David Wilson. This sixteen pitch route begins by climbing a pedestal for two pitches. Move slightly right for four sustained pitches of 5.10 and 5.11 vertical to overhanging crack climbing. This leads to a huge open book that lacks a continuous crack. The right wall of this book features a 5- to 7-inch off-width crack (5.10d; bring large protection) with parallel sides and rounded edges. Above this obstacle, the route consists of 5.8 and 5.9 plates and knobs on a rib that stays to the left of the East Face route.

Southeast Face. III, Class 5. First ascent October 11, 1941 by John Mendenhall and Ruth Mendenhall. This route begins on the buttress that leans against the southeast face. Class 4 climbing on the buttress leads to a point where you can traverse to the right into a chimney (loose rock!) above an overhang. A thousand feet of class 4 then lead to the top.

Whitney-Keeler Couloir. Class 5 and A. First ascent September 6, 1964 by Jim Servais and John Mendenhall. This is dangerously loose. Three climbers were killed here in the 1950s and 1960s. The first-ascent party encountered class 5 climbing on the walls around the numerous chockstones, and used aid to bypass steep ice near the top of the couloir.

The John Muir Trail. Class 1. This requires nothing more than stamina.

Further Reading: Paul Hellweg and Scott McDonald. *Mount Whitney Guide for Hikers and Climbers.* Canoga Park, Calif.: Canyon Publishing Co., 1990; Walt Wheelock and Tom Condon. *Climbing Mount Whitney.* Glendale, Calif.: La Siesta Press, 1970; Stephen F. Porcella and Cameron M. Burns. *Hiking and Climbing: California's Fourteeners.* Evergreen, Colo.: Chockstone Press, 1996, p. 1, pp. 23–29; Stephen F. Porcella and Cameron M. Burns. *Climbing California's Fourteeners.* Seattle: The Mountaineers Books, 1998, pp. 54–83.

Mount Young   4016 m; 13,177 ft

South Slopes. Class 1. First ascent September 7, 1881 by Frederick Wales, William Wallace, and James Wright. A mixture of sand and easy talus leads to the summit.

Traverse from Mount Hale. Class 1. If climbing Mount Young and Mount Hale, it is easier to ascend Mount Hale first and then traverse to Mount Young.

Mount Hale   4113 m; 13,440 ft+

The author is a proud graduate of George Ellery Hale (for whom the peak was named) Elementary School, Class of 1968.

South Slopes. Class 1. First ascent July 24, 1934 by J. H. Czock and Mildred Czock. These slopes are sandy.

Northeast Face. V, 5.9, A3. First ascent July 1973 by Dennis Hennek and Galen Rowell. Begin climbing in the center of the tallest of the two east faces of Mount Hale. Climb a right-leaning crack system for five pitches of continuously difficult climbing. Direct aid is needed to overcome an overhanging off-width crack. The upper half of the climb has several short but difficult sections.

Hale Pinnacles. First ascent June 1973 by Galen Rowell. There are two 100-foot pinnacles on the ridge between Mount Hale and Mount Russell. They are due north of Arctic Lake. The southern pinnacle is 5.6 and the northern one is 5.8.

West Face. II, 5.8. First ascent September 1991 by Claude Fiddler, Bob McGavren, and Danny Whitmore. Follow gully and face ending a few feet from the summit.

Northwest Ridge. III, 5.9. First ascent September 1991 by Claude Fiddler, Bob McGavren, and Dan Whitmore. Follow the ridge from Peak 3899m (12,790 ft).

Peak 3940m+   12,880 ft+; 0.4 mi S of Mount Hale

Arctic Dreams. IV, 5.10b. First ascent July 27, 1988 by Pat O'Donnell and Galen Rowell. This vertical face is next to Arctic Lake. Keep just left of center while climbing the face.

Peak 4245m   13,920 ft+;
0.5 mi W of Mount Russell

The northeast slope is class 2 until the class 3 summit rocks are reached. The east ridge from Mount Russell is class 3 if you keep well off the ridge when difficulties are encountered.

East Ridge Direct. II, 5.8. First ascent September 1979 by Claude Fiddler and Vern Clevenger. Follow the crest of the ridge from Mount Russell.

West Ridge. III, Class 5. First ascent September 1991 by Claude Fiddler, Bob McGavren, and Dan Whitmore. Follow the ridge from Mount Hale.

Mount Russell   4294 m; 14,086 ft

This is the finest peak in the Mount Whitney region. It is high and beautiful—and none of its routes is easy. The peak has two summits; the west peak is the high point.

East Ridge. Class 3. First ascent June 24, 1926 by Norman Clyde. Ascend the north side of the ridge from Russell-Carillon Pass to the east summit of Mount Russell. It is easy to traverse to the west peak.

Southeast Face, Right Arête. III, 5.10. First ascent July 1984 by Vern Clevenger, Claude Fiddler, and Bob Harrington. Climb the second arête east of the south buttress on the southeast face.

Southeast Face, Left Arête. III, 5.8. First ascent September 2, 1984 by John Cleary and Colin Fuller. Follow the left-hand arête to the east ridge. This route ends on the east ridge just before reaching the east peak of Mount Russell.

South Ridge to East Peak. II, 5.7. First ascent September 15, 1974 by Greg Thomsen, Ed Ehrenfeldt, and Fred Beckey. This ridge follows the Sierra crest from the low point between Mount Whitney and Mount Russell to the top of Mount Russell's east peak. The route involves climbing over and around the serrated ridge crest. It is simple to leave the ridge at any point by traversing or rappelling off it to the left.

South Face, Right Side. Class 3. First ascent 1928 by A. E. Gunther. Ascend easy talus slopes immediately left (west) of the south ridge to the headwall beneath the top of the ridge between the east and west peaks. Climb the second chimney to the right of the headwall to the top of the ridge. *Variation:* Class 3. First ascent August 7, 1931 by Howard Sloan, Frank Noel, and William Murray. Climb the headwall by following a ledge that rises diagonally to the left. *Variation:* Class 4. First ascent July 29, 1932 by James Wright. Climb the first chimney to the right of the headwall, then pass over a loose overhang near its top. Traverse right on a ledge, and then climb to the ridge between the two peaks.

South Face, Direct. III, 5.7. First ascent June 25, 1961 by Tom Condon and Grant Radden. Second ascent June 1977 by Tom Walter and Andy Selters. This route climbs the triangular face on the southern side of Mount Russell. The route starts at the bottom of this face and goes directly up, consisting of seven pitches of steady,

Mount Russell, South Face. Photo by R. J. Secor.

moderate class 5 climbing with long jam cracks and/or laybacks over good, sound rock. At the top of the face the route traverses to the left and ascends the South Face, Left Side.

South Face, Left Side. I, 5.0. First ascent July 1932 by Jules Eichorn, Glen Dawson, Walter Brem, and Hans Leschke. Follow the talus slopes as in the description of South Face, Right Side, but take the left branch, which leads to the left of the triangular face. Near the top of the left branch, climb a short chimney above a large ledge to the ridge, meeting it just east of the west peak.

Fishhook Arête. III, 5.8. First ascent June 1974 by Gary Colliver and John Cleare. This is the prominent, curved arête that drops immediately below the west peak of Mount Russell. Follow the arête to the summit. *Variation:* Climb onto the prow of the arête and follow it until progress is stopped by a headwall. Bypass the headwall by going up and left to a ledge, then follow a 5.8 pitch up and right that ends at a notch on the crest of the arête.

Further Reading: John Cleare. *Mountains.* New York: Crown Publishers, 1975, pp. 116–27; John Moynier and Claude Fiddler. *Sierra Classics.* Evergreen, Colo.: Chockstone Press, 1993, pp. 46–47; *Rock & Ice.* No. 73 (May–June 1996), pp. 66–75.

Direct South Face. III, 5.10. First ascent July 1986 by Rich Romano and Fred Yakulic. This and the next two routes are on the south face of the west peak of Mount Russell. Scramble into the recess between Fishhook Arête and the Southwest Buttress. This route starts by climbing a hand crack below a large right-facing dihedral. Later, a left-facing dihedral is entered, which is the crux of the climb.

Pilgrimage. III, 5.9. First ascent September 1979 by Allan Pietrasanta and Alan Bartlett. Low on this face is a left-facing broken dihedral. Climb a crack on the left side of this and go past a small roof. Continue up the face for several pitches to easier climbing and the summit.

The Mithral Dihedral. III, 5.10b. First ascent July 1976 by Alan Bartlett and Alan Roberts. This route has also been called the "Direct South Face." It climbs the large left-facing dihedral just to the right of the Southwest Buttress route. This route involves five pitches of sustained, difficult jamming. Climb some broken ledges up and right (5.7) to the bottom of the lower left-facing dihedral. Climb the dihedral (up to 5.8) to a ledge. The third pitch starts from the right side of the ledge and climbs the upper part of the lower dihedral

(5.9); finish by face climbing up and right to a ledge at the base of the large, left-facing dihedral. This diagonal traverse passes a dangerous, loose block. The next two pitches are truly vertical, involve up to 5.10b climbing, feature a real hanging belay, and finish with a wild stem followed by a slightly overhanging hand crack. Blocky ledges (mostly class 3 with a few 5.7 and 5.8 moves) lead up to the summit.

Further Reading: John Moynier and Claude Fiddler. *Sierra Classics.* Evergreen, Colo.: Chockstone Press, 1993, pp. 48–49.

Southwest Buttress. III, 5.8. First ascent September 1, 1974 by Gary Colliver, TM Herbert, and Don Lauria. This route ascends the face and the buttress to the left of The Mithral Dihedral. There are two prominent cracks at the base of this buttress. Climb the left crack (loose rock!). Three more pitches of 5.7 to 5.8 on better-quality rock lead to the crest of the buttress, and easier climbing then leads to the summit.

Bloody Corner. III, 5.10. First ascent September 1979 by Alan Bartlett and Allan Pietrasanta. This is the shallow dihedral to the left of the Southwest Buttress. Climb progressively more difficult rock for a few hundred feet to the dihedral. Two pitches in the dihedral lead to easier climbing and the crest of the southwest buttress.

West Face. IV, 5.10 or 5.9, A2. First ascent June 1971 by Galen Rowell and Chris Jones. First free ascent 1974 by Mark Moore and Julie X. First winter ascent March 1983 by Galen Rowell and Jack Tackle. Climb the crack system on the center of the west face. A landmark for this crack system is a square belay ledge 150 feet above the start of the route. There have been many variations done on this route, notably by Fred Yakulic, Alan Kouzmanoff, Rich Romano, Steve Untch, and Patrick Brennan. All of these variations are very close to the main crack system.

Beowulf's Revenge. IV, 5.8. First ascent October 1978 by Marie Grayson, Mark Fielding, and Fred Beckey. This route climbs the left side of the west face. Begin by climbing among some ledges in a loose chimney about 100 feet to the left of an obvious right-leaning arch. The first three pitches go up and left, with climbing becoming gradually better. The remaining portion of the climb is exposed, and has high-quality rock and roomy belay ledges. The last pitch traverses left on smooth rock and ends with a 5.7 layback.

West Chimney. III, 5.10. First ascent September 5, 1988 by Steve Porcella and Cameron Burns. This steep

Mount Russell, West Face. Photo by R. J. Secor.

chimney is on the left side of the west face, but right of the west couloir. The first pitch ends beneath an enormous roof. Climb the face on the left wall (5.8), then climb over the roof (5.9) to a steep hand crack above. This crack is 5.8, and it leads to a rubble-covered ledge. Continue climbing the main chimney for two more pitches. This is followed by a sustained pitch that climbs a face (loose rock and little protection!) to bypass a rotten roof. The next pitch continues up the chimney over some loose blocks. The seventh pitch is the crux of the climb. It goes up a shallow dihedral and features 5.10 face moves with no protection. One more pitch leads to the summit.

West Couloir. Class 4. Descended July 1932 by Jules Eichorn, Glen Dawson, Walter Brem, and Hans Leschke. This is the deep couloir between the west face and the west arête. Pass a chockstone on its left side and continue up to the west arête, which leads to the west peak.

West Arête. Class 3. Descended July 1932 by Norman Clyde. Follow the north side of the ridge leading from Peak 4245m (13,920 ft+).

Northwest Face. Class 3–4. First ascent 1935 by J. H. Czock, Mildred Czock, and Mary Luck. From the small lake near the base of the north ridge, ascend the northwest face near its east side. Go over easy rock to the first ledge that leads out onto the middle of the northwest face. Follow the ledge to the middle of the face and climb directly to the summit ridge midway between the east and west peaks.

North Arête. Class 3. Descended June 24, 1926 by Norman Clyde. Climb onto the ridge from Tulainyo Lake. Difficulties can be avoided by keeping to the right of the arête along the ends of the ledges on the northwest face. This route ends atop the east peak.

Northeast Face. III, class 5. First ascent June 10, 1971 by Reed Cundiff and Fred Beckey. Climb steep snow and rock slabs to the right of the main face. This climb ends on the east peak.

Further Reading: Stephen F. Porcella and Cameron M. Burns. *Hiking and Climbing: California's Fourteeners.* Evergreen, Colo.: Chockstone Press, 1996, pp. 30–31; Stephen F. Porcella and Cameron M. Burns. *Climbing California's Fourteeners.* Seattle: The Mountaineers Books, 1998, pp. 84–103; John Moynier and Claude Fiddler. *Sierra Classics.* Evergreen, Colo.: Chockstone Press, 1993, pp. 44–45.

Mount Carillon   4120 m+; 13,552 ft

From Russell-Carillon Pass. Class 2. First ascent 1925 by Norman Clyde. Either ascend directly from the pass, or from the slopes to the south of the peak.

Northeast Ridge. Class 3. Follow the ridge from Cleaver Col.

East Face. III, 5.8. First ascent July 1968 by Fred Beckey and Chuck Haas. This climb is between a deep crack on the right side of the face and a broad gully on the left. Climb up and left over slabs to an open book that slants up and right. Climb the book to a slab that leads to a narrow crack. A squeeze chimney in a corner and a jam crack lead to a traverse to the left to a cave with orange rock. One more pitch leads to the southeast ridge of Mount Carillon.

The Impala, South Face. II, 5.7. First ascent June 1968 by Chuck Ray and Brad Fowler. This formation is the sloping pyramid at the base of the long southeast ridge of Mount Carillon. It is due north of Clyde Meadow on the North Fork of Lone Pine Creek. Climb the obvious chimney in the middle of the south face for two pitches. Cross a left-ascending diagonal chimney system, then climb straight up to a false summit. Easy scrambling leads to the summit of The Impala.

The Impala, Diagonal Route. II, 5.7. First ascent November 1968 by Fred Beckey and Charlie Raymond. Fol-

low the diagonal chimney system that starts at the lower left side of the south face and goes up to the right. Once on the southeast face, go up to the false summit.

The Winged Horse. III, 5.8, A3. First ascent November 17, 1970 by Jack Miller and Fred Beckey. This formation is east of The Impala. The climb begins at the base of the south face, near a pine tree. After a pitch of tricky friction (5.8), go up and left. Aid climbing leads to a ledge at the base of a groove, and a pitch of mixed climbing goes up the groove. This is followed by chickenheads, a traverse left, and chimneys to the summit.

"The Cleaver"   4079 m; 13,355 ft;
0.7 mi SE of Tunnabora Peak

Northwest Ridge. Class 3. First ascent July 16, 1931 by Norman Clyde, who described it as "a good rubber-soled shoe climb." Climb easy class 3 ledges to the summit.

Southwest Ridge. II, 5.6. First ascent July 1973 by Galen Rowell, Dennis Hennek, and Dave Lomba. Most of this ridge from Cleaver Col is class 4.

South Face. III, 5.9. First ascent September 1961 by Arthur Killian and Tom Condon. First free ascent June 1980 by Bill St. Jean, Allan Pietrasanta, and Alan Bartlett. This route climbs just left of the center of the south face. The first pitch is a strenuous off-width, and four more pitches lead to the lower left end of a gold-colored band high on the face. One pitch along the band leads to the summit pitch, going up cracks and over a roof.

Tunnabora Peak   4134 m; 13,565 ft

South Slope. Class 2. First ascent August 1905 by George Davis. This is a talus hop from Tulainyo Lake.

Northwest Face. Class 2. First ascent 1958 by Bud Bingham, Barbara Lilley, and Fred Bressel. From George Creek, hike cross-country to the base of the northwest face. Ascend a chute to the summit.

"Tunnabora Pinnacles"   3900 m+/-; 12,800 ft+/-;
0.8 mi NW of Tunnabora Peak

These pinnacles are on the Sierra crest between Mount Carl Heller and Tunnabora Peak. Tulainyo Tower is one of these pinnacles. These pinnacles were traversed on August 9, 1970 by Charles Bell from northwest to southeast. Class 3–4. These can be approached from George Creek, via Vacation Pass, or by descending the northeast ridge of Tunnabora Peak to a gully that leads down to the upper George Creek drainage.

"Tulainyo Tower"   3920 m+; 12,800 ft+;
0.6 mi SE of Vacation Pass

This is the most prominent crag among the Tunnabora Pinnacles. It is the first tower south of Mount Carl Heller (UTM 841522). There is a class 2–3 gully on the west side that leads to the summit.

East Face. IV, 5.9. First ascent October 1972 by Galen Rowell and Marek Glogoczowski. This climb starts on the right side of the east face. Climb a wide chimney for two pitches to an area of red, broken rock. Traverse left to the main crack system of the face. Three pitches of 5.9 lead to an off-width crack. Traverse right onto easier climbing, then scramble up to the summit.

East Face Direct. IV, 5.8, A3 or IV, 5.10+. First ascent September 1973 by Bill Stronge and Arold Green. First free ascent July 1992 by Steve Untch and Patrick Brennan. This route follows the 1,000-foot crack system on the east face leading directly to the summit. The route starts directly beneath the crack system, and passes the lowest arch by going up and right (5.6) to a ledge. Climb over a roof (5.9) and pass to the right of a loose block to another ledge. A 5.9 move to the right of a flake leads up and left to a thin seam. Climb the seam, keeping to the right of a loose flake, with some 5.10 face moves ending at a ledge. Easy climbing then leads to the start of the crack system. A 5.8 pitch in the main crack leads up and right to a nice ledge. Climb up and then left across a 5.10 sloping hand traverse and climb a clean 3-inch crack. The crack becomes a chimney, with a 5.9 roof followed by a 5.10 roof leading to a good ledge/alcove to the right of a loose flake on the face. The next pitch is the crux, climbing a run out 5.10+ squeeze chimney, over a bulge, followed by another 4-inch, 5.10 off-width/layback to another ledge/alcove. Go up and left to a 5.8 chimney that leads to a death flake. Pass the flake by climbing up and right along a ramp and then climb a 5.7 face leading back to the left to a big alcove above the death flake. A clean crack on the left wall (5.8) then leads up and slightly right to a series of ledges interspersed with some easy class 5 moves to the summit. Protection to 4 inches is needed.

"Mount Carl Heller"   4031 m; 13,211 ft;
0.2 mi SE of Vacation Pass

This peak used to be unofficially known as "Vacation Peak." The name "Mount Carl Heller" has been proposed to the U.S. Board of Geographic Names in

memory of the late founder of the China Lake Mountain Rescue Group. The southeast peak is the high point. It is a magnificent piece of granitic sculpture.

East Ridge. Class 3–4. First ascent August 16, 1964 by Don Clarke and Harvey Hickman. Second ascent August 14, 1966 by Carl Heller and other members of the China Lake Mountain Rescue Group. This is a fine climb, once the approach up George Creek is completed. There is a horn about every 100 feet along the ridge, providing quick belay anchors.

Further Reading: John Moynier and Claude Fiddler. Sierra Classics. Evergreen, Colo.: Chockstone Press, 1993, pp. 50–51.

Northwest Ridge. Class 4. First ascent August 14, 1966 by Andy Smatko, Bill Schuler, Tom Ross, and Ellen Siegal. Climb a narrow and steep gully that leads to the northwest ridge from the western side of the peak. The knife edge ridge requires belays in three places: one to climb over a block sitting astride the ridge, another at a 20-foot vertical chimney, and the third along the ridge just below the summit.

West Rib (North). II, 5.9. First ascent 1984 by Claude Fiddler, Vern Clevenger, and Bob Harrington. Follow the prominent rib on the north side of the west face.

West Rib Center. II, 5.6. First ascent September 1979 by Claude Fiddler and Vern Clevenger. Follow the southern-most arête on the west face. This arête leads directly to the summit, and it is more enjoyable than the West Rib (North).

West Face. Class 3. First ascent 1940 by Olson and Roberts. Climb a broad chute on the southern side of the west face. The lower portion of this chute consists of smooth granite slabs. Go to the right along a ledge that leads to another gully, and follow this to the top.

Peak 3880m+   12,723 ft; 1.5 mi NE of Vacation Pass
South Slope. Class 2. Climb talus from the eastern approach to Vacation Pass.

North Face. Class 4. First ascent July 1963 by Arkel Erb and Sy Ossofsky. This peak is an impressive sight from the upper reaches of George Creek.

Mount Barnard   4264 m; 13,990 ft
Southwest Slopes. Class 1. First ascent September 25, 1892 by John Hunter, William Hunter, and C. Mulholland. Hike up scree slopes from Wallace Creek.

Northwest Face. III, 5.8. First ascent July 1986 by

Claude Fiddler and Nancy Fiddler. Follow the rib directly to the summit.

Traverse from Trojan Peak. Class 2. It may be preferable to drop down to approximately 13,000 feet on the east side of the ridge between the two peaks when making this traverse. Those who insist on remaining on or near the ridge crest can bypass two prominent gaps on their eastern sides.

From George Creek. Class 2. First winter ascent February 24, 1972 by John Smeson. From the head of the south branch of George Creek climb the broad couloir to the gentle slope northeast of the summit.

East Dihedral. III, 5.10a. First ascent June 1990 by Ken Kenaga and Patrick Brennan. Seven pitches in the dihedral lead to the summit.

East Face. III, 5.9. First ascent April 1972 by Tim Auger and Galen Rowell. This climbs the impressive face of the lower, eastern summit of Mount Barnard, Peak 4180m+ (13,680 ft+). This is an excellent but seldom-done route. The arduous approach and bighorn sheep restrictions of George Creek keep most people from doing this climb.

Two pitches (5.6) lead up the center of the lower face to a prominent ledge, which may be covered with snow.

Mount Carl Heller from the southwest. Photo by R. J. Secor.

Continue up to a ceiling, where a 50-foot horizontal traverse across a smooth wall leads to the base of a dihedral. Climb the dihedral directly to the summit. The fifth pitch follows the corner over a roof, followed by a jam crack on the left. The next lead ends at a nice ledge. Two more steep pitches lead to the base of a right-facing dihedral. One more pitch leads to the summit. Most of the pitches of this route are 5.7 to 5.8, with the last pitch having a short 5.9 section.

Shaw Spire. III, 5.8. First ascent March 1971 by Galen Rowell and Jerry Gregg. This is the freestanding pinnacle beneath the east face of Mount Barnard. Seven pitches on the southeast arête lead to the summit.

Trojan Peak   4251 m; 13,950 ft

From George Creek. Class 2. Climb the broad couloir that leads to the basin between Trojan Peak and Mount Barnard.

Traverse from Mount Barnard. Class 2. Descend to about 13,000 feet on the east side of the ridge between the two peaks when making this traverse. The two prominent gaps on the ridge can be passed on their eastern sides.

West Face. Class 3. First ascent June 26, 1926 by Norman Clyde. Ascend the loose face to the southwest ridge from the Wright Creek basin. Follow the ridge to the summit.

Northwest Face. Class 2. First ascent July 5, 1996 by Al Conrad and Xin Gong. Climb to the saddle between Mount Williamson and Trojan Peak from Williamson Bowl. From the saddle, traverse up and right over the northwest side of the peak and cross over a false summit before reaching the true summit. A variation from Williamson Bowl circles Lake Helen of Troy on its eastern shore, and then climbs to the saddle between Mount Barnard and Trojan Peak and on to the summit.

Mount Versteeg   4100 m+; 13,470 ft

North Slope. Class 2–3. Descended 1964 by John Robinson and Andy Smatko. Ascend directly to the summit from Lake 3733m (12,160 ft+) in Williamson Bowl.

Northeast Ridge. Class 2–3. First ascent 1964 by John Robinson and Andy Smatko. From Williamson Bowl head to the saddle just north of Lake Helen of Troy. From the saddle follow the northeast ridge to the summit.

Southwest Slope. Class 2. Climb a talus-filled chute that leads to the ridge south of the peak from the upper portion of Wright Creek. About 300 feet below the ridge crest, a steep, sandy chute with several chockstones leads to the crest just north of the summit. Climb the chute and scramble to the summit.

Northwest Ridge. Class 3. Follow the ridge from Tyndall Col.

Mount Williamson   4380 m+; 14,375 ft

California's second highest peak is an impressive sight from the Owens Valley. It has three summits: the high point, on the southwestern side of the summit plateau, and two lower peaks high along the northeast ridge, which are known as the "East Horn" (4280 m+; 14,125 ft) and the "West Horn" (4300 m+; 14,160 ft+). Mount Williamson is surrounded by the California Bighorn Sheep Zoological Area. The southeastern side of the peak (i.e., George Creek and the southeast ridge) is open only from December 15 to January 1 and from April 15 to May 15. The north and west sides of the peak are only open from December 15 to July 15.

Further Reading: *Summit.* October–November 1970, pp. 6–9; Stephen F. Porcella and Cameron M. Burns. *Climbing California's Fourteeners.* Seattle: The Mountaineers Books, 1998, pp. 104–123.

Southeast Ridge from George Creek. Class 2. First ascent 1884 by W. L. Hunter and C. Mulholland. First winter ascent December 22, 1954 by Leigh Ortenburger and Bill Buckingham. After the long and arduous approach up George Creek, leave the stream at approximately 11,200 feet near a small meadow. Go north up the slope to the basin southeast of the summit plateau. A landmark for this slope is a large rock pinnacle sticking out of the slope about two-thirds of the way up. From the basin, either climb the ridge immediately to the left or go north past a small lake to the ridge on the right, then climb to the summit plateau.

Bairs Creek. Class 3. First ascent 1958 by Rick Jali, John Harding, and Dick Cowley. Leave the George Creek Road 7.5 miles from Highway 395 and go right. Go 1.0 mile through a gate to a junction. Go left for 0.3 mile to the tiny trailhead. Follow a use trail on the south side of Bairs Creek, remaining high above the stream, for about ¼ mile to a small cliff. Climb the cliff via a ledge and a class 3 crack that passes through a small notch. The route stays high on the south side of the stream but eventually meets the creek. Follow the creek upstream to where several gullies meet in the cirque at the head of

Bairs Creek. Follow the south fork of Bairs Creek to the cirque at its head. Climb out of the cirque via a chute that leads up and right and follow the southeast ridge to the summit plateau. The North Fork of Bairs Creek can also be ascended.

Further Reading: John Moynier. *Backcountry Skiing in the High Sierra.* Evergreen, Colo.: Chockstone Press, 1992, p. 168.

Northeast Ridge. Class 4. First ascent June 13, 1970 by Dick Beach and Steve Rogero. This route ascends the northeast ridge from the mouth of the canyon of Shepherd Creek. This 8,000-foot, waterless ascent is one hell of a hard climb. Over 2,000 feet of sand, brush, and loose rock lead to talus and blocks along the crest of the ridge. Obstacles along the ridge are passed on their southern sides before regaining the ridge crest beyond some gendarmes. This class 3–4 ridge leads to the broad northeast slope of the East Horn. Climb to the top of the East Horn, then descend to the saddle between it and the West Horn. Climb to the top of the West Horn via a shallow gully on its northeast side (class 3). Descend the northwest side of the West Horn for 200 feet, then ascend diagonally toward the summit plateau of Mount Williamson to a small notch. Descend a short distance to another notch located between the West Horn and the summit plateau (class 4). Descend the southern side of this notch about 200 feet, and then traverse across the east side of the summit plateau to where it is possible to gain the summit plateau easily.

Northeast Ridge from Williamson Creek. Class 4. First ascent 1925 by Homer Erwin. First winter ascent December 29, 1954–January 2, 1955 by John Ohrenschall and Warren Harding. Hike up Shepherd Creek and then Williamson Creek to approximately 9,700 feet. The extreme eastern end of the north side of Mount Williamson features two waterfalls, one above the other. There is a red buttress to the left of these waterfalls. This buttress comes all the way down to the canyon floor. Climb this buttress (class 3) to a steep wall, then bypass this wall via a chute to the left. Regain the buttress above the wall and continue up to another obvious chute on the left. Climb this chute for a short distance and leave it on its left side and climb onto a loose, red slope. Ascend this slope to the crest of the main northeast ridge. The crest is gained at a small saddle that is to the left of a small, sharp peak. Continue up the northeast ridge, over the East Horn and West Horn, to the summit plateau of Mount Williamson.

Golden Eagle Buttress. Class 4. First ascent May 4, 1988 by Dave Haake, Chris Keith, and Pete Lowery. This buttress leads from Williamson Creek to the summit of the East Horn.

The Long Twisting Rib. III, 5.4. First ascent 1984 by Claude Fiddler and Jim Keating. This is the rib that leads to the summit of the West Horn from Williamson Creek. Climb onto the lower portion of the rib from the west and follow its crest upward to a prominent tower. Pass the tower on its right side, and then continue up the crest of the ridge to the top.

Further Reading: John Moynier and Claude Fiddler. *Sierra Classics.* Evergreen, Colo.: Chockstone Press, 1993, pp. 56–57.

North Rib. IV, 5.7. First ascent July 1972 by Edgar Boyles and Lito Tejada-Flores. This rib ascends the far left side of Mount Williamson's north face, ending at the northeastern end of the summit plateau. The upper third of this rib consists of ten pitches of 5.5–5.7 climbing.

North Face. III, Class 4–5. First ascent July 6, 1957 by John Mendenhall and Ruth Mendenhall. This is one of the more imposing north faces of the Sierra. From approximately 11,100 feet on Williamson Creek, ascend the chute that leads directly to the northeastern end of the summit plateau. There is a short, difficult chimney in the lower portion of this chute, followed by easier climbing to about 500 feet below the summit plateau. At this point the chute begins to steepen. A short traverse over an ice couloir within the chute is followed by three pitches over steep, loose rock. The last pitch ends atop the summit plateau. *Variation:* First ascent August 23, 1970 by Steve Rogero and Wally Henry. The short, difficult chimney in the lower portion of the chute can be bypassed by climbing the buttress to the right.

North Couloir. IV, 5.4, A1. First ascent May 30–31, 1976 by John Mendenhall, Tim Ryan, and Fred Wing. This route climbs the snow couloir that slants up the right side of the north face. Climb the couloir to its head and ascend the rocks to the summit plateau. A short pitch of aid is encountered above the top of the couloir.

Northwest Buttress. Class 5. First ascent October 1970 by Galen Rowell. From the west face of Mount Williamson, traverse up and left to a prominent notch behind a pinnacle at approximately 13,000 feet. Follow the buttress to the summit.

Mount Williamson, North Face. Photo by R. J. Secor.

West Face. Class 3. First ascent 1903 by Joseph LeConte, Edward Parsons, and five others. The west face of Mount Williamson is a confusing maze of chutes, many of which lead to dead ends. The following route description may not be of much help. Nevertheless . . .

Go southeast from Shepherd Pass to the saddle leading to Williamson Bowl. Descend to the bowl, but stay on top of the ridge in the middle of the bowl; there are two lakes on both sides of the ridge. Stay slightly to the right on top of the ridge to avoid a small cliff, and go to the second of the two lakes right of the ridge (Lake 3733m; 12,160 ft+). Head toward Mount Williamson from this lake. Climb talus to the largest, most prominent black stains on rock (there are some smaller black stains farther south on the west face; avoid these). Above

the larger black stains, enter the chute that leads up and slightly left (north). (Avoid a smaller chute that goes up and slightly right.) Follow this chute almost all the way to the crest of the northwest buttress. Traverse right (south) about 100 feet to a 60-foot class 3 crack, which leads to the summit plateau. The true summit is a short distance to the south. *Variation:* Class 3. First ascent July 19, 1929 by Walter A. Starr, Jr. Near the top of the main chute on the west face, instead of traversing right (south), go left and up a small crack that appears to go nowhere. This crack turns into a chimney with a chockstone in it. Climb under the chockstone and emerge out onto the summit plateau.

Further Reading: Stephen F. Porcella and Cameron M. Burns. *Hiking and Climbing California's*

Mount Williamson, West Face. Photo by R. J. Secor.

Fourteeners. Evergreen, Colo.: Chockstone Press, 1996, pp. 32–38.

Bolton Brown Route. Class 3. First ascent July 1896 by Bolton Brown and Lucy Brown. From Williamson Bowl, head toward red talus at the southern portion of the west face of Mount Williamson. Above this talus, climb the southernmost of the chutes on the west face to a notch on the southwest arête. Cross onto the south face and enter a broad chute in its upper portion. Climb ledges in a zigzag route to the summit plateau.

Direct South Arête. IV, 5.8. First ascent June 14, 1989 by Steve Porcella and Cameron Burns. This route ascends the most prominent arête on the south face. The route starts on the right-hand side of a large, triangular tower in the middle of the south face. Climb a dihedral for three pitches (5.8, 5.6, and 5.5) to where it disappears. Move left and climb the wildly exposed arête for three pitches of moderate class 5 climbing to the Sun Deck, a wide, sloping ledge. Climb a short, right-facing dihedral above the Sun Deck (5.8). Another pitch traverses around a wall (class 4) to a notch. Continue up the arête above for many class 4 pitches (with a few class 5 moves). This route ends close to the true summit of Mount Williamson.

South Face, Central Arête. Class 4+. First ascent May 2, 1989 by Pete Lowery and Chris Keith.

West Horn (Peak 4300m+; 14,160 ft+). Class 3–4. First ascent by Leroy Jeffers. This peak can be climbed via Mount Williamson's northeast ridge (see the Northeast Ridge route, above) or directly from the summit plateau. Descend about 150 feet on the east side of the summit plateau, then traverse north to the chute leading up to the notch between the West Horn and the summit plateau. From the notch, go up and left (north) 40 feet to another notch. Descend diagonally across the north side of the West Horn for 120 feet, and then climb up to the summit.

East Horn (Peak 4280m+; 14,125 ft). Class 3–4. Descend a shallow gully on the northeast side of the West Horn to the saddle between the two horns. Traverse a short distance across the west face and then climb the face to the summit.

East Horn, South Face. Class 4. First ascent June 8, 1978 by Carl Heller, Dennis Burge, Arold Green, Dianne Lucas, Terry Moore, Bob Rockwell, and Bob Westbrook. Descend from the summit plateau to the chute that leads to the notch located west of the West Horn. Descend this chute approximately 400 feet to where it joins the chute leading to the notch between the West Horn and East Horn. Ascend this chute 100 feet and climb another chute, which leads up the south face of the East Horn. Easy class 4 rock across the south face leads to a buttress on the right side of the face. Climb the buttress (class 3) to the summit of the East Horn.

Mount Tyndall   4273 m; 14,018 ft

Northwest Ridge. Class 2. First winter ascent January 1930 by Orland Bartholomew. This is the obvious ridge to the right of the north face, as viewed from Shepherd Pass.

Further Reading: Stephen F. Porcella and Cameron M. Burns. *Hiking and Climbing: California's Fourteeners.* Evergreen, Colo.: Chockstone Press, 1996, pp. 39–40.

North Rib. Class 3. First ascent July 6, 1864 by Clarence King and Richard Cotter. A shallow rib can be seen on the north face of Mount Tyndall. Climb the rib to the summit ridge, then go left (east) along the ridge to the summit. This is a good climb.

Further Reading: John Moynier and Claude Fiddler. *Sierra Classics.* Evergreen, Colo.: Chockstone Press, 1993, pp. 58–59.

East Face. Class 4. First ascent August 13, 1935 by Marjory Farquhar and William F. Loomis. The name of this route is a misnomer as it is actually a variation of the north rib. Climb the prominent, open chute on the extreme right-hand side of the east face. A short class 4 pitch in the chute leads to easier climbing. The chute ends on the lower portion of the north face. Climb the north face or the north rib to the summit ridge.

The Tyndall Effect. II, 5.6. First ascent 1994 by Daniel Roitman, Gus Benner, and Sergio Aragon. This route ascends the face located between the chute of the east "face" and the buttress of the northeast arête. Ascend the middle of this face, up right-facing layback cracks, to the north face of Mount Tyndall, where class 3 scrambling leads to the summit.

Northeast Arête. III, 5.9. First ascent June 12, 1989 by Cameron Burns and Steve Porcella. There is a large broken crack that ascends vertically and splits, forming a large Y at the base of this arête. Climb broken class 3 rocks to a small ledge at the base of this crack. The crack narrows, and there is an overhang about 35 feet above the ledge. This is immediately followed by a 5.9 face move onto a sloping triangular block on the left side of the crack. Another pitch leads up to a broken, snow-filled chimney (5.7). Increasingly easier pitches follow the left crack, and pass the remains of a small deer. The upper part of the route ascends class 4–5 slabs.

The Climbing Art. III, 5.7. First ascent June 1977 by David Mazel. This route climbs the second rib north of the rib of the Direct East Face route. It has little loose rock, protection is good, and the route is very aesthetically pleasing. Begin by ascending a band of orange rock to a large ledge. Rope up here, and head up and slightly left for three pitches. Then head slightly right, aiming for the left side of a large gendarme that is visible on the skyline; it is located immediately to the right of a big roof. The route ends atop the northeast arête. Either continue up the arête or up the north face of Mount Tyndall to the summit.

Direct East Arête. IV, 5.10. First ascent August 27, 1994 by Dave Nettle and Holly Samson. This route climbs the first rib north of the Direct East Face route; the rib is immediately left of the most prominent couloir on the east face of Mount Tyndall. Two pitches (5.6 and 5.8) lead up orange rock to the right of a prominent, right-leaning corner system, but left of the arête, ending at the edge of the arête overlooking the prominent couloir. Go left and climb a 5.10 chimney, move left past a roof and climb a 5.10 right-facing corner and then traverse horizontally to the right to the base of a left-facing corner. Climb the corner (5.8) and a flake, go diagonally left to a 1-to 1½-inch crack on a steep wall, ending at the base of a small tower on the crest of the arête. Pass the tower on its right side but go left of the arête and climb a white dike (5.6) to a ledge. Face climb straight up (5.9) and move to the right into a clean inside corner. Move to the right side of the arête at the top of the corner and continue to a big blocky ledge at the base of a large tower. Climb around the tower on its right side and cross back to the left side of the arête underneath a big flake. Go under and left of a small roof (5.6) to a small ledge. Traverse left and up (5.7) into an area of black rock. Continue up the loose black rock (5.9) and move right onto a flake. Climb a series of thin 5.10 cracks and pass through an improbable overhanging slot (5.10). A hand crack leads up to the last overhang, which is blocked by a flake (5.8). Scramble over blocks to the summit.

Direct East Face. IV, 5.10, A2. First ascent September 1983 by Steve Brewer, David Wilson, and Galen Rowell. This route ascends the east face directly beneath the summit. Difficult, vertical climbing (free and aid) for the first few pitches leads to moderate difficulties in the middle portion of the face. The final headwall has 5.8 to 5.10 cracks before reaching the summit.

Selters-Knight Route. IV, 5.10. First ascent July 1996 by Andy Selters and Bobby Knight. Start by climbing the East Chimney route, but move to the right from the top of the first, overhanging chimney. This is followed by easier class 4 and 5 climbing, gradually moving to the right with 5.7 climbing across grooves to within a couple of hundred feet of the Direct East Face route. Then go up and left; 5.9 face climbing leads to a 5.9 corner pitch that ends at the summit register.

East Chimney. IV, 5.8. First ascent August 1972 by Michael Heath and Bill Sumner. This route climbs the subtle chimney system to the right of the east couloir. Overhangs in the bottom of the chimney are bypassed to the right, and then the East Couloir route is followed to the summit ridge.

East Gully. III, 5.8. First ascent May 31, 1970 by Charles Raymond and Fred Beckey. This route climbs the deep couloir that splits the east face. The final, rotten headwall is the crux of the climb. It ends just south of the summit.

Southeast Ridge. Class 4. First ascent August 11, 1939 by Ted Waller and Fritz Lippmann. Climb the third large chute south of Mount Tyndall's great east face. Five hundred feet of class 4 climbing leads to the southeast ridge. Follow the ridge to the summit.

Southwest Slopes. Class 2. Descended July 6, 1864 by Richard Cotter and Clarence King. First winter ascent 1951 by Norman Goldstein, Al Steck, Jim Wilson, and Bill Dunmire. This is a simple talus hop from the Wright Lakes basin.

Further Reading: Stephen F. Porcella and Cameron M. Burns. *Climbing California's Fourteeners.* Seattle: The Mountaineers Books, 1998, pp. 124–133.

Peak 4120m+   13,540 ft+;
0.8 mi WSW of Mount Tyndall

The northwest face of this peak presents an interesting work of sculpture to those viewing it from the Shepherd Pass Trail. The southern slopes are class 2 from Wright Lakes.

Tawny Point   3740 m; 12,332 ft

First ascent July 12, 1946 by A. J. Reyman. Class 1 from the Bighorn Plateau.

WRINKLES

Alternatives to the Mount Whitney Trail. The Mount Whitney Trail is one of the most heavily used trails in this area. It has a strict quota, and many people have been turned away from the summit because they did not make reservations. An alternate approach is to start an extended hiking trip from Horseshoe Meadows, across Cottonwood Pass to the Pacific Crest Trail. This trail is followed down lovely Rock Creek, and then north to where it meets the John Muir Trail near Crabtree Meadow. The John Muir Trail is then followed to the summit of Mount Whitney. This alternate route is much longer than the standard Whitney approach, but it has the advantage of fewer people, tremendous scenic vistas of the west side of the Sierra crest, and access to lakes that can offer fantastic fishing.

Another alternative is to cross spectacular New Army Pass before joining the Pacific Crest Trail along Rock Creek. The approach to New Army Pass goes by way of Cottonwood Lakes, however, and this area also suffers from overuse.

Other alternatives are hiking to the west side of Mount Whitney from Shepherd Pass, Kearsarge Pass, or

Giant Forest. But as the old joke goes, every place is within walking distance if you have enough time.

Perhaps the best option is to get into excellent physical condition and hike up Mount Whitney in a day from Whitney Portal. A permit is required to day hike the trail, but the demand for day hike permits is less than that for overnight permits. Some people have done the 22-mile round trip (with 6,100 feet of gain) in remarkably fast time—although others have become altitude-sick just sleeping at Whitney Portal.

The East Face of Mount Whitney. This has become a "classic" climb, and now suffers from overcrowding. A large part of this route is class 3, with a few intervening roped pitches. There is also quite a bit of loose rock.

The East Buttress of Mount Whitney is a far better climb. The roped climbing is continuous, not difficult, but exposed, and the setting on the crest of the buttress is awe-inspiring (far preferable to the alcoves on the East Face route). Glen Dawson participated on the first ascents of both the East Face and the East Buttress, and after sixty years the East Buttress is still his favorite climb, one he has repeated many times.

A one-day (from Whitney Portal) ascent of the East Face or East Buttress is not a realistic possibility for most rock climbers. The climbing begins after 4,500 feet of gain in a mostly trailless approach. I know a handful of individuals who have done this successfully, but they had an intimate knowledge of the approach and climbing routes. Even so, for them it was a predawn to postdusk affair.

Hale, Young, and Hitchcock Traverse. Leave the John Muir Trail between Guitar and Timberline Lakes and climb Mount Hale and then Mount Young. Descend the south slope of Mount Young, cross the John Muir Trail near Timberline Lake, and climb onto the class 3 west shoulder of Mount Hitchcock. Descend Mount Hitchcock via its southeast saddle over loose scree to Hitchcock Lakes.

Mount Tyndall from the northeast. Photo by R. J. Secor.

The Kaweahs and the Great Western Divide

This prominent subrange is every bit as impressive as the Sierra crest itself. Located west of the Kern River, it follows the Great Western Divide south from Table Mountain to Vandever Mountain. It is bounded on the north by Sentinel Ridge (the southern rim of Kings Canyon). The Kaweah Peaks Ridge branches off from the Great Western Divide at Triple Divide Peak. The Kaweahs are high, consist of very loose rock, and feature the walk-up of Mount Kaweah and the sinister Black Kaweah.

HISTORY

Shepherds drove their flocks high into the Kern River and Kaweah River basins in the 1860s. They were the first to explore the high passes and the cirques at timberline, always searching for the perfect meadow. A prominent early explorer was William B. Wallace, a judge and prospector who searched for gold, silver, and copper following the 1879 mining excitement in Mineral King. In 1881 he crossed the Kern River and made an early ascent of Mount Whitney. Returning to the west, he and James Wright and the Reverend Frederick H. Wales climbed Mount Kaweah.

For many years it was thought that the Kaweah River originated near the Kaweah Peaks. In 1896 William R. Dudley climbed Sawtooth Peak and could easily see that the Kaweahs were not on the crest of the Great Western Divide, but instead were far into the Kern River watershed. The next year he climbed Mount Kaweah and named the Kern-Kaweah River, Milestone Bowl, Red Spur, and Picket Guard Peak.

The first significant mountaineering for sport occurred in 1912. That summer Charles Michael climbed

Michael's Pinnacle in the Kaweahs, and farther north, Robert Price, William Colby, and Francis Farquhar climbed Milestone Mountain.

The greatest prize of all was the first ascent of the Black Kaweah. This happened in 1920, when James Hutchinson, Duncan McDuffie, and the horse packer Onis Imis Brown reached the summit via the long west ridge.

MAPS

USGS. *7.5-minute series:* Chagoopa Falls, Mineral King, Silver City, Mt. Kaweah, Triple Divide Peak, Lodgepole, Giant Forest, Mt. Brewer, Sphinx Lakes, Mt. Silliman, Muir Grove. *National park maps:* Sequoia and Kings Canyon National Parks and Vicinity (1:125,000). *30 x 60–minute series:* Mount Whitney.

USFS. A Guide to the John Muir Wilderness and the Sequoia–Kings Canyon Wilderness (1:63,360); A Guide to the Golden Trout Wilderness/South Sierra Wilderness (1:63,360).

Tom Harrison Cartography. Mount Whitney High Country.

Map Link 15-minute series. Mount Whitney, Kern Peak, Mineral King, Triple Divide Peak, Giant Forest, Tehipite Dome.

Wilderness Press 15-minute series. Mount Whitney, Mineral King, Triple Divide Peak.

ROADS

Mineral King Road

Mineral King Road leaves Highway 198 3.9 miles east of the community of Three Rivers. It is a narrow,

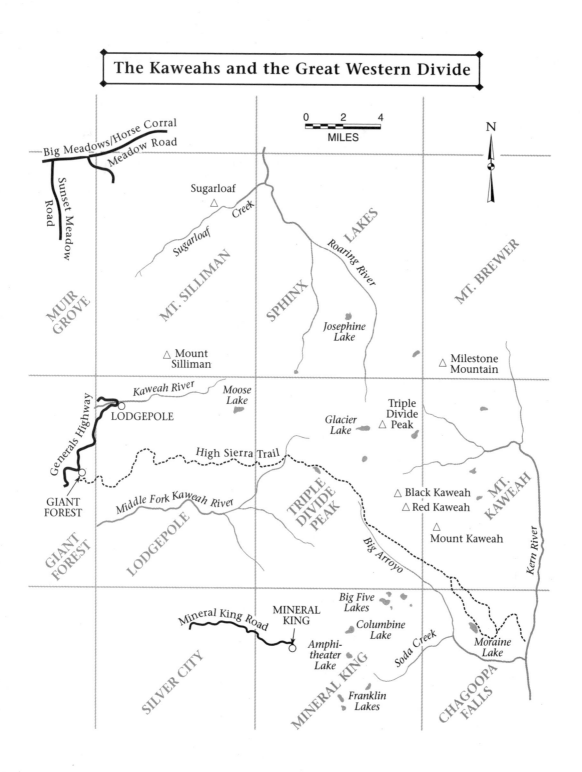

The Kaweahs and the Great Western Divide

0   2   4
MILES

N

Big Meadows/Horse Corral Meadow Road

Sunset Meadow Road

Sugarloaf △

Sugarloaf Creek

MUIR GROVE

MT. SILLIMAN

SPHINX

LAKES

Roaring River

Josephine Lake

MT. BREWER

△ Mount Silliman

△ Milestone Mountain

Kaweah River

Moose Lake

LODGEPOLE

Generals Highway

GIANT FOREST

High Sierra Trail

Glacier Lake

Triple Divide Peak △

GIANT FOREST

Middle Fork Kaweah River

LODGEPOLE

TRIPLE DIVIDE PEAK

△ Black Kaweah
△ Red Kaweah

△ Mount Kaweah

MT. KAWEAH

Kern River

Big Arroyo

Mineral King Road

MINERAL KING

Big Five Lakes

Columbine Lake

Amphitheater Lake

Franklin Lakes

SILVER CITY

MINERAL KING

Soda Creek

Moraine Lake

CHAGOOPA FALLS

steep road with many curves, paved for the most part. After 20.4 miles it reaches the summer home community of Cabin Cove. Silver City is 0.7 mile farther, and Mineral King itself is 2.7 miles beyond Silver City. Facilities at Mineral King are minimal: a ranger station, a pack station, and two hiker parking lots. The town of Mineral King disappeared many years ago, the victim of fires and avalanches. Mineral King is now a beautiful, unspoiled, tranquil valley.

Warning: The marmots of Mineral King like to chew on automobile radiator hoses, fan belts, and insulated electrical wires. Be sure to bring spares and tools for replacement, along with enough water to fill the vehicle's cooling system. This is not a joke—after one weekend, a friend of mine drove back to Los Angeles with a live marmot under the hood of her car! (This problem is most severe in early summer, and gradually diminishes towards autumn.)

Generals Highway

Generals Highway (Highway 198) leads from Lake Kaweah to Giant Forest and Grant Grove in Sequoia and Kings Canyon National Parks. At 6.2 miles east of Three Rivers, the road enters Sequoia National Park, and at 12.0 miles it meets another road leading to Buckeye Flat Campground; the trailhead for the Middle Fork Trail is 1.9 miles down this road, and the Paradise Creek Trailhead is at nearby Buckeye Flat Campground. The highway goes on, passing Hospital Rock, and at 10.4 miles from the turnoff it reaches Giant Forest. The Crescent Meadow Road leads south and then east from Giant Forest for 2.4 miles to the trailhead for the High Sierra Trail. The Generals Highway continues from Giant Forest another 1.7 miles to the junction with the road leading to Wolverton; the trailheads for the trails leading to Pear Lake and Alta Peak are along the loop at the end of this road, 1.4 miles from the highway. The Generals Highway continues another 1.6 miles beyond the junction with the Wolverton Road to Lodgepole. The trailhead for the Twin Lakes Trail is in this area.

From Lodgepole, the Generals Highway goes 18.7 miles farther to the junction with the Big Meadows/ Horse Corral Meadow Road. The Generals Highway continues toward Grant Grove and meets Highway 180 6.8 miles beyond the Big Meadow/Horse Corral Meadows Road junction.

Big Meadows/Horse Corral Meadow Road

Big Meadows/Horse Corral Meadow Road starts along the Generals Highway 18.7 miles from Lodgepole (or 6.8 miles from the junction with State Highway 180 near Grant Grove). It goes east (past Big Meadows) for 9.4 miles to a junction with the road leading to Sunset Meadow; the trailhead for the Sugarloaf Trail is 2.2 miles beyond the junction, along Sunset Meadow Road. The Horse Corral Meadow Road continues east from the junction another 1.3 miles to Horse Corral Meadow. Here it meets a road that goes south, leading to the trailhead for the Marvin Pass Trail; the trailhead is 4.2 miles beyond this junction. From this junction, the Horse Corral Meadow Road continues another 3.8 miles to Summit Meadow. This is the upper trailhead for the Don Cecil Trail, which comes up from Kings Canyon (described in Chapter 6, Monarch Divide and the Cirque Crest). There is also a trail that leads from this trailhead to the summit of Lookout Peak, where an outstanding view of Kings Canyon can be had for only ½ mile of hiking with approximately 500 feet of gain.

TRAILS

Farewell Gap Trail   4½ miles

A non-quota trail. From the pack station (0 mi; 7,840 ft+) near Mineral King, the Farewell Gap Trail goes south up the valley, passing the trail leading to Franklin Pass (2¼ mi; 9,538 ft), to the summit of Farewell Gap (2¼ mi; 10,680 ft+). The trail continues south from Farewell Gap to the headwaters of the Little Kern River. Wood campfires are prohibited north of Farewell Gap. Bears prowl through this area.

Franklin Pass Trail and Soda Creek Trail   12¾ miles

A quota trail. This trail starts from its junction with the Farewell Gap Trail, 2¼ miles from Mineral King (0 mi; 9,358 ft). It heads northeast from the junction to Franklin Lakes (2 mi; 10,400 ft). It then crosses the Great Western Divide at Franklin Pass (1½ mi; 11,720 ft+). Wood campfires are prohibited west of Franklin Pass. Bears prowl through this area. The trail descends the east side of the pass to the junction with the Shotgun Pass Trail (1¼ mi; 10,728 ft). The Franklin Pass Trail continues east from the junction to meet the Rattlesnake Creek and Soda Creek Trails (½ mi; 10,240 ft+). The Soda Creek Trail heads northeast from here to Little Clare Lake (1½ mi; 10,420 ft), then descends Soda Creek to a junction with the Sawtooth Pass Trail (6 mi; 8,604 ft) near the lower end of Lost Canyon.

Rattlesnake Creek Trail and the Kern River Trail   11¾ miles

This trail begins at its junction (0 mi; 10,240 ft+) with the Soda Creek Trail, 7½ miles from Mineral King via Franklin Pass. It descends Rattlesnake Creek to a junction with the Big Arroyo Trail (6¾ mi; 8,044 ft). A steep descent follows, ending with a junction along the Kern River Trail (2½ mi; 6,560 ft+). The Kern River Trail leads north to Upper Funston Meadow to meet the High Sierra Trail (2½ mi; 6,720 ft+).

Sawtooth Pass Trail   12¾ miles

This trail starts by heading north from the Mineral King hikers' parking area (0 mi; 7,800 ft+) before meeting the Timber Gap Trail (½ mi; 8,320 ft+). The Sawtooth Pass Trail turns southeast away from the junction and ascends the Monarch Creek drainage to "Groundhog Meadow" (½ mi; 8,757 ft; UTM 580355), where cross-country hikers can leave the trail and climb directly uphill toward the Sawtooth Pass Trail, which crosses the basin 1,500 feet above. From Groundhog Meadow the proper Sawtooth Pass Trail switchbacks up the slope to the south to meet a side trail (1¼ mi; 10,024 ft) leading to Crystal Lake, 2 miles away. The Sawtooth Pass Trail traverses east just below Monarch Lakes, then goes north across sandy slopes and switchbacks back to the southeast before climbing over Sawtooth Pass (3 mi; 11,720 ft+). Wood campfires are prohibited west of Sawtooth Pass. The trail descends the east side of the pass to Columbine Lake (1 mi; 10,970 ft). Bears prowl through this area. After a short climb out of this basin, it descends Lost Canyon and meets the Big Five Lakes Trail (4 mi; 9,580 ft). It continues down Lost Canyon to the Soda Creek Trail (1¾ mi; 8,604 ft) followed by a steep descent to the Big Arroyo Trail (¾ mi; 8,000 ft+).

Timber Gap Trail   9 miles

A quota trail. This trail starts approximately ½ mile above Mineral King along the Sawtooth Pass Trail (0 mi;

8,320 ft+). It climbs to the north to Timber Gap (2 mi; 9,520 ft+) before descending to its junction with the Black Rock Pass Trail (3½ mi; 7,124 ft). The trail continues down Cliff Creek (to 6,160 ft+) before ascending (to 6,400 ft+) and descending again to Redwood Meadow (3½ mi; 6,040 ft+). Wood campfires are prohibited south of Timber Gap and above 9,000 feet north of Timber Gap. Bears prowl through this area.

Black Rock Pass Trail   11½ miles

This trail begins along the Big Arroyo Trail about ¼ mile below the junction of the High Sierra Trail and the Big Arroyo Trail (0 mi; 9,520 ft). After crossing the Big Arroyo, the Black Rock Pass Trail climbs to a bench on the southwest wall of the canyon, then makes a gentle ascent to Little Five Lakes (3 mi; 10,476 ft) where it meets the northern end of the Big Five Lakes Trail. Wood campfires are prohibited above 10,400 feet in this basin. Bears prowl through this area. The Black Rock Pass Trail then climbs to Black Rock Pass (2 mi; 11,680 ft+), which features splendid views of the Kaweah Peaks Ridge. A long, rough descent with many switchbacks follows—along Cliff Creek, past Pinto Lake, and between the walls of the canyon, to the junction with the Timber Gap Trail (6½ mi; 7,124 ft). Wood campfires are prohibited above 9,000 feet along Cliff Creek. Bears prowl through this area.

Big Five Lakes Trail   5 miles

This trail connects Little Five Lakes with the Sawtooth Pass Trail in Lost Canyon by way of Big Five Lakes. It starts in the Little Five Lakes basin at its junction with the Black Rock Pass Trail (0 mi; 10,476 ft). Bears prowl through this area. It traverses around a spur of the Great Western Divide before descending to Big Five Lakes (2 mi; 10,450 ft); a 2-mile trail leads southwest from here to the lake basin. It then climbs a steep wall to the southeast before circling around to the southwest to meet the Sawtooth Pass Trail in Lost Canyon (3 mi; 9,580 ft).

Paradise Ridge Trail   9 miles

A quota trail. This trail is also known as the "Redwood Meadow Trail." The Paradise Ridge Trail starts near Atwell Mill Campground, at 19.5 miles along Mineral King Road from Highway 198. The trail climbs north to Paradise Ridge dividing the East and Middle Forks of the Kaweah River (3 mi; 8,440 ft+). (A trail traverses the ridge to the west, ending near the summit of Paradise Peak.) It then descends to Redwood Meadow (6 mi; 6,040 ft+).

The Paradise Ridge Trail involves slightly more elevation gain than the Timber Gap Trail. But the tradeoff is that it passes through the Atwell Grove of sequoias, and so has more shade, giving relief on a hot day.

Paradise Creek Trail   3¼ miles

The trailhead for this trail is at Buckeye Flat Campground, across from site No. 23 (0 mi; 2,800 ft+). It crosses the Middle Fork of the Kaweah River on a bridge (¼ mi; 2,840 ft+) and continues up Paradise Creek to where it ends (3 mi; 4,000 ft+). At one time the trail went all the way to the upper reaches of Paradise Creek, but the upper portion of the trail has not been maintained for many years and is very faint.

Middle Fork Trail   15 miles

A quota trail. At a point near Hospital Rock along the Generals Highway, 5.8 miles beyond the Sequoia National Park boundary, a road to Buckeye Flat Campground branches to the right. The road forks 0.6 mile from the Generals Highway; take the left fork 1.3 miles to the trailhead for the Middle Fork Trail (0 mi; 3,160 ft+). The trail follows the drainage of the Middle Fork of the Kaweah River on the north side of the canyon to Redwood Meadow (15 mi; 6,040 ft+). A trail descends to the river near Mehrten Creek.

An alternate route to Redwood Meadow leaves the Middle Fork Trail just beyond the crossing of the Middle Fork of the Kaweah River. This trail continues upstream before turning to the south, crossing Eagle Scout and Granite Creeks before descending to Redwood Meadow, adding 3 miles to the hiking distance and about 600 feet of elevation gain.

The Middle Fork Trail begins at an elevation of approximately 3,300 feet and ends at Redwood Meadow, about 6,000 feet above sea level. Accordingly, it could be a viable option for an early-season hike in the High Sierra while snow is still choking the higher elevations of the mountains. Caution must be exercised, however, while crossing Moro, Panther, Mehrten, and Buck Creeks during the spring. The Middle Fork itself must

be crossed just below Redwood Meadow. This may be impassable during the early season of a heavy snow year.

High Sierra Trail   49 miles

A quota trail. The High Sierra Trail starts in Crescent Meadow at Giant Forest, crosses the Great Western Divide at Kaweah Gap, and descends to the Kern River before meeting the John Muir Trail at Wallace Creek. This trail can be considered the trans-Sierra equivalent of the John Muir Trail. It crosses a beautiful region of the Sierra Nevada.

The trailhead is at the end of Crescent Meadow Road in Giant Forest (0 mi; 6,680 ft+). It meets several tourist trails leading back to the Giant Forest area before starting its main traverse high above the Middle Fork of the Kaweah River, 3,000 feet below. The trail eventually meets the southern branch of the Alta/Wolverton Trail (6¾ mi; 7,680 ft+). The High Sierra Trail continues east to Bearpaw Meadow (5 mi; 7,880 ft+); a branch of the Elizabeth Pass Trail leads northeast from here, while another trail heads southwest past Little Bearpaw Meadow to meet the Middle Fork Trail. As the name implies, bears prowl through this area. Camp only in designated campsites at Bearpaw Meadow. The High Sierra Trail goes east to meet another branch of the Elizabeth Pass Trail (2 mi; 7,400 ft+), and continues east to Hamilton Lake (3 mi; 8,235 ft), a magnificent amphitheater surrounded by big walls; this is a miniature Yosemite Valley. There is a two-night camp limit in the Hamilton Lakes basin, and wood fires are prohibited. Bears prowl through this area. The trail continues east over Kaweah Gap (4 mi; 10,680 ft+) where the High Sierra Trail goes south, down the Big Arroyo to a three-way junction (2¼ mi; 9,560 ft+). From the junction, a trail goes a short distance to the stream, where the Big Arroyo Trail goes southeast, and the Black Rock Pass Trail heads southwest. Wood campfires are prohibited above 10,000 feet in the Big Arroyo and in Nine Lake Basin. The High Sierra Trail climbs slightly from the junction to the junction with the Moraine Lake Trail (5 mi; 10,200 ft+). Leave the High Sierra Trail here and hike to Moraine Lake (2½ mi; 9,302 ft). Bears prowl through this area. Continue east on the trail to rejoin the High Sierra Trail (1¼ mi; 9,162 ft). (Alternatively, you can remain on the High Sierra Trail for 3½ miles, meeting the eastern end of the Moraine Lake Trail just above Funston Creek, but you should not miss a visit to beautiful Moraine Lake just to save ¼ mile of hiking.) The High Sierra Trail makes a steep descent to the Kern River canyon, ending just above the level of Upper Funston Meadow (4 mi; 6,720 ft+). Bears prowl through this area.

The junction with the Big Arroyo Trail and the Rattlesnake Creek Trail is 2½ miles to the south, but the High Sierra Trail continues north to Junction Meadow (9 mi; 8,071 ft+), passing through the giant Kern River canyon along the way. Bears prowl through this area. At Junction Meadow the Colby Pass Trail comes in from the west, and the High Sierra Trail goes north, leaving the upper Kern River Trail (1 mi; 8,793 ft+) and going east (into the realm of Chapter 2, The Whitney Region). It then ascends Wallace Creek to the John Muir Trail (3¼ mi; 10,403 ft).

Big Arroyo Trail   12 miles

From the three-way junction in the Big Arroyo (High Sierra Trail, Black Rock Pass Trail, and the Big Arroyo Trail) (0 mi; 9,520 ft+), this trail goes downstream, first on the north side and then on the south side, to the junction with the Soda Creek and Sawtooth Pass Trails (7 mi; 8,000 ft+). It continues downstream before climbing to the southeast and descending to meet the Rattlesnake Creek Trail (5 mi; 8,044 ft).

Cross-country hikers may be tempted to descend the Big Arroyo directly to the Kern River canyon, but this involves many steep drops and waterfalls; the Big Arroyo turns into a hanging valley in this area.

Wolverton/Alta Trail and the Moose Lake Trail   10 –11¾ miles

A quota trail. This is also known as the "Alta Peak Trail." From Wolverton (0 mi; 7,080 ft+) this trail follows Wolverton Creek to a junction with the Pear Lake Trails (2 mi; 8,040 ft+). The trail then heads south from the junction to Panther Gap (3 mi; 8,480 ft+). The trail goes east from Panther Gap to meet a side trail (1¼ mi; 8,760 ft+) that leads down to the High Sierra Trail. The Wolverton/Alta Trail continues east from the junction, passes Mehrten Meadow, then meets the Alta Peak Trail (1¼ mi; 9,280 ft+). As the name suggests, the Alta Peak Trail goes to the summit of the peak (2½ mi; 11,204 ft),

from which there is a splendid view of the Great Western Divide. The Wolverton/Alta Trail continues east to Alta Meadow (1¾ mi; 9,040 ft+). At one time a trail continued north from Alta Meadow over the ridge to desolate Moose Lake, but it has been abandoned.

Camping is prohibited along Wolverton Creek from the parking area to 8,000 feet. Wood fires are prohibited above 9,000 feet. Bears prowl through this area.

Pear Lake Trail   5 miles

A quota trail. This trail follows Wolverton Creek for 2 miles from Wolverton, where it leaves the Wolverton/Alta Trail (0 mi; 8,040 ft+). The Pear Lake Trail goes north and then east, passing Heather Lake, Emerald Lake, and Aster Lake to arrive at Pear Lake (5¼ mi; 9,520 ft+), nestled in a bowl beneath the steep cliffs north of Alta Peak. An alternate route goes farther to the north along the southern rim of Tokopah Valley before turning to the southeast and meeting the main Pear Lake Trail west of Heather Lake; this alternate trail adds only ¼ mile of hiking, and offers splendid views. Camp only in designated campsites at Emerald Lake and Pear Lake.

The Pear Lake Hut serves as a ranger station in the summer, and during the winter months it is a popular destination for cross-country skiers. It was constructed in the 1930s by the Civilian Conservation Corps. Reservations are required to use the hut; contact Sequoia Natural History Association for more information: HCR 89, Box 10, Three Rivers, CA 93271; tel: 559-565-3759.

Camping is prohibited along Wolverton Creek from the parking area to 8,000 feet. Wood fires are prohibited above 9,000 feet. Bears are active throughout this area.

Twin Lakes Trail   17½ miles

A quota trail. This is also known as the "Silliman Pass Trail." Bears are active along this entire trail. The Twin Lakes Trail leaves Lodgepole Campground (0 mi; 6,720 ft+) and goes north, past Cahoon Meadow and over Cahoon Gap (5 mi; 8,640 ft+) to a junction with the J.O. Pass Trail (1 mi; 8,434 ft). The Twin Lakes Trail goes east, past Twin Lakes and over Silliman Pass, to Ranger Lake (5½ mi; 9,200 ft+). From Ranger Lake the trail heads north (side trails go to Lost Lake and Seville Lake) to Comanche Meadow (6 mi; 7,889 ft). From Comanche Meadow you can follow trails to either Marvin Pass or Scaffold Meadows.

Marvin Pass Trail and J.O. Pass Trail

7 miles

A quota trail. From Horse Corral Meadow a road winds south for 4.2 miles to the trailhead for the Marvin Pass Trail (0 mi; 8,360 ft+). The trail heads east from the trailhead before turning south to cross Marvin Pass (1¼ mi; 9,080 ft+) and descend to a junction with the Sugarloaf Trail at Rowell Meadow (1¼ mi; 8,855 ft). The J.O. Pass Trail continues south, over J.O. Pass (4½ mi; 9,414 ft) to the junction with the Twin Lakes Trail (2¼ mi; 8,434 ft).

Sugarloaf Trail   16 miles

A quota trail. This trail starts near the end of Sunset Meadow Road (0 mi; 7,880 ft+), which is off Horse Corral Meadow Road. After a gentle climb it crosses Rowell Meadow and meets the Marvin Pass Trail and J.O. Pass Trail junction (2½ mi; 8,855 ft). The Sugarloaf Trail continues east over a small pass (2¼ mi; 9,320 ft+) and into Kings Canyon National Park. It continues to a junction with the Twin Lakes Trail near Comanche Meadow along Sugarloaf Creek (2¼ mi; 7,889 ft). The trail goes east through rolling terrain to Scaffold Meadows along Roaring River (9 mi; 7,400 ft+). Bears prowl through this area.

Three trails lead from Scaffold Meadows: the Elizabeth Pass Trail, the Colby Pass Trail, and the Sphinx Creek Trail. The Sphinx Creek Trail is described in Chapter 4, The Kings-Kern Divide.

Colby Pass Trail   22 miles

Bears prowl through this area. From Scaffold Meadows (0 mi; 7,400 ft+) the Colby Pass Trail ascends beautiful Cloud Canyon (with impressive views of Whaleback), then goes past Cement Table Meadow and Big Wet Meadow (also known as "Big West Meadow") to a junction with a side trail (9 mi; 9,040 ft+), which goes up Cloud Canyon. (This side trail, approximately 3 miles long, serves as the approach for ascents of Glacier Ridge and Whaleback, and is used for crossing Triple Divide Pass, Lion Lake Pass, and Coppermine Pass.) The Colby Pass Trail starts to climb toward the southeast, past Colby Lake, and up to Colby Pass (4 mi; 11,960 ft+). The upper portion of this trail is very rough and steep. From the pass, the trail descends to Gallats Lake (which is now almost a meadow; 3 mi; 10,040 ft+) along the Kern-Kaweah River, another beautiful canyon.

The trail continues downstream to Junction Meadow (6 mi; 8,070 ft+), where it meets the High Sierra Trail.

Elizabeth Pass Trail   16 miles

The Elizabeth Pass Trail goes south from Scaffold Meadows (0 mi; 7,400 ft) and up Deadman Canyon (a shepherd was killed here in the 1800s) to cross the Kings-Kaweah Divide. This is an easy, gradual ascent through forests and meadows. Big Bird Lake (which has also been called "Dollar Lake") can be reached by scrambling up its outlet stream. In the upper reaches of the canyon the trail becomes steep and rough, and Elizabeth Pass is finally attained (10 mi; 11,360 ft+). The descent of the southern side of the pass is easy. The trail comes to a three-way junction above Lone Pine Creek (3 mi; 8,160 ft+). (One trail goes east, up to Tamarack Lake, and another descends about 2½ miles to meet the High Sierra Trail.) The Elizabeth Pass Trail (the middle trail at the junction) at first climbs to the southeast and then descends to Bearpaw Meadow (3 mi; 7,840 ft+).

CROSS-COUNTRY ROUTES

Glacier Pass   11,080 ft+; 11,080 ft+; 0.6 mi ESE of Empire Mountain

Class 3. This route connects the Sawtooth Pass Trail with the Black Rock Pass Trail via Spring Lake. It is the easiest and fastest one-day route for experienced cross-country hikers traveling from Mineral King to the Big Arroyo. From "Groundhog Meadow" along the Sawtooth Pass Trail (at an elevation of 8,757 ft; UTM 580355), leave the trail and hike directly up the slope above. (Alternatively, you can remain on the Sawtooth Pass Trail beyond Monarch Lake.) You eventually regain the Sawtooth Pass Trail below Sawtooth Pass. At the point where the trail switchbacks to Sawtooth Pass, leave the trail and head for the saddle to the north. The north side of Glacier Pass is a short, steep cliff, which usually has a small snowfield until late in the summer; in the spring there may be a cornice blocking the way. Descend on the north side of the pass and go down to Spring Lake, circling it on its north side. Remain above the 10,000-foot contour and make a level traverse to the Black Rock Pass Trail.

When approaching Glacier Pass from the north, follow the north side of the stream that feeds Spring Lake to the tarns in the meadows below the pass. During low snow years it may be possible to skirt the snow on the right (west) side of the pass by climbing steep talus.

"Crystal Pass" 11,400 ft+; 11,360 ft+;
0.7 mi S of Sawtooth Peak; UTM 606343

Class 3. This pass leads between Crystal Lake and Amphitheater Lake. It is class 2 from the west, and class 3 from the east on huge granite slabs and benches.

"Cyclamen Lake Pass" 11,145 ft; 11,040 ft+;
0.5 mi NE of Cyclamen Lake

Class 3. This pass has also been called "Hands and Knees Pass" and "Bunny Ears Pass." This difficult cross-country route leads from Columbine Lake to Big Five Lakes. (It is the author's experience that it is easier and faster to hike down the Sawtooth Pass Trail through Lost Canyon and then take the Big Five Lakes Trail.) From Columbine Lake, cross the shallow pass to the north and descend steep slabs and talus to the east shore of Cyclamen Lake. Make an ascending traverse from the lake to Cyclamen Lake Pass; this involves more steep slabs and talus. From the top of the pass either descend to Big Five Lakes or traverse north around the east ridge of Peak 11,680ft+ (11,600 ft+) to the Black Rock Pass Trail above Little Five Lakes.

"Bilko Pass" 11,480 ft+; 11,360 ft+;
1.1 mi NNW of Needham Mountain

Class 3. This name commemorates Bill Croxson, Bill Schuler, and Andy Smatko, who crossed this pass on August 26, 1969. This is the pass just to the east of Peak 11,760ft+ (11,772 ft). It is a variation of the Cyclamen Lake Pass route. From Columbine Lake, make an ascending traverse to the pass and descend to Big Five Lakes. Only the very top portion of this pass is class 3.

"Kaweah Pass" 3760 m+; 12,320 ft+;
0.5 mi NE of Mount Kaweah

Class 2. This pass leads from the High Sierra Trail to Chagoopa Plateau, across beautiful Kaweah Basin, and down the west side of Picket Creek to the Colby Pass Trail along the Kern-Kaweah River. This is a very nice cross-country route through magnificent scenery. From the High Sierra Trail follow Chagoopa Creek to the basin northeast of Mount Kaweah. Cross Kaweah Pass at its low point, and descend (loose rock!) to Kaweah Ba-

sin. Go north through Kaweah Basin to the low point of the shallow ridge dividing Kaweah Basin and Picket Creek (Pass 3300m+; 10,800 ft+; 1.1 mi SE of Picket Guard Peak; UTM 693473). Descend Picket Creek to Lake 3320m+ (10,560 ft+; 1.0 mi ESE of Picket Guard Peak; UTM 699483). At this point, leave Picket Creek and descend class 2 terrain to the north down to the Colby Pass Trail. Don't follow Picket Creek down to the Colby Pass Trail; there are some waterfalls along the lower end of Picket Creek that bar the way. *Variation:* Class 3. An unnamed creek is about ½ mile to the southeast of Picket Creek. It is possible to ascend or descend the west side of the creek. Two short sections of class 3 are encountered.

"Pyra-Queen Col" 12,840 ft+; 12,800 ft+;
0.2 mi S of Kaweah Queen

Class 2. This pass provides access to Kaweah Basin from Nine Lake Basin in the upper part of the Big Arroyo. Pass Lake 11,705ft (11,680 ft+; the lake at the base of the north face of the Black Kaweah) on its north shore. Climb a chute that leads up diagonally from right to left to the easier, southernmost saddle, the one closest to Pyramidal Pinnacle. Differences as great as 8 degrees from the normal compass variation may be encountered near Pyra-Queen Col.

"Eagle Scout Pass" 11,600 ft+; 11,600 ft+;
0.2 mi SSE of Eagle Scout Peak

Class 3. This pass has been used to approach the upper Eagle Scout Creek drainage from the Big Arroyo. It is necessary to descend the west side of the pass by heading southwest to keep the difficulty down to class 3.

"Pants Pass" 11,960 ft+; 12,000 ft+;
1.4 mi S of Triple Divide Peak; UTM 634484

Class 2. This is a difficult cross-country pass that provides access between Nine Lake Basin and the Kern-Kaweah River. It is also known as "Kern-Kaweah Col," but anyone who has crossed it will appreciate the name Pants Pass. From Nine Lake Basin, climb loose scree and talus to the pass. There are actually two notches atop the pass. The correct notch is the higher one to the north; the southern, lower notch is class 3 on its western side, and heavily laden hikers may be forced to slide on their bottoms when crossing this notch from east to west.

From the Kern-Kaweah River proceed to the tarn just

north of Lake 11,360ft+ (11,380 ft+), then climb the steep chute leading to the easier northern notch atop the pass.

You may be tempted to take the next pass to the north, Pass 11,775ft (11,760 ft+). This pass has a vertical cliff on its eastern side. Pants Pass is the best route.

"Lion Rock Pass"   11,760 ft+; 11,680 ft+;
0.5 mi E of Lion Rock

Class 2. Lion Rock Pass, in combination with Lion Lake Pass, provides a direct route between Nine Lake Basin and Cloud Canyon. Actually, there are two passes that may be used for Lion Rock Pass: the lower pass, and the higher pass 0.2 mile to the west at 11,840 feet+ (11,760 ft+). Both passes are class 2.

"Lion Lake Pass"   11,600 ft+; 11,520 ft;
0.4 mi W of Triple Divide Peak

Class 2. This is the route between Cloud Canyon and Lion Lake. When traversing from Triple Divide Pass to Lion Lake Pass it is necessary to drop below the level of Glacier Lake to avoid a cliff to the east of Lion Lake Pass. When approaching Lion Lake Pass from the south, it is better to angle up to the pass from the west end of Lion Lake over talus. Those descending the southern side of Lion Lake Pass may want to slide down the scree slope that leads to the eastern end of Lion Lake.

There are several cliffs (surrounded by thick brush) along upper Lone Pine Creek between Tamarack Lake and Lion Lake. These can be avoided by following an abandoned trail that heads north from near the outlet of Tama-

Pants Pass from Nine Lake Basin. Photo by R. J. Secor.

rack Lake. It soon fades into brush at a gully located about 100 feet above the creek. The trail, which is overgrown in places with flowers and grass, switchbacks up the slope and then heads east over some fallen trees before leading to the swamp above the cliff northeast of Tamarack Lake. (Those looking for this trail from above can locate it at a small saddle at UTM 601497.) The route from here to Lion Lake keeps to the south side of the stream, crossing slabs and talus to the outlet of the lake.

Triple Divide Pass   12,200 ft+; 12,160 ft+;
0.4 mi NE of Triple Divide Peak

Class 2. This is the route between upper Cloud Canyon and the Kern-Kaweah River. From Glacier Lake go across the small bowl immediately north of Triple Divide Peak to the pass. From here there are two routes. One crosses the basin east of the pass to the south shoulder of Peak 12,560ft+ (12,600 ft+). Cross the shoulder at the 12,000-foot contour and descend to the Colby Pass Trail. The other route from Triple Divide Pass traverses around the east side of Triple Divide Peak to the southeast side of the peak. A steep descent, heading almost due south, leads to a break in the steep wall surrounding this side of Triple Divide Peak. From here it is easy to follow the Kern-Kaweah River downstream.

"Talus Pass"   3500 m+; 11,520 ft+;
0.1 mi NE of Talus Lake; UTM 661568

Class 2. This pass serves as a cross-country route between the Colby Pass Trail and Table Creek. Leave the Colby Pass Trail below the outlet of Colby Lake and go north before turning northeast towards Talus Lake. The pass is just beyond the lake, and it is necessary to drop down to 11,200 feet to bypass a cliff on the northeast side of the pass.

Copper Mine Pass   11,960 ft+; 11,920 ft+;
1.4 mi NW of Triple Divide Peak

Class 2. The name of this pass has been misplaced atop Peak 12,345ft (12,340 ft+) on some editions of the Triple Divide Peak 7.5-minute quadrangle. This pass crosses Glacier Ridge just north of the divide that separates the Kings River basin from the Kaweah River. This is a steep and difficult route, but it has spectacular views of the Kaweahs and Palisades, and this makes the route worthwhile.

This is one of the passes of the Sierra High Route, a trans-Sierra ski tour going from Shepherd Pass to

Wolverton. Depending on the snowfall and winds during the previous winter, this pass can be either easy or extremely difficult, with floating cornices and steep, icy slopes on its western side. Some ski mountaineers have referred to this pass as "Deadman Pass."

The official name commemorates a mine that was located along the ridge east of Elizabeth Pass. At one time a trail went from upper Cloud Canyon and along the east and west ridges of Peak 12,345ft (12,340 ft+) to the Elizabeth Pass Trail. The trail has been abandoned for a long time, and the mine has been abandoned for even longer than that.

"Horn Col"   11,280 ft+; 11,280 ft+;
0.5 mi NW of Elizabeth Pass

Class 1. Also known as "Fin Pass," this is the small pass just to the north of Peak 11,760ft+ (11,830 ft). It is one of the passes used on the Sierra High Route trans-Sierra ski tour.

"Pterodactyl Pass"   10,880 ft+; 10,880 ft+;
1.1 mi SW of Big Bird Lake

Class 2. This pass has also been called "Lightning Pass." This is technically not a pass, but a crossing of the south ridge of Big Bird Peak. This is one of the passes used on the Sierra High Route.

"The Right Pass"   9,680 ft+; 9,680 ft+;
0.3 mi E of Pear Lake Hut

Class 1. This is the small pass which must be crossed before dropping down to the Pear Lake Ranger Station on the Sierra High Route. With religious use of the map, compass, and altimeter, it is possible to ski "down" (i.e., no stopping to put on climbing skins) to this pass from Table Meadows.

Milestone Creek

At one time a trail ascended Milestone Creek to Lake 3620 m+ (11,840 ft+), but it has been abandoned. You may still find traces of it, however. The trail began at an elevation of 3240 meters+ (10,640 ft+; UTM 719563) along the Lake South America Trail. After crossing the Kern River on a large log at the south end of Lake 3240m+ (10,640 ft+; UTM 719566) it contoured to meet Milestone Creek. It continued up this drainage to approximately 11,100 feet, where it turned up the main stream of Milestone Creek. The best route for cross-country hikers is to follow the north branch of the creek in a west-northwesterly direction past a small lake, and proceed directly to Lake 3620m+ (11,840 ft+), which is in the cirque between Table Mountain and Midway Mountain. Wood campfires are prohibited above 10,400 feet in Milestone Creek basin.

"Milestone Pass" 3980 m+; 12,960 ft+;
0.2 mi SE of Milestone Mountain; UTM 676550

Class 2. This is actually a crossing of the southeast ridge of Milestone Mountain; the low point of the saddle has a cliff on its northeastern side. From Milestone Creek, approach the pass on its far right (north) side, then traverse to the left (south) down into the pass.

From Milestone Bowl, climb to the low point of the saddle and follow the ridge on the left (north) until it is possible to descend easily to Milestone Creek.

"Midway Col" 3920 m+; 12,880 ft+;
0.3 mi S of Midway Mountain

Class 2–3. This is a direct route between Cloud Canyon and Milestone Creek. Leave the Colby Pass Trail at Colby Lake and climb to Lake 3512m (11,523 ft), which is southwest of Midway Mountain. From the lake, cross talus and then follow a ledge that slightly ascends to the right (south). This is followed by approximately 20 feet of steep climbing to the summit. (A direct approach to the summit of the col from the west, i.e., avoiding the ledge, is class 4.) The east side of the col is gentler than the west.

PEAKS

Vandever Mountain 11,947 ft; 11,047 ft
From Farewell Gap. Class 1.

North Face. II, 5.6. First ascent August 1985 by Claude Fiddler and Nancy Fiddler.

Northwest Couloir. II, 5.0. First ascent September 1971 by Bruce Rogers. Climb the couloir that leads to the saddle just north of the summit. There is much loose rock on this route.

Northwest Ridge. Class 3. This is the ridge immediately right of the couloir.

Florence Peak 12,432 ft; 12,432 ft
Northeast Ridge. Class 2. This is a straightforward climb from Franklin Pass. Keep well to the left of the crest of the ridge.

The Ramp. II, 5.1. First ascent August 1972 by Bruce

Florence Peak, Northwest Face. Photo by R. J. Secor.

FLORENCE PEAK

The Ramp

Rampant

The Great Chimney

Direct Northwest Face

Rogers and Carl Boro. Climb the prominent, right-ascending ramp on the northwest face of Florence Peak to the northeast ridge.

Rampant. II, 5.7. First ascent August 22, 1976 by Bob Olson and Doug Meyer. Climb a 5.7 pitch to a large ledge below a broad ramp. Climb up and right to a ledge on the right margin of this ramp. A long pitch up some blocks ends on a ledge system, which is followed up and right to the broad gully above The Great Chimney.

The Great Chimney. III, 5.6. First ascent September 1968 by Jack Delk and Bill Sorenson. There is an obvious chimney on the northwest face. Climb the right wall of the chimney for three pitches, then move right onto easier terrain when difficulties increase. A bit of scrambling leads to a headwall, and two pitches on this lead to the summit ridge.

Direct Northwest Face. III, 5.8. First ascent August 1972 by Gary Kirk and Craig Thorn. This route begins in the middle of the face, directly above Franklin Lakes. Go to the left of a small tower. A huge ledge is reached after four pitches. Two more pitches lead to another ledge. Go right on this for about 100 feet and climb a right-leaning diagonal crack to the summit ridge.

Southwest Slope. Class 3. From Bullfrog Lakes, south of the peak, ascend the slope to the west ridge of Florence Peak. Climb over large blocks along the ridge to the summit.

Some may be tempted to make a direct ascent along the west ridge from Farewell Gap. There are many false summits along the way, resulting in some unnecessary elevation gain and loss.

East Side. Class 3. Ascend directly to the summit from the upper reaches of Rattlesnake Creek. Large blocks are encountered near the summit; careful routefinding is required. The Northeast Ridge is the preferred route.

Rainbow Mountain   12,043 ft; 12,000 ft+
Class 2 from the Franklin Pass Trail.

Peak 12,019ft   12,045 ft; 1.4 mi S of Sawtooth Peak
Class 2 from either the Franklin Pass Trail or Crystal Lake.

Mineral Peak   11,615 ft; 11,550 ft
Class 2 from Crystal Lake on the south or from Monarch Lake to the north. The summit rocks are best approached from the south.

Sawtooth Peak   12,343 ft; 12,343 ft
Northwest Ridge from Sawtooth Pass. Class 2. First ascent 1871 by Joseph Lovelace. Follow the sandy, southwest side of the ridge to the summit. The magnificent view from the summit makes it a worthwhile detour for hikers on the Sawtooth Pass Trail.

North Face. III, 5.8, A1. First ascent June 1970 by Ben Dewell, Dale Kruse, and Gary Goodson. There is a shallow rib on the face above Columbine Lake. Either climb the rib or the face to the right of the rib. When difficulties increase, traverse to the left and then go straight up to the summit.

Traverse from Needham Mountain. Class 2–3 along the ridge connecting the two peaks. It is easiest to drop down to 11,500 feet on the south side of this ridge beneath the pinnacles while traversing. Those doing this traverse who must return to Sawtooth Pass will have to reclimb Sawtooth Peak.

South Ridge. Class 2. First ascent July 12, 1929 by Walter A. Starr, Jr. A good use trail leads from lower Monarch Lake to upper Monarch Lake. From the upper lake, climb south over slabs, grass, and boulders until it is possible to turn east and climb over more slabs, sand, and grass to reach the low point of the ridge between Sawtooth Peak and Peak 11,600ft+ (11,440 ft+) at UTM 606346. Follow the south ridge to the top of Sawtooth Peak. *Variation:* Class 2. The south ridge can also be reached from the Soda Creek drainage.

Needham Mountain   12,520 ft+; 12,467 ft
South Slope. Class 2. First ascent July 1916 by Marion Randall Parsons, Agnes Vaile, H. C. Graham, and Edmund Chamberlin. This is usually done from the upper reaches of Soda Creek.

From Monarch Lakes. Class 3. First ascent 1994 by Matthias Selke. Go south from upper Monarch Lake over slabs, grass, and boulders until it is possible to turn east and ascend over more slabs, sand, and grass to the low point between Peak 11,600ft+ (11,440 ft+) and Sawtooth Peak at UTM 606346. Follow the south ridge of Sawtooth Peak until one is almost exactly halfway between the summit of the peak and the low point of the ridge, at an elevation of 11,900 ft. Cross the south ridge toward the northeast, aiming for a grassy ledge that at first goes up slightly for 10 feet, then descends for 30 feet (class 3) to the scree slopes that are east of the south ridge of Sawtooth Peak. From the end of the ledge, cross tedious boulders and slabs to the sandy west slope of Needham Mountain. Ascend the west slope to the first saddle west of Needham Mountain, then follow the ridge to the summit.

Traverse from Sawtooth Peak. Class 2–3. The pinnacles on this ridge can be avoided by traversing at the 11,500-foot level on their southern sides.

North Slope. Class 3. First ascent July 28, 1949 by R. R. Breckenfeld, Emily Frazer, and Donald Scanlon. From Lost Canyon, climb to the notch on the ridge between Sawtooth Peak and Needham Mountain. Follow the ridge to the summit of Needham Mountain.

Northwest Face. IV, 5.7. First ascent November 1968 by Gary Kirk and Bernard Hallet. The route is reportedly somewhere on this face.

Northwest Buttress. III, 5.6. First ascent by Claude Fiddler and Nancy Fiddler.

North Face. Class 3. First ascent July 28, 1949 by Howard Parker and Helen Parker. Climb the couloir that leads to the east ridge. Follow the ridge to the summit.

Southeast Slope. Class 2. First ascent August 8, 1951 by A. J. Reyman on a traverse from Peak 12,360ft+ (12,320 ft+).

Peak 12,360ft+   12,320 ft+;
0.8 mi ESE of Needham Mountain

South Ridge. Class 3. First ascent August 8, 1951 by A. J. Reyman on a traverse from Peak 12,168ft (12,172 ft).

Southwest Slope. Class 2. There is a lot of scree on this slope.

North Buttress. III, 5.9. First ascent June 1973 by Vern Clevenger and Jon Ross. This buttress ends about ½ mile from the peak along the northwest ridge. Make a left-ascending traverse to the crest of the buttress and follow it to the top.

Peak 11,880ft+   11,861 ft;
1.5 mi NE of Needham Mountain

Northeast Ridge. Class 3. First ascent 1966 by W. K. Jennings and friend.

The Wall Above Big Five. V, 5.11. First ascent by Claude Fiddler and Nancy Fiddler. Folow a crack system up the center of the face for seventeen pitches. Note that this is a long route on steep rock, and once you start on it, it is difficult to turn back.

"Two Fingers Peak"   11,760 ft+; 11,680 ft+;
1.3 mi NE of Needham Mountain

First ascent by Claude Fiddler and Nancy Fiddler on a traverse from Peak 11,880ft+ (11,861 ft). The summit blocks of this peak are composed of semisolid scree, and are class 3. The peak has a class 1 scree slope on its south side; the north face is class 3.

Peak 11,760ft+   11,772 ft;
1.2 mi NE of Sawtooth Peak

Northwest Ridge. II, 5.6, A0. First ascent August 25, 1985 by Claude Fiddler. Follow the north ridge to the summit from Cyclamen Pass. A rope was thrown over the summit block and was climbed hand-over-hand on the first ascent.

Peak 11,480ft+   11,440 ft+;
1.0 mi E of Empire Mountain

This little peak has a 1,000-foot sheer north face that drops down to Spring Lake. The south side of the peak is class 2.

"That's a Sheer Cliff" Route. IV, 5.9. First ascent 1975 by Vern Clevenger and Galen Rowell. This route ascends the dihedral to the right of center on the north face. Four pitches of 5.9 are followed by five pitches of 5.7 to 5.8.

North Face, Left Side. III, 5.6. First ascent July 14, 1974 by Rob Dellinger, Debbie Winters, and Fred Beckey. This route follows a crack and dihedral system directly to the summit.

Empire Mountain   11,550 ft+; 11,509 ft
Class 2 from Glacier Pass. The east face is class 2–3.

Mount Eisen   12,160 ft+; 12,160 ft+; UTM 596402
Southeast Ridge. Class 2. This is a long, tedious hike from Black Rock Pass. It features loose scree, a lot of side-hilling, a false summit, and a shallow angle—it isn't any fun coming down.

From Little Five Lakes. Class 3. First ascent August 23, 1984 by Dale Van Dalsem and Jim Murphy. A use trail branches off the Black Rock Pass Trail just north of where the trail crosses the stream-draining Lake 10,410ft (10,410 ft). Follow the use trail to Lake 10,410ft, circle on its south shore, and go to the cirque on the peak's southeast side. Go up, and then left, of a water-stained headwall located above the small, upper tarn and make a diagonal, right-ascending traverse to the south ridge of the peak. The southernmost summit is the high point.

Northeast Face. Class 3. First ascent July 15, 1949 by Howard Parker, Mildred Jentsch, Ralph Youngberg, and Martha Ann McDuffie. There is a lake immediately northeast of Mount Eisen with a small island in it. From this lake, climb the higher of two notches to the southwest, and then up to the summit.

Peak 11,680ft+   11,760 ft+;
0.8 mi S of Lippincott Mountain

Northeast Ridge. Class 4. First ascent August 30, 1969 by Andy Smatko and Bill Schuler. Most of this ridge is class 3; only the last 50-foot portion below the (higher) southwest peak is class 4.

Peak 11,800ft+   11,830 ft;
0.5 mi SE of Lippincott Mountain

Southwest Ridge. Class 2. First ascent August 30, 1969 by Carl Heller and Bill Stein.

North-Northwest Ridge. Class 2. First ascent 20 minutes later on August 30, 1969 by Andy Smatko and Bill Schuler.

Lippincott Mountain   12,265 ft; 12,260 ft
Southeast Slope. Class 3. First ascent July 1936 by Jules Eichorn and party. Leave the Black Rock Pass Trail at an elevation of approximately 10,400 feet, just north of Little Five Lakes. Contour north and northwest into the basin southeast of the peak. Climb either the southeast slope or the upper part of the east ridge to the class 3 summit rocks.

East Ridge. Class 3. First ascent 1922 by Norman Clyde. The crest of the east ridge can be attained from the basin north of the east ridge. Head for the shallow saddle immediately east of the summit of Lippincott Mountain. There is a chute that leads up to the saddle from the north. Avoid this chute, and instead ascend a class 2 ramp system immediately left of the chute. This ramp zigs and zags up and through the vertical to over-hanging headwall. Follow the crest of the ridge to the summit, with some detours to the left (south) side of the ridge.

North Face. III, 5.10. First ascent August 1985 by Claude Fiddler and Nancy Fiddler. Follow a beautiful crack system in the center of the face. A 5.10 finger crack leads to the summit.

Northwest Ridge. Class 3. First ascent August 30, 1969 by Bill Schuler and Andy Smatko. This was climbed during a traverse from Peak 12,200ft+ (12,250 ft). They traversed the west side of both peaks well below the saddle connecting Lippincott Mountain with Peak 12,200ft+ (12,250 ft) and then gained the northwest ridge.

Peak 12,200ft+   12,250 ft;
0.6 mi N of Lippincott Mountain

East Ridge. Class 2. The ridge can be attained either from the Big Arroyo or from the lake basin north of the peak.

South-Southwest Ridge. Class 2 from the saddle to the south of the peak.

West Face. Class 2. Descended August 30, 1969 by Andy Smatko and Bill Schuler. A steep chute on the face provides the key to this route.

Eagle Scout Peak   12,000 ft+; 12,040 ft
Class 2 from the Big Arroyo. It is best to head for the saddle just south of the peak, and then go directly to the summit. First ascent July 15, 1926 by Francis Farquhar and Eagle Scouts Frederick Armstrong, Eugene Howell, and Coe Swift. There is a wonderful view of the Hamilton Lakes area from the summit.

Dancing Deer Direct. III, 5.7. First ascent 1984 by Dave Nettle and Cindy Nettle. Begin by climbing the gully that is immediately to the right of the prominent north rib of the peak. Go up and right for six pitches of 5.6 to 5.7, reaching the ridge about 100 feet to the left of the summit block.

Further Reading: John Moynier and Claude Fiddler. *Sierra Classics.* Evergreen, Colo.: Chockstone Press, 1993, pp. 86–87.

North Face. II, 5.7. First ascent August 1985 by Claude Fiddler and Vern Clevenger. Follow the left of center crack system to the summit.

"Granite Creek Dome"   9,326 ft; 9,326 ft;
1.8 mi NW of Lippincott Mountain

The west ridge is 5.6, and was first climbed in June 1992 by Bart O'Brien and Peter Cummings.

EAGLE SCOUT PEAK

North Face

Dancing Deer
Direct

Eagle Scout Peak, North Face. Photo by R. J. Secor.

"Eagle Scout Towers"   10,880 ft+; 10,800 ft+;
1.0 mi SW of Eagle Scout Peak; UTM 589447

These towers are on the south side of the canyon containing Eagle Scout Creek. They were climbed by the Rock Climbing Section, Loma Prieta Chapter, Sierra Club, in 1953.

"Wallace Stegner Spire"   9,520 ft+; 9,550 ft+;
1.6 mi W of Eagle Scout Peak; UTM 577453

East Arête. II, 5.9. First ascent September 5, 1993 by Bart O'Brien and Richard Swayze. Begin by climbing a steep jam crack that leads to a horizontal crack, followed by 5.9 climbing to a belay at the base of a shallow corner. Then a long pitch of face climbing leads past two bolts to a belay at the base of a steep jam crack. This short crack (5.9) leads to the moderate slopes just below the summit area.

"Periscope Dome"

This dome is on the ridge between Wallace Stegner Spire and Eaglette Pinnacle.

East Side. II, 5.8. First ascent June 1992 by Peter Cummings and Bart O'Brien. This route starts just left of a big chimney. Climb a 5.7 face up to a brushy ledge at the base of an overhanging chimney. A short 5.8 pitch up the chimney leads to a blocky ledge. Follow the ledge around to the south side of the dome, where a 5.6 ramp leads to a steep 5.9 jam crack. This is followed by the spectacular summit block. The first-ascent party descended by means of two rappels down the east ridge.

"Eaglette Pinnacle"

This 200-foot pinnacle is located between Periscope Dome and Eagle Scout Creek Dome. It was first climbed in June 1992 by Peter Cummings and Bart O'Brien by way of a 5.7 off-width crack on the west side.

"Eagle Scout Creek Dome"   9,520 ft+;
1.7 mi W of Eagle Scout Peak; UTM 576453

East Face. I, 5.5. First ascent June 1992 by Bart O'Brien and Peter Cummings. This route ascends two pitches of flakes in corners on the left side of the east face.

"Hamilton Towers"   9,680 ft+–10,040 ft+; 9,680 ft+–10,000 ft+

These towers are on the ridge between Hamilton Creek and Eagle Scout Creek. There are nine towers in all, and their difficulty ranges from class 4 to 5.8. Some of the towers were first climbed by the Rock Climbing Section, Loma Prieta Chapter, Sierra Club, in 1953. The most difficult tower was first climbed in September 1970 by Greg Henzie, Chris Jones, and Galen Rowell.

"Hamilton Dome"   9,745 ft; 9,770 ft;
1.9 mi WNW of Eagle Scout Peak

This is the beautiful dome at the western end of Hamilton Towers.

East Gully. I, 5.6. First ascent 1936 by Dick Johnson and party. Second ascent June 1969 by Curt Chadwick, Chuck Kroger, and Norm Weeden.

North Arête. II, 5.7. First ascent 1971 by Don Lauria and

Hamilton Towers and Hamilton Dome. Photo by R. J. Secor.

TM Herbert. Climb seven pitches directly up the arête.

Before the Jury. IV, 5.10c. First ascent September 1996 by Dave Nettle and Richard Leversee. This route climbs the flake system directly up the center of the west face. Climb onto the ridge between the Middle Fork of the Kaweah River and Eagle Scout Creek and then drop down and cross the bowl on the west side of the dome. Class 2 and 3 climbing then leads to the top of the Black Pedestal. Three hundred feet of class 3–4 friction leads up and right. This is followed by some run out face moves (5.8) ending at a ledge on a horizontal black dike underneath a clean, blank left-facing corner. Go to the far right-hand end of the dike and go up and left underneath two roofs to the top of a flake, followed by 5.10a face climbing horizontally left to a grassy layback (5.10b). This pitch leads to the Wheat Thin Flake. Pass underneath the Wheat Thin and climb its right side (5.10c) to a sloping ledge. Go up and pass a chimney/flake on its right side before face climbing left to a 5.10c layback and passing to the left of a dark, triangular roof to a belay stance with a block. Pass to the left of a small tower and climb through a rounded slot to a crack that is left of a scooped-out hole. A tricky 5.10+ pitch goes up and left underneath a diagonal roof to the ledge beneath the cap of the dome.

"Thor Pinnacle"   10,040 ft+; 10,080 ft+;
1.2 mi NW of Eagle Scout Peak; UTM 587466

South Face. I, 5.7. First ascent August 1983 by Alan Swanson and friend. This two-pitch route has good rock.

"Angel Wings"   10,360 ft+; 10,252 ft;
1.6 mi W of Mount Stewart; UTM 585485

The south face of this peak is the biggest rock wall in Sequoia National Park; and, unlike Yosemite walls, it is 16 miles from the nearest road.

Further Reading: Greg Vernon, Sally Moser, and David Hickey. *Southern Sierra Rock Climbing: Sequoia/Kings Canyon.* Evergreen, Colo.: Chockstone Press, 1993, pp. 234–237.

North Side. Class 3–4. First ascent August 1980 by Bob Ayers and party. Leave the trail leading to Tamarack Lake at around 8,000 feet and climb gullies leading through the huge cirque on the north side of Angel Wings. Leave the cirque via an easy chute that goes through its headwall. (A landmark for this chute is a pair of large pine trees growing at its head in a small notch; don't go to the larger western notch in the headwall.)

From the top of the headwall, cross over large talus blocks to the lower northern summit, drop down a bit, then climb some large talus blocks to the summit. The very last section has two class 4 moves.

West Side. Class 3–4. Descended June 1971 by Galen Rowell and Chris Jones. Climb slabs from Lone Pine Creek to a gully that leads to the summit area.

Wings Over Sequoia. Grade V. First ascent May 1977 by Fred Beckey, Alan Neilfel, Bill Lahr, and Craig Martinson. This route climbs the rounded buttress on the left side of the face. Difficult aid and free climbing was required on the first ascent.

The Lorax. V, 5.10, A3. First ascent June 1996 by Phil White and Kirk Bland. This route starts to the right of the two ramps that form a huge X on the lower left-hand side of the south face. Go up and left over a brushy ramp system and climb a right-facing open book (A1, 5.7). A tension traverse to the right under a dike then leads up some flakes (5.8, A1+) to a brushy ramp that goes up and right. Follow the ramp up and climb a wide and plumb vertical right-facing book. Face climb to the left of a wide crack (5.8R) to the Lair of the Lorax, a cave at the intersection of the X on the face. Climb a wide crack (7 inches, A2) up and right and traverse to the right under a roof. Go up, traverse to the left under another roof, and up again to a pendulum that leads left to a shallow chimney. Climb the cracks (A3) in the back of the chimney. Aid then leads to a bush at the bottom of a 5.6 chimney that leads to Dagger Ledge. Easy aid cracks lead to the class 4 Kitty Litter traverse followed by a tension traverse to the left and up a ramp. Climb a 5.7 chimney with no protection, followed by a tension traverse left. A discontinuous left-facing open book (A2) leads to a loose trough ending at a boulder. Another 500 feet of class 2 and 3 leads to the true summit.

Just a Rock in the Park. VI, 5.10, A3+. First ascent June 1996 by Richard Leversee, Ron Felton, and E. C. Joe. This route starts to the left of the two ramps that form a huge X on the lower left-hand side of the south face. Two pitches lead to the right side of a heart-shaped ledge. Pendulum to the right and climb two difficult aid pitches to a stance beneath a sloping ledge. Aid climbing up and left ends at a small stance beneath the overhanging headwall. Difficult aid climbing (including some bathooking) leads to the right of an ugly chimney, followed by a long pitch up and left to a right-facing inside corner ending at another sloping ledge. Climb a crack on the inside wall of a wide black chimney to a roof and a pendulum to the right, followed by hooking leads to a discontinuous mixed crack. Two pitches up this crack end at a sloping ledge, followed by a long off-width crack (5.10; protection to 7 inches needed) ending at a cave. A 5.10 squeeze chimney out of the cave is followed by 5.8 to a terrace, and 5.7 slabs lead up and left to a slot just below the top.

South Face, Right Side. V, 5.8, A4. First ascent July 28–August 2, 1967 by Les Wilson, Jim Wilson, Dick Long, and Allen Steck. This route ascends the most massive part of the south face. High on this face is a huge dihedral; the route starts directly underneath this feature. Begin by climbing a rounded buttress, and then go up the right side of a sickle-shaped ledge to a large crack. Climb the crack; it eventually turns into a chimney. From the top of the chimney, traverse right to some broken rock, then to a sandy alcove at the bottom of a deep chimney. The chimney features a huge, detached finger of rock, which is gradually separating from the right-hand wall. From the tip of the finger, climb an open book that gradually slants back to a horizontal system of ledges that leads to Upper Bearpaw Meadow, a 45° patch of wet grass that slopes up to an alcove filled with ferns and dripping water. Instead of climbing the chimney above, climb the face to a flake and move right 40 feet to a flaring chimney, which leads to the base of a tower of vertical slabs known as the House of Cards. One pitch goes up from

Angel Wings, South Face. Photo by R. J. Secor.

here, and another diagonals left back into the chimney. Continue climbing the chimney to the top.

Hell on Wings. V, 5.10, A3. First ascent July 1989 by E. C. Joe, Richard Leversee, and Kim Grandfield. This route ascends an obvious crack system to the left of the south arête. This ten-pitch route involves some nailing, nutting, and hooking at the ends of the third and fifth pitches. The route ends atop the arête, a long way from the summit.

South Arête. IV, 5.11+. First ascent June 1971 by Galen Rowell and Chris Jones. First free ascent 1984 by the Hope Valley Fun Hogs. This route climbs the curving arête that leads to the summit of Angel Wings. Scramble up talus and slabs (some class 4) to the big gully that separates the main south wall from the south arête. Ascend the gully before moving up and to the right over ledges and slabs to the highest ledge at the base of the arête. Climb the main crack system (up to 5.10) above the ledge for three pitches crossing four black dikes. Above the fourth dike, go up and to the right to the 10-foot Black Ceiling. Climb over the roof (5.11+) and traverse to the right (5.9) to the base of a chimney/gully. Follow this chimney/gully, passing over two chockstones up and left to the top. Talus then leads to the summit.

South Arête Direct. IV, 5.11. First ascent October 1991 by Dave Nettle and Jim Nowak. This route continues up the South Arête of Angel Wings from the chimney and gully exit. Leave the chimney above the second chockstone and go up and right over a run out face (5.10) that is to the left of the crest of the arête. Go up and to the right across the arête, past a large flake, and up a pair of cracks (5.10) before moving back to the left to a ledge on the crest of the arête. The route continues up the left side of the crest of the arête for four more moderate (up to 5.7) pitches, followed by class 3 to the top.

Further Reading: John Moynier and Claude Fiddler. *Sierra Classics.* Evergreen, Colo.: Chockstone Press, 1993, pp. 90–92.

"Cherubim Dome"　10,440 ft+; 10,240 ft+;
1.2 mi W of Mount Stewart; UTM 589484

This peak is class 2 via slabs from the 8,800-foot level of the High Sierra Trail; approach the summit from the east ridge.

Angel Wings from the southeast. Photo by R. J. Secor.

Archangel. IV, 5.10c, A0. First ascent October 1985 by Richard Leversee and E. C. Joe. This route ascends the south buttress of the dome. Slabs and brush lead up from the High Sierra Trail to the base of the buttress. Difficult (5.10) climbing leads up and right to The Harp, a left-facing inside corner topped by a roof. Scary 5.10 face climbing leads left and up to a system of thin flakes. Pendulum left, make a short horizontal traverse to the left to a right-facing inside corner, and then climb up and left before going up and right to another right-facing open book beneath a roof system. Make a horizontal 5.10c traverse to the left across the face to the prow of the buttress. Crack and face climbing (to 5.9) leads up the prow to the top.

Further Reading: John Moynier and Claude Fiddler. *Sierra Classics.* Evergreen, Colo.: Chockstone Press, 1993, pp. 90–93; Greg Vernon, Sally Moser, and David Hickey. *Southern Sierra Rock Climbing: Sequoia/Kings Canyon.* Evergreen, Colo.: Chockstone Press, 1993, pp. 238–239.

Mount Stewart　12,200 ft+; 12,205 ft

There is an outstanding view of the Black Kaweah from the summit.

From Nine Lake Basin. Class 2. From the north end of Lake 10,440ft+ (10,400 ft+) climb a grassy gully to the slabs and ramps of the summit area. The high point of the peak is at the far western end of the high ridge atop the peak.

North Face. III, 5.6. First ascent August 19, 1973 by Michael Graber, Jack Roberts, and Hooman Aprin. Two buttresses drop down the north face, directly beneath the summit. From the large bench at the base of the north face, climb to the left of the eastern buttress directly up to a point just east of the summit.

West Pillar. III, 5.9. First ascent 1984 by Dave Nettle and Cindy Nettle. Second ascent June 17, 1986 by David Wilson and Michael Graber. This route climbs the western buttress on Mount Stewart's north face. It begins by climbing a jam crack in a left-facing dihedral on the left side (east) of the buttress. Continue up corner systems for six pitches to the top of the west buttress, and then make a tricky traverse along the broken west ridge to the summit.

South
Arête
Direct

ANGEL WINGS

Just a Rock
in the Park

Hell on
Wings

South
Arête

Wings Over
Sequoia

The
Lorax

South Face,
Right Side

Further Reading: John Moynier and Claude Fiddler. *Sierra Classics.* Evergreen, Colo.: Chockstone Press, 1993, pp. 88–89.

Lion Rock   12,360 ft+; 12,320 ft+

West Ridge. Class 3. First ascent July 7, 1927 by Dave Winkley, William Curlett, and Earl S. Wallace. From approximately 10,500 feet, between Tamarack Lake and Lion Lake, traverse southeast and diagonally upward across a talus slope into the bowl between the two west ridges of Lion Rock. Aim for the obvious ledge system leading to the southern west ridge. Follow the top of the ridge to the summit. The pitch just below the summit is loose, exposed class 3. The north peak is the high point.

South-Southwest Slope. Class 2–3. First ascent September 9, 1968 by John Fredlund. From Tamarack Lake ascend the slopes leading to the bowl south of the peak; this involves tedious routefinding through brush around small cliffs. From the bowl, climb the broad slope to the summit. *Variation:* First ascent August 22, 1994 by Matthias Selke, Bob Wyka, and Al Conrad. It is also possible to reach the South-Southwest Slope from the top of the Northeast Chute. Contour left (northwest) from the top of the chute, cross a rib, and continue up class 2 slabs to the south ridge, which is easily followed to the top. It is also feasible to reach this bowl from Nine Lake Basin by crossing the south ridge of the peak.

South Ridge. Class 4. First ascent August 20, 1984 by Ron Hudson, R. J. Secor, and Jim Murphy. From Nine Lake Basin, follow the south ridge to the summit of Lion Rock. Two class 4 moves are encountered on this ridge.

East Chute. Class 4. From the western Lion Rock Pass climb the first chute north of the pass and then ascend the rock rib on its right (north) side to the summit.

Northeast Chute. Class 3. This is the next chute north of the east chute. It leads to the saddle between the two peaks of Lion Rock. From a point about halfway up this chute, climb the southeast face of the north peak to the summit of Lion Rock. Snow and ice remain in these chutes for most of the summer; ice axes may be required.

Lawson Peak   13,120 ft+; 13,140 ft;
1 mi N of Black Kaweah

First ascent July 11, 1924 by Gerald Gaines, C. A. Gaines, and H. H. Bliss. The southwest slope and the northeast ridge are class 2.

Kaweah Queen   13,382 ft; 13,360 ft+

Northwest Ridge. Class 3. First ascent July 11, 1924 by Gerald Gaines, C. A. Gaines, and H. H. Bliss, on a traverse from Lawson Peak. This traverse is accomplished by remaining about 50 feet below the ridge crest on its western side. There is a lot of loose rock on this traverse.

Southwest Slope. Class 2. Loose rock is encountered while climbing the peak from the western approach of Pyra-Queen Col.

North Slope. Class 2. Some extraordinarily loose rock is encountered while climbing this peak from the upper reaches of Picket Creek.

Peak 4033m   13,232 ft;
0.5 mi E of Kaweah Queen; UTM 658464

South Face. Class 3. First ascent July 2, 1967 by Andy Smatko, Bill Schuler, and Ellen Siegal. Climb a chute on the south face that leads to a point approximately 150 feet west of the summit. The upper portion of the chute is loose class 3.

The northeast ridge is reportedly easy class 3.

The Black Kaweah   13,680 ft+; 13,765 ft

Differences as great as 8 degrees from the normal compass variation may be encountered in the vicinity of the Black Kaweah.

The Black Kaweah is one of the great peaks of the High Sierra. It is high and remote, looks good from a distance, and is in a scenic area. Plus, even its easy routes are challenging. But it is perhaps the least known of the more difficult peaks in the range. During the sixty years after its first ascent, fewer than 100 parties visited the summit. It deserves more attention.

The Black Kaweah has a well-deserved reputation for loose rock, as do the rest of the Kaweah peaks. But the rock is not as loose as that encountered on some other peaks, such as the Devil's Crags or Mount Morrison. Nevertheless, caution is advised. The party attempting this ascent should be small (no more than six climbers) and constantly vigilant. As my friend Dave Dykeman once said: "This peak demands intelligent risk management."

West Ridge. Class 3. First ascent August 11, 1920 by Duncan McDuffie, Onis I. Brown, and James Hutchinson. From the Big Arroyo, climb to the top of the west ridge and follow it toward the summit. At approximately 13,200 feet a deep notch bars further progress. Descend

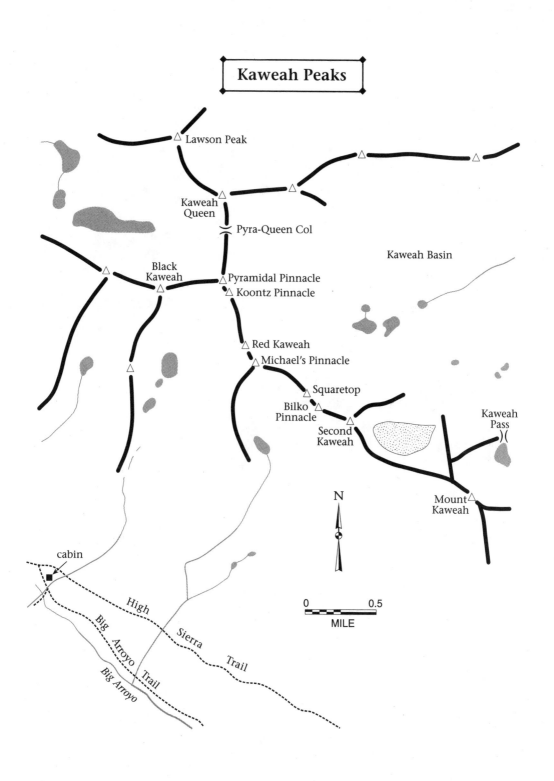

Kaweah Peaks

△ Lawson Peak

Kaweah
Queen

≋ Pyra-Queen Col

Black
Kaweah

Kaweah Basin

△ Pyramidal Pinnacle
△ Koontz Pinnacle

△ Red Kaweah
△ Michael's Pinnacle

△ Squaretop
Bilko
Pinnacle

Second
Kaweah

Kaweah
Pass
)(

N

Mount
Kaweah △

cabin

High

Sierra

Big
Arroyo

Trail

Trail

Big Arroyo

0   0.5
MILE

The Black Kaweah from the southwest. Photo by R. J. Secor.

about 100 or 200 feet on the south side of the ridge and traverse to the chute of the Southwest Face route. Climb the chute to where it joins the west ridge, approximately 100 feet beneath the summit. Scramble up the remaining class 3 to the top. *Variation: Southwest Ridge. Class 3. First ascent August 1928 by Albert Ellingwood and Carl Blaurock. Ascend the southwest ridge from the Big Arroyo to where it meets the west ridge. Follow the West Ridge route to the summit.*

Southwest Face. Class 3. First ascent July 26, 1921 by Philip E. Smith, Marian Simpson, and Irene Smith. First winter ascent January 4, 1970 by Eric Adelberger, Paul Emerson, and Lowell Smith. This is the most direct route to the summit of the Black Kaweah. Although it is not as technically easy as the West Ridge route, this seems to be the preferred route of ascent for most climbers. From the Big Arroyo, hike to the cirque immediately southwest of the peak. Pass over some loose talus to the base of the southwest face, and head for the right-hand chute. Climb the chute for about 100 feet, and then cross over to the left-hand chute via a ledge that goes diagonally up and to the left. A landmark for the crossover point is a black waterfall in the right-hand chute; the crossover point is 50 feet below this. Climb the left-hand chute to the summit. Most of this climb is moderate class 3, and there is a lot of reaching across delicately perched rocks. In early season both of these chutes are likely to be filled with hard snow and/or ice. Should this be the case, full ice-climbing regalia may be necessary. The angle averages 40°.

Further Reading: John Moynier and Claude Fiddler. *Sierra Classics.* Evergreen, Colo.: Chockstone Press, 1993, pp. 84–85.

South Face. IV, 5.7. First ascent 1968 by David Beck, Nick Hartzell, and Gary Kirk. Head toward a prominent dihedral on the south face of the peak from the cirque between the Black Kaweah and Red Kaweah. Climb to the left of the dihedral and continue up and left for fourteen pitches to the summit. Protection is hard to come by on the loose rock.

East Ridge. Class 4. First ascent June 1935 by Neil Ruge and James Smith. From the lake basin south of the Black Kaweah climb the small chute that leads to the notch between Pyramidal Pinnacle and Koontz Pinnacle. Before reaching the notch, traverse diagonally up and to the left along a convenient, broad ledge to the low point of the ridge connecting the Black Kaweah with Pyramidal Pinnacle. Follow the arête westward to where a yellow gendarme blocks progress. Traverse left via a ledge and regain the east ridge by climbing a short, loose chimney. Head for a sloping ledge that goes around the south side of the peak. From the end of the ledge, climb either a chimney or an outside corner (easier but more exposed than the chimney) to the top. *Variation:* Class 4. First ascent August 1, 1968 by John Mendenhall and Ruth Mendenhall. This is the preferred variation.

The Black Kaweah from the southeast. Photo by R. J. Secor.

Ascend the chute that leads directly to the low point of the east ridge of the Black Kaweah from the lake basin south of the peak. Leave this chute about 250 feet below its top and climb a class 4 chute to the left to the crest of the east ridge of the Black Kaweah. (The upper portion of the chute, which leads to the low point of the east ridge, consists of loose, dangerous class 3+ crud; it is only safe when the chute is full of snow.) *Variation:* Class 4. First ascent August 1955 by Carl Heller and Robert Stein. The east ridge can also be reached from Lake 11,682ft (11,705 ft), which is just north of the Black Kaweah. Head for the low point of the ridge connecting the Black Kaweah with Pyramidal Pinnacle.

"Pyramidal Pinnacle"   13,665 ft; 13,600 ft+;
0.4 mi E of Black Kaweah

West Face. Class 4. First ascent August 1, 1932 by Glen Dawson and Jules Eichorn. From the cirque between Red Kaweah and the Black Kaweah, climb the small couloir (loose rock!) that leads to the notch be-

tween Pyramidal Pinnacle and Koontz Pinnacle. Before reaching the notch, traverse up and left to the ridge connecting Pyramidal Pinnacle with the Black Kaweah. From the top of the ridge climb the west face (three pitches of class 4) to the summit of Pyramidal Pinnacle. *Variation:* Class 4. First ascent August 1955 by Carl Heller and Robert Stein. The west face of Pyramidal Pinnacle can also be reached from Lake 11,682ft (11,705 ft), which is north of the Black Kaweah.

"Koontz Pinnacle"   13,600 ft+;
0.5 mi E of Black Kaweah; UTM 652452

For some reason, this pinnacle does not appear in the contours of the Triple Divide Peak 7.5-minute map.

West Face. Class 4. First ascent August 26, 1953 by Jim Koontz, Pete Murphy, and Fred Peters. From the cirque between Red Kaweah and the Black Kaweah, climb the chute leading to the notch between Pyramidal Pinnacle and Koontz Pinnacle. The upper part of this chute is very loose, and it may be best to climb it

Pyramidal Pinnacle and Koontz Pinnacle from the south. Photo by R. J. Secor.

on the right side. From the notch, climb the northern side of the west face to the summit. The first pitch from the notch is extraordinarily loose.

East Face. IV, 5.9. First ascent by Claude Fiddler and Nancy Fiddler. This route is not recommended due to loose rock.

Red Kaweah   13,720 ft+; 13,760 ft+

West Face. Class 3. First ascent 1912 by Charles W. Michael. From the Big Arroyo, hike cross-country to the basin west of Red Kaweah. Pass Lake 11,795ft (11,825 ft) on its east side on a bench, and go through small rocks and talus to a prominent chute (big, loose rocks!), which leads to a ramp just beneath the summit. Follow the ramp to the right (south) and up to the ridge. Follow the ridge back to the left to the summit.

"Michael's Pinnacle"   13,680 ft+; 13,680 ft+;
0.1 mi SE of Red Kaweah; UTM 654446

Charles W. Michael made the first ascent of this pinnacle in 1912, via an unknown route.

Southeast Ridge. Class 4. First ascent August 28, 1953 by Jim Koontz, Pete Murphy, and Fred Peters. Climb to the saddle between Michael's Pinnacle and Squaretop. From the saddle, follow the ridge to the fourth major pinnacle from the saddle. Descend the southeast side of this pinnacle, then traverse across its west face along a ledge that ends in a steep chute. Descend this chute about 30 feet to where it joins another chute. Climb this next chute to the ledge at its top. Follow the ledge to the saddle immediately southeast of Michael's Pinnacle. From the saddle climb a broad ledge on the northern side of the ridge to some easy rock that leads to the summit.

"Squaretop"   4120 m+; 13,520 ft+;
1.3 mi NW of Mount Kaweah; UTM 659442

The rock on this peak is rather solid, at least when compared to the other Kaweah peaks.

Southeast Face. Class 4. First ascent June 26, 1935 by Jim Smith and Neil Ruge. From Lake 11,840ft+ (11,885 ft) climb loose scree and talus to the saddle between Squaretop and Bilko Pinnacle. Go straight up the southeast face (far to the left of a huge chute) to a wide ledge that ascends diagonally to the right. The ledge ends in a shallow chute. Climb the chute a short distance, to where it is possible to traverse left on some ledges ending on the summit ridge. *Variation:* It is also possible to

reach the saddle southeast of Squaretop from Kaweah Basin.

Southeast Ridge. I, 5.7. First ascent August 13, 1981 by Vern Clevenger. This route climbs the ridge to the right of the huge chute rising from the saddle southeast of the peak.

Northwest Face. Class 4. First ascent July 7, 1970 by Dick Beach and Barbara Lilley. From Lake 11,840ft+ (11,885 ft) ascend to the notch just northwest of Squaretop. Just before reaching the notch, leave the chute at a large chockstone and climb two class 4 pitches to the summit.

"Bilko Pinnacle"   4080 m+; 13,360 ft+;
1.2 mi NW of Mount Kaweah; UTM 661441

The second-ascent party (Bill Schuler and Andy Smatko) named this peak after themselves.

Northwest Face. Class 3. First ascent August 27, 1953 by Jim Koontz, Fred Peters, and Pete Murphy. This is supposed to go class 3 directly from the saddle between Squaretop and Bilko Pinnacle.

Southwest Ridge. Class 4. First ascent August 28, 1969 by Andy Smatko and Bill Schuler. From the saddle between Bilko Pinnacle and Squaretop, descend 40 feet to the southwest and go around a sharp buttress. Ascend a steep chute to the southwest ridge; one 30-foot class 4 pitch is encountered. Follow the southwest ridge to the top.

"Second Kaweah"   4164 m; 13,680 ft+;
1.0 mi NW of Mount Kaweah

This peak is also known as "Gray Kaweah." First ascent 1922 by Norman Clyde. The south slope from the High Sierra Trail is class 2, as is the traverse from Mount Kaweah. The high point is the southeastern summit.

The three pinnacles on the northwest ridge are loose class 3; they were first climbed on August 29, 1953 by Jim Koontz, Fred Peters, and Pete Murphy.

East Spur. IV, 5.9. First ascent August 1985 by Claude Fiddler and Nancy Fiddler. This is a loose and undesirable climb.

Mount Kaweah   4207 m+; 13,802 ft

This mountain has also been called "Big Kaweah" and "Great Kaweah." It is the highest point in the southwestern High Sierra.

South Slopes. Class 1. First ascent September 1881 by Judge William B. Wallace, Captain James Albert

Wright, and the Reverend Frederick H. Wales. This is a simple cross-country hike from the High Sierra Trail. Leave the trail at its high point (10,600 ft+) between the trail junction in the Big Arroyo and the junction with the trail leading to Moraine Lake. This is near a pond that is usually dry.

East Ridge. Class 3. First ascent August 17, 1966 by Bill Schuler. This is a direct route to the summit of Mount Kaweah from the southern approach to Kaweah Pass. Don't climb the ridge leading directly up from Kaweah Pass. Instead, approach the east ridge from the southern end of the lake near the top of the pass. As with other routes in the Kaweahs, caution must be exercised due to loose rock.

North Ridge. Class 4. First ascent September 1964 by Eduardo Garcia and Carlos Puente, two guys from Chile. Climb the ridge leading directly from Kaweah Basin.

Peak 4049m   13,285 ft; 1.4 mi NE of Mount Kaweah

First ascent July 17, 1936 by Jules Eichorn, Virginia Adams, Jane Younger, and Carl P. Jensen. The south slope from Chagoopa Plateau is class 2.

Red Spur   4019 m; 13,183 ft

Southwest Ridge. Class 3. First ascent July 17, 1936 by Jules Eichorn, Virginia Adams, Jane Younger, and Carl P. Jensen, on a traverse from Peak 4049m (13,285 ft). Stay below the crest of the ridge on its southern side.

Picket Guard Peak   3750 m; 12,302 ft

First ascent August 1, 1936 by C. Dohlman, H. Manheim, and B. Breeding. The east ridge is class 2 and the north ridge is class 3. The class 2–3 west ridge was ascended September 2, 1996 by Erik Siering, Brian Smith, and Larry Tidball.

Kern Point   3880 m; 12,789 ft

First ascent July 25, 1924 by William Horsfall and C. Laughlin. First winter ascent April 12, 1995 by Greg Colley, Brad Jensen, and R. J. Secor. The southwest slope is class 2, as is the traverse from Kern Ridge.

Triple Divide Peak   12,634 ft; 12,634 ft

This peak divides the Kern, Kaweah, and Kings Rivers.

East Ridge. Class 2 or 3. First ascent 1920 by James Hutchinson and Charles Noble. Follow the class 3 ridge

from Triple Divide Pass to the summit, or cross class 2 talus and slabs along the southern side of the ridge to the top.

North Face. Class 3. First ascent August 31, 1975 by Walton Kabler, Betty Kabler, Barbara Reber, and R. J. Secor. From Glacier Lake ascend steep talus directly to the summit of the peak.

West Ridge. Class 3. First ascent 1963 by John Wedberg, Bill Engs, and party. Follow the crest of the ridge from Lion Lake Pass, making an occasional detour from the crest to its north side.

Southwest Face. Class 2–3. Climb any of several chutes and gullies to the summit from Lion Lake.

South Ridge. Class 3. First ascent by Don Clarke. Follow the ridge to where progress is impeded by a gendarme. Detour and lose 200 feet of gain on the ridge's eastern side. Traverse across the peak's eastern side to the east ridge, and follow this to the top.

Peak 12,640ft+   12,640 ft+; 0.7 mi NE of Triple Divide Peak

First ascent July 21, 1926 by George R. Bunn and R. C. Lewis. The southwest slope is class 3.

Peak 12,560ft+   12,600 ft; 0.4 mi SW of Colby Pass

Southwest Ridge. Class 2. First ascent 1936 by Howard Gates and Carl P. Jensen.

Northeast Ridge. Class 3. First ascent 1936 by Jules Eichorn, Kenneth May, and A. Tagliapietra.

Peak 4129m   13,520 ft+; 0.6 mi SE of Milestone Mountain

This peak has been referred to as "Milestone Mesa." First ascent August 3, 1897 by W. F. Dean, Otis Wright, Harry C. Dudley, and W. R. Dudley. The south slope is class 2; the northwest ridge from Milestone Pass is class 3.

Northeast Ridge. Class 3–4. First ascent May 1981 by Claude Fiddler, Nancy Fiddler, and Dieter King.

Centennial Peak   4032 m; 13,255 ft; 0.6 mi SW of Milestone Mountain

This peak was named in honor of Sequoia National Park's 100th anniversary in 1990.

Southwest Slope. Class 1. First ascent 1912 by Francis Farquhar, William E. Colby, and Robert M. Price.

Southwest Ridge. Class 2. First ascent September 3,

The Black Kaweah · Pyramidal Pinnacle · Koontz Pinnacle · Red Kaweah · Michael's Pinnacle · Squaretop · Bilko Pinnacle · Second Kaweah · West Ridge · Southwest Ridge · Big Arroyo

Kaweah Peaks Ridge from the southwest. Photo by R. J. Secor.

1992 by Pete Yamagata. Follow scree and talus from Colby Pass to the summit.

East Face of the South Ridge. Class 3. First ascent September 12, 1967 by Bill Schuler and Andy Smatko. From the highest lakes of Milestone Bowl, gain the south ridge via a gully. From the ridge, head west to the plateau and then to the summit.

Milestone Mountain 4157 m; 13,641 ft

The summit pinnacle of this peak is an impressive sight from the upper Kern River basin. The view of the Kern River and Kings River basins from the summit is equally impressive.

East Side. Class 3. First ascent July 28, 1927 by Norman Clyde. From the upper reaches of Milestone Creek climb the steep, scree-filled gully that leads to the notch just north of the summit pinnacle. Cross over the notch, descend about 75 feet on the western side of the peak, go south across the west face around a buttress, and climb the west face and ridge to the summit.

Further Reading: John Moynier and Claude Fiddler. *Sierra Classics.* Evergreen, Colo.: Chockstone Press, 1993, pp. 70–71.

Southeast Arête. II, 5.6. First ascent August 1964 by Steve Thompson and Jeff Dozier. Climb over and around gendarmes along the arête from Milestone Pass.

Southwest Ridge. Class 3. First ascent July 14, 1912 by Francis Farquhar, William E. Colby, and Robert M. Price. From Milestone Bowl traverse across the south face of the peak toward the southwest ridge. Much loose rock is encountered just before reaching the ridge. Follow the ridge to the summit.

Northwest Face. Class 3. First ascent September 19, 1931 by Walter A. Starr, Jr. The northwest face of Milestone Mountain consists of many chutes. From Lake 3512m (11,523 ft) climb the second chute west of the summit; this chute appears to be reversed-S shaped when viewed from the lake. Leave the chute on the left side near its top at an altitude of 13,300 feet, just beyond a large buttress that separates the first chute west of the summit from the second chute. Traverse left to the west face of the summit pinnacle.

Northwest Ridge. I, 5.7. First ascent August 3, 1987 by Jean Baptiste Raqeeoir. This route begins from the notch just north of the summit of Milestone Mountain. Drop down and to the right 40 feet from the notch, and then climb back to the left (5.6). Continue up the buttress that is 150 feet to the left of the west ridge (5.7).

Midway Mountain 4165 m; 13,666 ft

West Slope. Class 2. First ascent July 1912 by Francis Farquhar, William E. Colby, Robert M. Price, and four others. Climb the west slope of the peak from Lake 3512m (11,523 ft). Approach the summit from the northwest.

East Ridge. Class 2. First ascent July 30, 1927 by Norman Clyde. Climb the north side of the east ridge from Milestone Creek. The crest of the east ridge can also be reached from Milestone Mountain by means of a deep notch in the east ridge.

South Face of the East Ridge. I, 5.7. First ascent July 1987 by Robin Ingraham, Jr., Mark Hoffman, and Mark Tuttle. This route starts 30 feet to the right of a prominent right-facing dihedral. Stemming and jam cracks lead to a belay slab, and two more pitches lead to the east ridge of the peak, at an elevation of 13,000 feet.

South Ridge and Southeast Face. Class 4. First ascent August 18, 1978 by Bill T. Russell and party on a traverse from Milestone Mountain. Climb the south ridge to where difficulties increase, and traverse out onto the southeast face. One class 4 pitch is encountered just below the summit.

South Ridge. Descended August 3, 1987 by Jean Baptiste Raqeeoir. This ridge has been reported as being 5.7 in places.

Peak 4149m 13,600 ft+; 0.7 mi SE of Table Mountain

First ascent August 18, 1949 by Jim Koontz and Jim Griffin. The east slope is class 3. Begin climbing from the left end of the ramp on the southeast side of Table Mountain.

Table Mountain 4155 m; 13,630 ft

This flat-topped mountain is a popular ascent by . . . helicopters.

Northeast Couloir. AI1 or WI2, class 4. First ascent July

Milestone Mountain from the northwest. Photo by R. J. Secor.

MILESTONE MOUNTAIN

Northwest Face

26, 1927 by Norman Clyde, Glen Dawson, and party. This is a 700-foot, 50° snow/ice couloir on the northeast side of the mountain. It is posssible to climb the class 4 rocks on the right side of the couloir in late season.

East Face. Class 4. First ascent 1932 by Norman Clyde, Alice Carter, Dorothy Baird, Emily Lillie, William Duley, and Rose M. Pischel. From the small lake due east of the summit plateau (at UTM 688575), climb the broken face to the top. A class 4 chockstone must be overcome. There is a lot of loose rock on this route.

Southeast Side. Class 3. First ascent July 29, 1927 by Norman Clyde. Even though this is listed as a class 3 route, a rope should be carried, because many parties have had difficulty locating the easiest route on the broad face on this side of the peak. From Lake 3620m+ (11,840 ft+) along the main drainage of Milestone Creek, climb to a right-ascending ramp on the left side of the southeast face of Table Mountain. There is a V-shaped notch on the southeast ridge, marked by a gendarme on its left side. The left (south) end of this ramp is directly beneath this notch. Zigzag up towards this notch to a point above and left of this ramp. Traverse downward to the right (east) onto and then along the ramp, passing a vertical face, to where it is possible to scramble to the summit plateau.

Further Reading: John Moynier and Claude Fiddler. *Sierra Classics.* Evergreen, Colo.: Chockstone Press, 1993, pp. 72–73.

West Ridge, South Side. Class 3. First ascent August 25, 1908 by Paul Shoup, Fred Shoup, and Gilbert Hassel. From the cirque southwest of Table Mountain, ascend the easternmost chute on the southern side of Table Mountain's west ridge. Approximately 100 feet below the crest of the west ridge, traverse up and right a short distance to another large chute. Follow this chute to the summit plateau.

West Ridge, North Side. Class 3–4. First ascent August 1978 by David Vandervoet, Geof Glassner, Bob Hozelton, and Ella Hozelton. From the cirque northwest of Table Mountain, climb the easternmost chute on the northern side of Table Mountain's west ridge. This chute, which may be filled with snow, is marked by a short class 4 rock cliff in the middle. Once atop the ridge, descend about 100 feet on the southern side of the ridge, and traverse east to another chute. Follow this chute to the summit plateau.

Whaleback   11,717 ft; 11,726 ft

This is the beautiful peak rising above Big Wet Meadow in Cloud Canyon.

Southwest Face. Class 3. First ascent August 5, 1936 by May Pridham and Adel Von Lobensels. From Cloud Canyon, climb through a prominent patch of small trees to a point about ¼ mile south of the summit along the peak's south ridge. (The south ridge can be followed directly to the summit, but this is class 4 in places.) Descend 300 feet on the east side of the ridge. Traverse north across the east side of the peak on some ledges to a broad chute. Climb the chute towards a reddish headwall, featuring a left-facing open book along its right side. At the base of the headwall turn right and go around the corner to a bottomless chute. Ascend the chute to the south ridge, meeting it at a notch about 200 yards south of the summit. Follow the ridge to the summit.

North Ridge. Class 4. First ascent 1951 by Fred Davenport and others. One piton was used on the first ascent.

East Face. Class 3. First ascent August 1971 by Frank Meyers and Jack Wolfe. Leave the Colby Pass Trail at approximately 10,000 feet and hike up the valley east of Whaleback. Climb onto the east face of the peak and ascend a broad chute that leads toward a reddish headwall that is south of and beneath the summit. This headwall is marked by a left-facing dihedral on its right side. From the base of the headwall, turn right and traverse north to a seemingly bottomless chute that leads up to a notch on the south ridge of the peak. An easy scramble along the ridge leads to the summit. *Variation:* Class 3. First ascent 1978 by David Vandervoet. It is apparently possible to zigzag up the east face via a series of connecting ledges which lead to the summit.

Glacier Ridge   12,360 ft+; 12,416 ft;
1.8 mi SW of Whaleback

Glacier Ridge is about 4 miles long. This description refers to the high point of the ridge.

South Side. Class 2, with a class 4 summit block. From Cloud Canyon ascend slabs and talus to the summit block. The summit block is about 15 feet high and is easy class 4.

North Face. II, 5.7. First ascent September 1971 by Galen Rowell and Jeanne Neale. Climb a diagonal crack system for five pitches to the summit.

There are two routes on the "Grave Site Wall," which is located on the east side of Deadman Canyon (UTM 603590). *Once Upon a Time in the West* is rated II, 5.11. *We Jammin* is II, 5.10b. Two ropes are needed to rappel these routes. These were climbed by Randy Judycki and Eric Fogel in 1986.

Peak 11,760ft+   11,830 ft;
0.6 mi NW of Elizabeth Pass

This peak has been called "Horn Peak," "The Horn," or "The Fin" by skiers on the Sierra High Route trans-Sierra ski tour.

Southeast Ridge. Class 2. First ascent 1936 by May Pridham and party. Follow the ridge from the top of Elizabeth Pass.

North Arête. III, 5.8. First ascent September 1970 by Greg Henzie, Galen Rowell, and Chris Jones. Four pitches on the arête lead to the summit.

Peak 11,600ft+   11,602 ft;
1.0 mi SE of Big Bird Lake

First ascent 1936 by May Pridham and party. The southwest slope is class 2, and it is a good ski run.

"Big Bird Peak"   11,600 ft+; 11,598 ft;
1.0 mi SW of Big Bird Lake

This peak has also been called "Bird Peak" and "Ghost Mountain." First ascent 1936 by May Pridham and party. It is class 2 from the west.

Northeast Face. III, 5.8. First ascent September 1970 by Chris Jones, Greg Henzie, and Galen Rowell. Relatively easy climbing leads to a dihedral system left of the center portion of the face. Climb the dihedrals to the summit.

Sugarloaf   7,995 ft; 8,002 ft
East Chute. Class 3–4. First ascent October 18, 1975 by two Basic Mountaineering Training Course students. The chute is on the left side of the east face and features a short, exposed move up a small flake.

Great West Chimney. Class 4. First ascent July 5, 1936 by Carl Jensen, Howard Gates, and John Poindexter. Leave the Sugarloaf Trail and climb on to the low, southwest ridge of the peak. Follow the crest of the ridge and climb into the chimney that splits the peak. When the difficulties in the chimney increase, crawl under a chockstone. Two more chockstones follow through narrow, cavelike passages. These secret passages lead to a large, dark room. A chimney within the Great West Chimney leads up and out of the room to the south. Scramble north to the high point of the peak. Headlamps are recommended!

West Face. III, 5.8. First ascent October 1979 by Alan Roberts and Fred Beckey. This climb involves thin crack problems, a committing overhang, and challenging friction climbing.

Ball Dome   9,435 ft; 9,357 ft
The southwest buttress is class 4. The north face, which was first climbed by John Moynier in 1985, consists of two 5.7 pitches.

Mount Silliman   11,188 ft; 11,188 ft
First ascent June 28, 1864 by Clarence King, James Gardiner, Richard Cotter, and William Brewer. There is a swell view from the summit. The south slope is class 2. It is also class 2 from Silliman Pass: traverse to the east ridge from the pass and follow the ridge to the summit.

There are two rock-climbing routes on the southern side of the west ridge of Mount Silliman. One consists of five pitches of 5.7, the other of seven pitches of 5.8. These were climbed in June 1981 by Guy McClure and Peter Cummings. The northeast ridge, a fun two-pitch 5.6 route, was first climbed in 1985 by John Moynier.

"Santa Cruz Dome"   9,520 ft+; 9,520 ft+;
1.1 mi NNW of Tokopah Falls; UTM 481543

Funky Neurosis. II, 5.9. First ascent November 1980 by Alan Swanson, Nick Badyrka, and Val LeCon. This route is on the southwest face. Begin by climbing a 5.7 chimney to the base of a smooth ramp. Continue by smearing up a smooth ramp protected by two bolts (5.9). The third pitch features some wild, overhanging chickenheads (5.6) to a steep face. The last pitch continues up the face (5.8) with two bolts, to the rounded summit.

"Winter Alta"   11,328 ft; 11,200 ft+;
0.7 mi NE of Alta Peak

This is a popular destination for skiers touring out of the Pear Lake Hut. Beautiful ski runs can be done on the northern and southern sides of this peak from January through May.

Alta Peak   11,204 ft; 11,204 ft
First ascent 1896 by William R. Dudley. The trail from Panther Gap is class 1.

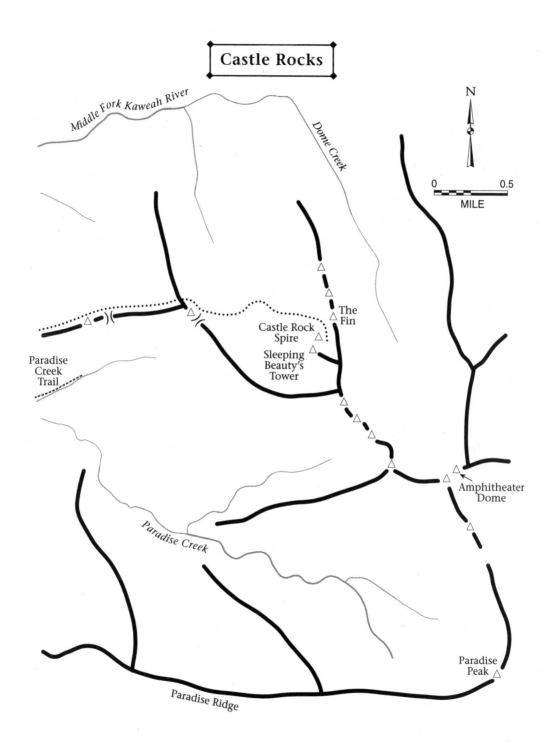

Castle Rocks

Middle Fork Kaweah River

Dome Creek

N

0   0.5
MILE

The Fin

Castle Rock Spire

Sleeping Beauty's Tower

Paradise Creek Trail

Amphitheater Dome

Paradise Creek

Paradise Peak

Paradise Ridge

"Castle Rock Spire"   7,600 ft+; UTM 462415

This incredible blade of rock, visible from Moro Rock and Generals Highway, is the most spectacular spire in California outside Yosemite Valley. In the first thirty-eight years after its first ascent in 1950, it was climbed only fourteen times. A long, difficult approach discourages most climbers from attempting an ascent. But the climbing is superb, and the setting is wild.

Further Reading: *Rock & Ice.* No. 28, November–December 1988, pp. 52–53; Greg Vernon, Sally Moser, and David Hickey. *Southern Sierra Rock Climbing: Sequoia/Kings Canyon.* Evergreen, Colo.: Chockstone Press, 1993, pp. 270–277.

There are two approaches to Castle Rocks. One leaves Mineral King Road at Atwell Mill Campground and follows the trail to a point near Paradise Peak. At this point, the trail disappears, and much tortuous bush-whacking is needed to reach the gully that leads to the notch between Castle Rock Spire and The Fin.

Most climbers use the Paradise Creek approach. From the Buckeye Flat Campground near Generals Highway, follow the Paradise Creek Trail for 1½ miles. At this point the trail starts to leave Paradise Creek and ascend a small, unnamed tributary leading east. Leave the trail and head directly up to the top of a large, grassy ridge to the east. Follow the crest of this ridge upward, past a huge, scorched oak, to meet the old, abandoned Castle Rocks Trail. Follow this *faint* trail east toward Dome Creek for about 4 miles. Leave this trail at the second rock gully encountered, then follow the gully to the notch between Castle Rock Spire and The Fin. This 4,000-foot approach has poison oak, a lot of brush and downed trees, as well as seasonal ticks, rattlesnakes, and wild bears.

The Wilson Route. III, 5.9, A2 or 5.11b. First ascent April 27, 1950 by Jim Wilson, Allen Steck, Phil Bettler, Will Siri, and Bill Long. First free ascent September 7, 1983 by Rob Raker and Richard Leversee. From the notch, traverse out onto the east face; this involves two horizontal class 4 pitches. These lead to a crack (to 5.8), which eventually turns into a gully (loose blocks!), and then eventually goes behind a large flake. Climb through a slot near the top of this flake, then descend about 50 feet to an outside corner. Climb the corner to an overhang, then pass this on the left side (5.11b or A2). Climb a crack to a cramped belay stance beneath another overhang. The Traverse Pitch then goes up and right, crosses an exposed face to an indistinct corner (5.8 to 5.9), and

traverses horizontally left to a left-slanting jam crack that leads to a belay alcove. After surmounting an overhang (5.8), climb an easy chimney. A long pitch (5.11 or A1) goes up and to the left, ending on a good ledge in a notch below a gendarme. The final pitch is easy, except for a steep corner, which requires two A1 placements or goes free at 5.10. *Variation:* First ascent May 15, 1988 by Miguel Carmona and Alois Smrz. The two horizontal class 4 pitches can be avoided by climbing directly to the flake from the approach gully. This involves one pitch of 5.10 and one pitch of 5.9. *Variation:* Face climb up and right above the easy chimney, past a small bush, to the crest of the north ridge of Castle Rock Spire. Continue up and right to the notch behind the gendarme, then descend a short distance down to a good ledge. This variation is reportedly 5.8.

Further Reading: *Summit.* June 1978, pp. 26–27; *Sierra Club Bulletin.* 1951, pp. 133–36.

Northeast Face. V, 5.8, A4. First ascent September 1967 by Tom Frost and TM Herbert. This route follows a crack system that eventually joins the Wilson Route behind the large flake. The first two pitches ascend a rotten corner that rises above the approach gully. The third, fourth, and fifth pitches go free, and the sixth pitch is mixed. Follow the rest of the Wilson Route to the summit.

West Face. IV, 5.9, A4. First ascent May 1969 by Mort Hempel, Ben Borson, Fred Beckey, and Galen Rowell. Some creative aid climbing is needed to reach the main crack system on the west face. At one point it is necessary to tie off manzanita bushes for direct aid! This 200-foot section took the first-ascent party 3 days to climb. The remainder of the climb is pleasant crack and chimney climbing.

Further Reading: *Summit.* May–June 1970, pp. 8–13.

Spiked Hairdo. III, 5.10, A3. First ascent March 18, 1996 by Bruce Bindner and Eric Coomer. This route starts from the notch of the Wilson Route and climbs the steep, narrow south arête/face. Begin by climbing a 5.7 chimney to a good stance inside the chimney. Continue up the chimney and a 5.10 off-width crack to another good stance on the arête. Mixed climbing then leads up and left to a hanging belay. A series of bolts and hook placements leads straight up to an A3 crack that ends at a good belay stance. Class 4 leads up and right across the arête to an exposed, run out 5.8 face; this is followed by a 5.7 ascending traverse back left that leads behind a block. A 5.5 slab then leads to the south summit, followed by a class 4 down-and-up climb to the higher, north summit. The first-ascent party used two 60-meter ropes and protection to 5 inches. Some of the bolts may need to be reinforced.

Descent Route. With two 60-meter (200-foot) ropes, only two rappels are needed to descend Spiked Hairdo. Down climb the 5.5 slab near the top of the south summit (a ¼-inch bolt atop the south summit facilitates this maneuver) to a large block. A 180-foot rappel leads to a hanging belay marked by a bad ¼-inch bolt, which must be backed up with one or two more bolts. The last 200-foot rappel passes over the top of the tower and down to the notch.

"The Fin"   7,641 ft; UTM 464417

This is the next formation east of Castle Rock Spire. Some of the finest rock climbs in the High Sierra are on its west face.

Further Reading: *Rock & Ice.* No. 28, November–December 1988, p. 52; Greg Vernon, Sally Moser, and David Hickey. *Southern Sierra Rock Climbing: Sequoia/Kings Canyon.* Evergreen, Colo.: Chockstone Press, 1993, pp. 270–277.

Silver Lining. IV, 5.9. First ascent May 26, 1985 by Patrick Paul, Ron Carson, Eve Laeger, and Herb Laeger. This route starts at a pine tree at the lower edge of the apron at the base of the west face of The Fin. Nine pitches of beautiful face climbing on excellent rock (with a lot of run outs) lead to the summit. The route passes the prominent block on its right side during the seventh pitch. Some 5.9 climbing is found on every pitch, and there are some serious chimneys.

Aspire. IV, 5.9. First ascent May 1986 by Richard Leversee and Herb Laeger. This route starts about 150 feet above and to the right of the pine tree at the base of the preceding route. It goes up and slightly right for nine pitches, parallel to Silver Lining.

Charley Knapp Route. III, 5.9. First ascent May 23, 1984 by Ron Carson, Patrick Paul, and Herb Laeger. This route is across from Castle Rock Spire, on the southern side of the west face of The Fin. The route goes directly up for four pitches before moving up and left to the crest of The Fin.

North Buttress. III, 5.10. First ascent June 26, 1997 by Dave Nettle, Richard Leversee, and Kevin Daniels. This route starts up the wide chimney and crack system

Castle Rocks from the northwest.

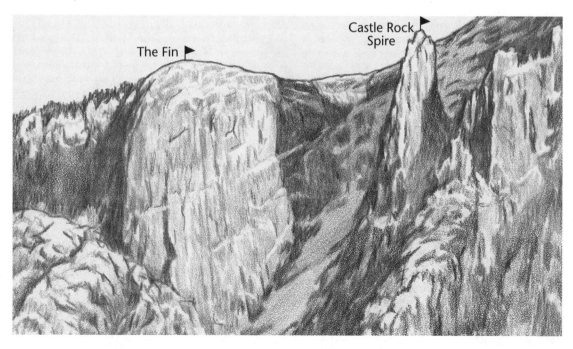

directly on the crest of the North Buttress. Go past an old bolt with a sling, overcome Bushy Roof (5.10), and continue to the highest ledge. Continue up the long, off-width squeeze chimney (5.10), go past a roof and up an inside corner, then move left 10 feet to a stance. Climb a 5.8 crack beneath a blank, vegetated, inside corner, then face climb (5.10+) to the left beneath the corner to a big ledge beyond a small pillar. Cross the face to the left to a big, dead tree, climb the face behind the tree and go right and slightly up to a dirty 5.10 right-facing corner. A horizontal traverse to the right across a 5.10 face leads to a short left-facing inside corner and another traverse to the right ends at a small ledge. A run out 5.8 face then leads to a couple of hundred feet of walking to the summit.

Rappel Route. This begins near a manzanita bush at the top of the narrow summit ridge, near the top of Aspire. Two 165-foot ropes and twelve runners are needed to complete the rappels.

"Sleeping Beauty's Tower"   7,680 ft+; UTM 461414

This tower is high above and slightly southwest of Castle Rock Spire.

The Gargoyle Route. III, 5.9, A0. First ascent July 1983 by Herb Laeger, Eve Laeger, and Rich Smith. This route starts low in a gully on the northwest side of the tower. It traverses right on a ramp system onto the vertical west face. It then follows a crack-and-corner system directly to the summit. These six pitches consist of beautiful climbing. A 10-foot tension traverse to the left on the second pitch is the only aid; it leads to a crack system. Descend to the southwest with a few rappels to gain the gully south of the tower.

"Amphitheater Dome"   9,081 ft; 9,180 ft

This dome is best approached from Paradise Peak.

Southeast Side. Class 3–4. First ascent 1946 by Ted Knowles, DeWitt Allen, and Anton Nelson.

North Buttress. II, 5.8, A2. First ascent June 23, 1968 by Fred Beckey, Roger Briggs, Jim Jones, and Dave Leen. The crux of this climb is an overhang (overcome with aid) followed by difficult free climbing.

Paradise Peak   9,362 ft; 9,360 ft+

A side trail leads almost to the top of this peak from the Paradise Ridge Trail.

WRINKLES

Mineral King to the Upper Big Arroyo. There are many options for this route, and many cross-country hikers have argued over which is the best approach. In my experience, the easiest route is the following: Cross Glacier Pass (the only obstacle is a short class 3 cliff with seasonal snowfields) and descend to meet the Black Rock Pass Trail near the headwaters of Cliff Creek. Follow the Black Rock Pass Trail to the Big Arroyo. The other passes may be technically easier, but they also involve hiking across miles of talus, which is hardly a pleasant prospect, especially with a heavy pack.

The Black Kaweah's Local Magnetic Disturbance. Differences as great as 8 degrees from the normal compass variation may be encountered in the vicinity of the Black Kaweah.

High Sierra Trail. The vast majority of the trails in the High Sierra were created by the Native Americans and the shepherds. In other words, they just happened. Many of these trails have been rerouted and graded by the NPS and the USFS, but the vast majority still maintain their original steep pitches. Exceptions to this are a few built specifically for recreation. These include the High Sierra Trail and parts of the John Muir Trail. The High Sierra Trail is a trans-Sierra trail that begins at Giant Forest and eventually meets the John Muir Trail along Wallace Creek; the John Muir Trail then goes to the summit of Mount Whitney. The High Sierra Trail traverses scenic terrain at a relatively gentle grade. There are tremendous views across the Middle Fork of the Kaweah River to Castle Rocks. The trail then passes through Valhalla, with its impressive cliffs, before descending the Big Arroyo to the canyon of the Kern River. Anyone hiking this section should not miss visiting Moraine Lake, which requires a slight detour. The High Sierra Trail then ascends the Kern River drainage to meet the John Muir Trail, at which point it offers views to the west of terrain it has traversed.

Of all the High Sierra trails, the John Muir Trail receives the vast majority of attention in the public imagination. But its rival, the High Sierra Trail, should not be ignored.

Junction Meadow. There are two Junction Meadows in the High Sierra, and they are located just close enough together to cause confusion. Prudent hikers should specify Junction Meadow—Kern River or Junction

Meadow—Bubbs Creek before making ironclad arrangements for a rendezvous or food drops.

Approaches to Triple Divide Peak, Whaleback, Glacier Ridge, Milestone Mountain, Midway Mountain, and other hard-to-reach places in this vicinity. Many people assume that the best approach to the northern portion of the Great Western Divide is from the east over Shepherd Pass, and that Triple Divide Peak and points north should be approached via the High Sierra Trail or by a cross-country route from Mineral King. An often neglected alternative is to approach these places from the west via the Sugarloaf Trail from Big Meadows/Horse Corral Meadow Road. Granted, this approach is long (25 miles+) but it has none of the severe ups and downs of the other alternatives. Besides, the view of Whaleback rising above Big Wet Meadow is worth the long hike. (Although it is outside the territory of this chapter, this is also a viable alternative to ascents of North Guard, Mount Brewer, South Guard, and other peaks at the northern end of the Great Western Divide. After all, Mount Brewer was first climbed by this approach and route.)

Thunder, Table, Midway, and Milestone Traverse. A major barrier to climbing all four of these peaks in a day is overcoming the technical Northeast Couloir or by-passing the long east ridge of Table Mountain. After climbing Thunder Mountain, cross to the west side of the Great Western Divide at MacLeod Pass (described in Chapter 4, The Kings-Kern Divide). Then climb the West Ridge, North Side of Table Mountain. This may require an ice axe as well as a rope to overcome a short class 4 section, but it is feasible to circle around the relatively short west ridge of Table Mountain and climb the class 3 West Ridge, South Side. Descend the Southeast Side of Table Mountain and then climb the East Ridge of Midway Mountain, descending the West Slope. Finish by climbing the Northwest Face of Milestone Mountain. Those camped in the upper reaches of the Kern River should descend the East Side, while those camped west of the Great Western Divide should retrace their steps down the Northwest Face and cross Talus Pass.

Chapter 4

The Kings – Kern Divide

The Kings-Kern Divide is a major barrier of the southern High Sierra. This wall of mountains extends for 6 miles west from Junction Peak on the Sierra crest to Thunder Mountain on the Great Western Divide.

This chapter covers the area bounded on the north by Bubbs Creek and Kearsarge Pass, on the south by Shepherd Pass and Tyndall Creek, on the west by the Kern River and Thunder Mountain to the Roaring River and Avalanche Pass.

For years, the only trail that crossed this divide was the old sheep route over Harrison Pass. One of the last sections of the John Muir Trail to be constructed, Forester Pass, was completed in 1932, making a crossing of the Kings-Kern Divide possible for mere mortals. Before this, travelers on the John Muir Trail had to bypass the divide entirely, and had to cross Junction Pass and Shepherd Pass instead. This compact area features rugged terrain, awesome scenery, and beautiful lakes and streams.

HISTORY

Clarence King and Richard Cotter crossed the Kings-Kern Divide twice during their epic journey to Mount Tyndall in 1864. King described this adventure in his American classic, *Mountaineering in the Sierra Nevada*. In the dramatic style so popular in the nineteenth century, King tells of crossing the divide somewhere between Thunder Mountain and Mount Jordan, where he and Cotter lassoed a loose spike of rock and climbed the rope hand over hand. He also describes rope-downs where retreat was impossible and continued descent uncertain. On their return to their camp along Roar-

ing River, somewhere in the vicinity of Lake Reflection, King attempted a steep climb and failed. Cotter succeeded, however, and called down to King to say that he had a secure stance and that King shouldn't be afraid to use the rope for tension. King's pride insisted that he climb the pitch free; after having done so, he discovered that Cotter was precariously balanced and the slightest tug on the rope would have caused them both to catch big air.

John Muir visited the Kings-Kern Divide in 1873 and, as was his practice, climbed several peaks—but he neglected to record which peaks he ascended. Shepherds were active in this region in the latter part of the nineteenth century, particularly on the southern part of the divide. Mountaineers such as Bolton Brown and Joseph LeConte began to climb some of the peaks in the late nineteenth and early twentieth centuries.

MAPS

USGS. *7.5-minute series:* Mt. Williamson, Mt. Brewer, Sphinx Lakes, Kearsarge Peak, Mt. Clarence King, The Sphinx, Mt. Kaweah. *National park maps:* Sequoia and Kings Canyon National Parks and Vicinity (1:125,000). *30 x 60–minute series:* Mount Whitney.

USFS. A Guide to the John Muir Wilderness and Sequoia–Kings Canyon Wilderness (1:63,360).

Tom Harrison Cartography. Mount Whitney High Country, Kings Canyon High Country.

Map Link 15-minute series. Mount Whitney, Mt. Pinchot, Triple Divide Peak, Marion Peak.

Wilderness Press 15-minute series. Mount Whitney, Mt. Pinchot, Triple Divide Peak.

ROADS

Onion Valley Road

Onion Valley Road heads west from Independence for 14.1 miles to Onion Valley, one of the highest trailheads in the eastern High Sierra. Trails leading out of Onion Valley are the Kearsarge Pass Trail, the Robinson Lake Trail, and the Golden Trout Lake Trail. There is a campground, a pack station, and hiker parking at Onion Valley.

Pinyon Creek Road

Pinyon Creek Road leaves Onion Valley Road 4.7 miles from Independence. The road heads southwest and goes right at 0.2 miles at a fork. It forks again 0.7 miles later; go right. The road ends in the desert after another 0.3 miles, next to Pinyon Creek. This is the trailhead for the cross-country hike up Pinyon Creek and the eastern approach for Mount Bradley and the Center Basin Crags.

Kings Canyon Highway   (Highway 180)

This road and trailhead are described in Chapter 6: Monarch Divide and The Cirque Crest. The Bubbs Creek Trail starts 2 miles from the end of Highway 180 in Kings Canyon.

TRAILS

Shepherd Pass Trail   12 miles

This trail, along with either the John Muir Trail or the Lake South America Trail, provides access to the southern portion of the Kings-Kern Divide. The Shepherd Pass Trail is described in Chapter 2, The Whitney Region.

Tyndall Creek Trail   5 miles

The Tyndall Creek Trail, which may be considered part of the Shepherd Pass Trail, begins about ¼ mile south of where the John Muir Trail crosses Tyndall Creek (0 mi; 10,826 ft+). After passing the Tyndall Creek Ranger Station, the trail follows a long, wet meadow. After crossing the creek, it passes through a lodgepole forest before making a slight climb. This climb ends at the edge of the Kern River canyon, where there are excellent views of the Great Western Divide (3 mi; 10,498 ft+). The trail then makes a steep descent with many switchbacks before meeting the Lake South America Trail along the Kern River (2 mi; 9,252 ft+), 4½ miles north of Junction Meadow.

John Muir Trail   14¼ miles

After meeting the Shepherd Pass Trail on the south side of Tyndall Creek (0 mi; 10,826 ft+), the John Muir Trail crosses the creek and heads north to meet the Lake South America Trail (¾ mi; 11,089 ft+). The John Muir Trail continues north, passes some lakes, and switchbacks up the cliff on the south side of Forester Pass to its summit (4¼ mi; 13,057 ft+). (The John Muir Trail and the Pacific Crest Trail are the same trail in this area; Forester Pass is the high point of the entire 2,400-mile Pacific Crest Trail.) The trail descends the gently sloping north side of the pass to the junction with the Center Basin Trail (4 mi; 10,630 ft+). Bears prowl through this area. The John Muir Trail continues as it descends Bubbs Creek, and then passes through beautiful forests and meadows to the junction with the Bubbs Creek Trail below Vidette Meadow (3 mi; 9,514 ft+). The John Muir Trail leaves Bubbs Creek here, climbs to the north, and meets the Bullfrog Lake Trail (1½ mi; 10,564 ft+). The John Muir Trail continues climbing to the north, passing the side trail leading to Charlotte Lake (½ mi; 10,630 ft+) before meeting the Kearsarge Pass Trail (¼ mi; 11,155 ft+).

Lake South America Trail   12¾ miles

The Lake South America Trail starts along the John Muir Trail ¾ mile north of the John Muir Trail junction with the Shepherd Pass Trail (0 mi; 11,089 ft+). The Lake South America Trail climbs and goes west to a junction (1 mi; 11,352 ft+) with a trail that continues west 2¼ miles directly to the Kern River. From this junction, the Lake South America Trail goes north and ascends a basin with a short cliff at its head to the top of the ridge overlooking Lake South America (2 mi; 12,139 ft+). The trail descends to the northwest and leads to a use trail that leads to the west shore of the lake (¾ mi; 11,942 ft+). Wood campfires are prohibited above 10,400 feet in the headwaters of the Kern River.

The trail continues southwest, down a lovely wooded and grassy basin—the headwaters of the Kern River—to

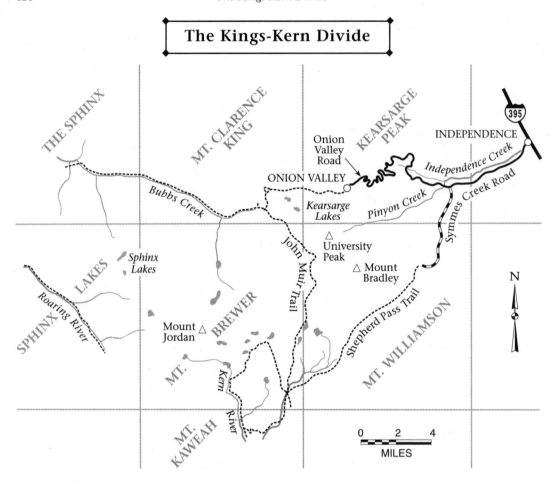

The Kings-Kern Divide

meet the trail that leads back to Tyndall Creek (3 mi; 10,630 ft+). The trail continues down the Kern River canyon to a junction with the High Sierra Trail (5 mi; 8,793 ft+), one mile north of Junction Meadow.

Center Basin Trail   3 miles

The Center Basin Trail starts along the John Muir Trail (0 mi; 10,630 ft+), 4 miles north of Forester Pass and 4 miles south of the John Muir Trail junction with the Bubbs Creek Trail. The trail climbs up into Center Basin and circles Golden Bear Lake on its north shore before disappearing in fields of talus (3 mi; 11,220 ft+).

This is one of the original routes of the John Muir Trail. It was used until the trail over Forester Pass was

constructed in 1932. Traces of the trail may still be found in the upper reaches of Center Basin and over Junction Pass, but this is now more of a cross-country route than a trail. It is described under Junction Pass.

Bubbs Creek Trail   11½ miles

A quota trail. The Bubbs Creek Trail begins 2 miles from the end of the Kings Canyon Highway along the Woods Creek Trail (0 mi; 5,120 ft+). Bears are active all along this trail. The trail crosses the South Fork of the Kings River on a bridge and switchbacks up the north bank of Bubbs Creek. It meets another trail descending from Avalanche Pass via Sphinx Creek (2 mi; 6,240 ft+). The Bubbs Creek Trail continues up the north bank of the creek to meet the East Lake Trail at Junction Meadow (6½ mi; 8,136 ft+), then goes upstream to meet the John Muir Trail near Vidette Meadow (3 mi; 11,483 ft+).

Sphinx Creek Trail   12½ miles

The Sphinx Creek Trail starts along the Bubbs Creek Trail 4 miles from the end of the road in Kings Canyon (0 mi; 6,220 ft+). It switchbacks up the east side of Sphinx Creek, crossing to its west bank at a prominent meadow (3 mi; 8,520 ft+). (From this point, a use trail continues up the west side of the creek to Sphinx Lakes; Mount Brewer can be climbed from here.) The Sphinx Creek Trail makes a gradual ascent to the west and leaves the drainage before reaching Avalanche Pass (3 mi; 10,080 ft+). The trail descends from the pass to Scaffold Meadow along Roaring River (6½ mi; 7,400 ft+).

East Lake Trail   5 miles

The beautiful East Lake Trail passes through forests of aspen and pine and meadows with flowers and willows. The sound of East Creek adds to the ambiance, and the views of Mount Brewer and the peaks of the Kings-Kern Divide are outstanding.

The East Lake Trail leaves the Bubbs Creek Trail at Junction Meadow (0 mi; 8,136 ft+) and crosses Bubbs Creek before ascending East Creek. At first the trail follows the western bank of the creek, but soon it crosses over it and ascends the east side of East Creek to East Lake (3 mi; 9,468 ft). Bears prowl through this area. The trail continues up the east side of the creek to Lake Reflection, one of the most beautiful lakes in the High Sierra (2 mi; 10,029 ft).

Kearsarge Pass Trail   6½ miles

A quota trail. The Kearsarge Pass Trail is one of the most heavily used trails in the High Sierra. Bears prowl through this area. Wood campfires are prohibited in the basin east of Kearsarge Pass and above 10,000 feet in Kings Canyon National Park.

The trail goes west out of Onion Valley (0 mi; 9,192 ft) and switchbacks up to overused Gilbert Lake; just beyond Gilbert Lake a trail heads south to Matlock and Slim Lakes, which offer more privacy. The Kearsarge Pass Trail continues climbing to the west and passes north of well-named Big Pothole Lake to reach the barren plateau just east of the pass. A gradual climb across the plateau brings you to the summit of Kearsarge Pass (4 mi; 11,811 ft+). The trail makes a steep descent on the western side of the pass to the junction with the Bullfrog Lake Trail (¼ mi; 11,352 ft+). The Kearsarge Pass Trail goes west from this junction, making a gradual descent, to meet the John Muir Trail (2¼ mi; 10,827 ft+). About ¼ mile before this junction, there is a Y-shaped fork: Those heading north on the John Muir Trail toward Glen Pass should go right; those bound for Charlotte Lake or Bubbs Creek must go left. It is about ¼ mile in each case.

Bullfrog Lake Trail   2½ miles

This was the original route of the Kearsarge Pass Trail, but Bullfrog Lake became so scarred and polluted from too many thoughtless campers that the NPS constructed a new trail to the north to divert traffic away from this site. Bullfrog Lake is closed to all camping, and Kearsarge Lakes has a one-night limit on camps. Bears prowl through this area.

The Bullfrog Lake Trail starts approximately ¼ mile west of Kearsarge Pass (0 mi; 11,352 ft+). Soon after it begins, it forks; the left fork goes for ½ mile to the Kearsarge Lakes. The main trail continues to the west, passing north of Bullfrog Lake, with outstanding views of East Vidette, Deerhorn Mountain, and West Vidette. From Bullfrog Lake, the trail contours southwest to meet the John Muir Trail (2½ mi; 10,564 ft+).

Robinson Lake Trail   2 miles

A non-quota trail. This short hike leads to an extremely popular overnight camping destination. Campfires are prohibited in the Robinson Lake basin.

From the eastern end of Onion Valley Campground (0 mi, 9,186 ft+), a trail leads through aspen and climbs the steep hillside to the entrance of the hanging valley. The trail goes south and, after climbing a slight rise, leads to Robinson Lake (2 mi; 10,499 ft+).

CROSS-COUNTRY ROUTES

Junction Pass   4020 m+; 13,200 ft+;
0.4 mi NE of Junction Peak; UTM 785617

Class 2. This is the original route of the John Muir Trail. It has not been maintained since 1932, but traces of the old trail are still visible. From The Pothole on the eastern side of Shepherd Pass, head northwest. Cross the meadow on the bench above The Pothole. Ascend the west side of the stream that leads into the meadow and head into the valley between Junction Peak and Junction Pass. Stay on the north side of the valley and ascend sand and scree to the plateau near the summit of Junction Pass. (The correct pass is 0.3 mile west of the name "Junction Pass" that appears on some editions of the Mount Williamson 7.5-minute quadrangle.) The route on the north side of the pass descends into Center Basin and remains west of the lakes in the upper portion of the basin. The Center Basin Trail is met southeast of Golden Bear Lake.

"Ski Mountaineers Pass"   4000 m; 13,120 ft+;
0.3 mi ESE of Forester Pass

Class 1–2. This pass consists of sand, scree, and talus, but during moderate to heavy snow years it provides a means for skiers to cross the Kings-Kern Divide without having to negotiate the cliffs on the south side of Forester Pass.

"Andy's Foot Pass"   4160 m+; 13,600 ft+;
0.2 mi SSE of Gregory's Monument

Class 2; ice axe required. This is a direct route between Lake South America and the upper regions of Bubbs Creek. From the top of Harrison Pass, hike east to the top of Andy's Foot Pass, which is the first pass south-southeast of Gregory's Monument. There is a permanent snowfield in the couloir on the northeast side of the pass, and the angle is quite steep. This pass is easiest to tackle in the late spring or early summer, when the snow is consolidated but not too icy and covers the huge talus northeast of the pass.

Harrison Pass   3880 m+; 12,720 ft+
Class 2. Some maps show a trail over Harrison Pass. Be forewarned: This trail has not been maintained for many years, and the especially critical section of it leading up the north side of the pass has all but disappeared. With snow, the north side of the pass is steep and icy; no snow reveals steep and loose rock.

From the East Lake Trail, climb into the basin north of Harrison Pass and the Ericsson Crags. The upper portion of this basin is composed of huge pieces of talus. From the highest lake, either climb the ledges toward

Mount Ericsson that lead back to the top of the pass or ascend a loose rock chute directly to the summit of the pass. The south side of the pass is easy.

"Ericsson Pass"   3840 m+; 12,560 ft+;
0.4 mi NE of Mount Ericsson

Class 2–3. This is an alternative to Harrison Pass. Only the upper portion of the northern side of this pass is difficult.

"Deerhorn Saddle"   3840 m+; 12,560 ft+;
0.4 mi SE of Deerhorn Mountain

Class 2. This pass is used to gain access between Vidette Creek and the basin north of Harrison Pass.

Lucy's Foot Pass   3780 m+; 12,400 ft+
Class 2. This pass was first crossed by Lucy Brown and Bolton Brown in 1896 during their exploration of the Kings-Kern Divide. Difficult talus is encountered on the north side of the pass. A short cliff just below the top on the north side can be bypassed by moving 150 feet to the east. The south side of the pass is easy.

Milly's Foot Pass   3740 m+; 12,240 ft+
Class 3. This is the most direct route between Lake Reflection and the upper Kern River Basin. This pass was first crossed in July 1953 by Mildred Jentsch and Sylvia Kershaw. Class 2 talus leads to the prominent slot that marks the pass on its northwestern side. Near the top, this slot narrows, and the climbing becomes class 3 for about 100 feet. The southeast side of the pass is easy.

"Thunder Pass"   3860 m+; 12,640 ft+;
0.2 mi ESE of Thunder Mountain

Class 2; ice axe required. This pass is also known as "Thunder Col." It was probably first crossed by Clarence King and Richard Cotter in their quest for Mount Tyndall in 1864. Some huge talus is encountered on the lower northern portion of the route. This can be minimized by going south from Lake 3540m+ (11,600 ft+; UTM 700610) before turning southwest to the southern shore of Lake 3560m+ (11,680 ft+; UTM 696603). Also, care must be taken on the northern slopes to ensure that the easiest route is followed. Further, there is a lot of talus along the stream draining the large lake to the southeast of the pass. This can be avoided by keeping northeast of the stream until near

Lake 3600m+ (11,640 ft+; UTM 694584). Make a descending traverse from here to the next small valley to the northeast, then make another descending traverse to the east.

"MacLeod Pass" 3980 m+; 13,040 ft+;
0.1 mi S of Thunder Mountain; UTM 683583

Class 2. This pass is named in honor of Gordon MacLeod. It leads between Table Creek and the upper Kern River Basin, and has been used to approach Thunder Mountain from the west. Climb a loose chute on the west side of the pass. The eastern side of the pass is easier.

"Thunder Ridge" 3660 m+; 12,000 ft+;
0.6 mi W of Thunder Mountain

Class 2. This pass provides access to Cunningham Creek from Table Creek, west of the crest of the Great Western Divide.

Longley Pass 3780 m+; 12,400 ft+

Class 1. This is the first pass south of South Guard. The west side of the pass is easy, but the east side is a little more difficult. In early season, the east side of the pass may be blocked by a cornice. This can be bypassed on the north by means of a short class 3 section.

"Brewer Pass" 3860 m+; 12,640 ft+;
0.5 mi SE of Mount Brewer

Class 2. Also known as "Brewer Col," this pass connects Brewer Creek with East Lake. The east side of this pass may be impassable due to steep snow. If this is the case, it can be bypassed by climbing the south ridge of Mount Brewer and descending the peak's east ridge to East Lake. In other words, it can be bypassed by traversing Mount Brewer.

"Cinder Col" 3680 m+; 12,080 ft+; 0.7 mi SW
of Mount Brewer

Class 2. This pass has been called "Brewer Ridge." It extends from Cunningham Creek to Brewer Creek, and is usually crossed with Sphinx Col for climbs of South Guard from Sphinx Lakes.

"Sphinx Col" 12,040 ft+; 12,000 ft+;
0.9 mi SW of North Guard; UTM 657637

Class 2. This pass is usually used to approach Mount Brewer from Sphinx Lakes. Leave the Sphinx Creek Trail where it crosses to its west bank at a prominent meadow at 8,520 ft+. Hike up the west side of the creek to Sphinx Lakes. Head south from Sphinx Lakes and then turn southeast, climbing up to this hidden pass, the notch northeast of Peak 12,360ft+ (12,393 ft). Descend the southeast side of the pass first by heading east and then southeast into the Brewer Creek drainage. The northwest slopes of Mount Brewer can be easily reached from here.

Vidette Creek

Class 1. Cross Bubbs Creek just east of the stream draining Bullfrog Lake that flows into Bubbs Creek. There is a large log at this crossing (UTM 743689). Follow a good use trail southeast from this crossing to one of Shorty Lovelace's tiny log cabins (UTM 746687). (Lovelace ran trap lines through this area before Kings Canyon National Park was created in 1940. This cabin is now a historical site, and camping is prohibited near the cabin.) Approximately 100 feet west of this cabin, next to two parallel downed trees, follow the use trail that ascends the west side of Vidette Creek to Vidette Lakes. Cross-country travel is easy in the upper basin until just beneath Deerhorn Saddle.

Pinyon Creek

Class 2. A non-quota trail. This serves as the eastern approach to Mount Bradley and the Center Basin Crags. From the trailhead, a use trail ascends the north side of the stream to the base of the diamond-shaped hill in the middle of the valley, which is best passed on its dry, left side. Regain the stream above the hill, and follow it to the basin north of Mount Bradley.

"University Pass" 3840 m+; 12,640 ft+;
0.6 mi SE of University Peak

Class 2. This is the most direct approach to Center Basin and the Kings-Kern Divide from Onion Valley, but it is a rough, cross-country route. Only experienced cross-country hikers should attempt it. From Robinson Lake, hike up the creek to the lowest point between University Peak and Peak 3926m (12,910 ft). There is a steep snow gully here for most of the summer (an ice axe may be helpful), and huge boulders at the base of the pass can make the approach rather tedious. The southwest side of the pass is a long chute with loose rocks.

"University Shoulder"　　3700 m+; 12,160 ft+;
0.6 mi NW of University Peak; UTM 773678

Class 2. This high-level route has been used by cross-country skiers to avoid losing altitude by way of Vidette Meadow or Onion Valley. Make an ascending traverse across the southwest side of University Peak to the northwest shoulder of the peak, which is southeast of Kearsarge Pinnacles. The north side of the shoulder is rather steep (with huge talus in the summer), but it leads directly to the Kearsarge Lakes basin.

PEAKS

Thunder Mountain　　4120 m+; 13,588 ft

East Ridge. Class 3 with a class 4 summit block. First ascent August 1905 by George Davis of the USGS. Gain Thunder Pass from either Lake Reflection or the Kern River Basin. Follow the east ridge of the peak (or the talus slope to the southeast) to the south summit of the peak. Cross over the south summit and descend about 20 feet to the notch between the south and middle summits. Cross to the north side of the notch on an airy bridge and traverse across the east face of the middle summit to the notch between it and the north summit. The north summit, the high point, can be climbed via a crack with natural chockstones on the southern side of the block, or by means of a jam crack on its southwest side. Either way is class 4. *Variation:* It is also possible to reach the southeast slope of the peak from Table Creek by crossing MacLeod Pass.

Further Reading: John Moynier and Claude Fiddler. *Sierra Classics*. Evergreen, Colo.: Chockstone Press, 1993, pp. 74–75.

Peak 3840m+　　12,560 ft+;
1.3 mi W of Thunder Mountain

South Slope. Class 2. First ascent 1940 by a Sierra Club party.

North Face and West Ridge. Class 3–4. First ascent July 1958 by Phil Arnot and party.

Peak 3980m+　　13,040 ft+;
0.5 mi NNW of Thunder Mountain

Southeast Face. Class 2–3. First ascent 1940 by Oliver Kehrlein and party.

Peak 3960m+　　12,960 ft+; 0.3 mi S of Longley Pass

First ascent 1925 by Norman Clyde. The peak is class 2 from Longley Pass.

South Guard　　4033 m; 13,224 ft

North Ridge. Class 2–3. First ascent 1864 by Clarence King and Richard Cotter. Follow the ridge from Brewer Pass. *South Slope*. Class 2 from Longley Pass.

Peak 3940m+　　12,960 ft+;
0.9 mi SE of Mount Brewer

Northeast Ridge. Class 3. First ascent July 26, 1916 by Walter L. Huber, Florence Burrell, Inezetta Holt, and James Rennie. Climb the northeast ridge from the south fork of Ouzel Creek. This ridge is loose and knife edge.

North Face. Class 3. The climb is made by following a series of ledges.

South Face. Class 2. Climb to the ridge west of the summit and follow it to the top.

Peak 3904m　　12,805 ft; 1.2 mi ESE of Mount Brewer

The west ridge is class 1–2.

Peak 12,640ft+　　12,683 ft;
1.1 mi W of South Guard

South Slope. Class 2. First ascent July 1959 by Phil Arnot, Shel Arnot, Harry Pancoast, Dale Nelson, and Charlie Backus. The north summit is the high point of the peak.

Mount Brewer　　4136 m; 13,570 ft

Mount Brewer is separate from the Sierra crest and the Kings-Kern Divide, and so has a wide, unobstructed view in all directions from its summit.

East Ridge. Class 2. First ascent 1895 by A. B. Clark and Bolton Brown. First winter ascent February 15, 1971 by Paul Emerson, Rick Rieder, Mike Lee, and Tim Duffy. From East Lake, follow Ouzel Creek upstream to where it is possible to climb onto the ridge that leads directly up Mount Brewer. Follow the ridge to where it ends against the south ridge of the peak; go left (south) through a small notch, and climb the south ridge to the summit.

South Ridge. Class 2. First ascent July 2, 1864 by William H. Brewer and Charles F. Hoffman. From Brewer Creek or South Guard Lake, ascend to Brewer Pass and follow the south ridge to the summit. The south ridge can also be ascended from East Lake, but the east ridge is an easier route.

Northwest Slopes. Class 2. Cross into the Brewer Creek basin from Sphinx Lakes via "Sphinx Col," the notch northeast of Point 12,360ft+ (12,393 ft). Traverse and climb into the bowl between North Guard and Mount Brewer and climb the northwest slope of Mount Brewer.

Northeast Couloir. Class 2–3. First ascent August 4, 1940 by Oliver Kehrlein, August Fruge, Grete Fruge, E. Hanson, L. West, R. Leggett, and A. Mulay. Climb the prominent snow-and-ice couloir just north of the northeast face of Mount Brewer. The couloir ends along the north ridge. Climb the north ridge to the summit.

Northeast Face. III, 5.7. First ascent September 1963 by Kenneth Boche and Russ McLean. This route begins by climbing the first chimney to the right of the rib that leads directly to the summit of the peak. Climb the chimney for about 200 feet to an overhang. Traverse right for 10 feet (5.7) into the next chimney. Climb this second chimney, passing a chockstone on its left side. Go up and right for about 40 feet to some class 4 slabs. Climb toward the higher of two notches that are to the right of the summit. The top of the climb is reached by climbing between the two notches.

Further Reading: John Moynier and Claude Fiddler. *Sierra Classics.* Evergreen, Colo.: Chockstone Press, 1993, pp. 76–77.

Central Rib Direct. IV, 5.9+. First ascent September 25, 1995 by Todd Vogel and Dave Nettle. Start by climbing a 5.9 squeeze chimney that is 25 feet to the right of the chimney of the Northeast Face route. The squeeze chimney leads to a left-facing corner (5.9) and the second pitch ends at a sandy, flat ledge. Move down and left onto the face of the rib, then continue up (5.6), climbing a 6-inch crack. Next encounter easy class 5 climbing to some white flakes where the rib narrows. Many beautiful hand cracks on the face of the rib (5.7 to 5.8) lead up and slightly right to a big, sloping ledge on the right side of the rib. A tricky move up and left, across the crest of the rib to its left side, leads to some 5.9+ stemming, with a belay on a flake. Another 5.9+ pitch on the left side of the rib leads to class 4 and the summit.

Peak 3520m+ 11,520 ft+;
1.9 mi ENE of Mount Brewer

This is a long ridge that overlooks East Lake. This peak has been called "Peak Corbel" and "Peak Korbel."

South Face. Class 3. First ascent May 28, 1934 by David Brower and Hervey Voge. The first-ascent party described this as "an entertaining climb, just below the difficulty requiring a rope."

Southwest Ridge. Class 3. Descended May 28, 1934 by Hervey Voge and David Brower. This traverse is among towers, blocks, and knife edges.

North Guard 4026 m; 13,327 ft

Mount Brewer may have a swell view from its summit, but North Guard is the better climb, hands down.

Mount Brewer, North Guard, and Mount Francis Farquhar from the southeast. Photo by R. J. Secor.

South Face. Class 3. First ascent July 12, 1925 by Norman Clyde. There are three chutes on the southern side of North Guard. Climb the middle chute and from its top, traverse up and left to a saddle along the west ridge of the peak. The traverse along the ridge to the summit involves some impressive scrambling and bouldering. Most impressive of all, however, is the large, sloping summit block overhanging the east face. *Variation:* It is also possible to traverse to the right onto the crest of the south ridge from the top of the middle chute.

Further Reading: John Moynier and Claude Fiddler. *Sierra Classics.* Evergreen, Colo.: Chockstone Press, 1993, pp. 78–79.

East Face. III, 5.8. First ascent June 1981 by Fred Beckey and Rick Nolting. Climb the center portion of the east face to an exposed edge. Make a difficult exit to the right and climb an outside corner that lacks holds and protection. The rest of the climb has better holds and protection.

East and North Faces. Class 4. First ascent May 28, 1934 by Hervey Voge and David Brower. Climb to the col north-northeast of the summit from the Ouzel Creek drainage. From the col, climb a 30-foot, V-shaped crack on the north ridge to a ledge. Traverse right (west) across broken ledges on the north face to a crack, which leads to easier rocks and the summit.

North Peak of North Guard. First ascent August 10, 1948 by James Koontz and party.

Peak 3840m+   12,600 ft+;
0.5 mi NW of North Guard

The northeast face is class 3; it was first climbed September 1973 by Andy Smatko and Bill Schuler.

Mount Francis Farquhar   3929 m; 12,893 ft;
1.0 mi NW of North Guard

This is a beautiful peak, and all of its routes are splendid. Before it was named officially, this peak was informally called "Notch Peak" for the prominent notch seen in the northwest ridge of the peak when viewed from the east. The new, official name, "Mount Francis Farquhar," is appropriate to both the memory of the man and the stature of the peak.

South Ridge. Class 3. First ascent July 17, 1932 by Alice Carter, Julie Mortimer, Dorothy Baird, Patricia Goodhue, Katherine Lindforth, D. R. Brothers, Glen Dawson, Thomas Rawles, Lincoln O'Brien, Arthur Neld, Norman Clyde, William Dulley, John Schager, and Alfred Weiler. Climb to the saddle south of the peak from Sphinx Lakes, and follow the ridge to the summit.

Northwest Ridge. Class 3. First ascent September 24, 1972 by Doug Mantle, Barbara Lilley, Diana Dee, Rick May, and R. J. Secor. From Sphinx Lakes, ascend the chute that leads to the notch on the northwest ridge. The chute divides just below the notch with two branches leading to the right. Take the right higher, narrow branch and follow it almost to the ridge crest. Go to the right onto a face and up to the summit. A nice climb.

Blank Stair Route. IV, 5.10+. First ascent July 31, 1997 by Dave Nettle and Mark McDaniel. This route climbs the northeast face of the lower, northwest summit of Mount Francis Farquhar. Start either by climbing a 5.10 right-facing open book with a roof or an easy class 4–5 ramp that leads up and left. Continue up the broken, right-facing corner and pass some loose flakes by going up and left. Climb to a sandy ledge and go up and left from a left-facing inside corner. Tip-toe to the left for 30 feet from a roof and climb a 5.10 face, protected by two bolts, to the Scud Rocket Pillar. Climb the left side of the pillar and traverse left from the first roof (5.10-) to Heart Flake. Go up and right above the second roof, then go up and left past Look, Don't Touch Flake, under and past the third roof, and to a small ledge. Continue up and left to the Blank Stair and climb through the break in the roof. Continue up a left-facing inside corner (5.10) and face climb up and right to a nice, yet sloping, ledge. Layback the thin, left edge of the arête (5.10, protected with tri-cams) to Big Sandy Ledge. Walk left 50 feet and climb a 90-foot hand crack on Gong Flake (5.9+). A left-facing inside corner (5.10) leads to a pedestal; this is followed by a tricky mantle that leads up and left for 80 feet to a 2- to 3-inch left-facing crack and ends on a ledge. One more 5.7 pitch leads to the top.

Northeast Face. IV, 5.8. First ascent September 1971 by Jeanne Neale and Galen Rowell. This route begins by climbing a dihedral on the right side of the face, following it to a ledge system in the middle of the face. Traverse left for two pitches to a prow, which leads directly to the summit. The first-ascent party encountered much ice on this route.

Cross Mountain   12,160 ft+; 12,185 ft
This insignificant peak is class 2 from Sphinx Lakes.

Peak 11,927ft   11,920 ft+;
0.6 mi N of Cross Mountain

Peak 11,927ft was once known as "Cross Mountain" until that name was placed in its correct location on the map. This peak is even less significant than the real Cross Mountain, and is class 2 from the Sphinx Creek drainage.

The Sphinx   9,143 ft; 9,146 ft

This is the rock formation with two summits, as seen to the southeast from the end of the road in Kings Canyon. The easiest approach is to hike up the Sphinx Creek Trail until you are south of Peak 9,721 ft (9,721 ft). Leave the trail here and hike cross-country to the rock.

South Side. I, 5.2. First ascent July 26, 1940 by Art Argiewicz and Bob Jacobs. From the higher southern summit descend to the notch between the two summits. Descend to the right to a ledge from the notch, then ascend a 20-foot vertical pitch at the far end of the ledge. This pitch ends near the ridge on the south side of the peak. Follow the ridge to the summit.

North Buttress. II, 5.7. First ascent October 18, 1970 by Greg Donaldson, Walt Vennum, and Fred Beckey. This climb ascends the slabs west of the north buttress. Two pitches across the slabs lead to the buttress itself. Follow the buttress to the north summit of The Sphinx.

Peak 4032m   13,231 ft;
0.7 mi ENE of Thunder Mountain

The southwest face and the east face are both class 2.

Peak 3980m+   13,090 ft;
0.4 mi SW of Mount Jordan

East Face. Class 4. First ascent September 9, 1967 by Andy Smatko, Dennis McAllister, and Tom Ross. Climb a left-ascending diagonal chute on the east face of the peak. Pass a big chockstone in this chute on the right. The chute ends on the south ridge. Two class 4 pitches along the ridge lead to the lower south summit. A short traverse leads to the higher north summit.

There are several interesting pinnacles between this peak and Mount Jordan.

Peak 3813m   12,513 ft; 1.0 mi SE of Mount Jordan

Class 3 from the south. First ascent August 1939 by Fritz Lippman, Dave Nelson, Don Woods, and Ed Koskinen.

Mount Jordan   4060 m+; 13,344 ft

East Slope. Class 3 with a class 4 summit block. First ascent July 1936 by parties led by Lewis Clark and Carl Jensen. Climb to the saddle between the north summit and the higher south summit. Easy class 3 leads to the summit block. It can be climbed either by friction on its east side or by making a delicate step-across on its northern side. The step-across is more sporting, but either way is class 4.

North Face. Class 3 with a class 4 summit block. First ascent August 3, 1940 by Art Argiewicz and party. Gain the north face from the basin southeast of Lake Reflection and northwest of Milly's Foot Pass. Climb the north face and traverse south to the summit block.

West Slope. Class 3 with a class 4 summit block. Descended August 3, 1940 by Art Argiewicz and party. Most of this climb is class 2, except for the summit area.

Mount Genevra   3979 m; 13,055 ft

First ascent July 15, 1926 by Norman Clyde. An ascent of this peak from the west or east consists of sand, talus, and class 2 summit rocks. The southern side is blocked by a band of cliffs, and is at a minimum class 3.

North Face. Class 3. First ascent July 19, 1951 by Barbara Lilley, Bill Bade, and Franklin Barnett. Climb a snow chute that leads to the ridge west of the summit. Follow the ridge to the summit.

Mount Ericsson   4120 m+; 13,608 ft

West Ridge. Class 2. First ascent August 1, 1896 by Bolton Brown and Lucy Brown. Follow the easy ridge from Lucy's Foot Pass to the summit.

South Ridge. Class 3. First ascent 1936 by Lewis Clark and Carl Jensen. This is a long climb around a lot of gendarmes and over many false summits. Climb onto the crest of the ridge from the east.

Further Reading: John Moynier and Claude Fiddler. *Sierra Classics.* Evergreen, Colo.: Chockstone Press, 1993, pp. 64–65.

East Face. Class 3. First ascent June 29, 1993 by Harry Marinakis and Yorgos Marinakis. This route ascends the right (north) side of the east face directly, and ends by passing through the notch of the northeast ridge.

Northeast Ridge. Class 3. Descended August 1, 1896 by Bolton Brown and Lucy Brown. Ascend the northeast ridge from Harrison Pass and gradually move into a chute that leads to a narrow notch near the summit. Pass through the notch to the west side of the peak, then traverse north to the summit.

Northwest Couloir. Class 4. First ascent July 1946 by Norman Clyde, Robert Breckenfeld, Jules Eichorn, Joe Brower, and Danny Kaplan. Climb the rocky chute between Mount Ericsson and Ericsson Crag 1A; this chute is best approached from low down on the north slope of Lucy's Foot Pass. Approximately 100 feet below the top of this chute, go right (south) and climb a steep, icy couloir. The couloir ends atop the west ridge of the peak. Follow the ridge to the summit.

Ericsson Crags

These are the crags to the north of Mount Ericsson. They were traversed in July 1991 by Claude Fiddler and Jim Keating.

"Ericsson Crag No. 1A"   3960 m; 13,040 ft+; UTM 736622

Class 4. This is the smallest, but most spectacular, of the Ericsson Crags. The first ascent, in August 1939 by Hervey Voge, Ted Waller, and Don Woods, was made from the shoulder between Ericsson Crag 1A and Ericsson Crag No. 1. One can also climb the western gully between Crag No. 1A and Mount Ericsson to a point about 300 feet below the notch. Climb up and left over class 4 rock to the summit.

"Ericsson Crag No. 1"   4000 m; 13,120 ft+; UTM 735623

West Chute and Southeast Face. Class 4–5. First ascent August 4, 1939 by Don Woods, Edward Koskinen, and DeWitt Allen. Ascend the west chute between Mount Ericsson and Ericsson Crag No. 1. About two-thirds of

Mount Ericsson and the Ericsson Crags from the northeast. Photo by R. J. Secor.

the way up, the chute branches; take the left (north) branch to the broad shoulder just south of Ericsson Crag No. 1. Climb a chimney on the southeast face of the crag. The overhanging portion of the chimney can be by-passed by making a downward traverse from a small rib just left of the chimney and then climbing above the overhang into the chimney. Climb over several large steps in the chimney; the summit block is climbed on its northwest side.

South Ridge. I, 5.8. First ascent July 1991 by Claude Fiddler and Jim Keating. Follow the south ridge from the broad shoulder between Ericsson Crags No. 1 and No. 1A.

"Ericsson Crag No. 1W"

This is the impressive crag on the west ridge of Ericsson Crag No. 1. First ascent July 1991 by Claude Fiddler and Jim Keating. Follow the classic class 3 ridge from Crag No. 1.

"Ericsson Crag No. 2" 3980 m+; 13,120 ft+; UTM 735625

West Chute. Class 4. First ascent August 3, 1939 by Hervey Voge and David Brower. From the west, ascend the main chute between Ericsson Crags No. 2 and No. 3. Climb the right-hand branch of the second-highest chute, which enters the main chute from the south. This second-highest chute leads to the northwest face of Ericsson Crag No. 2. Climb out of this chute just to the left of some caves by means of a class 4 pitch. Scramble to the top from here.

North Ridge. Class 3–4. First ascent July 1991 by Claude Fiddler and Jim Keating.

"Ericsson Crag No. 3" 3940 m; 13,040 ft+; UTM 735629

West Chute. Class 4. Ascend the major rocky chute that descends to the west between Ericsson Crags No. 2 and No. 3. When you near the top of this chute, cross a rib to the left (north) by means of a chimney at the top of this chute. Follow the east side of this ridge to the arête that is east of the summit. Follow the arête to the top.

Brujo Dihedral. III, 5.9. First ascent August 18, 1980 by Ti Neff and David Wilson. This route ascends the prominent dihedral on the right side of the north face of Ericsson Crag No. 3. An off-width crack (5.7) leads to 300 feet of scrambling to the base of the dihedral. Two pitches in the dihedral end at a ledge beneath an over-

hanging block. Go up and right from the ledge on a face (5.8) to a hanging belay on a sharp edge. Climb to the gentler summit slabs (class 4) and up to the summit.

Vinland. IV, 5.9. First ascent July 1987 by Alan Bartlett and Fred Beckey. This route is on the north face of the crag. The climb follows the obvious cracks and chimneys to the right of the prow that descends the north face. These lead to a ledge that goes left to the edge of the prow. The remaining portion of the climb is on the prow itself.

North Face. IV, 5.7. First ascent May 25, 1972 by Reed Cundiff and Fred Beckey. This route climbs the bowls and depressions to the left of the prow on the north face.

South Ridge. Class 5. First ascent July 1991 by Claude Fiddler and Jim Keating.

Deerhorn Mountain 4048 m; 13,265 ft

This fine-looking peak has some classic routes, none of which are trivial. The southeast summit is the high point.

Northeast Buttress. Class 3. First ascent July 8, 1927 by Norman Clyde. This is the buttress that rises directly from the Vidette Creek drainage to the lower northwest summit of the peak. From the largest of the Vidette Lakes, climb a talus ramp that leads up to the toe of the buttress. Climb the buttress to a point approximately 100 feet below the northwest peak and 30 feet above the level of the notch between the two peaks of Deerhorn Mountain. Traverse left over, down, and across broken ledges to the notch. Traverse across the southwest side of the small peak in the notch. From here, the higher southeast peak can be attained either by traversing across the southwest side of the peak over broken rock to the southeast ridge just below the summit, or by ascending the northwest arête, or by climbing a ramp on the north face. The summit itself is very small; there is room for about four climbers on the very top.

Northeast Couloir. Class 3. First ascent May 25, 1975 by Carl Heller, Fred Camphausen, Bob Joy, Jim Dixon, Dave Crosby, and Bob Rockwell. Second ascent July 4, 1980 by Bill T. Russell, Jim Erb, Gene Mauk, and party. This couloir leads from Vidette Creek to the notch between the peaks of Deerhorn Mountain. It has much loose rock, and it is only safe from rockfall when the couloir is full of snow. Ice axes and crampons will be needed in this case.

Northeast Ridge. Class 3–4. First ascent by Arkel Erb, Andy Smatko, Frede Jensen, Tom Ross, David Oyler, and Mike McNicholas. This ridge leads directly to the higher southeast peak from Vidette Creek. Gain the ridge from the base of the northeast couloir, climbing rock to the left (south) of the snow to reach the crest of the ridge about halfway up. Follow the ridge to the summit. A class 3–4 pitch is encountered just below the top. This is a very nice climb.

Southwest Chute. Class 4. First ascent August 3, 1939 by DeWitt Allen and Fritz Lippmann. This chute leads to the notch between the two peaks of Deerhorn Mountain. Only the very bottom and very top of this chute are difficult. *Variation:* First ascent July 2, 1989 by Don Borad. The lower, difficult portion of the chute can be avoided by climbing the next chute to the left before entering the main chute.

Southwest Face. Class 3–4. First ascent July 1946 by Norman Clyde, Jules Eichorn, Robert Breckenfeld, and party. Climb the southwest face of the mountain, aiming for a point just west of, and about 300 feet below, the northwest peak. Climb the northwest peak by traversing across the north side of the northwest ridge and climb to the top by means of some ledges.

West Ridge. Class 3. First ascent August 5, 1939 by Ted Waller, Hervey Voge, and Norman Clyde. Gain the saddle between Deerhorn Mountain and The Minster from either the north or south; a southern approach to this saddle is easier if it is approached from the left (west). From the saddle proceed up a wide scree chute, then move right into another scree chute and climb up to the ridge, meeting it to the right of a small peak. Climb the ridge until progress is stopped by a gendarme. Drop down about 60 feet on the northeast side of the ridge and traverse southeast before climbing up to the notch behind the gendarme. Go to the left of the pillars in this notch to reach the ridge crest. Continue up the ridge to the northwest peak, which is climbed by means of ledges on its north side. Descend to the notch between the peaks, and climb the southeast peak. *Variation:* First ascent July 2, 1989 by Don Borad. The northwest peak can be bypassed easily on its southwest side via some rock slabs. This is followed by a horizontal traverse to the notch between the two peaks.

Subsidiary Peaks of Deerhorn Mountain. There are two small peaks on the southeast ridge. The southeast peak was first climbed August 3, 1939 by DeWitt Allen and Fritz Lippman via a chute/chimney on its southeast side. Class 4.

The Minster   3740 m+; 12,240 ft+
This ridge of pinnacles was traversed from east to west on August 3, 1939 by Ted Waller, Don Woods, and Edward Koskinen.

West Spur   3817 m; 12,640 ft+
First ascent August 8, 1940 by William Morrison, Richard Kauffman, and Norman Roth, from East Lake.

From Vidette Creek. Class 2. First ascent by Arkel Erb, Andy Smatko, Tom Ross, Frede Jensen, David Oyler, and Mike McNicholas. Climb to the saddle north of the peak, and follow the ridge to the summit.

West Vidette   3820 m+; 12,560 ft+
East Slopes and South Ridge. Class 2. First ascent 1926 by Norman Clyde. Climb the chute that leads to the saddle south of the peak and follow the ridge to the summit. *Variation:* Class 2–3. First ascent September 6, 1992 by Larry Tidball, Barbee Hoffman, Mario Gonzalez, and Tom Sakowych. Climb an obvious right-angling ramp from the basin southeast of West Vidette. Then traverse a slope that continues up and right to the south ridge. Follow the ridge to the summit.

East Face. Class 3. Descended August 6, 1988 by Frank Meyers, Ralph Meyers, and Kurt Moeller. Begin by climbing a chute that ascends diagonally to the right (north). From the top of the chute, continue up the east face to the summit.

Northeast Chute. Class 2. Climb the loose chute to the saddle north of the summit and follow the ridge to the top.

East Vidette   3766 m; 12,350 ft
East Ridge. Class 3. First ascent 1910 by a Sierra Club party. Hike to the basin southeast of the peak from the John Muir Trail and climb the east ridge. This is a nice class 3 climb. *Variation:* Class 3. First ascent September 5, 1992 by Larry Tidball, Bill Oliver, Mario Gonzalez, Delores Holladay, Barbee Hoffmann, Paula Peterson, Bruce Peterson, Tom Sakowych, and Charlie Knapke.

Deerhorn Mountain from the northeast. Photo by R. J. Secor.

DEERHORN MOUNTAIN

Northeast
Buttress

Northeast
Ridge

Northeast
Couloir

Climb the gully that is just north of the east ridge, gaining the ridge beyond a gendarme. Follow the ridge to the summit.

North Side. Class 3–4 routes can be found on this side of the peak.

West Chute. Class 4. First ascent by Arkel Erb and Mike McNicholas. Climb a steep, shallow chute (loose rock!) that ends about 300 yards south of the summit on the south ridge. Follow the ridge to the summit.

Southeast Chute. Class 1–2. A scree chute leads from the basin southeast of the peak to the summit. This is a good descent route.

Mount Stanford from the northwest. Photo by R. J. Secor.

East Spur   3886 m; 12,735 ft

First ascent July 14, 1940 by Jim Harkins and Pat Goldsworthy.

Mount Stanford   4259 m; 13,963 ft

This is the "shyest" major peak in the High Sierra. Most of the other major peaks can be seen from great distances. In contrast, Mount Stanford is prominent only from Vidette Creek, a short section of the John Muir Trail south of Glen Pass, and the top of Gregory's Monument. The peak can be seen from the John Muir Trail north of Forester Pass; it is the tall, dark cliff to the west.

It makes up for its lack of prominence by the quality of its climbing.

The south peak is Gregory's Monument, and the higher north peak is Mount Stanford.

South Ridge. Class 3. First ascent August 1, 1896 by Bolton Brown. Gregory's Monument is reached by going east from Harrison Pass over easy slopes. Descend the north side of Gregory's Monument by making a delicate class 3 move over a chockstone. Descend to a ledge on the east side of the south ridge; the ledge is about 100 feet below the ridge crest. Traverse the ledge to a point east of the summit and scramble to the top. (This is much easier than it looks from the summit of Gregory's Monument.)

Further Reading: John Moynier and Claude Fiddler. *Sierra Classics.* Evergreen, Colo.: Chockstone Press, 1993, pp. 62–63.

West Face. Class 3. Descended August 1, 1896 by Bolton Brown. From the north side of Harrison Pass climb the first chute north of Gregory's Monument. This follows a steep ramp, which goes up and left to a small waterfall. Follow this upward for about 500 feet to a narrow chute filled with talus. This chute ends on the south ridge of Mount Stanford.

West Face and North Ridge. Class 3. First ascent August 1940 by Art Argiewicz and party. The northern portion of the west face can be ascended to the north ridge. Follow the north ridge to the summit.

North Ridge. Class 3. First ascent August 4, 1939 by David Brower and Norman Clyde. Climb to the ridge north of Mount Stanford from Deerhorn Saddle. The most difficult portion of the north ridge is the upper part. It is necessary to traverse across the east side of the summit before climbing to the top. *Variation:* The north ridge can also be reached from Bubbs Creek. Gain the crest of the East Spur at UTM 754644 and follow the long ridge south to Mount Stanford.

East Face. Class 3. First ascent August 1947 by James Harkins and others. First winter ascent March 20, 1973 by Roger Gocking, Geert Dijkhuis, Giovanni Columbo, and Darien Hopkins. A steep chute descends directly from the summit to the south of the east arête. Climb either the chute or the face to the left. A class 4 pillar must be traversed directly on the crest of the east arête.

Peak 4200m+ 13,760 ft+;
0,8 mi SE of Mount Stanford; UTM 755621
West Ridge. Class 3. First ascent June 3, 1934 by

Hervey Voge and David Brower. Attain the west ridge of this peak from the south and follow the west ridge to the summit.

Southeast Face. Class 4. Descended June 3, 1934 by David Brower and Hervey Voge. This follows the shallow chute that descends from the east ridge at a point near the summit. There is a 20-foot class 4 pitch in this chute.

Caltech Peak 4216 m; 13,832 ft
Southeast Slopes. Class 2. First ascent June 22, 1926 by Norman Clyde.

East Ridge. Class 3. First ascent June 8, 1963 by Arkel Erb, Gordon MacCleod, Tom Ross, and Andy Smatko.

West Face. Class 2–3 via any of the many chutes.

Junction Peak 4220 m+; 13,888 ft
West Ridge. Class 3. First ascent August 15, 1932 by Walter A. Starr, Jr. First winter ascent March 21, 1973 by Roger Gocking, Geert Dijkhuis, Giovanni Columbo, and Darien Hopkins. Follow the ridge from Forester Pass, either crossing over or traversing south of the peak that separates Forester Pass from Ski Mountaineers Pass. Once on the main peak, stay south of the ridge and climb any combination of chutes or gullies to the summit.

North Buttress. III, 5.7. First ascent June 17, 1972 by John Rupley and Fred Beckey. Climb just to the right (west) of the crest of the buttress. There is some extremely loose rock on this route.

East Couloir. Class 3–4. Descended 1956 by Carl Heller, Kermit Ross, and Bob Stein. Climb the northernmost of the two couloirs on the east side of the peak.

Southeast Ridge. Class 4. First ascent August 21, 1929 by Albert Ellingwood. Follow the ridge from Shepherd Pass to the summit.

South Face. Class 3. First ascent July 17, 1982 by Nancy Gordon, Dave Dykeman, Ruth Armentrout, and David Lesikar. From Lake 3806m (12,460 ft) ascend toward a U-shaped notch on the southeast ridge of the peak. Follow the southeast ridge to the summit.

South Ridge. Class 3. First ascent August 8, 1899 by E. B. Copeland and E. N. Henderson. Follow the knife edge ridge from Diamond Mesa to the summit of Junction Peak. The easiest route onto Diamond Mesa is at its extreme southern end. It is necessary to drop down approximately 100 feet on the west side of the south ridge just before reaching the summit.

Further Reading: John Moynier and Claude Fiddler.

Mount Stanford from the east. Photo by R. J. Secor.

Sierra Classics. Evergreen, Colo.: Chockstone Press, 1993, pp. 60–61.

Mount Keith   4260 m; 13,977 ft

Northwest Face. Class 2. First ascent July 6, 1898 by Robert Price, C. B. Bradley, Jennie Price, and J. C. Shinn. Climb loose boulders and scree from the upper lakes of Center Basin.

Southwest Ridge. Class 3. First ascent 1916 by a Sierra Club party. This ridge rising from Junction Pass is a nice climb.

South Face. Class 2. First ascent 1922 by Norman Clyde. A chute descends the south face of Mount Keith from a point just west of the summit. The chute is full of loose scree, and it makes a nice descent route. In the early season, when the chute is full of snow, it is a fine climb.

Northeast Slopes. Class 2. Begin by climbing the rocks that are left of some steep black rocks and then follow a ramp into the bowl above. Continue up the bowl and then head to the right towards the summit.

"Courte-Echelle"   4020 m+; 13,189 ft
0.7 mi NE of Mount Keith

This peak has also been called "Bat Pinnacle." It is quite prominent from the Shepherd Pass Trailhead. It can be reached by traversing from the summit of Mount Keith or by ascending directly from either Center Basin or the upper part of the Shepherd Pass Trail. The summit block was first climbed August 10, 1963 by Arkel Erb and Sy Ossofsky, who used a shoulderstand and a piton to overcome a slight overhang.

Center Peak   3880 m+; 12,760 ft

East Face. Class 2. First ascent July 5, 1898 by C. G. Bradley. Climb the broad chute from Center Basin.

North Face. Class 3. First ascent May 22, 1934 by David Brower and Hervey Voge. There are three talus chutes on the north side of Center Peak. Climb the center chute and leave it via the chute that leads up to the northwest buttress of the peak. Follow the buttress to a saddle. From the saddle, stay on the west side of the northwest buttress to a point about 200 feet below the summit. Zigzag to the summit from here.

Northwest Face. Class 3. First ascent July 26, 1952 by Phillip Berry and Frank Tarver. This climb begins about 100 yards south of the steepest part of the north face. Climb the northwest face to a tunnel at its top. From the tunnel, ledges lead to the summit.

Northwest Arête. III, 5.6. First ascent June 1983 by

Vern Clevenger and Claude Fiddler. There are three arêtes on the northwest side of Center Peak. This route climbs the center arête with crack climbing along its crest.

Further Reading: John Moynier and Claude Fiddler. *Sierra Classics.* Evergreen, Colo.: Chockstone Press, 1993, pp. 66–67.

Northwest Ridge. II, 5.7. First ascent June 1997 by Dave Harden, Don Palmer, and Bart O'Brien. This route follows the right-hand arête for six pitches, then involves lots of class 3 to the summit.

Mount Bradley   4043 m; 13,289 ft

West Face. Class 2. First ascent July 5, 1898 by Robert Price, Jennie Price, J. Shinn, and Lalla Harris. This climb follows the talus chute that descends directly from the summit, as seen from Center Basin. The chute forks

about three-quarters of the way up. Take the right branch, which leads to the saddle between the two summits of Mount Bradley. The high point is the northern summit; it is reached by climbing a narrow chute on its southeast side.

South Ridge. Class 2. First ascent 1966 by Steve Rogero, Gary Bowen, and Dick Beach. Follow the ridge from Courte-Echelle.

East Ridge. Class 3. First ascent October 27, 1948 by Fred L. Jones. This long climb begins along Symmes Creek in the Owens Valley. Stay on the southern side of the ridge, passing many saddles and pinnacles, for 8,000 feet of gain to the summit. There is an incredible amount of brush on this ridge.

North Slope. Class 2. Climb the long, barren north slope from the head of Pinyon Creek.

Northwest Ridge. Class 2–3. First ascent August 31,

Center Peak from the north. Photo by R. J. Secor.

1948 by Fred L. Jones. Follow the ridge from Center Basin Crag No. 5.

Center Basin Crags

3820 m+–3840 m+; 12,480 ft+–12,598 ft+

The Center Basin Crags are on the Sierra crest north of Mount Bradley. There are five crags, and they are numbered from north to south. They are composed of loose rock. The notch north of Crag No. 2 has been reached by traversing across the western side of the ridge south of Crag No. 1. The notch between Crags No. 3 and No. 4 is reached by traversing to it from the large scree gully that leads from Center Basin to the saddle north of Crag No. 5.

"Center Basin Crag No. 1" 3820 m+;
UTM 797664
South Ridge. Class 5. First ascent August 29, 1953 by Phillip Berry and party.

North Ridge. Class 4. First ascent September 1, 1984 by Dick Beach and Bob Good. Traverse the west side of the ridge from Peak 3926m (12,910 ft).

"Center Basin Crag No. 2" 3820 m+;
UTM 799661
South Ridge. Class 4. First ascent July 1940 by David Brower and Bruce Meyer.

North Face. II, 5.6. First ascent September 1, 1984 by Dick Beach and Bob Good. Climb the crack that leads directly to the summit.

"Center Basin Crag No. 3" 3820 m+;
UTM 799661
North Ridge. I, 5.8. First ascent July 1940 by David Brower and Bruce Meyer. One steep, exposed pitch leads to the summit from the notch between Crags No. 2 and No. 3.

South Ridge. I, 5.6. First ascent August 1953 by David Brower and Phil Berry. A 50-foot 5.6 pitch is encountered; climb from the notch between Crags No. 3 and No. 4.

"Center Basin Crag No. 4" 3840 m+;
UTM 799660
North Ridge. I, 5.6. First ascent July 1940 by David Brower and Bruce Meyer. Two pitches over some big, loose rocks lead to the summit from the notch between Crags No. 3 and No. 4.

"Center Basin Crag No. 5" 3840 m+;
UTM 800659
This is a class 2 scramble from the north.

Peak 3926m 12,910 ft; 0.7 mi SE of University Peak
First ascent September 4, 1984 by Bob Good and Dick Beach via the long class 3 northeast ridge.

University Peak 4142 m; 13,632 ft
Southeast Ridge. Class 2. Follow the southern side of the ridge from University Pass. *Shortcut Variation:* Class 2. There is a steep, V-shaped snow chute leading to the crest of the southeast ridge approximately ¼ mile northeast of the chute that leads up University Pass. The left branch of this chute has been used to climb the southeast ridge from the Robinson Lake basin.

South Slopes. Class 1. First ascent July 12, 1896 by Joseph LeConte, Helen M. Gompertz, Estelle Miller, and Belle Miller. Follow the easy southern slopes from Center Basin.

Northwest Side. Class 2. First ascent 1899 by Vernon L. Kellogg and others. First winter ascent March 1933 by Oliver Kehrlein and Norman Clyde. Climb to the top of University Shoulder from Kearsarge Lakes. Traverse southeast and follow the easy southwest or south slopes to the top. *Variation:* Class 3. First ascent August 14, 1932 by Walter A. Starr, Jr. Climb the northwest ridge from University Shoulder.

North Face. Class 3. First ascent by Norman Clyde. Climb the slabs southeast of Bench Lake, then pass Lake 3460m+ (11,360 ft+) on its eastern shore. Continue up scree and talus on the left side of the north face to the summit ridge. A short traverse along the northern side of the ridge leads to the summit block.

Direct North Face. III, 5.8. First ascent July 1994 by Mingo Morvin, Barbara Presteridge, and Matt Graham. Leave the right side of Lake 3460m+ (11,360 ft+) and ascend 1,000 feet of scree to a large gendarme. Pass the gendarme on its right side. Continue up steep class 4 to the right of the rock outcrop. From the top of the rock outcrop, move left to a prominent arête just east of three prominent gullies. Two 5.8 pitches on the arête lead to easier climbing and the summit.

Northeast Face. III, 5.7. First ascent July 1968 by Fred Beckey, Joe Brown, and Dan Clements. This route climbs the prominent wall above Slim Lake. Class 3 gullies lead to the massive part of the face. Six hundred

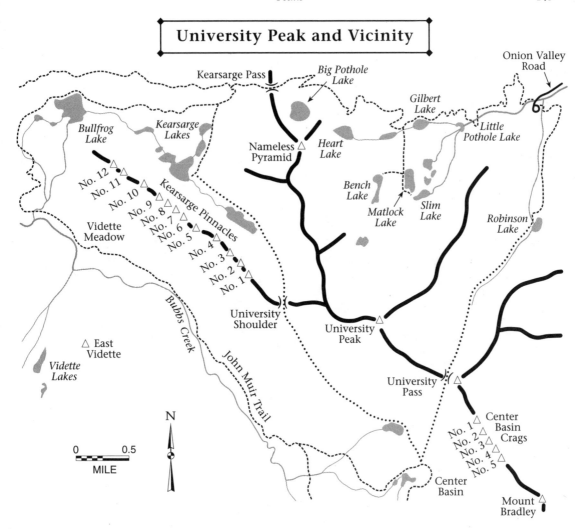

University Peak and Vicinity

feet of moderate rock climbing lead to the upper part of the northeast ridge.

Northeast Ridge. Class 4. The best approach for this ridge is from Robinson Lake.

East Slope. Class 3. First ascent 1994 by Matthias Selke. This climb begins from the flat, prominent moraine in the basin just north of University Pass. Climb up and right, across scree, sand, and talus for 200 to 300 vertical feet to a small, flat plateau on the east slope of University Peak. Continue directly up sandy ledges from the plateau toward the northeast ridge; avoid the shallow chute that leads up and right to a point low along the northeast ridge. The correct route leads to a cliff, which is overcome by climbing diagonally left over ledges, boulders, and slabs to a small, ill-defined rib. From the rib, go up and slightly right (northeast) over easy class 3 rock to a broad notch on the northeast ridge. Pass through the notch to its northern side, then follow a wide ledge or ramp system toward the summit, remaining 20 to 30 feet below the crest of the northeast ridge. This ledge system leads to a small snow patch that is just beneath the summit. Either climb the snow patch (an

University Peak from the southeast. Photo by R. J. Secor.

ice axe is helpful) or bypass it by means of class 3 rock that surrounds it.

Independence Peak   3579 m; 11,744 ft

South Ridge. Class 3. Climb any of the class 2–3 talus chutes on the southern side of the west face to the south ridge. Follow the crest of the south ridge to the last notch, located about 100 feet below the summit. Stay on the right (east) side of the ridge from this notch until the summit is reached.

West Face. Class 3. Leave the Robinson Lake Trail at approximately 10,000 feet, then follow a sandy use trail straight up to the first notch south of the summit. A few class 3 moves are encountered just below the notch. This is an excellent descent route.

North Ridge. Class 4. This is a nice climb from Onion Valley. Only the upper part of this ridge is class 4. The class 4 can be avoided by traversing across the west face from a point about 200 feet below the summit. This leads to the class 3 rock of the south ridge.

Southeast Chute. Class 3. Descended August 27, 1993 by Steve Thaw. This chute is best approached from Pinyon Creek by means of a bench that leads northeast then north to end in this chute at the 8,000-ft level. This bench starts on the north side of the diamond-shaped hill in the Pinyon Creek drainage.

"Nameless Pyramid"   3669 m; 11,920 ft+; 0.2 mi S of Big Pothole Lake

This is a contradictory name for a small peak that is easily seen from the Owens Valley.

North Ridge. Class 3. First ascent July 1952 by Ted Matthes, Frank Tarver, and Phillip Berry. Follow the ridge from Kearsarge Pass.

Northeast Ridge. Class 3. First ascent June 8, 1988 by Peter Lowery and Chris Keith.

East Face. III, 5.8. First ascent May 1968 by Burt Turney and Chuck Ray. This route follows the prominent crack system that diagonals up the face from left to right. The crack system ends at a notch high on the north ridge of the peak.

Further Reading: *Summit.* October–November 1975, pp. 10–13.

East Face Direct. III, 5.9, A1. First ascent October 1993 by Richard Swayze and Bart O'Brien. Climb the regular route on the east face to the second horizontal ledge system. Traverse up and left for two pitches (some 5.8), aiming for a spectacular crack that leads to a point just below the summit. Climb this right-leaning crack, which ranges in size from fingers to off-width and features ceilings, flakes, and hidden holds. The last pitch had some munge in the crack, and the first-ascent party was forced to use a point of aid.

Kearsarge Pinnacles
3560 m+–3660 m+; 11,680 ft+–12,000 ft+

These interesting pinnacles are located south of Kearsarge Lakes. The quality of rock varies from excellent to extremely rotten. On July 6, 1981, Dick Beach

and Dave King traversed every single bump on this ridge from northwest to southeast. Many more pinnacles in the vicinity are more interesting and beautiful than the "official" twelve listed here.

"Kearsarge Pinnacle No. 1"   3640 m+; 12,000 ft+; UTM 769682
Northwest Ridge. Class 3. First ascent July 28, 1935 by May Pridham, Niles Werner, and Pam Coffin. Approach this ridge from the top of the chute between Pinnacles No. 1 and No. 2, or traverse from the top of the chute between Pinnacles No. 3 and No. 4.

"Kearsarge Pinnacle No. 2"   3640 m+; 12,000 ft+; UTM 768683
Northwest Ridge. Class 3. First ascent July 28, 1935 by May Pridham, Niles Werner, and Pam Coffin. Ascend the ridge from the top of the gully between Pinnacles No. 3 and No. 4.

"Kearsarge Pinnacle No. 3"   3640 m+; 11,920 ft+; UTM 767684
Northwest Ridge. Class 4. First ascent August 1, 1939

University Peak from the north. Photo by R. J. Secor.

by Ted Waller, Don Woods, David Nelson, and Edward Koskinen. Climb the ridge from the top of the notch between Pinnacles No. 3 and No. 4.

"Kearsarge Pinnacle No. 4" · 3660 m+; 12,000 ft+; UTM 766686

Southeast Ridge. Class 3. First ascent August 1, 1939 by Ted Waller, Don Woods, David Nelson, and Edward Koskinen. Climb the ridge from the notch between Pinnacles No. 3 and No. 4.

"Kearsarge Pinnacle No. 5"   3580 m; 11,760 ft+; UTM 763687

This pinnacle can be climbed from the notch between Pinnacles No. 5 and No. 6.

"Kearsarge Pinnacle No. 6"   3580 m+; 11,760 ft+; UTM 762688

Southeast Ridge. Class 3. First ascent August 18, 1954 by Dwight Ericsson from the notch between Pinnacles No. 5 and No. 6.

West Face. II, 5.6. First ascent July 1970 by Liesl Day and Richard Hechtel. From the top of the gully between Pinnacles No. 6 and No. 7, traverse east into a gully and climb over an overhang and up ledges and cracks to the base of a prominent open book. Ascend this book about halfway and traverse right on a small ledge until another, higher ledge can be reached via a shallow crack. Follow the ledge to a large shoulder south of the summit. Steep rock then leads to the top of the pinnacle.

"Kearsarge Pinnacle No. 7"   3620 m+; 11,840 ft+; UTM 761690

This pinnacle is class 2 from the notch between Pinnacles No. 6 and No. 7.

Northeast Face. II, 5.4. First ascent June 13, 1971 by Scott Evans and Doug Kinzy. There is a prominent gully on this face that is visible from Kearsarge Lakes. Begin by climbing the less prominent gully 30 feet to the east of this main gully. The first pitch (5.4) follows this gully and passes an overhang on the right. After about 200 feet the route crosses the main gully and continues up

University Peak from the northeast. Photo by R. J. Secor.

KEARSARGE PINNACLES

No. 3 No. 4 No. 5 No. 6 No. 7 No. 8 No. 9

Kearsarge Pinnacles. Photo by R. J. Secor.

on the right for several class 4 pitches. Aim for the chute that separates the two summits of Pinnacle No. 7. A class 4 pitch on the right side of this chute leads to a point directly beneath the western summit. A short traverse left leads to the notch between the two summits. Either summit is class 3 from here.

"Kearsarge Pinnacle No. 8"   3620 m+; 11,920 ft+; UTM 759690

In the words of Dick Beach, "This pinnacle stops the traffic!"

Southeast Face. Class 5. First ascent July 1932 by Glen Dawson, Thomas Rawles, and Hans Leschke. Climb the steep face rising above the notch between No. 7 and No. 8.

Northwest Face. II, 5.8. First ascent July 6, 1981 by Dave King and Dick Beach. Climb a crack system above the notch between Pinnacles No. 8 and No. 9. Most of this climb is easy class 5; there is one 30-foot 5.8 pitch.

"Kearsarge Pinnacle No. 9"   3620 m+; 11,920 ft+; UTM 759691

Northwest Ridge. Class 2 from the notch between Pinnacles No. 9 and No. 10.

Southeast Ridge. Class 4. First ascent July 25, 1924 by R. Howard. From the top of the chute between Pinnacles No. 8 and No. 9, climb the south side of the small pinnacle rising above the notch. It is an easy scramble from the top of the pinnacle to the top of Pinnacle No. 9.

"Kearsarge Pinnacle No. 10"   3645 m; 11,680 ft+; UTM 757693

First ascent 1932 by Hans Leschke, Glen Dawson, and Owen Ward. Class 2 from the notch between Pinnacles

No. 9 and No. 10, or by traversing from Pinnacles No. 11 and No. 12.

"Kearsarge Pinnacle No. 11"   3560 m+;
11,680 ft+; UTM 754695

First ascent 1932 by Hans Leschke, Glen Dawson, and Owen Ward. Class 2 from either Pinnacle No. 10 or No. 12.

"Kearsarge Pinnacle No. 12"   3560 m+;
11,680 ft+; UTM 753695

First ascent 1932 by Owen Ward, Glen Dawson, and Hans Leschke. Class 2 from Pinnacle No. 11 or via the northwest slopes from Bullfrog Lake.

WRINKLES

Junction Meadow. Or perhaps I should say Junction *Meadows.* There are two Junction Meadows in the High Sierra, just close enough together to cause confusion. If you are making arrangements to meet someone, or pick up a cache of food, it is prudent to specify either Junction Meadow—Bubbs Creek or Junction Meadow—Kern River.

Skiing across the Kings-Kern Divide. Those skiing from Mount Whitney to Yosemite will find this to be either a minor inconvenience or an impassable barrier. This depends how much snow fell the previous winter. Light snow years may leave the south side completely bare, but a winter with heavy snow can build up cornices atop the passes. On the other hand, a friend of mine skiing across the Kings-Kern Divide during a light snow year went through a few minutes of stark terror of an intensity not experienced before in his thirty-year mountaineering career. The "snow" slope turned out to be a huge sheet of ice!

Ski Mountaineers Pass has scree on both of its sides during the summer, but the angle is moderate, and it may be passable in the winter or spring; a cornice has formed here before, however, so exercise caution. Forester Pass has a trail over it, but the south side of the pass is a cliff. The north side, on the other hand, is rather gentle. Andy's Foot Pass is dramatically steep on its north side, but it has been skied. Harrison Pass is very steep and icy on its north side. Ericsson Pass is not as steep as Harrison Pass, and this combined with Deerhorn Saddle may be a good alternative route. Lucy's Foot Pass and Milly's Foot Pass, both class 3, are dramatically steep for skiers. Thunder Pass will probably be passable, but it is far away from the Sierra crest.

The best alternative may be to bypass the entire Kings-Kern Divide by crossing Shepherd Pass and then Junction Pass.

University Pass. This route appears to offer a one-day direct route from Onion Valley to Center Basin, but this is only the case for experienced cross-country hikers. Others will find it much quicker and easier to approach Center Basin via the Kearsarge Pass and John Muir Trails.

Chapter 5

The High Passes

This region covers the Sierra crest from Kearsarge Pass to Taboose Pass. It is bounded on the west by the South Fork of the Kings River.

The title of this chapter refers to Baxter Pass, Sawmill Pass, and Taboose Pass. These passes are not the highest in the Sierra, but they *seem* to be the highest because each requires gaining over 6,000 feet of elevation to reach the summits from the trailheads. The Sierra crest divides the Great Basin from the Pacific Ocean watersheds, and a hike up one of these passes moves the hiker from desert to Arctic conditions. A hiker can be walking across a plain of brush and sand and soon thereafter be following the trail through barren talus fields. But at the summit of these high passes, the world comes alive again, with meadows and wonderful vistas.

HISTORY

Indians had crossed Kearsarge Pass and descended Bubbs Creek long before a party of prospectors, including a man named Bubbs, followed this route in 1863. The following year the California Geological Survey crossed the Sierra crest via this route after their exploration of Kings Canyon. John Muir visited this region in 1873, and shepherds overran the area over the next twenty years. Taboose and Sawmill Passes were used to move sheep between the Owens Valley and High Sierra meadows. Bolton Brown descended the South Fork of the Kings River in 1895, and climbed Mount Clarence King and explored Rae Lakes in the following years.

It seems to stand to reason that a region featuring passes with 6,000 feet of gain must have some mountain ridges with 8,000 to 9,000 feet of gain—and it does.

These ridges are east of the Sierra crest, face the desert, and are therefore dry. They were first explored by Fred L. Jones in the late 1940s and early 1950s during his studies of the Sierra Nevada bighorn sheep. These routes have not been retraced often, but the few individuals to climb these ridges have the utmost respect and admiration for Fred L. Jones.

MAPS

USGS. *7.5-minute series:* Kearsarge Peak, Mt. Clarence King, The Sphinx, Aberdeen, Mt. Pinchot, Marion Peak, Fish Springs. *National park maps:* Sequoia and Kings Canyon National Parks and Vicinity (1:125,000). *30 x 60–minute series:* Bishop, Mount Whitney.

USFS. A Guide to the John Muir Wilderness and the Sequoia–Kings Canyon Wilderness (1:63,360).

Tom Harrison Cartography. Kings Canyon High Country.

Map Link 15-minute series. Mt. Pinchot, Marion Peak, Big Pine.

Wilderness Press 15-minute series. Mt. Pinchot.

ROADS

Onion Valley Road

Onion Valley Road provides access to the Kearsarge Pass Trail and the Golden Trout Lake Trail. It is described in Chapter 4, The Kings-Kern Divide.

Fish Hatchery Road

Fish Hatchery Road leads to the trailhead for the Baxter Pass Trail. Leave Highway 395 2.3 miles north

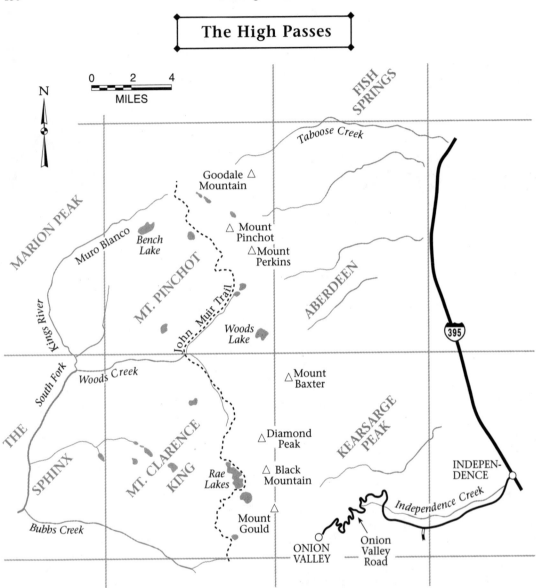

The High Passes

of Independence or 23.7 miles south of Big Pine. From here, Fish Hatchery Road goes west 1.3 miles, across Oak Creek Road and past the Mount Whitney Fish Hatchery, to a fork. Go right, pass Oak Creek Campground, and drive another 4.5 miles to the end of the road near the North Fork of Oak Creek.

Division Creek Powerhouse Road and Scotty Spring Road

This maze of roads leads to the trailheads for Sawmill Pass and Armstrong Canyon. Leave Highway 395 8.6 miles north of Independence or 18.0 miles south of Big Pine. Go west on the Black Rock Springs Road for 0.8

mile to its junction with Tinemaha Road. Turn right and go north on Tinemaha Road for 1.2 miles to the junction with Division Creek Powerhouse Road. Go left onto the road leading to the Division Creek Powerhouse; after 1.5 miles you come to the powerhouse and the hikers' trailhead for the Sawmill Pass Trail.

There is also a stock trailhead for the Sawmill Pass Trail. Leave Tinemaha Road 0.7 mile north of its junction with Sawmill Creek Road. The road goes left for 2.0 miles to the trailhead along Sawmill Creek.

The trailhead for Armstrong Canyon is beyond the Division Creek Powerhouse. Continue up the road for another 2.0 miles to a fork. Go right and drive another 0.5 mile to Scotty Spring. This is the limit for most cars. There is a difficult four-wheel-drive road that climbs up into Armstrong Canyon from this point.

Taboose Creek Road

Taboose Creek Road is the approach to the trailhead for the Taboose Pass Trail. Leave Highway 395 13.7 miles north of Independence or 12.1 miles south of Big Pine. Take Taboose Creek Road west to a four-way junction 0.4 mile from Highway 395. Go straight through this junction another 0.8 mile to another four-way junction. Go straight through this second junction another 0.5 mile to a fork, passing Taboose Campground along the way. Go right at the fork, through a gate (be sure to leave it as you found it, either open or closed) to another fork 2.1 miles beyond the previous fork. Take the right fork 1.9 miles to the trailhead for Taboose Pass. This last section of the road is rough, but most two-wheel-drive vehicles should be able to reach the trailhead with little trouble.

Kings Canyon Highway   (Highway 180)

The Woods Creek Trail starts from the end of Highway 180 in Kings Canyon. This trailhead is described in Chapter 6, Monarch Divide and the Cirque Crest.

TRAILS

Kearsarge Pass Trail   7 miles

The Kearsarge Pass Trail leads from Onion Valley over Kearsarge Pass to meet the John Muir Trail between Charlotte Lake and Bullfrog Lake. It is described in Chapter 4, The Kings-Kern Divide.

Golden Trout Lake Trail   2¼ miles

A quota trail. This is a popular day hike from Onion Valley. Golden Trout Lake is a heavily used camping area. Wood campfires are prohibited anywhere in this drainage. Bears prowl through this area.

The Golden Trout Lake Trail goes north out of Onion Valley (0 mi; 9,192 ft) starting next to the ruins of the old store. A wide, rocky path goes up to the base of the waterfall. The trail crosses the creek and climbs the slope east of the waterfall; this part is steep and loose and it is easy to miss the trail. At the top of the cliff the trail crosses the stream again before climbing a small ridge south of the stream. The trail eventually descends to the stream and follows it to a wet meadow. Skirt the meadow on the south side and head up a small canyon to Golden Trout Lake (2¼ mi; 11,388 ft).

From the meadow, a trail goes north to the two unnamed lakes in the basin north of Golden Trout Lake. This trail, which is approximately 1¾ miles long, is the approach for North Dragon Pass.

John Muir Trail   23 miles

The John Muir Trail heads west and then north from its junction with the Kearsarge Pass Trail and the Charlotte Lake Trail (0 mi; 10,695 ft+). (Charlotte Lake is 1 mile west of this junction; bears prowl through this area.) The John Muir Trail climbs to the top of Glen Pass (2¼ mi; 11,942 ft+). The trail descends the rough and difficult northern side of the pass to a junction with the Sixty Lake Basin Trail near the highest of the Rae Lakes (2 mi; 10,564 ft+). (The Rae Lakes are beautiful, but heavily used. There is a one-night camp limit along the John Muir Trail between Glen Pass and Woods Creek, and at Dragon Lake. Bears prowl through this area. Wood fires are prohibited anywhere in Kings Canyon National Park above 10,000 feet.) The trail crosses to the eastern side of Rae Lakes, passing the Rae Lakes Ranger Station. It gradually descends the South Fork of Woods Creek to the unsigned junction with the Baxter Pass Trail (2¾ mi; 10,170 ft+), north of Dollar Lake. The John Muir Trail descends to meet the Woods Creek Trail at Woods Creek (4 mi; 8,492 ft). Bears prowl all along Woods Creek.

The John Muir Trail crosses Woods Creek via a very nice suspension bridge and goes upstream to the junction with the Sawmill Pass Trail (3½ mi; 10,346 ft). Bears prowl through this area. The trail climbs to a use trail

(1 mi; 10,892 ft+) that leads down to beautiful Twin Lakes, below Mount Cedric Wright. The John Muir Trail climbs to a high, rocky basin, where there are occasional small meadows, and then to the top of Pinchot Pass (3 mi; 12,138 ft+). The trail, with many steep switchbacks, descends the north side of the pass to Lake Marjorie (1½ mi; 11,132 ft), which is located in the middle of a scenic basin with many smaller lakes. The trail descends to the junction with the Bench Lake Trail (1½ mi; 10,794 ft), fords the stream, and then meets the Taboose Pass Trail (¼ mi; 10,761 ft+). The John Muir Trail then makes a steep descent to the South Fork of the Kings River to meet what is left of the Cartridge Pass Trail (1¾ mi; 10,039 ft+).

Sixty Lake Basin Trail   4 miles

Sixty Lake Basin is one of the most beautiful places in the High Sierra. It is heavily used, however. The NPS has a one-night camp limit in the basin, and wood fires are prohibited. Bears prowl through this area.

The Sixty Lake Basin Trail leaves the John Muir Trail at the northwest shore of the highest of the Rae Lakes (0 mi; 10,564 ft+), climbs over the ridge just south of Fin Dome (to 11,220 ft+), and drops into Sixty Lake Basin. The trail gradually descends the basin and eventually disappears along the eastern shore of the northernmost lake (4 mi; 10,564 ft+).

Bench Lake Trail   2 miles

The Bench Lake Trail leaves the John Muir Trail just south of the Taboose Pass Trail junction (0 mi; 10,794 ft+). The trail crosses a meadow, descends slightly, and then contours across the bench from which the lake gets its name. Bears prowl all along this bench. The trail makes two easy stream crossings before reaching the north shore of Bench Lake. The view of Arrow Peak from the lake is one of the classic views in the Sierra. The trail ends at the western shore of the lake (2 mi; 10,558 ft).

Woods Creek Trail   15 miles

A quota trail. The Woods Creek Trail follows the South Fork of the Kings River to the mouth of Woods Creek, and then follows Woods Creek to the John Muir Trail. Bears are active all along this trail.

The trail starts at the end of Highway 180 in Kings Canyon (0 mi; 5,036 ft+). It goes upstream to meet the Bubbs Creek Trail (2 mi; 5,120 ft+). The Woods Creek

Trail continues up the South Fork of the Kings River, passing by Mist Falls and passing through Paradise Valley before crossing the river upstream from the mouth of Woods Creek (8 mi; 6,880 ft+). Camp only in designated sites in Paradise Valley; there is a two-night limit in Paradise Valley. The trail ascends the north side of the Woods Creek drainage to meet the John Muir Trail (5 mi; 8,492 ft).

Baxter Pass Trail   13 miles

A quota trail. Dogs are prohibited on this trail due to bighorn sheep restrictions. This is a long, hard hike. Fortunately, the first part of the trail is in the shade; this makes it unique among the trails that lead over the Sierra crest from the floor of Owens Valley. The Baxter Pass Trail starts at the end of Fish Hatchery Road (0 mi; 5,971 ft+) and follows an old road on the north side of Oak Creek. After a short distance the road forks; the trail goes right and makes a steep ascent. It soon crosses to the south side of the creek, switchbacks up the canyon floor, goes around a rocky rib, and crosses to the north side of the creek. The trail continues to climb, reaching the alpine basin of Summit Meadow at approximately 10,800 feet (Summit Meadow is incorrectly placed on some maps). The last part of the ascent goes through an area of red, green, and black metamorphic rock to the summit of Baxter Pass (8 mi; 12,270 ft+).

The trail makes a steep descent on the north side of the pass before skirting the north shore of the largest of the Baxter Lakes. The trail continues down the rocky basin and crosses a small stream. It later fords Baxter Creek before turning south and contouring far above the South Fork of Woods Creek to meet the John Muir Trail at an unsigned junction just below Dollar Lake (5 mi; 10,170 ft+).

Sawmill Pass Trail   13½ miles

A quota trail. Dogs are prohibited on this trail due to bighorn sheep restrictions. This is another long, hard hike. The hikers' trail begins near Division Creek Powerhouse (0 mi; 4,586 ft+) and climbs to meet the stock trail (1¾ mi; 5,708 ft+) that rises steeply from Sawmill Creek, 1½ miles below. The trail then climbs a steep, brush-covered slope before contouring into the Sawmill Creek drainage. (You can see the remains of the old sawmill at the lower end of The Hogsback.) The trail crosses the small stream north of The Hogsback and goes south over The Hogsback to Sawmill Meadow. The trail zigzags up a headwall, crosses the bench of Mule Lake, and makes two stream crossings while climbing up to beautiful Sawmill Lake (6½ mi; 10,023 ft). Above the lake, the trail crosses a timberline basin and makes a steep ascent to the top of Sawmill Pass (1¾ mi; 11,347 ft). The trail makes a gentle descent from the pass across fields of talus and sand before leading to the alpine basin of the headwaters of Woods Creek, with beautiful Woods Lake. At the lower end of this basin, the trail turns north and meets the John Muir Trail (3½ mi; 10,346 ft).

Armstrong Canyon   5 miles

A non-quota trail. Armstrong Canyon is used as the approach for climbing Mount Perkins and Colosseum Mountain and for crossing Armstrong Col. It is a dry canyon, i.e., it has no running water. Most visits to the canyon are during the spring, when snow can be melted for water. This "trail" is actually a four-wheel-drive road.

The trailhead is beyond the Division Creek Powerhouse at Scotty Spring, the limit for most automobiles (0 mi; 5,774 ft+). The road makes one big zig and another big zag before climbing and contouring to the abandoned mines in Armstrong Canyon. A fork is encountered along the way; take the right fork. The road ends once it reaches the canyon itself (5 mi; 8,268 ft+), but it is an easy cross-country hike to the upper reaches of the canyon and from there to the base of Mount Perkins.

Taboose Pass Trail   8¾ miles

A quota trail. The long, hard hike up Taboose Pass starts in the desert, passing through a seeming wasteland of talus with only the occasional bit of vegetation. But then you reach the summit of the pass, with its breathtaking view of the headwaters of the South Fork of the Kings River, Bench Lake, and Arrow Peak. You enter another world atop Taboose Pass.

From the end of Taboose Creek Road (0 mi; 5,380 ft+) the trail crosses the sandy desert floor before going left into the Taboose Creek drainage. The trail remains on the north side of the creek for a considerable distance, and then crosses the stream before climbing onto a small bench. The trail then traverses west before crossing the creek just below a small waterfall. It continues to ascend the canyon, before passing through some small meadows with tarns just before reaching Taboose Pass (6¼ mi; 11,352 ft+).

The trail descends gently down the west side of the pass, through meadows with wildflowers in early season, to a junction (1¼ mi; 10,941 ft). The left fork meets the John Muir Trail just below its junction with the Bench Lake Trail (1¼ mi; 10,761 ft+). The right fork meets the John Muir Trail along the South Fork of the Kings River before it makes its climb into Upper Basin (4 mi; 10,203 ft).

CROSS-COUNTRY ROUTES

Gardiner Pass   3429 m; 11,200 ft+

Class 2. At one time there was a trail over Gardiner Pass, but it has been abandoned for a long time. Traces of it may still be seen, however.

The route begins at the western end of Charlotte Lake. Cross the outlet stream, skirt a small meadow on its southern side, and then cross the stream again to its northern side. Those headed for Gardiner Pass make a gradual descent through this basin, leaving Charlotte Creek far below, while those headed for Charlotte Dome remain close to Charlotte Creek. At approximately 10,000 feet go right, then cross the northern tributary stream of Charlotte Creek before making the zigzag climb to Gardiner Pass. It seems ironic that you cross barren scree and talus in order to reach the forested summit of this pass. The route descends the steep, northern side of the pass and leads from ledge to ledge in the basin below. From the large lake at the bottom of this basin, climb a small rise and then make a steep descent to Gardiner Creek.

To reach Gardiner Basin, follow Gardiner Creek upstream. Cliffs are avoided by first climbing to the south and then traversing east to cross to the north side of Gardiner Creek at UTM 684763. It is best to approach Gardiner Basin from this point, staying high on the northern side of the basin to avoid the many small cliffs.

"King Col"   3540 m; 11,600 ft+;
1.0 mi W of Mount Clarence King; UTM 695744

Class 2. This has also been referred to as "Moulthrop Pass" after Paul Moulthrop, who crossed it in 1940. King Col provides direct access between Gardiner Basin and Woods Creek. From the lower end of Gardiner Basin, climb steep slopes to the gentle sandy slope leading northeast to the top of King Col. Descend the northeast side of the pass on steep, loose rock and sand. Descend the basin below by keeping west of the three lakes and stream. The big difficulty is crossing Woods Creek. If the water level is low, you may be able to ford the creek near the meadow opposite Castle Domes. If the water is high, remain on the south side of Woods Creek and hike 1½ miles upstream to where the John Muir Trail crosses Woods Creek on a bridge.

"Sixty Lake Col"   3560 m+; 11,680 ft+;
1.0 mi S of Mount Cotter

Class 2. This pass provides access to Gardiner Basin from Sixty Lake Basin. Leave the Sixty Lake Basin Trail where the trail makes an abrupt turn to the north (at UTM 729751). Follow a use trail to the western side of narrow Lake 3304m (10,800 ft+). From the lake, climb over talus and slabs to the low gap in the ridge south of Mount Cotter. Just below this gap, follow ledges to cross the divide just north of the low point. Make a careful descent from the top of the ridge, picking your way through talus and ledges to skirt the east and north shores of Lake 3477m (11,394 ft). Before reaching the outlet of this lake, climb over the low ridge to the north and descend to the bowl just west of Mount Cotter. Keep to the west of the lakes in this bowl. A direct descent of Gardiner Basin is best accomplished by keeping to the north and above the lakes in the basin to avoid the many small cliffs. Of course, you can descend to any of the lakes in the basin by careful routefinding.

"Basin Notch"   3260 m+; 10,720 ft+;
0.9 mi NNW of Fin Dome

Class 1. This is an easy cross-country route between Arrowhead Lake and Sixty Lake Basin. Leave the John Muir Trail at the outlet of Arrowhead Lake and go southwest to the little pass on the ridge north of Fin Dome. Cross-country travel is easy in Sixty Lake Basin.

"Rae Col"   3560 m+; 11,680 ft+;
0.7 mi NNW of Glen Pass

Class 2. This is a direct route from the basin north of Glen Pass to Sixty Lake Basin.

Rixford Pass   3760 m+; 12,480 ft+;
0.6 mi ESE of Mount Rixford

Class 2. This pass has been used by skiers on high-level ski tours. The north side of this pass is dramatically steep.

Further Reading: John Moynier. *Backcountry Skiing in the High Sierra.* Evergreen, Colo.: Chockstone Press, 1992, p. 29.

"Gould Pass"   3820 m+; 12,800 ft+;
0.5 mi N of Gould Peak

Class 2. This provides a direct route between Onion Valley and Rae Lakes. From Golden Trout Lake climb west and then north to the small notch on the ridge between Mount Gould and Dragon Peak. The west side of the pass is descended by means of a steep chute over loose rock to the lakes in the basin west of Dragon Peak. Boulder hop north to Dragon Lake to meet a use trail on its north shore that leads down to the Rae Lakes.

When approaching this pass from the west, you will see two talus slopes; make the final approach via the southern one.

There are two eastern approach variations. One is from the summit of Kearsarge Pass by skirting the summit of Mount Gould and descending the ridge to the pass. The other is Dragon Pass. Climb the broad talus gully that leads west from Lake 3460m+ (11,360 ft+) toward the ridge crest. This gully eventually ends among cliffs below the crest. From the top of the gully head southwest and climb class 2 ledges and talus to the Sierra crest. Either continue south along the crest to Gould Pass or go north a couple of hundred feet to a class 2 chute that descends the west side of the crest to Lake 3640m+ (12,000 ft).

"North Dragon Pass"   3640 m+; 11,920 ft+;
0.7 mi N of Dragon Peak; UTM 775733

Class 3. This pass is typically approached from Onion Valley via the unnamed lakes east of and below Dragon Peak. With this approach, it is necessary first to climb to 12,400 feet on the Sierra crest and then to descend to North Dragon Pass. From the unnamed lakes, head for the V-shaped notch just north of Dragon Peak. Before reaching this notch, go right (north) toward the square-shaped Dragon's Tooth. Pass this peak to the right (east) and remain on the eastern side of the crest while moving north to the actual pass. Pass another minor peak on its right (east) side, and then descend on scree down to Dragon Lake. A use trail on the north side of the lake leads to the John Muir Trail at Rae Lakes.

Both Gould Pass and North Dragon Pass are difficult cross-country routes, and should only be undertaken by

Gould Pass, North Dragon Pass, and Vicinity

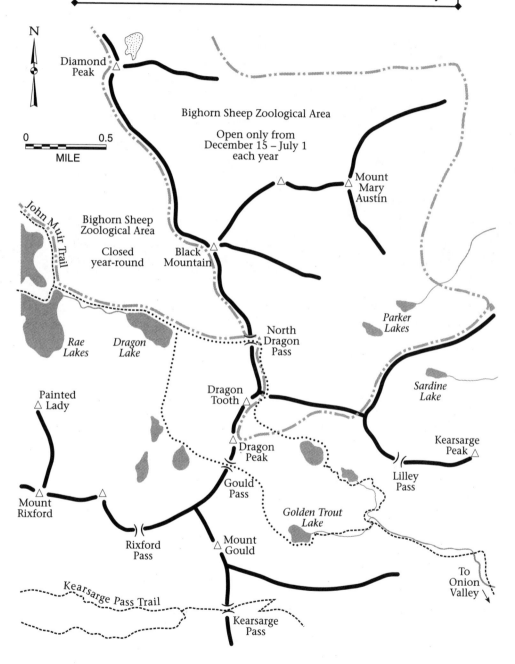

N

0   0.5
MILE

Diamond Peak

Bighorn Sheep Zoological Area

Open only from
December 15 – July 1
each year

Mount Mary Austin

John Muir Trail

Bighorn Sheep Zoological Area

Closed year-round

Black Mountain

Rae Lakes

Dragon Lake

North Dragon Pass

Parker Lakes

Dragon Tooth

Sardine Lake

Painted Lady

Dragon Peak

Kearsarge Peak

Gould Pass

Lilley Pass

Mount Rixford

Golden Trout Lake

Rixford Pass

Mount Gould

To Onion Valley

Kearsarge Pass Trail

Kearsarge Pass

North Dragon Pass, Dragon Tooth, and Dragon Peak from the northwest. Photo by R. J. Secor.

experienced hikers. Many who have crossed these passes prefer the trails over Kearsarge Pass and Glen Pass as the easiest one-day route to Rae Lakes from Onion Valley.

North Dragon Pass is only open from December 15 to July 1 due to bighorn sheep restrictions.

"Lilley Pass" 3660 m+; 11,920 ft+;
0.5 mi W of Kearsarge Peak

Class 2. Named in honor of Barbara Lilley, this pass is typically used by skiers who wish to ski Sardine Canyon with the minimum amount of climbing and the maximum amount of vertical feet skied. Leave the Golden Trout Lake Trail below the unnamed lakes east of Dragon Peak and climb to the lowest saddle west of Kearsarge Peak. A chute leads to the saddle; it is filled with disagreeable loose rock and dirt during the height of the summer.

Further Reading: John Moynier. *Backcountry Skiing in the High Sierra.* Evergreen, Colo.: Chockstone Press, 1992, p. 169.

Sardine Canyon

Sardine Canyon is a barren, desolate place during the height of the summer, but in the spring it is a fantastic ski run. It is approached by leaving Onion Valley Road approximately 8 miles from Independence, where a dirt road blocked by a locked gate leads north. Hike up the road to where it forks. Take the left fork, which soon turns into a long-abandoned trail that gets fainter as it approaches Sardine Lake. (This lake, despite its name, has no fish.)

Further Reading: John Moynier. *Backcountry Skiing in the High Sierra.* Evergreen, Colo.: Chockstone Press, 1992, p. 169.

Parker Lakes

These lakes are within the California Bighorn Sheep Zoological Area, which is open only from December 15 to July 1. The approach is the same as for Sardine Canyon, except that you continue hiking north where the gated road forks. This leads to Little Onion Valley. After crossing the South Fork of Oak Creek, the route goes up the canyon to the lowest of the Parker Lakes. The upper lake is reached after ½ mile of talus hopping.

"Black Diamond Pass" 3720 m+; 12,240 ft+ ;
0.7 mi NW of Black Mountain

Class 2. This pass has been used by skiers to cross the Sierra crest between Rae Lakes and the Baxter Pass Trail. The west side of this pass is closed year-round and the east side of the pass is open only from December 15 until July 1 due to bighorn sheep restrictions. The east side of the pass is steep.

Further Reading: John Moynier. *Backcountry Skiing in the High Sierra.* Evergreen, Colo.: Chockstone Press, 1992, p. 31.

"Grasshopper Pass" 3900 m+; 12,480 ft+;
0.3 mi E of Acrodectes Peak

Class 3. This pass has also been named "Baxter Col," but Grasshopper Pass is used here to avoid confusion with Baxter Pass. If open to cross-country travel, it would provide direct access between Woods Lake and the Baxter Lakes. The pass is class 3 on its northern side (loose rock!) and class 2 on the south.

This pass is included only for the record, as it is in an area of Kings Canyon National Park that has been closed to all cross-country travel due to bighorn sheep restrictions.

"Arrow Pass" 3540 m+; 11,600 ft+;
0.7 mi SE of Arrow Peak; UTM 684874

Class 2. This is the direct route between Bench Lake and Paradise Valley. From Bench Lake head for the *second* saddle southeast of Arrow Peak (the first saddle has a cliff on its northern side). From the top of the pass, traverse west above the lake at the head of Arrow Creek before descending the creek to the lowest lake in the basin. Climb over the southwest spur of Pyramid Peak and descend the slabby east side of the unnamed creek (known as "Window Creek") that leads down to Woods Creek.

Further Reading: *Summit*, Summer 1994, p. 83.

An alternate route is to descend the east side of Arrow Creek to where it meets the South Fork of the Kings River and Woods Creek, in the upper part of Paradise Valley. A short pitch of class 3 is encountered at the waterfalls at the lower part of Arrow Creek; this is followed by thick brush. Window Creek is the better route.

"Explorer Pass" 3720 m+; 12,160 ft+;
0.9 mi NE of Pyramid Peak

Class 3; ice axe required. This route leads to upper Woods Creek from Bench Lake. From Bench Lake traverse southwest to the valley east of Arrow Pass. Ascend the valley to its head, then climb to the saddle immediately southwest of Peak 3891 m (12,773 ft). The route involves ascending a steep chute, which usually contains hard snow well into the summer. An easier route ascends the slope to the east of the chute and ends about 100 feet east of and above the low point of the pass. Descend the basin, staying east of the stream and lakes, to the large lake east of Window Peak. Go southeast, passing a small lake on its south shore before crossing its outlet. Descend the east side of the creek, through a lot of brush, to the John Muir Trail along Woods Creek.

"Colosseum Col" 3520 m+; 11,520 ft;
0.4 E of Mount Cedric Wright

Class 2. This pass extends from the Woods Lake drainage to the Twin Lakes drainage.

Further Reading: John Moynier. *Backcountry Skiing in the High Sierra.* Evergreen, Colo.: Chockstone Press, 1992, p. 31.

"Armstrong Col" 3660 m+; 12,000 ft+;
0.8 mi N of Colosseum Mountain

Class 2. This is the approach for climbing Colosseum Mountain, Mount Cedric Wright, Mount Wynne, and Mount Pinchot from Armstrong Canyon. Climb the chute at the head of Armstrong Canyon to the east shoulder of Peak 3705 m (12,080 ft+), which leads to the plateau north of Colosseum Mountain. Descend from the plateau to the southwest before turning northwest to the John Muir Trail near Twin Lakes.

Further Reading: John Moynier. *Backcountry Skiing in the High Sierra.* Evergreen, Colo.: Chockstone Press, 1992, p. 170.

Muro Blanco

Class 2. To be precise, "Muro Blanco" actually refers to the great white wall that descends from Arrow Ridge to the South Fork of the Kings River. The description here refers to a descent of the canyon. This trailless descent involves numerous varieties of brush, talus, and rock slabs—but also some beautiful little meadows and forests, along with superb scenery. This is one of the classic bushwhacks of the High Sierra.

The entire route remains on the northwest side of the South Fork of the Kings River. From the John Muir Trail north of the river, follow the trail downstream past the Cartridge Pass Trail junction. The trail disappears when it passes through some boulders, but reappears in a grove of trees on the other side of the boulders. The trail soon disappears for good in a small meadow. The rest of the route is impossible to describe. General comments: Before crossing Kid Creek you have a choice of beating through brush near the river or traversing across talus high above the river. The worst brush of the entire route is encountered 1½ miles before reaching the Woods Creek Trail, near the mouth of the creek.

PEAKS

Mount Bago   3618 m; 11,868 ft

East Slope. Class 1 from Charlotte Lake. First ascent July 11, 1896 by Joseph LeConte and W. S. Gould. The south summit is the high point.

South Arête. IV, 5.7. First ascent September 1, 1974 by David Boyd and Paul Hurd. This route climbs the right-hand skyline (as seen from Junction Meadow) of an orange dihedral. One thousand feet of excellent rock is found on this climb.

The Parapet. III, 5.8. First ascent May 1982 by Rick Nolting and Fred Beckey. This climb is on the central portion of the south face of Mount Bago. Begin by climbing a long chimney-and-gully system to a vertical, overhanging headwall which consists of flakes. This headwall leads to a long, easy ramp that in turn leads to an outside corner. Zigzag up another headwall, then traverse left across small holds to a shallow crack system. Easier climbing follows.

"Bubbs Creek Wall"   3237 m; 10,617 ft;
1.4 mi NW of Mount Bago

This massive wall is about ½ mile southwest of Peak 3237m (10,617 ft). It is approached by leaving the Bubbs Creek Trail about 1 mile east of the Charlotte Creek crossing, where the first full view of the wall can be seen. Scramble over talus and slabs to the base. Descend from the top by aiming for Charlotte Dome, keeping a big slab on the right (looking down), then angle to the left across a talus field until intersecting the ancient sheep trail that is on the southeast side of Charlotte Creek. Continue down the trail, beating your way through brush occasionally, to the Bubbs Creek Trail.

Further Reading: Greg Vernon, Sally Moser, and David Hickey. *Southern Sierra Rock Climbing: Sequoia/Kings Canyon.* Evergreen, Colo.: Chockstone Press, 1993, pp. 181–183.

Aquaman. III, 5.10+. First ascent July 1983 by Bill McConachie and Richard Leversee. The east side of the Bubbs Creek Wall has two obvious crack systems. This route climbs the right crack. Eight pitches of 5.7 and 5.8 lead to a 5.10 off-width inside corner, which ends 200 feet below the top.

Beckey Route. V, 5.8, A2. First ascent June 8–9, 1974 by Fred Beckey, Mike McGooey, and Mark Losleben. This route ascends the left-hand crack system.

Crystal Bonsai. VI, 5.11, A3. First ascent August 1986 by Richard Leversee and Eddie Joe. One of the few grade VI routes in the High Sierra, this climbs the highest section of the Bubbs Creek Wall just to the left of center, following a band of white crystal from bottom to top. The route begins at a large pine tree about 100 yards up and right of a huge left-facing dihedral that marks the beginning of the crystal band. Climb up and left to a ramp that leads to Crystal Palace ledge. Climb the dihedral to its top and then follow the Crystal Corner up and left, using bat hooks and bolts, to a small stance with two bolts. Climb up and slightly right to the main crack-and-corner system to Bombs Away Ledge. Continue up the corner system for four pitches to Zero Point Ledge, immediately above the Seagull Roof. Two pitches of cracks lead up and left to a good ledge. A pitch to the right leads to a right-facing dihedral. Instead of climbing the dihedral, face climb to the left for 20 feet to a large flake; climb this and a thin crack to Dead Tree Ledge. Climb diagonally left to a blank, right-facing corner. From the corner, traverse left to easy knobs, which lead to the top. This seventeen-pitch route requires two complete sets of nuts (from tiny to 4-inch), skyhooks, bat hooks, and hammocks. *Variation: Samurai Wind Start.* V, 5.11, A0. First ascent October 1996 by Dave Nettle and Hunter Sibbald. Traverse right and up from the initial ramp of Crystal Bonsai to a sling belay on a large knob. Go up and left (past an old ¼-inch bolt; 5.10 face) to Fish Taco Flake. Climb the right-hand side of the flake and continue left to a right-facing inside corner. From the top of the corner, traverse left across knobs and then go up and left (pull on a bolt; A0) to a short right-facing inside corner. Pendulum 50 feet to the left to the crystal band and then continue up and left to Bombs Away Ledge of Crystal Bonsai.

Samurai Warriors. V, 5.11, A1. First ascent September 1997 by Dave Nettle and Brandon Thau. Start by climbing the Samurai Wind Start to the very top of the right-facing inside corner above Fish Taco Flake. Pendulum 20 feet to the right, then climb the Big Kahuna, a 5.11 hand crack. Continue up the Brown Headwall via a thin crack and then steep knobs to a roof, where the first-ascent party had a hanging bivy. Go to the right and then up with mixed climbing, protected by bolts and bat hooks. Move up and left to a dike, ending at a small ledge. Three bat hook moves from the belay are followed by a 5.10 face to the left. Next go up and right, then make a slightly ascending traverse left to the right edge of the Seagull Roof. Continue left and face climb the left side of a dike to a two-bolt belay on a small ledge. Traverse horizontally to the right, then go up and climb over the three Rocket Roofs, ending with some 5.10 mantles. Go up and left to a belay stance in a block in an alcove to the right of a huge, dirty inside corner. A long (200-foot; 5.10) pitch leads to the right and then up to a belay stance on a ledge with some small pine trees. Go left, down, and then up a 5.10 layback crack ending with a traverse to the left before dropping down and passing a bushy tree. The last pitch, the free crux, climbs a thin, smooth, layback corner, ending on a ledge marked by a lonesome tree. The first-ascent party used 60-meter ropes.

Charlotte Dome   3253 m; 10,690 ft

This beautiful piece of rock was one of the earliest Sierra domes to be discovered outside of Yosemite Valley. In 1864, when the California Geological Survey camped along Charlotte Creek, Charles Hoffman sketched this dome. It was first climbed 102 years later. Then in 1970 one of the world's finest rock climbs was discovered on its south face.

Charlotte Dome can be approached from either the west (from the end of Highway 180 in Kings Canyon) or the east (from Onion Valley over Kearsarge Pass via Charlotte Lake). The western approach is easier. Those approaching from the west should note that a use trail has appeared about 100 to 200 feet to the northwest of,

and parallel to, Charlotte Creek. Bears have been known to raid food caches in this area.

Further Reading: Greg Vernon, Sally Moser, and David Hickey. *Southern Sierra Rock Climbing: Sequoia/Kings Canyon.* Evergreen, Colo.: Chockstone Press, 1993, pp. 184–188.

North Ridge. Class 3. First ascent August 1966 by Ed Lane from Gardiner Pass. This is the usual descent route for climbs on the south face. Many parties make the mistake of descending too soon from the summit. It is better to go well north, beyond and above the small saddle behind the dome, before turning right and descending to the unnamed tributary of Charlotte Creek.

Neutron Dance. IV, 5.10d. First ascent 1985 by Jack Wenzel and Elizabeth Ammon. This ten-pitch route starts at a prominent orange dike on the southeast face. The first pitch is the crux. The rest of the climb is moderate, except for the summit pitch, which is 5.10a.

The Epicureans. IV, 5.7+. First ascent June 30, 1988 by Todd Swain and Peggy Buckey. This route starts about 200 yards up and right from E. B. White. There are two left-facing corners or grooves here. The first two pitches climb the right-hand corner to the top of a pillar (5.7); belay on a good ledge to the right. Traverse right (5.2) to a belay stance in a mossy alcove. Continue to the right from the alcove, then move up (5.4) a poorly protected golden slab that is next to a right-leaning dike; this pitch ends at a sloping belay ledge with a bolt. Continue up the slab to a shallow left-facing corner. Climb the corner to where it meets a white dike with a bolt, and then continue up the slab (5.6) to a belay stance at some exfoliated flakes. Go straight up (5.5) over numerous flakes to a stance at a shallow left-facing corner. This is followed by a left-facing flake that leads to an obvious left-facing corner (5.7+) just below a roof. Continue up the corner (scary 5.7) for one and a half pitches to a ledge. Climb the crack system above the ledge, then go up a huge right-facing flake (5.6) to a hanging belay. The next pitch climbs a crack and a wide, white dike (5.5) to a belay in a tree. The last two pitches follow a crack system (5.2) to the top. Chocks from micronuts to 3 inches are needed to protect this route.

E. B. White. IV, 5.9. First ascent August 1979 by Allan Pietrasanta and Alan Bartlett. This route is on the eastern side of the south face of Charlotte Dome. There are two parallel black water marks to the right of the Classic South Face. Follow the left-hand water

CHARLOTTE DOME

Charlotte's Web

Classic South Face

E.B. White

Charlotte Dome, South Face. Photo by R. J. Secor.

mark, past two bolts to a one-bolt belay anchor at the top of the first pitch. Two more pitches lead to the Classic South Face route. Go left and continue up cracks to where the angle lessens. Climb the headwall to the summit.

Sea of Granite. III, 5.8. First ascent August 17, 1988 by Chris Keith and Pete Lowery. This twelve-pitch climb is to the right of the Classic South Face. There are many run outs on this route.

Classic South Face. III, 5.7. First ascent October 1970 by Galen Rowell, Chris Jones, and Fred Beckey. First winter ascent April 1992 by Rich Henke, Nancy Jensen, and Alois Smrz. This justifiably popular route climbs the highest part of the south face. Start climbing from the top of the large recess at the lowest portion of the face. Two class 4 pitches up and right lead to a steep section, which is climbed by the most prominent crack for two pitches to a big belay ledge. This is followed by some easy knobs to the Slot Pitch. Climb to the very top of the Slot and belay from a small ledge on its left side. Climb a knobby face above the Slot Pitch to a wide ramp that leads to the right. Follow the ramp around an outside corner to the Furrow Pitch. The Furrow Pitch ends on a steep headwall with a belay in a little nook. A long pitch in a left-facing corner is followed by a pitch up a steep, left-leaning crack, which ends on a huge ledge with a dead tree. One more easy pitch up and left leads to the top. A common mistake made on this route is not taking enough runners; six is not enough, and a dozen (with some doubles and triples) is not too many. Also, there are many possible variations on this climb; it seems that many parties end up too far to the right. But the quality of the rock and magnificent surroundings usually make up for any routefinding errors.

Further Reading: Allen Steck and Steve Roper. *Fifty Classic Climbs of North America.* San Francisco: Sierra Club Books, 1979, pp. 294–299; John Moynier and Claude Fiddler. *Sierra Classics.* Evergreen, Colo.: Chockstone Press, 1993, pp. 95–99.

Charlotte's Web. IV, 5.8. First ascent August 1976 by Bart O'Brien and Dave Harden. This route is left of the Classic South Face route. Start climbing from near a solitary pine tree between a small recess on the south face and the larger recess of the Classic South Face route. About 100 feet of class 3 climbing ends on a flat ledge. Four pitches up and right lead to the base of a steep, shallow crack. Two long (165-foot) pitches are needed to climb the crack. The route continues straight up over

beautiful knobs and chickenheads for several hundred feet to a large, sandy ledge with a dead tree. Climb the knob-covered face directly above the ledge. One more pitch of easy climbing leads to the summit.

Further Reading: *Summit.* June 1978, pp. 28–32.

Southwest Arête. IV, 5.9. First ascent May 1973 by Dave Lomba and Galen Rowell. This climb consists of eleven pitches on excellent rock along the narrow ridge.

Charlito Dome, The Artesian Route. III, 5.10b. First ascent June 1986 by E. C. Joe and Richard Leversee. This is a large slab facing southwest, just south of Charlotte Dome. This route climbs the right-facing corner on the upper half of the slab. There is a spring beneath the corner bypassed by a long, circular pitch to the left—the crux. There are four run out 5.8 to 5.9 pitches to beneath the spring.

Glacier Monument   11,154 ft; 11,165 ft
First ascent September 1972 by Andy Smatko, Tom Ross, and Bill Schuler, on a traverse from Gardiner Pass.

Mount Gardiner   3934 m; 12,907 ft
This would be one of the classic peaks of the High Sierra, except for all of that darned climbing! (This peak requires a long slog up a scree-and-talus slope from the south to reach a classic knife edge.)

South Slope. Class 4. First ascent July 1896 by Bolton Brown and Joseph LeConte, who met by chance on the south summit of the peak. Climb almost interminable scree-and-talus slopes from the Charlotte Creek drainage to the south summit of the peak. From the south summit, a 300-foot class 4 knife edge leads to the higher north summit. For variation, you can also climb the southeast ridge to the south summit.

Northeast Chute. Class 4. First ascent July 9, 1940 by a party led by Norman Clyde. Climb the shallow class 2 chute just south of Mount Gardiner's northeast ridge from Gardiner Basin. This chute leads to the southeast ridge and the south summit. Climb the class 4 knife edge ridge to the north summit.

Further Reading: John Moynier and Claude Fiddler. *Sierra Classics.* Evergreen, Colo.: Chockstone Press, 1993, pp. 100–101.

Mount Cotter   3875 m; 12,721 ft
The south peak is the high point.

Southeast Slope. Class 2–3. First ascent August 6, 1922 by Bob Fitzsimons. Climb the slope rising from

Sixty Lake Basin. Only the summit rocks are difficult.

South Ridge. Class 3. Follow the ridge rising from Sixty Lake Col.

Southwest Slope. Class 2–3. Climb the slope from Lake 3477m (11,394 ft) in Gardiner Basin.

North Ridge. I, 5.3, A0. First ascent July 8, 1940 by a party led by David Brower. The key to this route is to stay on or very close to the ridge crest. The ridge is dramatically exposed, but most of it is class 3 to 4, and involves two short rappels to get around the two largest notches on the ridge.

North Cotter, Northeast Buttress. Class 4–5. First ascent June 23, 1984 by Dick Beach and Steve Rogero. This exceptionally fine climb leads to the lower, north summit of Mount Cotter. Approach the buttress from Sixty Lake Basin by staying on ledges on the north (right) side of the lower part of the buttress. Climb to a notch that is on the crest of the buttress. Climb the buttress from the notch, keeping to its north (right) side, to the summit of the north peak. Protection is scarce on many of the leads, but this is balanced by incredible hand- and footholds.

North Cotter, East Face. IV, 5.9, A1. First ascent June 1972 by Tony Qamar, Marek Glogoczowski, and Galen Rowell. This route begins just right of the center portion of the east face. The second pitch includes a gigantic pendulum traverse to the left. On the first ascent, one piton was used for aid at the beginning of a 5.9 jam crack higher on the wall. This route ends atop the north summit of Mount Cotter.

Mount Clarence King   3934 m; 12,905 ft

This beautiful peak dominates the entire Woods Creek drainage. Its first ascent was the hardest rock climb in nineteenth-century American mountaineering history.

South Face. I, 5.4. First ascent August 1896 by Bolton Brown. From either Gardiner Basin or Sixty Lake Basin, climb to the saddle on the south ridge of the peak. The final approach to the saddle from Sixty Lake Basin

Mount Gardiner from the north. Photo by R. J. Secor.

Mount Cotter and North Cotter from the northeast. Photo by R. J. Secor.

uses either a ledge in the cliff on the eastern side of the saddle or a scree-and-talus slope farther south. Climb talus and sand from the saddle to the highest rocks, which are near the eastern cliff. A jam crack and squeeze chimney (located just right of a guillotine flake of rock) are climbed to gain access to the final summit block. The summit block is climbed via a crack on its eastern side, and then by standing on the edge of a subsidiary block before making the delicate move onto the highest rock. Alternatively, you can climb the southern face of the summit block (with the aid of a shoulderstand or it goes free at 5.7) before making the delicate move. *Starr's Variation:* First ascent July 27, 1929 by Walter A. Starr, Jr. There is a prominent overhang around the corner to the right of the jam crack and squeeze chimney. Climb up a *very small* hole under the overhang to the summit block. This hole is in line with the summit of Mount Clarence King, Mount Cotter, and Mount Stanford.

Further Reading: John Moynier and Claude Fiddler. *Sierra Classics.* Evergreen, Colo.: Chockstone Press, 1993, pp. 102–103.

Northwest Face, Right Side. III, 5.4. First ascent August 25, 1975 by Bill Stronge, Scott Charlton, and Mike Walters. Ascend the west ridge of Mount Clarence King to approximately halfway up the ridge. Traverse left onto the northwest face via a talus ledge. Climb directly to the summit via cracks and chimneys that begin in a broken area on the right side of the center of the face. This is a six-pitch climb.

Northwest Face, Left Side. IV, 5.7. First ascent September 1971 by Gilles Corcos and Graeme Wilson. This climb starts on the left side of the face. Ascend a 200-foot class 4 ramp to a shallow spur on the face. Climb the inside corner of the spur (5.7) for one pitch, then climb up and right for another lead. Continue climbing up and right, with alternate horizontal traverses, to a point about 300 feet west of the summit, where it is possible to climb up to the west ridge. Follow the west ridge to the summit block.

North Ridge. I, 5.4. First ascent September 3, 1972 by George Oetzel, Dick Brown, Stu Langdoc, and Pat Buchanan. This climb begins from near the top of Peak 3760m+ (12,356 ft). From this point, the ridge appears to be more of a face, with some small arêtes to the east. Climb the face, keeping within 50 to 100 feet of its junction with the northwest face. Some steep slabs near the top can be bypassed by going to the left of a 20-foot sloping ledge at their base. A 50-foot class 4 pitch, up cracks at the top of the slabs, leads to a bowl where the north ridge joins the east ridge. From the bowl, an easy but exposed scramble along the top of the northwest face leads to the summit block (5.4).

Mount Clarence King, Southeast Face. Photo by R. J. Secor.

East Ridge. I, 5.4. First ascent August 1948 by Fred Davenport and Standish Mitchell. First winter ascent April 1972 by Dan Eaton and Doug Kinzy. Follow the ridge from Sixty Lake Basin to the summit block. A difficult section on the lower part of the ridge is bypassed on its south side via a series of narrow cracks and ledges. The upper part of the ridge features a "large wafer"—or thin block of rock. This is bypassed (5.2) on the northern side of the ridge. The summit block is 5.4.

Southeast Face, Chimney Route. III, 5.9. The name of the route is something of a misnomer, as it just barely touches the prominent chimney system on this face. Begin by ascending a left-facing open book (5.9) that is topped by a roof. This open book is to the right of the chimney. Face climbing leads left into the chimney, and the chimney is ascended to a belay stance to the right of a chockstone. Two pitches of face and crack climbing (up to 5.8), interspersed with ledges, lead left from the chimney to a 5.9 off-width crack that ends atop the ramp system on the left side of the face. A 5.7 crack then leads to a ledge, followed by 5.8 cracks (loose rock!) that end on a sandy ledge almost directly below the summit. This is followed by a 5.8 crack system that ends at a notch to the right of the summit block.

Further Reading: John Moynier and Claude Fiddler. *Sierra Classics*. Evergreen, Colo.: Chockstone Press, 1993, pp. 104–105.

Southeast Face, Ramp Route. III, 5.8. First ascent August 1970 by Greg Henzie and Galen Rowell. This route climbs the right-trending ramp-and-crack system to the left of the prominent chimney system on this face. Two pitches of 5.8 crack climbing along the ramp lead to a class 3 section in the middle of the route. This class 3 section is to the right of a gray patch on the face and ends on the sandy ledge of the Chimney Route, where a 5.8 crack system leads up to the top.

Further Reading: John Moynier and Claude Fiddler. *Sierra Classics*. Evergreen, Colo.: Chockstone Press, 1993, pp. 104–105.

Peak 3620m+   11,870 ft; 0.7 mi W of Mount Clarence King

South Face and East Ridge. Class 3. First ascent September 11, 1972 by Bill Schuler, Tom Ross, and Andy Smatko. Climb a chute on the south face and follow the east ridge to the summit.

Peak 3722m   12,160 ft+; 1.1 mi N of Mount Clarence King

First ascent July 6, 1940 by Jim Harkins, Bob Jacobs, Art Argiewicz, and Bruce Meyer. The two summit blocks are class 4.

Fin Dome   3558 m; 11,693 ft

West Face. Class 3. First ascent 1910 by James Rennie. From the top of the talus fan on the southwest side of the dome, contour left (west) and slightly upward on the west face. The route zigzags on sandy ledges and over boulders between large slabs. It is easy to get off route and onto class 4 terrain.

South Ridge. Class 4. First ascent July 7, 1940 by David Brower and party.

East Face. I, 5.7. First ascent June 1972 by Marek Glogoczowski and Galen Rowell. Two pitches lead to the summit.

East Face, Left Side. I, 5.6. First ascent August 1975 by Rick Spittler, Don Spittler, and Kevin Babich. This route starts on the left side of the face. Traverse up and right to a left-facing corner. Climb the corner to a large ledge in the middle of the face; one more pitch then leads to the top.

North Buttress. Class 4. First ascent June 16, 1966 by Arkel Erb, Ken McNutt, and Dick Beach. Approach this ridge from the west, and keep to the right side of the buttress for five pitches to the summit.

Painted Lady   3694 m; 12,126 ft

First ascent 1931 by Robert Owen. Class 2 from the John Muir Trail north of Glen Pass.

West Rib. III, 5.7. First ascent August 1975 by David Babich and Rick Spittler. This nine-pitch route ascends a prominent rib that is seen on the right side of the peak when viewed from Rae Lakes. Start by climbing the center of the rib and then emerge onto the west face after four leads. Continue up the face as directly as possible to the summit.

Mount Rixford   3928 m; 12,890 ft

First ascent 1897 by Emmet Rixford and two others, via an unknown route. First winter ascent March 1933 by Oliver Kehrlein and Norman Clyde. This peak is class 1 from Bullfrog Lake. It is class 2 from Mount Gould, as long as you remain low on the southern side of the ridge connecting the two peaks. The northeast side of this peak has loose rock.

This peak is class 3 from Glen Pass. Traverse across the southwest slope of the pinnacle that is east of the pass to a small notch. Continue from the notch to the main saddle west of Mount Rixford. Climb the west ridge to the summit. This route was climbed by Larry Tidball, Richard Fritsen, and party on August 19, 1988.

Peak 3912m   12,800 ft+; 0.4 mi E of Mount Rixford
This peak is class 3 via its southwest face, southeast ridge, or east face.

Mount Gould   3964 m; 13,005 ft
The summit rocks of this peak are class 3.

From Kearsarge Pass. Class 1. First ascent July 2, 1890 by Joseph LeConte, Hubert P. Dyer, Fred S. Pheby, and C. B. Lakeman. First winter ascent March 1933 by Oliver Kehrlein and Norman Clyde. The south ridge is an easy talus hop.

Southeast Ridge. Class 1. Ascend the southeast slope from the eastern side of Kearsarge Pass to the southeast ridge. Stay south of the crest of the ridge while climbing to the summit to keep the difficulties to a minimum.

North Side. Class 2. The plateau north of Mount Gould can be reached from Golden Trout Lake, Dragon Peak, or from the Kearsarge Lakes basin.

Kearsarge Peak   3846 m; 12,598 ft
This peak is class 1 from Sardine Canyon and from the old mining trails that climb the southeastern side of the peak from Onion Valley Road. This peak has also been climbed from Golden Trout Lake via Lilley Pass: class 2.

BIGHORN SHEEP

The eleven peaks mentioned below are in areas that have restricted access due to bighorn sheep habitat. These sheep once roamed throughout the High Sierra, but the herds were decimated with the introduction of domestic sheep in the nineteenth century. Domestic sheep have not grazed in the High Sierra since the 1940s, but the remaining herds of bighorn sheep are so tiny that it is still considered an endangered species. (It is estimated that there are fewer than twenty ewes in the Mount Baxter population.) The California Department of Fish and Game's long-range plans call for bighorn sheep to repopulate the entire High Sierra, so these areas of restricted access may again someday be completely open to the public. In the meantime, please respect these closed areas, and give the bighorn sheep a fighting chance at a comeback.

The eleven peaks are Dragon Peak, Dragon Tooth, Mount Mary Austin, Black Mountain, Diamond Peak, Peak 3984m (13,070 ft), Mount Baxter, Acrodectes Peak, Peak 3914m (12,852 ft), Peak 3903m (12,804 ft), and Indian Rock.

All cross-country travel above 11,000 feet is prohibited east of the John Muir Trail and west of the Sierra crest from North Dragon Pass on the south to the Sawmill Pass Trail on the north, year-round. Also, cross-country travel is prohibited in the basin south of Woods Lake, and a mile-long section north along the Sierra crest from Sawmill Pass and the 11,000-foot contour to the west. Cross-country travel is also prohibited east of the Sierra crest between Dragon Peak and Sawmill Pass from July 1 to December 15.

Dragon Peak   3940 m+; 12,955 ft+
South Ridge. Class 3. First ascent 1920 by Fred Parker and J. E. Rother. This ridge can be approached from either Mount Gould or from the unnamed lakes north of Golden Trout Lake. Climb the broad talus slope that leads west from the unnamed lakes toward the ridge crest. This slope eventually ends among cliffs below the crest. At the right (north) side of the slope, a short, narrow chute leads up and to the right. This chute ends after 100 feet and leads to a chimney that features an awkward class 3 move over the right side of a boulder. This is followed by the col immediately south of the peak. From the col, traverse the western side of the south ridge over many minor ribs and buttresses to the summit gendarme. This is climbed on its west side via a ledge that lacks handholds. The ledge is class 3 with a lot of exposure. This is a nice climb that can be done easily in a day from Onion Valley.

Southwest Slope. Class 3. First ascent 1920 by Norman

Clyde. The summit gendarme can be approached directly from the western approach to Gould Pass.

Northwest Ridge. II, 5.8. First ascent June 1985 by Vern Clevenger and Claude Fiddler. This route climbs the left of two arêtes on the northwest side of the peak. This climb, which consists of six pitches, begins above Dragon Lake.

Further Reading: John Moynier and Claude Fiddler. *Sierra Classics.* Evergreen, Colo.: Chockstone Press, 1993, pp. 106–107.

"Dragon Tooth" 3803 m; 12,480 ft+;
0.3 mi N of Dragon Peak

This is the large square-topped peak that is passed during the eastern approach to North Dragon Pass.

North Face. I, 5.6, A1. First ascent July 26, 1944 by Parker Severson. Second ascent June 22, 1984 by Dick Beach and Steve Rogero. This route is open from December 15 to July 1. The climb begins on the northern side of the east face. The first pitch is followed by a 15-foot aid crack. The route then goes through a prominent notch to the north face; this features a large flake with a narrow walkway. Descend the walkway and traverse onto the north face. At the far side of the north face, climb a series of cracks to the summit.

Mount Mary Austin 3978 m; 13,040 ft+

First ascent May 3, 1965 by Andy Smatko, Tom Ross, Ellen Siegal, and Eric Schumacher. The southeast slope is class 2. The entire peak is open only from December 15 to July 1.

Black Mountain 4051 m; 13,289 ft

South Slope. Class 2. First ascent 1905 by George Davis. This route is closed year-round.

North Slope. Class 2. First ascent August 20, 1948 by Fred L. Jones. This route is open only from December 15 to July 1. Climb the slope from the Baxter Pass Trail. A short, steep section is encountered when approaching the basin immediately north of the summit. (It is easier to climb Black Mountain first, and then climb Diamond Peak via the southeast slope from the 11,800-foot or 3600-meter level.)

East Ridge. Class 2. Descended August 19, 1948 by

Dragon Peak from the north. Photo by R. J. Secor.

Fred L. Jones. This route is open only from December 15 to July 1. The large blocks just below the summit are class 2. This ridge can be approached from the Baxter Pass Trail, from the summit of Mount Mary Austin, or from Parker Lakes.

South Ridge. Class 2. The Sierra crest can be followed from North Dragon Pass to the summit of Black Mountain. This route is open only from December 15 to July 1.

Diamond Peak   4001 m; 13,126 ft

Black Diamond Traverse. Class 2. First ascent August 20, 1948 by Fred L. Jones. This route is open only from December 15 to July 1. The southeast slope of Diamond Peak is a splendid snow climb in the spring. Those traversing from Black Mountain should drop down to the 11,800-foot or 3600-meter contour before climbing Diamond Peak.

Northeast Couloir. Class 3. Descended May 30, 1960 by Henry Mandolf, Charles Bell, and Rowland Radcliffe. This route is open only from December 15 to July 1. The route ascends the left-hand (eastern) 40° snow couloir on the north side of the peak. This is a classic early-season snow climb.

West Slope. Class 2. First ascent August 1922 by Norman Clyde. This route is closed year-round.

Peak 3984m   13,070 ft; 0.6 mi N of Diamond Peak

First ascent 1925 by Norman Clyde. The southeast slope is class 2. This route is open only from December 15 to July 1.

East Ridge. Class 3. First ascent August 6, 1948 by Fred L. Jones. This route is open only from December 15 to July 1. Follow the ridge from Baxter Pass. Traverse the chutes and ribs on the south side of the ridge until beneath the summit.

Mount Baxter   4004 m; 13,125 ft;
0.5 mi E of Acrodectes Peak

For some reason, this peak is unnamed on some editions of the Kearsarge Peak 7.5-minute quadrangle. The west peak is the high point.

South Ridge. Class 3. Descended August 5, 1948 by Fred L. Jones. This route is closed year-round.

Southwest Slope. Class 2. This route is closed year-round.

From the Northwest. Class 3. This route is closed year-round.

Northwest Face. Class 4–5. First ascent July 1986 by Dave Scheven and Steve Porcella. This route is closed year-round.

North Ridge. Class 2. First ascent 1905 by George Davis. This route is closed year-round.

North Face. Class 3. First winter ascent 1975 by Doug Mantle, John McKinley, and three others. Ascend a wide chute that ends near the top of the lower eastern peak of Mount Baxter. This route is open only from December 15 to July 1.

Northeast Ridge. Class 3. Descended July 25, 1948 by Fred L. Jones. This route is open only from December 15 to July 1. This traverse begins atop Peak 3795m (12,400 ft+), about 1 mile northeast of Mount Baxter. This peak can be reached from the Sawmill Pass Trail. From this peak, make a direct traverse on the northwest side of the ridge to the base of two pinnacles on the ridge crest. Continue traversing to a small col, then cross the col to the southeast side of the ridge. Climb the southeast side of the ridge to the ridge crest, climb over a small peak, and descend to a notch. Traverse the northwestern side of the ridge across large talus blocks to the lower, eastern peak of Mount Baxter.

The entire northeast ridge of Mount Baxter, from Sawmill Creek to the summit, was climbed by Dick Beach and Bob Good on June 11, 1988. (This route is open only from December 15 to July 1.) The ridge rises 9,500 feet from the floor of Owens Valley to the summit of Mount Baxter. Dick Beach said after completing this ascent, "It is important not to become overwhelmed by the length of this ridge or the complexity of the routefinding. This ridge above all others puts all the ingredients of challenging mountaineering into play. That's why doing a ridge like this becomes an element of high adventure and not one of an arduous slog."

Southeast Slope. Class 2. Climb to the basin southeast of Mount Baxter from the Baxter Pass Trail and ascend the southeast slope of the peak to the summit. This route is open only from December 15 to July 1.

Acrodectes Peak   4018 m; 13,183 ft

The name of this peak is misspelled on some maps. First ascent July 1935 by a party led by Norman Clyde on a traverse from Mount Baxter. This entire peak is closed year-round.

North Buttress of West Peak. III, 5.10a. First ascent 1988 by Galen Rowell and Vern Clevenger.

Peak 3914m   12,852 ft;
0.9 mi W of Acrodectes Peak

North Ridge. Class 2. First ascent July 1935 by a party led by Norman Clyde, on a traverse from Acrodectes Peak. This entire peak is closed year-round.

Peak 3903m   12,804 ft;
1.0 mi NW of Acrodectes Peak

This is the prominent peak seen to the south of Woods Lake. It has been referred to as "Woods Peak." This entire peak is closed year-round.

Northeast Ridge. Class 3. First ascent July 6, 1929 by Vance Hopkins, Tom Bundy, R. L. Worden, W. F. Angbauer, Bill Widney, Earl Wallace, and Toni Freeman.

From the Northwest. Class 2. First ascent July 21, 1948 by Fred L. Jones.

Southeast Ridge. Class 3. First ascent July 1935 by a party led by Norman Clyde on a traverse from Peak 3914m (12,852 ft).

Indian Rock   3712 m; 12,160 ft+;
1.5 mi NE of Mount Baxter

This is the prominent spire seen from Highway 395 between Big Pine and Independence.

Southwest Arête. Class 3. First ascent October 16, 1948 by Fred L. Jones. This entire peak is open only from December 15 to July 1. Ascend the brush-choked canyon of Thibaut Creek to its head, and climb a talus chute to the saddle on the northwestern side of Indian Rock. Climb over a series of rubble-covered ledges and ascend a 50-foot section of class 3 to the southwest arête. Follow the southwest arête to the flat summit.

West Face. Class 4. First ascent June 11, 1988 by Dick Beach. Approximately 200 feet of class 4 climbing over solid rock leads to the summit.

Castle Domes   3200 m+; 11,360 ft+
These are class 1 from Woods Creek via the east slope and northeast ridge. Jack Roberts and friend climbed a route dubbed "Sillmarillion" (IV, 5.11) in the 1980s.

Window Peak   3684 m; 12,085 ft
First ascent July 5, 1940 by Art Argiewicz and Bob Jacobs, via an unknown route. The east face is class 3. The blocky southeast ridge is class 3. The crest of the north ridge from Pyramid Peak was traversed in 1998 by Alec Isabeau, who reported many stunning class 4

sections. The crux of the north ridge route is a short 5.4 down climb into the prominent notch north of the "window."

Peak 3764m   12,350 ft; 1.1 mi SE of Pyramid Peak
First ascent June 27, 1940 by Jed Garthwaite, Jim Quick, and Howard Leach. The west slope and the south ridge are class 2–3.

Pyramid Peak   3895 m; 12,777 ft
South Ridge. Class 3. First ascent July 21, 1942 by Art Reyman. Climb to the first notch south of the peak from either the west or the east, and follow the knife edge to the summit. An alternative route is to traverse from Window Peak.

West Ridge. Class 2. From the upper part of Arrow Creek, head southeast to where a scree-and-talus gully breaks through the cliffs along the west ridge of the peak. This gully leads to the ridge at an elevation of approximately 11,500 feet, where there is a small tarn. Follow the west ridge to the summit.

Northeast Ridge. Class 3. Gain this ridge from the basin south of Explorer Pass and follow the knife edge ridge to the summit.

Arrow Ridge   12,188 ft; 12,188 ft
First ascent August 8, 1945 by Art Reyman. Class 1 from Arrow Peak.

Arrow Peak   3950 m; 12,958 ft
The view of Arrow Peak from Bench Lake is one of the finest in the High Sierra. And the view from the summit isn't bad either.

Southeast Slope. Class 2. First ascent August 20, 1930 by Walter A. Starr, Jr. This is an easy climb over talus from the head of Arrow Creek, or from the top of Arrow Pass. Be sure to head for the higher, northeastern summit.

Southwest Ridge. Class 3. First ascent June 1902 by Joseph LeConte, Tracey Kelley, and Robert Pike. Ascend the south slope from Arrow Creek to the top of the ridge. There is a knife edge ridge between the false summit (Peak 3921m; 12,800 ft+) and the true summit; bypass the knife edge on its southern side.

Northeast Spur. Class 3. First ascent August 8, 1895 by Bolton Brown from the South Fork of the Kings River. This route is now commonly approached from Bench

Arrow Peak from Bench Lake. Photo by R. J. Secor.

Lake. This spur has some narrow knife edges near its top.

Further Reading: John Moynier and Claude Fiddler. *Sierra Classics.* Evergreen, Colo.: Chockstone Press, 1993, pp. 109–111.

Peak 3681m 12,000 ft+; 0.5 mi SE of Bench Lake
First ascent August 12, 1922 by W. and J. Sloane. *Bench Lake Boogie.* III, 5.9. First ascent July 1973 by Vern Clevenger and Jon Ross. Climb a left-facing dihedral for two pitches; a few more pitches lead to the top.

Mount Ickes 3942 m; 12,968 ft
First ascent July 25, 1939 by a party led by Art Argiewicz, via the west ridge. The west ridge and the northeast ridge are class 2.

Peak 3891m 12,773 ft; 1.1 mi NE of Pyramid Peak
First ascent July 13, 1970 by Doug Sabastion, Jack Dozier, Eric Ratner, and Steve Ratner, via the class 2 northeast ridge. The southwest ridge is class 1.

Crater Mountain 3924 m; 12,874 ft
Class 2 from the east and northeast. First ascent July 19, 1922 by W. H. Ink, Meyers Butte, and Captain Wallace.

Mount Cedric Wright 3761 m; 12,372 ft
First ascent August 25, 1935 by Norman Clyde. The southeast slope is class 1. The peak is class 3 between the saddle and Colosseum Mountain.

Colosseum Mountain 3794 m; 12,473 ft
Southwest Slope. Class 1. First ascent August 5, 1922 by Chester Versteeg. Leave the Sawmill Pass Trail in the vicinity of Woods Lake and hike up sand to the summit. Be sure to keep below 11,000 feet (3350 meters) for

1 mile north of Sawmill Pass to avoid disturbing bighorn sheep habitat.

West Ridge. Class 1. The saddle between Colosseum Mountain and Mount Cedric Wright can be reached from either the north or south. From the saddle, ascend the west ridge to the summit.

Northwest Chute. Class 2. There are many gullies and chutes on the northwest side of the peak. Ascend the chute that leads to the north ridge just north of the summit. Cross over the north ridge and climb a small bowl to the summit plateau of Colosseum Mountain.

North Ridge. Class 3. Follow the Sierra crest south from Armstrong Col. There are many knife edges on this ridge, and care must be used to ensure that the easiest route is followed. The final part of the climb leaves the north ridge on its east side and ascends a small bowl to the summit plateau.

Peak 3578m   11,765 ft;
1.5 mi NNE of Mount Perkins

The southwest ridge, which is class 2, was first climbed by Fred L. Jones on July 31, 1948. An ascent from Division Creek is class 3; this was first climbed by Jones on May 11, 1951. He descended via the class 2 chute on the northeast face.

Further Reading: John Moynier. *Backcountry Skiing in the High Sierra.* Evergreen, Colo.: Chockstone Press, 1992, p. 170.

Mount Perkins   3830 m; 12,591 ft
South Ridge. Class 2. Follow the Sierra crest north from Armstrong Col.

West Slope. Class 2 from the John Muir Trail north of Twin Lakes.

North Ridge. Class 2. First ascent 1972 by Dave King. First winter ascent March 1978 by Brian West and Sam Roberts. Gain the north ridge from Armstrong Canyon, then follow the ridge to the summit.

Mount Wynne   4017 m; 13,179 ft
First ascent 1935 by a Sierra Club party. The west ridge from Pinchot Pass is class 2, as is the southeast slope.

East Ridge. Class 2. First ascent August 15, 1972 by Natalie Smith, Dick Beach, Elton Fletcher, Gordon MacLeod, and Jerry Keating. This was done as a one-day round trip from the end of the road in Armstrong Canyon.

North Ridge. Class 3. First winter ascent December 29, 1990 by Doug Mantle. The traverse from Mount Pinchot goes best by staying on top of the ridge that connects both peaks, with some detours on each side of the crest.

Mount Pinchot   4113 m; 13,495 ft
South Ridge. Class 3. The traverse from Mount Wynne involves some loose rock. It is best to stay on top of the ridge, making minor variations onto the sides of the crest when necessary.

Southwest Chute. Class 2. First ascent June 30, 1996 by R. J. Secor. This chute leads to the lower, western summit of Mount Pinchot. Traverse across the north side of the ridge to the higher, eastern summit.

East Ridge. Class 2. First winter ascent December 29, 1990 by Doug Mantle.

Peak 4043m   13,259 ft;
0.6 mi S of Striped Mountain

First ascent September 26, 1965 by Ed Lane and Gary Lewis, via the class 3 north face. The class 2 east ridge from Goodale Creek was climbed June 9, 1968 by Tom Ross, Ellen Siegal, Bill Schuler, and Andy Smatko.

Peak 3905m   12,720 ft+;
0.9 mi SW of Striped Mountain

First ascent July 23, 1939 by Madi Bacon and Tom Noble, via an unknown route. The northwest ridge is class 3. The class 3 east face was climbed by Tom Ross, Bill Schuler, and Andy Smatko on September 13, 1970.

Striped Mountain   (4017 m; 13,120 ft+)
From Taboose Pass. Class 2. First ascent July 1905 by George Davis. First winter ascent February 20, 1995 by Bob Rockwell, Tom Sakai, Daryl Hinman, and R. J. Secor. Head southeast from Taboose Pass to the cirque between Striped Mountain and Goodale Mountain. Climb the northeast slope to the summit.

West Ridge. Class 2. First ascent August 1, 1948 by Fred L. Jones. This ridge is most easily climbed on its northern side.

From Goodale Creek. Class 2. First ascent August 11, 1948 by Fred L. Jones. Climb to the saddle between

Striped Mountain and Goodale Mountain from Goodale Creek. Ascend the east slope of the peak to the summit. This route was originally climbed from the Woods Creek drainage, which crosses the Sierra crest east of Peak 4043m (13,259 ft); this variation is class 3.

Goodale Mountain   3893 m; 12,790 ft

West Slope. Class 2. First ascent July 23, 1939 by Norman Clyde, Allan MacRae, and Albion J. Whitney. First winter ascent January 12, 1969 by Jim Jenkins, Art Wester, and Ed Lane. Climb to the saddle between Goodale Mountain and Striped Mountain from either Taboose Pass or Goodale Creek. The summit block is class 3.

East Slope. Class 2. This is a long climb from the Owens Valley. The starting point is between Taboose Creek and Goodale Creek.

Peak 3744m   12,285 ft;
0.8 mi NW of Goodale Mountain

The class 3 west face of this peak was climbed on September 18, 1970 by Andy Smatko, Bill Schuler, and Tom Ross.

WRINKLES

Alternatives to Kearsarge Pass. Kearsarge Pass is the easiest crossing of the Sierra crest in this region, and it receives the bulk of the traffic; impact on both the east and west sides is severe and there are a lot of domesticated bears. North Dragon Pass is a difficult cross-country route suitable only for experienced mountaineers, and the bighorn sheep restrictions make it legally impassable between July 1 and December 15. Baxter Pass is the most pleasant of the other three high passes, with water over most of its 8 miles (to the summit) and 6,300 feet of gain; this trail also has the most shade. Sawmill Pass starts in the desert and climbs a long way before reaching water; but Sawmill Meadow and Sawmill Lake may balance out the discomfort suffered during the start of this 10-mile, 6,761-foot hike. Taboose Pass is the shortest of the three trails leading to the Sierra crest (6¼ miles, 5,972 feet of gain), but it seems to be in the desert all the way to the summit of the pass. On the other hand, the view from the summit is outstanding, and it will rejuvenate any hiker who has just ascended its barren east side.

Monarch Divide and the Cirque Crest

The words "Kings Canyon" may bring to mind images of the great valley along the South Fork of the Kings River, the village of Cedar Grove, and the hordes of car campers who traveled there by driving along Highway 180. But there is another great valley to the north that few people ever see. This is the Middle Fork of the Kings River—a wild, roadless area, with difficult access. If Kings Canyon is the rival of Yosemite Valley, then the Middle Fork of the Kings River is the rival of Kings Canyon. The Middle and South Forks are separated by a great ridge that extends westward from the Sierra crest at Mount Bolton Brown and Mather Pass. This ridge is known by two names: the Monarch Divide and the Cirque Crest.

This region is bounded by Sentinel Ridge on the south, the South Fork of the Kings River on the east, Palisade Creek on the north, and the Middle Fork of the Kings River on the west. The rock climbs in Kings Canyon itself are not described here. They are covered in the excellent book, *Southern Sierra Rock Climbing: Sequoia/Kings Canyon*, by Greg Vernon, Sally Moser, and David Hickey (Evergreen, Colo.: Chockstone Press, 1993).

HISTORY

The Monarch Divide proved to be an impassable barrier to the California Geological Survey in 1864. After their adventures on Mount Brewer and Mount Tyndall, survey members moved north in an attempt to climb Mount Goddard. Their pack animals were unable to descend the north side of the divide to the Middle Fork of the Kings River, however, so they moved east up Bubbs Creek and temporarily left the High Sierra via Kearsarge Pass.

The shepherds moved into this area in the 1870s and created the Granite Pass Trail across the Monarch Di-

vide to reach the ample pasturage available in the vast Middle Fork drainage. Bolton Brown followed this trail in 1895, and ascended Mount Ruskin and crossed Cartridge Pass before returning to Kings Canyon via the South Fork of the Kings River.

The rock towers of the Grand Dike and in the Gorge of Despair were first climbed in the early 1950s. Few parties visit these areas, and there has been comparatively little exploratory climbing in this region. There are still unclimbed spires and pinnacles in the gorges branching away from the crest of the Monarch Divide.

MAPS

USGS. *7.5-minute series:* The Sphinx, Cedar Grove, Wren Peak, Tehipite Dome, Slide Bluffs, Marion Peak, Mt. Pinchot, Split Mtn., North Palisade. *National park maps:* Sequoia and Kings Canyon National Parks and Vicinity (1:125,000). *30 x 60–minute series:* Bishop, Mount Whitney.

USFS. A Guide to the John Muir Wilderness and the Sequoia–Kings Canyon Wilderness (1:63,360).

Tom Harrison Cartography. Kings Canyon High Country.

Map Link 15-minute series. Marion Peak, Tehipite Dome, Mt. Goddard, Big Pine, Mt. Pinchot.

Wilderness Press 15-minute series. Mt. Goddard, Mt. Pinchot.

ROADS

Kings Canyon Highway (Highway 180)

The Kings Canyon Highway goes east from Fresno and enters Kings Canyon National Park near Wilsonia

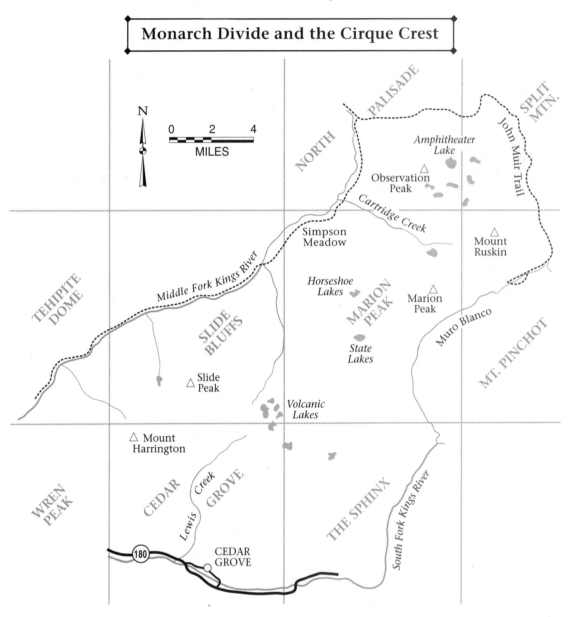

Monarch Divide and the Cirque Crest

and Grant Grove. From the junction with the Generals Highway, the Kings Canyon Highway turns north, passes by Wilsonia, passes through Grant Grove Village, and then leaves Kings Canyon National Park. The road is open year-round as far as the turnoff to Hume Lake, 7.5 miles from its junction with the Generals High-

way. Beyond this point, the road is closed from late October or early November to approximately the first week of May.

The Kings Canyon Highway descends into Kings Canyon and goes east, following the South Fork of the Kings River to reenter Kings Canyon National Park

36.1 miles from the junction with the Generals Highway. The road continues another 1.1 miles to Cedar Grove, which features campgrounds, a ranger station, a lodge, and a grocery store. Kings Canyon Highway continues another 5.8 miles to Road's End, the trailhead for the Woods Creek Trail, and the Granite Pass Trail.

TRAILS

Deer Cove Trail 5 miles

A non-quota trail; in fact, at time of writing, a wilderness permit was not required to visit the Sequoia National Forest section of the Monarch Wilderness. Those who plan to enter the Sequoia–Kings Canyon Wilderness from the Monarch Wilderness must obtain a wilderness permit from Sequoia and Kings Canyon National Parks. The trailhead for this trail is 35.1 miles from the Generals Highway on Highway 180, approximately 1 mile west of the national park boundary (0 mi; 4,400 ft+). The trail climbs the north side of Kings Canyon and crosses Deer Cove Creek (1½ mi; 5,600 ft+) and continues to Deer Cove Saddle (1½ mi; 6,520 ft+). The trail continues its climb, with excellent views, passing Wildman Meadow (bears prowl through this area) to a trail junction (2 mi; 7,640 ft+). The trail on the left heads west for 4 miles to its end just beyond Happy Gap and serves as the approach to the upper end of the Grand Dike. The Deer Cove Trail continues its climb and soon meets another trail on top of the ridge serving as the Kings Canyon National Park boundary (¼ mi; 7,800 ft+). The side trail leads right to Frypan Meadow, while the Deer Cove Trail continues to another trail junction (½ mi; 8,000 ft+). The right branch leads to Frypan Meadow and the Kennedy Canyon Trail, while the left branch continues its climb to eventually disappear above Grizzly Lakes (3¾ mi; 9,800 ft+).

Don Cecil Trail 6 miles

A non-quota trail. The Don Cecil Trail leads from the floor of Kings Canyon to the saddle just south of Lookout Peak on the south rim of the canyon. (A splendid view of Kings Canyon is available from the top of Lookout Peak.) This hike is mostly downhill when begun from Summit Meadow at the end of the Big Meadow/Horse Corral Meadow Road (described in Chapter 3,

The Kaweahs and the Great Western Divide). The following description starts on the floor of Kings Canyon at Cedar Grove.

Head south from the Cedar Grove Ranger Station and cross the Kings Canyon Highway (0 mi; 4,600 ft+). The trail climbs through the forest and soon crosses a dirt road, and then continues its ascent to Sheep Creek. It crosses the creek on a bridge and climbs to the west fork of Sheep Creek. In this area the trail passes through some beautiful flower gardens with views across the canyon to the Monarch Divide; Mount Clarence King dominates the up-canyon view. The trail climbs to a ridge before turning south across the east side of Lookout Peak to the saddle south of the peak. At the saddle, the trail meets the Big Meadows/Horse Corral Meadow Road (5½ mi; 7,960 ft+). A trail leads from here to the top of Lookout Peak, which has an outstanding view of Kings Canyon (½ mi; 8,480 ft+).

Kennedy Canyon Trail 18 miles

A quota trail. This is also known as the Lewis Creek and Kennedy Pass Trails. This long, hard hike is made bearable by the sound of Lewis Creek, ample forest cover, wildflowers in meadows, and changing views of the High Sierra as you gain elevation from the floor of Kings Canyon.

The preferred starting point for this trail is where Lewis Creek crosses the Kings Canyon Highway, approximately 1½ miles west of Cedar Grove (0 mi; 4,560 ft+). (The alternate route is the Hotel Creek Trail, which starts at Cedar Grove, makes a steep 4-mile ascent of the north wall of Kings Canyon, and then descends to meet the Lewis Creek Trail.) The trail makes a steep ascent of the west bank of Lewis Creek to meet the Hotel Creek Trail (2 mi; 5,640 ft+) and continues climbing to the north to Frypan Meadow (4 mi; 7,800 ft+). Bears prowl through this area. The Kennedy Canyon Trail goes east from Frypan Meadow. It gradually turns northeast and then north on the final climb to the top of Kennedy Pass (4 mi; 10,800 ft+), where there is an outstanding view. The trail descends the north side of the pass to Kennedy Canyon, passing through its meadows to the east bank of Kennedy Creek (4 mi; 8,520 ft+). The trail climbs onto Dead Pine Ridge and traverses south along the ridge before turning east and descending to Volcanic Lakes (2½ mi; 9,600 ft+). It climbs out of this basin on the eastern side and descends to the middle fork of

Dougherty Creek, where it meets the Granite Pass Trail (1½ mi; 9,520 ft+), 2½ miles north of Granite Pass.

Granite Pass Trail   23 miles

A quota trail. This trail is also known as the Copper Creek or Simpson Meadow Trail. It goes from the floor of Kings Canyon over the Monarch Divide at Granite Pass to beautiful Simpson Meadow. The strenuousness of this hike is made up for by the rewarding views available from both sides of the Monarch Divide. Bears are active all along this trail.

The trailhead is at Road's End of the Kings Canyon Highway (0 mi; 5,040 ft+). The trail goes north on the western side of Copper Creek, then climbs to Lower Tent Meadow (4 mi; 7,825 ft), where there are a few level campsites. It continues its climb, passes the even steeper Upper Tent Meadow, goes over a ridge (to 10,347 ft), and descends to the first level terrain at Granite Basin (5½ mi; 10,000 ft+). Wood campfires are prohibited in Granite Basin. The trail goes north to a junction with a trail that leads to Granite Lake (1½ mi; 10,080 ft+). The trail continues north to Granite Pass (1 mi; 10,674 ft) and descends the north side of the pass to meet the Kennedy Canyon Trail (2½ mi; 9,520 ft+), which provides access to Volcanic Lakes. Continuing north, a trail branches off to the west (½ mi; 9,480 ft+), descending to the Lake of the Fallen Moon. The trail makes a short, steep climb (to 9,800 ft+) and then meets the State Lakes Trail (½ mi; 9,640 ft+). The trail to Simpson Meadow descends toward the north and leads to Dougherty Meadow (to 9,480 ft+), from where a short ascent meets the Horseshoe Lakes Trail (1 mi; 9,920 ft+). The Granite Pass Trail goes north from this junction and descends the crest of the ridge between Dougherty Creek and Horseshoe Creek to Simpson Meadow, along the Middle Fork of the Kings River (6½ mi; 5,960 ft+).

State Lakes Trail and Horseshoe Lakes Trail   7 miles

This trail leaves the Granite Pass Trail 3½ miles north of Granite Pass (0 mi; 9,640 ft+). It goes east to the lower State Lake (2 mi; 10,250 ft), where wood campfires are prohibited. The trail turns north, passes the upper State Lake, and then turns west to a junction (2 mi; 10,480 ft+). From here, the Horseshoe Lakes Trail goes north to Horseshoe Lakes (1 mi; 10,480 ft+); the other trail

goes west to meet the Granite Pass Trail (2 mi; 9,920 ft+), 5 miles above Simpson Meadow.

The Middle Fork Trail   8½ miles

The description of this trail from Crown Valley to Simpson Meadow is given in Chapter 7, Kettle Ridge and The LeConte Divide. From Simpson Meadow (0 mi; 5,960 ft+), the trail ascends the Middle Fork of the Kings River on the south bank to meet the last traces of the Cartridge Pass Trail just north of where it crosses Cartridge Creek (4¼ mi; 6,400 ft+). The trail continues north, passing through the narrow canyon with many small waterfalls, to meet the John Muir Trail on the north side of Palisade Creek (4¼ mi; 8,040 ft+). The bridge across Palisade Creek is missing, making the crossing of Palisade Creek a hazardous and difficult undertaking.

CROSS-COUNTRY ROUTES

"Harrington Pass"   10,680 ft+; 10,640 ft+;
0.5 mi NE of Mount Harrington; UTM 459824

Class 2. This pass is also known as "Despair Pass." It is the approach to the Gorge of Despair. After reaching Frypan Meadow via the Kennedy Canyon Trail, take the west branch of the trail. This leads to Grizzly Lakes after 4 miles. Head northwest from the lakes to the high pass immediately northeast of Mount Harrington. Descend the Gorge of Despair on the northeastern side of the stream. (It is really difficult to descend the Gorge of Despair its entire distance to the Middle Fork of the Kings River due to some huge cliffs and waterfalls. But this has been done; the team that did it wore wet suits in addition to using rock climbing gear.) *Variation:* The Gorge of Despair has also been reached by crossing the Monarch Divide just west of Hogback Peak. Traverse west across the northern side of the divide to the upper part of the Gorge of Despair.

Further Reading: H. Warren Lewis. *You're Standing on My Fingers!* Berkeley, Calif.: Howell-North Books, 1969, pp. 188–202.

"Gimme Pass"   10,440 ft+; 10,400 ft+;
0.6 mi S of Slide Peak

This class 2 pass leads between Lost and Slide Canyons north of the Monarch Divide.

"Grouse Lake Pass" 11,040 ft+; 11,040 ft+;
0.5 mi N of Grouse Lake

Class 2. This pass, immediately northeast of Peak 11,320ft+ (11,354 ft), is the first pass crossed as part of a cross-country route between upper Copper Creek and State Lakes. Leave the Granite Pass Trail at approximately 10,300 feet, just below the lip of Granite Basin. Ascend the west side of Copper Creek to the meadow at the south shore of Grouse Lake. Cross the outlet of the lake, and circle the lake on its east shore. The south side of the pass is easy, but there are talus blocks on the north side.

Further Reading: Steve Roper. *Sierra High Route.* Seattle: The Mountaineers Books, 1997, pp. 90–91, 104.

"Goat Crest Saddle" 11,440 ft+; 11,440 ft+;
1.5 mi NE of Granite Pass

Class 1. This pass is also known as "Goat Pass." It is between Peaks 11,822ft and 12,000ft+ (11,797 ft and 12,059 ft). The south side of the pass is easy, but careful routefinding is needed on the upper portion of the northern side of the pass. It is best to begin the descent to Glacier Valley well to the west of the lowest of the Glacier Lakes.

Further Reading: Steve Roper. *Sierra High Route.* Seattle: The Mountaineers Books, 1997, pp. 91–92, 104.

"Glacier Saddle" 11,240 ft+; 11,200 ft+;
2.0 mi SW of Dougherty Peak

Class 2. This pass extends from Glacier Lakes to the north fork of Kid Creek.

Further Reading: John Moynier. *Backcountry Skiing in the High Sierra.* Evergreen, Colo.: Chockstone Press, 1992, p. 68.

"State Peak Ridge" 12,080 ft+; 12,000 ft+;
0.4 mi NE of State Peak

Class 2. This steep pass has been used on ski tours of the Cirque Crest.

Further Reading: John Moynier. *Backcountry Skiing in the High Sierra.* Evergreen, Colo.: Chockstone Press, 1992, p. 68.

"Cirque Ridge" 11,840 ft+ ; 11,920 ft+;
0.8 mi SSW of Marion Peak; UTM 643897

Class 2–3. This "pass" actually crosses the steep southeast ridge of Peak 12,400ft+ (12,400 ft+). The easi-

est crossing is a little further southeast than what would be expected from studying the Marion Peak 7½-minute quadrangle.

Further Reading: John Moynier. *Backcountry Skiing in the High Sierra.* Evergreen, Colo.: Chockstone Press, 1992, p. 68.

"Gray Pass" 10,760 ft+; 10,000 ft+;
2.8 mi ESE of Windy Peak

Class 1. Gray Pass, White Pass, and Red Pass are the three passes used on the cross-country route between Horseshoe Lakes and Marion Lake. From Horseshoe Lakes hike north, past the largest Horseshoe Lake, to the steep slope that drops into Windy Canyon. Go northeast from this point, crossing the crest of Windy Ridge, and descend to the small lake at UTM 605918. Traverse east along a small bench from the pond to Gray Pass, which overlooks the south fork of Cartridge Creek. Descend the southeast side of the pass by means of a shallow, grassy gully to the stream at the bottom of this canyon.

Further Reading: Steve Roper. *Sierra High Route.* Seattle: The Mountaineers Books, 1997, pp. 94, 104.

"White Pass" 11,680 ft+; 11,680 ft+;
0.7 mi NW of Marion Peak

Class 2. The western approach to this pass starts where the description for Gray Pass ends. Continue up the stream a short distance to a round lake. Head east-northeast from the lake to the basin immediately northwest of Marion Peak. White Pass is the almost-level saddle low on Marion Peak's northwest ridge; the saddle is marked by white talus. From the top of the pass, climb the ridge leading toward Marion Peak a very short distance in order to bypass a small cliff on the north side of the pass. Make a level traverse to the east across talus before making a gradual descent through some loose chutes until you are immediately west of and below Red Pass.

Further Reading: Steve Roper. *Sierra High Route.* Seattle: The Mountaineers Books, 1997, pp. 94–95, 104.

"Red Pass" 11,560 ft+; 11,600 ft+;
0.2 mi S of Red Point

Class 2. After traversing and descending from White Pass, climb the easy but loose western side of Red Pass to its summit. Descend the eastern side of the pass and head toward Marion Lake. There is a cliff above the southwestern side of Marion Lake; this is bypassed by means of a gully on its northern side.

Further Reading: Steve Roper. *Sierra High Route.* Seattle: The Mountaineers Books, 1997, pp. 94–95, 104.

"Marion Pass"   12,040 ft+; 12,080 ft+;
0.5 mi ENE of Marion Peak

Class 2. This pass leads from Lake Basin to the southeast side of Cirque Crest.

Further Reading: John Moynier. *Backcountry Skiing in the High Sierra.* Evergreen, Colo.: Chockstone Press, 1992, p. 68.

"Pete's Col"   3520 m+; 11,520 ft+;
0.7 mi SW of Cartridge Pass; UTM 669922

Class 3. This pass, named here in honor of Pete Yamagata, is a shortcut across the Cirque Crest from the basin south of Cartridge Pass to Marion Lake. It has been used while making the Ruskin-Marion traverse. The east side of the pass is easy; the west side features loose class 3 rock and sand.

Cartridge Pass   3560 m+; 11,680 ft+

Some maps may show a trail leading up Cartridge Creek, going over Cartridge Pass, and descending to the South Fork of the Kings River. But this trail has not been maintained for more than fifty years—if it was ever maintained at all. This is an old sheep route which was once the route for the John Muir Trail, until the trail was constructed up Palisade Creek and over Mather Pass in 1938. The Cartridge Pass "Trail" is for all intents and purposes a difficult cross-country route. On a more positive note, this route takes the hiker to beautiful Marion Lake, Lake Basin, and the unnamed lakes on the bench south of Cartridge Pass.

Leave the Middle Fork Trail approximately ¼ mile north of Cartridge Creek and ascend the brushy north side of the stream. Climb a steep, broken cliff to the north of Triple Falls, then cross to the south side of Cartridge Creek. Stay on the south side for about ¼ mile, then cross to the north side; stay on the north side for about 1 mile before crossing back to the south side again. Difficult cross-country travel leads you across the outlet stream of Marion Lake and up to the lower part of Lake Basin. For the easiest approach to Marion Lake, traverse south across the lowest bench in Lake Basin.

Anyone who is in this area should not miss a visit to this beautiful lake.

After the climb through the brush, dust, and loose talus of Cartridge Creek, the meadows and lakes of Lake Basin may at first appear to be mirages. The route follows the north shores of the lakes to the highest lake in the basin, which is located north of Cartridge Pass. From the eastern shore of this lake go south, first ascending a steep cliff with loose rock and then an easier talus slope, to the top of Cartridge Pass. Descend the south side of the pass over talus past a small lake to the larger lake at the south end of the bench below. Skirt the eastern shore of this lake and descend to the South Fork of the Kings River, keeping to the east of the outlet stream. You can either ascend the South Fork to the John Muir Trail (easier) or descend Muro Blanco (harder). (See the description of Muro Blanco in Chapter 5, The High Passes.)

"Vennacher Col"   3780 m+; 12,320 ft+;
0.2 mi S of Vennacher Needle

Class 3. This pass has also been referred to as "Upper Basin Pass." It provides access between Lake Basin and the John Muir Trail in Upper Basin. From the lake north of Cartridge Pass in Lake Basin, ascend the stream that leads to the cirque southwest of Vennacher Needle. Ascend a steep, loose chute to a point about 100 feet below the top of the pass. The class 3 section that follows is best climbed via a left-ascending traverse so that the pass is crossed just north of the actual low point. Descend the east side of the pass and follow the stream southeastward to meet the John Muir Trail east of Mount Ruskin and The Saddlehorn.

Further Reading: Steve Roper. *Sierra High Route.* Seattle: The Mountaineers Books, 1997, p. 105.

"Frozen Lake Pass"   3760 m+; 12,320 ft+;
2.1 mi SW of Mather Pass; UTM 682964

Class 2–3; ice axe required. This pass has also been called "Lake Basin Pass." This is the direct cross-country route between Lake Basin and Upper Basin. From Lake Basin, ascend to Lake 3540m+ (11,600 ft+) in the cirque northwest of Vennacher Needle. Climb steep talus to the left-hand notch visible to the northeast. Descend the steep, loose northeast side of the pass to the permanent snowfield below. Pass the frozen lake and then make a diagonal descent through a

Lake Basin and Vicinity

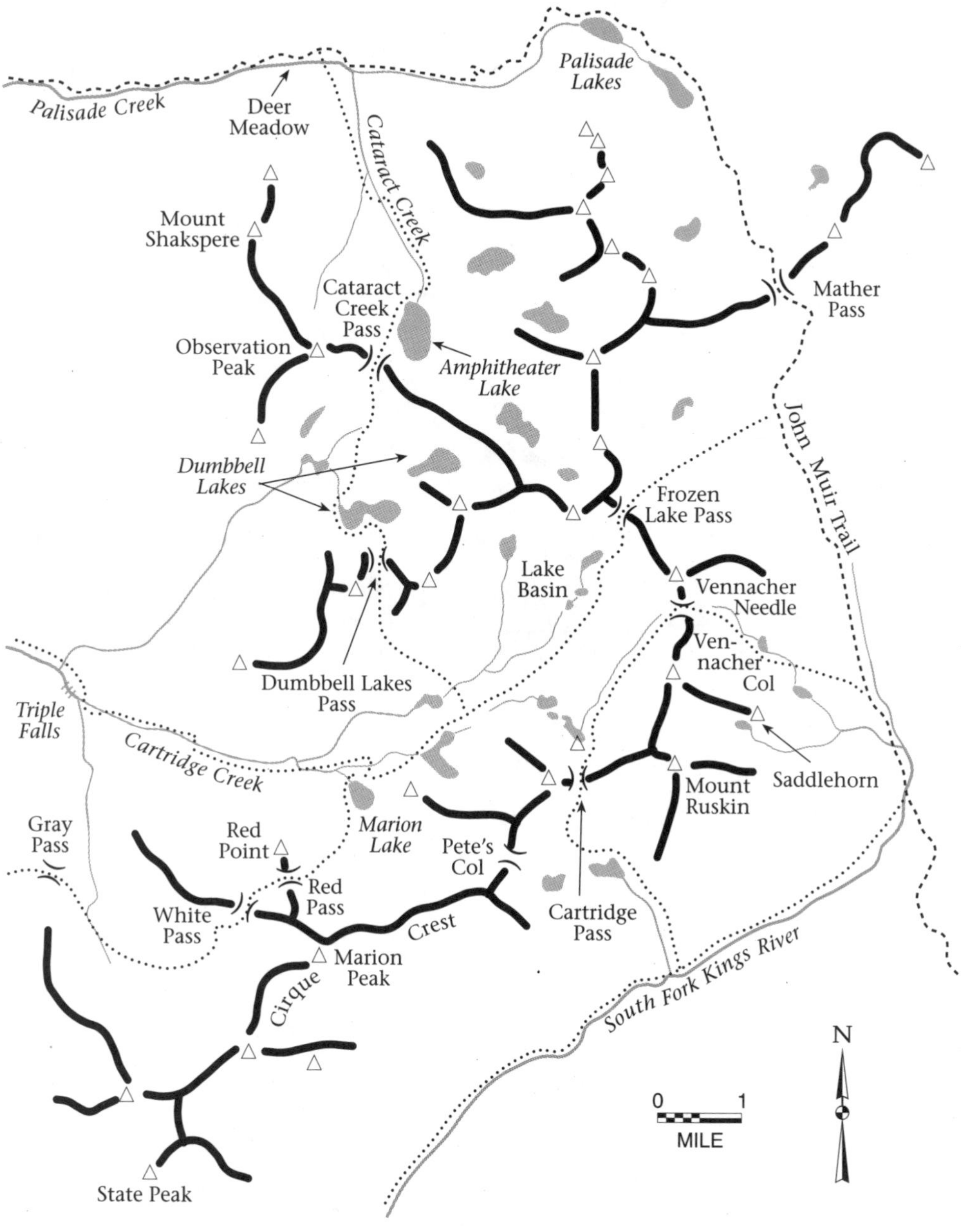

Palisade Creek

Deer Meadow

Palisade Lakes

Cataract Creek

Mount Shakspere

Cataract Creek Pass

Mather Pass

Observation Peak

Amphitheater Lake

John Muir Trail

Dumbbell Lakes

Frozen Lake Pass

Lake Basin

Vennacher Needle

Vennacher Col

Dumbbell Lakes Pass

Saddlehorn

Triple Falls

Cartridge Creek

Mount Ruskin

Gray Pass

Red Point

Marion Lake

Pete's Col

White Pass

Red Pass

Crest

Cartridge Pass

Marion Peak

Cirque

South Fork Kings River

State Peak

0   1
MILE

N

Vennacher Needle and Frozen Lake Pass from Upper Basin. Photo by R. J. Secor.

steep talus slope to nearly perfectly round Lake 3500 m+ (11,520 ft+) in Upper Basin. Easy cross-country travel east across Upper Basin leads to the John Muir Trail south of Mather Pass.

Further Reading: Steve Roper. *Sierra High Route.* Seattle: The Mountaineers Books, 1997, pp. 96–98, 103.

"Dumbbell Lakes Pass"   11,640 ft+; 11,680 ft+; 1.5 mi N of Marion Lake; UTM 652954

Class 2. Also called "Dumbbell Pass" and "Sheep Pass," this is the direct cross-country route between Lake Basin and Dumbbell Lakes. It is necessary to pass Lake 11,108ft (11,120 ft+) on its western shore.

The Dumbbell Lakes basin can also be reached from Cartridge Creek by following the stream that drains Dumbbell Lakes. Leave Cartridge Creek downstream from Triple Falls and remain on the southeast side of the stream all of the way up.

"Cataract Creek Pass"   11,520 ft+; 11,520 ft+; 0.4 mi ESE of Observation Peak; UTM 652982

Class 2. This pass has also been called "Observation Pass." At one time there was a trail up Cataract Creek to Amphitheater Lake, but it has long been abandoned. Leave the John Muir Trail at Deer Meadow, ford Palisade Creek, and hike through the forest west of Cataract Creek. The route eventually follows the west bank of the creek and crosses a tributary stream uphill from a small lake. The route then crosses to the east bank of Cataract Creek. Easy cross-country hiking in the upper part of Cataract Creek leads to Amphitheater Lake.

From the north side of Amphitheater Lake, hop over talus on its western shore to where it is possible to make a diagonal ascent to the southwest. Cataract Creek Pass may be blocked by a snow cornice; this can be passed by climbing above the level of the pass on its northern side.

Further Reading: *Summit.* Summer 1994, pp. 84–85.

PEAKS

The rock climbs in Kings Canyon are described by Greg Vernon, Sally Moser, and David Hickey in *Southern Sierra Rock Climbing: Sequoia/Kings Canyon* (Evergreen, Colo.: Chockstone Press, 1993).

Grand Dike
8,600 ft+-7,440 ft+

This impressive ridge contains many jagged towers. The Grand Dike is on the north side of Kings Canyon; the best approach is from the Deer Cove Trail. The towers are numbered starting from the lower, southeastern end of the ridge.

"Tower No. ½"   7,440 ft+; 7,520 ft+; UTM 450772
This small pinnacle is on the south side of Tower No. 1.
Northwest Face. I, 5.3. First ascent November 26, 1954 by Kim Malville, John Ohrenschall, and Richard Smyth. From the notch immediately south of Tower No. 1, descend to the southwest and go through a keyhole formed by a chockstone. Climb a small ledge on the face of Tower No. 1 and climb to the top of the chockstone. Crossover to the northeast side of Tower No. ½ and traverse a ledge on the northwest face to the base of a small chimney. Rope up here, then climb the chimney to the summit, passing a chockstone on its right side. Descend via rappel over the southeast corner of the tower.
East Face. Class 5. First ascent August 11, 1956 by John Ohrenschall and Russ Hoopes. From the notch between Tower No. 1 and Tower No. ½, traverse onto the east face, and climb it to the summit.

"Tower No. 1"   7,560 ft+; 7,680 ft+; UTM 449772
First ascent July 28, 1951 by David Hammack and Anton Nelson. Climb the east face of Tower No. 2 for about 70 feet to a broad, horizontal ledge (avoid the diagonal ledge). The horizontal ledge leads to the notch between Towers No. 1 and No. 2. Traverse out onto the west face from the notch, then climb the class 4 west face to the summit. The horizontal ledge can also be reached from the notch between Towers No. 2 and No. 3 by following a wide ledge.

"Tower No. 2"   7,480 ft+; 7,680 ft+; UTM 449773
East Face. Class 4. First ascent July 28, 1951 by David Hammack and Anton Nelson. Climb a class 4 chimney from the broad ledge that leads across the east face of the tower.
Northwest Face. Class 4. First ascent August 12, 1956 by John Ohrenschall and Russ Hoopes. From the notch between Towers No. 2 and No. 3, climb a chimney on the northwest face to the summit.

"Tower No. 3"   7,760 ft+; 7,760 ft+; UTM 448774
Southeast Face. I, 5.5. First ascent July 28, 1951 by Anton Nelson and David Hammack. From the notch between Towers No. 2 and No. 3, traverse across the southeast face. When difficulties increase, go up and back to the right on a steep face with good holds to a large ledge. Go left and climb the northwest corner of the tower. This leads to the crux of the climb: a 70° face with few holds. Climb this on its right side to an undercling. The next pitch, which leads to the summit, is easy. *Variation:* I, 5.4. First ascent November 27, 1954 by Kim Malville, John Ohrenschall, and Richard Smyth. Traverse across the southeast face to a ledge with a tree on it. Climb the tree to get started, then go toward some bushes. Traverse to the right around a corner and climb to the summit.

"Tower No. 4"   7,720 ft; 7,680 ft; UTM 448775
Northeast Face. I, 5.3. First ascent June 15, 1952 by David Hammack, Bob Smith, George Larimore, and Bob Purington. Ascend a large chimney on the northeast face for 30 feet. Traverse to the right onto the face and climb to some small ledges. Continue straight up and then traverse slightly left to a large, detached flake. Climb the flake and the face above it on good holds. Ascend a tight chimney to a ledge with a tree. Continue climbing the face to the north shoulder. A class 3 pitch leads to the summit from here. The best descent route is a 110-foot rappel from the shoulder to the notch between Towers No. 4 and No. 5.

"Tower No. 5"   7,760 ft+; 7,760 ft+; UTM 447776
Southeast Face. Class 4. First ascent July 28, 1951 by Anton Nelson and David Hammack. Climb the broken southeast face from the notch between Towers No. 4 and No. 5. The only difficult section of the face is about halfway up, where a short, slightly overhanging wall must be climbed to get out of an alcove. Follow the main arête to the summit.

North Face. Class 3. First ascent November 27, 1954 by Kim Malville, John Ohrenschall, and Richard Smyth.

"Tower No. 6" 7,928 ft; 7,929 ft

First ascent July 28, 1951 by Anton Nelson and David Hammack. The face above the notch between Towers No. 5 and No. 6 is blocked by an overhang, which is overcome by descending the west side of the notch for about 30 feet and climbing a small tree. Traverse across the wall to easier climbing. Continue up the face to the summit.

The north side of this tower is class 3.

"Tower No. 7" 8,560 ft+;
8,400 ft+; UTM 442784

"Tower No. 8" 8,600 ft+;
8,400 ft+; UTM 442785

Both of these towers were first climbed July 28, 1951 by Anton Nelson and David Hammack. They are easily climbed by class 2 and class 3 routes.

Mount Harrington 11,009 ft; 11,005 ft

North Ridge. Class 3. First ascent July 27, 1951 by David Hammack and Anton Nelson. This short but steep climb has many excellent holds. And there is a great view from the summit.

The south arête, which is class 4, was first climbed

by Arkel Erb and friend. There is also a class 3 route on the west face.

The Gorge of Despair

This outstanding rock-climbing area is hard to get to, so solitude is easy to find in the gorge. The rock on these towers, which features many knobs, horns, and chickenheads, is similar to that found on the south face of Charlotte Dome.

Further Reading: H. Warren Lewis. *You're Standing on My Fingers!* Berkeley: Howell-North Books, 1969, pp. 188–202.

"Bushmaster"

This pinnacle is above The Python, along the Silver Spur.

Northwest Ridge. I, 5.4. First ascent June 1991 by Bart O'Brien and Peter Cummings. Follow the ridge from The Python for two pitches.

"The Python" 9,936 ft; 9,840 ft+; UTM 439831

Class 2 from Fang Turret; class 4 from the south. First ascent June 1955 by Fred Martin, Kim Malville, and Robert Tambling.

"Fang Turret"

This 75-foot rock spire is just east of Silver Turret. *Northeast Notch.* I, 5.7. First ascent July 27, 1951 by

Silver Spur from the north. Photo by R. J. Secor.

Gorge of Despair and Vicinity

Fascination Turret

Frustration Turret

El Corporale
El Comandante

Cobra
Turret

Crystal
Turret

Tehipite
Valley

Kings River

Middle Fork

Gorge of
Despair

Tenderfoot
Peak

Silver
Spur

Silver Turret

Friday's
Folly

Fang Turret

Silver
Maiden

N

Silver Creek

Harrington
Pass

Mount
Harrington

Grizzly
Lakes

0   0.5
MILE

Anton Nelson and David Hammack. First free ascent September 1955 by John Ohrenschall and Russ Hoopes. Ascend vertical cracks on the northeast corner past a bolt and two fixed pitons.

"Silver Turret"   9,880 ft+; 9,913 ft; UTM 435832

This is the most impressive rock formation on the Silver Spur, the ridge serving as the southern boundary of the Gorge of Despair.

Southeast Ridge. Class 4. First ascent July 27, 1951 by David Hammack and Anton Nelson. This is an enjoy-able and straightforward climb from the notch southeast of the rock. Two pitches of easy class 4 are encountered.

West Face. Class 3. First ascent September 1973 by Gary Valle and Phil Warrender. This is a very intricate yet enjoyable route on the west face that leads to the northwest arête near the summit. Careful routefinding is needed to keep the difficulty down to a class 3 level.

North Buttress. III, 5.8, A1. First ascent July 1972 by Mike Cohen and Mort Hempel. This route starts on a slab that gradually steepens. After a few pitches, climb a chimney to the top of an inconspicuous green wall.

Climb up and left to some more chimneys, which lead to an overhang. Ascend the overhang directly and climb several class 4 pitches to the summit. A tension traverse low on the route is the only direct aid on this climb.

Desperadoes. III, 5.12a. First ascent July 1996 by Kris Solem, Guy Keesee, and Chelsea Griffie. Climb the left-arching crack system on the east face. Four pitches (up to 5.11+) end at a hanging belay under the large "monkey face" in the center of the face. The crux fifth pitch climbs a bolted face and a thin crack before moving left under the large roof of the monkey's brow. Three more wandering 5.10 pitches lead to the top.

"Silver Maiden"   9,280 ft+; UTM 436828

This formation is in the Silver Creek drainage, about 500 feet below the notch between Fang Turret and Silver Turret.

Northeast Arête. Class 5 and A. First ascent August 3, 1962 by Bruce Edwards, Howard Lewis, Bob Smith, James Smith, and Ed Sutton. Ascend the broken wall to the edge of the northeast arête. A traverse on the exposed left side of the arête leads to a ledge. The next pitch traverses 50 feet to the south to the base of a prominent rib. Ascend the rib to an alcove under a large block. Ascend the chimney directly above the alcove. This chimney eventually turns into a classic layback, and a bolt and some aid climbing is needed to reach the shoulder just below the summit. A class 4 pitch on large knobs leads to the summit.

Further Reading: H. Warren Lewis. *You're Standing on My Fingers!* Berkeley, Calif.: Howell-North Books, 1969, p. 201.

"Friday's Folly"   9,411 ft; 9,388 ft; UTM 431832

This is the large, wedge-shaped formation west of Silver Turret.

East Face. I, 5.3. First ascent July 8, 1955 by Felix Knauth, Harold Sipperly, and John Whitmer. Climb the overlapping flakes in the middle of the east face.

"Tenderfoot Peak"   10,600 ft+; 10,621 ft; UTM 452836

This gray peak dominates the view from the lake near the head of the Gorge of Despair. First ascent June 1955 by Fred Martin, Kim Malville, and Robert Tambling. The right-hand ridge above the lake is class 2.

Southwest Face. II, 5.6. First ascent 1971 by Steve DeVoto and party. This route ascends the large open book on the face. Climb the book for 80 feet, then traverse right into a gully. Ascend the gully for about 200 feet, traverse left, and climb to the top.

"Crystal Turret"   9,608 ft; 9,520 ft+; UTM 442848

This is the highest crag on the north rim of the Gorge of Despair.

East Face. I, 5.4. First ascent July 25, 1951 by David Hammack and Anton Nelson. From the Gorge of Despair, hike through brush to the notch east of Crystal Turret. Before reaching the notch, ascend a layback crack on the east face. (This crack is about 50 feet left of a "window" below some huge overhanging blocks.) Traverse to the right from the top of the crack to another jam crack. Pass through the window, turn right, and climb an arête to a huge ledge. Go to the far, southern edge of the ledge, then climb the southeast edge of the summit block.

East Buttress. I, 5.7. First ascent August 1971 by Steve DeVoto and Bill Oldfield. This route starts at the notch that is east of Crystal Turret. Climb a patch of dark rock to its end, then traverse to the prow of the buttress. Climb the buttress to the huge ledge just below the summit.

Southwest Face. I, 5.8. First ascent July 1972 by Steve Roper and Tom Gerughty. Climb the obvious chimney that ascends the face diagonally. Most of this route is class 4. A short, difficult section is found in a flared chimney immediately above a big ledge.

"Cobra Turret"   9,097 ft; 9,040 ft; UTM 438849

This is the bulky tower down the ridge from Crystal Turret.

Northwest Face. I, 5.8. First ascent July 26, 1951 by David Hammack and Anton Nelson. Start climbing from the highest point of the forest on the northwest side of the rock. Approximately 75 feet of class 3 climbing leads to a large tree. Go right for 25 feet, then ascend a left-facing corner that leads into the obvious right-facing ramp. Follow the ramp for a rope length past two fixed pins to a belay at two bolts. Continue up the crack, or the knobby face on the left, to the summit.

Direct Northwest Face. I, 5.9. First ascent September 1973 by Phil Warrender and Gary Valle. This route climbs a thin, vertical crack that is about 100 feet to the

Crystal Turret, East Face. Photo by R. J. Secor.

left of the Northwest Face route. Follow the crack to the summit cairn for three pitches of crack and face climbing on large knobs.

Prow of Cobra. III, 5.9. First ascent 1979 by Gary Valle and Phil Warrender. This route ascends the prow of the west buttress of Cobra Turret, passing between the left- and right-facing arches in the middle of the face. A 165-foot rope is needed for this climb. Approach the route by scrambling to the left edge of the prow at its base. Climb up and left to a notch in the first overhang, followed by friction climbing (5.6) up and right to a huge ledge and a belay bolt. Climb a 30-foot-long jam crack and traverse left or right and then up to an obvious knobby area with a rib (5.5) to a two-bolt belay. Go up from this belay to a depression, traverse right and up (5.8) to another knobby area. Eighty feet of easy but unprotected climbing then leads to another bolt belay among some knobs. Continue up on knobs to a large edge, and then move right to a large flake with a fixed pin. Climb over the flake (5.9) to a tiny ledge and step to the right onto the knobby face to a two-bolt belay. The fifth pitch goes up and right at first, then back left to a depression with shallow potholes. Easy climbing leads up for 70 feet (unprotected) to another two-bolt belay at the right edge of the overhang. Overcome the roof on knobs and then go up and right to the Wanderland, an area of huge solution tubs. This pitch ends along the left side of the Wanderland at a single-bolt belay at a large pothole or ledge. Class 4 climbing goes left to a trough that gradually turns into a low-angle cleft, followed by the broken summit arête, which features a few class 5 moves.

From Afar. II, 5.11c. First ascent July 1992 by Kris

Cobra Turret from the southeast. Photo by R. J. Secor.

Solem and Guy Keesee. This two-pitch route on the south face starts to the right of a huge alcove. Climb past three bolts to a crack to a bolted belay stance at the end of the crack. The second pitch goes left and then up another crack.

Descent Route. Walk west 50 feet to two fixed pitons. A 165-foot rappel leads to two bolts. Another 165-foot rappel ends at class 3 rock just above the large tree at the start of the Northwest Face route.

"El Comandante Turret" 8,640 ft+; 8,530 ft; UTM 434854

Hammack-Nelson Route. I, 5.7. First ascent July 25, 1951 by David Hammack and Anton Nelson. There is a large chimney on the south side of the turret which leads to a large ledge. Ascend the chimney for about 30 feet, then traverse left and climb knobs to the large ledge. Follow the ledge up to where it ends, overlooking the north face. Zigzag up the steep face to just below the summit block. A 5.7 friction traverse across the face of the block leads to the southwest corner. Ascend the corner to the summit.

South Chimney. I, 5.6. First ascent July 19, 1952 by a Sierra Club party of nine. Follow the chimney on the south side of the peak to where it ends on the large ledge. Go right to a steep chimney and climb it to its top. Traverse right, then climb a steep layback crack to a ledge just below the summit. A narrow, steep ledge leads to the summit block.

Southwest Face. II, 5.7. First ascent July 1972 by Mort Hempel, Steve Roper, and George Sessions. This route begins on the lower right side of the face at a small, orange dike. Ascend the dike and the face to its left to a slot. Ascend up and left from the top of the slot and follow a left-ascending crack and ledge underneath an overhang. Go to the right above the overhang, then traverse up and right to a sloping belay ledge. A long but easy pitch over many fine knobs leads to a ledge; follow the ledge to where it ends, overlooking the north face. Continue to the summit as described under the Hammack-Nelson Route.

"El Corporale Turret"   8,480 ft+; 8,400 ft+; UTM 433854

This small turret is on the north side of El Comandante Turret.

South Face. Class 4. First ascent July 25, 1951 by David Hammack and Anton Nelson. Climb the gully or the ridge to its left to the summit.

"Frustration Turret"   7,480 ft+; 7,280 ft+; UTM 428855

This turret is about ½ mile from El Comandante Turret.

East Face. II, 5.7, A1. First ascent June 18, 1952 by David Hammack, Jules Eichorn, Clinton Kelley, and Bob Smith. This climb starts from below the notch that separates the turret from the hillside. Go straight up the face for 100 feet to a small tree. Ascend another 15 feet to a small ledge. Traverse across the face to the right, passing underneath an overhanging slab, to a broken shoulder on the northeastern side of the turret. Ascend the shoulder to a large friction ledge above. From the upper end of the ledge ascend a crack/chimney and go right up a steep slab on the northwest corner of the

The northeast rim of the Gorge of Despair. Photo by R. J. Secor.

turret. Climb a vertical jam crack from the slab, then go up and right to a small ledge. Either go left and ascend small holds, or go right and climb a steep trough (using friction) to a narrow ledge under a vertical face about 100 feet below the summit. One or two aid placements in a small crack are needed to overcome a short wall. Continue up and to the left, using hidden holds with long arm pulls. This leads to the northeast shoulder at the summit block. Traverse around the block to its south side and climb to the top.

Two rappels are needed to descend the north face to the large friction ledge. Down climb the route from the ledge to the small tree. One more rappel is needed from the tree.

"Gendarme Turret"

This is the small needle on the ridge between Frustration Turret and Fascination Turret. First ascent June 1955 by Kim Malville, Fred Martin, and Robert Tambling. Descend the steep talus gully leading north from the base of the east face of Frustration Turret. Ascend the first gully rising to the left toward the gendarme. A few aid placements are needed to reach the top.

"Fascination Turret"   7,120 ft+; 7,120 ft+; UTM 427858

This is the last turret on the ridge north of the Gorge of Despair. Its north face drops 3,000 feet to Tehipite Valley.

East Face. Class 3. First ascent June 16, 1955 by Kim Malville, Fred Martin, and Robert Tambling. Descend the steep talus gully leading north from the base of the east face of Frustration Turret. After dropping about 300 vertical feet, contour north to the second gully. Climb over loose rock to the base of the turret. Ascend the east face to the summit.

Hogback Peak   11,080 ft+; 11,077 ft; UTM 473823

Class 2 over huge talus blocks from the saddle to the west. Class 2 from south or east. The west summit is the high point. First ascent September 10, 1955 by John Ohrenschall and James M. Carl.

Slide Peak   10,915 ft; 10,915 ft

First ascent May 29, 1960 by George Whitmore. The east slope is class 1.

Kennedy Mountain   11,433 ft; 11,433 ft

This peak is class 1–2 from Kennedy Pass.

Comb Spur   11,618 ft; 11,618 ft

Class 2. This was traversed by Robert Owen in July 1931.

Mount Hutchings   10,785 ft; 10,785 ft

Class 2 via the north ridge from the Granite Pass Trail. First ascent April 1, 1933 by Norman Clyde and Oliver Kehrlein.

Goat Mountain   12,207 ft; 12,207 ft

First ascent July 22, 1864 by James T. Gardiner and Charles F. Hoffman. The northwest ridge is class 2. The south ridge is class 2–3.

Munger Peak   12,040 ft+; 12,076 ft;
0.5 mi NW of Goat Mountain

The northeast ridge is class 2.

Kid Peak   11,458 ft; 11,458 ft

First ascent July 2, 1940 by a party led by Norman Clyde and David Brower, from Paradise Valley. This was Clyde's *last* first ascent.

This peak can be climbed from Kid Lakes by ascending one of the chutes that lead to a point just west of the summit.

Dougherty Peak   12,241 ft; 12,244 ft

Class 2 from State Lakes. First ascent 1935 by a Sierra Club party.

Further Reading: John Moynier. *Backcountry Skiing in the High Sierra.* Evergreen, Colo.: Chockstone Press, 1992, p. 68.

State Peak   12,620 ft; 12,620 ft

Class 2 from State Lakes. The best route goes up the obvious broad, shallow chute on the northwest side of the peak. The peak is also class 2 from the south and east.

"Windy Point"   11,200 ft+; 11,150 ft;
1.5 mi N of Horseshoe Lakes

This is not a peak, but rather a point from which there is a fantastic view of the Middle Fork of the Kings River. It can be reached easily during the approach to Gray Pass by following the crest of Windy Ridge out to the point. The NPS also recognizes this as a great viewpoint—a line-of-sight radio repeater has been installed on the summit!

Marion Peak   12,719 ft; 12,719 ft

The northeast ridge is class 2 and was first climbed from Marion Lake on July 22, 1902 by Joseph LeConte and Curtis Lindley.

The northwest ridge, rising from White Pass, is class 3. First ascent August 11, 1945 by Art Reyman.

Marion Peak has been climbed down on its southern side; this descent is made directly down to the South Fork of the Kings River. This is class 2, with a lot of nasty brush along the floor of the canyon.

Red Point   11,884 ft; 11,840 ft+

First ascent August 11, 1945 by Art Reyman. Class 1 from Red Pass.

Peak 11,440ft+   11,553 ft; 0.4 mi E of Marion Lake

There is an excellent view from the top of this small peak. First ascent August 6, 1895 by Bolton Brown. It is class 2 from Marion Lake. Ascend to the basin southeast of Marion Lake, and climb talus and slabs toward the northeast to the summit.

Mount Ruskin   3938 m; 12,920 ft

All of the routes on this peak are classic climbs. There is an outstanding view from the summit.

From Cartridge Pass. Class 3. First ascent August 7, 1895 by Bolton Brown. Follow the ridge from the pass to the northwest arête. Either continue along the arête to the summit, or traverse across the west face to the south ridge, and then climb to the top.

Southwest Face. Class 3. First ascent August 13, 1945 by Art Reyman. From the basin south of Cartridge Pass, ascend the southwest face via a rock chute to a point on the south ridge just below the summit. A gendarme along the south ridge is passed on its left (west) side.

East Ridge. Class 3. First ascent 1961 by Andy Smatko, Tom Ross, and Arkel Erb. The best approach onto the crest of the east ridge is from the southeast, from Lake 3500m+ (11,520 ft+). Once on the ridge, follow it to the summit, passing a block near the top on its north side.

North Ridge. Class 4. First ascent August 21, 1997 by Craig Clarence and party, on a traverse from The Saddlehorn.

"The Saddlehorn"   3722 m; 12,080 ft+; 0.5 mi NE of Mount Ruskin

This is the first peak to catch a rock climber's eye from the summit of Taboose Pass. It is frequently mistaken for Vennacher Needle.

East Ridge. Class 4. First ascent July 22, 1939 by Bruce Meyer, Charlotte Mauk, and David Brower. From the base of the east ridge, traverse across the south side of the ridge for about 200 feet. This traverse ends in an area of broken rock. Climb up and over the crest of the east ridge, then ascend a system of ledges to the summit.

South Face. II, 5.8. First ascent May 1972 by Galen Rowell and Steve Roper. Three steep pitches of crack climbing lead to the summit. A shallow crack above an overhang is the crux.

West Ridge. Class 4. First ascent August 21, 1997 by a group led by Craig Clarence. The party traversed to the north ridge of Mount Ruskin.

Vennacher Needle   3961 m; 12,996 ft

This poorly named peak is class 2 from the southeast.

North Arête. III, 5.8. First ascent July 12, 1988 by Galen Rowell. This route begins above a dark, holelike overhang near the base of the wall.

Peak 3855m   12,640 ft+; 0.6 mi NW of Vennacher Needle; UTM 684963

The south ridge and southwest slope are class 2. First ascent September 15, 1970 by Andy Smatko, Bill Schuler, and Tom Ross.

Peak 12,882ft   12,860 ft; 1.6 mi SE of Observation Peak

Southeast Face. Class 3. First ascent August 12, 1945 by Art Reyman. Ascend a chute with loose rocks from the lake southeast of the mountain.

Cyclorama Wall. V, 5.10, A1. First ascent September 1979 by Claude Fiddler, Vern Clevenger, and Galen Rowell. This route climbs the impressive north face of this peak. Start by climbing a difficult crack system. Four 5.10 pitches with some aid and tension traverses lead to a steep dihedral. Follow the dihedral directly to the summit.

Observation Peak   12,362 ft; 12,322 ft

There is a swell view of the Palisades from the summit of Observation Peak. The south slopes from Dumbbell Lakes or Cataract Creek Pass are class 2; first ascent

July 25, 1902 by Joseph LeConte and Curtis Lindley. The northwest ridge is class 2 and was climbed by Marjory Hurd in 1926. The class 2 northeast ridge can be reached from the west branch of Cataract Creek.

Mount Shakspere   12,174 ft; 12,151 ft
First ascent July 20, 1930 by Francis Farquhar, Mary Lou Michaels, Doris Drust, Lorna Kilgariff, and Robert Lipman. Class 2 from Observation Peak. The northwest slopes from Palisade Creek are also class 2.

Windy Cliff   11,151 ft; 11,132 ft
The class 2 east ridge was climbed by Douglas Dooley on August 29, 1970.

Peak 11,998ft   11,948 ft; 0.7 mi ESE of Windy Cliff
The north ridge is class 2–3. First ascent August 29, 1970 by Douglas Dooley.

WRINKLES

Cross-country routes from the Monarch Divide to the Middle Fork of the Kings River. All the canyons that lead north from the Monarch Divide turn into hanging valleys before dropping precipitously into the Middle Fork.

The Saddlehorn from the south. Photo by R. J. Secor.

The only reasonable route is the Granite Pass Trail. The Gorge of Despair has been descended, but it is so hazardous that the party who did so wore wet suits, in addition to rock climbing regalia, to protect them from the cold, running water. A trail leads up and over Happy Gap, then ends abruptly. The rest of the route to the Middle Fork consists of brush and cliffs.

Marion Peak to State Peak. This traverse is typically done on the southeast side of the Cirque Crest, crossing Cirque Ridge and State Peak Ridge before climbing over the peak and descending to State Lakes.

Further Reading: John Moynier. *Backcountry Skiing in the High Sierra.* Evergreen, Colo.: Chockstone Press, 1992, p. 68.

Mount Ruskin to Marion Peak. Although these peaks are on two different maps, they are only 3 miles apart as the Clark's nutcracker flies. This traverse is typically done by ascending the east ridge of Mount Ruskin, descending the southwest face to the basin south of Cartridge Pass, then ascending the Cirque Crest to Pete's Col. From this point either follow the Cirque Crest or cross Pete's Col, then traverse the basin north of the Cirque Crest to Marion Peak's northeast ridge. Descent down the south side of Marion Peak leads to the South Fork of the Kings River, which is followed upstream to return to the starting point of the traverse.

Kettle Ridge and the LeConte Divide

At first glance, this region may appear to be rather dull to the experienced hiker or climber. There is little of the great relief seen in the other areas of the High Sierra, glaciers are absent, and you have to walk a long way to reach timberline. A journey in this area would seem to be better suited for stock users than for self-propelled individuals. The long walk to Kettle Ridge and the LeConte Divide is worthwhile, however. There are outstanding views of the High Sierra from the crest. Those who prefer a close-up view of the timberline country will be delighted with Blackcap Basin, and moving farther south, Blue Canyon is a sight to behold. Blue Canyon Creek drops into the Middle Fork of the Kings River, which turns downstream to Tehipite Valley, a miniature Yosemite Valley that features the largest dome in the entire Sierra Nevada, Tehipite Dome. Rock climbers can find excellent climbing in complete solitude on Kettle Dome and the Obelisk.

This region is bounded by Rodgers Ridge, Tombstone Ridge, and the Middle Fork of the Kings River on the south; by Goddard Creek and Goddard Canyon on the east; by the South Fork of the San Joaquin River on the north; and by Florence Lake, Courtright Reservoir, and Wishon Reservoir on the west.

HISTORY

Frank Dusy and Bill Helm set up a partnership in sheep raising at Dinkey Creek in 1869. Later that year Dusy wounded a grizzly bear during a hunting trip near Crown Creek. He followed it down to the Middle Fork of the Kings River, where he discovered Tehipite Valley and Tehipite Dome. He continued upstream and found abundant forage at Simpson Meadow. In the next few years Dusy and Helm built the Dinkey Trail to Crown Valley, and the Tunemah Trail to Simpson Meadow.

Comparatively little mountaineering has been done in this area. Tehipite Dome's first recorded ascent was in 1896, and Kettle Dome was climbed by Hermann Ulrichs in 1920. The Obelisk was first climbed in 1947, and some of the peaks along Kettle Ridge and the LeConte Divide were first climbed as late as the 1950s.

MAPS

USGS. *7.5-minute series:* Ward Mountain, Mt. Henry, Blackcap Mtn., Courtright Reservoir, Mt. Goddard, Slide Bluffs, Tehipite Dome, Rough Spur. *National park maps:* Sequoia and Kings Canyon National Parks and Vicinity (1:125,000). *30 x 60–minute series:* Bishop, Mount Whitney.

USFS. A Guide to the John Muir Wilderness and the Sequoia–Kings Canyon Wilderness (1:63,360).

Tom Harrison Cartography. Kings Canyon High Country, Mono Divide High Country.

Map Link 15-minute series. Marion Peak, Tehipite Dome, Blackcap Mtn., Mt. Goddard.

Wilderness Press 15-minute series. Mt. Goddard.

ROADS

Dinkey Creek Road and McKinley Grove Road

Dinkey Creek Road leaves Highway 168 at Shaver Lake. It goes east for about 12 miles to just short of Dinkey Creek; turn right onto McKinley Grove Road.

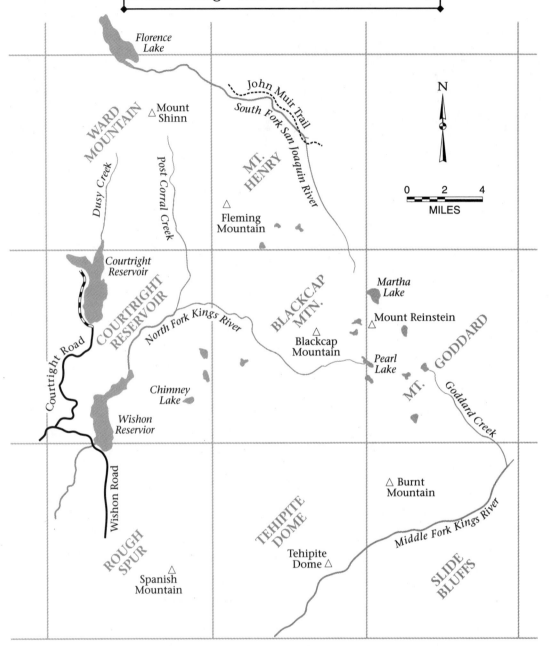

Kettle Ridge and the LeConte Divide

Florence Lake

John Muir Trail

South Fork San Joaquin River

WARD MOUNTAIN

△ Mount Shinn

Dusy Creek

Post Corral Creek

MT. HENRY

△ Fleming Mountain

N

0   2   4
MILES

Courtright Reservoir

COURTRIGHT RESERVOIR

North Fork Kings River

BLACKCAP MTN.

Martha Lake

Mount Reinstein △

Courtright Road

Blackcap Mountain △

MT. GODDARD

Goddard Creek

Chimney Lake

Pearl Lake

Wishon Reservoir

Wishon Road

Burnt Mountain △

ROUGH SPUR

TEHIPITE DOME

Middle Fork Kings River

SLIDE BLUFFS

△ Spanish Mountain

Tehipite Dome △

After approximately 15 miles the road ends at the junction of Wishon Road and Courtright Road.

Wishon Road

Wishon Road heads east from a three-way junction with McKinley Grove and Courtright Roads. It crosses the dam that forms Wishon Reservoir after 3.3 miles, and passes the Woodchuck Trailhead at 4.1 miles. At 6.6 miles, it comes to the junction with the road leading to the Crown Valley Trailhead; go left if headed for the Rancheria Trailhead. Another junction is encountered 1.8 miles farther up Wishon Road. Turn left, and the Rancheria Trailhead is 0.7 mile beyond.

To reach the Crown Valley Trailhead, turn right at the junction of Wishon Road 2.5 miles beyond the dam (6.6 miles from the junction with McKinley Grove and Courtright Roads). The Crown Valley Trailhead is 1.1 miles farther.

Courtright Road

Courtright Road goes left from the three-way junction of McKinley Grove and Wishon Roads. There is a junction just before Courtright Reservoir after 7.9 miles; go right. Drive across the spillway and the dam 0.4 mile farther; the Maxson Trailhead is 0.9 mile beyond the dam.

Florence Lake Road

This road is described in Chapter 10, The Mono Recesses.

TRAILS

Spanish Lake Trail and Geraldine Lakes Trail   8 miles

A non-quota trail. This trail starts at the Crown Valley Trailhead (0 mi; 6,720 ft+) and goes east to where it branches south from the Crown Valley Trail (¾ mi; 6,960 ft+). The trail to Spanish Lake descends to and crosses Rancheria Creek twice and comes to Statham Meadow (2½ mi; 8,080 ft+). Instead of crossing the meadow (which is private property) the trail climbs the ridge to the north to a junction (¼ mi; 8,320 ft+). The left branch leads to Crown Valley; the right or southern branch goes toward Spanish Meadow and meets the abandoned four-wheel-drive track that at one time led

to Spanish Lake and Little Spanish Lake (1 mi; 8,400 ft+). The trail to Geraldine Lakes goes east across the four-wheel-drive track, past Spanish Meadow and Spanish Lake to a trail junction (1¼ mi; 8,623 ft+). A trail leads north from here to Wet Meadow and Crown Valley; the Geraldine Lakes Trail goes east, then south along the western edge of a meadow, and eventually into the forest. The trail climbs slightly, and crosses a small pass (locally known as "Spanish Pass"; 1¼ mi; 9,200 ft+) before descending to Geraldine Lakes. (Just beyond this pass another trail branches off the main trail and heads southwest to the top of Spanish Mountain.) The trail eventually comes to the eastern shore of the lower Geraldine Lake (1 mi; 8,718 ft). From Geraldine Lake a trail goes northeast to Crown Valley; another trail goes southeast and ends north of the Obelisk.

There is also a four-wheel-drive track (the Spanish Off-High-Vehicle [OHV] route) that climbs to the top of Rodgers Ridge from Rancheria Creek. At one time the track went by Spanish Lake and almost to Chain Lakes, but the road has been blocked at the point where it leaves Rodgers Ridge and descends to Spanish Lakes. (This was done because of an enlargement of the John Muir Wilderness in 1984.) The four-wheel-drive route has many ups and downs, and most hikers will find it tedious walking. The Spanish Lake Trail is preferable. Also, it is an OHV route, not a *road*, and it is only suitable for *real* high-clearance four-wheel-drive vehicles.

Crown Valley Trail   7½ miles

A non-quota trail. This trail leaves the Crown Valley Trailhead and goes east for ¾ mile to the junction with the trail to Spanish Lake (0 mi; 6,960 ft+). The Crown Valley Trail goes left, climbs past Three Springs, and meets a trail that leads north to the Rancheria Trail (1½ mi; 8,160 ft+). The Crown Valley Trail continues east to meet the old four-wheel-drive track between Spanish Lake and Chain Lakes (2½ mi; 8,480 ft+). The trail goes southeast over a small pass (to 8,560 ft+) and down to another trail junction near Cow Meadow (¾ mi; 8,440 ft+). The trail leading west meets the Spanish Lake Trail above Statham Meadow. The Crown Valley Trail continues east, passing Wet Meadow, two side trails leading south to Spanish and Geraldine Lakes, and the Crown Valley Ranger Station before descending to Crown Valley (2¼ mi; 7,881 ft).

Tehipite Valley Trail and Middle Fork Trail   21 miles

These trails descend to and travel along the floor of the canyon of the Middle Fork of the Kings River. This is one of the great canyons of the Sierra Nevada, rivaling in grandeur Kings Canyon (South Fork of the Kings River) and Yosemite Valley. But what makes this canyon unique is that no roads approach it. It is as wild today as when the shepherd Frank Dusy first traveled this route in 1869.

This trail leaves Crown Valley (0 mi; 7,881 ft) and goes south past a side trail that heads southwest to Geraldine Lakes. It then passes through the forest to Gnat Meadow (5 mi; 7,360 ft+; some maps incorrectly name this as Hay Meadow). From Gnat Meadow the trail climbs to the top of a ridge (to 7,440 ft+) and makes a gradual descent before descending more than 3,000 feet with many switchbacks to Tehipite Valley (4 mi; 4,120 ft+). The Middle Fork Trail ascends the canyon floor on the north side of the stream to Simpson Meadow, where it crosses the Middle Fork on a large log high above the Kings River and meets the Granite Pass Trail (12 mi; 6,000 ft+). There is a waist-deep ford across the Middle Fork upstream from Simpson Meadow.

Blue Canyon Trail   12 miles

Although this trail has not been maintained for many years, it is still serviceable for a visit to beautiful Blue Canyon.

The trail goes east from Crown Valley (0 mi; 7,881 ft) to Crown Creek (3½ mi; 6,960 ft+), which is a dangerous crossing at high water. Across the stream, the trail climbs around the south side of Kettle Dome (to 8,640 ft) before descending to Blue Canyon (5 mi; 7,200 ft+). The trail follows the west bank of Blue Canyon Creek, and then crosses the stream and ascends its east bank to where the trail ends in the lake basin above (3½ mi; 9,200 ft+). Cross-country travel is easy among the lakes.

Rancheria Trail   5¾ miles

A non-quota trail. This trail goes east from the Rancheria Trailhead (0 mi; 7,600 ft+). It climbs slightly at first and then contours before meeting a side trail that leads south to the Crown Valley Trail (1¾ mi; 8,000 ft+). The Rancheria Trail continues its gentle climb to another trail junction east of Finger Rock (2 mi; 8,840 ft+). One trail branches south from here and leads to Crown

Valley; another trail goes east to Duck Lake. The Rancheria Trail continues north (climbing to 9,040 ft+) to meet the Chuck Pass Trail (1½ mi; 8,720 ft+). The Rancheria Trail goes north to meet the Woodchuck Lake Trail (½ mi; 8,640 ft+).

Chuck Pass Trail   5½ miles

The Chuck Pass Trail starts along the Rancheria Trail about ½ mile from the Woodchuck Trail (0 mi; 8,640 ft+). It goes east past Indian Springs and over Chuck Pass (9,600 ft+) to meet the Crown Pass Trail (5½ mi; 9,280 ft+) approximately four miles north of Crown Valley.

Crown Pass Trail   9 miles

The Crown Pass Trail connects Crown Valley with the summit of Crown Pass. From Crown Valley, follow the Blue Canyon Trail approximately ½ mile to meet the Crown Pass Trail (0 mi; 7,840 ft+). The trail goes north, and soon meets a trail that leads northeast to Mountain Meadow and Coyote Pass (½ mi; 8,000 ft+). The Crown Pass Trail continues north, passes Elizabeth Lake, and meets the Chuck Pass Trail (3 mi; 9,280 ft+). The trail continues north, passing Scepter Lake and Crown Lake on the way to the top of Crown Pass (5½ mi; 10,188 ft), where it meets the Woodchuck Trail.

Woodchuck Trail   14 miles

A non-quota trail. This trail leaves the Woodchuck Trailhead (0 mi; 6,680 ft+) and goes south, then north, and finally to the east up the Woodchuck Creek drainage to meet the Rancheria Trail (5 mi; 8,640 ft+). The Woodchuck Trail climbs to the north and meets the side trail leading to Woodchuck Lake (½ mi; 8,880 ft+). The Woodchuck Trail continues east, passing a side trail to Chimney and Marsh Lakes and the Woodchuck Lake Trail before climbing to 10,400 feet and descending to Crown Pass (5 mi, 10,188 ft). Strictly speaking, Crown Pass is not a pass at all, but a crossing of the shoulder of an unnamed peak. The Crown Pass Trail descends the south side of the pass to Crown Valley; the Woodchuck Trail continues north, down to Halfmoon Lake (½ mi; 9,400 ft+), where the trail branches. The north branch descends to meet the Blackcap Basin Trail near Big Maxson Meadow (2½ mi; 8,440 ft+). The east branch crosses the outlet of Halfmoon Lake to meet the Blackcap Basin Trail (3 mi; 9,120 ft+) approximately 3½ miles upstream from Big Maxson Meadow.

Woodchuck Lake Trail   3½ miles

This side trail, which leaves the Woodchuck Trail about ½ mile from the Rancheria Trail junction (0 mi; 8,880 ft+), leads to Woodchuck Lake (2½ mi; 9,950 ft). It then circles the lake on its eastern shore and goes south to meet the Woodchuck Trail again (1 mi; 10,000 ft+).

Blackcap Basin Trail   22½ miles

A quota trail. The Blackcap Basin Trail starts from the Maxson Trailhead near Courtright Reservoir (0 mi; 7,920 ft+). The trail, a dirt road at first, turns into a proper trail just before reaching Maxson Meadows. It then crosses a small pass and meets the Burnt Corral Meadow Trail (4½ mi; 8,480 ft+). The Blackcap Basin Trail goes east and meets another branch of the Burnt Corral Meadow Trail (1½ mi; 8,480 ft+). The Blackcap Basin Trail gradually descends Post Corral Creek to meet the Hell-For-Sure Pass Trail (3½ mi; 8,240 ft+). The Blackcap Basin Trail goes south to the junction with the Meadow Brook Trail, along the North Fork of the Kings River (5 mi; 8,200 ft+). The Blackcap Basin Trail remains on the north bank of the river; it continues upstream to meet the branch of the Woodchuck Trail that descends from Halfmoon Lake (2 mi; 8,440 ft+). The Blackcap Basin Trail goes upstream to meet the Bench Valley Trail (1 mi; 8,600 ft+), then continues to a crossing of the river, and a junction with the other branch of the Woodchuck Trail (1½ mi; 9,120 ft+). The Blackcap Basin Trail remains on the south side of the river and gradually climbs to where the trail forks (3 mi; 10,160 ft+). The east branch leads to Portal Lake (½ mi; 10,320 ft+); the west branch goes over a small pass (to 10,320 ft+) to Crown Basin.

Bench Valley Trail   7 miles

At one time a trail ascended the south bank of Fall Creek, but it has not been maintained for many years. The best route ascends a trail that leaves the Blackcap Basin Trail about 1 mile east of Big Maxson Meadow (0 mi; 8,600 ft+). The trail makes a steep ascent before gradually climbing around and up to the hanging valley that holds McGuire Lakes (6 mi; 9,660 ft+). The trail goes around the north and east sides of the lakes and makes a short climb to Guest Lake (½ mi; 10,160 ft+). It then goes north over a small pass to Horsehead Lake (½ mi; 10,400 ft+). There are many use trails that lead to the small lakes in this basin.

Meadow Brook Trail   7 miles

This trail leaves the Blackcap Basin Trail about 5 miles downstream from Big Maxson Meadow (0 mi; 8,200 ft+). It makes a steep ascent to the west of Meadow Brook to Devil's Punchbowl (6 mi; 10,098 ft) and continues north to meet the Hell-For-Sure Pass Trail (1 mi; 10,200 ft+).

Hell-For-Sure Pass Trail   12½ miles

This trail leaves the Blackcap Basin Trail 9 ½ miles from the trailhead near Courtright Reservoir (0 mi; 8,240 ft+). The Hell-For-Sure Pass Trail goes east, climbing over a small ridge and passing southeast of Fleming Lake to meet the Indian Lakes Trail (5½ mi; 9,720 ft+). The trail makes a gradual ascent to the east to meet the Meadow Brook Trail coming from Devil's Punchbowl (1½ mi; 10,200 ft+), then continues climbing to the east to the summit of Hell-For-Sure Pass (2½ mi; 11,320 ft+). The pass was named by Joseph LeConte and Karl Grove Gilbert when they crossed it in 1904, after failing to find a route for pack animals across the Goddard Divide. The trail makes a steep descent down the northeast side of the pass and comes to a bench leading southeast across the wall of Goddard Canyon. It then makes a gradual descent to meet the Goddard Canyon Trail (3 mi; 9,880 ft+) at an unsigned junction.

Indian Lakes Trail   2½ miles

The Indian Lakes Trail leaves the Hell-For-Sure Pass Trail just east of Fleming Lake (0 mi; 9,720 ft+). It goes north, meeting a branch trail (¼ mi; 9,880 ft+) leading to Rae Lake. The main trail continues north to the west shore of Lower Indian Lake, becoming rather faint north of the lake but continuing through the meadows and sand flats upstream to Upper Indian Lake (2¼ mi; 10,480 ft+).

Burnt Corral Meadow/Thompson Lake Trail   11 miles

This trail leaves the Blackcap Basin Trail 4½ miles from the Maxson Trailhead (0 mi; 8,480 ft+). It goes north, passes Hobler Lake, and meets the trail's other branch near Burnt Corral Creek (1 ¾ mi; 8,720 ft+). The trail goes up the west bank of the creek and crosses to the east side before reaching Burnt Corral Meadow (2½ mi; 9,520 ft+). It then continues upstream and crosses an unnamed pass (to 10,240 ft+) before descending to

Thompson Lake (3 mi; 9,520 ft+). The trail goes north from the lake and gradually descends to meet the Blayney Meadows Trail south of Florence Lake (3¾ mi; 7,600 ft+).

Blayney Meadows Trail   9¼ miles

The Blayney Meadows Trail provides access to the northern portion of the LeConte Divide. It is described in Chapter 10, The Mono Recesses.

CROSS-COUNTRY ROUTES

Tunemah Trail

This is an old sheep and cattle route that leads from Crown Valley to Simpson Meadow. The trail has not been used for many years, and it is now an adventurous and historic cross-country route.

Leave Blue Canyon at the 8,000-foot level and ascend to the saddle north of Burnt Mountain. Descend and traverse east to cross Alpine Creek, and reach Bunchgrass Flat on a level traverse from Alpine Creek. Make a steep ascent to the northeast, climbing over Peak 10,987ft (10,985 ft), which is the real Tunemah "Pass." (Some maps erroneously place the name on the saddle 0.4 mile northwest of the peak.) From the top of the "pass" you can see Simpson Meadow far below. The word "Tunemah" is a Chinese obscenity. This section is the Tunemah part of the cross-country route: Descend (i.e., plunge down) the east side of the pass to a point along Goddard Creek approximately ½ mile upstream from its junction with the Middle Fork of the Kings River. After finding a safe place to cross the river, you have access to the Middle Fork Trail or the Granite Pass Trail.

Coyote Pass   10,071 ft; 10,000 ft+

At one time a trail went over this pass, providing access between Crown Valley and the upper part of Blue Canyon. Only traces of the trail may still be seen, however.

From Crown Valley take the Crown Pass Trail north for ½ mile to a trail junction. The trail goes east and then northeast across many small creeks and big Crown Creek to Mountain Meadow. Alternatively, it is possible and perhaps easier to hike up Crown Creek to the meadow. From Mountain Meadow, go east to the sum-

mit of the pass atop Kettle Ridge. The descent of the east side of the pass is steep in places; the route eventually breaks out of the forest and into the beautiful meadows of Blue Canyon.

"Dykeman Pass"   11,040 ft+; 11,046 ft; 2.0 mi SSW of Blue Canyon Peak

Class 2. Dykeman Pass, named here in memory of Dave Dykeman, provides access between the upper reaches of Blue Canyon Creek and Alpine Creek. It is used to approach Tunemah Peak.

"Alpine Pass"   11,160 ft+; 11,120 ft+; 0.1 mi S of Tunemah Lake

Class 2. This pass is at the head of the Alpine Creek drainage; it provides access to Tunemah Lake.

"Mantle Pass"   10,960 ft+; 10,880 ft+; 1.2 mi WSW of Finger Peak

Class 2. Mantle Pass, named here in honor of Doug Mantle, crosses Kettle Ridge and provides access between Crown Basin and the upper part of Blue Canyon. It is best to go around the lake east of the pass on its northern shore.

"Midway Pass"   11,640 ft+; 11,600 ft+; 0.7 mi WNW of Finger Peak; UTM 451997

Class 2. This pass crosses Kettle Ridge and leads between Blue Canyon Creek and Midway Lake. Strictly speaking, it is not a pass but rather a ridge crossing. Climb steep slabs interspersed with sand on the south side of the pass. From the top of the pass, follow the ridge crest northwest to where Cathedral Lake and Midway Lake can be seen to the north. Descend the southeast side of this small ridge over rock and sand, then gradually contour around to the north to meet Midway Lake.

"Blue Canyon Pass"   11,480 ft+; 11,440 ft+; 0.5 mi E of Finger Peak

Class 2. Blue Canyon Pass leads between Blue Canyon Creek and the upper part of Goddard Creek. The southern approach to the pass is made from the southwest by ascending a series of chutes to the top of the pass. The north side of the pass consists of large talus, and it is best to traverse across the north side of Finger Peak before going north and then northeast to Goddard Creek.

"Finger Col"   11,560 ft+; 11,520 ft+;
0.4 mi NNW of Finger Peak; UTM 459000

Class 2. This pass provides access between the headwaters of the North Fork of the Kings River and Goddard Creek. Ascend the south side of the stream between Portal Lake and Midway Lake; this is over steep slabs and talus. Pass Midway Lake on its northern side and head for the north shore of Cathedral Lake. Ascend northeast, away from Cathedral Lake, on slabs and talus, and then traverse south, gradually ascending to the first, small col north of Finger Peak. Descend the east side of the pass by following a ledge that leads south, and then descend slabs to a gully that descends northeast. Stay south of the small lake east of the pass, and continue descending to Goddard Creek.

North Fork of the Kings River

This is a difficult descent of the gorge of the North Fork between the Blackcap Basin Trail and Wishon Reservoir. It is for experienced cross-country hikers only.

Leave the Blackcap Basin Trail at the point where the trail descends from Post Corral Meadows and meets the North Fork. Descend the north bank of the river for ¼ mile, then go right to avoid a precipitous, but beautiful, series of cascades. After this the route remains near the north side of the river, but with occasional, minor detours to avoid small cliffs and domes. You eventually come to more cascades, which end in a large pool. Contour west from here to Post Corral Creek and follow it downstream to where it meets the North Fork. Cross over to the south bank of the river at this point, then make a level traverse across the southeast side of the gorge, above the steep cliffs. Continue southwest and downstream, gradually moving away from the North Fork drainage to the drainage north of Cape Horn. Follow this creek downstream to where it meets the North Fork. Follow the North Fork downstream, through loose rock and brush, to where Wishon Reservoir (or its mud flats, if the water level is low) becomes visible. Shortly after this you come to a small creek. Descend the south side of the creek, staying south and west of its steep sections, to the boat campsite on the northeast shore of Wishon Reservoir.

The easiest way from here is by boat. If none is available, it is necessary to go south, climb over a ridge, and descend to the Woodchuck Trail. During the winter and early spring, it may be possible to hike along the bottom of the reservoir to the road leading to Shaver Lake—but watch out for deep mud!

Nichols Canyon

The trail that once descended this canyon is long gone. For the cross-country route, descend the north slope of Crown Pass and keep to the east of the stream in the canyon. There is a meadow where the stream from Old Pipe Lake meets the main stream of Nichols Canyon. Continue downstream, keeping to the east of the creek, to where the canyon drops off above the North Fork of the Kings River. Continue down to the North Fork, then cross on any of the many fallen logs.

"Blackcap Pass"   11,160 ft+; 11,120 ft+;
0.5 mi NE of Blackcap Mountain

Class 2. This pass is between Blackcap Basin and Guest Lake in Bench Valley. The ascent of the pass from Blackcap Basin is easy. From the top of the pass, make a steep, rocky descent on its west side to a sandy bench. Descend the north side of the stream to Guest Lake.

"Reinstein Pass"   11,880 ft+; 11,840 ft+;
0.2 mi NE of Mount Reinstein; UTM 459052

Class 2. Although this pass crosses the Goddard Divide and connects Goddard Creek with Goddard Canyon, it has come to be known as Reinstein Pass by cross-country hikers.

From Goddard Creek climb into the basin southeast of Mount Reinstein. Then go north over ledges and boulders to the summit of the pass. Descend the north side of the pass, over talus and slabs, to Martha Lake. The next pass to the northeast has a cliff on its northern side.

"Valor Pass"   11,760 ft+; 11,760 ft+;
1.0 mi NNW of Mount Reinstein

Class 2–3. This pass has also been called "Reinstein Saddle." It connects Blackcap Basin with the lake at the head of Goddard Canyon (Martha Lake), and is commonly used by climbers on their way to Mount Goddard. From Blackcap Basin ascend to Ambition Lake and make the steep ascent to the cirque that holds Valor Lake. Steep talus leads to the surprisingly flat summit of the pass. Descend the northeast side of the pass by first going east and then north to Martha Lake.

"Confusion Pass"   11,360 ft+; 11,360 ft+;
2.5 mi NE of Blackcap Mountain

Class 2. This pass crosses the LeConte Divide between Blackcap Basin and Goddard Canyon. The name of the pass comes from the lake very near to the top of the crest of the LeConte Divide. This eastern shore of the lake is actually a huge cliff overlooking Goddard Canyon; the north, west, and south shores of this lake are composed of gigantic blocks of talus. Valor Pass is a preferable route.

Ascend to Rainbow Lake in Blackcap Basin and continue northward to a broken granite bench. Enter a shallow chute or gorge, hopping from block to block to where the chute ends at the southwest corner of Lake Confusion. Follow the western shore of the lake northward over much broken talus to Confusion Pass, which is located at the northwest corner of the lake. The descent into Goddard Canyon consists of much steep, loose talus.

"Gunsight Pass"   11,600 ft+; 11,600 ft+;
1.0 mi E of Bullet Lake

Class 2. This pass, also known as "Wild West Pass," leads from the lakes in the upper reaches of Bench Valley, over the LeConte Divide, and into Goddard Canyon. A direct ascent to the pass from Bullet Lake encounters much talus. It is better to begin the ascent from the north and east shores of Holster Lake. Go east, between the rocky canyon on the right (south) and the long recesses on the left; avoid the recesses themselves. At the last recess, go left (east) and ascend some slabs to the top of the pass. A lot of loose, steep talus is encountered while descending the east side of the pass to Goddard Canyon.

"Hutton Pass"   11,480 ft+; 11,440 ft+;
0.3 mi E of Mount Hutton

Class 2. This has also been called "Hutton Col." It is best to descend the north side of the pass by heading northeast.

Further Reading: John Moynier. *Backcountry Skiing in the High Sierra.* Evergreen, Colo.: Chockstone Press, 1992, p. 73.

"Lucifer's Saddle"   11,000 ft+; 10,960 ft+;
1.0 mi SE of Devil's Punchbowl

Class 2. This was previously named "Two Passes," but

Jim Watter's imaginative name is now used here. Lucifer's Saddle and the next pass to the southeast (Pass 11,120 ft+; 11,120 ft+) connect Red Mountain Basin with the lakes in Bench Valley. Head southeast from the north shore of Devil's Punchbowl, passing Little Shot Lake and Big Shot Lake on their northern shores. Go north a short distance to a small meadow. Leave this meadow from its southern side, then climb a granite face of slabs and blocks toward a low notch visible above and to the left. Eventually you will reach a chute that leads away from the notch, to the right. Follow this chute to the top of the ridge and cross the sandflat, keeping to its right, to a meadow. Leave the meadow at its eastern side, next to the stream, and climb up and right to another face of granite slabs. Climb this face to the top of the first pass.

From here the second pass, to the southeast, is an easy climb. From the top of the second pass you have two options. You can traverse north and then east to Schoolmarm Lake. Or you can descend directly southeast on sand and then traverse south down the Fall Creek drainage.

"Fleming Pass"   10,560 ft+; 10,560 ft+;
0.4 mi N of Fleming Mountain

Class 1. Fleming Pass is an easy climb from Lower Indian Lake. It is best to descend the western side of the pass by first going north and then west.

"Post Corral Pass"   10,240 ft+; 10,240 ft+;
2.5 mi NNE of Post Corral Meadows; UTM 327166

Class 1. This pass leads to the upper reaches of Post Corral Creek from the meadows northwest of Fleming Mountain. It was used by cowboys to move stock that grazed these meadows over the summer.

Mosquito Pass   10,440 ft+; 10,400 ft+

Class 2. This route leads from Upper Indian Lake to the South Fork of the San Joaquin River. Follow the eastern shore of Upper Indian Lake northward and ascend a short chute. At its top, traverse left (west) to the top of Mosquito Pass. Descend the north side of the pass by traversing west across sandy chutes and broken granite to a small stream choked with willows. An area of huge boulders is bypassed by going to the east. Descend through the forest to the stream that drains the lake north of Mosquito Pass. Continue hiking downstream by any number of routes to the river. The Blayney Meadows

Trail is easily reached once the South Fork of the San Joaquin River is crossed.

PEAKS

Finger Rock   9,606 ft; 9,606 ft
The north side is class 3.

South Face. III, 5.8, A3. First ascent 1981 by Rick Nolting and Fred Beckey. Begin by climbing the chimney that splits the center of the pillar on the south face. Two pitches in the chimney lead to a ledge that angles right and ends at a blank wall. This wall is overcome by climbing from an isolated ledge using tiny holds and cracks and one aid move. Continue up cracks and then traverse left across a steep friction slab. Then ascend a rib and climb slabs to the summit.

Further Reading: Greg Vernon, Sally Moser, and David Hickey. *Southern Sierra Rock Climbing: Sequoia/Kings Canyon.* Evergreen, Colo.: Chockstone Press, 1993, p. 152.

Spanish Mountain   10,051 ft; 10,051 ft
First ascent 1921 by Hermann F. Ulrichs. A trail leaves the Geraldine Lakes Trail and leads almost to the very top. Class 1.

A more interesting (class 2) route ascends the southeast ridge from the highest of the Geraldine Lakes. Many small cliffs and boulders must be overcome, but this route offers the most outstanding view of Kings Canyon.

Obelisk   9,705 ft; 9,700 ft
This landmark peak serves as the extreme western boundary of Kings Canyon National Park. It has excellent rock (reminiscent of Charlotte Dome), but the long approach keeps it from being overwhelmed by climbers. From Geraldine Lakes, the best approach is on top of the ridge between the Obelisk and Spanish Mountain. The final approach is made from near the top of Peak 9,628 ft (9,600 ft+; 0.2 mi NE of the Obelisk). A direct approach from the west requires much bushwhacking. Routes on the east and south faces are best approached from the small peak northeast of the Obelisk.

Further Reading: *Rock & Ice.* No. 30, p. 54; Greg Vernon, Sally Moser, and David Hickey. *Southern Sierra Rock Climbing: Sequoia/Kings Canyon.* Evergreen, Colo.: Chockstone Press, 1993, pp. 146–151.

South Face. II, 5.7. First ascent 1947 by Jim Wilson and Allen Steck. This route goes up a long, broken chimney on the right-hand side of the south face. The first short class 4 pitch in the chimney leads through some vegetation to an alcove. Continue up the chimney to where it ends at the foot of a steep wall, the crux of the climb. This pitch, about 100 feet long, climbs a vertical wall of chickenheads. Traverse to the left across the large ledge at the base of the final headwall. Climb a right-trending white chute before traversing left across a seemingly "blank" face (a 5.7 move) to a belay stance in a shallow right-facing corner. The last pitch climbs the inside corner to where it turns into the chute that pierces the upper headwall, followed by 200 feet of class 3 to the top.

Poultry in Motion. II, 5.7. First ascent September 25, 1994 by Ellen Holden and R. J. Secor. This route ascends the knobby face between Los Pollos Locos and the chimney of the South Face route. It consists mostly of vertical class 4 climbing with a few moderate class 5 moves between patches of knobs, horns, and chickenheads. Climb the chimney of the South Face route to the alcove and then go up and left across a face of knobs and chickenheads to a point beneath the roof of Los Pollos Locos. Next, climb up and right across knobs and chickenheads to an exposed belay stance at an obtuse, outside corner. The fourth pitch goes straight up the dead-vertical chickenheaded face above the corner to the large ledge at the base of the final headwall. Continue up the South Face route to the summit.

Los Pollos Locos. II, 5.9. First ascent August 13, 1989 by Greg Vernon, Mike Baca, and R. J. Secor. A crack splits the middle of the south face (between the deep chimney to the left and the right-hand chimney of the South Face route), passes through a small roof, and ascends a vertical headwall. Bushwhack up the chimney of the South Face route to an alcove (class 4) and then go up and left across knobs and chickenheads to the crack. Climb the face left of the crack to a point above the roof, move to the right across the crack, and then move left across the crack again to a tiny belay stance. Go straight up from the stance, keeping to the right of a black watermark and left of the crack. The top of this headwall is blank, and the crack assumes a wicked overhanging flare at this point (5.9). The last pitch is easier, but features high quality climbing, followed by 300 feet of class 3 to the top.

Wasabi Man. II, 5.8. First ascent July 1990 by Barry

OBELISK

rappel

Los Pollos Locos

Poultry
in Motion

Southeast
Buttress

South
Face

Chambers and Leni Reeves. This route, on the south-west side of the Obelisk, climbs between two dihedrals that form an arch. (This is not the system that leads to a deep cleft, but the next one to the left.) Scramble up the blocky right dihedral to a ledge. Climb the dihedral for about 30 feet, then move left out onto the face and up over good holds to a ledge in the middle of the face. Continue up from the ledge to where climbing gets harder. An undercling to the left is followed by a small flake, and then more face climbing leads up to the roof at the apex of the two dihedrals. Climb the big crack that splits the roof, then continue up and slightly right for four more pitches to the summit.

Rock Solid. II, 5.8. First ascent September 2, 1990 by Bart O'Brien, Richard Swayze, and Mike Jaurequi. This route follows the crack system that is 40 feet to the right of the chimney on the West Face route. The route starts from a narrow ledge at the base of the crack system, about 50 feet above the talus. A nice pitch with one 5.8 move leads to a belay alcove in a chimney. Step to the right and climb a full rope length of outstanding 5.8 face climbing. Three more pitches on big knobs lead to the summit.

West Face. II, 5.7. First ascent April 1971 by Fred Beckey and Hooman Aprin. Climb a chimney on the left side of the face before moving to the right onto the face. This is followed by six pitches of excellent climbing on knobs and chickenheads to the summit.

Handle With Care. III, 5.8. First ascent June 19, 1990 by David Harden, Jack Bedell, and Don Palmer. This route is close to the northwest corner of the Obelisk, and consists of seven pitches of excellent face climbing. Begin by climbing the left side of the west face for four pitches of delightful face climbing (5.5–5.7). These pitches lead to a notch behind an obvious pillar on the northwest corner. A beautiful hand crack goes up and slightly left across a white wall on the north face for 200 feet. Sustained, steep face climbing (5.8) leads along the crack over some eroded and friable knobs. Traverse a few feet to the right from the top of the crack onto a steep prow. Follow the prow to easier climbing.

The Flake Route. II, 5.9. First ascent September 1983 by Herb Laeger, Eve Laeger, and Rick Smith. This route ascends the overhanging flakes on the right side of the north face. The climb continues up the left-facing corner system above the cracks.

North Face. II, 5.7. First ascent June 1951 by Anton Nelson, David Hammack, John Salathé, and Alice Ann Dayton. The north face has a 45° ridge near its center. Either climb the ridge for 100 feet to its end (class 4) or climb to the left of the ridge (5.3). From the top of this ridge, traverse right on a small, exposed ledge. This traverse ends at two short dihedrals. The one on the left is off-width, the right is a hand jam, and they both are 5.7. After this, go up and right to climb a tight chimney (5.4) to the west face. It is class 3 from the upper west face to the summit.

The Bacanal. II, 5.9, A1. First ascent August 1988 by Mike Baca and Greg Vernon. This route climbs the dihedral directly above the 45° ridge on the north face. Two aid placements are needed at the start of the dihedral. Go up and left just below the top of the dihedral to the summit.

Hands of Fate. II, 5.10. First ascent September 1976 by Alan Bartlett and Robb Dellinger. This route follows the obvious crack system that is to the left of The Time Warp. An easy pitch leads to the base of the crack, where two small overhangs bar the way. Bypass the first by traversing right, then follow a difficult arch up and left. Surmounting the second overhang is the crux of the climb.

East Face. II, 5.5. First ascent March 1972 by Chuck Kroger and Ben Dewell. Descend about 200 feet from the small peak northeast of the Obelisk. Walk through some brush, then climb class 3 ledges to the bottom of a large chimney on the east face. The route goes up 100 feet on the poorly protected face left of the chimney to a ledge system. Traverse left 100 feet on easy ledges. Climb to the summit from these ledges.

Southeast Buttress. II, 5.8. This route ascends the buttress to the right of the chimney of the South Face route.

Descent Route. The south face requires six rappels to reach the ground. The northeast shoulder requires two rappels: a short one from the summit to a ledge above the great overhang and a 165-foot free rappel from above the overhang to the notch northeast of the Obelisk. Care should be taken when placing the rappel anchor in order to prevent rope jams. (There are at least two ropes tangled among the horns above the great overhang; the ⅜-inch twisted nylon rope has been there since September 1975.) From the notch, it is class 3 over the small peak northeast of the Obelisk to the ground.

Obelisk, Southeast Face. Photo by R. J. Secor.

OBELISK

Handle With Care

West
Face

Wasabi Man

Rock
Solid

Obelisk, West Face. Photo by R. J. Secor.

OBELISK

rappel

The Bacanal

Hands of Fate

North Face

Handle With Care
(from West Face)

Flake Route

Obelisk, North Face. Photo by R. J. Secor.

Kettle Dome   9,451 ft; 9,446 ft

Northeast Face. Class 4. First ascent July 20, 1920 by Hermann Ulrichs. A short class 4 move is followed by a traverse across slabs to two class 4 pitches, which lead directly to the flat summit.

West Face. II, 5.7. First ascent October 20, 1974 by Phil Warrender, Walt Vennum, and Fred Beckey. Climb a long, poorly protected crack to the center of a shallow bowl on the west face. Two pitches of friction in the bowl are followed by a traverse right for 100 feet to a flared outside corner. Climb the corner to the crest of the southwest ridge, then follow the ridge to the summit.

Further Reading: Greg Vernon, Sally Moser, and David Hickey. *Southern Sierra Rock Climbing: Sequoia/Kings Canyon.* Evergreen, Colo.: Chockstone Press, 1993, p. 152.

Tehipite Dome   7,708 ft; 7,708 ft

This is the largest dome in the Sierra Nevada. There is an outstanding view from its summit.

Further Reading: Greg Vernon, Sally Moser, and David Hickey. *Southern Sierra Rock Climbing: Sequoia/Kings Canyon.* Evergreen, Colo.: Chockstone Press, 1993, pp. 152–155.

North Ridge. Class 3. First ascent July 25, 1895 by Ernest C. Bonner (with Theodore S. Solomons in support); second ascent July 31, 1896 by Allan L. Chickering and Walter A. Starr, Sr. Many parties make the mistake of leaving the Blue Canyon Trail too early and end up traversing across duff and brush to Tehipite Dome. It is better to follow the Blue Canyon Trail to where it starts its descent to Blue Canyon at UTM 420896, at an elevation of 8,600 feet. Head south-southeast to Point 8,401 ft (8,369 ft), where there is a fantastic view of the Middle Fork of the Kings River. Head south and then southwest, over the top of Point 7,719 ft (7,680 ft+), to the north base of the dome. Stay on the east side of the ridge a short distance below its crest before making the short class 3 move onto the ridge. An easy scramble leads to the summit of the dome. The spectacular view of the Middle Fork canyon during the approach and on the summit is ample reward for the modest effort expended to reach the summit.

The Time Warp. IV, 5.9. First ascent June 1963 by Fred Beckey, Herb Swedlund, John Ahern, and Ken Weeks. First free ascent June 1983 by Bob Harrington, Dale Bard, and Richard Leversee. The crux of this climb

is the approach. An approach from the floor of the Middle Fork canyon is not recommended due to the difficulty of crossing the river. The best approach is from the base of the north ridge of the dome and down the dome's east side, through trees and brush; it also requires rappels from hanging trees, and some creative down climbing.

The approach ends on a tree- and brush-covered ledge about halfway up the south face of the dome. Ascend a crack behind a pillar that leans against the wall, then follow a crack system that is to the right of the nose. Traverse left and climb a long, difficult flaring chimney and off-width crack. One pitch on the very nose leads to another traverse left into a chimney. Climb an unprotected sloping ramp that leads to a shallow chimney. One more pitch leads to the Huge Ledge, which traverses across the southwest face of the dome. (This ledge can be used as an escape route, if necessary.)

From the Huge Ledge, climb the overhanging, brush-filled crack left of a wide tower that leans against the dome. This pitch ends with some wide stemming. Climb flakes and cracks on the main part of the dome; this leads to a dihedral system, which is followed to just below the summit. The route ends with pleasurable climbing on knobs and solution pockets.

Further Reading: *Summit.* September 1963, pp. 1, 31; *Summit.* November 1963, pp. 14–19.

Southwest Face. VI, 5.9, A4. First ascent July 1970 by Chuck Kroger, Curt Chadwick, and Norm Weeden. This climb begins several hundred feet below and left of The Time Warp. Climb some ramps (some are difficult, but short) to a gigantic hollow flake. Ascend the left edge of this to a terrace just left of the start of The Time Warp. Above the terrace, climb a left-facing dihedral, which leads to a difficult, narrow chimney. This chimney ends on the Huge Ledge that crosses the southwest face of the dome. Follow The Time Warp to the summit from here.

In the Niche of Time. VI, 5.10, A3+. First ascent October 22, 1997 by Ron Felton, Guy Zielski, and E. C. Joe. This route starts to the left of the Southwest Face route at the left side of a prominent pyramid. Go left and up over some wet, slimy shelves (some A2) to a ledge with a tree. This is followed by A2 nailing up and right along a thin ramp that crosses a prominent arête. The second pitch ends by passing underneath a roof and a bat hook traverse left to a small ledge (A3+). Another aid crack is followed by a loose 5.10 off-width crack ending at the base of The

Tehipite Dome from the southeast. Photo by R. J. Secor.

Pillar. Climb behind The Pillar (off-width 5.10, thin A3) and then traverse to the left underneath a roof (A2) back to the arête. Climb steep, thin cracks along the arête, and then go up the distressingly blank ripples that mark the sixth pitch. Overcome the blank sixth pitch by means of rivets, bat hooks, bolts, and beaks (A3+), ending just short of a good crack system (the first-ascent party had 60-meter ropes). More blank climbing leads up and to the right to a mixed pitch (5.9, A1) with hand cracks and nailing, and ends with a scary mantle onto the belay stance. More nailing leads up. This is followed by a tension traverse to the right and down climbing a class 4 diagonal ramp leading to the Sierra Sahara, a large ledge at the base of a huge, left-facing inside corner. Three long and difficult pitches—two 5.10 and one 5.9—up the left side of the corner lead to the Huge Ledge high on the southwest face of Tehipite Dome.

Walk left along the Huge Ledge to arrive underneath a flake. Go up and left underneath the loose flake and traverse left to a ledge with a tree and continue up to another ledge with a tree. A steep, difficult face (5.10+) leads up and right, then up and left, to an arête. This leads straight up before traversing left onto a blocky ledge beneath The Headwall. Overcome The Headwall by climbing straight, thin cracks through two major horizontal cracks/bands (5.9, A1) to a tension traverse to the left to a ramp leading to a belay stance beneath a right-facing inside corner/chimney. An awkward move up left and then right leads to the off-width chimney (5.10). The chimney ends at two ledges where a wide crack leads up and left. Climb the off-width 5.9, A1 crack to the further left of two ledges. A short pitch (80 feet) up a 5.8 crack and a pitch up an enjoyable 5.6 left-facing corner lead to face climbing, which ends on a ledge. Two easy class 5 pitches and one class 4 pitch end at blocky ledges beneath the summit. Hardware: the usual shoulder-bruising load.

Wilderness Serenity. II, 5.10b. First ascent August 1990 by Barry Chambers and Leni Reeves. This route is on the apron on the lower portion of Tehipite Dome. Begin by climbing a right-facing dihedral, then go up a crack (5.10a) to a belay from a tree. A minor variation here is to climb the crack about halfway up, then face climb up and right (5.9) to another crack that leads back to the tree. From the tree, continue up a groove, where an undercling leads left to a left-facing dihedral. Belay from two trees on top of the dihedral. Climb another groove from the two trees, at first leading left (5.8), then

bypassing a small roof on its right side, and continuing to the right to a belay beneath a large roof. The last part of this pitch, which consists of some 5.10b face moves beneath the roof, is the crux. Surmount the roof (5.10a) and continue up and right over a combination of face and crack climbing (5.8) to a large ledge. Climb diagonally right from the ledge and overcome another roof (5.8). This is followed by 5.6 face climbing to a tree and the end of the climb.

Burnt Mountain   10,608 ft; 10,608 ft
Class 1 from the saddle north of the peak.

Tunemah Peak   11,894 ft; 11,894 ft
The west and southwest slopes of this peak are loose class 2, anchored by small, branchy trees. The south ridge from Tunemah Pass is class 2.

Blue Canyon Peak   11,860 ft; 11,849 ft
First ascent August 27, 1959 by Robin J. McKeown and Frank Orme. This peak is class 2 from all directions.

Finger Peak   12,404 ft; 12,404 ft
The northwest ridge of this peak is class 3. From Cathedral Lake, climb either the obvious chute or the buttress (on its left side) to the crest of the northwest ridge. Stay on the southern side of the northwest ridge while traversing to the summit.

The south ridge is class 3; traverse to the right near the top.

The southwest couloir is class 3; the southeast slope and east ridge are class 2.

Mount Reinstein   12,586 ft; 12,604 ft
The northeast ridge from Reinstein Pass is class 3. The southeast ridge is also class 3. The south slope from Blackcap Basin is class 2.

Blackcap Mountain   11,600 ft+; 11,559 ft
The northeast slope from Blackcap Pass is class 1. The west ridge of this peak is class 2.

Peak 12,200ft+   12,265 ft;
2.8 mi NE of Blackcap Mountain
First ascent July 13, 1951 by Art Reyman, via the class 3, knife edge west ridge.

Mount Hutton   11,990 ft; 11,998 ft;
1.4 mi S of Hell-For-Sure Pass

The class 1 south slope was first climbed by Art Reyman on July 12, 1951.

The Cooked Walnut. II, 5.7, A2. First ascent August 31, 1973 by Walt Vennum, Curt Chadwick, and Rick Boyce. This 600-foot climb is on the north face of this peak. Climb a crack system immediately to the right of a pillar that splits the center of the north face. Most of this climb goes free, and is on excellent rock.

Red Mountain   11,963 ft; 11,951 ft

First ascent July 12, 1898 by J. N. LeConte and C. L. Cory. Class 1 from all directions.

Peak 12,120ft+   12,154 ft;
1.0 mi SSE of Mount Henry

The northeast ridge of this peak is an awesome sight from Mount Henry. First ascent July 10, 1951 by A. J. Reyman, via the class 2 northeast ridge.

Mount Henry   12,196 ft; 12,106 ft

North Ridge. Class 3. First ascent July 10, 1951 by A. J. Reyman. Follow the ridge from Peak 11,600ft+ (11,600 ft), keeping to its east side to pass blocks and notches.

Northeast Ridge. Class 2. First ascent July 7, 1939 by David Brower and party. This is a straightforward climb from Goddard Canyon.

The south ridge is class 2 and the southwest and west slopes are class 2.

Zingheim Heights   11,138 ft; 11,148 ft;
0.2 mi SW of Mosquito Pass

First ascent July 10, 1951 by A. J. Reyman. The south slope is class 1.

Fleming Mountain   10,796 ft; 10,796 ft
Class 2 from Fleming Pass.

Ward Mountain   10,840 ft+; 10,682 ft
The west slope is class 2.

Mount Shinn   10,960 ft+; 11,020 ft

This peak dominates Florence Lake. First ascent August 8, 1925 by Francis Corey. The steep west slope from Mount Shinn Lake is class 2.

WRINKLES

Goddard Canyon and Goddard Creek. The eastern boundary of the region described in this chapter may be confusing. Goddard Canyon is north of the Goddard Divide, and is the source of the South Fork of the San Joaquin River. Goddard Creek, south of the Goddard Divide, flows down an unnamed canyon to the Middle Fork of the Kings River.

Cross-Country Routes to the Middle Fork of the Kings River. The only route that goes here is the Tunemah Trail, which isn't really a trail, but a cross-country route. The Middle Fork has steep cliffs on both sides, and the only other way to get there is on the Tehipite Trail from Crown Valley to Tehipite Valley.

Chapter 8

The Palisades

This is the most alpine region of the High Sierra. These peaks are high—five summits exceed 14,000 feet in elevation. The Palisade Glacier is the largest glacier in the range, and most of the peaks in this region are steep on all sides, not just on one or two. The glaciers on the northeast sides of the Palisades are fed by some steep ice couloirs, which can complicate an ascent for a typical California climber who is at home on rock, but not on ice. A climber on the summit of North Palisade may have used all of his or her skills on snow, ice, and rock to get there, and will look out upon a tremendous panorama of tundra, cliff, glacier, forest, and desert.

This region covers the Sierra crest from Taboose Pass to Bishop Pass, and is bounded on the west by Palisade Creek and the Middle Fork of the Kings River.

Further Reading: *Summit.* September–October 1981, pp. 16–20; *Climbing.* No. 87, December 1984, pp. 32–41; *Off Belay.* No. 21, June 1975, pp. 8–29; Doug Robinson. *A Night on the Ground, A Day in the Open.* La Crescenta, Calif.: Mountain 'N' Air Books, 1996, pp. 77–97.

HISTORY

The Palisades were discovered and named in 1864 by the California Geological Survey. Frank Dusy explored the entire Middle Fork of the Kings River in the 1870s, searching for the perfect meadow for his sheep. He was probably the first white man to see the Palisade Glacier, from somewhere near what was later called Dusy Basin. During the same period, the Wheeler Survey triangulated Split Mountain and North Palisade from the east, and in 1879 Lil A. Winchell visited the region and named Mount Winchell (after his father's cousin, geologist Alexander Winchell) and Mount Agassiz (at the time named "Agassiz Needle"). Winchell gave the name "Dusy Peak" to North Palisade in honor of Frank Dusy, who had shown him the approaches to this region from the west. In 1895 Bolton Brown named it "Mount Jordan," after David Starr Jordan, the president of Stanford University, where Brown was a professor. (I assume that Brown's tenure decision was imminent at the time.) Eventually Joseph LeConte's admirably descriptive name, North Palisade, was accepted as official, after his first ascent of the peak in 1903.

Middle Palisade was attempted in 1919, but the climbers selected the wrong route and ended up atop Disappointment Peak. Two years later, Ansel F. Hall and Francis Farquhar repeated the mistake, but then descended and climbed another 2,000 feet to the true summit on the same day.

Norman Clyde moved to Independence in the 1920s, and proceeded to explore the eastern approaches to the Palisades. On June 7, 1930, he climbed the east face of Middle Palisade, which he reported as being "one of the best climbs in the Sierra." Two days later he climbed what came to be known as Norman Clyde Peak via the north face. Clyde moved to the other side of the Sierra crest later in the month and climbed Middle Palisade again on June 18 via the Farquhar Route, then the south face of Norman Clyde Peak the next day. On June 20 he climbed Disappointment Peak from the northeast. On July 5 he climbed the northeast face of Mount Agassiz, which he said was "one of the finest rock climbs in the Sierra." The next day he climbed the Clyde Couloir of North Palisade and called it, "One of the very best climbs in the Sierra." On July 9 he repeated part of this climb, ascending Starlight Peak instead, and called it "a superb climb." He also made nine ascents of Temple Crag that year, in addition to ascents of The Thumb, Mount Winchell, and Mount Bolton Brown. All of these climbs were done solo. As his friend Jules Eichorn once said, "For me there can never be another human being so completely in tune with his chosen environment—mountains—as Norman Clyde."

Robert L. M. Underhill of the Appalachian Mountain Club visited the High Sierra in 1931 at the invitation of Francis Farquhar, then the vice-president of the Sierra Club. Underhill taught selected members of the Sierra Club proper management of the rope for safe rock climbing during the High Trip that year, and a grand tour of the High Sierra was conducted afterwards. This tour included a visit to the Palisades, where the northwest face of Temple Crag was climbed, and the first ascent of the last 14,000-foot unclimbed peak in the High Sierra, Thunderbolt Peak. Throughout the 1930s, many routes were established on the high peaks of the Palisades by members of the Sierra Club's Rock Climbing Sections from various cities in California.

Larry Williams opened the Mountaineering Guide Service in 1959, which he operated under a permit from the Inyo National Forest. This was the first mountain-based climbing school in California. It was a popular school, and its guides and instructors (and a few students) soon put up many difficult routes in the Palisades. For many years, the school had its base camp at Third Lake, beneath Temple Crag, and Don Jensen established many fine routes on this peak's massive north face. After Larry Williams' untimely death in an airplane crash in 1968, the Mountaineering Guide Service was purchased by Mountain Travel and its name changed to the Palisade School of Mountaineering (PSOM; pronounced "possum"), first under the direction of Bob Swift, then Smoke Blanchard, and then Jack Miller. John Fischer purchased and directed the school in 1976. Unfortunately, PSOM stopped operation in 1989, the victim of rogue guides who operated without permits. PSOM's presence in the Palisades will be missed.

MAPS

USGS. *7.5-minute series:* Fish Springs, Aberdeen, Mt. Pinchot, Split Mtn., North Palisade, Mt. Thompson, Coyote Flat. *National park maps:* Sequoia and Kings Canyon National Parks and Vicinity (1:125,000).

30 x 60-minute series: Bishop, Mount Whitney.

USFS. A Guide to the John Muir Wilderness and the Sequoia–Kings Canyon Wilderness (1:63,360).

Tom Harrison Cartography. Kings Canyon High Country.

Map Link 15-minute series. Mt. Pinchot, Big Pine, Mt. Goddard.

Wilderness Press 15-minute series. Mt. Goddard.

ROADS

Taboose Creek Road

This is the road leading to the trailhead for the Taboose Pass Trail. It is described in Chapter 5, The High Passes.

Tinemaha Creek Road

Tinemaha Creek Road leads to the trailhead for the Red Lake Trail. This could serve as the eastern approach for climbing Split Mountain; however, the road passes through private property and is not open to the public. McMurry Meadows Road is the current approach to the Red Lake Trailhead.

McMurry Meadows Road

McMurry Meadows Road leads to the trailhead for Birch Lake and to the Red Lake Trailhead. From Big Pine, go west up Glacier Lodge Road for 2.4 miles to the McMurry Meadows Road. Turn left onto the road and take the left fork (the lower road). A short distance later the road forks again; take the right fork. Continue up the road another 5.6 miles to a junction; those headed for the Birch Lake Trailhead turn right, then turn left at a fork 0.7 mile later. High-clearance vehicles are recommended beyond this point.

If headed for the Red Lake Trailhead, go left at the 5.6-mile junction. Go straight through a four-way intersection after 1.5 miles, then go through a gate after another 0.5 mile (leave it as you found it, either open or closed). Go left at a fork 0.7 mile beyond the gate and, after a couple of difficult fords (four-wheel drive recommended), go left at the next fork. Go through another gate a short distance later (leaving it either open or closed) to another fork 0.8 mile later. Go right. After 1.0 mile the road meets a fence and stays to the right of the fence for 0.7 mile to a road marked "10S01-A"; go right.

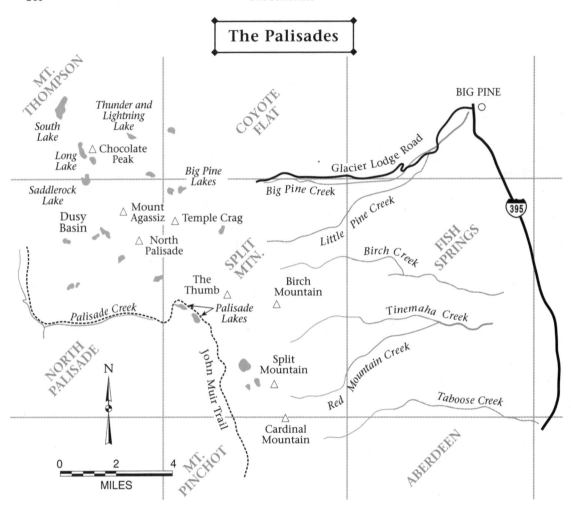

The Palisades

Take a right fork after another 0.5 mile, and another right fork again after 0.2 mile. Then go left on the road marked "10S01." Continue to the second fork and turn right. You eventually come to the last fork. The right branch leads to Tinemaha Creek and the left fork leads to the Red Lake Trailhead.

Glacier Lodge Road

Glacier Lodge Road leads from Big Pine to the trailheads for trails leading up the North and South Forks of Big Pine Creek. The road goes west from Big Pine and passes the McMurry Meadows Road after 2.4 miles. It continues west, with much climbing, to the hikers' parking area at 13.9 miles. This is the trailhead for trails leading up the North and South Forks. The road ends near Glacier Lodge, another 0.5 mile farther.

At one time this road continued up the canyon to a point along the North Fork of Big Pine Creek between First Falls and Second Falls. This section of the road was wiped out by a flood in 1982.

South Lake Road

This road is described in Chapter 9, The Evolution Region.

TRAILS

Taboose Pass Trail   10½ miles
This trail provides access to the southern part of the Palisades. It is described in Chapter 5, The High Passes.

Red Lake Trail   6 miles
A non-quota trail. The Red Lake Trail, which leads to Red Lake, serves as the eastern approach to Split Mountain. Contrary to what many maps may indicate, the trail is on the north side of Red Mountain Creek. The trail starts by following a dirt road to the north from the sign marking the trailhead (0 mi; 6,568 ft). The trail climbs over 600 feet to a prominent rock outcrop high on the northern side of the canyon. It then traverses before climbing many short switchbacks to Red Lake (6 mi; 10,459 ft). This steep trail hasn't been maintained for many years, and care must be taken to ensure that you are on the correct path.

John Muir Trail   20 miles
This section of the John Muir Trail begins along the South Fork of the Kings River at its junction with the remains of the Cartridge Pass Trail (0 mi; 10,039 ft+). The John Muir Trail goes north and passes a side trail leading to the Taboose Pass Trail (½ mi; 10,203 ft). The John Muir Trail continues north and eventually climbs to Upper Basin, one of the most beautiful lake basins in the Sierra Nevada. At the northern end of the basin, the trail has some switchbacks that lead to the top of Mather Pass (4¾ mi; 12,073 ft+). The north side of the pass has some rough talus, and the trail zigzags through it before descending across slabs past upper Palisade Lake and then traversing across the top of the cliffs north of the Palisade Lakes to the lower lake (4 mi; 10,613 ft). The trail descends a steep cliff (this was the last portion of the John Muir Trail to be completed) to Deer Meadow, which seems to consist of more timber than grass (3 mi; 8,840 ft+). The trail continues down the north bank of Palisade Creek to meet the Middle Fork Trail, which comes upstream from Simpson Meadow (3½ mi; 8,040 ft+). The John Muir Trail goes west a short distance to the mouth of Palisade Creek, where it turns north and leads to Grouse Meadows (1 mi; 8,240 ft+). The John Muir Trail goes north through LeConte Canyon to meet the Bishop Pass Trail descending from Dusy Basin (3¼ mi; 8,720 ft+). The LeConte Canyon Ranger Station is west of this junction.

Birch Lake Trail   6 miles
A non-quota trail. This steep trail starts by following an old jeep road that heads west from the trailhead near McMurry Meadows (0 mi; 6,561 ft+). Go to the right at the first fork, where the road soon turns into a trail and then goes to the crest of the ridge on the north side of Birch Creek. The trail continues west, passing a watering trough and crossing two gullies and ridges before turning south and following Birch Creek upstream in a broad valley. Cross the stream and contour up through talus to a meadow just below Birch Lake (6 mi; 10,761 ft+).

South Fork Big Pine Creek Trail   5 miles
A quota trail. Wood campfires are prohibited in this entire basin. The South Fork Trail has also been called the Brainard Lake Trail. From the hikers' parking lot along Big Pine Creek (0 mi; 7,677 ft+), follow the road past Glacier Lodge to its end. Follow the trail along the north bank of the stream, below some cabins. The trail crosses a bridge beneath First Falls, and then meets the old dirt road. Go down the dirt road a short distance and meet the trail where it crosses a brush-covered plain (1¼ mi; 8,005 ft+). The trail soon fords the South Fork of Big Pine Creek and begins to switchback up beneath a steep cliff. It then makes a slight descent towards Willow Lake. Those headed for Willow Lake and the cross-country route to Elinore Lake and Glacier Notch should go right at the first stream past Willow Lake. The main trail goes left and climbs up to Brainard Lake (3¾ mi; 10,256 ft).

Finger Lake is ¼ mile west of Brainard Lake. Follow a good use trail around the north shore of Brainard Lake, climb a steep talus slope, and then traverse across granite slabs to the northern end of Finger Lake. There is a splendid view of Middle Palisade from the lake.

North Fork Big Pine Creek Trail   9½ miles
A quota trail. The North Fork Trail passes through the most alpine scenery of the High Sierra. There are outstanding views of Temple Crag and the northern Palisade peaks. This trail ends at Seventh Lake—it does not cross the Sierra crest, contrary to the opinion of many misinformed yet enthusiastic trans-Sierra hikers met at the trailhead. Wood campfires are prohibited in this entire basin.

From the hikers' parking area (0 mi; 7,677 ft+), follow the trail west (past a fork leading to Brainard Lake). Then go north into the canyon of the North Fork of Big

Pine Creek to meet the old trail coming up from the old trailhead (wiped out by a flood in 1982) and another trail, which leads uphill to Baker Lakes (1¾ mi; 8,596 ft+). The North Fork Trail continues upstream and passes the cataract of Second Falls to the remarkably flat terrain above. The trail then passes Cienaga Mirth (misspelled as "Cienega" on some maps); the stone cabin south of the trail was built by actor Lon Chaney in 1925. The North Fork Trail continues up the canyon to meet the Black Lake Trail (3½ mi; 9,974 ft+). The North Fork Trail turns southwest, passing First Lake, Second Lake, and Third Lake, then climbs to the junction with the Sam Mack Meadow Trail (2½ mi; 10,600 ft+). The North Fork Trail continues north to a four-way junction (¼ mi; 10,760 ft+). The Black Lake Trail comes in from the east, and another trail leads to Fifth Lake, ¼ mile to the west. The North Fork Trail passes the west shore of Fourth Lake and then meets a side trail leading to Summit Lake (½ mi; 10,840 ft+); Summit Lake is ½ mile to the east. The North Fork Trail gradually turns west, climbing over a small rise and passing Sixth Lake before arriving at Seventh Lake (1 mi; 11,160 ft+).

Black Lake Trail   2 miles

This trail leaves the North Fork Trail 3½ miles from the junction of the Baker Lake Trail and the old trail leading to the former trailhead in the canyon of the North Fork of Big Pine Creek (0 mi; 9,974 ft+). It gradually switchbacks up the northern slope of the canyon and turns west, passing the southern shore of Black Lake (1 mi; 10,649 ft). It continues west to rejoin the North Fork Trail (1 mi; 10,760 ft+). There are some outstanding views of North Palisade, Mount Sill, and Thunderbolt Peak along this trail. Wood fires are prohibited in this basin.

Sam Mack Meadow and Glacier Trail
2½ miles

This trail has also been called the Glacier Trail because its upper portion leads to the Palisade Glacier. Leave the North Fork Trail approximately 1 mile beyond Third Lake (0 mi; 10,600 ft+). The trail descends to a small meadow, crosses the stream, and ascends a forested boulder field to Sam Mack Meadow (1½ mi; 11,000 ft+). Wood campfires are prohibited in the vicinity of Sam Mack Meadow.

From Sam Mack Meadow the Glacier Trail crosses the creek, goes south, and ascends benches to the ridge above the meadow. The trail turns south and traverses under and just east of the terminal moraine of the Palisade Glacier (1 mi; 11,700 ft+). A use trail then heads southwest across a short stretch of loose boulders to some slabs. Follow the slabs to the toe of the northwest ridge of Mount Gayley, where there is an outstanding view of the Palisade Glacier.

Bishop Pass Trail   12 miles

The Bishop Pass Trail provides access from South Lake to the western approaches of the Palisades. It is described in Chapter 9, The Evolution Region.

CROSS-COUNTRY ROUTES

"Red Lake Pass"   3940 m+; 12,960 ft+;
0.4 mi N of Split Mountain

Class 3. This is not really a pass, but instead a traverse across the north slope of Split Mountain between Red Lake and Upper Basin. Head northwest from Red Lake, but stay low and go to the far left side of the snowfield before climbing a chute that leads to the top of the ridge between Peak 3832m (12,627 ft) and the Sierra crest. A short class 3 traverse along this ridge leads to the "pass" at the base of the north slope of Split Mountain. The west side of the pass is easy; horses climbed it from Upper Basin in 1943.

"Bolton Brown's Shoulder"
4020m+; 13,200ft+;
0.3 mi WNW of Mount Bolton Brown

Class 2. This high pass has been used by skiers when cornices blocked Mather Pass.

Further Reading: John Moynier. *Backcountry Skiing in the High Sierra.* Evergreen, Colo.: Chockstone Press, 1992, p. 69.

Tinemaha Creek

The Tinemaha Creek canyon has been used as an early-season approach for climbs of Mount Prater and Mount Bolton Brown. Take McMurry Meadows Road or Tinemaha Creek Road to the last fork below the start of the Red Lake Trail. Hike the right branch of the fork and climb onto the ridge just south of the creek and follow it upstream, bypassing some willows on the south side.

"Lane Pass" 3980 m+; 13,120 ft+;
0.6 mi NE of Mount Bolton Brown

Class 2. This pass has been used to climb Mount Bolton Brown from Birch Lake; it also provides access to the upper part of the Palisade Creek drainage. The name commemorates Ed Lane.

From Birch Lake, go south to the saddle southwest of Birch Mountain. Traverse west from the saddle across the plateau to the pass along the Sierra crest. The west side of the pass is class 2.

"Birch Creek Pass" 3900 m+; 12,800 ft+;
0.4 mi S of The Thumb; UTM 716031

Class 3. This pass provides access between Birch Lake and the upper portion of the Palisade Creek drainage. From Birch Lake, ascend the class 3 cliff that is southeast of The Thumb. Turn left (southwest) at the top of the cliff and pass through a narrow notch located along The Thumb's southeast ridge. The southwestern side of the pass consists of a narrow class 2 chute.

Southfork Pass 3800 m+; 12,560 ft+

Class 3. Southfork Pass is used to gain access to the Palisade Creek drainage from the South Fork of Big Pine Creek. This is a difficult cross-country route, and should only be undertaken by experienced mountaineers. An ice axe and perhaps crampons and a rope may be needed, depending on the previous winter's snowfall and the time of year.

The easiest northern approach to the pass starts from the south side of Finger Lake. Follow the inlet stream uphill to where it forks. Take the left (southeast) fork, and pass two small lakes while traversing over a sea of talus and small cliffs to Pass 3660m+ (12,000 ft+; UTM 707037). Descend the east side of the pass to the small glacier beneath the north side of Southfork Pass.

From this point, the best route is almost impossible to describe. Nevertheless . . . two passes are visible, each with a chute/couloir that leads to the top of Southfork Pass. "East Southfork Pass" (UTM 709032) usually has a passable bergschrund, but its lower portion is usually a steep, narrow ice funnel; the middle portion of the chute is gentler and broader, but it has loose rock, unless it is covered with snow or ice. "West Southfork Pass"

(UTM 708032) is not quite as steep, and may be the best route. Pass the bergschrund on its right side, climb through the moat, and climb the chute to its top. But the 'schrund may be impassable, and the middle and upper portions of this chute consist of scree and loose rock, unless there is sufficient snow cover. Both chutes must be examined beforehand, preferably from the north.

The south side of the pass consists of easy scree and talus down to Lake 3589m (11,767 ft).

"Chimney Pass" 3840 m+; 12,560 ft+;
0.5 mi S of Palisade Crest; UTM 676041

Class 2. This pass has been used by climbers exploring the western side of Palisade Crest. Hikers will find Chimney Pass a preferable route between the Palisade Lakes and the Glacier Creek drainage. There are no steep slabs and the route is more obvious than Cirque Pass.

"Cirque Pass" 3680 m+; 12,000 ft+;
0.9 mi SW of Palisade Crest; UTM 667036

Class 3. This pass, in combination with Potluck Pass and Knapsack Pass, is a popular cross-country route between Mather Pass and Bishop Pass. Leave the John Muir Trail just below the lowest of the Palisade Lakes and make a gradual ascent to the west to bypass a cliff in the cirque above the level of the trail. Ascend the western edge of the cliff on a series of ledges. Beyond this barrier, pass a tarn on its western side, then ascend rock slabs and gullies to the broad saddle to the north. Descend a few feet on the north side of Cirque Pass and then traverse northwest across ledges to the outlet stream of Lake 3559m (11,672 ft) in the Glacier Creek drainage.

Further Reading: Steve Roper. *Sierra High Route.* Seattle: The Mountaineers Books, 1997, pp. 99–100, 103.

Potluck Pass 12,120 ft+; 12,080 ft+

Class 2. From Glacier Creek, either traverse or ascend to the cliff that marks the southeastern side of Potluck Pass. This cliff is bypassed by ascending a scree slope southwest of the cliff, and then climbing a series of rock ledges, which lead diagonally upward to the summit of the pass. Make a very gradual descending traverse from Potluck Pass, at first going north, and then west, to a flat saddle just northwest of Point 12,005ft (12,000 ft+;

UTM 654051). Descend from here to the largest of the Barrett Lakes (Lake 11,523ft; 11,440 ft+), and circle the lake on its eastern and northern shores.

Further Reading: Steve Roper. *Sierra High Route.* Seattle: The Mountaineers Books, 1997, pp. 100–101, 103.

"Scimitar Pass"   4100 m+; 13,451+ ft
0.4 mi SE of Mount Jepson; UTM 675052

Class 3. This pass provides access between the South Fork of Big Pine Creek and the Glacier Creek drainage. It crosses the Sierra crest north of Palisade Crest. Technically, it is not a pass but a ridge crossing. Leave the

Scimitar Pass and Palisade Crest from the east, August 24, 1972. Photo by Austin Post, No. 72R2-155, USGS Ice and Climate Project, GeoData Center, University of Alaska, Fairbanks.

cross-country route to Glacier Notch at UTM 689069, where the stream from Elinore Lake meets the stream descending from the cirque between Temple Crag and Mount Gayley. Hike up the open chute west of the stream that descends from Elinore Lake; the easiest route is on the eastern side of the chute. Continue south from Elinore Lake, aiming for the flat spot on the ridge leading west up to the Sierra crest. Follow the ridge up to the "pass," skirting the permanent snowfield northeast of Palisade Crest.

From the west, climb to the northeast from Lake 3559m (11,672 ft). Instead of going to the low point immediately southeast of Mount Jepson, climb onto the northwest shoulder of Palisade Crest. The correct crossing is approximately 200 feet above the saddle; it can be easily identified once the ridge leading down to the east is seen.

"Glacier Notch" 13,080 ft+; 13,120 ft+;
0.3 mi N of Mount Sill

Class 3; ice axe required. This pass is between Mount Sill and Mount Gayley. From Willow Lake along the South Fork of Big Pine Creek, cross the meadow upstream from the lake and follow the south side of the stream descending from the cirque between Mount Gayley and Temple Crag. Cross to the north side of the stream at the outlet of a meadow, then continue west through talus to the junction with the stream descending from Elinore Lake. Continue following the stream west to the cirque between Temple Crag and Mount Gayley. Skirt Mount Gayley on its south side, then head directly to Glacier Notch.

From the eastern side of the Palisade Glacier, cross the bergschrund (difficulty varies with the season and snow year) and climb a chute with much loose rock to the top of Glacier Notch.

Contact Pass 3580 m+; 11,760 ft+
Class 2. This pass provides access between the North and South Forks of Big Pine Creek. Leave the North Fork Big Pine Creek Trail near Second Lake and follow a good use trail that leads to two bridges across the outlet of the lake. Hike along the south shore of Second Lake and climb onto the bench above Third Lake. Follow the contact zone of light and dark rock to the top of the pass east of Temple Crag. Descend the south side of the pass to a small tarn on a bench; descend the southeast side

of the bench to the stream that descends to Willow Lake. This section of the route is described above under Glacier Notch.

"The U Notch" 13,880 ft+; 13,920 ft+;
0.1 mi SE of North Palisade

Class 4; ice axe and perhaps crampons required. This is a climbers' route, and it is not suitable for cross-country hikers without climbing equipment and experience. It has been used by climbers to gain the southwest side of the North Palisade massif from the Palisade Glacier. For details, see the climbing descriptions of The U Notch and LeConte routes for North Palisade, later in this chapter.

Knapsack Pass 11,680 ft+; 11,673 ft
Class 1. Knapsack Pass leads from Dusy Basin to the Barrett Lakes in Palisade Basin. Leave the Bishop Pass Trail near the lowest lakes in Dusy Basin and head southeast to the saddle south of Columbine Peak, which is Knapsack Pass. Rock slabs and shallow gullies lead to the summit of the pass. Traverse east beneath the southern cliffs of Columbine Peak to where it is possible to make a short, easy descent to the Barrett Lakes.

Further Reading: Steve Roper. *Sierra High Route*. Seattle: The Mountaineers Books, 1997, pp. 100–101, 103.

If you are headed toward Deer Meadow along Palisade Creek, make a direct descent from the summit of Knapsack Pass over many tedious class 2 cliffs. It is best to remain on the western bank of the stream for most of the time during the descent to the John Muir Trail.

"Isosceles Pass" 12,080 ft+; 12,000 ft+;
0.1 mi S of Isosceles Peak

Class 3. This pass has been used as an alternative to Knapsack Pass. It is class 3 on the Dusy Basin side and class 2 on the Barrett Lakes side. Knapsack Pass is much easier and is preferable.

"Thunderbolt Pass" 12,360 ft+; 12,320 ft+;
0.4 mi WSW of Thunderbolt Peak

Class 2. This is another route between Dusy Basin and Palisade Basin. Leave the Bishop Pass Trail south of Bishop Pass and contour southeast above the level of Lake 11,400ft+ (11,393 ft) to the obvious saddle southwest of Thunderbolt Peak. Much tedious talus is encountered before reaching the summit of the pass. From

Palisade Glacier and Vicinity

Jigsaw Pass

Aperture Peak

Mount Robinson

Sam Mack Meadow

Third Lake

Second Lake

Bishop Pass

Mount Agassiz

Sam Mack Lake

Temple Crag

Contact Pass

Agassiz Col

Palisade Glacier

Dusy Basin

Mount Winchell

Mount Gayley

Thunderbolt Peak

Glacier Notch

Elinore Lake

Thunderbolt Pass

North Palisade

Isosceles Peak

Mount Sill

Columbine Peak

Polemonium Peak

Mount Jepson

Barrett Lakes

Scimitar Pass

Knapsack Pass

N

Palisade Basin

Potluck Pass

Palisade Crest

0   0.5

MILE

the top of the pass, either descend to the south over talus and many small cliffs to the largest of the Barrett Lakes, or traverse southeast across talus beneath North Palisade to Potluck Pass.

"Winchell Col"   13,040 ft+; 12,960 ft+;
0.2 mi S of Mount Winchell

Class 4, A0. This col is to the south of the pinnacle (the "Dolphin Fin") near the saddle between Thunder-

bolt Peak and Mount Winchell. This pass has been used by climbers to approach the west sides of Mount Winchell and Thunderbolt Peak from the Thunderbolt Glacier. This involves a 100-foot rappel when going from east to west, so it is a route used by climbers only.

Agassiz Col   13,080 ft+; 13,040 ft+

Class 3. This pass leads between Sam Mack Meadow and Dusy Basin. Leave Sam Mack Meadow at its western end and go north (the snow chute at the western end of Sam Mack Meadow is frequently too icy to climb, especially with heavy packs). Follow a good use trail up and right to a point approximately 100 feet below a waterfall, the outlet of Sam Mack Lake. Traverse right (east) and then go up sandy ledges to the ridge above. Go west across boulders to Sam Mack Lake. From the western shore of the lake go west to the cirque and glacier between Mount Winchell and Mount Agassiz. Cross the glacier and approach the col from the northeast, making a diagonally ascending traverse across the base of the south face of Mount Agassiz to the top of the col. Descend the west side of the col over scree and talus to Dusy Basin.

When crossing Agassiz Col from the west to east, ascend the largest chute between Mount Winchell and Mount Agassiz to the top of the col.

Jigsaw Pass   12,720 ft+; 12,720 ft+;
0.1 mi NW of Aperture Peak; UTM 639090

Class 3. Jigsaw Pass is between Fifth Lake (in the drainage of the North Fork of Big Pine Creek) and the Bishop Creek basin (just north of Bishop Pass). From the south shore of Fifth Lake, ascend talus and slabs south of the inlet stream that flows from Mount Agassiz. Take the north branch from where the stream forks and then go left over easy terrain to Jigsaw Pass, which is south of the lowest point on the crest of the ridge leading northwest from Aperture Peak. Descend the west side of the pass via an easy chute and cross boulders to meet the Bishop Pass Trail.

It is difficult to identify the correct chute leading to Jigsaw Pass when crossing the pass from west to east. Jigsaw Pass is south of the lowest point northwest from Aperture Peak, and is separated from the low point by a small peak. Ascend the southern of two chutes, over scree, grass, and broken rock. The ascent is easier than it appears from below.

PEAKS

Peak 3917m   12,851 ft;
1.0 mi SW of Cardinal Mountain

First ascent August 5, 1945 by A. J. Reyman, via the class 1 southeast ridge.

Cardinal Mountain   4083 m; 13,397 ft

First ascent August 11, 1922 by George Downing, Jr. Ascend a chute on the south side of the mountain from the vicinity of Taboose Pass. The chute is class 2, and it is filled with disagreeably loose rock.

The east ridge from Stecker Bench is class 2, and was first climbed February 7, 1971 by Tom Ross.

County Line. Class 2. First ascent 1993 by Paul Richins and his daughter, Sierra Richins. Head northwest from Taboose Pass to the spur ridge that is to the east of Lake 3620m+ (11,840 ft+). Follow this ridge to the north and then to the northeast to some towers. Move to the southern side of the ridge crest, then traverse across three or four gullies before climbing back onto the crest. Follow the ridge to the summit.

Peak 4180m+   13,803 ft;
0.5 mi SSW of Split Mountain

Southeast Couloir. Class 4. First ascent October 3, 1965 by Gary Lewis and Ed Lane. Hike up the south branch of Red Mountain Creek and head for a huge pillar on the southeast side of the peak. Ascend the couloir just west of this pillar. The couloir is blocked at one point; this obstacle is easily bypassed by a short class 4 move on its right side. The couloir goes west and then southwest to the summit rocks.

Horseshoe Ridge. Class 4. First ascent August 28, 1989 by Steve Porcella and Cameron Burns. Gain the crest of the northwest ridge immediately west of Lake 3650m (11,599ft) and follow it south, southeast, and east to the summit. Most of this ridge is class 3, but a few class 4 sections are encountered where the ridge gradually turns to the east. The first-ascent party traversed the peak and continued on to Split Mountain via its south ridge.

Split Mountain   4280 m+; 14,058 ft

This mountain was once known as "South Palisade." It is easily identified from the Owens Valley by the large East Couloir, which leads to the notch between its two summits. The north summit is the high point. After Mount Whitney, this is the easiest 14,000-foot peak in the Sierra. First ascent July 1887 by Frank Saulque and party, via an unknown route.

Further Reading: Stephen F. Porcella and Cameron M. Burns. *Climbing California's Fourteeners.* Seattle: The Mountaineers Books, 1998, pp. 134–147.

North Slope. Class 2. First ascent July 23, 1902 by Joseph LeConte, Helen LeConte, and Curtis Lindley. Ascend to the saddle between Mount Prater and Split Mountain from Upper Basin and climb the easy talus slopes to the summit.

North Slope from the East. Class 3. The north slope can be reached from Red Lake by crossing Red Lake Pass.

Further Reading: Stephen F. Porcella and Cameron M. Burns. *Hiking and Climbing: California's Fourteeners.* Evergreen, Colo.: Chockstone Press, 1996, pp. 41–45.

St. Jean Couloir. Class 3–4. First ascent December 1981 by Bill St. Jean. This route is also known as "Ice None" and "Ice Nein." This couloir is on the northeast side of Split Mountain and ends along the north slope. This couloir is deeper than the East Couloir, and it retains snow longer during the summer. The bottom part of the couloir consists of 35° to 40° névé to a steep step. Bypass the step by climbing rocks on the right, gained by a small but prominent recess or chimney. Continue up the couloir over rock (mostly class 3 with a few class 4 steps) to the top.

East Arête of North Summit. III, 5.8. First ascent October 1976 by Galen Rowell. This arête is immediately right of the East Couloir. After 20 feet of loose rock, a 5.8 squeeze chimney is encountered before the angle of the arête eases. Continue following the arête to where it is blocked by some large gendarmes. An impossible-appearing gendarme is climbed on its left side from a small ledge via a 5.8 layback. Follow the crest of the gendarmes to where the arête ends just north of the north summit.

East Couloir. III, AI2 or WI3, class 4. First ascent May 1964 by Arkel Erb. This 1,300-foot gully has been reported as being one of the better ice climbs in the High Sierra. The couloir begins by climbing a narrow, 20-foot 65° section of ice. Class 3 and 4 climbing for 300 feet then leads to a 100-foot headwall. This is overcome by means of a snow-filled chimney on the left. Continue ascending the couloir to where it ends between the two summits of Split Mountain. A short class 4 pitch leads to the higher north summit. *Variation:* 5.4. First ascent December 1981 by Bob Harrington. The headwall can be bypassed by means of a short rock pitch on the far left.

Variation: First ascent early 1980s by Yvon Chouinard, Richard Leversee, and James Wilson. The headwall can also be overcome by means of a 70-foot pitch of water ice on its right side.

Further Reading: John Moynier and Claude Fiddler. *Sierra Classics.* Evergreen, Colo.: Chockstone Press, 1993, pp. 113–117.

East Arête of South Summit. IV, 5.9. First ascent February 1976 by David Belden and Galen Rowell. This arête is immediately south of the East Couloir of Split Mountain. Cross the snowfield beneath the East Couloir and head left onto easy rock to the base of a sheer wall. Some 5.9 climbing is needed to climb the wall. The route eventually leads to the narrow crest of the arête. Follow the crest to a small headwall, which is overcome by some 5.8 climbing. The arête ends atop the lower south summit. *Variation:* First ascent by Dean Hobbs and Bob Harrington. The sheer wall on the lower part of the route can be bypassed by traversing left and gaining the crest of the arête earlier.

Hobbs-Slate Route. IV, 5.9. First ascent September 1984 by Dean Hobbs and Gary Slate. This route climbs the arête farthest left on the east side of Split Mountain. More than twenty pitches of varied climbing lead to the south ridge, which is then followed to the south summit.

Southeast Chute. Class 3. Head southwest from Red Lake and cross the long, east ridge of Split Mountain to the basin that is southeast of the peak. A large chute leads up from this basin directly to the south summit. Ascend the chute, crossing between its sides to avoid steep rock, to the south summit. Descend the class 3 north face of the south summit, then go left (northwest) from the notch to a class 2 gully that leads to the north summit.

South Ridge. II, 5.6. First ascent 1932 by Jules Eichorn and Glen Dawson. Follow the ridge north from Peak 4180m+ (13,803 ft), bypassing gendarmes to the left and right as needed. This ridge is dangerously loose. The crux is at the notch beneath Peak 4180m+; climb straight up the opposite wall of loose bricks.

West Face. Class 3. Descended by Norman Clyde. The west side of Split Mountain is marked by ribs and chutes. It is better to ascend the ribs, as there are many small cliffs in the chutes. This climb can become class 4 if the best route isn't chosen.

Split Mountain from the east. Photo by John Moynier.

SPLIT MOUNTAIN

South
Summit

North
Summit

East Arête
of North Summit

North Slope

Hobbs-Slate
Route

East Arête
of South Summit

St. Jean
Couloir

East
Couloir

Mount Tinemaha   3186 m; 12,561 ft

West Ridge. Class 2. First ascent July 1, 1937 by Chester Versteeg. From Tinemaha Creek, ascend to the west ridge of the peak and follow the ridge to the summit. This ridge can also be followed from Red Lake Pass. Follow the south side of the ridge over many class 3 ribs and chutes.

South Slope. Class 1. This is an easy ascent from Red Lake.

The south and east ridges are class 3.

Mount Prater   4106 m; 13,329 ft

Southeast Ridge. Class 1. First winter ascent March 7, 1971 by Peter Lewis and Tom Ross. Gain the southeast ridge from Upper Basin and follow the ridge to the summit. A short knife edge is easy but scary.

Hidden Couloir. II, 5.2. First ascent September 1980 by Del Johns and Wayne N. Sawka. This 800-foot, 45° ice couloir leads to the southeast ridge of Mount Prater from Tinemaha Creek.

Obvious Chute. Class 3. First ascent March 19, 1972 by Ed Treacy, Karl Bennett, Dave Gladstone, Vi Grasso, Dave King, and Doug Mantle. From Tinemaha Lake, climb the chute leading to the plateau between Mount Bolton Brown and Mount Prater. Turn south to the deep notch north of Mount Prater, where a 100-foot class 3 pitch leads to the summit.

North Ridge. Class 3. First ascent October 6, 1948 by Fred L. Jones. Ascend to the plateau north of Mount Prater from the northernmost part of Upper Basin. It is best to ascend the largest chute south of the pinnacles that are south of Mount Bolton Brown. Traverse south from the top to the deep notch north of Mount Prater. It is class 3 to the summit from there.

Mount Bolton Brown   4112 m; 13,538 ft

South Ridge. Class 3. First ascent March 19, 1972 by Ed Treacy, Karl Bennett, Dave Gladstone, Vi Grasso, Dave King, and Doug Mantle. Follow the ridge from the plateau southeast of Mount Bolton Brown. Drop down on the west side of the ridge before reaching the lower, southeast summit. Then climb to the true summit via the northwest ridge.

North Slope. Class 2. First ascent October 6, 1948 by Fred L. Jones. It is best to ascend the slope to the northwest ridge and follow the ridge to the summit.

Southwest Slope. Class 3. Descended August 14, 1922 by Chester Versteeg and Rudolph Berls. The slope directly beneath the summit has much loose rock.

Birch Mountain   4146 m; 13,665 ft

First ascent 1887 by J. W. Bledsoe. First winter ascent February 22, 1961 by Tom Ross. The southwest ridge is class 2 from the saddle between Birch Creek and Tinemaha Creek. The south slope is class 2 from Tinemaha Creek. Ribs and gullies on the west and northwest sides of the peak are class 2–3.

Further Reading: John Moynier. *Backcountry Skiing in the High Sierra.* Evergreen, Colo.: Chockstone Press, 1992, p. 171.

Peak 4138m   13,520 ft+;
1.0 mi N of Mount Bolton Brown

This peak has been referred to as "Ed Lane Peak."

Northwest Ridge. Class 3. First ascent June 14, 1930 by Norman Clyde. First winter ascent March 12, 1972 by Dick Beach, Bob Thornburg, and Dan Dunaway. Climb to the saddle south of The Thumb from either the east or west and ascend the western side of the north ridge to the summit. Only the last portion of this climb is class 3.

West Chute. Class 3. First ascent August 7, 1971 by John and Louise Clark. Ascend a chute or gully on the west side of the peak to a point on the north ridge just north of the summit.

South Ridge. Class 4. First ascent June 13, 1971 by Carl Heller and Dennis Burge. A short headwall must be overcome before climbing onto the ridge from Lane Pass.

North Couloir. Class 4. First ascent June 16, 1979 by Peter von Gaza and Lars Mollor. Ascend a 40° to 50° snow couloir on the north-northeast face to the north ridge of the peak. Follow the western side of the north ridge to the summit.

The Thumb   4071 m; 13,388 ft

Southeast Slope. Class 2–3. First ascent December 12, 1921 by W. B. Putnam. This is a straightforward climb from Birch Lake. A small cliff low on the slope is bypassed on its southwest side by climbing a ramp with some loose class 3 moves. The rest of the climb is easy.

From Southfork Pass. Class 2. This climb begins from the top of "East Southfork Pass." Contour toward the east to a broad, scree-filled chute. Ascend it to where it narrows and then cross into the next chute to the right.

Follow this chute to the gentle slopes southeast of the summit.

Northwest Couloir. Class 4. First ascent June 5, 1930 by Norman Clyde. Climb the large, recessed couloir at the far right-hand side of the northwest face of The Thumb. The couloir gradually narrows and is blocked by a large chockstone, which is bypassed by climbing the wall on the right. You eventually reach the crest of the rib between the couloir and the next chute south. Enter the next chute south, then follow it to the gentle slope south of The Thumb.

Northwest Corner. III, 5.7. First ascent June 1965 by Hank Abrons, Peter Carman, and C. Bickel. This route ascends an outside corner high on the northwest side of The Thumb. This corner is flanked by two faces marked by prominent black dikes.

Black Dike. IV, 5.9. First ascent July 1979 by Eve Laeger, Herb Laeger, and Dick Saum. Second ascent 1983 by Karl McConachie and Charlie Jenkowitz. This route ascends a conspicuous vein of black diorite on the northwest face.

North-Northeast Ridge. Class 5. First ascent September 12, 1957 by Leigh Ortenburger and Irene Ortenburger. Climb the deep couloir (loose rock!) on the west side of The Thumb that ends closest to the summit along the north-northeast ridge. Three chockstones in the couloir are easily bypassed. Leave the couloir on its right side and ascend an arête to the main north-northeast ridge. Follow the north-northeast ridge to the summit. Turn the last obstacle just below the top on its left side, then climb a series of class 5 ledges to a point near the summit.

The Thumb from the northwest. Photo by R. J. Secor.

Peak 3994m   13,365 ft; 0.9 mi NNE of The Thumb

First ascent November 14, 1926 by Norman Clyde. The broad hour-glass–shaped couloir on the north side of the peak was climbed winter 1996 by Tom Sexton and Bob Rockwell. This couloir leads to the north ridge, which is then followed to the top.

"Balcony Peak"   4220 m+; 13,840 ft+;
0.1 mi SE of Disappointment Peak

This small peak is a landmark for those ascending Disappointment Peak. The east ridge and the southeast slope are class 2.

Disappointment Peak   4242 m; 13,917 ft

This is the second peak south of Middle Palisade, and the first peak north of Balcony Peak. Its name reflects the feelings of the first-ascent party, who thought they were climbing Middle Palisade only to find themselves separated from it by class 4 cliffs. There is much loose rock

on this peak, and extreme caution is advised.

Northeast Couloir. Class 4. First ascent June 20, 1930 by Norman Clyde. There are two couloirs on the northeast side of Disappointment Peak. Climb the right-hand (north) couloir, which leads to the notch north of the peak. Ascend the couloir part way, then traverse to the notch south of the peak. The summit is an easy scramble from here.

Doug's Chute. Class 4. First ascent August 1971 by Don Anderson, Dave King, and Ed Treacy. This route is named after Doug Mantle, who climbed it shortly after the first-ascent party. It follows the left-hand (south) side of the two couloirs on the northeast side of Disappointment Peak; this couloir leads to the notch south of the summit. Climb the chute to the right of a band of red rock intruded into the cliffs beneath the peak. This class 4 chute has some extraordinarily loose rock; it is more akin to climbing vertical seashells than rock. At the top of the chute, go right and climb the couloir to the

Balcony Peak, Disappointment Peak, and Middle Palisade from the southeast. Photo by R. J. Secor.

notch south of the summit. The summit is easily reached from the notch.

East Ridge. Class 4. First ascent September 1953 by Bill Dunmire and Allen Steck, who in reality bypassed the summit of Disappointment Peak on their way to the summit of Middle Palisade. The name of this route actually refers to the east ridge of Balcony Peak. From the Middle Palisade Glacier, climb one of the snow or ice couloirs to the crest of the east ridge. Ascend the crest of the ridge to the point where the ridge crest appreciably steepens, which is about 300 feet below the summit of Balcony Peak. Traverse down and across the north face of Balcony Peak to a small notch in a rib. Traverse horizontally from the notch across three loose chutes to the main couloir between Balcony Peak and Disappointment Peak. Climb the couloir to the notch, and then on to the summit.

Traverse from Balcony Peak. Class 4. This traverse starts by going *south* from the summit of Balcony Peak for approximately 150 (horizontal) feet. Descend a narrow chute, which is blocked by a chockstone, to the main southwest chute of Disappointment Peak. Ascend the southwest chute to the notch south of the summit, then follow the ridge north to the top of Disappointment Peak.

Southwest Chute. Class 4. First ascent July 20, 1919 by J. M. Davies, A. L. Jordan, and H. H. Bliss. There is a large buttress that descends southwest from the summit of Balcony Peak toward the Palisade Lakes. Ascend the first chute left (north) of this buttress to the notch south of Disappointment Peak. There are four roped pitches in this chute, mostly over and around some huge chockstones. The summit is class 3 from the notch.

West Face. IV, 5.10, A2. First ascent September 1986 by Galen Rowell and Dan Frankl. This route begins by climbing the arête to the left (north) of the Southwest Chute route. Leave the arête via a crack that leads left to the main west face of Disappointment Peak. Continue up the face to the summit.

Traverse from Middle Palisade. Class 4. This route does not follow the ridge south from Middle Palisade, but rather descends from the summit of Middle Palisade, moving gradually southeast to a point approximately 200 vertical feet below the first peak south of Middle Palisade (known locally as "Excitement Peak"). Traverse horizontally from this point, across two small chutes and ribs to the couloir leading to the notch north of Disap-

pointment Peak. Either ascend the couloir to the notch, or leave the couloir and traverse beneath Disappointment Peak to the notch south of the peak. *Variation:* 5.6, A0. You can also traverse along the crest of the ridge (or very close to it) from the summit of Middle Palisade.

Middle Palisade   4271 m; 14,040 ft

The top of Middle Pal is a knife edge fin, approximately 300 feet long.

Further Reading: Stephen F. Porcella and Cameron M. Burns. *Climbing California's Fourteeners.* Seattle: The Mountaineers Books, 1998, pp. 148–161.

Northeast Face. Class 3. First ascent June 7, 1930 by Norman Clyde. First winter ascent January 2, 1960 by John Mendenhall and Tom Condon. You can approach the start of this route either from the top of the moraine that divides the Middle Palisade Glacier, or by climbing the southern half of the glacier. Gain a ledge that climbs diagonally up and right. This leads to a wide couloir, which is followed to where it is possible to traverse into the next couloir to the right (this point is marked by a patch of white or lightly colored reddish brown rock, depending on one's mood, it seems). Follow the left branch of this couloir to the summit. *Variation:* From reading Clyde's account of the climb (published in the magazine *Touring Topics,* August 1931, p. 32) it appears that he climbed directly to the first couloir from the northern half of the Middle Palisade Glacier.

Further Reading: Stephen F. Porcella and Cameron M. Burns. *Hiking and Climbing: California's Fourteeners.* Chockstone Press, Evergreen, Colo., 1996, pp. 46–50; John Moynier and Claude Fiddler. *Sierra Classics.* Evergreen, Colo.: Chockstone Press, 1993, pp. 124–125. *Summit.* July–August 1987, p. 12.

East Face. III, 5.4. First ascent August 31, 1975 by Tim Ryan and John Mendenhall. This climb begins at the highest point of the south Middle Palisade Glacier. Climb straight up to a 60-foot horizontal ledge. Move to the left end of the ledge and ascend a loose chimney. Go left from the top of the chimney, then ascend to a belay ledge beneath an overhang. Continue up for another pitch, and then traverse left into the broad chute that leads to the notch immediately south of the summit. From the notch, traverse right, across the east side of the peak, before climbing to the summit.

Norman Clyde Peak, Middle Palisade, Disappointment Peak, and Balcony Peak from the southwest. Photo by R. J. Secor.

Traverse from Disappointment Peak. Class 4. First ascent July 20, 1939 by David Brower, Bruce Meyer, and Keith Taylor. Descend the north side of the summit of Disappointment Peak to the first notch. Descend the eastern side of the peak, down the chute approximately 300 feet, and traverse left (north) across two ribs and chutes. Make a diagonal ascent up and across the east side of Middle Palisade to the summit. *Variation:* 5.6, A0. You can traverse close to the ridge crest on its eastern side at first, then on its western side near the summit of Middle Palisade.

Farquhar Route. Class 4. First ascent August 26, 1921 by Francis Farquhar and Ansel F. Hall. This route is exposed and has much loose rock, and it is easy to get off-route. Only experienced climbers should attempt this climb. When viewing Middle Palisade and Disappointment Peak from the Palisade Lakes, you see a chute leading to the notch between Disappointment Peak and Bal-

cony Peak. There is another chute north of this one, followed by yet another, which leads to Middle Palisade. If the wrong chute is chosen, then this will result in . . . Disappointment.

Ascend this steep, loose chute to about three-fourths of the way up, where it becomes more difficult. Traverse left and climb an exposed, broken face, then move slightly to the right to climb a class 4 chimney meeting the summit ridge just south of the top.

Smoke Buttress. IV, 5.9, with a rappel. First ascent July 10, 1990 by Steve Porcella and Cameron Burns. This route has been named in memory of Smoke Blanchard. It climbs the steep buttress in the center of Middle Palisade's west face; it is immediately left of the chute marking the Farquhar Route. Climb the crest of the buttress for nine pitches of 5.5–5.8 to a steep headwall (5.9). One more pitch on the buttress ends at its top, where a rappel is necessary. Climb a class 3 ridge to a class 4 chimney on the right; two pitches in the chimney end on the summit ridge. Climb the summit ridge to the top of the peak.

Northwest Ridge. III, 5.6, A0. First ascent July 30, 1933 by Jules Eichorn and Glen Dawson. This traverse starts from the summit of Norman Clyde Peak.

Norman Clyde Peak   4223 m; 13,920 ft+

This is the impressive peak seen from Glacier Lodge along Big Pine Creek. The southeast summit is the high point.

North Face. II, AI1 or WI2, class 3. First ascent June 9, 1930 by Norman Clyde. First winter ascent April 1959 by Jon Shinno, Jim Eslinger, and Ricky Tejada-Flores. Ascend the 40°, 700-foot snow/ice couloir that leads to the col between Norman Clyde Peak and Mount Williams (Peak 4152m; 13,659 ft). Pass through the col to its south side. Traverse east across the south side of the peak to a chute that leads to the crest of the ridge; the crest is marked by a chockstone. Ascend this chute, but go right when another broad, easy chute appears to the right. This leads to a notch behind a low tower. Pass

Balcony Peak, Disappointment Peak, and Middle Palisade from the northeast, August 24, 1972. Photo by Austin Post, No. 72R2-156, USGS Ice and Climate Project, GeoData Center, University of Alaska, Fairbanks.

NORMAN CLYDE
PEAK

Firebird
Ridge

North-Northeast
Ridge

North Face

Norman Clyde Glacier

through the notch to another large chute that descends to the south. Climb to the bowl at the head of this chute, where a ledge system leads up and right to the higher, southeast summit.

North-Northeast Ridge. Class 3–4. First ascent September 21, 1958 by Bill Sanders and Bud Bingham. Second ascent July 22, 1961 by Arkel Erb and Mike McNicholas. This is the preferred route from the north, but the routefinding is tricky, and many outstanding climbers have been defeated. From Finger Lake, ascend scree and talus west to the crest of the ridge that runs north and south from Peak 3862m (12,640 ft+). Follow the ridge south to the start of Norman Clyde Peak's north-northeast ridge. Cross onto the north face, where the ridge begins to steepen at two large boulders on the ridge crest. Zigzag on ledges on the north face, always remaining between 50 and 200 feet of the north-northeast ridge. Aim for a series of black, watermarked slabs about 300 feet below the apparent summit ridge. A narrow crack system to the right of these slabs leads to the top of the false summit. Scramble southeast to the true summit. *Variation:* The north-northeast ridge can also be reached from the east by ascending a ledge and chute that lead to the saddle between Peak 3862m (12,640 ft+). *Variation:* The north-northeast ridge has also been approached from the Norman Clyde Glacier. Ice axes and crampons may be needed to cross the glacier, and there is much loose rock on the lower portion of the north face. A better alternative may be to bypass the glacier on its northern side and climb to the north ridge of Peak 3862m (12,640 ft+) before turning south to the start of the north-northeast ridge of Norman Clyde Peak.

Further Reading: *Summit.* July–August 1987, p. 12.

Firebird Ridge. IV, 5.9. First ascent July 1975 by Fred Beckey, Mike Graber, and Dave Black. This route has also been referred to as "Primrose Ridge." This climb is accomplished by religiously staying on the very crest of the ridge.

Eagle Face. II, 5.4. First ascent August 1961 by John Sharsmith, Larry Williams, and Allen Steck. From the point where the north-northeast ridge begins to steepen, traverse left across the northeast side of Norman Clyde Peak to the large, circular snow patch on the northeast face. Left of this snow patch is Twilight Pillar, the steep buttress that drops directly from the true summit of

Norman Clyde Peak. From the upper left-hand edge of this snow patch, enter a chimney about 100 feet to the right of Twilight Pillar. Ascend the chimney for 80 feet, then traverse right onto the face and ascend it for several pitches. Cross the face to the left over some loose rock to a small snow patch. Continue climbing up and left over the steep wall to the summit, taking care that the easiest and safest route is followed.

Twilight Pillar. III, 5.9. First ascent July 1966 by Don Jensen and Frank Sarnquist. First winter ascent February 1986 by David Wilson and Galen Rowell. This is the prominent, steep outside corner leading directly to the summit on Norman Clyde Peak's northeast side: a beautiful route.

The buttress can be reached directly from the Middle Palisade Glacier by climbing one 5.7 pitch, or from the circular snowfield described under the Eagle Face route, above. The route starts to the right of the prow by climbing a 5.9 chimney requiring jamming and stemming that ends atop the crest of the prow. The next pitch starts by climbing a 5.9 crack to the left of the prow, then traverses to the right across the crest of the prow. Ascend the face that is left of a right-facing open book for 80 feet of 5.8 face and crack climbing before traversing back into the open book to a comfortable belay ledge in an alcove. Climb the alcove (loose rock!) and then a 5.8 crack that ends on a ledge. The next pitch climbs 90 feet above the book on cracks, and includes a delicate move to the right (5.9) over a slight overhang. The remainder of the climb follows a shallow trough on the crest of the pillar for four pitches to the summit.

Further Reading: John Moynier and Claude Fiddler. *Sierra Classics.* Evergreen, Colo.: Chockstone Press, 1993, pp. 126–127; *Rock & Ice.* No. 73 (May–June 1996), p. 70.

Thunderbird Wall. III, 5.7. First ascent June 1965 by Hank Abrons and Peter Carman. This route climbs a prominent crack-and-chimney system on the wall to the left of Twilight Pillar. This system can be reached by traversing from Twilight Pillar, or from the north Middle Palisade Glacier by climbing ledges that are below and left of the crack system. Four pitches in the crack system lead to the southeast ridge of the peak, approximately 200 feet from the summit.

Southeast Ridge. III, 5.6, A0. First ascent July 30, 1933

Norman Clyde Peak from the northwest. Photo by R. J. Secor.

Norman Clyde Peak, North Face. Photo by R. J. Secor.

by Jules Eichorn and Glen Dawson. Traverse the ridge from Middle Palisade. The first small peak encountered on the traverse is locally known as "Dent du Dent," and the second as "Bivouac Peak."

South Face. Class 3. First ascent June 19, 1930 by Norman Clyde. A buttress curves down to the southwest from the ridge between Mount Williams (Peak 4152m; 13,659 ft) and Norman Clyde Peak. Ascend the inside curve of this buttress to a chute that leads up and slightly right to the crest of the ridge; this chute eventually leads to a narrow notch with a chockstone bridging it on the ridge crest. Ascend this chute about two-thirds

of the way up and then go to the right over easy terrain to a notch behind a low, squat tower. Pass through the notch to another large chute, which drops off to the south. Ascend this large chute to the bowl at its head, where a ledge system leads up and right to the higher, southeast summit of Norman Clyde Peak. *Variation:* Class 4. First ascent 1978 by Frank Meyers, Bill Lipps, and Mark Fincher. After passing through the notch to the second large chute, climb a class 4 ledge followed by another class 4 pitch to the lower, northwestern summit of Norman Clyde Peak. Follow the ridge southeast to the high point.

"Mount Williams"   4152 m; 13,659 ft;

0.3 mi WNW of Norman Clyde Peak

This peak is unofficially named after Larry Williams, the founder of the mountaineering school and guide service in the Palisades. There is a 40°, 700-foot ice couloir on the north face of the peak. Doug Adams and John Fischer traversed this peak from south to north, and gave it a 5.2 rating.

Palisade Crest   4131 m; 13,520 ft+

This is the impressive row of twelve pinnacles rising above Elinore Lake. The pinnacles have been named af-

ter characters from J. R. R. Tolkien's book, *The Hobbit*. The high point, known as "Gandalf Peak," is the northwesternmost pinnacle.

Northwest Ridge. Class 4. First ascent 1969 by Don Jensen, Rex Post, and Joan Jensen. From the top of Scimitar Pass, traverse at first on the west side of the ridge, then between flakes on top of the ridge. Descend the eastern side of the ridge to the notch immediately northwest of the summit pinnacle. This traverse is class 3, with diligent routefinding. From the notch, climb a 160-foot class 4 slab to just below the summit. It is class 3 from the top of this pitch to the summit.

Middle Palisade and Norman Clyde Peak from the northeast, August 24, 1972. Photo by Austin Post, No. 72R2-156, USGS Ice and Climate Project, GeoData Center, University of Alaska, Fairbanks.

Traverse. III, 5.5. First ascent 1969 by Don Jensen, Rex Post, and Joan Jensen. This traverse has been described as not too difficult, with high-quality climbing.

Northeast Face. Class 4. First ascent 1967 by Don Jensen and Stu Dole. Climb a rib on the northeast face of Palisade Crest. This route ends atop one of the central pinnacles.

Southeastern Pinnacles. II, 5.7. First ascent July 4, 1954 by John Mendenhall and Ruth Mendenhall. From the western lobe of the Norman Clyde Glacier, climb the snow couloir leading to the notch southeast of Palisade Crest. The first pitch up from the top of the notch is 5.7, and the rest of the climb to the top of the southeast pinnacle has been described as having some interesting class 4 and class 5 pitches. The two pinnacles northwest from the southeast pinnacle are class 4 from the southeast pinnacle.

Mount Jepson   4081 m; 13,390 ft

This peak was once unofficially known as "The Pine Marten."

From the South. Class 2. First ascent July 3, 1939 by Don McGeein, Chet Errett, and Evelyn Errett. This is an easy climb from either the Glacier Creek drainage or the top of Scimitar Pass.

Northeast Face. III, 5.8. First ascent August 1970 by Doug Robinson and Don Jensen. There are two chimneys on the northeast face. Begin climbing 40 feet to the right of the left-hand chimney. After one pitch of 5.7, go left into the chimney. Continue climbing in the chimney into an immense cave. Difficult chimney climbing leads out under the lip of the cave. One more pitch leads to the summit.

The Steeple. II, 5.8. First ascent by Richard Dobeman and John Fischer. This route climbs the far left-hand side of the northeast face. Climb a prominent pillar that is split by a crack.

Giraud Peak   12,608 ft; 12,585 ft

First ascent September 1925 by Norman Clyde. First winter ascent April 15, 1996 by Colin Fuller. The southeast slope is class 2. The southeast slope can be reached from Dusy Basin by following the north ridge of Peak 12,265ft (12,240 ft+). This ridge steepens at approximately 11,400 feet, and it is best to traverse to the right into a gully and climb it to the top of the east ridge of Giraud Peak. Alternatively, the right side of the crest of the northwest ridge of Peak 12,265ft (12,240 ft+) can be ascended. Descend the south side of the east ridge almost to the northwestern shore of Lake 11,080ft+ (11,040 ft+; UTM 611038) before ascending the southeast slope. In 1995 Tina Stough descended the north side of the stream-draining Lake 11,080ft+ (11,040 ft+) to Grouse Meadows: class 2, brush, with a couple of easy class 3 moves over slabs.

North Face. II, 5.4. First ascent July 1979 by David Mazel. Climb the prominent snow couloir on the north face. This consists of several hundred feet of 45° snow/ice climbing, followed by two pitches of rock climbing, which lead directly up to the summit.

There is also a chute on the far right side of the north face that is full of loose class 2 rock.

Columbine Peak   12,662 ft; 12,652 ft

This peak is class 2 from nearby Knapsack Pass; a scree chute on the west side of the peak provides a good descent route. The northeast ridge is class 2. There is an outstanding view of the Palisades (and other peaks) from the summit.

Isosceles Peak   12,321 ft; 12,240 ft+

Northeast Face. Class 3 with a class 4 summit block. First ascent July 1938 by Wear and Morse.

West Face. II, 5.9. First ascent August 1978 by Alan Bartlett and Allan Pietrasanta. Climb the central crack-and-chimney system in the middle of the face.

West Face, Right Side. II, 5.7. First ascent October 24, 1988 by Chris Keith and Peter Lowery.

West Chute. II, 5.7. First ascent July 1991 by Don Palmer and David Harden. Climb the chute (5.5) that leads to the notch just south of the summit. Climb through a tunnel in the ridge and climb a steep crack (5.7) on the east side to gain the summit block.

Southwest Buttress. II, 5.6. First ascent August 1995 by Reese Martin, Sharon Reynolds, and Steve Reynolds. This route starts by climbing the large ramp just to the left of center on the buttress. Easy class 5 climbing leads to a corner beneath a blocky roof. At the end of the corner, an undercling to the right (5.6) ends atop the crest of the buttress. Three more pitches along the blocky crest of the buttress end on top.

Southwest Face. Class 5. First ascent July 1939 by Chet Errett and Don McGeein.

Isosceles Peak. Photo by R. J. Secor.

Kid Mountain   3615 m; 11,896 ft

This is the second biggest pile of rubble in the High Sierra. The north slope is class 1–2. Tom Sexton has climbed it from the large saddle that is south of the peak, approached via the South Fork of Big Pine Creek Trail.

Mount Alice   3541 m; 11,360 ft

This is the biggest pile of rubble in the High Sierra. The south side is class 2.

"Church of the Poisoned Mind"

This 200-foot-high triangular tower is on the southeast side of the amphitheater north of Contact Pass.

The Temple of Doom. I, 5.10. First ascent 1984 by Scott Ayers and Mike Strassman. This route ascends the left-facing dihedral that crosses the face diagonally from left to right.

Sustained Chapel. I, 5.10. First ascent 1984 by Scott Ayers and Howard Cohen. This route is to the right of the Temple of Doom. It climbs a right-facing corner that goes through an overhang to a crack. Sustained hand and fist jamming is encountered.

Temple Crag   3955 m; 12,999 ft

This is the beautiful peak seen above the North Fork of Big Pine Creek. When viewed from Third Lake, its most impressive feature is the north buttress. This buttress has three summits: the top of the Lower Buttress, the North Peak, and the true summit of Temple Crag. The northeast face is cut by two deep, narrow chimneys with many thin arêtes. The northwest face is marked by a broad couloir, a narrow chute farther right, and many indistinct ribs far out on the face. Some of the finest rock climbs in the High Sierra are on the northern side of the peak. Temple Crag has a summit cairn that is 1 foot high, to make it a 13,000-foot peak. Its new metric elevation, however, makes the summit equal to 12,975 feet above sea level. It will be interesting to see how the summit cairn grows over the years!

Further Reading: *Climbing.* No. 178, August 1998, pp. 62–69.

Southeast Face. Class 3. First ascent 1909 by the United States Geological Survey. Climb the chute that leads up the southeastern side of the peak; the entrance to this chute is approximately 300 feet below the south side of Contact Pass. The chute leads to a large talus slope, which is followed to its top. A short section of class 3 follows, and a few hundred feet of scrambling leads to the top. There is a 50-foot section of class 3 just beneath the summit. *Variation:* Class 3. First ascent September 1, 1994 by Paul Graff and Janet Graff. Go approximately 200 feet to the west of the chute, then ascend a talus slope to the base of a cliff marked by some ill-defined ledges. Ascend the ledges (class 3) up and to the right to the chute on the southeast side of Temple Crag. *Variation:* There is a prominent chute further to

Temple Crag, Northeast Face. Photo by R. J. Secor.

the left (southwest). Climb the chute to its top, then descend and traverse across another chute to the large talus slope.

Contact Crack. I, 5.2. First ascent November 1926 by Norman Clyde. This crack is west of the very top of Contact Pass. Climb the 30-foot class 4 inside corner to the talus slope above. Continue following the southeast face route to the summit.

Eclipsed Arête. III, 5.3. First ascent 1970 by Bob Swift, Pete Kennedy, and Tom Thayer. There are four arêtes to the left of the left-hand couloir on the northeast face. The first arête (Moon Goddess Arête) starts from the lowest portion of this face. The other three arêtes start much higher on the face. The second arête is rather minor, and not as prominent. The third arête (Venusian Blind Arête) is to the left of the minor arête, and starts with a large slab about 200 feet high. The last arête (Eclipsed Arête) is marked by a short, steep tower.

Climb onto a ledge from the snowfield below the left-hand couloir on the northeast face. This ledge leads horizontally left, out to the edge of the Moon Goddess Arête. Easy climbing up and left leads around the large slab marking the start of the Venusian Blind Arête. Traverse left to the start of the Eclipsed Arête, where about fifteen easy class 5 pitches lead to the talus slope on the southeast side of Temple Crag.

Venusian Blind Arête. IV, 5.7. First ascent August 1969 by Don Jensen, S. Petroff, and A. Walker. From the snowfield beneath the left-hand couloir, climb out onto the horizontal ledge (class 3–4; locally known as "The Traverse of Death") that leads across the Moon Goddess Arête. Climb up and left over easy terrain to the large slab that appears farthest to the left, bypassing a minor slab to its right. Climb an open book on the left side of the slab, and remain on the left-hand edge of the slab to the prow of the arête above. Climb through a ceiling that is by a class 4 pitch. Pass through a notch and climb a 100-foot tower on the right. (Escape route: From the top of the tower, go to the right into the class 4 gully between the Venusian Blind and Moon Goddess Arêtes.) From the top of the tower, go left and climb the major tower of the arête for three pitches. Climb over gendarmes to the base of the next tower on the arête. (This tower is 160 feet high.) Continue climbing the arête for several more pitches to the talus slopes on the southeast side of Temple Crag.

Moon Goddess Arête. IV, 5.8, A0. First ascent of lower part July 1969 by Don Jensen and J. Conners; first ascent of upper part September 1969 by Carl Dreisbach and Pat Armstrong. This is a fabulous twelve-pitch climb—exposed, yet not continually difficult. Climb onto the horizontal ledge from the snowfield beneath the left-hand couloir on the northeast face. Climb up and left from the lower end of the arête for approximately 200 feet. Go to the right to the start of the Moon Goddess Arête and climb several class 4 and 5 pitches to a large gendarme. Bypass this by means of an exposed 40-foot, 5.6 traverse to the right to the notch behind the gendarme. Continue up another pitch to the flawless 200-foot-high Ibrium Tower. (Escape route: You can move into a class 4 gully to the left when near the base of this tower.) Climb either a steep hand crack or the face (both options are 5.8 sustained) up the prow of the tower. Then climb up and to the right around the prow (5.6), passing over a large block to the right. Drop down behind the block and follow ledges to the right for about 120 feet to a belay stance in a corner (5.6). Climb steep cracks straight up for 150 feet (5.6) toward the top of the tower and the obvious horizontal flake at the base of the upper arête. Climb the arête and then rappel into another notch. Climb out of the notch via the obvious first crack (5.8) on the arête. Follow the arête for four more pitches upward (up to 5.6; most of the difficulties are passed on the right side of the arête) to the talus slope on the southeast side of Temple Crag. *Variation:* Instead of traversing the right side of the gendarme, climb to its top (5.7) and either down climb or rappel to the first notch.

Further Reading: John Moynier and Claude Fiddler. *Sierra Classics.* Evergreen, Colo.: Chockstone Press, 1993, pp. 128–129.

Sun Ribbon Arête. IV, 5.9, A0. First ascent of lower part July 1969 by Don Jensen, W. Miller, and R. Schwartz; first ascent of upper part September 1969 by John Fischer and Don Jensen. First winter ascent February 1982 by George Lowe and Brock Wagstaff. This is a difficult eighteen-pitch climb that ascends the first arête to the right of the left-hand couloir on the northeast face. Climb the snowfield beneath the couloir, then traverse right over easy terrain to the base of a left-facing open book. Climb the book (5.7) and scramble up 200 feet to the notch behind the small gendarme at the base of the arête above. Climb the edge of the arête for five pitches of 5.5–5.7—the obvious alcove on top of the prow. There is a notch just beyond the alcove. This notch is most easily crossed by lassoing a block across the 15-foot gap (or rappel into the notch and climb up the right side of the arête: 5.7). After the Tyrolean traverse, cross the left side of the arête to another notch. (Escape route: The gully on the left can be reached from this point.) Belay from a point 10 feet below the notch. Climb the left-facing crack above this point, either from its base (5.9) or by making a delicate traverse from the left (5.8). Continue climbing the arête (5.5–5.6) to a notch; climb down into this and up the other side (5.4). Bypass a smooth, steep wall on its right side and regain the crest of the arête. This is followed by two more pitches, and scrambling leads to the talus slope.

Further Reading: John Moynier and Claude Fiddler. *Sierra Classics.* Evergreen, Colo.: Chockstone Press, 1993, pp. 129–131; *Rock & Ice.* No. 73 (May–June 1996), p. 71.

Northeast Face. III, 5.4. First ascent June 9, 1957 by John Mendenhall and Ruth Mendenhall. This route starts from the snowfield beneath the right-hand couloir on the northeast side of Temple Crag. Climb a right-facing chimney from the left side of the snowfield. From the top of the chimney, climb up and right toward the notch behind the North Peak. Before reaching the notch, go left, encountering a few class 4 pitches before reaching the true summit.

Mendenhall Couloir. III, Class 4–5. First ascent July 7, 1940 by John Mendenhall and Ruth Mendenhall. This follows the right-hand couloir on the northeast face. Steep snow is encountered low, followed by a narrow slot choked with chockstones. Follow the couloir almost to the notch behind the North Peak, then go left toward the true summit.

26th of July Arête. III, 5.8. First ascent July 1970 by Don Jensen and Chuck Kroger. There are two arêtes on the northeast side of the North Peak of Temple Crag. This route follows the right-hand arête. Begin by climbing the wall to the right of the arête for two pitches (5.8) to the base of the prominent gully. Go left onto the arête (5.8) and follow the crest (some 5.7) to its top. Go up and right through the small notch to the top of the Lower Buttress (one 5.5 move). The climb ends here, but it is possible to continue via the upper part of the Dark Star route or via the North Peak, Right Side route.

Communion Route. III, 5.8. First ascent 1966 by Tom Higgins and Bud Crouch. Ascend the first two pitches of the 26th of July Arête to the base of the prominent gully. Climb the wall to the right of this gully to the notch just north of the Lower Buttress.

Dark Star. V, 5.10c or 5.10, A0. First ascent of lower part September 1970 by Don Jensen and John Fischer; first ascent of upper part July 1971 by Don Jensen and Keith Brueckner. First winter ascent by Jay Smith and Charlie Jenkowitz (date unknown). This is the longest technical route in the Palisades (thirty-three pitches). It ascends the north buttress of the peak. Approximately 500 feet of climbing (up to 5.6) from the toe of the buttress leads to the most prominent right-facing dihedral (5.10c) on the very prow of the buttress. (An alternate approach to the start of the serious climbing is via the ledge from the base of the northeast face of Temple Crag.) One and a half pitches in the dihedral lead to a ledge that is left of the corner. Traverse left a short distance to a difficult layback (5.9+). After this, ascend directly up over corners to some small ledges. Go slightly left and then up to a large flake. An easy pitch and then a moderate pitch lead to the base of a deep chimney. Ascend this chimney from deep inside to a ledge behind some chockstones. This is followed by scrambling and some easy class 5 moves to the top of the Lower Buttress. (Escape route: You can descend the North Peak, Right Side route from here.) Traverse left and up from the notch behind the Lower Buttress for 75 feet and then go straight up (5.7) for another 50 feet. Go to the right into a shallow gully and climb it a short way to a small ceiling, which is overcome by a 5.9 crack. This is followed by many pitches of free climbing with several significant gendarmes, and then a scramble to the top of the North Peak. Continue directly up the north ridge to the true summit of Temple Crag. *Variation:* 5.10. There is a sandy gap just beyond the top of the upper buttress. Go to the right side of the arête and climb a 5.10 crack that ends on a ledge. Then 5.5 face climbing leads to the notch behind the North Peak.

Further Reading: *Climbing.* No. 132, June–July 1992, p. 82, p. 144; John Moynier and Claude Fiddler. *Sierra Classics.* Evergreen, Colo.: Chockstone Press, 1993, pp. 132–134.

Barefoot Bynum. IV, 5.10b. First ascent September 1970 by Doug Robinson and Chuck Kroger. Climb the right-facing dihedral that is 40 feet to the right of the dihedral used for the start of Dark Star. Leave the dihedral on its right side after three pitches and aim for a large roof. A 5.10b move over the roof is followed by a crack-

and-chimney system, which is followed to its end after four pitches. Scrambling, with some technical moves, leads to the top of the Lower Buttress.

Planaria. IV, 5.10, A1. First ascent 1977 by Gordon Wiltsie and Jay Jensen. This route climbs the blank, steep face to the right of Dark Star and Barefoot Bynum. It leads into the shallow dihedral seen high on the face.

North Peak, Right Side. III, 5.4. First ascent August 18, 1963 by John Mendenhall, Vivian Mendenhall, Roy Coates, and Ed Lane. Begin by climbing the northwest couloir on Temple Crag. Leave the couloir after a few hundred feet via a class 4–5 pitch on its left side. Scramble upward, then go left and up (some class 4) to the top of the Lower Buttress. Traverse right on a ledge for 150 feet to a crack system that is to the left of the prominent open book on the northwest side of the North Peak. Climb the crack system (5.4) and then go right, scrambling to the top of the North Peak.

Northwest Chimney. III, 5.7. First ascent 1970 by Les Roberts and Joe Herbst. Ascend the northwest couloir for a few hundred feet and leave it on its left side via a class 4–5 pitch. Scramble up the North Chute for 500 feet to the prominent, right-facing dihedral on the western side of the North Peak. Five long pitches in a chimney in this dihedral lead almost to the top of the North Peak.

North Chute. Class 4. First ascent August 11, 1931

Temple Crag from the north. Photo by R. J. Secor.

by Norman Clyde, Robert Underhill, Glen Dawson, and Jules Eichorn. Go a few hundred feet up the northwest couloir and climb out of it on its left side via a class 4–5 pitch. Scramble up, then ascend the prominent rock chute on the west side of the North Peak to the notch between the North Peak and the true summit of Temple Crag. Pass through the notch and continue to the true summit, either via the exposed north ridge or on the easier left side of the north ridge. *Variation:* The first-ascent party climbed the deep crack left of the mouth of the northwest couloir.

The Surgicle, East Side. II, 5.7. First ascent 1969 by Don Jensen and Joan Jensen. This is the pinnacle on the rib to the left of the deep chute marking the start of the Northwest Face route. Climb the east face beneath the pinnacle, and then the east face of the pinnacle itself. Rappel the route to descend.

The Surgicle, North Rib. II, 5.8. Three pitches lead to the top of The Surgicle.

Northwest Face. Class 4. First ascent May 1930 by Norman Clyde. This route climbs the deep chute that is right (southwest) of the northwest couloir. Climb the left-ascending chute to where it joins the northwest couloir. There is a 15-foot class 4 move approximately 200 feet above the base of the chute; the remainder of the climb is class 3. Climb the northwest couloir to where it forks. Take the left branch of the couloir to the headwall beneath the summit. Go to the right to a prominent notch, then follow the arête to the true summit. *Variation:* Class 4. The northwest couloir itself can also be climbed from the very bottom. Before it meets the deep chute, the couloir narrows and has some chockstones; bypass the chockstones on their right sides.

Rabbit Ears. II, 5.5. First ascent 1968 by Chuck Pratt, Bob Swift, and friends. There is a sloping bench to the right of the chute used to ascend the Northwest Face route. There are three ribs above this bench. The Rabbit Ears is the large pinnacle on the central rib; its north face is split by a large crack. From the bench, climb the gully that leads to the right side of the Rabbit Ears. The large crack on its north side is the crux. Rappel the route.

Red Eye Pillar. III, 5.9. First ascent August 1970 by Don Jensen and Chuck Kroger. This pillar is to the right (across a narrow chute) from the bench beneath the Rabbit Ears. There is a patch of red rock about three-fourths of the way up this pillar. The climb starts about 50 feet to the right of the narrow chute and goes

up and to the left of a left-facing dihedral topped by a roof. Go to the right into the dihedral, then climb the roof via a 5.8 crack. Four pitches of easier climbing follow; they lead to the base of a large block with smooth, steep walls on both sides. Traverse right for 30 feet to a narrow crack; climb this (5.9) to the top of the pillar. Continue to the crest of the ridge between Mount Gayley and Temple Crag. To descend, continue along the crest of the ridge toward Mount Gayley, then descend the northwest side of the ridge on ledges to the snowfields north of Mount Gayley.

Cirith Anodyne. III, 5.10. First ascent by Doug Robinson, Jay Jensen, and Gordon Wiltsie. This climb consists of five pitches of difficult free climbing from the very bottom of the Red Eye Pillar.

Traverse from Mount Gayley. II, Class 5. First ascent 1969 by Don Jensen and friend. This is an enjoyable but long traverse with many exposed places. Approach the ridge crest by descending the east face of Mount Gayley. There is one vertical rappel on the traverse from Temple Crag to Mount Gayley.

Mount Gayley   4118 m; 13,510 ft

There is a fine view of the peaks of the North and South Forks of Big Pine Creek from the summit.

Southwest Ridge. Class 3. First ascent June 10, 1927 by Norman Clyde. First winter ascent January 1961 by Tom Condon and John Mendenhall. This route has also been called "Yellow Brick Road." From Glacier Notch ascend a system of wide ledges on the right side of the ridge to the summit.

West Face. Class 3. First ascent July 1949 by Norman Clyde and party. Climb the rib that is left (northeast) of the approach to Glacier Notch from the Palisade Glacier. Traverse left and up across some ledges from a point approximately 200 feet below the level of the notch. Go across the west face to the arête leading up to the summit, then follow the arête to the top.

Northwest Ridge. I, 5.2. First ascent July 4, 1960 by John Mendenhall and Ruth Mendenhall. Second ascent July 10, 1971 by Wally Henry, Steve Rogero, and Jon Inskeep. The crest of the northwest ridge is followed most of the way, with occasional detours onto the north face.

North Face, Center Arête. III, 5.8. First ascent 1984 by James Eakin and Rick Todd. This route follows the curving arête in the center of the face, just right of a narrow gully. The crux is on the third pitch. Move down and right from a flake on the crest of the ridge to a crack system. Follow the cracks up and to the right to a left-facing corner with two cracks. Climb this corner to a small belay ledge. Continue up the arête, with short deviations to the right and left, until it is possible to traverse into the gully. Head left into the gully, climb it to its top, and go to the right through the notch that separates the lower and upper portions of the arête. This leads to a large bowl. Climb the left side of the bowl for two pitches to a belay beneath a short, wide chimney. After you climb the chimney, make a hand traverse left

to a ledge. Climb the short corner from the left end of the ledge to the crest of the upper arête. Class 3 and 4 climbing then leads to the north summit.

Northeast Ridge and East Face. I, 5.2. First ascent by Smoke Blanchard. Traverse left across the north face to a small notch on the northeast ridge. Pass through the notch and climb the east face to the summit.

South Side. Class 3. Descended September 28, 1931 by Walter A. Starr, Jr. This involves climbing over some huge boulders and small cliffs from the South Fork drainage.

Palisade Glacier from the northeast, August 24, 1972. Photo by Austin Post, No. 72R2-151, USGS Ice and Climate Project, GeoData Center, University of Alaska, Fairbanks.

Mount Sill   14,153 ft; 14,162 ft

Mount Sill has the best summit view of any peak in the Sierra. It is a sacred mountain to the Paiute, who call it *Nee-na-mee-shee* (the Guardian of the Valley) and worship it in their religious ceremonies.

Further Reading: Stephen F. Porcella and Cameron M. Burns. *Climbing California's Fourteeners.* Seattle: The Mountaineers Books, 1998, pp. 162–174.

Southwest Slope. Class 2–3. First ascent July 24, 1903 by Joseph LeConte, James K. Moffitt, James S. Hutchinson, and Robert D. Pike. Ascend the Glacier Creek drainage to where it is possible to go left (northwest) into the cirque between Mount Sill and Polemonium Peak. Cross the snowfield at the head of the cirque, keeping to its right, and follow the west ridge of the peak to the summit. The upper part of the west ridge consists of large talus; this is the only difficulty. *Variation: South Headwall.* Class 4, with one rappel. First ascent July 15, 1975 by Woody Stark and Richard Webster. From the Glacier Creek drainage, instead of turning left toward the cirque southwest of Mount Sill, climb the headwall that is visible from Lake 3559m (11,672 ft). The first-ascent party used one rappel to avoid aid. From the top of the headwall, follow the southeast ridge to the summit.

Further Reading: Stephen F. Porcella and Cameron M. Burns. *Hiking and Climbing: California's Fourteeners.* Chockstone Press, Evergreen, Colo., 1996, pp. 58–59.

Traverse from The U Notch and Polemonium Peak. I, 5.2. First ascent August 2, 1933 by Lewis Clark, Ted Waller, Julie Mortimer, and Jack Riegelhuth. This route is described under Polemonium Peak. The ridge west of Mount Sill to the gap before Polemonium Peak is class 2–3.

Northwest Face. Class 4. First ascent June 10, 1927 by Norman Clyde. There is a small pyramid-shaped peak (locally known as the "Apex Peak") just north of Mount Sill (at UTM 664065). From the Palisade Glacier, climb the snow/ice couloir leading to the notch between this small peak and Mount Sill, then continue up the North Couloir route to the summit. There is much loose rock on this side of Mount Sill; the North Couloir route from Glacier Notch is the preferred route.

North Couloir. Class 4. First ascent September 25, 1931 by Walter A. Starr, Jr. From Glacier Notch, ascend the L-shaped snow/ice couloir leading to the notch between Mount Sill and Apex Peak (on the north side of Mount Sill). (Alternatively, you can ascend the class 3 rocks on the right side of the couloir.) Climb toward Mount Sill from the notch for 80 feet and then traverse to the right across the northwest face. This leads to a small, scree-covered rib. Ascend the rib to the west ridge, then follow the ridge to the summit. *Variation:* I, 5.2. First ascent by George Wallerstein. Climb straight up from the start of the traverse for five short pitches. Some leader protection is needed on the third pitch.

Further Reading: *Summit.* July–August 1987, p. 10; Stephen F. Porcella and Cameron M. Burns. *Hiking and Climbing: California's Fourteeners.* Chockstone Press, Evergreen, Colo., 1996, pp. 53–55.

North Couloir, Descent Route. Class 4. This is commonly used as a descent route after climbs of the Swiss Arête, east face, or the V Notch of Polemonium Peak. At an approximate elevation of 13,900 feet on the west ridge of Mount Sill (near a prominent rock spike along the ridge), descend the north side of the ridge about 200 feet. Traverse down and across the northwest face of Mount Sill to a point just above the notch between Mount Sill and Apex Peak to the north. Descend to the notch and go down the 35° North Couloir (or the class 3 rocks on its north side) to Glacier Notch.

Swiss Arête. II, 5.7. First ascent July 3, 1938 by Spencer Austin, Ruth Dyar, Ray Ingwersen, Richard M. Jones, and Joe Momyer. This ascent of the north buttress of Mount Sill is one of the classic climbs of the High Sierra. It is in a spectacular location and has little loose rock. From Glacier Notch, traverse up and left, across the North Couloir, to the north buttress of Mount Sill. The climb begins at a point where the buttress flattens out a bit, at an approximate elevation of 13,500 feet. After two pitches (5.5 and 5.6), a 5.5 pitch leads to an impasse. Traverse to the right on ledges to an exposed outside corner (5.6). This is followed by a 5.7 move up an open book. The rest of the climb is mostly class 4, with a few class 5 moves over and around huge blocks to the summit.

Further Reading: *Summit.* September–October 1988, pp. 24–29; Allan Bard. *Swiss Arête of Mount Sill.* Bishop, Calif.: Shooting Star Guides, 1991 (a route card); John Moynier and Claude Fiddler. *Sierra*

Mount Sill from the northeast. Photo by R. J. Secor.

MOUNT SILL

(route continues
on other side
of the notch)

Apex
Peak

Swiss
Arête

North
Couloir

East
Couloir

East
Face

Larry's
Pillar

Glacier Notch
to Palisade Lake

East
Chimney

start of
Larry's Pillar

Sill
Glacier

To Willow Lake

Classics. Evergreen, Colo.: Chockstone Press, 1993, pp. 136–137.

Variation. Continue directly up the buttress from where the impasse is met; this is 5.9.

East Chimney. III, 5.8. First ascent July 4, 1960 by Tom Condon and Fred Kipfelsberger. The glacier on the eastern side of Mount Sill has been called "Sill Glacier." This route starts by climbing the prominent chimney on the right side of the east face of Mount Sill. The chimney widens after two pitches, turning into a bowl. Climb up and right over broken ledges for four pitches to a chimney system heading up and left. Climb the chimneys to a ramp leading up and left, meeting the ridge about 100 feet southeast of the summit.

East Face. III, 5.7. First ascent September 1, 1963 by John Mendenhall, Rich Gnagy, Burt Turney, and Genevieve Turney. This route ascends the chimney/gully system in the middle of the east face. Climb the class 4 chimney on the right side of the east face to a large, overhanging chockstone. Climb a thin crack (5.7) behind the chockstone. This is followed by a 5.6 pitch, and then a 5.7 pitch. Easier climbing leads to a steep gully, which is ascended for four pitches on its right side (5.2). Continue up the gully that becomes a steep chimney and climb its right wall (5.4–5.7) to its top, where an exposed traverse to the left leads to the southeast ridge about 200 feet from the summit. *Variation:* From the top of the gully, climb up and to the right around a small buttress to a chute. Ascend the chute and then follow a ramp system left to a point about 100 feet southeast of the summit. *Variation:* III, 5.9. First ascent July 1991 by Kevin Malone and Patrick Brennan. From the top of the gully, continue straight up for five pitches. The last three pitches are 5.9.

Larry's Pillar, Center. III, 5.10. First ascent 1978 by Mike Farrell and Mike Graber. This prominent pillar is on the southern half of the east face of Mount Sill. It was affectionately named by the guides of the Palisade School of Mountaineering after their late director, Larry Williams. Ascend a left-leaning, overhanging crack from the Sill Glacier. Once above the overhang, go to the right and climb the center of the pillar.

Larry's Pillar, Left Side. III, 5.9. First ascent August 1986 by Ken Davenport, David Wilson, and Michael Graber. After surmounting the overhanging crack, climb the left side of the pillar.

East Couloir. Class 3. Descended June 16, 1934 by Norman Clyde, Hervey Voge, and David Brower. First winter ascent January 1957 by John Mendenhall and Henry Mandolf. From the Sill Glacier ascend the left-hand snow/ice couloir to where the two couloirs join. Follow the main couloir to the notch on the southeast ridge, then ascend the ridge to the summit.

Polemonium Peak   14,080 ft+; 14,000 ft+; 0.15 mi SE of North Palisade

This is the small peak immediately southeast of The U Notch. On some maps, the name Polemonium Peak has been erroneously placed on Peak 13,962ft (13,920 ft+), 0.3 mile southeast of the correct peak.

Further Reading: Stephen F. Porcella and Cameron M. Burns. *Climbing California's Fourteeners.* Seattle: The Mountaineers Books, 1998, pp. 176–183.

From The U Notch. I, 5.2. First ascent August 2, 1933 by Lewis Clark, Ted Waller, Julie Mortimer, and Jack Riegelhuth. The top of The U Notch is attained by ascending either the Southwest Chute or The U Notch Couloir on North Palisade. From the top of The U Notch, climb up and right onto a ledge on the northwest face of Polemonium Peak for 60 feet of easy class 4. Then traverse diagonally upward to the right for about 100 feet toward the obvious notch that is just above the prominent gendarme on the southwest arête. Go up from the notch; several class 5 moves are followed by class 4 climbing to the summit.

V Notch Couloir. III, AI2 or WI3. First ascent September 1957 by John Mathias and John Ohrenschall. This is one of the classic ice climbs of the High Sierra. The route ascends the left branch of the obvious couloir east of The U Notch and features 50° snow/ice for 900 feet. The bergschrund is usually passable on its left side, and most parties belay from rock on the right side of the couloir to avoid being overexposed to rockfall. It is possible to climb the rocks in the upper part of the couloir, but this is seldom done in this age of modern ice-climbing equipment and *sangfroid.*

Further Reading: Doug Robinson. *A Night on the Ground, A Day in the Open.* La Crescenta, Calif.: Mountain 'N' Air Books, 1996, pp. 71–76; *Summit.* April 1975, pp. 2–3, 16–19; John Moynier and Claude Fiddler. *Sierra Classics.* Evergreen, Colo.: Chockstone Press, 1993, pp. 138–139.

Southeast Side. Class 4. First ascent July 27, 1930 by Jules Eichorn, Glen Dawson, John Olmstead, and

Charles Dodge. Ascend to the top of the snowfield southwest of Mount Sill, or follow the west ridge of Mount Sill west to the gap just before the true summit of Polemonium Peak. Down climb into the gap and follow the knife edge ridge to the summit of the peak. This last section consists of two short pitches of easy class 4.

Further Reading: Stephen F. Porcella and Cameron M. Burns. *Hiking and Climbing: California's Fourteeners.* Chockstone Press, Evergreen, Colo., 1996, pp. 60–64.

North Palisade   14,242 ft; 14,242 ft

North Pal is *the* classic peak of the High Sierra. It is striking from a distance, and it has routes that will challenge climbers of all abilities and preferences. The true summit is the higher, southeast peak. The lower, northwest peak is known as "Starlight Peak."

Further Reading: Stephen F. Porcella and Cameron M. Burns. *Climbing California's Fourteeners.* Seattle: The Mountaineers Books, 1998, pp. 184–213.

U Notch Couloir. II, AI1 or WI2, Class 4–5. First ascent June 1928 by Norman Clyde. First winter ascent March 17, 1940 by David Brower and Fred Kelley. This route climbs the couloir leading to The U Notch from the Palisade Glacier. The U Notch is unmistakable; it is the most prominent gap on the ridge between Mount Sill and North Palisade. The couloir is a 700-foot, 42°, snow/ice climb. The bergschrund itself is frequently impassable, but may be bypassed by climbing a short, easy class 4–5 chimney on its right side. Keep to the far right side of the couloir when ascending to avoid being overexposed to the rockfall, which seems to prefer the lower right-center portion of the couloir; the first three to four pitches are the most exposed to rockfall. There is a

North Palisade, North Face. Photo by R. J. Secor.

peninsula of loose rocks about halfway up the couloir; pass this to its left and continue up snow/ice to easy scree, which leads to the top of The U Notch. From here you have two choices: the Chimney Variation and the Clyde Variation.

Chimney Variation: 5.4. Climb the steep chimney leading up the northwest wall of The U Notch for two pitches; the second pitch is especially strenuous. From the top of the chimney, follow the southeast arête, at first keeping to its right side and then moving to its left side. Traverse across the top of the bowl that drops toward the southwest, then follow a band of light-colored rock before heading directly for the huge boulders that make up the summit of the peak.

Clyde Variation: Class 4. Descend the southwest side of The U Notch 120 feet to the base of a large crack that leads up to a ledge. Climb the wall to the right of the crack (40 feet of easy class 4) to the ledge and follow the ledge left, around an arête, and into the next chute north. Climb the chute (class 3) to the southeast arête of North Pal, meeting it right next to the top of the Chimney Variation. Follow the southeast arête to the summit.

The U Notch Couloir with the Chimney Variation is the classic route, but most parties climb the Clyde Variation.

Further Reading: *Summit.* July–August 1987, p. 10.

Northeast Buttress. II, 5.6. First ascent July 2, 1961 by Larry Williams, John Sharsmith, Burt Turney, and Genevieve Turney. This route climbs the obscure, obtuse open book above and right of the bergschrund of the U Notch Couloir. The book consists of light-gray rock. Climb it for 300 feet to a prominent vein running horizontal across the face. Traverse to the left for 20 feet and proceed upward over broken blocks to a wide ledge. Traverse right over a slightly overhanging portion of the wall to a narrow ledge. Climb straight up for two pitches to the class 3 slabs on the upper portion of the north face. These slabs lead to the southeast arête and the summit.

The Doors of Perception. II, 5.8. First ascent July 1970 by Allen Steck and Doug Robinson. This route ascends the obvious, gigantic dihedral to the right of the U Notch Couloir. Three pitches of crack and chimney climbing lead to the gentler upper portion of the north face of North Palisade.

North Buttress. II, 5.8, A2. First ascent July 12, 1970 by Ken Boche and Lee Panza. This route ascends the broad right-hand buttress of the three buttresses between the U Notch and Clyde Couloirs. Begin by climbing the center of the buttress for a long pitch to a ledge. Go up to the right from the ledge, using some aid to pass some loose blocks, to a small ledge beneath a prominent overhang. Climb the overhang by means of a strenuous crack to a sloping ledge. Go up and left from the ledge (one 5.8 move) to the class 3 slabs beneath the summit snowfield.

Clyde Couloir. II, Class 4–5. First ascent July 6, 1930 by Norman Clyde. The Clyde Couloir is the narrow snow/ice couloir to the right (west) of the U Notch Couloir; it leads to the notch between North Palisade and the lower, northwest summit, Starlight Peak. In early season, the Clyde Couloir can be a 900-foot snow climb, with an average angle of 55°. Later in the summer it becomes a 300-foot ice climb surrounded by loose rocks, with some parts exceeding 60°. No matter what time of year you climb the Clyde Couloir, it is advisable to leave it for Starlight Buttress as soon as is practical. Norman Clyde described this as being "one of the very best climbs in the Sierra." Very few climbers have disagreed.

The bergschrund at the base of the couloir may be impassable, except by the strongest and most skilled ice climbers. Once past the 'schrund, climb the right side of the couloir for 300 feet and traverse diagonally right onto the upper part of Starlight Buttress. Ascend the crest of the buttress (class 3 and 4) to a point about 200 feet below the summit of Starlight Peak. From this point, you can traverse across the distinctive snowfield high on North Pal's north face to the southeast ridge, head directly for the summit of North Pal (taking care to avoid cul-de-sacs), or climb the northwest ridge and follow it to either the summit of North Palisade or Starlight Peak. (These options are listed in order of increasing difficulty.) *Variation:* First ascent September 1955 by John Mendenhall and Dick Franklin. This party followed the couloir almost to its top before moving right and out of the couloir. They experienced considerable rockfall, which is to be expected in the deteriorating ice conditions of late summer. (At one point, the belayer noticed that the leader was "wearing" his knapsack as if it were a helmet, as protection from falling rocks!) *Variation: The Narrows.* First ascent 1969 by Doug Robinson. Climb the Clyde Couloir from its very bottom to its very top.

Starlight Buttress. III, 5.5. This buttress is the first one right (west) of the Clyde Couloir. Cross the bergschrund of the Clyde Couloir, then immediately traverse to the right onto the crest of the buttress. Follow it up for four pitches of exhilarating class 3, 4, and 5 climbing to a large ledge. Climb up and to the right over flakes (5.5) to a steep, shallow gulley. Two long class 4 pitches in the gully end just south of the Milk Bottle, the summit of Starlight Peak. *Variation:* From the large ledge, go up and left over class 3 and 4 ledges with a few class 5 moves lead to the notch on the northwest ridge between Starlight Peak and North Palisade. Follow the ridge to either summit.

Piper at the Gates of Dawn. III, 5.7. First ascent June 1968 by Doug Robinson and Carl Dreisbach. The lower portion of the northeast face of Starlight Peak has a large, smooth slab: the Flatiron. From the bergschrund to the right of the Flatiron, climb the dihedral formed by its right edge for one pitch of snow/ice climbing and one pitch of rock. Climb left out of the dihedral and onto the Flatiron. Climb cracks over two ceilings (5.7) for two pitches to the top of the Flatiron. Ascend the right margin of a right-leaning snow patch (class 4). This is followed by a class 3 pitch, which ends 70 feet below a prominent large chimney (full of dangerous loose blocks) that leads to the summit. Traverse left onto a small arête (5.6). Two increasingly easier pitches lead to the summit ridge, which is at a point about 50 feet west of the summit of Starlight Peak. *Variation:* First ascent August 1970 by W. Katra and D. Summers. From the large, prominent chimney, go right and ascend steep flakes and cracks (5.7). The last pitch traverses out onto the face and turns an overhang on the right.

The X. II, 5.7. First ascent July 1968 by John Clark, Jon Lonne, Dick James, and Steve Roper. This is probably the most dangerous route in the Palisades. There are two diagonal crack systems on the right-hand side of the northeast face of Starlight Peak; these cracks form a huge X. Climb both right-hand segments of The X. The lower portion of this climb is 5.6–5.7 and the upper portion is easy class 5. There is much loose rock on this route.

Northwest Ridge. II, 5.5. First ascent June 29, 1934 by Norman Clyde, David Brower, and Hervey Voge. This is a spectacular climb, with great views, intricate routefinding, and moderate difficulties. The climb begins from the notch between Thunderbolt Peak and Starlight Peak, which is reached from the top of either the Underhill Couloir or Southwest Chute No. 2 of Thunderbolt Peak. Ascend the western side of the northwest ridge (class 3 and 4), passing around gendarmes and into notches. A steep chimney (5.4) leads close to the summit block of Starlight Peak. A class 4 chimney leads down to the notch between Starlight Peak and North Palisade. From the notch, traverse on the southwest side of the ridge to another notch. Pass through it, then down climb the northeast side of the ridge for about 30 feet (class 4). Traverse across this side of the ridge, bypassing the central gendarme, and climb up into another notch, with a flake on its south wall. Surmount the flake (easier said than done; some very experienced climbers have been embarrassed here). Next, traverse across the exposed northeast side of the ridge to a chimney. Ascend the chimney to the top of the northwest ridge; the second pitch on this ridge is especially difficult. From the top of the ridge descend about 15 feet on the southwest side to another chimney, which leads up the wall to the summit. *Variation:* The flake pitch has been bypassed by lowering the leader on tension to a point where it was possible for the leader to swing over the notch and flake to the large ledge on top of the flake. The rest of the party also followed on tension, with the help of protection placed by the leader.

Northwest Chute. Class 4. First ascent July 13, 1933 by James Wright. This is the first chute right (southwest) of the Southwest Chute No. 2 on Thunderbolt Peak. Ascend the chute towards the higher triangular headwall beneath Starlight Peak. Near the base of this headwall, traverse to the right, up a shallow class 3 gully and across a sloping slab to a notch that drops dramatically into Starlight Chute. Make a slightly descending class 3 traverse to the east, into the chute. Climb the chute to its top, then traverse up and left over class 4 rock to the crest of the west ridge of Starlight Peak. Follow the knife edge ridge crest to the summit block of Starlight Peak, known as the "Milk Bottle."

Further Reading: Stephen F. Porcella and Cameron M. Burns. *Hiking and Climbing: California's Fourteeners.* Chockstone Press, Evergreen, Colo., 1996, pp. 66–68.

Starlight Peak, West Rib. IV, 5.10b. First ascent July 4, 1990 by Cameron Burns and Steve Porcella. This rib connects the prows of two large, triangular buttresses on the west face of Starlight Peak. The lower triangular buttress is split by an enormous ledge. Start climbing just

Thunderbolt Peak and North Palisade from the west. Photo by R. J. Secor.

left of an obvious triangle of white quartzite. It goes up and slightly left for three leads (all about 5.8) to a large flake that is very obvious from the bottom. A beautiful pitch goes up behind this flake (5.9). This is followed by a ledge that leads through a small roof; this short, strenuous layback is the crux (5.10b). Follow the ledge up and left, following the line of least resistance. Another easy pitch goes up and around a corner and ends on the enormous ledge that splits the lower triangular buttress. Climb the White Dihedral pitch directly above the ledge for a long way. Continue up the rib above the dihedral, traverse right a few feet, and climb a shallow dihedral (5.8). One more lead (5.7) up blocks and cracks leads to the very prow of the first triangular buttress. Continue across a huge slab to a 40-foot 5.9 layback crack. This is followed by some unprotected mantles over blocks (5.8), and then an impasse. A rappel followed by two horizontal (more or less) class 4 pitches lead to the notch between the two triangular buttresses. A 5.8 pitch up the

very crest of the upper buttress leads to the base of a loose chimney. Climb the chimney on its tight, right side (5.8). Three more pitches straight up flakes, dihedrals, and corners (5.7–5.8) lead to the top of the ridge. A short class 4 descent leads into a gully. From there it is a few hundred feet to the summit block.

Further Reading: *Mountain.* No. 135, September–October 1990, pp. 36–41.

Starlight Chute. Class 5. Descended August 28, 1985 by Michael Feldman and Jim Shirley. This chute leads to the notch between North Pal and Starlight Peak from Palisade Basin. This chute contains a lot of dangerous loose rock, broken occasionally by polished slabs, and some difficult chimneys. The not very obvious start of the climb is marked by a black, watermarked stain 40 feet wide and 90 feet high, which is the chute outfall (the black watermarks for the west face route are hundreds of feet to the right, and are much higher and narrower). Ascend the wall and enter the chute. A vertical section is encountered and climbed by means of chimneys. This is followed by much class 3 and 4 to the notch south of Starlight Peak.

West Buttress. IV, 5.10. First ascent July 1982 by David Wilson and Galen Rowell. This route follows the buttress on the right (south) side of Starlight Chute. From the talus at the base of the west side of North Palisade, ascend three easy class 5 pitches to a smooth, slightly overhanging headwall. This headwall is overcome by means of four pitches of 5.9 and 5.10, followed by a steep arête, where a section of crackless towers forces you into a gully for a few hundred feet. The arête meets the northwest ridge between North Palisade and Starlight Peak. Follow the northwest ridge to the summit.

Es Lasst Sich Nicht Lesen. III, 5.10. First ascent July 3, 1989 by Steve Porcella and Cameron Burns. The name of this route is German for "It cannot easily be read." Climb the West Face route, but ascend the left side of the wide chute. From where the left side of this chute narrows, follow a horizontal band of light-colored rock for 200 feet to the right. Drop down onto class 4 rock at one point to avoid a difficult, unprotected traverse. This detour leads to a steep, snow-filled couloir. Climb the face on the right side of the couloir (5.10), then go up and left over a loose face to the top of a huge buttress. Climb several left-facing dihedrals to an enormous flat area: the Patio. Two easy class 5 pitches traverse around the Patio to the left and lead to an easy chimney system. One more pitch of easy class 5 leads to the summit ridge behind a tower. Drop down to the right to the bowl high on the southwest side of North Pal and climb to the summit.

West Face. II, 5.4. First ascent August 1936 by Richard M. Jones and Mary Jane Edwards. There are three white cliffs along the base of the southwest face of North Palisade. This climb starts to the left of a long, narrow black watermark on the left side of the northernmost cliff. Ascend straight up to where progress is stopped by a large slab. Traverse to the right on a sloping ledge, across the watermark, and then go up a short chimney to the top of the cliff (5.4). Continue up and right over slabs into a wide chute. Ascend the right side of this chute, which eventually becomes narrow and steep. Continue up the chute and traverse to the right on a horizontal white vein of rock across a ridge and into the bowl that is southwest of the summit. Ascend the bowl to the summit.

White Ship. II, 5.9. First ascent July 2, 1989 by Steve Porcella and Cameron Burns. This route climbs the middle of the northernmost of the three white cliffs at the base of the southwest face of North Palisade. Climb the dihedral to the right of a small, black watermark in the middle of the cliff. The first pitch ends with a difficult mantle (5.9) and the second pitch climbs a series of blocks (5.8) and ends on a large ledge. Climb another dihedral above this ledge, with a strenuous and sustained 5.9 crux. This is followed by a chimney; then you move right and into a trough. This is followed by easy face climbing. The next pitch climbs to a ledge, and is followed by a short dihedral to another ledge. Then move left up a right-slanting flake to the top of the cliff. Continue up the West Face route to the summit.

Putterman Couloir. I, 5.5. First ascent July 2, 1989 by Cameron Burns and Steve Porcella. This couloir is on the southern side of the northernmost of the three white cliffs at the base of the southwest face of North Palisade. Climb loose talus in the couloir to a steep section of crumbling mud and blocks. A gully branches off to the left; stay in the main couloir and climb past a narrow section of extraordinary loose rock. An orange wall can be seen on the left. Climb the right side of this wall and go up and left to a ledge that leads to the left to the top of the cliff.

Southwest Buttress. IV, 5.11c. First ascent June 29, 1990 by Cameron Burns and Steve Porcella. This is the buttress that is left of the lower southwest chute, or LeConte Route. This route starts from the upper right-hand side of the large slab that is at the base of the middle cliff on the southwest face of North Palisade. A pitch up an easy crack system, followed by some ledges, leads to a steep headwall. This headwall features a choice of three steep off-width cracks. Take the off-width crack farthest right; bring some big pieces of protection (5.11c). The next three pitches are class 3 and 4, and lead to the base of the proper southwest buttress. Four pitches up the buttress lead to a sustained fingertip crack (5.10). Stay close to the crest of the arête from here for another seven pitches (nothing harder than 5.8) to a notch. Either down climb or rappel 20 feet into the notch and scramble up to the summit, which is nearby. Take off-width protection for this sixteen-pitch climb.

Further Reading: *Mountain.* No. 135, September–October 1990, pp. 36–41.

The LeConte Route. Class 4. First ascent July 25, 1903

by Joseph LeConte, James Hutchinson, and James Moffitt. This route ascends the large chute between the middle and southernmost cliffs at the base of the southwest face of North Palisade. This chute leads to the top of The U Notch. Approximately halfway up (at an elevation of 13,100 feet) this chute widens out in an area of slabs and rubble. The chute branches in this area. A vague left branch goes almost due north; this is a rock wall on its right side. Climb this left branch for 100 feet to where a ledge appears on the rock wall. This narrow ledge leads left, and from its end go up and right across a large ledge system, pass around an outside corner to a chute. Ascend this chute to where it narrows, at an elevation of 13,500 feet. This narrow chute has two chockstones, which are both overcome by means of two class 4 moves; it is easier when it is filled with snow. Continue ascending this chute to its top and traverse to the right into a broad chute. Climb this chute to the

bowl that is southwest of the summit of North Palisade. Continue up the bowl to the crest of the southeast ridge, just right of the summit. Class 3 climbing over blocks near the drop-off over the Palisade Glacier leads to the summit.

Further Reading: Stephen F. Porcella and Cameron M. Burns. *Hiking and Climbing: California's Fourteeners.* Chockstone Press, Evergreen, Colo., 1996, pp. 66–68.

Southwest Chute. Class 4. First ascent July 19, 1921 by Hermann Ulrichs. Climb the chute for the LeConte Route to the top of The U Notch. There may be quite a bit of loose rock if there isn't any snow in the upper portion of this chute. From the top of The U Notch, climb either the Chimney Variation (the route of the first ascent) or the Clyde Variation to the summit. *Moore Variation:* Class 4. First ascent July 3, 1988 by Kathy Moore and R. J. Secor. Ascend the chute to an elevation of

North Palisade from the southwest. Photo by R. J. Secor.

13,700 feet; the floor of the chute is wall-to-wall scree at this point. Climb up and left via a narrow ledge to the next chute left. This chute leads up to the bowl on the southwest side of the summit.

Starlight Peak from North Palisade. 5.4. First ascent August 9, 1931 by Norman Clyde, Elmer Collet, Lewis Clark, Bestor Robinson, Robert Underhill, Neill Wilson, Jules Eichorn, Glen Dawson, and Francis Farquhar. Descend a chimney on the northwest side of the summit of North Palisade, either by down climbing or by means of a long rappel. Go north along a wide, sloping ledge to a notch. Down climb the flake in the notch (or rappel over it) and traverse across the northeast side of the ridge to a chimney that leads back over the ridge to its southwest side. Continue north to the notch between North Pal and Starlight Peak. Climb a chimney leading up from the notch to the summit block of Starlight Peak. The summit block, known as the "Milk Bottle," is climbed by means of a delicate mantle (5.4). It is the best-looking summit block in the Palisades, and it is situated in a good location for dramatic photographs.

Thunderbolt Peak   14,003 ft; 14,000 ft+

This is another classic peak of the High Sierra, and the last 14,000-foot peak to be climbed in the range. The summit block (on the higher, south peak) is difficult, and has defeated many climbers. Some really creative rope tricks are needed to pass a rope over it for aid or an upper belay; the east side of the block goes free at 5.9, and the west face is 5.8. The lower, north peak (locally known as "Lightning Rod") is class 5 from the notch between it and the south peak. The name "Thunderbolt Peak" commemorates an incident during the first ascent, when a nearby lightning strike temporarily broke Jules Eichorn's stride.

Further Reading: Stephen F. Porcella and Cameron M. Burns. *Climbing California's Fourteeners.* Seattle: The Mountaineers Books, 1998, pp. 214–229.

The Underhill Couloir. Class 4. First ascent August 13, 1931 by Robert Underhill, Norman Clyde, Bestor Robinson, Francis Farquhar, Glen Dawson, Lewis Clark, and Jules Eichorn. First winter ascent December 1962 by Leigh Ortenburger and Jerry Halpern. There are two couloirs that lead from the Palisade Glacier to the notch south of Thunderbolt Peak. Ascend the right-hand couloir to where progress is blocked by a chockstone. Bypass this by climbing the wall to its right before returning to the couloir and climbing it to the notch. Go north from the notch and ascend slabs to a chimney. There are two options from the top of the chimney. Either follow a ledge left to an exposed mantle, or continue up the face and chimney to the small notch next to the flat-topped pinnacle at the southern edge of the summit ridge. Follow the ridge to the summit. *Variation: Left Underhill Couloir.* Class 4. This is the route of the first-ascent party. The left couloir is full of loose rocks, unless there is sufficient snow cover—then it may be the preferable route. Ascend the left couloir approximately halfway up, then move right and ascend the crest of the arête to the notch south of Thunderbolt Peak. *Variation:* 5.4. The arête between the two couloirs can also be followed from the bottom.

Further Reading: *Summit.* July–August 1987, p. 10.

East Face. II, 5.5. First ascent August 1965 by Charles Ray and Ulrich Brosch. Traverse right on scree-covered ledges from the base of the Underhill Couloir for approximately 200 feet. Scramble up loose talus for about 200 feet to the base of a shallow open book. Climb the book for four pitches of class 4 and 5 climbing (one 5.5 move) to the top of a narrow ridge. Approximately 400 feet of class 3 lead to the base of the summit block. This has been described as an enjoyable climb on relatively good rock.

East Couloir. Class 5. First ascent July 4, 1959 by Ellen Wilts and Rich Gnagy. This narrow couloir ascends the east face of Thunderbolt Peak from the Palisade Glacier. Ascend the couloir, then go up and right, toward the crest of the upper northeast buttress. At one point there is a choice of two cracks to climb; the crack on the right is the correct choice. Ascend the headwall to the crest of the buttress, then follow the crest around the west side of Lightning Rod to the notch between the two summits of Thunderbolt Peak.

The Prow. III, 5.6. First ascent August 1970 by W. Katra and D. Sommers. This route ascends the great northeast buttress that almost divides the Palisade Glacier. The glacier north and west of this point has been called the "Thunderbolt Glacier." The route begins 50 feet to the left of the lowest tip of the buttress. Ascend a short, steep chimney to where class 4 and 5 climbing leads to the top of the long upper part of the northeast buttress.

Northeast Couloir. III, 5.6. First ascent August 1968

THUNDERBOLT
PEAK

Lightning
Rod

East
Face

Upper Northeast
Buttress

East
Couloir

Underhill
Couloir

Palisade Glacier

Thunderbolt Peak, East Face. Photo by R. J. Secor.

by Bob Lindgren and Brad Fowler. Ascend the first small couloir west of the prow of the northeast buttress. Keep to the left side of the couloir and climb onto a broken-rock ledge. Climb straight up from the ledge for one pitch (5.6). Continue up gentler rock for a few pitches (mostly class 4) to the top of the buttress. Follow the crest of the buttress around the west side of the north peak to the notch between the two summits of Thunderbolt Peak.

North Couloir. Class 3. Descended August 13, 1931 by Norman Clyde, Robert L. M. Underhill, Bestor Robinson, Francis Farquhar, Lewis Clark, Glen Dawson, and Jules Eichorn. This route climbs the large, Y-shaped snow and ice couloir west of the great northeast buttress of the peak. Cross Thunderbolt Glacier (the western lobe of the Palisade Glacier, north of Thunderbolt Peak) to the bergschrund at the base of the couloir. Cross the bergschrund on its left side, then head for ledges on the left side of the couloir. (Alternatively, you can directly ascend the 35°, 1,000-foot couloir; this may be preferable in early season.) Ascend the left side of the

couloir, and then its left branch where it divides, to the crest of the upper northeast buttress. Go to the right from the northeast buttress around the north side of Lightning Rod to a prominent notch, approximately 100 feet below the north peak. Drop down about 30 feet and traverse across the west side of the peak on a series of ledges to a chute that leads up to the notch between the higher, south peak and the north peak. Traverse to the right from the notch across the west side of the ridge to a steep class 3 face with ample holds and continue up to the summit block.

Northwest Ridge. Class 5. First ascent August 11, 1938 by W. K. Davis and Jack Riegelhuth. Follow the ridge from Winchell Col to the summit. The first one-third of this route is class 3, and the rest is class 4 and 5.

West Face. Class 4. First ascent September 3, 1949 by Oscar Cook, Sylvia Kershaw, Mildred Jentsch, Hunter Morrison, and Isabella Morrison. Ascend the first chute north (left) of Thunderbolt Pass from Dusy Basin. Follow the right branch of this chute to where it ends in an ice-filled chimney. Traverse to the right to an arête. Climb the arête for a while, and then leave it at a vein of rotten quartz by traversing to the right into a chute. A chockstone in this chute is passed on its left side (class 4). Ascend the chute to a spur and follow it to where it ends on the northwest ridge of Thunderbolt Peak. Follow the ridge to the base of Lightning Rod and drop down and traverse across its west side to the notch between the two summits of Thunderbolt Peak. Traverse to the right from the notch, across a class 3 face, and then climb to the summit.

Southwest Buttress. Class 5. First ascent August 28, 1964 by Kim Tucker, Sten Hedberg, and Alan Jedlicka. Follow the crest of the buttress upward from Thunderbolt Pass. Traverse left near the top and follow a chute to bypass some gendarmes to where it is possible to regain the buttress. The buttress ends atop the northwest ridge, which is followed to the southeast, to the notch between the two summits of Thunderbolt Peak. A traverse to the right from the notch leads to the summit block of the higher, south peak.

Southwest Chute No. 1. Class 3. Descended September 3, 1949 by Oscar Cook, Sylvia Kershaw, Mildred Jentsch, Hunter Morrison, and Isabella Morrison. This is the easiest route on Thunderbolt Peak. Ascend the first chute to the right (south) from Thunderbolt Pass. Approximately one-third of the way up, the chute narrows and is filled with chockstones. This section is bypassed by traversing to the right on a 3-foot-wide, scree-covered ledge. Continue up the chute to where it divides repeatedly; always take the right fork. These forks lead to the notch between the north and south summit of Thunderbolt Peak. Move south from the notch and traverse up and right across a steep face with horizontal cracks, then up to the base of the summit

Thunderbolt Peak and North Palisade from the northwest. Photo by R. J. Secor.

block. *Variation:* Class 5. Pass through the notch. A short, easy class 5 move to the left leads to less exposed climbing and the summit block.

Further Reading: John Moynier and Claude Fiddler. *Sierra Classics.* Evergreen, Colo.: Chockstone Press, 1993, pp. 142–143; Stephen F. Porcella and Cameron M. Burns. *Hiking and Climbing: California's Fourteeners.* Chockstone Press, Evergreen, Colo., 1996, pp. 76–77.

Southwest Chute No. 2. Class 4. First ascent August 3, 1933 by Norman Clyde, John Poindexter, and Philip Von Lubken. This is the largest chute that climbs from Palisade Basin to the notch south of Thunderbolt Peak. The main obstacle in this chute is a large chockstone. It may be possible to crawl underneath it; otherwise, a short class 4 pitch on its right side is used. It is possible to continue up the chute to the notch south of Thunderbolt Peak, but a better route is to take a steep, loose, short chute leading left into the next major chute, and follow this to the slabs above the notch. Ascend the slabs to a chimney. From the chimney's top, either follow a ledge left to an exposed mantle or continue up the face and chimney to the small notch next to the flat-topped pinnacle at the southern edge of the summit ridge.

Lightning Rod. Class 5. This is the lower, north summit of Thunderbolt Peak. The route starts from the notch between the two summits of Thunderbolt Peak. Climb to a wide, sloping ledge on the east side of the north summit. At the far end of this ledge, go right to a notch in the ridge with a chockstone in it. Pass through the notch to a narrow ledge with a lot of exposure. Ascend straight up from the ledge over small ledges to a 2-inch-wide crack, which leads to the summit.

Mount Winchell   13,775 ft; 13,768 ft

East Arête. Class 3. First ascent June 10, 1923 by W. B. Putnam, J. N. Newell, and H. C. Mansfield. First winter ascent January 10, 1938 by Norman Clyde, Morgan Harris, and David Brower. When viewing the southern side of the east arête from the Thunderbolt Glacier, you can see two chutes leading up to the arête. Climb the right-hand chute to the crest of the arête. Follow the arête to where it becomes a knife edge, and then traverse left into a steep chute that leads to the summit. This route is not especially difficult, and the summit is spectacular, with an impressive view down the magnificent sculp-

tures on the west face. *Variation:* Class 3. First ascent September 1953 by George Bloom, Kay Bloom, and Glenn Cushman. The east arête can also be approached from the north. Go to the north of a large buttress at the end of the east arête and climb a broken face to the crest of the arête. Follow the arête to the knife edge just below the summit.

Further Reading: John Moynier and Claude Fiddler. *Sierra Classics.* Evergreen, Colo.: Chockstone Press, 1993, pp. 144–145.

North Face. Class 4. First ascent August 14, 1955 by Robert Stebbins, Bill Rogers, and G. Ledyard Stebbins. Climb to the top of the glacier on the north side of Mount Winchell and continue upward between the northeast buttress and the north couloir. At one point there is a long diagonal traverse. The route ends on the east arête just below the summit.

Further Reading: John Moynier and Claude Fiddler. *Sierra Classics.* Evergreen, Colo.: Chockstone Press, 1993, pp. 144–145.

Northwest Ridge. IV, 5.8. First ascent August 1971 by Chris Fredericks and Tim Harrison. Climb onto the ridge at a point just south of Agassiz Col and follow the ridge to the summit. A long rappel is needed to descend into the major notch in the ridge. This is followed by a steep headwall, the crux of the climb.

West Chute. Class 4–5. First ascent July 29, 1930 by Jules Eichorn, Glen Dawson, and John Olmstead. From Dusy Basin, climb a chute with some difficult chimneys and then go up and right to a notch high on the northwest ridge.

West Arête. III, 5.8. First ascent May 1976 by Galen Rowell and Warren Harding. Climb the broad face that is to the left of the two chutes in the center of the southwest face of Mount Winchell. Gradually move to the right onto the crest of the arête, then follow the arête to where it ends on the northwest ridge, about 100 feet from the summit. Most of this route is moderate class 5.

Southwest Chute. Class 4–5. First ascent August 11, 1938 by W. K. Davis and Jack Riegelhuth. This route is also known as the Southwest Arête. Climb the left-hand chute of the two chutes on the southwest face of Mount Winchell. Ascend the chute to its top. Traverse left to the top of the west arête. Follow the arête to the northwest ridge, then follow the ridge to the summit. *Variation:* Class 4. First ascent 1966 by Steve Roper and Gordon Waddell. Climb the face that is several hundred feet left of the left-hand chute. Ascend this face for approximately 400 feet, then traverse to the right across the west arête and into the southwest chute. *Variation:* Class 4. First ascent 1962 by Tom Mathes and Jim Eder. Ascend the chute to where it narrows. After climbing over a large boulder, a steep, yellow gully is seen on the right wall. Climb the class 4 gully to the crest of the arête that separates the two chutes on the southwest side of Mount Winchell. Four more class 4 pitches lead to the summit.

Further Reading: John Moynier and Claude Fiddler. *Sierra Classics.* Evergreen, Colo.: Chockstone Press, 1993, pp. 146–147.

Southwest Buttress. III, 5.7, A2. First ascent September 1977 by David Mazel. This is the first major buttress to the left (northwest) of Winchell Col. Climb two pitches in a left-facing dihedral and then move right (A2) and climb a prominent chimney. Move right again from the top of the chimney over class 3–4 rock. Some more technical climbing leads to a shallow notch at the top of the buttress. Several hundred feet of class 3–4 climbing along the south arête leads to the summit.

Southeast Face. Class 5. First ascent June 21, 1959 by Don Dohrmann and Don Harmon. Class 3 climbing from Winchell Col leads to a prominent chute.

Thunderbolt Glacier from the northeast, August 24, 1972. Photo by Austin Post, No. 72R2-151, USGS Ice and Climate Project, GeoData Center, University of Alaska, Fairbanks.

MOUNT WINCHELL

Northwest Ridge

Winchell
Col

West
Arête

Southwest
Chute

Southwest
Buttress

West
Chute

Three class 4 pitches over loose rock in the chute end on a broad ledge. A long class 5 pitch leads over a small overhang and up a crack to a ledge beneath a second overhang. Turn this overhang on its right side, then climb out onto the east face of the peak. Some class 4 then leads to the top of the south arête a short distance from the summit.

Mount Agassiz   13,893 ft; 13,891 ft

This is the easiest major peak of the Palisades, and the ascent from Bishop Pass is very popular. There is a splendid view of the peaks surrounding the Palisade Glacier from the summit.

West Slope. Class 2. First ascent August 30, 1925 by Norman Clyde. First winter ascent March 20, 1967 by Rich Gregersen and Gary Vogt. Ascend a shallow chute that rises above Bishop Pass to the summit.

Southeast Face and South Ridge. Class 2. First ascent June 13, 1927 by Norman Clyde. From the northern moraine of the glacier east of Agassiz Col, climb a scree chute to the crest of the south ridge of Mount Agassiz. Follow the ridge to the summit. The east side of the south ridge can also be followed from Agassiz Col; this is mostly talus, and may be preferable to the loose scree in the chute.

East Ridge. Class 4. Climb the left-hand couloir of the two couloirs that lead onto the east ridge from the glacier northeast of Mount Agassiz. Ascend the east ridge to the summit.

Northeast Face. II, 5.2. First ascent July 5, 1930 by Norman Clyde. Cross the glacier northeast of Mount Agassiz and ascend the Y-shaped couloir that leads onto the north ridge of the peak. Ascend halfway up the Y, and then traverse left onto class 2 rocks. Climb the face diagonally to the left; when about halfway up the face, traverse to the right to an arête which overlooks the Y-shaped couloir. Ascend the left side of the arête (5.2), then either continue up the east face to the summit or cross the arête and the upper part of the couloir to the gentler slopes to the right.

Mount Robinson   12,967 ft; 12,800 ft

Northeast Face. Class 3. First ascent July 4, 1930 by Norman Clyde. Pass numerous pinnacles on the face and climb the long northeast ridge to the summit.

Mount Winchell, West Face. Photo by R. J. Secor.

The Lichen Arête. II, 5.7. First ascent August 1969 by Don Jensen, D. Kennedy, and R. Davis. There are three couloirs on the right-hand side of the northeast face of Mount Robinson. The two right-hand couloirs join halfway up. There is an arête between these two couloirs and the left-hand couloir. Climb the broad face, with increasingly difficult climbing, to the start of the arête. Ascend an easy chimney and traverse right to a ledge on the prow of the arête. Climb a vertical 5.7 open book to a small ledge left of the prow, then continue climbing to a good belay ledge a few feet higher. Climb several pitches to a notch with a steep, red tower on its opposite side. Make a delicate ascending traverse on its left side. One more pitch leads to the summit of the arête. The true summit of Mount Robinson is a long scramble along the northeast ridge.

West Ridge. Class 3. First ascent June 14, 1934 by David Brower and Hervey Voge. Follow the jagged ridge from the broad saddle between Mount Robinson and Mount Agassiz.

South Face. II, 5.7. First ascent July 1968 by Steve Roper, John Clark, Jon Lonne, and Dick James. Ascend the second arête from the right-hand arête on the south side of Mount Robinson.

Southeast Face. Class 3. Descended June 14, 1934 by David Brower and Hervey Voge. Ascend any of the many chutes above Sam Mack Lake.

Aperture Peak   13,265 ft; 13,200 ft+

First ascent June 1934 by David Brower and Hervey Voge. This peak is class 3 from Jigsaw Pass or from the glacier northeast of Mount Agassiz.

Gendarme Peak   13,252 ft; 13,241 ft

First ascent August 13, 1967 by Bill Schuler and Andy Smatko, via the southwest ridge. They descended a snow couloir on the southeast face. The summit rocks are easy class 3. There are four spectacular gendarmes on the northeast ridge.

Two Eagle Peak   12,966 ft; 12,880 ft+

This peak is actually a spur extending northeast from Gendarme Peak. It rises above Fifth Lake.

East Ridge. Class 3. First ascent July 6, 1929 by Norman Clyde. Follow the north side of the east ridge from Fifth Lake. The summit block is a smooth slab.

South Buttress. II, 5.6. First ascent July 1972 by Grant Hoag and Don Jensen. There are many small arêtes and gullies to the right of a smooth face on the south side of this peak. Begin by climbing a class 4 chimney just right of the face. Climb the left wall of the chimney for four pitches to the top of the buttress. Traverse across the flat ridge atop the buttress to a large, red tower. This is climbed via a chimney on its right side. Follow a sharp arête to the summit.

The Diamond. III, 5.6. This excellent route consists of ten pitches with wild exposure. Go a few hundred feet up and left from the very bottom of the south face and follow an improbable ledge/crack system up and right. Then climb a pitch left to the crest of the south buttress, above the flat ridge.

North Couloir. Class 3. First ascent May 27, 1993 by Yorgos Marinakis and Harry Marinakis. This narrow couloir cuts through the cliffs at the base of the moun-

tain and meets the east ridge a few hundred feet below the summit.

Picture Puzzle   13,280 ft+; 13,278 ft

North Slope. Class 3. First ascent 1937 by Norman Clyde from Ruwau Lake.

Northeast Couloir. Class 3. First ascent August 13, 1967 by Andy Smatko, Bill Schuler, Frank Yates, and Tom Ross. Ascend the 40° snow couloir on the northeast face to easy class 3 rock.

Southwest Face. Class 4. First ascent 1962 by Mike Loughman.

Cloudripper   13,525 ft; 13,501 ft

First ascent June 15, 1926 by Norman Clyde. First winter ascent April 3, 1966 by Tom Ross. The summit rocks are easy class 3. This peak is class 1 from Seventh Lake via the east ridge. The north slope is class 2 from Green Lake. The west slope from Chocolate Lakes is

Mount Agassiz, Northeast Face. Photo by R. J. Secor.

MOUNT AGASSIZ

Northeast
Face

Mount Robinson, South Face. Photo by R. J. Secor.

class 3 and was climbed by Ted Waller in 1932. The west chute from Chocolate Lakes was climbed by Tony Watkin on June 22, 1997. This steep chute starts above a large scree fan and takes the right branch about halfway up. Go to the left at the top of the chute where it broadens. This chute ends on the south ridge of the peak. Go left, following the ridge to the summit.

"Vagabond Peak" 13,374 ft; 13,356 ft;
0.5 mi N of Cloudripper

The north and south slopes are both class 2. There is a great ski descent off the north side of this peak down to Green Lake.

Chocolate Peak 11,682 ft; 11,658 ft

The class 2 southeast side was climbed by Don McGeein on July 4, 1932.

WRINKLES

The Palisade Glacier and Its Couloirs. The Palisade Glacier is the largest in the High Sierra, but it should not be confused with the type of glaciers found in the Cascade Range. There are crevasses in the Palisade Glacier, but these are not the same types of obstacles that are encountered on Mount Rainier, for example. During a typical snow year, the crevasses are small, narrow cracks that do not impede progress. During drought years, however, the crevasses may be 10 feet wide and perhaps 100 feet deep. But under these conditions, the Palisade Glacier is a "dry" glacier (i.e., no névé, only bare ice) and the crevasses can be easily spotted and avoided, or crossed at convenient places. Climbers seldom rope up while crossing the Palisade Glacier.

The bergschrunds at the bottoms of the V Notch, U

Notch, and Clyde Couloirs are another matter. These are always wide and deep, and their snow bridges (if present) seem to be only a few inches thick; climbers usually rope up. By mid-July these bridges may have collapsed, making the bergschrunds impassable unless the climber is skilled at climbing vertical ice. Sometimes these bridges collapse into a series of interconnected ramps, remaining that way until the next winter.

All of the couloirs above the Palisade Glacier can receive a phenomenal amount of rockfall. This can happen anytime, but in my experience it has been most frequent in the first half hour after sunrise in the spring and early summer. On the other hand, in Norman Clyde's experience, rockfall was most frequent in the afternoon during the middle of the summer. It is best to be out of these couloirs (either at their tops or on the buttresses on their sides) before sunrise. Next best is to delay the start of the climb at least until 1 hour after sunrise, but not much later, and not dawdle in the couloir. The snow or ice in the couloirs will be soft in the spring and early summer after midmorning, and a party cannot help but knock off some big pieces of ice. It is foolish to climb behind another party under these conditions.

These couloirs don't really get into shape until late September to October. During this time the ice is hard (in terms of both density and difficulty), and a long, cold morning keeps most of the rock from falling.

But all of this is a generalization, and the only way to find out exactly what conditions are in the couloirs is to climb them and see for yourself. One summer weekend my partner and I didn't get to the base of The U Notch until mid-morning, by which time other climbers were retreating because the bergschrund appeared to be impassable. The 'schrund was indeed impassable, but it had melted in such a way that we could find a way over the rock on the side of the couloir. It was a low snow year, and we expected the snow/ice in the couloir to be brick-hard. Instead, it was perfect Styrofoam, and we kicked steps to the top of the couloir without crampons. Yet two months earlier, another partner and I had attempted the Clyde Couloir only to find ourselves exposed to falling cannonades of rock and rime ice—the exact opposite of what would normally be expected at that time of year.

The "East Face" of North Palisade. North Palisade does not actually have an east face. The Sierra crest generally runs northwest–southeast, but between North Palisade and Mount Sill the crest runs west–east. The U Notch faces north, not east. Thunderbolt Peak does have an east face, however.

Traverses. Traversing peaks in the Palisades has a long tradition. It could be said that this began on August 11, 1938, when Ken Davis and Jack Riegelhuth made the first ascents of the Southwest Chute of Mount Winchell and the Northwest Ridge of Thunderbolt Peak on their way to the summit of North Palisade (in 13 hours!). Another notable traverse went from Southfork Pass to Jigsaw Pass along the entire Sierra crest. This traverse is 8 miles long, with 1½ miles of moderate class 5 and 3 miles of class 4, along with snow, mixed pitches, and acres of scrambling. It was first completed in July 1979 by Jerry Adams and John Fischer, in seven days. It was not repeated until 1993 and 1994 by Tom Birch, Jeff Jarvi, Dave Riggs, and Bela Vadasz, who reported over 160 pitches; the party stayed religiously along the crest itself.

Further Reading: John Moynier and Claude Fiddler. *Sierra Classics.* Evergreen, Colo.: Chockstone Press, 1993, p. 122.

A popular traverse goes from Thunderbolt Peak to Mount Sill; seasonal snow patches in the southwest bowl high on North Palisade can provide running water at a bivouac. The pinnacles that comprise Palisade Crest have been traversed in a day. Traverses between Norman Clyde Peak and Middle Palisade or Disappointment Peak have also been done.

Approach from Bishop Pass. The vast majority of climbers approach North Palisade and vicinity via the North Fork of Big Pine Creek. This is certainly an aesthetically pleasing route; it passes lakes and forests, and the approaches to climbs on the peaks loom over the Palisade Glacier. It seems that few climbers approach the peaks from the west, via Bishop Pass. It takes about the same amount of time to hike from South Lake to Palisade Basin as it does to hike from Glacier Lodge to a bivouac near the Palisade Glacier. The biggest rock faces are on the southwest sides of these peaks, and the easiest routes on North Palisade and Thunderbolt Peak are on their southwest sides. There is also a larger wilderness permit quota for the route from South Lake than for the route from the North Fork of Big Pine Creek. A western approach is not that difficult, and this side of the Palisades deserves more attention.

Chapter 9

The Evolution Region

If the wilderness of the High Sierra has a "destination resort," then Evolution Basin may be it. The John Muir Trail passes through this popular, lake-lined basin, but you only have to move a couple of miles to the west or south from the trail to find solitude. One of the wildest parts of the High Sierra is the area south of Muir Pass, which was not accurately charted until the 1950s. This remote area features rugged, trailless terrain, and place names that stir the imagination of all Sierra wanderers: Scylla, Charybdis, Disappearing Creek, Enchanted Gorge, Black Divide, and Devil's Crags.

This region covers the Sierra crest from Bishop Pass to Piute Pass. Its northern boundary is marked by Piute Creek, and it is bounded on the west by the South Fork of the San Joaquin River and Goddard Creek. The Middle Fork of the Kings River and the Dusy Branch serve as the southern border.

HISTORY

The California Geological Survey first attempted to climb Mount Goddard in 1864 from the south, from Kings Canyon via the Monarch Divide. This proved to be an impassable barrier for their pack animals, so they temporarily left the High Sierra via Kearsarge Pass, moved north through the Owens Valley, and reentered the range at Mono Pass (south). From their camp along Mono Creek they made a bold attempt to climb the mountain, 20 miles distant. Richard Cotter and a soldier by the name of Spratt got to within 300 feet of the summit before being turned back by hunger and exhaustion. John Muir visited the region in 1873, and may have climbed Mount Darwin. Lil A. Winchell explored the Middle Fork of the Kings River in the 1870s; in 1879, with Louis W. Davis, he made the first ascent of Mount Goddard.

It could be said that this area was "discovered" in 1895 by Theodore S. Solomons and Ernest C. Bonner. They shouldered heavy knapsacks at Florence Lake and hiked up the South Fork of the San Joaquin River. They then turned left at the mouth of Goddard Canyon and ascended Evolution Creek, which Solomons named on the spot. The pair continued upstream and bestowed place names honoring the evolutionists. They returned to Goddard Canyon and ascended it to its head, then climbed Mount Goddard. They then moved east through the Ionian Basin and descended Enchanted Gorge. The purpose of Solomons's explorations was to discover a high mountain route between Yosemite Valley and Kings Canyon. He succeeded in finding one, but his route has seldom been repeated.

For years, early Sierra explorers tried in vain to cross the Goddard Divide with their pack animals. George Davis of the United States Geological Survey finally succeeded in crossing the Goddard Divide via Muir Pass in 1907, probably thanks to the heavy snowpack that year, which made the talus on the east side of the pass passable. This feat was repeated in 1908 by Joseph LeConte, James Hutchinson, and Duncan McDuffie, but their mules just barely made it down into what is now called LeConte Canyon. Construction began on the John Muir Trail in 1915, and a humane route over Muir Pass was soon blasted through the talus.

There has been relatively little roped climbing practiced in this region. Exceptions to this are the ice couloirs on the north sides of Mount Mendel and Mount Darwin, and the rock faces and arêtes of the Devil's Crags. Devil's Crag No. 1 was first climbed by Charles Michael in 1913, a bold solo climb. The crag was not climbed again until 1930, when Jules Eichorn, Glen Dawson, and John Olmstead repeated Michael's route. Ascents of the other crags took place in 1933 and 1934, but they have been seldom visited since then; each of them probably has only a handful of ascents. Devil's Crag No. 1 has received most of the traffic, and in the 1960s and 1970s it averaged one ascent a year. With the increase of interest in climbing in the 1990s it now averages two ascents per year.

MAPS

USGS. *7.5-minute series:* Slide Bluffs, Marion Peak, North Palisade, Mt. Goddard, Blackcap Mtn., Mt. Thompson, Mt. Darwin, Mt. Henry, Mt. Tom, Mt. Hilgard. *National park maps:* Sequoia and Kings Canyon National Parks and Vicinity (1:125,000). *30 x 60-minute series:* Bishop, Mount Whitney.

USFS. A Guide to the John Muir Wilderness and the Sequoia–Kings Canyon Wilderness (1:63,360).

Tom Harrison Cartography. Mono Divide High Country, Kings Canyon High Country.

Map Link 15-minute series. Marion Peak, Mt. Goddard, Blackcap Mtn.

Wilderness Press 15-minute series. Mt. Goddard.

ROADS

South Lake Road

The South Lake Road leaves Highway 168 approximately 15 miles from Bishop. The South Lake Road goes up the South Fork of Bishop Creek, past some lodges and resorts, for 5.8 miles to South Lake and the trailhead for the Bishop Pass Trail and the Treasure Lakes Trail. Overnight parking is limited, and overflow parking is inconvenient for hikers to say the least: it's 1½ miles back down the road.

Lake Sabrina Road   (Highway 168)

The Lake Sabrina Road leads to Lake Sabrina at 18.7 miles from Bishop. Hiker parking is at the junction with the North Lake Road, 17.8 miles from Bishop and 0.7 mile from the trailhead for the Sabrina Basin Trails.

North Lake Road

The North Lake Road leads to the trailhead for the Piute Pass Trail and the Lamarck Lakes Trail. It leaves Highway 168 at 17.8 miles from Bishop. The partly paved and partly dirt road makes a steep climb up and past North Lake to the trailhead after 2.0 miles. Hiker parking is on the north side of North Lake, 0.8 mile from the trailhead.

TRAILS

Bishop Pass Trail   10 miles

A quota trail. The Bishop Pass Trail is one of the most popular trails in the High Sierra. It provides relatively quick and easy access to the backcountry of Kings Canyon National Park, and the views along it are terrific. And this is one of the few "downhill" trails—the start is at a higher elevation than the end. Wood campfires are prohibited in the entire Bishop Creek basin. Bears prowl through this area.

The trail leaves the parking area at South Lake (0 mi; 9,800 ft+) and climbs gently to meet the junction with the Treasure Lakes Trail (1 mi; 10,240 ft+). The Bishop Pass Trail goes left and continues to climb to the junction with a short side trail leading to Bull Lake and Chocolate Lake (1 mi; 10,680 ft+). The Bishop Pass Trail climbs to and then follows the eastern shore of beautiful Long Lake and meets the side trail leading to Ruwau Lake (1 mi; 10,800 ft+). The Bishop Pass Trail continues past Saddlerock Lake and Bishop Lake, then makes a steep ascent with many switchbacks to the summit of Bishop Pass (2 mi; 11,960 ft+). The trail descends into and eventually wanders out of Dusy Basin. Wood campfires are prohibited above 10,000 feet anywhere in Kings Canyon National Park, and this includes Dusy Basin; overnight camping with pack stock is also prohibited in Dusy Basin. The trail makes a steep descent into LeConte Canyon and meets the John Muir Trail (5 mi; 8,720 ft+); the LeConte Canyon Ranger Station is nearby.

Treasure Lakes Trail   3 miles

A quota trail. This trail leads to beautiful Treasure Lakes, a favorite spot for anglers, above South Lake. The trail leaves the Bishop Pass Trail approximately 1 mile

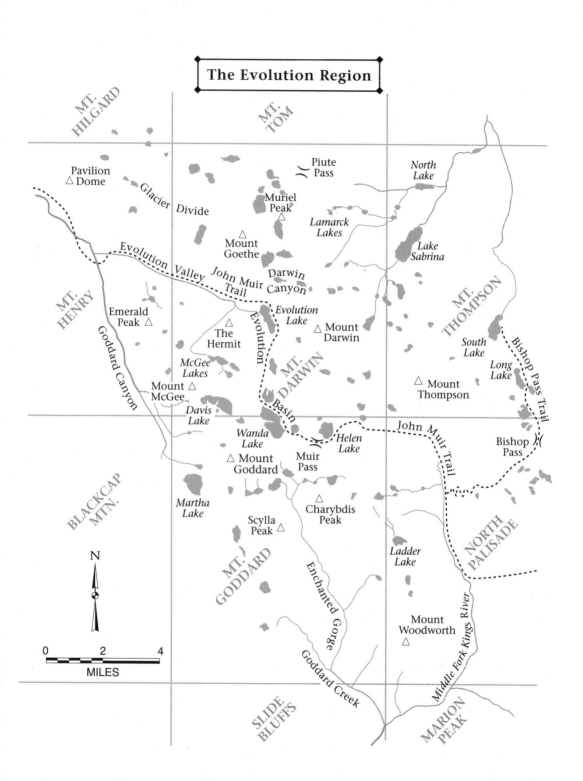

The Evolution Region

MT. HILGARD

MT. TOM

Pavilion △ Dome

Glacier Divide

Piute Pass

North Lake

Muriel Peak △

Lamarck Lakes

Lake Sabrina

Evolution Valley

John Muir Trail

Mount Goethe △

Darwin Canyon

MT. HENRY

Emerald Peak △

Goddard Canyon

The Hermit △

Evolution Lake

Evolution

△ Mount Darwin

MT. THOMPSON

South Lake

Long Lake

Bishop Pass Trail

McGee Lakes

MT. DARWIN

Mount McGee △

Davis Lake

Basin

△ Mount Thompson

Wanda Lake

Helen Lake

John Muir Trail

Bishop Pass

BLACKCAP MTN.

△ Mount Goddard

Muir Pass

Martha Lake

NORTH PALISADE

N

Scylla Peak △

△ Charybdis Peak

Ladder Lake

0   2   4
MILES

MT. GODDARD

Enchanted Gorge

Mount Woodworth △

Middle Fork Kings River

SLIDE BLUFFS

Goddard Creek

MARION PEAK

from South Lake (0 mi; 10,240 ft+). The Treasure Lakes Trail goes southwest and descends slightly before climbing to the largest of the Treasure Lakes (3 mi; 10,668 ft). The main trail ends here, but a faint path leads upward to the higher lakes above. Wood campfires are prohibited along this trail.

John Muir Trail   25 miles

The John Muir Trail goes north from the junction with the Bishop Pass Trail in LeConte Canyon (0 mi; 8,720 ft+), and leads to Little Pete Meadow, a heavily used campsite (½ mi; 8,840 ft+) and then Big Pete Meadow, which doesn't receive as much use (½ mi; 9,240 ft+). The John Muir Trail gradually turns to the west and climbs along the Middle Fork of the Kings River to Helen Lake (5¼ mi; 11,617 ft). The trail skirts the southeast shore of the lake and climbs through talus and many small cliffs to the summit of Muir Pass (1 mi; 11,960 ft+). There is a hut atop Muir Pass, but it should only be used in case of emergency.

The John Muir Trail descends the western side of Muir Pass and enters beautiful Evolution Basin. The trail passes Lake McDermand, then skirts the eastern shore of Wanda Lake and crosses its outlet before passing the western shore of Sapphire Lake and crossing the stream again just above Evolution Lake (4½ mi; 10,852 ft). The trail goes around the eastern shore of Evolution Lake. This lake is one of the finest in the High Sierra, but it has suffered from overuse due to many thoughtless campers. From the northern shore of Evolution Lake (1¼ mi; 10,852 ft), the John Muir Trail makes a steep descent into Evolution Valley and comes to Colby Meadow (3½ mi; 9,720 ft+). The trail continues to descend the valley, passes McClure Meadow and its ranger station (1 mi; 9,640 ft+), and then arrives at Evolution Meadow (2 mi; 9,240 ft+). After crossing Evolution Creek (the hikers' crossing is upstream and the stock crossing is downstream) the trail makes a steep descent out of the valley to the bridge across the South Fork of the San Joaquin River, where it meets the Goddard Canyon Trail (2 mi; 8,480 ft+). The John Muir Trail continues down the South Fork of the San Joaquin River and crosses it on another bridge (¾ mi; 8,360 ft+). The trail goes downstream to cross Piute Creek on a bridge and meet the Piute Pass Trail just beyond (2¾ mi; 8,050 ft).

Sabrina Basin Trails   4–6 miles

These trails lead to the scenic lakes above Lake Sabrina. Wood campfires are prohibited in this entire basin. Bears prowl through this area. The trailhead is just below the dam for Lake Sabrina (0 mi; 9,040 ft+). The trail traverses around and up above Lake Sabrina to the junction with the trail leading to George and Tyee Lakes where wood campfires are prohibited (1¼ mi; 9,400 ft+). The trail continues to Blue Lake, where it branches (1½ mi; 10,400 ft+). The south branch continues to Donkey Lake and Baboon Lakes (1½ mi; 10,976 ft). The other branch goes west past Emerald Lakes and Dingleberry Lake to a fork (2¼ mi; 10,840 ft+). The right-hand fork leads to Midnight Lake (½ mi; 10,988 ft); the left-hand fork leads to Hungry Packer Lake and Moonlight Lake (1 mi; 11,071 ft).

Lamarck Lakes Trail   2 miles

This short trail not only provides access to Upper and Lower Lamarck Lakes, but also serves as the approach for the Lamarck Col cross-country route. Wood campfires are prohibited along this trail. The trail starts at the North Lake Campground, next to the Piute Pass Trailhead (0 mi; 9,320 ft+). After crossing the stream, the trail climbs to a junction with a side trail leading to Grass Lake (¾ mi; 9,960 ft+). The right fork continues uphill to Lower Lamarck Lake. The main trail crosses the outlet stream, ascends a small canyon with trees, and crosses and recrosses a small stream (the route to Lamarck Col goes south in this area) before reaching Upper Lamarck Lake (1¼ mi; 10,918 ft).

Piute Pass Trail   17 miles

From the trailhead at North Lake Campground (0 mi; 9,320 ft+), this trail gradually climbs into the scenic basin east of Piute Pass. Wood campfires are prohibited along this entire trail east of Piute Pass. The trail passes Loch Leven and Piute Lake and then crosses Piute Pass, where there is a splendid view of Humphreys Basin (5 mi; 11,423 ft). The trail descends into the basin and goes past Lower Golden Trout Lake, where camping is prohibited. The trail eventually meets Piute Creek, then descends into a steep canyon before meeting the Pine Creek Pass Trail at Hutchinson Meadow (6 mi; 9,480 ft+). The Piute Pass Trail continues down Piute Canyon, where it climbs above and descends to the creek many times before meeting the John Muir Trail just west of the bridge across Piute Creek (6 mi; 8,050 ft).

Goddard Canyon Trail 6 miles

The Goddard Canyon Trail leaves the John Muir Trail at the bridge across the South Fork of the San Joaquin River, approximately 3½ miles upstream from Piute Creek (0 mi; 8,480 ft+). It ascends the western bank of the South Fork of the San Joaquin River to meet the Hell-For-Sure-Pass Trail at an unsigned junction (5 mi; 9,880 ft+). The Goddard Canyon Trail continues upstream and gradually disappears in the upper reaches of the canyon (1 mi; 10,000 ft+). Cross-country travel is easy to Martha Lake.

CROSS-COUNTRY ROUTES

"Rambaud Pass" 11,560 ft+; 11,553 ft;
0.6 mi W of Devil's Crags
Class 2. This is an old sheep route between Grouse Meadow and Simpson Meadow. The Middle Fork of the Kings River can be a difficult crossing in times of high water. The lower part of Rambaud Creek is choked with brush and manzanita close to the stream, so it is best to ascend from the southern end of Grouse Meadow and angle up to the 10,000-foot level of Rambaud Creek. Loose scree and talus lead to the saddle southeast of Wheel Mountain; the Devil's Crags and Mount Woodworth are accessible from the saddle. Descend the southwest side of the pass to Goddard Creek.

Enchanted Gorge

Class 3. The only thing "enchanted" about Enchanted Gorge is its name. This is a difficult cross-country route that descends Disappearing Creek almost 4,000 feet in 7 miles. (The creek gets its name when it disappears beneath some huge talus.) This route features gigantic boulders, cliffs, and icy snowbanks; it is for experienced cross-country hikers only.

From the Ionian Basin, traverse the eastern side of Chasm Lake on either snow or talus. Descend steep, loose talus south from Chasm Lake to the amphitheater at the head of the gorge. Continue downstream. Beyond some small tarns, the creek disappears. The creek reappears, disappears, and reappears yet again before it enters a small lake. At this point the gorge narrows, and the route enters its most difficult section. It is impossible to give an accurate description of the rest of the route. In general, it is necessary to climb up and down giant talus, bypass cliffs west of the creek, and cross the creek on seasonal snow bridges. The lower reaches of the gorge are choked with brush. The route eventually joins Goddard Creek.

Further Reading: *Sierra Club Bulletin.* 1924, pp. 7–20.

Goddard Creek

Class 2. This is another difficult cross-country route, but it is not as difficult as Enchanted Gorge. Goddard Creek is also a more pleasant area, with a few meadows, lakes, trees, and flowers. But these features are countered by almost impenetrable brush and talus at its lower level.

From Simpson Meadow along the Middle Fork of the Kings River, go north along the east bank of Goddard Creek for 3½ miles through some thick brush. This is followed by a lovely area of grass, trees, and flowers where Disappearing Creek meets Goddard Creek. (Cross-country hikers who have just descended Enchanted Gorge will find an ascent of Goddard Creek to be far more preferable than bushwhacking onto Simpson Meadow.) Continue ascending the east bank of Goddard Creek. Where the walls of the canyon close in, you are forced to cross much talus interspersed with thick willows. Eventually the canyon turns west, and beyond a fountainlike waterfall, the canyon opens up into a broad valley. Continue up the valley to Lake 10,232 ft (10,212 ft). After walking around the western shore of the lake, either cross Reinstein Pass, cross Goddard Creek Pass, or head northeast into the Ionian Basin.

Further Reading: *Sierra Club Bulletin.* 1924, pp. 7–20.

Ladder Lake

Class 2. Ladder Lake is approached from LeConte Canyon by making an ascending traverse from north to south. Avoid the stream that appears to drain Ladder Lake. Instead, climb through an area of brush and then forest far to the north of the stream to the band of cliffs at 10,000 feet. Pass through these cliffs via a loose class 2 chute that ends just west of Point 10,57ft (UTM 563037; this point does not appear on the 15-minute

Mt. Goddard map). The 15-minute Mt. Goddard map incorrectly shows a stream draining this chute; the 7.5-minute North Palisade map shows the correct drainage, however.

"Goddard Creek Pass"   12,240 ft+; 12,240 ft+;
0.7 mi S of Mount Goddard

Class 2. This route leads from Martha Lake to the Ionian Basin. From the South Fork of the San Joaquin River, skirt the north shore of Martha Lake and head for the lower, right-hand (south) saddle that is south of Mount Goddard. Go left (northwest) from the top of the saddle, skirting the north shore of a small lake, and then descend southeast, passing Lake 11,951 ft (11,920 ft+), to Lake 11,818 ft (11,804 ft). Cross the lake over the two peninsulas that almost touch. From the southern shore of this lake, you can either turn southwest toward Goddard Creek, or northeast into Ionian Basin.

Reinstein Pass is a more direct alternative route between Goddard Canyon and Goddard Creek. This is described in Chapter 7, Kettle Ridge and The LeConte Divide.

"Goddard Col"   12,280 ft+; 12,360 ft+;
0.5 mi S of Mount Goddard

Class 2. This has been used as an approach to climb Mount Goddard. It leads from Martha Lake to the bench lake that is high on the southeast side of Mount Goddard, Lake 12,240 ft (12,120 ft+). Circle the lake on its southeast side.

Further Reading: John Moynier. *Backcountry Skiing in the High Sierra.* Evergreen, Colo.: Chockstone Press, 1992, p. 73.

"Wanda Pass"   12,440 ft+; 12,400 ft+;
0.4 mi S of Wanda Lake

Class 2. This route leads from Evolution Basin into Ionian Basin. Leave the John Muir Trail at the outlet of Wanda Lake, and follow the western shore of the lake. Go south up a gradually steepening slope to the obvious saddle on the Goddard Divide. Descend the south side of the pass to the eastern shore of Lake 11,592 ft (11,520 ft+). Those headed for Goddard Creek should pass Lake 11,837 ft (11,824 ft) on its southern shore. Those headed for Enchanted Gorge should proceed southeast, making sure that Chasm Lake is passed on its eastern shore.

"Nietzsche Col"   12,440 ft+; 12,400 ft+;
0.3 mi NW of Mount Solomons

Class 2. This pass was formerly named "Solomons Pass." It leads to Ionian Basin from the vicinity of Muir Pass. Head southwest from Muir Pass, gradually ascending to the obvious saddle west of Mount Solomons. The north side of the pass is frequently covered with snow. Descend the south side of the pass to the eastern shore of Lake 11,592 ft (11,520 ft+).

"Black Giant Pass"   12,200 ft+; 12,160 ft+;
0.5 mi W of Black Giant

Class 2. This pass serves as the eastern access to the Ionian Basin. Leave the John Muir Trail anywhere between Helen Lake and Muir Pass and head south to the obvious saddle west of the Black Giant. Cross the pass and descend to the western shore of the lake that is south of the pass. Go west and after a short, steep descent, pass between many small lakes to the northern side of Chasm Lake.

Further Reading: *Summit.* Summer 1994, p. 85.

"Goode Pass"   12,680 ft+; 12,640 ft+;
0.4 mi S of Mount Goode

Class 2. This pass has been used by skiers traversing the Sierra crest. The west side of this pass consists of a steep couloir.

Further Reading: John Moynier. *Backcountry Skiing in the High Sierra.* Evergreen, Colo.: Chockstone Press, 1992, p. 36.

"Hurd Col"   11,720 ft+; 11,680 ft+;
0.6 mi SSW of Hurd Peak

Class 2. This pass leads between Treasure Lakes and Margaret Lake in the Bishop Creek drainage.

Further Reading: John Moynier. *Backcountry Skiing in the High Sierra.* Evergreen, Colo.: Chockstone Press, 1992, p. 110.

"Treasure Col"   12,000 ft+; 11,760 ft+;
0.3 mi NNW of Mount Johnson

Class 2; ice axe required. This pass leads between Treasure Lakes and Big Pete Meadow in LeConte Canyon. Head southwest from Treasure Lakes to the cirque north of Mount Johnson. Climb a snow/ice chute (bordered by loose rocks) on the southern side of the broad saddle north of Mount Johnson. The western side of the pass is a steep and loose class 2 chute. Stay on the southeastern side of the stream that descends from the western basin between Mount Gilbert and Mount Johnson. When the cliffs above Big Pete Meadow appear, traverse left (south) along the base of a small cliff for approximately 100 feet, and then gain the crest of the blunt ridge above the cliff. Descend the crest of the ridge to where an obvious route to the stream is seen to the right (southwest). Cross the stream and bushwhack down its western bank for about 300 feet. Cross the stream again and descend through talus and some small patches of manzanita to Big Pete Meadow.

"Powell-Thompson Col"   12,880 ft+; 12,720 ft+;
0.5 mi W of Mount Thompson; UTM 560115

Class 2; ice axe required. This is a convoluted cross-country route, leading to the easy southern routes on Mount Powell and Mount Thompson. Echo Col is preferred for those seeking a more direct cross-country route between Sabrina Basin and the John Muir Trail east of Muir Pass. Head south from the southernmost of the Baboon Lakes, aiming for the small pass north-northwest of Sunset Lake (Pass 11,560ft+; 11,520 ft+; UTM 564133). Go through the pass and bypass Sunset Lake on a bench above its western shore. Continue south and climb onto the glacier northeast of Mount Thompson. Three cols can be seen above the glacier. The highest, right-hand col is the Northeast Chute of Mount Powell. The lowest col is to the left. The correct col is the middle one, a little higher than the one on the left and much lower than the one to the right. The upper part of the chute leading to Powell-Thompson Col is filled with disagreeably loose rock. Descend the steep southern side of the col and turn southeast, passing Lake 12,120ft+ (12,132 ft) on its northeastern shore. Continue downstream to the 11,400-foot contour. Make a slightly ascending taverse to the right, going around Point 12,120ft+ (12,080 ft+), and hike up to Lake 11,725ft (11,710 ft). One can continue on to the John Muir Trail east of Helen Lake via Keating Pass.

"Keating Pass"   12,280 ft+; 12,240 ft+;
UTM 548103

Class 2. This pass has been named here in honor of Jerry Keating. It is used to climb Mount Powell from the vicinity of Helen Lake, and it is also used by skiers during high-level traverses of the Sierra crest. A steep gully is on its southwest side and benches are on the northeast side of the pass.

Further Reading: John Moynier. *Backcountry Skiing in the High Sierra.* Evergreen, Colo.: Chockstone Press, 1992, p. 36.

"Echo Col"   12,400 ft+; 12,400 ft+;
1.0 mi SE of Mount Wallace; UTM 541112

Class 3; ice axe required. This pass has also been referred to as "Echo Pass" and "Black Notch." This is the direct route between Lake Sabrina and Muir Pass. Hike cross-country from the western shore of Moonlight Lake to the eastern shore of Echo Lake. Gradually contour up and onto the bench above and south of Echo Lake. The correct pass is to the right (west) of the saddle, atop a chimney marked by black rock; it is *not* the easier-appearing pass to the left (east). Ascend straight up to the top of the pass and descend a short chute on its southern side. Go slightly left (east) and pass Lake 11,428ft (11,360 ft+) on its western shore. Go south over a low ridge before turning west. Descend a talus-filled chute to bypass a small cliff and meet the John Muir Trail at the 11,000-foot level, where it crosses a small stream descending from the northwest.

"Fiske Col"   12,640 ft+; 12,640 ft+;
0.3 mi SW of Mount Fiske

Class 2. This cross-country route leads between Helen Lake and Sapphire Lake.

Further Reading: John Moynier. *Backcountry Skiing in the High Sierra.* Evergreen, Colo.: Chockstone Press, 1992, p. 112.

"Wallace Col"   12,960 ft+; 12,960 ft+;
0.2 mi SSE of Mount Wallace

Class 2. This is a loose class 2 route across the Sierra crest between Moonlight Lake and Sapphire Lake in Evolution Basin. From Moonlight Lake hike toward Echo Lake but make an ascending traverse southwest to the bench high above the western shore of Echo Lake. Go west from the bench to the low point of the broad saddle south of Mount Wallace. Descend the west side of the pass over loose scree and talus. Go northwest and west, past benches, small meadows, and tarns, to the John Muir Trail near Sapphire Lake.

"Haeckel Col"   12,680 ft+; 12,640 ft+;
0.3 mi NW of Mount Haeckel

Class 3. This pass is north of Mount Haeckel and leads to Evolution Basin from the Sabrina Basin. Climb onto the long ridge between Midnight Lake and Hungry Packer Lake from near Topsy Turvy Lake. Follow the ridge to the cirque north of Mount Haeckel. Pass north of Lake 12,345ft (12,320 ft+) and head for a point to the right of a small, round peak on the crest; this point is about 300 feet northwest of the lowest point of the saddle. Traverse west from the top of the pass to a scree chute. Descend the chute to the northeast corner of Lake 11,808ft (11,822 ft). Follow the north shore of the lake around to its outlet, and then descend directly to Sapphire Lake.

The long ridge between Midnight Lake and Hungry Packer Lake has also been reached directly from the northwest shore of Hungry Packer Lake.

"Davis Lake Pass"   11,640 ft+; 11,600 ft+;
1.6 mi NE of Mount Goddard

Class 2. This pass leads from Evolution Basin to Goddard Canyon. Go southwest from the outlet of Wanda Lake to the obvious saddle to the west of the peninsula in the lake. Easy cross-country hiking leads over the saddle and down to Davis Lake. Circle around Davis Lake on its south shore, but cross to its north shore on the eastern peninsula; there is no crossing on the western peninsula. (You can remain on the south shore of the lake, but this involves a short, exposed class 3 climb over a buttress with a tricky descent as well as a traverse over a steep snowfield and then lots of talus.) Head for the low saddle that is north of the outlet portion of the lake (at UTM 458107). Pass through the saddle and make a steep descent along North Goddard Creek to the floor of Goddard Canyon.

Martha Lake can be reached from Davis Lake by heading southwest from the outlet of Davis Lake and climbing onto a bench at approximately 11,200 feet (UTM 453100). Turn south and climb onto another bench between 11,400 and 11,600 feet. Follow the series of lakes along this bench and then descend southwest to Martha Lake.

It is also possible to reach McGee Lakes from Davis Lake by crossing Pass 11,720ft+ (11,760 ft+; 1.3 miles ESE of Mount McGee). Class 2.

"McGee Lakes Pass"   11,560 ft+; 11,520 ft+;
1.5 mi SE of The Hermit

Class 2. This route leads from Sapphire Lake in Evolution Basin past McGee Lakes and down to McClure Meadow in Evolution Valley. Leave the John Muir Trail near Sapphire Lake and make a steep ascent to the obvious saddle southeast of Peak 12,245ft (12,260 ft). Descend the west side of the pass, keeping to the south of two small tarns and to the north of a small lake, to the northern shores of McGee Lakes. Continue down the outlet stream into McGee Canyon. Cross the stream immediately downstream of the fork that drains Lake 11,140ft (11,137 ft). Continue downstream to meet a trail that comes up from Evolution Valley. Follow the trail down, then make a difficult crossing of Evolution Creek at the eastern end of McClure Meadow.

Another approach to McGee Lakes is via Pass 11,800ft+ (11,840 ft+; 1.2 miles west of Mount Huxley). Leave the John Muir Trail north of Wanda Lake and ascend over talus to the saddle between Peaks 12,040ft+ and 12,262ft (12,086 ft and 12,290 ft). Descend west and then north past two lakes to the eastern shore of the easternmost of the McGee Lakes.

"Darwin Col"   12,800 ft+; 12,800 ft+;
0.3 mi NE of Mount Darwin

Class 2. This pass leads between Sabrina Basin and Darwin Canyon. A steep scree gully leads up the east side of this pass from Blue Heaven Lake.

Further Reading: John Moynier. *Backcountry Skiing in the High Sierra.* Evergreen, Colo.: Chockstone Press, 1992, p. 114.

Lamarck Col   12,960 ft+; 12,880 ft+

Class 2. This is probably the most popular cross-country route across the Sierra crest between Bishop Pass and Piute Pass. It has none of the loose rock found on the other passes, and the talus is not as severe. But this is still a long, arduous route, and it should only be attempted by hikers in good condition.

Leave the Lamarck Lakes Trail between Lower Lamarck Lake and Upper Lamarck Lake. The correct place to leave the trail is near where the trail crosses the stream (at UTM 542196). Head southwest along a faint path, past a small meadow with a tarn, and climb the steep slope above. From the top of this slope, the route

Lamarck Col

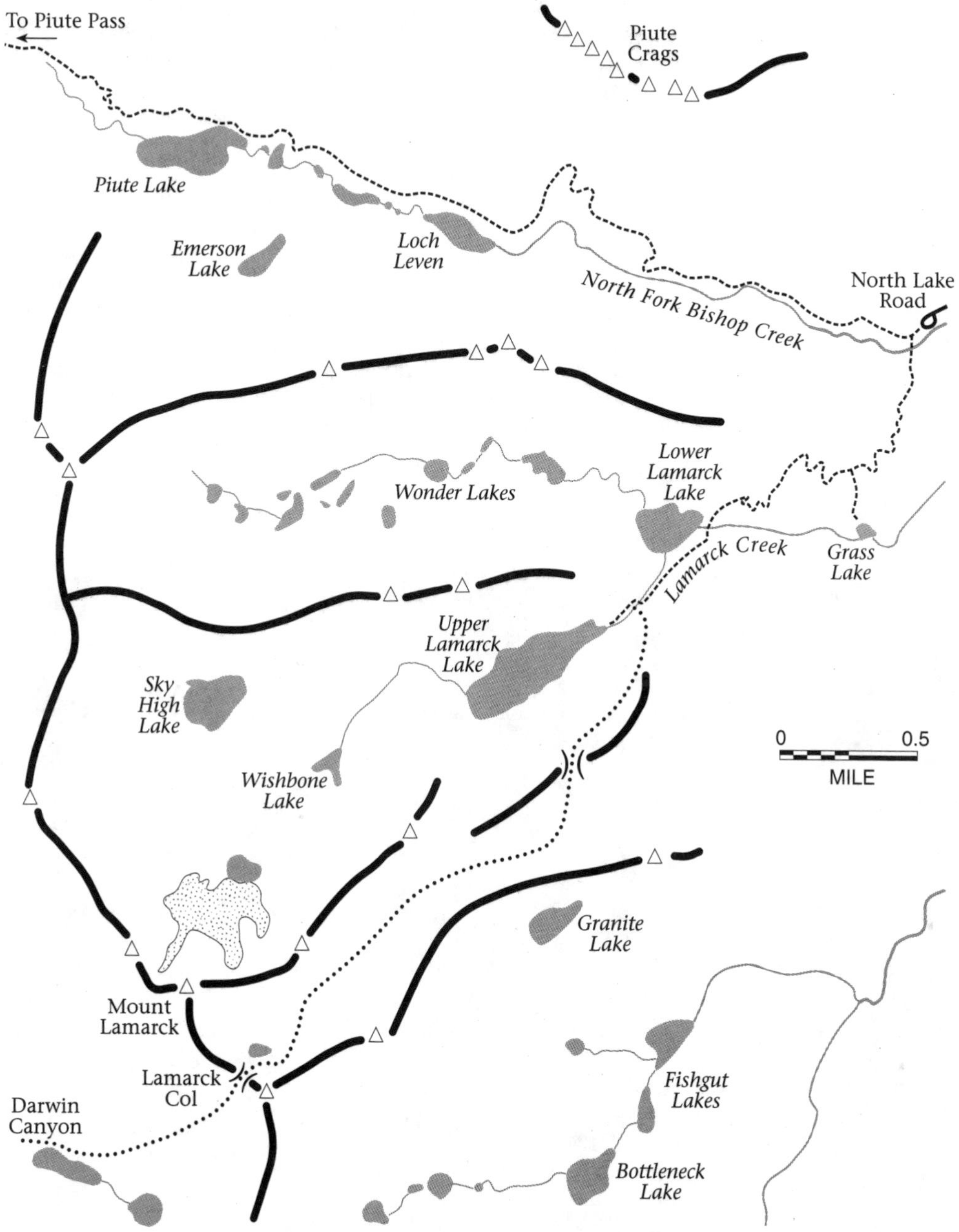

To Piute Pass

Piute Crags

Piute Lake

Emerson Lake

Loch Leven

North Fork Bishop Creek

North Lake Road

Wonder Lakes

Lower Lamarck Lake

Grass Lake

Lamarck Creek

Upper Lamarck Lake

Sky High Lake

Wishbone Lake

Granite Lake

N

0   0.5
MILE

Mount Lamarck

Lamarck Col

Darwin Canyon

Fishgut Lakes

Bottleneck Lake

goes southwest up a broad, sandy valley with some boulders to the small lake immediately beneath Lamarck Col. Cross the snowfields beyond the lake, and pass through the first notch to the right of a small, sharp peak (the most easterly of several notches on the crest). Descend the southwest side of Lamarck Col approximately 200 feet and follow sandy ledges down into upper Darwin Canyon. Descend the canyon on the northern side of the lakes, passing over a few talus fields, and drop down to Darwin Bench. From the southern side of Lake 11,160ft+ (11,200 ft+) descend east of the outlet stream on a good use trail to meet the John Muir Trail northwest of Evolution Lake.

When crossing Lamarck Col from west to east, it is important to head toward the higher pass to the left (north) of the low pass at the head of Darwin Canyon; the lower pass leads to the lakes above Lake Sabrina. And be sure to go left (northeast) at the end of the long, sandy valley (at UTM 538185) on the east side of Lamarck Col to reach the Lamarck Lakes Trail. The area beneath the long, sandy valley is a superb ski tour in the spring.

The Keyhole   12,520 ft+; 12,560 ft+

Class 3. This pass is so named because you can pass through it, rather than over it. It leads between Humphreys Basin and Darwin Bench, and involves a lot of talus hopping. Climb southeast from Muriel Lake to the highest of the Lost Lakes. Climb toward a small notch that is southeast of Muriel Peak, skirting the western edge of a small glacier along the way. The Keyhole is a 4-foot triangular gap in the talus atop the notch. A short class 3 pitch is encountered just below the southwestern side of The Keyhole. Descend steep talus to the eastern shore of the lake below, and stay above its eastern shore while hiking to its south end. Pass between Lake 11,540ft (11,520 ft+) and Lake 11,546ft (11,520 ft+) and head toward Darwin Bench to meet the Lamarck

Lamarck Col and Mount Lamarck from the north. Photo by Austin Post, No. 72R2-123, USGS Ice and Climate Project, GeoData Center, University of Alaska, Fairbanks.

Col route, which heads down to the John Muir Trail.

Further Reading: Steve Roper. *Sierra High Route.* Seattle: The Mountaineers Books, 1997, p. 127.

Alpine Col   12,320 ft+; 12,320 ft+

Class 2. Like The Keyhole, this pass also crosses the Glacier Divide between Darwin Bench and Humphreys Basin, and also has a lot of unpleasant talus. From Darwin Bench pass between Lakes 11,540ft and 11,546ft (11,520 ft+ and 11,520 ft+) to the western shore of Lake 11,910ft (11,840 ft+). Follow granite ledges above the lake to its northwest side. Ascend steep talus to the saddle southwest of Muriel Peak. The northwest side of Alpine Col consists of a wide chute filled with some huge boulders, which leads down to the eastern shore of Goethe Lake. Pass the lower lake on its western shore and descend to Muriel Lake.

Further Reading: Steve Roper. *Sierra High Route.* Seattle: The Mountaineers Books, 1997, p. 127.

"Snow-Tongue Pass"   12,200 ft+; 12,160 ft+;
1.5 mi NW of Mount Goethe

Class 2–3. This pass crosses the Glacier Divide between Peaks 12,477ft and 12,920ft+ (12,440 ft+ and 12,971 ft). Make a gradually ascending traverse northwest from the 10,680-foot level of the John Muir Trail northwest of Evolution Lake. This leads to the basin that holds Lake 11,092ft (11,106 ft). Bypass the lake and ascend the stream that enters the lake from the northeast. After heading north, go to the right to the summit of the pass. Instead of descending directly down the northwest side of the pass, climb up the ridge leading south for about 50 feet to a small notch, and make a right diagonal descent over loose rock. You can then descend either a snow couloir to the right (east) or the rocks on the side of the couloir. Descend talus to the Wahoo Lakes and hike cross-country to the Piute Pass Trail.

Further Reading: Steve Roper. *Sierra High Route.* Seattle: The Mountaineers Books, 1997, pp. 119–121, 126.

"Packsaddle Pass"   12,440 ft+; 12,400 ft+;
2.7 mi ESE of Pavilion Dome

Class 2. This pass crosses the Glacier Divide between Packsaddle Lake and Evolution Meadow. Head southwest from Packsaddle Lake to the saddle southeast of Peak 12,900ft (12,900 ft). The last 300 feet just below

the pass is steep class 2. The southwest side of the pass is easy. Head down to the stream, and follow it downhill to Evolution Meadow.

"Lobe Pass"   12,320 ft+; 12,320 ft+;
2.2 mi ENE of Pavilion Dome; UTM 432220

Class 2. This pass, also known as "Matthes Col," crosses the Glacier Divide between Lobe Lakes and Evolution Meadow. Go southwest from Lobe Lakes to the saddle southeast of Peak 12,560ft+ (12,591 ft). The northeast side of the pass is quite steep, but remains class 2. Go west from the summit of the pass before turning south to the large lake. Follow the outlet stream of this lake downstream to Evolution Meadow.

Lower Honeymoon Lake and Ramona Lake

Class 2. These two lakes are above Piute Creek, nestled in hanging valleys. Leave the Piute Pass Trail at the 9,760-foot level. Go south, across Piute Creek, and follow a good use trail upstream to Lower Honeymoon Lake. Go south around the western shore of the lake and turn to the northwest. Ascend granite slabs to the top of the rounded ridge to the west of Lower Honeymoon Lake. Go southwest to a small notch, which leads to the steep talus slope that leads down to Ramona Lake.

PEAKS

Mount Woodworth   12,219 ft; 12,219 ft

First ascent August 1, 1895 by Bolton Brown, via the class 2 southwest spur. The traverse from Rambaud Pass is class 3.

Devil's Crags
12,400 ft+–11,440 ft+

These impressive peaks are seldom visited. They deserve far more attention than they have received in the past, despite their remoteness and extremely abundant loose rock. The second ascent of Devil's Crag No. 5, made 37 years after its first ascent, gave the author (then 14 years of age) quite a thrill.

The Devil's Crags are numbered from the northwest to southeast, starting at the highest crag. But there are several different numbers in the registers atop the crags. For example, the small crag between Devil's Crag No. 1 and Devil's Crag No. 2 has been called "Devil's Crag

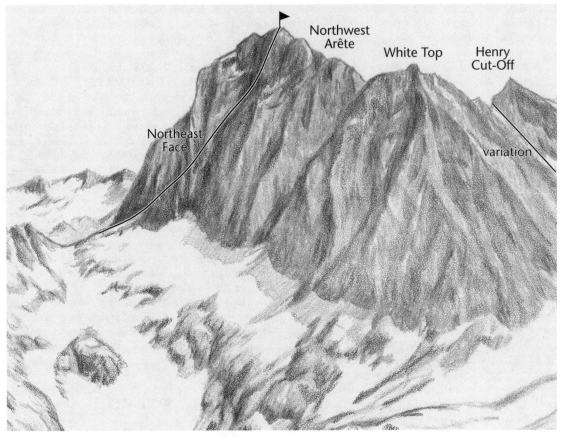

Devil's Crag No. 1 from the north.

No. 2." Jules Eichorn and Glen Dawson reported the first ascent of "Devil's Crag No. 11" in 1933; this turned out to be Devil's Crag No. 9 according to the system of numbers used here.

Most ascents of the Devil's Crags have utilized the chutes between the crags. The chutes that are relatively easy (class 4) to climb from the northeast are those between Crags No. 2 and No. 3, Crags No. 4 and No. 5, and Crags No. 8 and No. 9. From the southwest, only the chute between Crags No. 4 and No. 5 is difficult. The easiest chutes that cross the Devil's Crags are the northeast and southwest chutes between Crags No. 8 and No. 9 (class 2–3).

Further Reading: *Sierra Club Bulletin.* 1934, pp. 19–23.

"White Top"   12,262 ft; 12,240 ft+;
1.1 mi W of Rambaud Peak

First ascent August 18, 1924 by Rollin E. Ecke and Jack B. Rhodes. This small peak northwest of Devil's Crag No. 1 is class 3 from the saddle to the southwest. The white rock atop this peak contrasts with the prevailing black rock of the Black Divide.

"Devil's Crag No. 1"   12,400 ft+; 12,560 ft+;
UTM 567001

Michael's Chimney. Class 4. First ascent July 21, 1913 by Charles Michael. Go southeast from the top of Rambaud Pass to the first saddle west of the White Top. Descend a loose scree slope into the basin southwest of the Devil's Crags. On the southwest face of Devil's Crag

No. 1 there are two great chutes or chimneys that form a huge X. Climb the lower left-hand branch of the X. After passing a small chockstone, you come to the junction of the two chutes. Ascend the right-hand chimney to near the top, then go left onto the crest of the northwest arête. Follow the arête to the summit.

Diagonal Chute. Class 4. First ascent July 25, 1933 by Hans Leschke, John Poindexter, and Ted Waller. Ascend the lower left-hand branch of the X on the southwest face to the junction of the two chutes. Ascend the upper left-hand branch of the X to the northwest arête of Devil's Crag No. 1. Follow the arête to the summit. This route is technically easier than Michael's Chimney.

Northwest Arête. Class 4. First ascent July 25, 1933 by Jules Eichorn, Helen LeConte, and Alfred Weiler. This is a classic climb with much exposure. Not as much loose rock is encountered on this route compared to other routes on Devil's Crag No. 1. Reach the saddle west of the White Top from Rambaud Pass. Traverse across the southwest side of the northwest ridge for about 300 yards, gradually dropping 100 feet to the entry point of a prominent chute. Ascend the chute about 150 feet, then climb 100 feet of class 3–4 on the buttress to the right of the chute to the crest of the arête. Ascend the arête, passing between a pair of black rocks ("Black Rabbit Ears") to a notch where the Diagonal Chute meets the arête. A 60-foot class 4 pitch up from the notch is followed by class 3 to a dramatically exposed knife edge notch; this is where Michael's Chimney joins the northwest arête. The knife edge notch is crossed on the northeastern side of the arête. Much exposed class 3 then leads to the summit. *Variation:* Class 4. First ascent September 1, 1985 by Dave Dykeman, George Toby, Nancy Gordon, Bob Hartunian, and R. J. Secor. Instead of ascending the prominent chute and buttress to the crest of the arête, remain on the southwest side of the arête, passing a minor rib to a more prominent buttress farther south. Ascend this buttress to a point along the crest of the arête that is left (northwest) of where the Diagonal Chute joins the northwest arête. *Variation: Henry Cut-Off.* Instead of climbing to the top of Rambaud Pass, it is possible to turn left about 500 feet beneath the northeastern side of the pass and climb a loose class 2–3 chute to the saddle west of the White Top. A wide chute angles off to the right in the bottom part of the Cut-Off. Climb about 300 feet above the junction of these two chutes and then move to the left and climb over a rib and ascend the far left-hand side of the Cut-Off. This

is a good descent route, but caution must be exercised due to loose rock.

Further Reading: John Moynier and Claude Fiddler. *Sierra Classics.* Evergreen, Colo.: Chockstone Press, pp. 172–173.

Northeast Face. Class 4. First ascent August 5, 1938 by Raffi Bedayan, Kenneth Davis, and Jack Riegelhuth. This route has ample exposure, good belay stances, and relatively sound rock. From the head of Rambaud Creek climb to the saddle northeast of Devil's Crag No. 1. This saddle is immediately southwest of Peak 11,408ft (11,360 ft+). Rope up at the saddle, then traverse up and right over loose rock to the chute in the middle of the northeast face. (This traverse should be planned so that it ends above the lower, overhanging portion of the chute.) Ascend the chute to a point about 35 feet beneath the summit. Go right, where a short, steep pitch leads to the northwest arête. Follow the arête to the summit.

"Devil's Crag No. 2"   12,280 ft+; 12,320 ft+

Northeast Chimney. Class 4. First ascent July 26, 1933 by Jules Eichorn, Ted Waller, and Glen Dawson. Climb the narrow chimney south of Devil's Crag No. 1 and north of the intermediate crag between Crags No. 1 and No. 2. This chimney is rather narrow and steep; proper chimney technique ("back and feet") is needed in some places. Ascend the chimney to its top, then traverse over the small crag on the ridge to the true summit of Devil's Crag No. 2.

East Face. II, 5.8. First ascent 1992 by Claude Fiddler, Danny Whitmore, and Bob McGavin.

Southwest Chute. Class 3–4. Descended July 26, 1933 by Jules Eichorn, Ted Waller, and Glen Dawson. Climb the southwest chute between Devil's Crag No. 2 and the small crag to the north.

Further Reading: *Sierra Club Bulletin.* 1934, pp. 21–22.

"Devil's Crag No. 3"   12,240 ft+; 12,320 ft+

North to South Traverse. Class 4, A0. First ascent June 24, 1934 by David Brower, Hervey Voge, and Norman Clyde. Ascend the northeast chute between Crags No. 2 and No. 3. Remain on the floor of the chute, and pass under a huge chockstone to the notch at the top of the chute. From the notch, climb the left side of a broken face and then contour out and up a broad, sloping ledge on the north face to the north arête. Climb the left side of the arête to the northwest arête and follow this arête to the summit. Descend a sloping, broken ledge on the east side of the crag. Follow this around to the south, but traverse left and down (east) to a wide ledge along the way. This ledge leads around and beyond the southeast arête to its west side. Climb down another 60 feet. Rappel down overhangs to the notch between Crags No. 3 and No. 4. Descend the southwest chute (class 3) or northeast chute (class 4) from this notch.

To climb Devil's Crag No. 3 from the notch between Crags No. 3 and No. 4, you must overcome some vertical to overhanging rock.

Southwest Chute. Class 3. Climb the southwest chute between Crags No. 2 and No. 3 to the notch, and ascend to the summit from the notch.

"Devil's Crag No. 4"   12,240 ft+

Southwest Chute. Class 3. First ascent June 24, 1934 by Hervey Voge, David Brower, and Norman Clyde. Climb to the notch between Crags No. 3 and No. 4 from the southwest, and ascend the southwest side of the northwest arête to the summit.

Northeast Chute. Class 4. First ascent August 1971 by Connie Eaton and Wally Henry. Climb the chute leading to the notch between Crags No. 3 and No. 4 from the northeast, and follow the southwestern side of the northwest arête to the top.

The southeast face of Devil's Crag No. 4 is quite precipitous.

"Devil's Crag No. 5"   12,240 ft+

North to South Traverse. Class 4. First ascent June 25, 1934 by Norman Clyde, David Brower, and Hervey Voge. Climb the northeast chute that leads to the notch between Crags No. 4 and No. 5, passing a chockstone on its left side along the way. Climb a short chimney on the left-hand side near the top of the chute. Traverse and slightly descend across the western side of the crag and ascend the right side of the northwest arête to a point about 25 feet beneath the summit block. Go right, then walk up the south side to the summit. Descend the southeast arête to the notch between Crags No. 5 and No. 6.

"Devil's Crag No. 6"   12,240 ft+

North to South Traverse. Class 4. First ascent June 25, 1934 by David Brower, Norman Clyde, and Hervey

Voge. Traverse from Devil's Crag No. 5 to the notch between Crags No. 5 and No. 6, and ascend the west side of the northwest arête to the top.

"Devil's Crag No. 7"   12,160 ft+

Southwest Chute and Northwest Ridge. Class 4. First ascent June 25, 1934 by Hervey Voge, David Brower, and Norman Clyde. Climb the southwest chute to the notch between Crags No. 6 and No. 7. Alternatively, you may descend the southeast ridge from Crag No. 6 to the notch. Ascend the northwest ridge to the summit of Crag No. 7.

"Devil's Crag No. 8"   12,000 ft+

Southwest Chute. Class 3. First ascent June 25, 1934 by Norman Clyde, Hervey Voge, and David Brower. Climb the southwest chute between Crags No. 7 and No. 8, then follow the northwest slope (one short class 3 section) to the summit.

"Devil's Crag No. 9"   11,720 ft+

Northwest Arête, Right Side. Class 4. First ascent August 1, 1933 by Jules Eichorn and Glen Dawson. Gain the notch between Crags No. 8 and No. 9 from either the southwest or northeast. Ascend the right side of the northwest arête to the summit.

Northwest Arête, Left Side. Class 4. First ascent August 1988 by Mark Hoffman and Robin Ingraham, Jr. Ascend the left side of the arête to the summit.

"Devil's Crag No. 10"   11,640 ft+

Traverse from Crag No. 9. Class 4 with two rappels. First ascent June 23, 1934 by David Brower, Hervey Voge, and Norman Clyde. Down climb the southeast ridge of Crag No. 9 and rappel to the notch between Crags No. 9 and No. 10. Ascend the west side of the northwest ridge of Crag No. 10.

Southeast Arête. Class 2. Climb the northeast chute between Crags No. 10 and No. 11 and ascend the southeast ridge of Crag No. 10, passing over a smaller crag along the ridge.

"Devil's Crag No. 11"   11,440 ft+

Northeast Chute. Class 4. First ascent June 23, 1934 by David Brower, Hervey Voge, and Norman Clyde. Ascend the northeast chute to the notch between Crags No. 10 and No. 11. Climb to the summit of Crag No. 11 over exposed, broken rock.

Rambaud Peak   11,044 ft; 10,960 ft+

First ascent 1925 by Ruth Prager and Albert Tachet. This peak is class 2 from Rambaud Creek to the northwest. The northwest buttress, a short class 4 climb, was first done in August 1971 by Marc Leon and Ed Rose.

Wheel Mountain   12,774 ft; 12,781 ft

Northwest Slopes. Class 3. First ascent July 26, 1933 by Marjory Bridge, Lewis F. Clark, John Cahill, and John Poindexter. From the summit of Rambaud Pass traverse around the southwest and west sides of the mountain to the bench northwest of the peak. Ascend the northwest slope to the east ridge, and climb the east ridge to the summit.

Southeast Ridge. Class 3. First ascent August 1963 by Phil Clayton, Jess Logan, Tom Ross, and Andy Smatko. This is the preferred route. Ascend the southeast ridge rising from Rambaud Pass. There is a short detour off the ridge to the west just below the summit.

Southeast Arête. II, 5.4. First ascent August 1977 by Brian West and Sam Roberts. This route follows the prominent buttress and arête. It is necessary to cross over and bypass several gendarmes.

The Citadel   11,738 ft; 11,744 ft

West Ridge. Class 2. First ascent June 24, 1951 by Richard Searle and William Wirt. Ascend the ridge from Ladder Lake.

Northwest Chute. Class 4. First ascent 1952 by Charles Bay Locker, R. J. McKenna, S. Hall, D. E. Albright, and Karl G. Hufbauer. Ascend the chute rising from the eastern end of Ladder Lake to the ridge west of the summit.

Northwest Buttress. Class 5. First ascent August 1971 by Dave Gladstone and Marc Leon. Climb the broad buttress to the left (northeast) of the chute on the northwest side of the peak.

North Face. IV, 5.7, A3. First ascent 1968 by TM Herbert, Don Lauria, and Dennis Hennek. Ascend a dihedral with several overhangs. The crux is about 600 feet above the ground, where an overhang is overcome via difficult aid climbing. The rest of the route is easier.

The Edge of Time Arête. IV, 5.10+. First ascent August 1991 by Dave Nettle and Jim Howle. This is the striking arête on the left side of the north face. The route starts on the right side of the arête with two pitches (5.7) that lead up the left side of a pillar. From the top of the pillar, a 5.8 face leads up and left over a small ledge to

another ledge on the crest of the arête; the second ledge is marked by trees. Move to the left side of the arête, then ascend a left-facing open book (5.10) for two pitches. Go up and slightly right to a belay in slings beneath the first triangular roof on the crest of the arête. Pass the roof on its right side. The next pitch goes left across the crest of the arête, climbs a crack, and then goes to the right, back across the crest over flakes, before reaching a hanging belay beneath the second triangular roof. Pass the second roof on its left side, where a 5.10 slot leads to a prominent notch on the crest of the arête. Above the notch, one has a choice of either a steep 5.9 face on the left or a strenuous 5.10 corner on the right. The rest of the route remains on the right side of the arête and ends with class 3 climbing atop the east summit.

Further Reading: John Moynier and Claude Fiddler. *Sierra Classics.* Evergreen, Colo.: Chockstone Press, 1993, pp. 174–176.

Northeast Face. Class 4. First ascent June 24, 1951 by Donald Goodrich and Robert Means, who arrived at the summit several hours after the first ascent of the west ridge. Climb the northeast face via several gullies and chutes to the ridge east of the peak. Follow the ridge to the summit, passing over the lower eastern summit.

Mount McDuffie   13,282 ft; 13,271 ft

North Ridge. Class 3. First ascent July 23, 1951 by Charles Bays Locker, Karl Hufbauer, and Alfred Elkin. Climb from the west to the saddle between Mount McDuffie and Peak 13,04ft (13,046 ft). Just below the saddle, traverse south toward Mount McDuffie, keeping 150 to 200 feet below the crest of the north ridge. About 200 yards from the summit, ascend a shallow, broad chute to the crest of the north ridge, then follow the ridge to the summit.

Southeast Ridge. Class 2–3. First ascent July 15, 1952 by Charles Bays Locker, Don Albright, Gary Hufbauer, and Karl Hufbauer. Head west-southwest from Ladder Lake to Lake 12,040ft+ (12,000 ft+; 0.8 miles SE of Mount McDuffie). Climb to the southeast ridge of the peak from the lake, then ascend the ridge to the summit, keeping to its west side. There are a few class 3 moves while crossing chutes.

Southwest Ridge. Class 2. First ascent August 10, 1989 by Dave Helphrey, Ron Robson, and Reiner Stenzel. Follow the ridge from Enchanted Gorge.

West Chute. Class 3. First ascent August 2, 1974 by

THE CITADEL

Edge of Time
Arête

The Citadel, North Face. Photo by R. J. Secor.

Bob Rockwell. Head south from the lake west of the peak (Lake 11,520ft+; 11,680 ft+; UTM 532043), crossing the prominent rock rib to the next chute to the south. Ascend the chute, working up and back onto the rib over very loose rock and talus. After about 400 feet of class 3, the angle lessens, and the rib leads to the southwest ridge. Continue up the class 2 ridge to the summit.

Northwest Slope and West Ridge. Class 3. First ascent August 1971 by Dave Gladstone. Climb the slope to the right of the prominent snow couloir on the northwest side of Mount McDuffie to the broad west ridge, and follow the ridge to the summit.

Langille Peak   12,018 ft; 11,991 ft

West Ridge. Class 3. First ascent August 1926 by Nathaniel Goodrich, Marjory Hurd, and Dean Peabody. This ridge is best approached from Hester Lake.

Southeast Face. Class 4. First ascent Norman Brown, Susanne Marcus, John Pearson, and Paul Axinn. Ascend slabs on the southeast face, over the lower, southeast peak and on to the true summit.

East Buttress. Class 4–5. First ascent July 2, 1970 by Chris Jones and Fred Beckey. The east face of Langille Peak is marked by many deep gullies and spurs. This route ascends close to the crest of the east buttress that drops from the lower, southeastern peak. The climb starts over talus and ascends gradually steepening slabs.

East Buttress Direct. IV, 5.10b. First ascent July 14, 1988 by Galen Rowell and David Wilson. This route climbs the very prominent arête that leads to the lower, southeastern summit.

Black Giant   13,330 ft; 13,330 ft

West Slope. Class 1. First ascent 1905 by George R. Davis. This is a simple climb from Black Giant Pass. There is a swell view from the summit.

South Slope. Class 2. This slope is usually climbed during a traverse to or from the north ridge of Mount McDuffie.

Southeast Ridge. Class 3. First ascent August 19, 1971 by Wally Henry, R. J. Secor, and Jim Cervenka. Ascend the class 3 east ridge of Peak 12,800ft+ (12,804 ft) and follow the gentle southeast ridge to the summit.

Northeast Face. Class 4. First ascent August 1966 by Steve Roper. There are four small glaciers on the northeast side of Black Giant. Climb the northernmost gla-

cier to its top, and ascend a loose chute for 100 feet. Follow a diagonal ledge system to the summit ridge.

Charybdis   13,096 ft; 13,091 ft

Northeast Ridge. Class 3. First ascent July 7, 1931 by Anna Dempster and John Dempster. Follow the southern side of the northeast ridge to the summit.

Further Reading: John Moynier and Claude Fiddler. *Sierra Classics.* Evergreen, Colo.: Chockstone Press, 1993, pp. 178–179.

Southeast Ridge. Class 3. Descended August 1971 by Dave Gladstone. This route has been used to traverse to Mount McDuffie, but it involves much elevation gain and loss. It is better to descend the northeast ridge of Charybdis and then cross Pass 12,360ft+ (12,400 ft+; 1.0 mile south of Black Giant) to approach the north ridge of Mount McDuffie.

The north face was first climbed in July 1954 by Eric Smith.

The Three Sirens
(12,640 ft+; 12,640 ft+)

These three pinnacles are east of Scylla. The snowfields and couloirs north of The Three Sirens last long into the summer. Ice axes will probably be needed.

"West Siren"   12,520 ft+; 12,480 ft+

West Chimney. Class 4. First ascent August 4, 1962 by George Wallerstein, Don Wilson, and Mike Raudenbush. Ascend a snowfield to the notch between Scylla and the West Siren. Go to a platform from the saddle and climb a class 4 chimney to the summit of the West Siren.

"Central Siren"   12,640 ft+; 12,640 ft+

West Ridge. Class 4. First ascent August 4, 1962 by George Wallerstein, Don Wilson, and Mike Raudenbush. This climb begins from the notch between the Central and West Sirens. This notch can be reached by two rappels from the summit of the West Siren, or by climbing the snow chute on the northern side of the notch. An alternate approach is done by going around the southern side of the West Siren. From the platform on the West Chimney route, follow a ledge around West Siren to where it ends. Rappel 45 feet and then climb to the notch from the south.

Ascend a system of ledges up and right from the notch to the summit of the Central Siren.

East Siren   12,560 ft+; 12,480 ft+

West Ridge. Class 4. First ascent August 2, 1978 by Carl Heller, Dave Brown, and Peter Woodman. A short

walk from the Central Siren is followed by a short class 4 pitch to the summit.

Scylla   12,956 ft; 12,939 ft

First ascent July 3, 1934 by David Brower and Hervey Voge. First winter ascent March 30, 1984 by

Langille Peak from the southeast. Photo by R. J. Secor.

The Three Sirens and Scylla. Photo by R. J. Secor.

Peter Cummings and Ed Cole. The northwest slope is class 2.

Mount Hansen   12,975 ft; 12,960 ft+;
0.5 mi S of Scylla

This peak is named on some maps. The north ridge is class 1 and was climbed by Robin McKeown and Frank Orme on August 17, 1954.

Ragged Spur   12,843 ft; 12,841 ft

This entire ridge is class 1–2 and was traversed by Robin McKeown and Frank Orme on August 17, 1954.

Mount Solomons   13,034 ft; 13,016 ft

First ascent August 12, 1929 by M. H. Pramme and F. F. Harms, via the class 2 northeast shoulder from Muir Pass. The snow chute on the north face is also class 2. The west and south ridges are class 2 from Ionian Basin. The east ridge is class 3, and was climbed by Harry Marinakis and Yorgos Marinakis on June 17, 1993.

Mount Goddard   13,568 ft; 13,568 ft

Starr's Route. Class 2. First ascent August 1928 by Walter A. Starr, Jr., and companion. This is an interesting route on an otherwise dull mountain. Climb the north ridge of Peak 13,040ft+ (12,980 ft+) above Davis Lake (this is the first peak east of Mount Goddard along the Goddard Divide). The ridge becomes steep just below the crest; follow a ledge around the left side of the ridge to the top of the Goddard Divide. Ascend the tedious talus of the east slope to the summit of Mount Goddard. *Variation:* Class 3. First ascent by Charles Bell. Instead of taking the ledge, cross a gully and continue straight up to the crest on good holds. *Variation:* The glacier to the right (west) of the ridge can be ascended before moving left onto the ridge.

Further Reading: John Moynier and Claude Fiddler. *Sierra Classics.* Evergreen, Colo.: Chockstone Press, 1993, pp. 180–181.

East Slope. Class 2. Follow the Goddard Divide west from the summit of Wanda Pass. The Goddard Divide and the east slope of Mount Goddard can be reached from almost anywhere in the Ionian Basin.

Southwest Ridge. Class 2–3. First ascent September 23, 1879 by Lilbourne A. Winchell and Louis W. Davis. Go east from Martha Lake to Lake 11,960ft+ (11,920 ft+), a small lake that is surrounded by a cirque. Turn northeast and climb to Goddard Col, which leads to the next larger lake on a bench above the cirque, Lake 12,240ft+ (12,120 ft+). Go left from the southern shore of this larger lake and ascend a chute to the southwest ridge. The north summit is the high point, and a small bit of class 3 is encountered between the two summits.

West Side. Class 3. There is a steep, narrow snow gully directly east of Lake 11,520ft+ (11,440 ft+; UTM 462077). Climb the ridge that is immediately south of the snow gully. Loose rock along the ridge leads to the southwest ridge, which is followed to the top.

Northeast Face. 5.8. First ascent June 1986 by Steve Porcella and Kevin Sugar. There is a tremendous amount of loose rock on this route. Cross the glacier to the right of Starr's Route and climb the steep, loose rock

to the crest of the Goddard Divide. Follow the ridge to the summit.

The first-ascent party descended the chute above the glacier, where they found the conditions far worse than on the northeast face.

Peak 12,964ft 12,913 ft;

0.9 mi N of Mount Goddard

North-Northwest Ridge. Class 2–3. First ascent July 27, 1941 by R. S. Fink. This ridge is best approached from the west, avoiding cliffs on the northern and northwestern sides of the ridge. A chute leads onto the crest of the ridge. Follow the ridge to the summit.

Southeast Ridge. Class 3–4. First ascent September 2, 1942 by August Fruge, William A. Sherrill, and Neal Harlow. Climb the steep, blunt buttress that leads to the top of the ridge that connects this peak with Mount Goddard. Follow the ridge, passing a pinnacle to its right. Climb the left side of the ridge and then traverse out onto the south face of the peak. A narrow chimney leads up to several chutes, any of which can be followed to the top.

Mount Goddard from the northeast. Photo by R. J. Secor.

Hurd Peak   12,237 ft; 12,219 ft

First ascent 1906 by H. C. Hurd. The west face is class 3 from Treasure Lakes; the south ridge is class 4. There is a class 2–3 gully on the east side of the peak from Long Lake; this was first climbed by Pete Yamagata on September 28, 1991.

Mount Goode   13,085 ft; 13,092 ft

Southeast Slope. Class 2. First ascent July 16, 1939 by Chester Versteeg. This is an easy climb from Bishop Lake.

South Ridge. Class 2. First ascent August 12, 1939 by Jack Sturgeon. Follow the ridge north from Peak 12,916ft (12,916 ft).

North Buttress. III, 5.8. First ascent September 1974 by John Fischer, Dennis Hennek, Jay Jensen, and TM Herbert. Begin by climbing a left-facing open book (5.8) that is immediately to the right of the toe of the buttress. A horizontal traverse left leads across a prow, a chimney, and then another prow to a second chimney. Climb this second chimney to a notch behind a pillar. The next pitch, the crux, begins with a 5.9+ move around a small roof and finishes on a ledge above a 5.8 chimney. The route continues up the crest of the buttress and finishes with a 5.8 hand traverse to the right before manteling onto the summit.

Further Reading: John Moynier and Claude Fiddler. *Sierra Classics.* Evergreen, Colo.: Chockstone Press, 1993, pp. 150–153.

North Buttress, East Side. IV, 5.10. First ascent 1979 by Claude Fiddler and Vern Clevenger. This route starts just east of the buttress. Many pitches, four of which are 5.10, lead to join the North Buttress route approximately two-thirds of the way up.

Peak 12,916ft   12,916 ft; 0.5 mi S of Mount Goode

This peak is frequently climbed by parties with the mistaken belief that they are climbing Mount Goode. This peak has come to be informally named "Mount No Goode." The peak is class 2 from the southeast, and was first climbed by Chester Versteeg on July 12, 1939.

Peak 12,920ft+   12,960 ft+;
0.4 mi W of Mount Goode
This peak has been called "Trapezoid Peak."

Mount Goddard from the southeast. Photo by R. J. Secor.

West Ridge. Class 3. First ascent 1968 by Ed Lane. This is a straightforward climb from Mount Johnson.

Northwest Face. Class 3. First ascent July 19, 1969 by Andy Smatko, Bill Schuler, Dave Wallace, and Tom Ross. Climb a snow couloir on the northwest face from the cirque southeast of Mount Johnson. From the top of the couloir an easy class 3 wall leads to a short area of loose rock, which is followed by the sloping summit plateau and the summit block.

North Ridge. Class 3–4. First ascent July 1962 by a Sierra Club party. This is the long ridge that curves toward the east as it extends north from the summit. Gain the ridge from the east and follow it to the summit. Most of this route is class 3, with a few class 4 moves.

Mount Johnson   12,871 ft; 12,868 ft

North Ridge. Class 3 from Treasure Col.

Southeast Slope. Class 2. First winter ascent March 17, 1974 by Roy Keenan and party. Climb a sandy chute from the highest of the Treasure Lakes.

West Ridge. Class 3. First ascent August 14, 1939 by Jack Sturgeon. Climb to the bench beneath the west ridge. Easy class 2 leads up from the bench, passes a false summit on the left, and moves onto the sharp west

ridge. Climb the class 3 ridge, generally keeping to its right side, to an exposed catwalk. This is followed by easy boulder scrambling to the summit.

Mount Gilbert   13,106 ft; 13,103 ft

Southeast Slope. Class 2. First ascent September 15, 1928 by Norman Clyde. This route is usually climbed from Treasure Lakes. After climbing to the top of Treasure Col (ice axe required), ascend the easy southeast slope to the summit. This slope can also be reached from Big Pete Meadow. *Variation:* Class 3. First ascent October 30, 1994 by Matthias Selke. First winter ascent February 18, 1996 by Gregg Howard, Ellen Holden, Rick Beatty, and R. J. Secor. An ice axe is not usually required for this variation. Treasure Col can be bypassed by climbing up and to the left across the southeast slope of Peak 12,640ft+ (12,600 ft+; 0.5 miles ESE of Mount Gilbert). This diagonally ascending traverse leads to the Sierra crest. Remain about 100 feet below the crest, crossing some minor ribs and slabs, to an obvious notch that is just south of Peak 12,640ft+. Pass through the notch, descend about 100 feet on the other side, and ascend the southeast slope of Mount Gilbert to the summit.

Mount Goddard from the west. Photo by R. J. Secor.

MOUNT GOODE

North Buttress,
East Side

Mount Goode from the northeast. Photo by R. J. Secor.

North Couloir. III, 5.6, AI2 or WI3. First ascent September 3, 1972 by Al Fowler, Dan Eaton, and Ron Cale. The angle of ice in this 900-foot couloir varies between 50° and 65°. From the notch atop the couloir drop down 40 feet, then climb up and left to the summit ridge.

Further Reading: *Summit.* March–April 1984, pp. 34–35; John Moynier and Claude Fiddler. *Sierra Classics.* Evergreen, Colo.: Chockstone Press, 1993, pp. 154–155.

West Face. II, 5.7. First ascent 1985 by Claude Fiddler and Vern Clevenger.

Peak 12,960ft+ 12,993 ft;
1.6 mi NNE of Mount Thompson

First ascent November 7, 1931 by Norman Clyde. The summit block is class 4.

"Cheba Spire" 12,520 ft+; 12,400 ft+;
1.2 mi N of Mount Gilbert; UTM 561130

South Face. II, 5.9+. First ascent August 1988 by Alan Swanson and Cory Hicks. The pitches on this route are 5.9+, 5.8, and class 4.

Peak 12,640ft+ 12,560 ft+;
1.1 mi NE of Mount Thompson

West Ridge. Class 4. First ascent June 24, 1973 by Barbara Lilley, Ed Treacy, Tom Ross, Bill Schuler, and Andy Smatko. Gain the saddle on the west ridge from the south. Follow the west ridge to the impressive summit block, which is climbed via a monstrous flake.

Peak 13,000ft+ 12,880 ft+;
1.0 mi NNE of Mount Thompson

First ascent August 25, 1968 by Andy Smatko and party. Gain the plateau north of Mount Thompson via a class 2 chute on its southeastern side. The southwest summit is class 2. The northeast summit, a sliver of granite about 20 feet high, is rated 5.6.

"Ski Mountaineers Peak" 13,280 ft+; 13,323 ft;
0.4 mi NNE of Mount Thompson

This is the high point of Thompson Ridge. This peak is unofficially named after the Ski Mountaineers Section of the Sierra Club, who have skied off its summit for many years. (Dissident members of the Ski Mountaineers

Mount Thompson from the west. Photo by R. J. Secor.

Section call it "Motocross Peak.") The east slope is class 2 and was first climbed by Norman Clyde on September 6, 1931.

Mount Thompson   13,494 ft; 13,440 ft+

Southwest Face. Class 2. First ascent August 14, 1939 by Jack Sturgeon. A narrow chute north of Lake 12,120ft+ (12,132 ft) leads up to the small plateau south of the summit of Mount Thompson. *Variation:* Class 2. The southwest face can also be reached from Sunset Lake. Cross the glacier northwest of Mount Thompson (an ice axe may be needed). There are two chutes that lead to the ridge between Point Powell and Mount Thompson from the north. (Ignore the highest, right-hand col; this is the Northeast Chute of Point Powell.) Climb the right-hand chute to Powell-Thompson Col, then descend its south side about 200 feet. Traverse east from here along the bottom of the cliffs on the southern side of the west ridge of Mount Thompson to a chute, which leads to the summit plateau.

West Ridge. Class 3. Climb to the lower col between Mount Thompson and Point Powell. Those approaching from the north may need ice axes to cross the glacier northwest of Mount Thompson. Follow the west ridge to the summit.

Northwest Face. Class 3. First ascent June 30, 1931 by Norman Clyde. Ascend the glacier northwest of Mount Thompson from Sunset Lake to the base of a steep chute close to where the northwest face meets Thompson Ridge. This chute rises diagonally from right to left and ends at a notch high on Thompson Ridge. Ascend the chute, bypassing an obstruction to its left, to a notch on the ridge. Keep to the left side of the ridge while climbing to the summit.

Thompson Ridge. Class 3. First ascent September 1959 by Henry Mandolf, Charles Bell, and Stuart Ferguson. Follow the ridge south from Peak 13,240ft+ (13,323 ft) to the deep notch between it and Mount Thompson. Climb over broken benches on the east side of the ridge to the summit. *Variation:* Class 4.

First ascent July 16, 1986 by Vern Clevenger. The ridge can also be climbed directly along its crest.

Moynier Couloir. III, AI3 or WI4. First ascent August 1986 by John Moynier. This narrow, 900-foot couloir is on the far, right-hand side of the face rising above the glacier northeast of Mount Thompson. It cannot be seen until one is near the eastern base of Thompson Ridge. It has six pitches of moderately difficult ice climbing. The crux is passing a chockstone about two-thirds of the way up. This is followed by 70°+ ice.

Further Reading: John Moynier and Claude Fiddler. *Sierra Classics.* Evergreen, Colo.: Chockstone Press, 1993, pp. 156–157.

Harrington Couloir. III, AI2 or WI3. First ascent early 1980s by Bob Harrington. There are three moderately difficult ice couloirs that are visible on the northeast face of Mount Thompson. This route ascends the right-hand couloir. This 900-foot couloir is wide, straight, enclosed by sharp ridges, and increases in angle up to 70° at its top.

Smrz Couloir. III, AI3 or WI3, 5.6. First ascent August 1990 by John Moynier and Scott Andrews. Second ascent October 5, 1997 by Alois Smrz. This is the middle couloir on the northeast face of Mount Thompson. Overcome the bergschrund at its far, right-hand side, and once past its vertical lip, climb 600 feet of 55° to 60° snow/ice to a rock band. The rock band is about 12 feet wide, and is marked by a rock slab to the left of an overhanging boulder. Climb a 2-inch-wide crack on the left side of the boulder (5.6–5.8, depending on the amount of ice that can be hooked above the boulder). This is followed by steeper (up to 65°) snow/ice to the top.

Knudtson Couloir. III, AI3 or WI3. First ascent September 16, 1984 by Bruce Knudtson and Larry Cobb. This 800-foot couloir is the one of the far far left (southeast). It rises to the crest from the glacier northeast of Mount Thompson. It varies between 45° and 70° in angle, and ends at a point about ½ mile southeast of the summit of Mount Thompson.

Southeast Face. Class 3–4. Descended September 16, 1984 by Larry Cobb and Bruce Knudtson. There are many ledges and small cliffs on this side of the peak.

Peak 12,486ft 12,440 ft+;
1.1 mi NNW of Mount Thompson

First ascent July 15, 1961 by Kenneth Taylor and party. The summit rocks are class 3.

Peak 13,040ft+ 13,040 ft+;
0.6 mi WNW of Mount Thompson

First ascent August 14, 1971 by Dave King. A crack on the southeast face is class 4.

East Face. III, 5.10b. First ascent 1994 by Eric Tipton and Pat Brennan. This route ascends the vertical crack on the right side of the east face that ends just north of the summit. The third pitch, the crux, passes through three small roofs.

"Point Powell" 13,360 ft+; 13,360 ft+;
UTM 557115

Confusion has surrounded the naming of this peak, formerly called "Mount Powell." In 1911, the Board of Geographic Names named a peak in memory of John Wesley Powell, the noted western explorer and former director of the United States Geological Survey. Unfortunately, on the Mount Goddard 15-minute map, the name was placed incorrectly on the lower, western summit of this plateau (Peak 13,356ft; 13,360 ft+; UTM 554111), informally known as "Point Wesley." This error made its way into early editions of the Mount Darwin 7.5-minute map. The Board of Geographic Names detected this mistake in 1983 and directed the USGS Mapping Center to place the name Mount Powell on the third peak, previously called "Point John" (Peak 13,364ft; 13,360ft+; 1.4 mi SE of Mount Wallace; UTM 550113). While Point John may be the highest of the three points, it is not as prominent as Point Powell.

I hope that the Board of Geographic Names will reconsider its 1911 decision and return the name "Mount Powell" to Point Powell. Aside from being the high point of the plateau, this summit looks better and it is an aesthetic, challenging climb from the Powell-Thompson Col.

South Side. Class 2. First ascent August 1, 1925 by Walter L. Huber and James Rennie. Leave the John Muir Trail east of Helen Lake at the 11,000-foot level; this is the same departure point as for Echo Col. Climb a talus-filled chute to bypass a small cliff and proceed to the southern shore of Lake 11,428ft (11,360 ft+). Head northeast and climb a steep gully leading up the west side of Keating Pass. Descend benches on the east side of the pass and continue to Lake 11,725ft (11,710 ft). Climb talus to the plateau south of the summit.

West Ridge. Class 3. Cross the Powell Glacier and climb the obvious chute that leads to a notch on the west ridge. This chute is full of loose rocks, and it is only safe in early season when snow covers the hazards. Follow the west ridge to the lower southwest summit of the plateau, Point Wesley.

Northwest Chute. Class 3. First ascent June 29, 1931 by Norman Clyde. Climb the right-hand (south) chute of the two on the northwestern side of Point Powell. This chute ends atop the plateau, between the higher, northeast summit and the southwest summit.

East Face. III, 5.10. First ascent June 1969 by Fred Beckey, Galen Rowell, and Dan McHale. First free ascent September 1978 by Bob Harrington and Allan Pietrasanta. The first pitch involves 5.8 crack climbing in a steep dihedral; the rest of the climb is in easier corners. The first-ascent party used aid to avoid an icy squeeze chimney.

Armless Fun. III, 5.9. First ascent August 1990 by David Harden and Glenn Harden. Climb two pitches (5.8) in the left-facing corner on the East Face route. Then go up and left for three pitches (5.9) of loose rock, poor protection, and tricky routefinding. The quality of climbing improves above; the last pitch starts with a problematic overhang followed by easier climbing.

Broken Rainbow. III, 5.9. First ascent September 1978 by Kim Walker and Alan Bartlett. This route is also on the east face. Climb a crack to an obvious orange bulge about halfway up the face. Traverse left and ascend the crack that forms the left side of the bulge. Some 4-inch to 6-inch chocks are advisable.

Northeast Chute. Class 2–3; ice axe required. First ascent June 1961 by a Sierra Club party. Climb a steep, loose chute to the left of the east face of Point Powell. (This chute starts from the western edge of the glacier between Point Powell and Mount Thompson.) This is a fine snow climb in the spring; later in the year it may be icy, with loose rock.

Northeast Ridge. Class 3. First ascent by Norman Clyde. Ascend the southern side of the ridge from Powell-Thompson Col.

Southeast Chute. Class 2. This prominent chute leads to the plateau south of the summit of Point Powell. Climb the chute from the cirque south of Powell-Thompson Col. *Eckert Variation:* A sandy ledge leads from the top of Powell-Thompson Col to the southeast chute, dropping only 50 to 100 feet along the way.

Point Powell, East Face. Photo by R. J. Secor.

Mount Powell 13,364ft
13,360 ft+;
1.4 mi SE of Mount Wallace

This peak is informally known as "Point John."
North-Northwest Face. Class 3. First ascent August 27, 1967 by Andy Smatko and seventeen others. Leave the eastern shore of Echo Lake and climb onto the prominent 35° to 45° snow face on the north side of this peak. This leads to the col immediately west of the summit. Follow the easy class 3 ridge to the top.

Peak 13,000ft+
12,960 ft+;
1.3 mi ESE of Mount Wallace

The class 3–4 northwest ridge rising from Echo Lake was first climbed by Norman Clyde. Careful routefinding is needed to keep the difficulties to a minimum. The class 4 east face was first climbed in 1958 by Jay Holliday and Mike Loughman.

The southernmost peak is the high point.

Clyde Spires
13,240 ft+; 13,267 ft; UTM 535115

The name of these spires has been misplaced on some maps. The correct location is 0.6 mile southeast of Mount Wallace, atop the Sierra crest.
Southwest Side. Class 4. First ascent July 22, 1933 by Norman Clyde, Jules Eichorn, Theodore Waller, Helen LeConte, Julie Mortimer, Dorothy Baird, and John D. Forbes. Ascend a chute on the southwest side of the spires and traverse around the higher west spire on its north side to the east ridge. Climb the ridge to the top.

The lower east spire, a difficult slab climb, was first climbed by Norman Clyde, Jules Eichorn, and Ted Waller on July 22, 1933.
West Ridge. Class 4. Traversed June 20, 1959 by Ernest Bower and Carl Heller. The ridge between Clyde Spires and Mount Wallace has a lot of loose rock. A spire along this ridge is class 4 via a chimney on its southwest side. A notch west of this spire is bypassed on its north side. The peak at the west end of this ridge (Peak 13,240ft+; 13,200 ft+), which has become known as "Crumbly Spire," was first climbed June 23, 1937 by Smoke Blanchard, Hubert North, and Gary Leech.
North Couloir. III, 5.7. First ascent September 1978 by Marty Ross and Al Stone. Ascend the main couloir on the north face of Clyde Spires for several hundred feet, then traverse left to a small couloir on the left wall of the main couloir. Climb the small couloir to the summit ridge between the two spires.

North Arête. III, 5.10a. First ascent September 1986 by Alan Swanson and Steve Schneider. This route ascends the arête left of the north couloir. The climb consists of ten pitches, mostly 5.7–5.8. The crux on the third pitch is a 1¼-inch crack on a blank slab, which is capped by an awkward, bulging slot.
Northeast Ridge. Class 4. First ascent October 9, 1966 by Gary Lewis and Ed Lane. Ascend the ridge rising from Echo Lake. Leave the ridge where you encounter loose, black rock, and traverse left and climb a couloir to the summit of a black spire. Follow the ridge west over and around some smaller spires to the higher, west spire of the Clyde Spires. The final approach to the higher spire is made from the south, and then up the east ridge to the summit. *Direct Variation:* Class 5 with one aid pitch. First ascent July 27, 1967 by Roy Bishop, Curt Chadwick, and Ed Keller. This variation is achieved by staying atop the very crest of the northeast ridge.
South Ridge. Class 4. First ascent August 27, 1967 by Andy Smatko and a Sierra Club Sierra Peaks Section party. Approach the base of the south ridge from Echo Col, and ascend the ridge to a point about 50 feet below the summit. Go right and up to the small east arête that descends from the summit. Most of this route is class 2.

Mount Wallace
13,377 ft; 13,377 ft

Southwest Chute. Class 2. First ascent July 16, 1895 by Theodore S. Solomons. Climb a rubble-filled chute up and left across the southwest face to the northwest ridge and follow it to the summit.
Northwest Ridge. Class 3. The traverse between Mount Haeckel and Mount Wallace is done by keeping about 100 feet beneath the ridge on its northeastern side. Only the descent of Mount Haeckel is class 3.
North Slope. Class 2. Climb to the cirque between Mount Wallace and Mount Haeckel by making a gradual ascending traverse from Moonlight Lake to the bench that is high above Echo Lake. Turn northwest and climb into the cirque, which features a small tarn. Climb over talus blocks to the summit.
East Face. Class 3–4. First ascent June 14, 1987 by Mark Ledel, David Haake, and Chris Keith.
Southeast Slope. Class 2. Loose scree makes this a good descent route. Caution is needed when crossing loose blocks near the top.
South Ridge. Class 2. Climb over loose rock from the top of Wallace Col.

CLYDE SPIRES

Northeast
Ridge

North
Couloir

North
Arête

Clyde Spires, North Face. Photo by R. J. Secor.

Picture Peak from the northeast. Photo by R. J. Secor.

"Picture Peak" 13,120 ft+; 13,120 ft+;
0.6 mi E of Mount Haeckel

This is one of the most beautiful Sierra peaks. As its name implies, it is frequently photographed.

South Side. Class 4. First ascent June 13, 1987 by Mark Ledel, Dave Haake, and Chris Keith.

Southwest Side. Class 3. First ascent 1931 by Norman Clyde. There are three chutes on the southwest side of this peak. Climb the middle chute to within 100 feet of the summit, where easy class 3 leads to the top.

North Face. Class 4. First ascent 1960 by a Sierra Club party. Ascend scree on the north side of the peak for about two-thirds of the way up to the notch on the northeast buttress. Ascend diagonally right across a broken face with much loose rock to a chute, which goes to the summit.

Elphinston Buttress. IV, 5.10. First ascent August 1976 by Rick Mosher, Paul Landrum, and Chuck Fitch. This route climbs the prominent northeast buttress. Approach the toe of the buttress from the south shore of Hungry Packer Lake. Follow the buttress to the summit. The crux is about halfway up, where a thin crack leads to a slight overhang.

Northeast Rib. IV, 5.10. First ascent 1977 by Rick Wheeler and Tony Jennings. This rib is to the left of the preceding route, and forms the right-hand edge of the northeast face. Begin by climbing a hand-and-fist crack that runs parallel to a chimney for about 200 feet. A 5.9 roof is passed on the left. Continue up the rib to a notch. This is followed by an awkward corner that requires some wide stemming.

Northeast Face. III, 5.9. First ascent July 1967 by Gary Colliver and Steve Thompson. Class 3 and 4 chimneys on the lower part of the face lead to a smooth wall with

5.9 cracks that end about 75 feet below two flakes. Climb the squeeze chimney between the flakes (5.7) and ascend a face with a steep corner (5.9). Go up and left onto a ledge on the corner of a buttress. Climb left along a steep ramp (5.7), and then move to the right onto the edge of the buttress. Climb a clean crack (5.8), and end on a blocky ledge. Class 4 climbing leads to the top of the east spire of Picture Peak. Descend class 3 to the notch between the east spire and the true summit, then cross the south face of the true summit before climbing to the top.

Further Reading: John Moynier and Claude Fiddler. *Sierra Classics.* Evergreen, Colo.: Chockstone Press, 1993, pp. 158–159.

East Side. Class 5. First ascent 1958 by Mike Loughman, Bob Orser, Dick Grunebaum, and Rick Polsdorfer. Climb to the notch high on the northeast buttress from the east. Continue along the top of the northeast buttress to the summit. Several hundred feet of class 5 climbing was reported.

Mount Haeckel   13,418 ft; 13,435 ft

South Ridge. Class 3. First ascent July 14, 1920 by Edward O. Allen, Francis E. Crofts, and Olcott Haskell, just a few minutes after the first ascent of the west shoulder. Allen, Crofts, and Haskell were quite surprised to find that they had been beaten to the summit. An even greater surprise was that they were not on the summit of Mount Darwin, which was that day's objective!

The first-ascent party gained the ridge by climbing a chute to the saddle between Mount Haeckel and Mount Wallace from the southwest. Most parties approach this ridge from the northeast, or by traversing from Mount Wallace. Keep about 100 feet below the crest of the ridge

Mount Haeckel and Mount Wallace from the southwest. Photo by R. J. Secor.

on its northeastern side to a point close to the summit of Mount Haeckel. A system of easy class 3 ledges leads to the summit block.

West Shoulder. Class 3. First ascent July 14, 1920 by Walter L. Huber and party. This climb begins from the southern shore of Lake 11,808ft (11,822 ft), west of the mountain. (This lake is best approached from the northern side of the basin, between Mount Spencer and Mount Huxley, in order to avoid loose scree in the middle of the basin.) Go southeast and climb onto the bench marked by Lake 12,021ft (12,000 ft+). Turn northeast, heading towards Mount Haeckel and climb the second chute from the left; this chute leads to the crest just south of the summit. A vertical face of 30 to 40 feet (with excellent handholds) is surmounted before arriving at the summit block.

Northwest Arête. Class 4. First ascent 1933 by Jack Riegelhuth. The ascent of this arête is one of the beautiful climbs of the High Sierra. Ascend the crest of the arête from the first notch northwest of Mount Haeckel. An approach from Lake 12,345ft (12,320 ft+) may require an ice axe as there is a permanent patch of steep snow on the northeastern side of this notch. Climb the first chute from the left when approaching the notch from the southwest via Lakes 11,808ft and 12,021ft (11,822 ft and 12,000 ft+). *Variation:* First ascent August 4, 1984 by Jim Erb, Theresa Rutherford, Bill Gray, and Steve Nelson. The crest can also be followed from the top of Haeckel Col. This involves traversing a knife edge ridge and a rappel into the notch. It is better to ascend directly to the notch. *Variation:* It is easier to climb the chute left (northeast) of the arête. But the climbing is excellent on the arête itself, with solid rock and excellent views. It is much better to ascend the crest.

Further Reading: John Moynier and Claude Fiddler. *Sierra Classics.* Evergreen, Colo.: Chockstone Press, 1993, pp. 160–161.

North Face. Class 4. First ascent 1958 by Mike Loughman and Jay Holliday. Climb directly up steep snow and rock slabs from Lake 12,345ft (12,320 ft+). Traverse to the right through a notch in a rib to the chute that is left of the northwest arête.

North Couloir. Class 4. First ascent November 5, 1971 by Choong-Ok Sunwoo and Yvon Chouinard. This 50° snow/ice couloir provides about 800 feet of climbing.

East Ridge. Class 3. First ascent 1935 by Merton

Brown, Angus Taylor, and O. H. Taylor. Climb to the first saddle east of Mount Haeckel from the north over loose scree slopes. Traverse across the southeast face of the peak to class 3 ledges near the south ridge, which lead to the base of the summit block.

East Arête. III, 5.8. First ascent by Claude Fiddler and Leon Borowski.

Mount Fiske   13,503 ft; 13,524 ft

The west summit is the high point.

Southeast Ridge. Class 2. First ascent August 10, 1922 by Charles Norman Fiske, John N. Fiske, Stephen B. Fiske, and Frederick Kellet. Go north from Helen Lake to the southeast ridge. Ascend the southeast ridge over the lower, eastern summit to the true summit.

Southwest Ridge. Class 2. First ascent August 18, 1939 by Jack Sturgeon. Ascend the ridge from the saddle between Mount Fiske and Mount Warlow. As a variation, you can climb the broad class 1 slope to the right (east) of this ridge.

West Face. Class 2. First ascent August 25, 1993 by Dale Van Dalsem, Judy Ware, Mary Motheral, Rayne Motheral, and R. J. Secor. Climb the broad chute in the center of the face from the cirque between Mount Fiske and Mount Huxley. The chute ends just south of the summit.

North Ridge. Class 4. First ascent July 4, 1971 by Dick Irvin, Dave Madison, Jim Peterson, and Kirt Catanese.

Northeast Ridge. Class 2–3. First ascent August 20, 1958 by Andy Smatko, Peter Hunt, and John Robinson. Ascend the ridge from the basin west of Mount Wallace to the east peak of Mount Fiske. An easy walk leads to the higher, west summit.

Mount Warlow   13,206 ft; 13,231 ft

South Ridge. Class 1. First ascent 1926 by Nathaniel Goodrich and Marjory Hurd. This is an easy traverse along the ridge from Muir Pass.

Northwest Ridge. Class 3. Descended 1966 by Gordon Waddell. The ridge from the saddle south of Mount Huxley is class 2–3. This saddle can be reached via the class 3 south ridge of Mount Huxley, or via the class 4 rocks from the northeast.

Northeast Ridge. Class 4. First ascent 1966 by Gordon Waddell, during a 12-hour traverse from Mount Spencer to Mount Huxley. Follow the crest of the ridge from the saddle between Mount Fiske and Mount Warlow.

Mount Huxley 13,086 ft; 13,117 ft

West Shoulder. Class 3. First ascent July 15, 1920 by Norman Clyde. Leave the John Muir Trail at the northern end of the bench between Sapphire Lake and Wanda Lake and climb the left side of the west face. Head for a chute that has three branches at its top. Climb the left (north) branch to the crest of the northwest ridge, and follow the ridge to the summit. Most of this route is class 2, but a headwall just below the summit is class 3 with excellent handholds.

Southwest Chute. Class 3–4. This route is frequently climbed in error by those seeking the easier West Shoulder route. This left-ascending chute climbs the right side of the west face of Mount Huxley, and leads to a point south of the summit along the summit ridge.

South Ridge. Class 3. First ascent August 22, 1963 by Arkel Erb. Traverse the ridge from Mount Warlow. The saddle between Mount Warlow and Mount Huxley is class 3 from the southwest or class 4 from the northeast.

Northeast Ridge. Class 3. First ascent May 30, 1970 by Wally Henry and Steve Rogero. There are two ridges or buttresses on the north side of Mount Huxley, separated by a small cirque. Approach the left ridge from the east and follow it to the summit.

Northeast Buttress. III, 5.10a. First ascent July 1997 by Dick Duane and Galen Rowell. This route ascends the left side of the small cirque on the north side of Mount Huxley. Climb a series of perfect finger cracks to the fractured blocks atop the northeast ridge.

Northwest Buttress. III, 5.10a. First ascent July 1997 by Hans Florine and Jerry Dodrill. Climb the long, clean dihedrals on the right side of the cirque on the north side of Mount Huxley.

Northwest Ridge. Class 3. First ascent August 9, 1942

Mount Huxley from the west. Photo by R. J. Secor.

by A. J. Reyman. Approach the right buttress via the talus slope to the north, and go to the right onto the crest of the ridge. Follow the ridge to the summit.

There is a cliff low on the northwest ridge of Mount Huxley and above Sapphire Lake. A II, 5.11a route was climbed in July 1997 by Galen Rowell and Hans Florine. Climb the obvious cracks on the right side of the cliff; these cracks start beside a large block. Then traverse left on a ramp, and go up and left on a vertical wall to the top. The 5.11a face-climbing crux was on the last pitch. Traverse to the right onto the open face and back left again 30 feet higher to avoid an overhanging seam.

Mount McGee   12,944 ft; 12,969 ft

This is the dark, impressive peak seen to the northwest from Muir Pass. There are three summits, running east to west. The central summit is the high point.

South Chute. Class 2–3. First ascent July 11, 1923 by Roger N. Burnham, Robert E. Brownlee, Ralph H. Brandt, and Leonard Keeler. Climb the westernmost of two chutes on the south side of the peak. The correct chute leads to the notch between the west and central peaks. This chute is composed mostly of disagreeably loose scree, and some climbers have preferred climbing the class 3 rock on the sides of the chute. From the top of the chute, go right and follow the ridge to the summit.

West Face. Class 4. First ascent July 17, 1933 by Glen Dawson, Neil Ruge, and Bala Ballantine. Go northwest from the outlet of lower Davis Lake to the small lake—Lake 11,800ft+ (11,760 ft+), at UTM 447117—west of Mount McGee and southwest of Peter Peak. From the lake, climb talus to the north summit of the west peak. Descend northeast from the summit over class 2 rock until you are approximately 40 feet north of the notch between the west and central peaks of Mount McGee. Climb up and to the south (class 2–3) and cross the main rib that runs into the notch from the west peak. Descend south and then east over class 3–4 rock into the notch atop the south chute. Follow the class 2 ridge to the central peak.

North Chute. Class 4. First ascent July 16, 1930 by Glen Dawson, Charles Dodge, Jules Eichorn, and John Olmstead. This chute climbs to the notch between the west and central peaks of Mount McGee from the north. Head toward the chute on the right-hand side of the north face of the peak from upper McGee Canyon. Enter the chute from the right (west). There is usually snow in this chute, but it may be possible to climb along its

edge, where the snow has melted away. The last 800-foot section of this chute is class 4. From the notch atop the chute, traverse east to the central peak.

Northeast Spur. Class 4. First ascent August 30, 1970 by Wally Henry. Climb the northeast spur of the east peak from McGee Lakes. Climb over the east peak and traverse to the notch between it and the central peak. Climb a dihedral and a wide crack on the east face of the central peak. This is followed by easier climbing over loose rock to the summit.

Peter Peak   12,490 ft; 12,543 ft

Northeast Ridge. Class 2. First ascent July 11, 1936 by Peter Grubb and Richard G. Johnson. Climb to the notch in the northeast ridge from the east. The chute leading to this notch is loose, and you must "hold the mountain together with one hand while climbing it with the other." Follow the crest of the ridge to the summit.

South Slope. Class 2. This is a long talus walk from the lake southwest of the peak.

Emerald Peak   12,546 ft; 12,543 ft

Northwest Ridge. Class 2. First ascent August 8, 1925 by Norman Clyde, Julie Mortimer, and Eleanor Bartlett. Follow the northwest ridge from Peak 11,786ft (11,778 ft). There is a lot of loose, unstable talus along this ridge.

West Slope. Class 2. This side of Emerald Peak has been approached from Evolution Meadow and Goddard Canyon. It is generally preferred over the Northwest Ridge route. Approach the west slope from the 10,900-foot level of Peak 11,786ft (11,778 ft).

South Ridge. Class 3. First ascent June 30, 1968 by Barbara Lilley, Jess Logan, and Dick Beach. Gain the south ridge by climbing to the saddle south of Emerald Peak from the east. A class 3 diagonal ledge leads across the east side of the saddle to the south ridge of the peak. Keep to the west side of the south ridge to the summit.

Northeast Ridge. Class 3. First ascent July 4, 1971 by Jerry Keating and Elton Fletcher. Climb a shallow chute for approximately 50 feet and then ascend ledges southward to the crest of the northeast ridge. Follow the crest of the ridge to the summit.

North Chute. Class 2. Descended June 30, 1968 by Barbara Lilley, Jess Logan, and Dick Beach. This gully rises from the basin between Emerald Peak and Peak 11,786ft (11,778 ft). Climb the gully to the crest of the northwest ridge, then follow the ridge to the summit.

THE HERMIT

to Evolution
Lake

The Hermit from the northeast. Photo by R. J. Secor.

The Hermit   12,328 ft; 12,360 ft

This is the impressive peak seen from the upper reaches of Evolution Valley. The summit block is class 4 friction from the south; a jam crack on its east side is rated 5.6.

Further Reading: *National Geographic.* April 1989, pp. 484–85.

From Evolution Lake. Class 3. Cross the outlet of Evolution Lake and ascend rock slabs to the south to the first prominent notch on the ridge that is southwest of the lake. Pass through the notch and descend about 300 feet before traversing southwest to the meadow that is due east of The Hermit. Ascend a grassy chute southwest from the meadow to a bench directly beneath the peak. A diagonal chute leads across the east face and ends in a loose gully. Climb the diagonal chute, cross the loose gully, and ascend ledges to the summit. *Variation:* It is also feasible to climb to the saddle between The Hermit and Peak 12,342 ft (12,350 ft). Follow the ridge north from the saddle to the summit of The Hermit. *Variation:* You can also climb to the notch immediately south of The Hermit. From the notch, climb the east side of the ridge to the summit.

From McGee Canyon. Class 2. First ascent July 2, 1924 by Leonard Keeler, Ralph Brandt, Margaret Avery, and Marion Avery. Hike up to the lake that is southwest of The Hermit from McGee Canyon. Climb a loose chute that leads to the first notch south of the summit of The Hermit, and follow the east side of the ridge to the summit block.

Northwest Face. Class 3. First ascent July 9, 1939 by Harriet Parsons, Madi Bacon, and Maxine Cushing.

From Evolution Valley, climb to a ledge on the north shoulder of the peak. (This ledge usually has a snowbank.) Follow a broad ledge to the right, up and around the west face. This leads to a chute that goes up and left to a point on the north face that overlooks the cliffs that shelter the snowbank. Proceed over rock slabs to the summit block of The Hermit.

North Face. Class 3. First ascent July 9, 1936 by Richard G. Johnson and Peter Grubb. This climb starts from the snowbank ledge on the north shoulder of the peak, as described under the Northwest Face route. Go left from the ledge, under the cliffs that shelter the snowbank, to where it is possible to climb up and right over rock slabs to the summit block.

East Face. I, 5.8. First ascent July 1988 by Galen Avery Rowell (whose mother, Margaret, was a member of the first-ascent party—see above). This route climbs the steepest part of the east face. Three short hand cracks form the cruxes of this route.

Peak 12,342ft   12,350 ft; 0.5 mi SE of The Hermit

This peak is frequently confused with The Hermit. In fact, some editions of the Mount Goddard 30-minute quadrangle erroneously label this peak The Hermit. It was first climbed by Dr. Grove Karl Gilbert and Mr. Kanawyer (the packer) in July 1904. The southeast ridge and northwest ridge are both class 2.

Mount Spencer   12,431 ft; 12,400 ft+

First ascent August 20, 1921 by Robert M. Price, George J. Young, H. W. Hill, and Peter Frandsen. This peak has a swell view from its summit. It is class 2 from the saddle to the east.

Peak 13,322ft   13,280 ft+;
0.5 mi SE of Mount Darwin

First ascent July 19, 1933 by Glen Dawson, Neil Ruge, and Bala Ballantine, via the class 3 south ridge. The southeast slopes are class 2.

Mount Darwin   13,831 ft; 13,830 ft

Mount Darwin is the monarch of the Evolution region. Its flat-topped shape is easily recognizable from great distances and all its routes are challenging. The true summit, however, is a pinnacle detached from the southeast side of the summit plateau. The pinnacle may be ascended by climbing down off the plateau and tra-

versing around the pinnacle on its right side to a chute. Descend this chute a short distance, and then climb another chute to the far southeast side of the summit block. Climb either of two cracks that lead to a narrow ledge about 6 feet below the top of the pinnacle on its southeast side. The final move can be done by using either strength or technique, and most climbers will require a belay.

Further Reading: *Summit.* May 1971, pp. 6–9.

Darwin Glacier and West Ridge. Class 3. First ascent August 21, 1921 by Robert M. Price and Peter Frandsen. There is a large notch on the ridge between Mount Darwin and Mount Mendel, and a smaller notch lies about 300 feet to the east of the larger notch. Climb Darwin Glacier and cross the bergschrund (ice axes and crampons may be required). Climb up to the smaller eastern notch; a short, vertical section immediately beneath the notch can be bypassed by climbing the rock to the right. Instead of climbing the ridge crest from the notch, drop down to the right and follow the right-hand ridge to the summit plateau. As a variation, you can bypass the glacier on its western side and make a diagonally ascending traverse from right to left to the smaller notch; this variation may be preferable during icy conditions and/or with an impassable bergschrund.

Erin's Arête. II, 5.8. First ascent 1982 by Bruce Hendricks and Bruce Watts. This route climbs the right-hand rib on the north face. There are two ribs on the north face of Mount Darwin. Follow the crest of the right-hand rib for six pitches to the summit plateau.

North Face. Class 3–4. Descended July 14, 1930 by Jules Eichorn, John Olmstead, and Glen Dawson. Ascended July 5, 1934 by David Brower and Hervey Voge. Climb the left rib on the north face of Mount Darwin, keeping just to the left of the crest of the rib. A boulder blocks progress about halfway up; bypass this by dropping down a little and moving left. This rib eventually merges into the north face. Climb a crack to the left and reach the summit plateau via a chimney. *Variation:* The broad couloir to the left of the left rib can be climbed to the summit plateau. This 900-foot snow/ice couloir, which averages 45° in angle, is the preferred route in early season. In late season it is a fine WI2 ice climb.

Further Reading: John Moynier and Claude Fiddler. *Sierra Classics.* Evergreen, Colo.: Chockstone Press, 1993, pp. 162–163.

Northeast Ridge. Class 4. First ascent 1945 by Spencer

Mount Darwin, North Face. Photo by R. J. Secor.

Austin, Bill Pabst, and Chuck Wilts. The climbing starts from the top of Darwin Col, which is most easily reached from Darwin Canyon. The approach to Darwin Col from Blue Heaven Lake involves climbing a scree gully to the left of Peak 13,048ft (12,960 ft+); alternatively, you can climb class 4 rock to the flat saddle to the left of the scree gully. From the top of Darwin Col, follow the crest of the northeast ridge to the summit.

East Face, Right Side. Class 3–4. First ascent July 30, 1960 by Tom Condon, Bill Dixon, Don Groom, and Grant Raddon. Follow the crest of the lower northeast ridge and climb a 60-foot class 4 pitch in a chimney. Traverse left on easy ledges across two sharp ribs to the main chute in the middle of the east face. Climb the right side of the chute and then continue left across several more gullies to the base of the summit pinnacle.

Direct East Face. II, 5.5. First ascent October 6, 1968 by Ed Lane, Barbara Lilley, and Dave McCoard. This route starts by climbing a black band that ascends the face from left to right. The first 50 feet is class 5, with the crux being a traverse to the left under an overhang (5.6) followed by a climb to a large ledge. Continue climbing the black band (class 3–4), which ends at the chute separating the true summit pinnacle from the plateau, about 400 feet beneath the notch.

East Face, Left Side. Class 4. First ascent September

9, 1955 by Morrough O'Brien and Dick Leigh. This route starts below the left-hand rib of the main chute on the east face. Traverse up and left over a discontinuous ledge system for four pitches of class 4; the second pitch is the most difficult because the ledge system disappears. This traverse ends in a wide, ill-defined chute at the far left-hand side of the east face. Climb this chute to its head and traverse right on a wide ledge of dark rock over two ribs to the main chute. Climb the left side of the main chute to the notch between the summit plateau and summit pinnacle.

Southeast Ridge. III, 5.0. First ascent September 6, 1964 by Fred Martin, George Wallerstein, Herbert Weidner, Don Wilson, and Robert Wyman. From the southern end of Blue Heaven Lake climb about 700 feet of loose class 3–4 rock to a notch in this ridge where it starts its steady rise to the summit. Pass the first gendarmes on their west sides with several hundred feet of class 2–3 climbing to the base of a narrow, steep section. Ascend an easy class 5, 75-foot diagonal crack to a short knife edge leading to a ledge part way up the last gendarme. Go left and climb an exposed crack on the west face of the gendarme to an easy gully that leads to the summit pinnacle.

Mount Darwin from the north, August 24, 1972. Photo by Austin Post, No. 72R2-124, USGS Ice and Climate Project, GeoData Center, University of Alaska, Fairbanks.

Mount Darwin, East Face, August 24, 1972. Photo by Austin Post, No. 72R2-125, USGS Ice and Climate Project, GeoData Center, University of Alaska, Fairbanks.

Southwest Arête. III, 5.8. First ascent July 1997 by Galen Rowell. This arête is on the extreme left side of Mount Darwin's south face. Hike up to a bench above the inlet of Evolution Lake to the foot of the arête. Class 3 leads to a steep white buttress (5.8), followed by an exposed, easy ridge. The ridge leads to a headwall just beneath a prominent pinnacle. Traverse across the left side of the pinnacle (5.8) to its notch, and continue up to the summit plateau.

West Face. Class 3. First ascent August 12, 1908 by E. C. Andrews of the Geological Survey of New South Wales (Australia!) and Willard D. Johnson of the United States Geological Survey. This side of Mount Darwin is confusing, to say the least. The following route description may confuse many climbers. Nevertheless . . .

Go east from the southern end of Evolution Lake and hike to the base of the west face, avoiding the cirque between Mount Spencer and Mount Darwin. There are three chutes with talus fans on the west face of Mount Darwin. Climb the right-hand chute to where it branches. Take the left branch through the gap jut above a pinnacle and descend ledges to the middle chute. Ascend the right side of this broad middle chute almost to its head. Climb a shallow gully that goes to the right to a narrow knife edge ridge, which leads to the flat summit plateau of Mount Darwin. The high point of the plateau is at its southeastern end, next to the detached summit pinnacle, the true high point of the peak.

Mount Mendel   13,710 ft; 13,691 ft

Although this peak is overshadowed by nearby Mount Darwin, it is a worthwhile objective in its own right. None of its routes are trivial, and the hardest ice climbs in the High Sierra are found on its north face.

East Face. Class 3. From the western edge of Darwin Glacier, climb a ledge that rises diagonally to the right. Then go left onto another ledge that leads to a chute filled with loose rocks, with a chockstone at its head, just below the rim of the summit plateau of Mount Mendel. Climb the chute to just below the summit plateau, and then go to the right to a small saddle. Pass through the saddle, descend slightly, and then continue up to a 15-foot wall. Turn left and pass through a keyhole that leads up to the summit plateau, and walk north to the summit.

Northeast Ridge. Class 3. First ascent 1956 by Bud Bingham and Don Clarke. There is a deep chute on the lower western side of the northeast ridge. Climb the ridge on the left side of this chute. This leads to a shallow chute, which ends on the crest of the northeast ridge. Follow the ridge to the summit. This is a much more pleasant climb than the East Face route.

Ice Nine. IV, class 5+, AI4 or WI5. First ascent July 1967 by Mike Cohen and Roy Bishop; second ascent June 1976 by Dale Bard and Doug Robinson. This is also known as the Left Mendel Couloir. The first-ascent party climbed the rock face to the right of this couloir before traversing to the left into the couloir itself. They did so because of the absence of ice in the dark, narrow slot in the bottom lower portion of the couloir. The complete couloir (from the very bottom to top) was first climbed in June 1976 by Dale Bard and Doug Robinson, and many climbers consider their "Ice Nine" (made famous

Mount Mendel and Mount Darwin from the south. Photo by R. J. Secor.

by an article in an early issue of *Outside* magazine) an early-season direct-start variation. But considering the ephemeral nature of ice in the High Sierra, all ice routes are variations. Ice Nine is more than 1,000 feet long and averages 50° to 60° in angle. It has two short, overhanging sections lower in the couloir, the technical crux is passing a chockstone midway, and there is a 75° narrow ice chimney higher in the couloir.

Further Reading: *Outside.* December 1977, pp. 26–29; *Summit.* March–April 1982, pp. 30–32; Doug Robinson. *A Night on the Ground, A Day in the Open.* La Crescenta, Calif.: Mountain 'N' Air Books, 1996,

pp. 98–106; John Moynier and Claude Fiddler. *Sierra Classics.* Evergreen, Colo.: Chockstone Press, 1993, pp. 166–167.

The Mendel Couloir. III, 5.6, AI2 or WI3. First ascent June 21, 1958 by Felix Knauth and John Whitmer. This is the right-hand couloir on the north face of Mount Mendel, a highly coveted climb. It is well over 1,000 feet long, with some bulges exceeding 60° in angle. The first-ascent party climbed to the toe of the buttress that divides the two couloirs, climbing class 4 rock before entering the couloir itself. Today almost all parties climb the ice on the lower section of the couloir and belay from

Mount Mendel from the north, August 24, 1972. Photo by Austin Post, No. 72R2-124, USGS Ice and Climate Project, GeoData Center, University of Alaska, Fairbanks.

the rocks. The upper part of the couloir may be bare rock in late season, and a short rock pitch must be overcome in order to reach the crest of the northwest ridge. Follow the ridge (5.6) to the summit.

Further Reading: Yvon Chouinard. *Climbing Ice.* San Francisco: Sierra Club Books, 1978, pp. 82–83, 104–5; Jeff Lowe. *The Ice Experience.* Chicago: Contemporary Books, 1979, pp. 169–70; *Summit.* April 1975, p. 17; *Summit.* June 1975, p. 34; *Summit.* March–April 1982, pp. 30–32; John Moynier and Claude Fiddler. *Sierra Classics.* Evergreen, Colo.: Chockstone Press, 1993, pp. 164–165; *Climbing.* No. 167, March 1997, pp. 68–71.

North Rib. III, 5.8. First ascent September 1991 by Patrick Brennan and Ken Kenaga. This route follows the rock rib to the right of the Mendel Couloir. The rock is very loose and the first-ascent party wandered a lot.

Southwest Central Chute. Class 4. Descended 1966 by Gordon Waddell and Steve Roper. There are many ribs and chutes on the southwest face of Mount Mendel above Evolution Lake. Climb the central chute, which leads directly to the summit from the lower end of Evolution Lake. Many short class 4 sections are encountered in this chute.

Southwest Face. Class 3. First ascent July 18, 1930 by Jules Eichorn, Glen Dawson, and John Olmstead. Leave the John Muir Trail about ¼ mile south from where the peninsula enters Evolution Lake from its eastern shore. Climb onto a buttress of glaciated granite surrounded by talus on its north and south sides. Ascend the buttress for approximately 1,500 feet onto broken rock. Go right to a talus fan, and ascend the left branch of the chute above the fan to the crest of the ridge. Follow the ridge to the summit.

Peak 13,360ft+ 13,385 ft;
0.5 mi NW of Mount Mendel

Not much is known about this striking peak. First ascent August 23, 1964 by R. G. Dunn. A chute on the west side is class 2. The north side is class 3–4.

Peak 12,200 ft+ 12,011 ft;
0.4 mi E of Blue Heaven Lake

West Ridge. Class 3. First ascent August 1978 by Alan Swanson. This has been described as being an "interesting scramble to a cool summit."

"Mount Tom Ross" 13,253 ft; 13,248 ft;
1.0 mi NE of Mount Darwin

This peak is named informally after the noted climber, ski mountaineer, and photographer Tom Ross. First ascent 1925 by Norman Clyde. The southeast slope is class 2; the north ridge is class 3.

Mount Lamarck 13,417 ft; 13,417 ft
The southeast slope, the southern slope, and the ridge from Lamarck Col are all class 2.

North Couloir. Class 4. First ascent 1974 by John Fischer and Jay Jensen. There are several gullies on the right side of the north face. Climb the gully farthest to the left. This provides about 1,000 feet of 40° snow/ice climbing.

Peak 13,404ft 13,400 ft+;
1.8 mi NW of Mount Lamarck

This peak has been called the "Keyhole Plateau." First ascent 1925 by Norman Clyde, via the class 1 north slope. The west slope is class 2 and was climbed July 8, 1933 by Hervey Voge.

Muriel Peak 12,937 ft; 12,942 ft
The north summit is the high point. The southwest ridge from Alpine Col is class 2, and was first climbed July 8, 1933 by Hervey Voge. The southeast ridge from The Keyhole is class 2–3 over and around large blocks. Class 3 ledges above Lost Lakes lead to the summit plateau from the east.

Mount Goethe 13,264 ft; 13,200 ft+
First ascent July 6, 1933 by David R. Brower and George Rockwood. The south slope from the isthmus between Lakes 11,540ft and 11,546ft (11,520 ft+ and 11,520 ft+) is class 1. The northwest ridge is class 1. The northeast ridge from Alpine Col is class 3–4. A class 5 route has been done on the north face; climb from the highest reach of the glacier.

Peak 12,920ft+ 12,971 ft;
1.1 mi NW of Mount Goethe

North Ridge. Class 2. First ascent July 25, 1942 by R. S. Fink. Ascend large blocks from the top of Snow-Tongue Pass.

Southeast Ridge. Class 1. First ascent August 29, 1942 by

August Fruge, Neal Harlow, and William A. Sherrill. This is an easy climb from the saddle southeast of the peak.

East Couloir. Class 3. First ascent September 16, 1967 by Wayne Inman, Alan Leeds, John Williams, and Ron Hudson. Climb the far left-hand snow/ice couloir on the northeast face and follow the southeast ridge to the summit.

Peak 12,477ft   12,440 ft+;
1.8 mi NW of Mount Goethe
First ascent September 12, 1968 by Andy Smatko, Bill Schuler, Tom Ross, and Frank Yates. The southeast ridge is class 3; the southwest ridge is class 2.

Peak 12,488ft   12,498 ft;
0.8 mi S of Lower Golden Trout Lake
First ascent July 11, 1933 by Glen Dawson and Neil Ruge. The northwest ridge is class 3.

Peak 12,480ft+   12,873 ft;
0.9 mi SSE of Packsaddle Lake
The north ridge is class 4.

Peak 12,900ft   12,900 ft; 1.2 mi S of Lobe Lakes
The southeast ridge is class 2–3 and was first climbed September 11, 1968 by Andy Smatko, Bill Schuler, Tom Ross, and Frank Yates.

Peak 12,560ft+   12,591 ft;
0.7 mi S of Upper Honeymoon Lake
First ascent July 14, 1933 by Hans Helmut Leschke, Dr. Hans Leschke, and Helen LeConte, via the class 2 south ridge.

Pavilion Dome   11,856 ft; 11,846 ft
The south slope is class 2.

WRINKLES

Alternative approach to Mount Goddard. Most parties intent on climbing Mount Goddard from the west start the approach from Florence Lake, hike the Blayney Meadows Trail to the John Muir Trail, and then ascend Goddard Canyon to Martha Lake at the base of the peak. The trip is 24 miles (18¾ if the ferry across Flo-

rence Lake is used). A frequently overlooked alternative is to hike the Woodchuck Trail from Wishon Reservoir to Blackcap Basin, and then hike cross-country across Valor Pass to Martha Lake (described in Chapter 7, Kettle Ridge and the LeConte Divide). This distance is 21 miles, only slightly longer than an approach from Florence Lake, and Crown Pass (to 10,400 ft) must be crossed before arriving at Blackcap Basin. But the advantages include no quota on the Woodchuck Trail (while there is a quota on the Blayney Meadows Trail); the driving approach to the trailhead is easier than negotiating Kaiser Pass, and there is no delay waiting for the ferry.

Goddard Canyon, Goddard Creek, North Goddard Creek, Evolution Valley, Evolution Basin, Evolution Creek. The locations of these places can be confusing. Goddard Canyon is north of the Goddard Divide, and is the source of the South Fork of the San Joaquin River. Goddard Creek is south of the Goddard Divide, flowing down an unnamed canyon to the Middle Fork of the Kings River. But North Goddard Creek is north of the Goddard Divide; it drains Davis Lake and flows into the South Fork of the San Joaquin River. And Evolution Valley is downstream from Evolution Basin. Thankfully, Evolution Creek flows down both the basin and the valley.

Charybdis to Mount McDuffie to Black Giant. A loop trip or traverse of these three peaks is a reasonable day trip from the vicinity of Helen Lake. This is typically done by first climbing Charybdis and then climbing the northwest slope of Mount McDuffie. The north ridge of Mount McDuffie is then descended before climbing the south slope of Black Giant.

Mount Darwin to Mount Mendel. The ridge connecting these two peaks is difficult. Most parties who have traversed between these two peaks have had to drop off the ridge and onto Darwin Glacier or the west side of Mount Darwin/south side of Mount Mendel.

Lamarck Col vs. The Keyhole or Alpine Col. Lamarck Col is high, and some cross-country hikers may assume that it would be easier to approach Darwin Canyon via Piute Pass and Alpine Col or The Keyhole, as this involves less elevation gain. Alpine Col and The Keyhole are difficult cross-country routes, however, with a lot of unstable talus. Lamarck Col is much easier, and is a preferred route.

Chapter 10

The Mono Recesses

The Mono Recesses are the four valleys that drop precipitously into the Mono Creek Valley from the south. This is one of the most scenic regions of the High Sierra. South of the Mono Divide are the headwaters of Bear Creek—a fisherman's paradise. Northeast of Bear Creek is Rock Creek, with Mount Abbot and Bear Creek Spire dominating the skyline. Southeast of this area is Humphreys Basin, a desolate region dominated by isolated Mount Humphreys.

This region follows the Sierra crest from Piute Pass to Mono Pass (south), and is bounded on the north by Mono Creek. Its western boundary is the South Fork of the San Joaquin River, and it is marked on the south by Piute Creek.

HISTORY

Native Americans used Mono Pass (south) as a trading route for centuries. In 1864 the California Geological Survey followed the Indian trail up and over the pass to a camp along Mono Creek. The party attempted to climb Mount Goddard from here, but the peak was too distant, so the party left the region, moving west and northwest toward Yosemite.

Theodore Solomons explored the Mono Creek and Bear Creek regions in 1894 and 1895 during his search for a high mountain route from Yosemite to Kings Canyon. Solomons and Leigh Bierce climbed Seven Gables in 1894, and Solomons probably explored the entire upper Bear Creek drainage in June 1895 while waiting for the snow to diminish before moving south with Ernest Bonner on their epic journey to Kings Canyon.

James Hutchinson had an enviable series of first ascents in the High Sierra, and some of his greatest trophies were collected in the Mono Recesses region. In 1904, he and his brother Edward made the first ascent of Mount Humphreys. Four years later, accompanied by Joseph LeConte and Duncan McDuffie, James traveled from Tuolumne Meadows to Kings Canyon, and the trio bagged Mount Mills and Mount Abbot along the way.

Norman Clyde was active throughout the Sierra from the 1920s, but special mention should be made of his fondness for the Rock Creek region for backcountry skiing. With its combination of perfect snow, breathtaking scenery, and easy access, this was his favorite area during the spring for ski tours.

MAPS

USGS. *7.5-minute series:* Tungsten Hills, Mt. Darwin, Mt. Tom, Mt. Hilgard, Mt. Henry, Ward Mountain, Florence Lake, Graveyard Peak, Mt. Abbot, Mt. Morgan. *30 x 60–minute series:* Bishop.

USFS. A Guide to the John Muir Wilderness and the Sequoia–Kings Canyon Wilderness (1:63,360).

Tom Harrison Cartography. Mono Divide High Country.

Map Link 15-minute series. Mt. Goddard, Blackcap Mtn., Mt. Abbot, Mt. Tom.

Wilderness Press 15-minute series. Mt. Abbot, Mt. Goddard.

ROADS

Florence Lake Road

Highway 168 leaves Fresno, climbs into the Sierra foothills, and goes past Shaver Lake to end at a three-way

299

road junction east of Huntington Lake. Go to the right onto Kaiser Pass Road. After approximately 15 miles you come to a fork. The right fork will take you to Florence Lake and the trailhead for the Blayney Meadows Trail in 7 miles. There may be a water taxi service across Florence Lake, depending on the water level.

Lake Thomas A. Edison Road

Lake Thomas A. Edison Road takes the left fork that is approximately 15 miles from Huntington Lake along Kaiser Pass Road (the right fork goes to Florence Lake; see Florence Lake Road descripton, above). The road descends to the South Fork of the San Joaquin River and goes past Mono Hot Springs and the Bear Creek Trailhead to Lake Thomas A. Edison. The road turns west, goes across the dam, and ends at the trailheads near the far western shore of the lake. It is approximately 7 miles from Kaiser Pass Road to the trailheads. There is a twice-daily water taxi service across Lake Thomas A. Edison.

North Lake Road

North Lake Road leads to the Piute Pass Trailhead; it is described in Chapter 9, The Evolution Region.

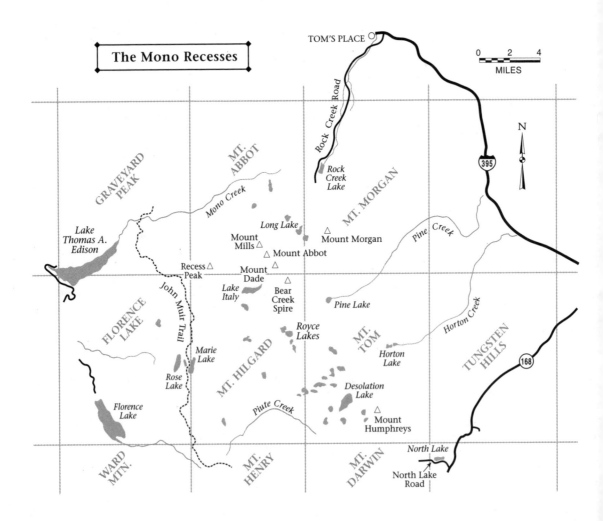

Buttermilk Road

Buttermilk Road leads to the Horton Lake Trailhead and the McGee Creek Trailhead, both located west of Bishop. Go west on Highway 168 from Bishop, and after 7.5 miles go right onto Buttermilk Road. The road, which leads through a major cattle-grazing area, has many side roads and trails; always follow the most heavily traveled road. After 1.7 miles a major fork is encountered; go right. Go straight through a cattle guard at mile 3.6 miles and continue to a fork at mile 6.1. Turn right. After another 0.8 mile over a rough road there is parking for a few cars in a nice wooded area. The Horton Lake Trailhead is 0.3 mile farther.

Those headed to the McGee Creek Trailhead should turn left at the last major fork, 6.1 miles from Highway 168. A rough road goes south for 2.3 miles across McGee Creek to a fork. Turn right, go straight at a junction 0.2 mile farther, and continue up the road another 0.6 mile to the trailhead.

An alternate approach to the McGee Creek Trailhead leaves Highway 168 approximately 10 miles west of Bishop. Turn right onto Dutch Johns Meadow Road and follow the rough road for 6.2 miles. Go left at the fork, and after 0.1 mile go left again. The trailhead is another 0.6 mile up the road.

Pine Creek Road

Pine Creek Road leaves Highway 395 approximately 10 miles north of Bishop. Go west from Highway 395 for about 10 miles to the Pine Creek Pass Trailhead. Those headed to the Morgan Pass Trail continue up the road to the tungsten mine. Park along the side of the road outside of the mine's boundary.

Rock Creek Road

Rock Creek Road leaves Highway 395 at Tom's Place. It goes south, past Tom's Place, and climbs up the canyon of Rock Creek approximately 9 miles to Rock Creek Lake. Those headed for the Tamarack Lake Trailhead turn left and drive to the trailhead on the eastern shore of this lake. The Davis Lake Trailhead, the northern terminus of the Hilton Creek Trail, is 0.6 mile farther up Rock Creek Road. The Rock Creek Road goes up the canyon another 1.2 miles to Mosquito Flat, which is the trailhead for the Morgan Pass/Little Lakes Valley Trail and the Mono Pass Trail.

TRAILS

Piute Pass Trail   11 miles

A quota trail. The Piute Pass Trail leads from the vicinity of North Lake over Piute Pass to Hutchinson Meadow, where it meets the Pine Creek Pass Trail. This trail is described in Chapter 9, The Evolution Region.

Blayney Meadows Trail   11¼ miles

A quota trail. The Blayney Meadows Trail starts from Florence Lake, goes past Blayney Meadows, and meets the John Muir Trail. The trail leaves the end of the road at the Florence Lake dam (0 mi; 7,350 ft) and traverses high above the southwestern shore of the lake to meet the Thompson Lake Trail (2¼ mi; 7,600 ft+). The trail gradually descends, crosses the South Fork of the San Joaquin River on a bridge, and meets the side trail coming up from the ferry landing along the southeastern shore of Florence Lake (3 mi; 7,583 ft). (Hikers who take advantage of the ferry service across Florence Lake save 5¼ miles of walking.) The trail continues up and down, passing Blayney Meadows. Soon the cabins of the Muir Trail Ranch (a resort) can be seen to the south. The trail goes left, over a small hill, away from the dude ranch, to a trail junction (4½ mi; 7,600 ft+). The trail to the south leads to the ranch, with a branch leading to the river. After a long ford, come to Blayney Meadows Hot Springs, a primitive site where hikers can soak for free. The Blayney Meadows Trail continues upstream to meet the John Muir Trail (1½ mi; 7,880 ft+).

There is an unmaintained and little-used trail that leaves the Blayney Meadows Trail approximately ¾ mile west of the Muir Trail Ranch and the hot springs (UTM 324236). The trail makes a steep ascent of the northeast side of the canyon along the west bank of Sallie Keyes Creek to meet the John Muir Trail just south of Sallie Keyes Lakes (UTM 336258). Those headed for Sallie Keyes Lakes and Selden Pass will save a lot of hiking by using this trail.

Horton Lakes Trail   4 miles

A non-quota trail. This "trail" is actually an abandoned road that once provided motor access to what is now a wilderness area. From the locked gate at the end of Buttermilk Road (0 mi; 8,000 ft+), hike up the road past some abandoned mining prospects to Horton Lake

(4 mi; 9,920 ft+). A trail continues upstream to Upper Horton Lakes. Another trail (really a road) ascends the north slope of the canyon to the hanging valley southwest of Mount Tom.

Gable Lakes Trail 3½ miles
A non-quota trail. This steep, unmaintained trail leads to an abandoned mine near Gable Lakes. The trail starts from the Pine Creek Trailhead along Pine Creek Road (0 mi; 7,440 ft+). The trail goes southeast before turning southwest and making some switchbacks. It eventually traverses upward along the west bank of Gable Creek, crossing the creek just below the lowest lake (3½ mi; 10,400 ft+). A good use trail leads up to the upper lakes to the southeast.

Pine Creek Trail 14 miles
A quota trail. This trail leaves Pine Creek Road (0 mi; 7,400 ft+) and makes a steep climb, with many switchbacks, to Pine Lake (3½ mi; 9,942 ft). The trail passes Pine Lake on its northern shore and, after a gentle climb, meets the Italy Pass Trail (1½ mi; 10,400 ft+). The Pine Creek Trail turns south from the fork and crosses Pine Creek Pass (2 mi; 11,120 ft+). The trail descends the southern side of the pass and meets a side trail leading to Moon Lake and L Lake (1 mi; 10.640 ft+). The Pine Creek Pass Trail continues down French Canyon, which has a spectacular view of the falls draining the Royce Lakes on the northwest wall of the canyon. The trail then meets the Piute Pass Trail at Hutchinson Meadow (6 mi; 9,280 ft+).

Italy Pass Trail 12½ miles
This trail has not been maintained for many years. The section leading over Italy Pass itself is in the worst shape, but many parts are still visible, and cross-country travel is relatively easy over this section. The trail starts along the Pine Creek Pass Trail at 5 miles from Pine Creek Road (0 mi; 10,400 ft+). The trail goes west into Granite Park to a creek crossing at UTM 434343 (3 mi; 11,580 ft+), where it soon disappears. From here, a faint use trail leads to the outlet of Lake 11,800ft+ (11,760 ft+; UTM 427345), where easy slopes and slabs pass north of this lake before traversing across the southern side of Mount Julius Caesar and climbing up to Italy Pass (1 mi; 12,400 ft+). The rough, vague trail descends the western side of the pass, passes the northern shore of Jumble Lake, and arrives at

the southern shore of Lake Italy (1½ mi; 11,202 ft). Follow the shore westward to the lake's outlet (1 mi; 11,202 ft+). The trail descends the Hilgard Branch of Bear Creek and meets the John Muir Trail (6 mi; 9,340 ft+). While this lower section of the Italy Pass Trail may be difficult to follow, it is in a delightful area, with a rushing stream, meadows, and trees.

John Muir Trail 22¾ miles
From its junction with the Piute Pass Trail (0 mi; 8,050 ft), the John Muir Trail descends the South Fork of the San Joaquin River to meet the Blayney Meadows Trail (1¾ mi; 7,880 ft+). The John Muir Trail takes the right fork, and climbs with many switchbacks, passing a side trail that descends to Blayney Meadows, to Sallie Keyes Lakes (5½ mi; 10,200 ft+). The trail continues north to the top of Selden Pass (1 mi; 10,880 ft+), which has a beautiful view of Bear Creek from its summit. The trail descends the north side of the pass and crosses the outlet of Marie Lake (2 mi; 10,560 ft+). The trail descends the eastern side of the West Fork of Bear Creek to Rosemarie Meadow, where it meets the junction with the Rose Lake Trail (1¼ mi; 10,000 ft+). It continues north to the junction with the Sandpiper Lake Trail (¼ mi; 10,000 ft+). The John Muir Trail continues downstream, crossing the West Fork of Bear Creek and the main fork of Bear Creek itself (this latter crossing may be a difficult ford) before meeting the Seven Gables Lakes Trail (¾ mi; 9,560 ft+). The trail continues down the east bank of Bear Creek to meet the Italy Pass Trail just beyond the crossing of the Hilgard Branch of Bear Creek (1¼ mi; 9,320 ft+). The trail continues down Bear Creek to meet the Bear Creek Trail (2¼ mi; 8,960 ft+). The John Muir Trail goes north from this junction and makes a steep ascent with many switchbacks to the top of Bear Ridge, where it meets the Bear Ridge Trail (2 mi; 9,840 ft+). The John Muir Trail goes northwest from the junction and at first makes a gradual descent before making a steep drop with many switchbacks to Mono Creek (4¾ mi; 7,880 ft+).

Rose Lake Trail 1 mile
The Rose Lake Trail leaves the John Muir Trail about 1½ miles north of Marie Lake. The Rose Lake Trail goes west across the West Fork of Bear Creek and turns southwest before arriving at the northwestern shore of Rose Lake (1 mi; 10,495 ft).

Sandpiper Lake Trail   2 miles

Leave the John Muir Trail at Rosemarie Meadow (0 mi; 10,000 ft+). The trail goes southeast before turning east around the southern shore of Lou Beverly Lake. It then continues southeast to the eastern shore of Sandpiper Lake (2 mi; 10,480 ft+). Cross-country travel is easy to Medley Lake, Flat Note Lake, and Three Island Lake (with its four islands), all in the basin above.

Seven Gables Lakes Trail   3 miles

This trail leaves the John Muir Trail below Upper Bear Creek Meadows and ascends the East Fork of Bear Creek to lovely Seven Gables Lakes and Bear Lakes Basin. Leave the John Muir Trail where the John Muir Trail fords Bear Creek (0 mi; 9,540 ft+). The Seven Gables Lakes Trail goes southeast before turning east and ascending the north bank of the stream. The trail crosses to the south side of the East Fork below the lowest of the Seven Gables Lakes (3 mi; 10,720 ft+). The trail ends at this lake, but cross-country travel is easy in the basin above.

Bear Creek Trail   6¾ miles

A quota trail. The trailhead for this trail is at the Bear Creek Diversion Dam, which is reached by leaving the road leading to Lake Thomas A. Edison approximately 1 mile north of Mono Hot Springs. A steep, difficult road (four-wheel drive recommended) goes east for 2½ miles to the trailhead; many hikers park their cars along the road leading to Lake Thomas A. Edison and hike along this road to the actual trailhead (0 mi; 7,320 ft+). The Bear Creek Trail follows the north bank of Bear Creek to meet the John Muir Trail south of Bear Ridge (6¾ mi; 8,960 ft+).

Bear Ridge Trail   5 miles

A non-quota trail. The trailhead for this trail is at the eastern end of the dam of Lake Thomas A. Edison (0 mi; 7,560 ft+). After an initial steep ascent, a moderate climb leads east through forests to meet the John Muir Trail (5 mi; 9,840 ft+).

Little Lakes Valley and Morgan Pass Trails   9¼ miles

A quota trail. Wood campfires are prohibited along this entire trail. Bears prowl through this area. The portion of this trail that passes through Little Lakes Valley

features beautiful lakes and is surrounded by impressive peaks. The trailhead is at Mosquito Flat, at the end of Rock Creek Road (0 mi; 10,200 ft+). The trail goes south to the Mono Pass Trail (½ mi; 10,440 ft+). It continues up the valley and crosses Morgan Pass (3½ mi; 11,080 ft+), then gradually widens and turns into an abandoned mining road. This road leads down Morgan Creek to the tungsten mine along Pine Creek (5¼ mi; 7,880 ft+). The section between Morgan Pass and Pine Creek is rather dull, compared to the Little Lakes Valley section.

Another abandoned mining road leaves the Morgan Pass Trail approximately 4 miles from the tungsten mine and leads north into the basin between Mount Morgan and Broken Finger Peak.

Mono Pass Trail   15 miles

A quota trail. This trail leaves the Little Lakes Valley Trail ½ mile from Mosquito Flat at the end of Rock Creek Road (0 mi; 10,440 ft+). It makes a gradual ascent and meets a side trail leading to Ruby Lake (1 mi; 11,040 ft+). Wood campfires are prohibited along this trail east of Mono Pass. Bears prowl through this area. The Mono Pass Trail goes to the right, up many switchbacks, to the summit of Mono Pass (1½ mi; 12,040 ft+). The trail descends the north side of the pass, and after many zigzags crosses Golden Creek (2½ mi; 10,440 ft+). A side trail climbs to the east to Golden Lake from here; the main trail continues downstream to meet a side trail that goes south to Fourth Recess Lake (¼ mi; 10,120 ft+). A short distance downstream, it meets the Pioneer Basin Trail (¼ mi; 10,040 ft+). The Mono Pass Trail continues downstream to meet a rough side trail (1½ mi; 9,600 ft+), which ascends the Third Recess to Third Recess Lake. Continuing downstream, it meets the Hopkins Creek Trail (¾ mi; 9,320 ft+). The Mono Pass Trail goes down the northern bank of Mono Creek to the Laurel Lake Trail (2¼ mi; 8,800 ft+). The Mono Pass Trail descends to meet the trail that ascends Second Recess (½ mi; 8,480 ft+). The Mono Pass Trail continues down beautiful Mono Creek before climbing out of the main drainage to meet the John Muir Trail along the North Fork of Mono Creek (4¼ mi; 8,320 ft+).

Tamarack Lakes Trail   4½ miles

A non-quota trail. The trailhead for this trail is on the eastern shore of Rock Creek Lake (0 mi; 9,700 ft+). The trail climbs to the east and eventually enters a forested

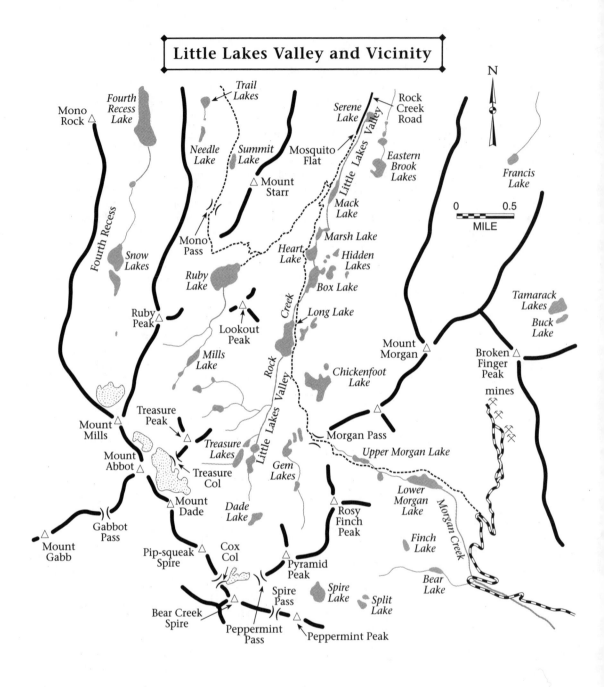

Little Lakes Valley and Vicinity

N

Mono Rock △

Fourth Recess Lake

Trail Lakes

Serene Lake

Rock Creek Road

Francis Lake

Needle Lake

Summit Lake

Mosquito Flat

Little Lakes Valley

Eastern Brook Lakes

△ Mount Starr

Mack Lake

0   0.5
MILE

Fourth Recess

Mono Pass

Heart Lake

Marsh Lake

Hidden Lakes

Snow Lakes

Ruby Lake

Box Lake

Tamarack Lakes

Ruby Peak △

△ Lookout Peak

Long Lake

Buck Lake

Mount Morgan △

Broken Finger Peak △

Mills Lake

Rock Creek

Chickenfoot Lake

mines

Mount Mills △

Treasure Peak
△

Treasure Lakes

Morgan Pass

Upper Morgan Lake

Mount Abbot △

Treasure Col

Little Lakes Valley

Gem Lakes

Lower Morgan Lake

△ Mount Dade

Dade Lake

△ Rosy Finch Peak

Finch Lake

Morgan Creek

△ Mount Gabb

Gabbot Pass

Mount Gabb

Pip-squeak Spire

Cox Col △

△ Pyramid Peak

Spire Lake

Split Lake

Bear Lake

Bear Creek Spire

Spire Pass

Peppermint Pass

△ Peppermint Peak

basin with many small lakes. A side trail leaves the main trail near Kenneth Lake and leads to Francis Lake. The trail continues upstream along the East Fork of Rock Creek to Tamarack Lakes (4½ mi; 11,600 ft+). Wood campfires are prohibited along this entire trail.

CROSS-COUNTRY ROUTES

McGee Creek

The title refers to the creek that drains into Buttermilk Country west of Bishop, not the creek of the same name that drains into Lake Crowley farther north. An abandoned road leaves the McGee Creek Trailhead (see the Buttermilk Road description, above) and ascends along the southern bank of the creek for about ½ mile before crossing the creek. It then makes a steep ascent before arriving at Longley Reservoir, beneath the north face of Mount Humphreys.

"Carol Col"   11,800 ft+; 11,760 ft+;
0.6 mi SE of Puppet Lake

Class 2. This pass has also been called "Puppet Pass," but the name in memory of Carol Kassler Ransford is used here. This pass connects Humphreys Basin with the bench lakes above the upper reaches of French Canyon. Easy hiking leads northwest from the outlet of Desolation Lake to the pass, which overlooks Puppet Lake. A steep slope with huge talus leads down the northwest side of the pass to the eastern shore of Puppet Lake. Easy cross-country travel leads east from here to Star Lake. A descent to the north then leads to L Lake and Moon Lake, where a good use trail provides access to the Pine Creek Pass Trail.

Further Reading: Steve Roper. *Sierra High Route.* Seattle: The Mountaineers Books, 1997, pp. 121–122, 126.

"Steelhead Pass"   12,080 ft+; 12,000 ft+;
0.6 mi SE of Steelhead Lake

Class 2. This pass connects Steelhead Lake with Desolation Lake. Climb onto the bench southeast of Steelhead Lake. Continue to ascend, passing two small lakes on the next bench above before climbing the steep slope leading to the pass. Cross the pass, then gradually descend to the east before traversing south, aiming for a small bench

northeast of Desolation Lake (the bench is located at UTM 496269). Descend the gully that goes south from this point to the southeastern shore of Desolation Lake.

Peak 11,840ft+   11,840 ft+;
0.7 mi SE of Three Island Lake

Class 2. This route provides access to the lakes at the head of West Pinnacles Creek. The "pass route" actually crosses over the top of a broad peak along the way from Three Island Lake to Old Squaw Lake in the West Pinnacles Creek drainage. Easy cross-country hiking leads from the end of the Sandpiper Lake Trail to the outlet of Three Island Lake (which, in reality, has four islands). Gradually ascend above the west shore of Three Island Lake to the saddle that is northeast of Mount Senger. Turn east from the saddle and hike across tedious slopes over the top of Peak 11,840ft+ (11,840 ft+). Descend the southern slope of the peak to Upper Turret Lakes. An easy gully leads down to Old Squaw Lake. Continue downstream past Big Chief Lake to Spearpoint Lake (there are a lot of 39-foot cliffs in this area that don't appear on the topo map). This basin is a hanging valley, and a descent of lower West Pinnacles Creek is not recommended. The lakes of upper East Pinnacles Creek can be reached by going east from the outlet of Spearpoint Lake to the southern shore of Pemmican Lake before climbing up and across the shallow ridge to the east and traversing northeast to the basin.

"Seven Gables Pass"   12,040 ft+; 12,000 ft+;
0.8 mi SE of Seven Gables

Class 2. This pass is used for ascents of Seven Gables and Gemini. It can also be used as an alternative approach to the lakes in the upper portion of West Pinnacles Creek. Easy cross-country hiking leads from the end of the Seven Gables Lakes Trail to Stub Lake. Go southeast from Stub Lake a short distance and climb onto the ridge that heads south to the low point between Seven Gables and Gemini. This ridge in reality ends above the pass, and it is necessary to descend a few feet down to the pass. Seven Gables Pass can also be approached directly from Seven Gables Lakes, but this involves talus; the slabs of the ridge provide easier climbing.

Those headed for West Pinnacles Creek must traverse up and across the west side of Gemini to the prominent shoulder before descending to Wampum Lake.

"Stough Pass"   11,920 ft+; 11,840 ft+;
0.6 mi NE of Gemini

Class 2. This pass is named here in honor of Tina Stough. There is an easy gully that leads to the top of this pass from the Seven Gables Lakes basin.

"Merriam Pass"   12,000 ft+; 11,920 ft+;
0.5 mi NW of Merriam Lake; UTM 404294

Class 3. This pass leads from Merriam Lake to Seven Gables Lakes. Ascend the steep slopes above the north-western shore of Merriam Lake to the small basin with two small lakes just below the pass. Climb to the summit of the pass from the western lake. The northern side of the pass consists of steep, loose rock, and snow or ice may be present. Ruskie Pass is longer but easier.

"Ruskie Pass"   12,040 ft+; 12,000 ft+ ;
0.7 mi NNW of Merriam Lake; UTM 405297

Class 2. This pass has been named here in honor of Ruskie Rush. An easy class 2 gully leads up the east side from Lake 11,160 ft+ (11,120 ft+), above Merriam Lake. The west side of this pass is class 1, and offers access to Seven Gables Lakes.

"La Salle Col"   11,960 ft+; 11,920 ft+;
0.4 mi SW of La Salle Lake

Class 2. This pass leads to the Bear Lakes Basin from the Merriam Lake area. Feather Pass is a better route.

Further Reading: John Moynier. *Backcountry Skiing in the High Sierra.* Evergreen, Colo.: Chockstone Press, 1992, p. 126.

"Feather Pass"   12,360 ft+; 13,320 ft+;
0.6 mi WNW of Royce Peak

Class 2. This pass provides access to the Bear Lakes Basin from Merriam Lake. Ascend the north inlet stream of Merriam Lake and keep to the eastern shores of the lakes in the sandy valley above. Go left at the highest lake in the basin and climb to the broad saddle southwest of Feather Peak. A short, steep section of talus is encountered just below the top of the pass on its northwest side. This is followed by sandy slopes down to Bearpaw Lake in Bear Lakes Basin.

Further Reading: Steve Roper. *Sierra High Route.* Seattle: The Mountaineers Books, 1997, pp. 124, 126; *Summit.* Summer 1994, p. 84.

"Royce-Merriam Saddle"   12,200 ft+; 12,160 ft+;
0.4 mi SSE of Royce Peak

Class 2; ice axe required. This pass, also known as "Merriam Col," is located between Royce Peak and Merriam Peak. There is a steep snow chute on the northeast side of this pass.

Further Reading: John Moynier. *Backcountry Skiing in the High Sierra.* Evergreen, Colo.: Chockstone Press, 1992, pp. 125–126.

"Royce Pass"   11,760 ft+; 11,680 ft+;
1.0 mi NE of Royce Peak

Class 1. This pass has also been called "Coco Col." It leads from Honeymoon Lake along the Italy Pass Trail to the Royce Lakes. Leave the Italy Pass Trail at the bench west of Honeymoon Lake, where the trail crosses a stream. Follow the stream uphill to where it disappears, and ascend easy terrain southwest to the top of the pass. Cross-country travel is easy from Royce Lakes southeast to Pine Creek Pass.

There are five Royce Lakes, numbered 0 to 4, counting upstream. Royce Lake No. 0 is 0.6 mile southeast of Merriam Peak, at UTM 444298. Royce Lake No. 1 (Lake 11,656ft; 11,600 ft+) is 0.5 mile northeast of Merriam Peak, UTM 441311. Royce Lake No. 2 is 0.5 mile east-northeast of Royce Peak, UTM 439317. Royce Lake No. 3 (11,725 ft; 11,680 ft+), the largest, is located 0.7 mile north-northeast of Royce Peak (UTM 437324). There is a tiny lake (thankfully not numbered) between Lakes No. 3 and No. 4. Royce Lake No. 5 is 0.5 mile northeast of Feather Peak (UTM 432327).

The next pass northwest of Royce Pass (Pass 11,840 ft+; 11,760 ft+) has been used as a direct route between Royce Lakes and Granite Park. It is a tricky pass, however, with many small cliffs on its southwestern side that impede progress. It is best to bypass this pass by climbing above it, over the southwest shoulder of Peak 12,470ft (12,400 ft+).

"Granite Bear Pass"   12,360 ft+; 12,320 ft+;
1.0 mi S of Italy Pass

Class 2. This pass provides a straightforward route across the Sierra crest between Granite Park and the upper part of Bear Lakes Basin. The east side features steep talus, while the west side has sandy slopes that lead down to Black Bear Lake.

"Ursula Pass" 11,840 ft+; 11,760 ft+;
0.4 mi S of Beartrap Lake

Class 2. This pass, named here in memory of Ursula Slager, provides access to Bear Lakes Basin from the Hilgard Branch of Bear Creek. Leave the Italy Pass Trail downstream from Lake Italy and ascend to the south, past Beartrap Lake and a smaller lake, to the broad saddle above. Descend the south side of the pass by going east to Coronet Lake.

"White Bear Pass" 11,880 ft+; 11,760 ft+;
0.1 mi NW of White Bear Lake

Class 2. This pass leads to White Bear Lake, and also to Bear Lakes Basin, from the Hilgard Branch of Bear Creek. Leave the Italy Pass Trail at the point where it crosses the Hilgard Branch downstream from Lake Italy. Contour south on the eastern bank of the stream before traversing up to the northern and eastern sides, then climb steep terrain to the broad saddle above. The final approach to the pass is made from the left (northeast). White Bear Lake is on the southeast side of the pass. Black Bear Lake can be reached by crossing a sandy saddle to the southeast of White Bear Lake.

Further Reading: Steve Roper. *Sierra High Route.* Seattle: The Mountaineers Books, 1997, p. 125.

"Dancing Bear Pass" 12,120 ft+; 12,080 ft+;
1.0 mi SW of Italy Pass

Class 2. This pass leads to Bear Lakes Basin from the western side of Italy Pass. The easiest route traverses south from the western side of Italy Pass before turning west and meeting the northeastern side of Dancing Bear Pass. (An alternate route leaves the eastern shore of Jumble Lake and ascends steep talus to the entrance of the pass.) The pass consists of a long gravel corridor. Descend the southwestern side of the pass by aiming for the sandy saddle between White Bear Lake and Black Bear Lake.

Further Reading: Steve Roper. *Sierra High Route.* Seattle: The Mountaineers Books, 1997, p. 128.

"Peppermint Pass" 12,360 ft+; 12,320 ft+;
0.4 mi NE of Bear Creek Spire

Class 2. This pass is used in combination with Spire Col to go from the Rock Creek drainage to the Pine Creek drainage. From Dade Lake in Little Lakes Valley climb to the pass between Pyramid Peak and Bear Creek Spire. The southeast side of the pass can be descended directly to Spire Lake; those headed for Peppermint Pass make a slightly descending traverse to the southeast before climbing to the top of Peppermint Pass.

"Spire Col" 12,400 ft+; 12,320 ft+;
0.5 mi E of Bear Creek Spire

Class 5. The easiest crossing of this pass is at the eastern side of the low point of the saddle between Bear Creek Spire and Peppermint Peak. A steep, 50-foot moderate class 5 chute (5.6) leads up from the north to the top of the pass. An exposed class 3 ledge system on the south side of the pass leads down to the Pine Creek drainage.

"Cox Col" 13,040 ft+; 12,960 ft+;
0.2 mi NW of Bear Creek Spire

Class 2. This pass is also known as "North Col." This is the only reasonable route from Rock Creek across the Sierra crest to Lake Italy. From the western shore of Dade Lake climb steep and loose slopes to the first saddle northwest of Bear Creek Spire. This saddle is marked by several notches on its eastern side; the first notch south of the lowest notch is preferred. The descent of the western side of the pass is easy. It is necessary to head northwest into the cirque that is west of Mount Dade and Mount Abbot and east of Mount Gabb before turning southwest and heading directly for Toe Lake and Lake Italy. Circle Lake Italy on its northern shore.

This pass has been named here in honor of Chris Cox, one of the pioneers of the Redline ski tour.

"Treasure Saddle" 12,480 ft+; 12,480 ft+;
0.4 mi ENE of Mount Abbot

Class 2. Steep cross-country hiking from Treasure Lakes, over many grassy benches and rubble-covered slabs, leads to the top of this pass between Mount Abbot and Treasure Peak. The west side of the pass features talus before easy ground on the way to Mills Lake and Ruby Lake is encountered.

Further Reading: John Moynier. *Backcountry Skiing in the High Sierra.* Evergreen, Colo.: Chockstone Press, 1992, pp. 128–130.

Gabbot Pass 12,240 ft+; 12,240 ft+;
0.6 mi SW of Mount Abbot

Class 2. Gabbot Pass is the easiest route across the

Mono Divide between the Second Recess and Lake Italy. Leave the Mono Pass Trail, cross Mono Creek, and ascend the trail that leads up the Second Recess. The trail remains on the northern bank of Mills Creek (it is hard to follow in places) to Lower Mills Creek Lake. A use trail continues upstream from here to the lovely meadows beneath Upper Mills Creek Lake. Head east from Upper Mills Creek Lake, then turn south-southeast to a small lake at the entrance of the valley leading up to Gabbot Pass. Ascend the valley over sand and talus to the top of the pass between Mount Gabb and Mount Abbot. The south side of the pass is easy, and the easiest route around Lake Italy is on its northern shore.

Further Reading: Steve Roper. *Sierra High Route.* Seattle: The Mountaineers Books, 1997, pp. 141–143, 155.

"Hilgard Pass"   12,480 ft+; 12,400 ft+;
0.6 mi NNE of Mount Hilgard; UTM 385371

Class 2. This route is much more difficult than Gabbot Pass. Leave the trail that ascends Mills Creek in the Second Recess. Cross Mills Creek and directly ascend the Second Recess. The headwall at the head of the recess is bypassed on its right (west) side on sloping ledges to the hanging valley above. Go to Lake 11,320ft+ (11,280 ft+; UTM 388378) and ascend the steep slope to the south, crossing over a small permanent snowfield to the top of the pass. Descend the south side of the pass to the outlet of Lake Italy and the Italy Pass Trail.

"Recess Pass"   11,920 ft+; 11,920 ft+;
0.5 mi NW of Recess Peak

Class 2. This route crosses the Mono Divide between the First Recess and the section of the John Muir Trail north of Bear Creek. Ascend the First Recess from the Mono Pass Trail to the highest of the First Recess Lakes. Go southwest to the saddle between Recess Peak and Peak 12,188ft (12,205 ft); the saddle has some steep sections on its northeastern side, so take care to ensure that the easiest route is selected. The southwestern side of the pass is easy. A gentle descent over meadows leads west to the John Muir Trail atop Bear Ridge.

Fourth Recess

This cross-country route goes from Fourth Recess Lake to Snow Lakes, near the head of the Fourth Recess. Take the trail that leads to Fourth Recess Lake from the Mono Pass Trail. Cross the outlet of the lake and traverse high above the western shore of the lake to the hanging valley that marks the upper part of the Fourth Recess. Cross-country hiking is easy in the valley above.

PEAKS

Piute Crags

The Piute Crags, the series of pinnacles southeast of Mount Emerson, are easily approached from the south via the Piute Pass Trail. These crags have abundant loose rock. The numbering system used here may or may not agree with the numbers in the summit registers.

"Piute Crag No. 1"

South Couloir and North Face. Class 5. First ascent September 2, 1950 by Charles Wilts and George Harr. Ascend the couloir leading to the notch between Crags No. 1 and No. 2. Approach Crag No. 1 from the northeast, and traverse diagonally upward across the 70° north face on excellent holds to the summit ridge. Follow the ridge to the summit.

"Piute Crag No. 2"

Northeast Face. Class 4. Descended September 3, 1950 by George Harr and Charles Wilts. Climb onto the northeast face from the notch between Crags No. 2 and No. 3. Loose, high-angle rock leads to the summit.

South Face. Class 5. First ascent September 3, 1950 by George Harr and Charles Wilts. Traverse onto the south face from a point below the notch between Crags No. 1 and No. 2. Some interesting, but easy class 5 pitches lead to the summit.

West Face. Class 5. First ascent August 27, 1949 by Ray Van Aken, George Harr, and Ray Osoling. Ascend the lower west face (class 4) to a belay ledge at the junction of the west face and the west arête. Climb up and right on a smooth slab for one class 5 pitch. Climb onto the west arête and ascend it to the summit.

"The White Tower"

This is the prominent point of white rock on the southern side of Piute Crag No. 2. It is a class 2 talus hop from the west, and was first climbed on August 27, 1949 by Ray Osoling, George Harr, and Ray Van Aken.

"Piute Crag No. 3"

West Arête. Class 4. Descended July 7, 1951 by Ray Van Aken, Wallace Hayes, and Lou Hayes. Ascend the arête rising from the notch between Crags No. 2 and No. 3.

East and North Faces. Class 4. First ascent July 7, 1951 by Ray Van Aken, Wallace Hayes, and Lou Hayes. There is a small crag to the west of the deep notch between Crags No. 3 and No. 4. Climb to the notch between this small crag and Crag No. 3. Climb over loose class 3 rock to the base of the east face. Traverse around the corner onto the north face. Go up and right across the north face to the summit ridge and follow it to the top.

"Piute Crag No. 4"

North Face. Class 5. First ascent September 1949 by Charles Wilts, Ellen Wilts, and George Harr. There is a small crag to the east of the deep notch between Crags No. 3 and No. 4; this small crag is high above the notch, closer to Crag No. 4. Climb to the notch between this small crag and Crag No. 4. From the notch, traverse across the north face to a large belay ledge. One class 5 pitch leads straight up from the ledge to the crest of the east ridge. Another one and a half pitches along the east ridge lead to the summit.

"Piute Crag No. 5"

South Ridge. Class 3. First ascent 1927 by Norman Clyde. Climb onto the south ridge from the notch between Crags No. 5 and No. 6. Follow the south ridge to the summit.

There is a minor crag between Crags No. 5 and No. 6. It is class 4 and can be traversed from either the east or west. This route was first climbed on June 17, 1950 by George Harr and Ray Van Aken.

"Piute Crag No. 6"

East Ridge. Class 2. Descended June 17, 1950 by George Harr and Ray Van Aken. Ascend talus and ledges from the notch between Crags No. 6 and No. 7.

West Ridge. Class 4. First ascent June 17, 1950 by George Harr and Ray Van Aken. Climb up and to the right from the notch between Crags No. 5 and No. 6.

"Piute Crag No. 7"

Class 3. This crag was traversed on October 12, 1974 by Dick Beach and Dave King.

"Piute Crag No. 8"

This is the prominent red pinnacle on the south face of Piute Crag No. 7.

Northeast Face. Class 3. First ascent July 21, 1951 by Ray Van Aken, George Harr, Charles Wilts, and Ellen Wilts. Climb the couloir to the east of Crag No. 7 and head for the notch north of Crag No. 8. Climb sound class 3 rock up the northeast face to the summit.

"Piute Crag No. 9"

This is the higher of the two pinnacles east of Crag No. 8.

North Arête. Class 3. Descended July 21, 1951 by Charles Wilts, Ellen Wilts, George Harr, and Ray Van Aken. Climb to the notch south of Crag No. 9 from the broad couloir to the east of the crag. Follow the arête from the notch to the summit.

South Ridge. Class 5. First ascent July 21, 1951 by Charles Wilts, Ellen Wilts, George Harr, and Ray Van Aken. Ascend the south ridge from the notch between Crags No. 9 and No. 10. This route is on solid rock.

"Piute Crag No. 10"

This is the lower of the two pinnacles east of Crag No. 8.

North Face. Class 3. First ascent July 21, 1951 by George Harr, Charles Wilts, Ellen Wilts, and Ray Van Aken. Ascend the south-facing gully between Crags No. 9 and No. 10 to the notch between the two crags. Loose rock on the north face leads to the summit.

"Piute Crag No. 11"

Southeast Buttress and North Face. Class 4–5. Climb the broken southeast buttress from the couloir east of the crag. This leads to a chute that goes up and left to a notch behind the crag. An easy pitch from the notch leads to the summit.

Mount Emerson   13,204 ft; 13,225 ft

The name of this peak has been misplaced on some maps. The true summit is on Peak 13,204ft (13,255 ft; UTM 534229), 0.4 mile southeast of the false summit.

West Ridge. Class 3. Head northeast from the summit of Piute Pass to the bench with many small lakes that is west of Mount Emerson. Scramble up to the lower, northwestern summit of the peak and traverse the south side of the ridge to the true summit.

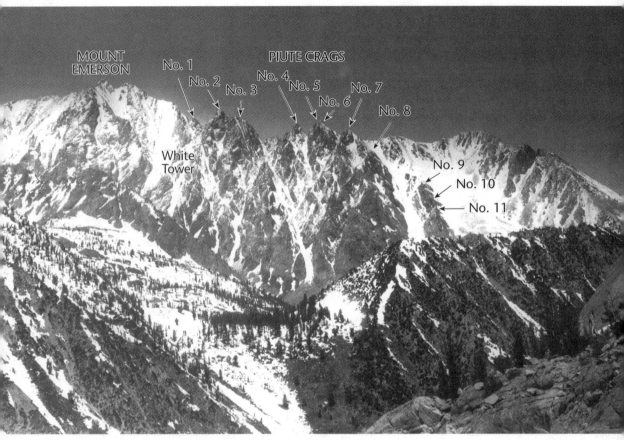

Mount Emerson and the Piute Crags from the southeast. Photo by R. J. Secor.

South Slope. Class 3. Leave the Piute Pass Trail about ¼ mile west of Loch Leven and ascend a rib that goes up the southern side of Mount Emerson. The summit is two small bumps on the skyline, left of the apparent high point. Head for the summit ridge, aiming for a point left (west) of a prominent overhang that is just below the crest. The rib eventually turns into ledges, then turns into a couloir, which leads onto the summit ridge a few hundred feet west of the summit.

A common mistake made on this route is to begin the ascent too far to the west; this leads onto the lower, northwestern summit of the peak. By the way, there is a fine view from this lower summit, but it is not the true summit.

Southeast Face. II, 5.4. First ascent August 1955 by G. Ledyard Stebbins and Robert Stebbins. This appealing route is on beautiful rock. Leave the Piute Pass Trail below Loch Leven and climb to the base of the southeast face. There are two prominent cracks on this face, which is left (southwest) of the couloir that separates the Piute Crags from Mount Emerson. Climb the 5.4 left-hand crack. Continue up class 4 slabs to the right of the crack, followed by 100 feet of class 3. Reenter the crack for another class 4 pitch. This leads to a broad chute, which is climbed for about 500 feet. Cross a rib to the left into another chute, which leads to a notch in the ridge above. Climb to the summit from the notch, passing the first gendarme on its right over class 4 ledges into another notch. Follow the class 3 ridge, passing over several gendarmes, to the summit.

Southeast Ridge. Class 3. First ascent October 12, 1974 by Dick Beach and Dave King. The first ascent of this route was accomplished after traversing the Piute Crags. This ridge can be reached from the Piute Pass Trail by climbing the couloir that separates the Piute Crags from Mount Emerson. Follow the ridge from the top of the couloir to the summit of Mount Emerson.

North Face. III, AI1, or WI2. First ascent July 1, 1926 by Norman Clyde. This route ascends a 1,400-foot snow/ice couloir with an average angle of 40°. This couloir is surrounded by loose rocks.

Further Reading: John Moynier and Claude Fiddler. *Sierra Classics.* Evergreen, Colo.: Chockstone Press, 1993, pp. 184–185.

"Checkered Demon"   13,121 ft; 13,112 ft; 1.1 mi SE of Mount Humphreys

First ascent July 7, 1926 by Norman Clyde. The western side of this peak and south ridge is class 2–3. The southeast slope is class 2. There are two snow/ice couloirs on its northeastern side. The left-hand couloir is known as "Kindergarten Chute:" III, AI1 or WI2 with 800 feet of 50-degree snow/ice climbing. The far, right-hand couloir is the Checkered Demon Couloir, rated IV, AI2 or WI3, class 4. This 1,400-foot couloir forks in its upper part. Take the right fork. The couloir narrows down to three feet and steepens to 55°, with class 4 mixed climbing above the narrows. It was first climbed by Doug Robinson and John Fischer in October, 1970.

"Mount Locke"   12,634 ft; 12,560 ft+; 1.4 mi SE of Mount Humphreys

This peak is informally named here after the late Bob Locke. The southeast slope is class 1–2. The 32° northeast chute, known as the "Wahoo Gully," is about 2,500 feet long and at least 50 feet wide.

Further Reading: John Moynier. *Backcountry Skiing in the High Sierra.* Evergreen, Colo.: Chockstone Press, 1992, pp. 122–123.

Mount Humphreys   13,986 ft; 13,986 ft

This is an impressive peak when viewed from either the east or west. The easy routes are challenging, the summit is high, and the scenery is outstanding.

Southwest Slope and Northwest Face. Class 4. First ascent August 3, 1919 by George R. Bunn and party. First winter ascent December 28, 1956 by Dick Long, Jim Wilson, Gary Hemming, Steve Roper, Fred Martin, and Terry Tarver. This has become the regular route on the peak. Most of this route is class 2, with a 100-foot easy class 4 section just below the summit. Climb onto the loose southwest slope from the highest of the Humphreys Lakes. Gain a scree-covered ledge that goes left (north) to the wide gully, which leads to the notch northwest of the summit. Ascend a trough from the notch (class 3) toward the summit of Mount Humphreys. A vertical wall is encountered after 200 feet. A short class 4 pitch to the right leads to the crest of the arête on the west side of the trough. Another short class 4 pitch (with excellent holds) up the crest of the arête leads to a short scramble to the summit. *Variation:* 5.5. First ascent July 1958 by John Dorsey, Jim Koontz, and Leif Thorne-Thomsen. Leave the gully leading to the notch and climb the southwest face via chimneys and broken ledges, crossing a sharp wedge beneath an overhang. Rejoin the regular route about halfway between the notch and the summit. *Variation:* 5.9. First ascent August 1988 by Mark Hoffman and Robin Ingraham, Jr. Climb the regular route to the crest of the arête just below the summit. Go right and ascend a vertical to overhanging inside corner with a thin finger crack. Small nuts are needed to protect the crux.

Further Reading: John Moynier and Claude Fiddler. *Sierra Classics.* Evergreen, Colo.: Chockstone Press, pp. 186–187.

Southwest Face. Class 5. First ascent July 29, 1938 by Jack Riegelhuth, Dick Cahill, George Wilkins, Bill Leovey, and Bruce Meyer. This route starts near a prominent pointed spire at the base of the southwest face of Mount Humphreys. Climb the face up and diagonally left to the summit. The last pitch is class 5.

Hutchinson Route. I, 5.4. First ascent July 18, 1904 by Edward C. Hutchinson and James S. Hutchinson. This route climbs the south couloir, which is high on the southwest face of Mount Humphreys. Climb the gully that leads to the deep notch southeast of the summit of Mount Humphreys. Leave this gully before reaching the notch and turn left (north) into the deep, south couloir. (This couloir passes between two black formations, and it may contain snow or ice.) Pass two chockstones on their left sides (both class 4). The south couloir leads to a notch that is just to the right of the summit. Some responsible members of the first-ascent party named this notch "Married Men's Point" and remained there while the Hutchinson brothers went on to bag the peak. Go left a few feet from Married Men's Point and climb a 50-foot 5.4 pitch up a ladderlike series of small ledges. The rest of the climb is a scramble to the summit. *Variation:* Descended August 1992 by Dabney Eastham. A gully directly descends from Married Men's Point to the talus at the base of the southwest face.

Triangle Face. II, 5.8. First ascent August 15, 1970 by Al Fowler, Mike Levine, and Jerry Snyder. This face rises above the south couloir; the top of the face is the southeast buttress. Climb the deep, south couloir of the Hutchinson Route to an area of light-colored rock. The route ascends a crack/ledge system directly up the face, climbing the left side of the triangle. Follow the Southeast Buttress route from the top of the face.

Southeast Buttress. II, 5.4. First ascent July 7, 1933 by Hervey Voge. Ascend the gully from Humphreys Lakes that leads to the deep notch southeast of the summit of Mount Humphreys. Climb four roped pitches on the left (southwest) side of the buttress before moving right onto the crest of the buttress. Follow the ridge to Married Men's Point, the notch just below the summit. Go left from this notch, climb a 50-foot 5.4 pitch, and then scramble onto the summit. *Variation:* Descended June 29, 1935 by Norman Clyde. The deep notch southeast of Mount Humphreys can be reached from the south fork of McGee Creek by climbing a loose class 3–4 gully.

South Pillar of the Southeast Face. III, 5.8. First ascent December 30, 1975 by Galen Rowell and Jay Jensen. This pillar is on the left side of the southeast face, above the south fork of McGee Creek. The pillar leads to the southeast ridge, which is followed to the summit.

East Arête. II, 5.4. First ascent June 29, 1935 by Norman Clyde. This is the most enjoyable route on Mount Humphreys. Ascend the south fork of McGee Creek and skirt the east side of a permanent snowfield on the southeastern side of Mount Humphreys. Climb the chute that is closest to the southeast face to the crest of the east arête. Follow the crest of the arête upward to a steep section, which is passed on its left side via a ledge that leads to a short, exposed 5.2 crack. Another 100 feet of climbing over and around the arête leads to the surprisingly flat plateau where the east arête and southeast ridge join. Follow the southeast ridge to Married Men's Point. Move left from the notch, where a short 5.4 pitch leads to easier climbing and the summit. *Variation:* The crest of the east arête can also be reached from the gla-

cier north of Mount Humphreys. Start climbing from the left (east) side of the glacier by keeping to the left of a couloir that leads to the crest of the east arête. Cross the couloir and follow a ledge that goes up and right. Leave the ridge after a few hundred yards and climb the face above to the crest of the east arête. With careful routefinding, this variation never exceeds class 4 to the crest of the arête. *Variation:* Climb to the saddle between Mount Humphreys and Peaklet (Peak 12,241ft; 12,160 ft+), then follow the crest of the ridge over the class 4 tower of Peak 13,151ft (13,040 ft+) before descending to the head of the chute.

Further Reading: John Moynier and Claude Fiddler. *Sierra Classics.* Evergreen, Colo.: Chockstone Press, 1993, pp. 188–189.

North Face. III, 5.7. First ascent May 1970 by Joe Faint and Galen Rowell. A snow/ice couloir ascends the right side of the north face. Go up and left from the bottom of this couloir over broken rock for about 500 feet. Then traverse up and right, following a ledge and eventually passing around a rib. Go straight up from here, and then go up and right to a dihedral, which leads to the summit ridge at a point about 40 feet east of the summit. The first-ascent party encountered much frozen snow on this route and needed ice axes and crampons.

Preconception Route. III, 5.8. First ascent 1990 by Andy Selters and Darla Heil. Climb half to two-thirds of the way up the couloir on the right side of the north face. Traverse to the right around a six-foot red roof (5.8), and continue up and left for three more pitches of run out 5.8 on good rock. This is followed by two pitches of 5.6 climbing up and right, ending via a sharp crack to the crest of the northwest arête near the summit.

North Couloir Direct. III, AI2 or WI3. First ascent 1979 by Craig Peer. This route makes a direct ascent of the main couloir on the right side of the north face. It features 900 feet of 50° to 60° snow/ice climbing.

North Couloir. Class 4. First ascent August 8, 1929 by Walter A. Starr, Jr. Ascend the snow/ice couloir on the right side of the north face. After about 300 feet the couloir forks. Take the right fork (or the rocks to the right) to the crest at a point northwest of the first small peak northwest of Mount Humphreys. Climb around this small peak on its southern side to the notch northwest of the summit. Ascend the class 3 trough leading up the northwest face to a vertical wall. Climb up and right over a short class 4 pitch to the crest of the arête, where another short, easy class 4 pitch leads to scrambling and the summit.

Northwest Ridge. Class 4. First ascent July 18, 1920 by C. H. Rhudy, L. C. Bogue, and J. L. Findlay. This long ridge can be gained from either McGee Creek or Desolation Lake. Follow the ridge from the large, flat area to the notch northwest of the summit. Climb the trough and right-hand arête on the northwest face to the summit.

Southeast Pinnacle. First ascent July 20, 1933 by Jules Eichorn and Marjory Bridge. This is the pinnacle that rises above the deep notch southeast of Mount Humphreys. The first-ascent party climbed its southwest face and descended its northwest ridge. The northwest ridge is class 3 from the notch.

"Peaklet"   12,241; 12,160 ft+;
1.2 mi NE of Mount Humphreys

This peak is also informally known as "Magic McGee." First ascent 1940s by Smoke Blanchard, via the class 2 south slope. The summit rocks are class 4. The west face from Longley Reservoir is class 3.

Peaklet Wall. III, 5.7. First ascent August 1975 by Galen Rowell, Jay Jensen, Gordon Wiltsie, and Helmut Kiene. This route climbs the north-northeast face of the peak. This route has been described as being slightly longer and more difficult than the East Face route of Mount Whitney. It includes some long class 4 sections. The crux is a 200-foot vertical dihedral with a bulge near its top, about halfway up the face.

Mount Humphreys from the southwest. Photo by R. J. Secor.

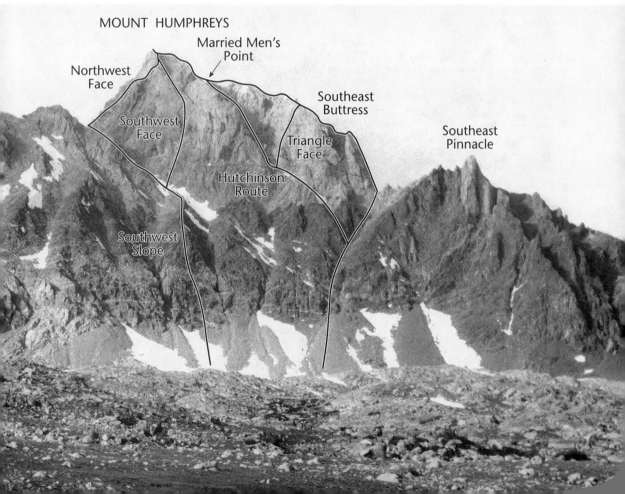

Basin Mountain   13,181 ft; 13,240 ft

North Slope. Class 2. First ascent November 9, 1930 by Norman Clyde. Head south from Horton Lake, following the main drainage to the two small lakes above. Head east and up from the higher lake towards the north ridge. Before reaching the ridge, go right and directly ascend the north slope to the higher, eastern summit.

East Chute. Class 4. First ascent October 1974 by Dick Beach and Dave King. This route climbs the large chute or basin that is visible from Owens Valley. A dirt road leaves the Horton Lakes Trail (which is actually a road) and switchbacks into the basin, ending at an aban-doned mine. Climb the chute to the rock slabs beneath the summit. Approximately 400 feet of clean class 4 rock lead to the summit. *Variation:* Climb the chute to the small saddle that is just to the southeast of the summit. A large couloir leads to the summit from the saddle.

Further Reading: John Moynier. *Backcountry Skiing in the High Sierra.* Evergreen, Colo.: Chockstone Press, 1992, p. 172.

Peak 13,240ft+   13,224 ft;
0.9 mi WSW of Basin Mountain
First ascent November 8, 1930 by Norman Clyde

Mount Humphreys from the northeast, August 24, 1972. Photo by Austin Post, No. 72R2-110, USGS Ice and Climate Project, GeoData Center, University of Alaska, Fairbanks.

from Upper Horton Lakes. The southwest ridge is class 3, and was first climbed September 20, 1953 by Barbara Lilley, John Wedberg, and Dick Woodward. The class 4 northeast ridge was climbed July 27, 1992 by Will Crjenko and Jim King.

Four Gables   12,720 ft+; 12,720 ft+; UTM 499299

South Slope. Class 1. First ascent 1931 by Norman Clyde. First winter ascent February 1979 by Mary Omberg and Sam Roberts. A sandy, class 2 chute leads up to the south slope from Steelhead Lake.

South Ridge. Class 2. First ascent August 27, 1978 by a party led by Bill Bradley. Climb from Upper Horton Lakes to the next basin to the south. Bypass the glacier in this cirque and climb a steep talus slope to the south, eventually reaching a saddle at 12,600 feet+ (12,640 ft+). Follow the south ridge from the saddle to the summit.

East Face, Left Side. Class 5. First ascent July 14, 1960 by Harvey Hickman, Tom Sadler, Bob Weakley, and Rich Gnagy. The east face is the wall that is above the cirque to the west of Upper Horton Lakes. This easy class 5 route is on the left side of the face. From the top of the face, turn right and ascend the south ridge to the summit.

East Face, Right Side. III, 5.8. First ascent June 1971 by Jeanne Neale and Galen Rowell. Climb a prominent buttress that is on the right side of the east face. Ten pitches in cracks and chimneys lead directly to the summit.

East Ridge. Class 3. First ascent 1963 by Rick Jali. Ascend the southern side of the east ridge from Upper Horton Lakes. A chute appears on the extreme right-hand side of the east face when you are within 100 feet of the headwall in the cirque. Climb the chute to another wall, then go left into another chute, which leads to the plateau just below the summit.

Northeast Buttress. II, 5.6. First ascent June 15, 1974 by Fred Beckey and Mike Levine. This buttress is on the face to the north of the east ridge of Four Gables. Ascend the prominent, sharp buttress to a point about 500 feet below the summit, where much loose rock is encountered. Traverse left into a steep snow gully, which leads to the summit plateau.

The Beagle. IV, 5.9R. First ascent 1978 by David Evans and Sibylle Hechtel. This route follows the crack system on the right side of the large pillar in the center of the face. Thirteen pitches lead to the top.

North Ridge. Class 2. First ascent May 27, 1973 by John Ripley, Fred Clements, John Halcomb, John Issac, and Bruce Masson. Follow the ridge from the saddle north of Four Gables. This saddle can be reached by traversing over Peak 12,808ft (12,825 ft), or from the west. The east side of the saddle is blocked by cliffs.

Northwest Ridge. V, Class 5. First ascent October 1991 by Will Crjenko, Andy Selters, and Claude Fiddler. This traverse starts at Peak 12,542ft (12,480 ft+).

Mount Tom   13,652 ft; 13,652 ft

This is the enormous mountain west of Bishop.

From Horton Lake. Class 2. An abandoned mining road leads north from Horton Lake to the old Tungstar Mine. Ascend a steep chute from the mine to the summit. *Variation:* One may be tempted to follow the long southwest ridge from the head of Hanging Valley. But there are many ups and downs along the crest, and intricate routefinding is needed to keep the difficulty from exceeding class 3. *Variation:* The couloirs and slopes directly south of the summit offer a direct route back to Horton Lake; these are usually glissaded in the spring with sufficient snow cover.

From Gable Creek. Class 2. This is a long, hard hike. Leave the Gable Lakes Trail at approximately 8,000 feet and follow the path of an abandoned tramway across Gable Creek and up the northwest slope of Mount Tom. Ugh!

North Ridge. Class 2. First ascent October 1971 by Steve Rogero and Dick Beach. First winter ascent March 8, 1997 by Brad Jensen, Greg Colley, and Doug Mantle. This ridge is best approached from Pine Creek Road. Follow the crest of the ridge, which has a lot of 20-foot bumps that must be climbed up and down to the summit. Ugh! Ugh!

Northeast Ridge. Class 4. First ascent March 1982 by Dean Hobbs, Gary Slate, and Andy Selters. This is the long ridge to the left of Elderberry Canyon.

Elderberry Canyon. Class 2. This is a popular ski tour in the spring. Leave Pine Creek Road at Rovana. Go south on this road for approximately 0.5 mile to a junction. Go south from this junction and follow a rough dirt road to the trailhead for Elderberry Canyon. A trail ascends the canyon to the abandoned Lambert Mine. Continue ascending the canyon to the north ridge of Mount Tom. Follow the ridge south to the summit. Elderberry Canyon is a dry canyon (i.e., there is no running water) during the summer and fall. But in the spring it is a great ski tour. Some parties arrange a car shuttle in order to climb the peak from Horton Lake and descend Elderberry Canyon—a ski descent with perhaps a 7,000-foot vertical drop. The upper part of the canyon is dramatically steep. If this were a ski area it would be rated with double black diamonds.

Further Reading: John Moynier. *Backcountry Skiing in the High Sierra.* Evergreen, Colo.: Chockstone Press, 1992, p. 173.

Pilot Knob   12,245 ft; 12,245 ft
This peak is class 2 from the saddle to the east of the peak. There is an outstanding view from the summit.

Turret Peak   12,091 ft; 12,000 ft+
A north or south traverse of this peak is easy.

Mount Senger   12,286 ft; 12,271 ft
First ascent 1907–09 by George R. Davis, T. G. Gerdine, C. F. Urquhart, and L. F. Biggs of the United States Geological Survey. This peak is class 1 from Sallie Keyes Lakes. It is also class 1 from Selden Pass; from here, traverse southeast from the northern side of the pass, then climb rock slabs and sand to the high saddle northeast of Peak 12,068ft (12,000 ft+), at UTM 348273. Go south of the intermediate peak and ascend the northwest ridge to the summit of Mount Senger. Mount Senger is class 2 from the east.

Peak 12,000ft+   12,014 ft;
0.9 mi SE of Mount Hooper
The southeast slope is class 1 from Sallie Keyes Lakes. *Northeast Ridge.* Class 2–3. First ascent July 15, 1954 by Oliver Kehrlein and Jim Koontz. Ascend the southern side of the northeast ridge to the small plateau beneath the summit. Go west across the plateau to a knifeedge ridge and follow this to the summit.

Peak 12,080ft+   12,080 ft;
0.4 mi SE of Mount Hooper
The west slope and south ridge are class 3.

Mount Hooper   12,349 ft; 12,349 ft
First ascent 1929 by Glen Dawson, William A. Horsfall, and John Nixon. This peak is class 2 from Selden Pass. Traverse west from the northern side of Selden Pass to the flat saddle southeast of Mount Hooper. Descend slightly while traversing westward

from the saddle and climb the easy southern slope to the summit block. The block is climbed by crossing its west side to the north face before reaching the top (class 4). A crack on the southern side of the block can also be climbed.

Bear Dome   9,945 ft; 9,947 ft
South Face. III, 5.8. First ascent July 1984 by Alan Swanson, Josh Starr, and Rich Kropp. This seven-pitch route involves some intricate routefinding.

The Pinnacles   12,320 ft+–12,080 ft+; 12,240 ft+–12,080 ft+
Not much is known about this ridge, which extends south from Gemini. Generally speaking, the northern pinnacles seem more difficult than those on the southern side of the ridge, and ascents seem to be easier on their eastern sides than on their western sides. The highest pinnacle (Peak 12,320ft+; 12,240 ft+; 1.0 mile south of Gemini) was first climbed July 14, 1933 by Glen Dawson, Neil Ruge, and Alfred Weiler. The two southernmost pinnacles (12,120 ft+; 12,122 ft; 0.5 mile east of Big Chief Lake) were first climbed July 5, 1939 by L. Bruce Meyer and Jim Harkins, from Hutchinson Meadow.

Gemini   12,880 ft+; 12,866 ft
The northwest summit is the high point. First ascent July 30, 1953 by Jim Koontz and Rosemarie Lenel. Class 2 from Seven Gables Pass. Go south from the saddle on the western slope of the north ridge. Gain the west spur of the northwest summit and ascend talus to the summit. This peak is also class 2 from Aweetsal Lake via the east slope and south ridge.

Seven Gables   13,080 ft+; 13,075 ft
The south summit is the high point. *South Slope.* Class 3. First ascent July 18, 1976 by R. J. Secor and party. Traverse west and northwest from Seven Gables Pass, well beneath Peak 12,440ft+ (12,400 ft+), onto the south slope of Seven Gables. Most of this approach is class 2, with a short class 3 chute passing through some cliffs. Ascend the south slope to a knife edge ridge just beneath the summit. Go left (west) over the ridge and into a chute that descends to the west. After a short distance turn right and climb a chimney/ wide crack for 100 feet until 20 feet below the summit.

Seven Gables from the east. Photo by R. J. Secor.

Go to the left around and under an overhanging block and then go right to the summit.

West Ridge. Class 2–3. First ascent September 20, 1894 by Theodore S. Solomons and Leigh Bierce. Go east from Sandpiper Lake, passing through some barely penetrable brush, to the rocky bowl northwest of Seven Gables. Make a left-diagonal ascent of the northern slope of the west ridge, passing a permanent snowfield on its left side, to the crest of the ridge. Follow the class 3 ridge to the summit. *Variation:* Class 3. Descended July 23, 1974 by Jerry Keating, Andy Smatko, Bill Schuler, and Barbara Lilley. First ascent July 1973 by Jon Inskeep, Al Conrad, Scott Sullivan, Barbara Cohen, Brian Smith, Rhoda Gilson, David Underwood, and Bahram Manahedgi. A scree chute from Lake 11,120ft+ (11,140 ft+) leads north to the West Ridge, which is then followed to the summit.

North Ridge. Class 2–3. This ridge can be reached from the approach to the west ridge, or from Seven Gables Lakes to the east. Go west from the oblong Lake 10,720ft+ (10,720 ft+) in the Seven Gables Lakes basin to the saddle north of Seven Gables. The saddle is best approached from the north. The ridge above the saddle ascends talus, ledges, and chimneys to the summit.

East Face. Class 4. First ascent August 1, 1970 by Steve Roper and Jani Roper. This route climbs the northern part of the east face, where a steep, broken wall leads to a point about 200 feet north of the north summit. The lower section of the route is class 4; the middle section consists of 700 feet of class 3, and the last section is class 4.

Direct East Face. IV, 5.9. First ascent August 1981 by Vern Clevenger and Claude Fiddler. Second ascent August 18, 1988 by Dick Duane and Sebastian Letemendia.

This route climbs the central portion of the huge east face of the north peak of Seven Gables. Ascend cracks in the central pillar on the face. Higher, the pillar becomes a knife edge arête that ends atop the north summit of the peak.

Further Reading: John Moynier and Claude Fiddler. *Sierra Classics.* Evergreen, Colo.: Chockstone Press, 1993, pp. 192–193.

East Face, Chimney Route. IV, 5.9. First ascent August 18, 1988 by Galen Rowell and Kevin Worral. As the name implies, this route climbs the chimney on the true east face of Seven Gables.

Peak 12,441ft   12,427 ft; 0.8 mi E of Gemini

First ascent July 12, 1933 by David Brower via an unknown class 2 route. The class 3 northwest ridge was first climbed by Peter Cummings on July 23, 1994.

Peak 12,400ft+   12,440 ft+; 0.3 mi SW of Merriam Lake

First ascent August 20, 1968 by John Pelkey, Scott Smith, F. J. Novak, and Tom Frost via the class 2 southwest gully that ends just north of the summit. The class 3 south ridge was first climbed by Peter Cummings on July 24, 1994.

"Mount Morrow"   12,402 ft; 12,432 ft; 0.7 mi S of Merriam Lake

The high point is at the southwest end of the summit ridge. First ascent July 7, 1940 by a Sierra Club burro trip via an unknown route. This peak is class 2–3 from Hutchinson Meadow. First ascent August 8, 1979 by a party from the Hillcrest Congregationalist Church of Berkeley, who have proposed that this peak be named after their late minister, Fred Morrow. The northwest slope is class 2.

Merriam Peak   13,103 ft; 13,077 ft

First ascent July 14, 1933 by Lewis Clark, Julie Mortimer, and Ted Waller. This peak has also been called "Isosceles Peak" and "Bastille Peak." It is class 2 from the Royce-Merriam Saddle; the east side of this saddle is usually composed of steep snow, and an ice axe may be needed. The east face is class 3 and was first climbed July 3, 1939 by Alan Bryant and Bob Helliwell; climb the solid, open chute immediately left of the prominent northeast ridge. The south slope and south-

west ridge are class 3; it is necessary to drop down below the crest of the southwest ridge on its northwest side to keep the difficulty to class 3.

North Buttress. III, 5.10b. First ascent August 1976 by Bob Harrington and Vern Clevenger. Climb directly up from the toe of the buttress up a 5.9 face to a belay stance underneath some roofs. Go left and up over some loose blocks to a slot (5.10 stemming) to the left-facing dihedral in the middle of the route. Climb a crack (5.8) that is to the left of the dihedral to a large flake and belay in an alcove. Continue up the dihedral before climbing a crack (5.9) that leads up and right, and ends. The next pitch follows a crack up and left to a ledge (5.8; 3- to 4-inch protection needed), followed by the crux pitch: a steep 5.10b layback up another left-facing dihedral. This pitch ends on a ledge in a notch behind a block that is atop the buttress. A 5.7 pitch leads up out of the notch followed by four or five class 4–5 pitches that lead to the summit.

Further Reading: John Moynier and Claude Fiddler. *Sierra Classics.* Evergreen, Colo.: Chockstone Press, 1993, pp. 194–197.

Silver Cloud. IV, 5.10+, with a rappel. First ascent July 22, 1994 by David Harden and Bart O'Brien. This route follows the prow on the left side of the north buttress for nine pitches before joining the North Buttress route for its final, easy traversing pitches. The route begins on the far left-hand side of the north face by scrambling above the talus for approximately 50 feet. An aesthetic 3-inch jam crack (5.8) leads up for 40 feet. The second pitch follows class 3 rock to the left of the prow for about 80 feet. From here it is possible to go back to the right onto the crest of the prow via easy cracks to the bottom of a wide crack. The third pitch climbs the face to the right of the wide crack to the top of the first spire on the prow. Next, rappel to the left to the gully, then climb broken rock and cracks (5.7) for 100 feet to a beautiful 5.9 fist crack that leads up 30 feet into a chimney. This chimney is located behind the most impressive spire along the prow. Climb over blocks and then chimney up to where run out 5.9 moves lead onto the smooth, beautiful headwall. From here a 5.10+ crack leads to a belay stance at a nice ledge. The sixth pitch is a classic hand and finger crack that leads up for about 120 feet to the second of two comfortable ledges at the base of a wide crack. Begin by climbing the crack, but then move out to the right across an easy face that leads to the Big Ledge

Merriam Peak, North Buttress. Photo by R. J. Secor.

(clearly visible from Royce Lakes). From the left end of the Big Ledge, climb up a 5.9 crack that leads to a horizontal traverse (5.10b) to the left. Down climb to the left for 30 feet to a gully at the base of a spectacular Yosemite-type crack. Climb this crack for 160 feet of sustained yet varied climbing that leads up to and around an imposing roof. This pitch ends abruptly on the same ledge in the notch behind the block that is atop the north buttress. Three moderate, traversing pitches across and along the arête lead to the true summit of Merriam Peak.

Royce Peak   13,280 ft+; 13,253 ft

The southeast ridge rising from the Royce-Merriam Saddle between Merriam Peak and Royce Peak is class 2 with some sandy sections; first ascent June 23, 1931 by Nathan Clark and Roy Crites. An ice axe may be needed to approach this saddle from the east. The best route from Merriam Lake is via the class 2 southwest ridge. The class 3 east face was first climbed in 1936 by Ellis Porter, Herbert Welch, and Frank Richardson. Climb an inconspicuous chute that starts between Royce Lakes No. 1 and No. 2 at UTM 439315. The bottom part of this chute consists of slabs and ledges. Loose rock and sand are found higher. Climb the left rib to the summit.

Feather Peak   13,240 ft+; 13,242 ft

Southwest Ridge. Class 3. First ascent July 13, 1933 by David Brower. Climb the ridge rising from the top of Feather Pass, keeping to its southern side to keep the difficulty down to class 3.

Southeast Slope. Class 2–3. Descended July 13, 1933 by David Brower. Ascend sand and talus from the saddle between Royce Peak and Feather Peak to the easy class 3 summit rocks.

Northeast Face. III, 5.8. First ascent August 1966 by Gary Colliver, Edward Keller, Mark Waller, and Andy Lichtman. Scramble up the lower part of the face to a large, sloping ledge beneath a large crack. Make a right-ascending traverse to where easier climbing leads to the base of a headwall. The 300-foot headwall is overcome by an inside corner to a belay stance beneath a ceiling. Go left into a jam crack (5.8) and climb this to the summit area.

Feather Couloir. III, AI2, or WI3, Class 4. First ascent December 1976 by Alan Bartlett and Michael Graber. This 700-foot snow/ice couloir never exceeds 60° in angle. The right side of the couloir is less steep, but is exposed to rockfall. The left side of the couloir is steeper, but there is less danger from rockfall. There are one to two pitches of class 4 rock between the top of the couloir and the summit.

Further Reading: John Moynier and Claude Fiddler. *Sierra Classics.* Evergreen, Colo.: Chockstone Press, 1993, pp. 198–199.

Peak 12,918ft   12,880 ft+;
0.6 mi NNW of Feather Peak

The class 2 northeast ridge was climbed by Andy Smatko and party on September 5, 1966. He said they "found a cairn and an old register left by the first-ascent party 25 years earlier."

Peak 12,470ft+   12,400 ft+;
1.0 mi NNE of Royce Peak

This has been called "Spire Peak." First ascent August 3, 1969 by Andy Smatko and Bill Schuler, via a loose chute on the south-southwest face. The summit block is class 4 on its north side. The class 4 northeast ridge was climbed by John Moynier in 1988.

Peak 12,563ft   12,563 ft; 1.1 mi NE of Royce Peak

West Slope. Class 3. First ascent 1938 by Norman Clyde. The spectacular summit block is climbed on its south side.

Northwest Face, Right Side. II, 5.7. First ascent August 1966 by Gary Colliver, Andy Lichtman, and Mark Waller. Climb an open book that ends in a bowl.

Northwest Face, Left Side. II, 5.8, A2. First ascent August 1966 by Andy Lichtman and Mike Cohen. Aid climbing on the face leads up a crack past an overhang. This is followed by free climbing to the top of a pinnacle high on the face.

Northeast Ridge. II, 5.6. First ascent July 1982 by Galen Rowell. Follow the ridge to the summit.

Peak 12,320ft+
12,287 ft; 0.5 mi SE of Beartrap Lake

First ascent July 1947 by W. J. Losh, via the class 2–3 west ridge.

Peak 12,760ft+   12,756 ft; 1.0 mi SW of Italy Pass

First ascent July 13, 1933 by George Rockwood and David Brower, who described the southeast slope as being one of the better sand climbs in the High Sierra. The northwest ridge is class 3.

Mount Julius Caesar   13,200 ft+; 13,196 ft

First ascent August 12, 1928 by A. H. Prater and Myrtle Prater. First winter ascent March 18, 1965 by Tom Ross and Peter Lewis. The west ridge is a classic class 3 climb; the southwest slope and south ridge from Italy Pass are both class 2. A party led by Steve Eckert climbed the class 2 southeast bowl above Chalfant Lake on August 8, 1997.

This peak has been climbed from the western cirque between Mount Julius Caesar and Bear Creek Spire. Climb south from the cirque up a class 2 slope to the top of the Sierra crest, then follow the crest (class 3) to the summit of Mount Julius Caesar. This was first done August 9, 1953 by Jim Koontz, Pete Murphy, Al Wolf, and Ed Toby.

Peak 13,160ft+   13,120 ft+;
0.6 mi S of Bear Creek Spire

South Slope. Class 2. First ascent August 2, 1969 by a party led by Andy Smatko. Climb the south slope to the summit of the east peak. The higher, west peak is easy from there. A convenient descent route goes south, down a chute between the two summits.

West Ridge. Class 3. Descended July 8, 1954 by Jim Koontz, Mike Loughman, Dan Popper, and Roger Popper. Climb a chute on the southern side of the cirque that is west of the peak. This chute leads to the Sierra crest. Follow the crest eastward to a point just below the summit. Climb onto a ledge that crosses the west face to a point about 200 feet below the summit. The ledge ends about 100 feet north of the summit.

West Face. Class 4. First ascent July 8, 1954 by Jim Koontz, Mike Loughman, Dan Popper, and Roger Popper. Climb up and right across the west face from the cirque west of the peak. Climb past the low point of the north ridge, and then climb up and left onto the north ridge. Follow the north ridge to the summit.

"Peppermint Peak"   12,680 ft+; 12,640 ft+;
0.6 mi ESE of Bear Creek Spire

West Ridge. Class 3. First ascent August 20, 1972 by Andy Smatko, Barbara Lilley, Bill Schuler, and Tom Ross. From the eastern end of Spire Col, climb around a large chockstone in a narrow chute. Climb up and

across the southern side of the peak, crossing some gullies and ribs, to the base of the eastern summit pinnacle. The high point is the summit of the east pinnacle, an easy scramble from its base.

Bear Creek Spire   13,720 ft+; 13,713 ft

This is the impressive peak at the head of Little Lakes Valley.

Ulrichs Route. Class 4. First ascent August 16, 1923 by Hermann F. Ulrichs. First winter ascent April 1941 by David Brower, Alex Hildebrand, Milton Hildebrand, Edmund Chambers, Lewis Clark, Nathan Clark, Fred Kelley, Paul Lafferty, Einar Nilsson, and Bestor Robinson. This route ascends the northwest slope of Bear Creek Spire; it can be approached from Lake Italy or from Little Lakes Valley (either way via Cox Col). Ascend the slope to the base of the final summit spire, which is climbed by a diagonal crack that is left of the high point. The crack leads to a squeeze chimney. An exposed boulder move leads to the high point.

North Arête. III, 5.8. First ascent August 1971 by Galen Rowell and Jeanne Neale. First winter ascent February 1987 by Greg Orton and Robert SP Parker. This is an enjoyable climb, consisting of about a dozen pitches of moderate technical climbing with spectacular surroundings. There are two short sections of 5.8 and two pitches of 5.7 on this climb; the remainder is easy class 5.

Start climbing from the very lowest point of the arête, where a 100-foot section of 5.6 leads to a large ledge. Go about 15 feet left of a large, left-facing dihedral, then climb a thin, steep crack (5.8). Continue up and right over flakes (5.7) to a ramp that leads up the right side of the north arête. Climb down and left and ascend a crack that eventually widens into a chimney; 5.8 off-width climbing leads out of the chimney and up a thin crack. The fifth pitch goes slightly left and ascends over many steps before returning to the crest of the arête. Continue climbing along the arête, moving right to bypass some short, steep walls, to the base of a gendarme. Go left across the gendarme, passing two difficult-looking cracks, to the third crack; this crack is steep, with sharp flakes in it (5.7). Walk about 10 feet to the right from the top of this pitch and squeeze through a triangular hole in the base of a wall to the left (east) side of the arête. The rest of the route diagonals slightly left and ascends the left side of the arête before crossing to its right (west) side, where a class 4 ramp leads to the base of the summit rocks. *Variation:* A thin crack (5.10c) is to the right of the off-width chimney.

Further Reading: John Moynier and Claude Fiddler. *Sierra Classics.* Evergreen, Colo.: Chockstone Press, 1993, pp. 209–212; *Rock & Ice.* No. 73 (May–June 1996), pp. 66–75.

Northeast Buttress. Class 4. First ascent May 27, 1932 by Norman Clyde. This is a very enjoyable route. This buttress, which is left (east) of the north arête, is marked by a tower on its lower section. Approach the buttress from the east and follow it to the summit. Some class 4 (approximately 200 feet) is encountered just below the summit.

Further Reading: John Moynier and Claude Fiddler. *Sierra Classics.* Evergreen, Colo.: Chockstone Press, 1993, pp. 208–209.

Northeast Face. Class 3–4. First ascent October 7,

1931 by Norman Clyde. Climb the wide face between the northeast buttress and east ridge of Bear Creek Spire. Many variations are possible.

Neurosis. III, 5.9. First ascent August 1978 by David Evans and Sibylle Hechtel. This route was formerly known as "Killer Pace." It is on the buttress on the far left side of the northeast face. Climb a crack system in the middle of the buttress for seven pitches. This route ends high on the east ridge.

East Ridge. IV, 5.8, A0. First ascent July 1977 by Sheari Taylor and John Vawter. Follow the crest of the ridge (more or less) from the top of Spire Col. This route is twenty-two pitches long.

Further Reading: John Moynier and Claude Fiddler. *Sierra Classics.* Evergreen, Colo.: Chockstone Press, 1993, pp. 206–207.

South Face. IV, 5.9. First ascent August 1971 by

Bear Creek Spire from the north. Photo by R. J. Secor.

Galen Rowell. The right side of the south face has two cracks that are separated by a steep, serrated fin. Climb the wall to the right of the right-hand crack, over steep, rough granite. The crux is located below the crest of the east ridge, where a short overhang with a discontinuous crack system must be overcome. This is followed by a traverse on a long ledge to a dihedral, which leads to the crest of the east ridge.

Further Reading: Galen Rowell. *High and Wild.* San Francisco: Lexicos, 1983, pp. 15–21.

Solar Eclipse Route. III, 5.10b. First ascent July 11, 1991 by Dave Nettle and Jim Quirk. There are three prominent towers with smooth right sides on the left side of the south face. There is a right-facing inside corner below and right from the three towers, starting about 60 feet above the ground. Start from a large flake and face climb up and left to the inside corner (5.8) to a hanging belay. Continue up the flared, vegetated groove of the corner (5.10b), then pass a square roof to a belay in an alcove. Go left on the first of several cracks out of the alcove, then go up for two pitches (5.8 and 5.6) to where easy class 5 climbing leads up and left across a gully to The Three Towers. Climb a 4-inch crack on the right side of the towers (5.8) to a belay stance in a notch. Go left and up (5.7) and left and up again (5.7 squeeze) before wandering up the face to a notch on the east ridge. About 250 feet of class 3 leads up the ridge to the summit.

British Chimney Route. IV, 5.9, A0. First ascent July 5, 1978 by Nigel Gifford and Galen Rowell. This route ascends the prominent chimney on the west side of the south face. Continue up the chimney to a steep headwall, which is bypassed by a short pendulum. Climb to the crest of the east ridge, meeting it near the summit.

South Face Direct. IV, 5.9. First ascent February 1988 by Bill Kerwin and Robert SP Parker. This climb begins from rock slabs at a point directly beneath the summit of Bear Creek Spire. The route ends 10 feet left of the summit block.

"Pyramid Peak" 12,840 ft+; 12,866 ft;
0.7 mi NE of Bear Creek Spire; UTM 445377

First ascent 1927 by Norman Clyde. The southeast ridge is class 2 from the top of Peppermint Pass. The northwest face is class 2–3, and was first climbed March 28, 1966 by Tom Ross. The north ridge is class 3.

"Pip-squeak Spire" 13,268 ft; 13,200 ft+;
0.6 mi SE of Mount Dade

First ascent 1957 by Andy Smatko, John Robinson, and Peter Hunt, via the class 2–3 southeast ridge. The north ridge from the top of The Hourglass on Mount Dade is class 3. The northwest ridge is class 2. The summit block is 15 feet of vertical class 5.

"Rosy Finch Peak" 12,744 ft; 12,744 ft;
0.5 mi SSW of Upper Morgan Lake

John Moynier made the first winter ascent in the early 1980s. The southeast slopes are class 2, the east ridge is class 3, and the north ridge from Morgan Pass is class 4.

Mount Dade 13,600 ft+; 13,600 ft+

The Hourglass. Class 2. This route has also been called the "Dade Couloir" and "East Couloir." This broad couloir leads from Treasure Lakes to the cirque south of Mount Dade. In early season, when it is filled with snow, it is a fine 1,000-foot climb, but the angle approaches 40° in places. Later in the summer it has patches of ice surrounded by much loose scree. *Variation:* It is possible to bypass the couloir by climbing rock ribs to the right of the couloir. There is a lot of loose rock on these ribs.

East Face. Class 4. First ascent August 20, 1960 by Frederick Roy Suppe. Climb the second chute from the northern end of the east face. Ascend the chute about two-thirds of the way up, go left a short distance, and climb toward a depression in the crest. Follow the crest to the summit. There is some extraordinarily loose rock in this chute.

Northeast Face. Class 4. First ascent September 1956 by Ray Van Aken and Kim Malville. Ascend a steep snow couloir that is to the left of a large rock face. Follow a ledge to the right to bypass some vertical sections. This leads to easier terrain and the summit. There is a lot of loose rock on this route.

North Face. Class 4. First ascent 1972 by Al Green, Dave Brown, and Bill Stronge. First winter ascent January 1986 by John Moynier and Tim Forsell. Ascend steep snow from the glacier north of Mount Dade to a rock rib which forks at the top of a broad couloir. Class 4 rock on the left side of the rib leads to the summit.

Further Reading: John Moynier and Claude

Fiddler. *Sierra Classics.* Evergreen, Colo.: Chockstone Press, 1993, pp. 214–216.

North Couloir. Class 4. This is a moderate snow/ice couloir. The couloir leads to the notch between the Cat's Ears and Mount Dade. Follow the northwest ridge to the summit.

Northwest Chute. Class 3. First ascent August 24, 1951 by Lloyd Chorley and Don Chorley. This chute leads from the basin southeast of Gabbot Pass to the northwest ridge of Mount Dade. Follow the northwest ridge to the summit.

West Chute. Class 2. First ascent August 19, 1911 by Liston and McKeen. This chute leads almost directly to the summit of Mount Dade from the basin southeast of Gabbot Pass. The rock rib immediately south of this chute is class 3.

South Slope. Class 2. This slope can be reached from the west side of the Sierra crest, or from the top of The Hourglass.

Mount Abbot   13,704 ft; 13,715 ft

North Couloir. Class 3. First ascent July 11, 1934 by David Brower, Hervey Voge, and Norman Clyde. First winter ascent December 30, 1967 by George Barnes,

Mount Dade and Mount Abbot from the east, September 2, 1965. Photo by Austin Post, No. F655-192, USGS Ice and Climate Project, GeoData Center, University of Alaska, Fairbanks.

Mount Dade from the northeast. Photo by R. J. Secor.

Lowell Smith, Margaret Young, Pat Buchanan, Bob Summers, and Dave Duff. This is the easiest route up Mount Abbot from Little Lakes Valley. Climb the prominent snow couloir that is north of the northeast buttress. Class 3 rock leads right from a point about halfway up the couloir. Go up and right to the north ridge, then follow the ridge south to where it becomes a knife edge. The first large boulder that blocks progress is passed on the left (east) side of the ridge. Then, cross to the right (west) side of the ridge and follow a ledge system (class 3 in places) below the crest. Climb back onto the crest of the ridge at the northern end of the summit plateau. *Variation:* Class 5. First ascent August 1984 by John Moynier. The north couloir can be followed all the way to the summit. This 1,000-foot couloir, with angles up

to 50°, is followed by a short rock wall, which is overcome by means of a blocky chimney.

Further Reading: John Moynier and Claude Fiddler. *Sierra Classics.* Evergreen, Colo.: Chockstone Press, 1993, pp. 216–217.

Northeast Buttress. Class 4. This buttress is left of the north couloir, and has much loose rock. But this may be the preferred route in early season as it is more direct, with snow covering most of the loose rock.

East Side. Class 3–4. Descended August 19, 1932 by Samuel W. French. Cross the glacier east of Mount Abbot and aim for a small, poorly defined ridge south of a prominent snow gully on the east side of the peak. (This snow gully is south of the northeast buttress.) Climb up and over ledges to the south of this small ridge. These

Mount Abbot from the northeast. Photo by R. J. Secor.

lead to the plateau beneath the summit. There is a lot of loose rock on this route. *Variation:* In early season it may be preferable to climb the snow gully to where it is possible to go left onto ledges to the north of the small ridge. This reduces, but does not entirely eliminate, exposure to rockfall.

Southeast Buttress. Class 3. First ascent August 19, 1932 by Samuel W. French. This route ascends the buttress at the left side of the east face of Mount Abbot. Climb the southern side of the buttress, making occasional detours onto its northern side. There is a lot of loose rock on this route.

Southwest Chute. Class 3. First ascent July 13, 1908 by James Hutchinson, Joseph LeConte, and Duncan McDuffie. Follow a talus slope east from the southern approach to Gabbot Pass and climb to the top of the talus beneath the summit of Mount Abbot. Three chutes are visible from this point. Climb the central chute; the entrance to this chute is just to the left of the top of the talus fan and close to the rock wall that descends directly from the summit. Ascend the right side of the chute to the class 3 headwall, which is much easier than it looks. The headwall ends at the summit plateau, and the true summit is a short talus walk to the left (north).

West Chimney. Class 4. First ascent July 22, 1953 by C. N. LaVene and Hervey Voge. This route ascends the farthest left of the three chutes that are visible from the top of the talus fan along the Southwest Chute route. A chockstone in this chute is passed on its left side, and the chute (or chimney) leads to a notch between Mount Abbot and an overhanging spire on the west ridge. Climb up and left from the notch to the summit plateau.

West Ridge. Class 4. First ascent August 30, 1927 by Robert Yatman and Maurice L. Higgins. Ascend the west ridge of Mount Abbot from Gabbot Pass. Some deviations from the crest of the ridge are needed to keep the difficulty within a class 4 range.

"Treasure Peak" Peak 12,920ft+; 12,975 ft;
0.6 mi NE of Mount Abbot

West Face and North Ridge. Class 3. First ascent August 19, 1972 by Andy Smatko, Barbara Lilley, Bill Schuler, and Tom Ross. First winter ascent March 1987 by John Moynier and Tim Forsell. Climb the west face on its northern side, and ascend easy class 3 rock on the face and ridge to the summit.

Band of Gypsies. I, 5.9+. First ascent 1994 by Alan Swanson and Urmas Franosch. This three-pitch route makes a direct ascent of the north face, up progressively looser, banded rock. The first and second pitches are 5.7 and 5.8 respectively, while the last pitch has been conservatively rated at 5.9+ due to loose rock and complicated routefinding.

Black Pyramid. I, 5.7. First ascent August 1979 by Kevin Rivett and David Babich. This route climbs the featureless wall to the left of a prominent, loose crack in the center of the east face. The first pitch goes up and left. The second pitch goes straight up to a small belay stance beneath a steep headwall. The next pitch goes up and left to the left edge of the headwall. This is followed by class 4 to the top.

"Petite Griffon" 13,040 ft+;
0.3 mi NNW of Mount Abbot; UTM 419395

This spire is between Mount Mills and Mount Abbot. It actually has two summits; the western one is the high point. Vertical climbing up the southeast side leads to the notch between the two summits, and a strenuous 5.7 crack ends atop the western summit; this was first climbed by Dave McDonald and David Harvey in June 1964. The north side of the western summit was climbed in July 1990 by John Moynier and Andy Selters via a three-pitch

Mount Abbot from the southwest. Photo by R. J. Secor.

5.9 route up a prominent left-facing corner.

The couloir that leads to the saddle between Mount Mills and Mount Abbot is 1,000 feet long and 40° steep.

Mount Mills   13,451 ft; 13,468 ft

East Couloir. Class 3. First ascent August 1921 by Norman Clyde. First winter ascent February 14, 1971 by Dick Beach, Bernard Hallet, Dave MacCoard, Charles Morfin, Frank Risely, and Mike Risely. This route ascends a large couloir that appears to be blocked by a large chockstone. The main difficulty is climbing over the chockstone; in early season the chockstone may be covered with verglas, and in late season it may be covered with sand. Continue up the loose couloir to the summit plateau. Move south over the plateau to the summit. *Variation:* Class 3. First ascent September 5, 1981 by Jackie Van Dalsem and Dave Heany. Go right (north) from the chockstone to an alcove. Climb up and

Mount Abbot and Mount Mills from the northeast. Photo by Austin Post, No. F655-191, USGS Ice and Climate Project, GeoData Center, University of Alaska, Fairbanks.

right from the alcove onto some ledges, then climb up and over the ledges to the top of the couloir. Cross the plateau to the summit. This variation avoids much of the loose rock found in the main couloir. *Variation:* Class 3. First ascent June 21, 1980 by Cuno Ranschau and Larry Machleder. Climb a chute located about 100 feet south of the chockstone. Continue up the chute, then climb from below and left of a large rock outcrop to gain the summit plateau.

South Notch. Class 4, A1. First ascent July 1960 by Rich Gnagy, Barbara Lilley, and Sy Ossofsky. Climb to the notch between Mount Abbot and Mount Mills from the east. Some aid climbing is needed to climb out of the notch and onto the ridge. Follow the ridge to the summit.

Southwest Face. Class 4. First ascent July 23, 1953 by Jim Koontz, Marian Steineke, Louis Christian, and Jim Carl. Climb avalanche chutes on the right side of the face. The last 200-foot section is class 4.

North Face. Class 3; ice axe needed. First ascent July 10, 1908 by James S. Hutchinson, Joseph LeConte, and Duncan McDuffie. From the Fourth Recess, climb onto the glacier that is north of Mount Mills. Ascend the couloir between the central and western rock ribs on the north face, then climb onto the central rock rib. Traverse to the right near the top of the central rib, then ascend the western rock rib to the summit plateau.

North Ridge. Class 3 with a rappel or a class 4 down climb. Follow the north ridge and either down climb or rappel to the top of the east couloir. Ascend the couloir a short distance to the summit plateau.

"Ruby Peak" 13,188 ft; 13,198 ft;
0.7 mi SW of Ruby Lake
"Ruby Wall" is the east face of the ridge between Peak 13,188ft (13,198 ft) and Peak 13,125ft (12,960 ft+).

The Gendarmes. Class 5. First ascent 1963 by Mike Loughman and Jay Waller. Traverse the gendarmes along the Sierra crest between Mount Mills and Ruby Peak.

West Couloir. Class 3. First ascent July 24, 1946 by Fritz Gerstaker and Virginia Whitacre. Climb the couloir and its side buttress, which is located immediately beneath the highest pinnacle.

West Wall and North Ridge. Class 5. First ascent August 17, 1953 by Jim Koontz, Ralph Perry, and Fred Peters. From Snow Lakes in the Fourth Recess, climb the chockstone-filled chimney that leads to the large col on

the north ridge of Ruby Peak. Leave the chimney partway up, and climb the face to the col. Traverse south along the north ridge, on its right (west) side for the most part, to the summit.

North Arête. Class 5. Traverse the ridge from Mono Pass.

Pteradon. III, 5.10, A1, or 5.11. First ascent October 1986 by Robert SP Parker and Bill Kerwin. First free ascent July 1989 by Richard Leversee, Kim Miller, and Roanne Miller. This route is on the wall that is to the right (north) of the main Ruby Wall, in the cirque that is hidden when viewed from Ruby Lake. Climb the farthest left outside corner of the four dihedrals on this hidden wall. The corner has a large roof halfway up its left side, followed by 3- to 8-inch widening crack. Take a double set of protection, from ½-inch to 5-inch.

Daphne. IV, 5.10b. First ascent by Robert SP Parker, Mark Houston, and Andy Selters. This route makes a direct ascent of the prominent crack that leads to the diamond-shaped headwall, but goes left into the dihedral on the left side of the headwall below the top.

Wide Sargasso Sea. IV, 5.10b. First ascent September 1988 by Robert SP Parker and Malcolm Ives. This route climbs the crack system to the left of the prominent crack, but finishes by following the crack directly up the headwall.

Central Route. IV, 5.10. First ascent July 10, 1982 by Galen Rowell and Mike White. The start of this route is beneath and slightly to the right of the two prominent dihedrals on the east face of Ruby Wall. Begin by climbing a pair of cracks (5.10), then pass through a slot, to a belay stance under a roof. Climb through another roof and up a flared corner (5.10) and up and left to a belay ledge; off-route cracks (marked with old rappel slings) lead up and left from the ledge. Go straight up from the ledge and climb a smooth corner that arches to the left (5.10) to another stance. Continue up a left-facing corner/chimney, passing a chockstone (5.8) to some big ledges. Climb up and under an overhanging ramp (i.e., an arch, 5.9+) and then move left to some ledges at the base of the first dihedral. Climb the dihedral (5.10-; large cams are needed) to the first ledge at its top; an off-route dihedral goes up from the ledge. Move left for 40 feet (class 4) to the bottom of a gritty, steep crack on the face. Climb the crack (5.10) and then move left and up to a belay stance on some blocks. This is followed by a 5.7 chimney and 200 feet of easy class 5 to the top.

RUBY PEAK

RUBY WALL

Wide Sargasso Sea

Daphne

East Arête

Pteradon

Daphne

Wide Sargasso Sea

Central Route

Ruby Wall from the southeast. Photo by R. J. Secor.

East Arête. IV, 5.10. First ascent August 1984 by David Wilson and Galen Rowell. This route ascends a buttress on the left side of the Ruby Wall. Eight long, steep pitches of fine climbing (5.7–5.9, with a couple of 5.10 spots) over steep rock lead to the summit. Cross a permanent snowfield and begin by climbing over loose, fluted overhangs. The sixth pitch is an exposed traverse to the right of, and then into the notch behind, a large overhanging block.

East Ridge. Class 3. There is a steep section at the bottom of the east ridge, which is bypassed on its left side.

East Couloirs. Class 3. First ascent August 1, 1946 by Lester Lavelle and Malcolm Smith. First winter ascent 1980s by John Moynier. These couloirs, which are south of the east ridge, have an angle of about 35°.

"Lookout Peak"   11,902 ft; 11,898 ft;
0.3 mi SE of Ruby Lake

This peak has also been called "Tempest Peak" and "Ruby Peak." The northeast ridge and east slope are class 2.

"Little Lakes Peak"   12,782 ft; 12,808 ft;
0.8 mi SW of Mount Morgan

First ascent October 2, 1947 by A. J. Reyman, via the class 2 scree slope on the south side of the peak. First winter ascent in 1980s by John Moynier.

The traverse from Mount Morgan is class 3, and the northwest ridge is an enjoyable class 4 route. The southwest side of the peak consists of class 5 slabs, which have been climbed from Morgan Pass. The west couloir consists of 35° snow in winter and early spring.

Mount Morgan   13,748 ft; 13,748 ft

First ascent 1870 by the Wheeler Survey. First winter ascent April 4, 1971 by Howard Stephens, Bill Britten, Bob Eakin, Greg Emigh, John Finn, Jurgis Gedaugas, Bill Houze, Don Inman, Paul Kellow, Stuart Long, Roy Magnuson, Jeff Moore, Ed Rose, Barbara Rosen, Ben Schiffrin, Ken Berger, Dick Ramirez, John Arden, and John Arden, Jr. This peak is class 1 from Francis Lake; keep to the far right-hand (north) side of the northeast slope for the easiest route. Class 2 from both forks of

Morgan Creek. The west slope from Little Lakes Valley is a loose, tedious class 2 climb. The southwest ridge is class 3 with many class 4 moves from Little Lakes Peak. There is a splendid view of Bear Creek Spire, Mount Dade, Mount Abbot, and Mount Mills from the summit.

Further Reading: John Moynier. *Backcountry Skiing in the High Sierra.* Evergreen, Colo.: Chockstone Press, 1992, p. 174; John Moynier and Claude Fiddler. *Sierra Classics.* Evergreen, Colo.: Chockstone Press, 1993, pp. 204–205.

Broken Finger Peak   13,080 ft+; 13,120 ft+

Northeast Couloir and Northwest Ridge. Class 3. First ascent October 28, 1967 by Frank Yates, Bill Schuler, and Andy Smatko (who broke a finger during an attempt on the southeast ridge earlier that year). Ascend steep snow and loose class 3 rock in the couloir that leads to the col northwest of the summit. From the col, traverse across the west side of the peak, climb over two ribs, and then ascend a gully that leads up to a false summit. Traverse southeast over another false summit to the true summit.

"Wheeler Peak"   13,000 ft+; 12,966 ft;
1.4 mi NE of Broken Finger Peak

This is the high point of Wheeler Ridge. The north summit is the true summit. The northeast and southwest ridges are class 2. First ascent August 14, 1945 by Don McGeein and Virgil Sisson.

Northwest Couloir. III, 5.4. First ascent December 1982 by Robert SP Parker. The angle in this couloir never exceeds 50°.

Northwest Arête. III, 5.8. First ascent May 1984 by Susan Williams and Robert SP Parker. Follow the arête that is left of the northwest couloir.

North Arête. Class 5. First ascent 1991 by Claude Fiddler and Jim Keating. This route starts from the junction of the north and northwest face.

Recess Peak   12,813 ft; 12,836 ft

Southwest Arête. Class 3. This is a straightforward climb up steeply tilted flakes along the arête. The problem is approaching the arête. Leave the John Muir Trail immediately south of the junction with the Bear Ridge Trail. A good use trail leads northeast to the meadows that are southwest of Volcanic Knob. Using a map (or maps) and compass, go southeast, either over or around an obtuse ridge leading southwest from Volcanic Knob, to the foot of the arête and follow it to the summit.

Southeast Ridge. Class 3. First ascent June 26, 1985 by Ron Jones, Norm Rohn, Nathan Wong, and Joy Fagert. Leave the Italy Pass Trail at the 9,680-foot level and follow the east bank of the outlet stream of Hilgard

Ruby Peak from the east. Photo by R. J. Secor.

Lake. Cross the stream before reaching Hilgard Lake, then ascend the easy southern scree slope of Peak 12,680ft+ (12,692 ft). Descend the northeast side of this peak, then follow the class 3 southeast ridge to the summit of Recess Peak. *Variation:* Class 2. First ascent 1997 by Barbara Cohen, Charlie Knapke, and Greg Gerlach. Descend the northwest side of Peak 12,680ft+ (12,692 ft) and climb a chute on the southern side of Recess Peak to the summit.

Northeast Arête. Class 3. Leave the upper reaches of the Second Recess and hike into the large cirque that is east of Recess Peak. Climb to the col on the northeast arête and follow it to the summit.

Peak 12,760ft+   12,720 ft+;
0.7 mi NNW of Mount Hilgard

Northeast Arête. Class 4. First ascent August 11, 1953 by Jim Koontz, Al Schmitz, George Wallerstein, and Fred Peters.

West Face. Class 2. First ascent July 6, 1954 by a Sierra Club Base Camp party. Ascend the west face diagonally to the apparent high point, which is the summit.

Mount Hilgard   13,361 ft; 13,361 ft

First ascent July 10, 1905 by Charles F. Urquhart. The south slope is class 2. The southeast face from the outlet of Lake Italy is class 2. A narrow gully on the southeast face leads to a headwall. Bypass the headwall by climbing a small chute to its left. The east face is class 2 via a loose chute located south of the broad east ridge. The northeast ridge is class 3–4, and was climbed on September 8, 1963 by Arkel Erb, Ed Lane, and Barbara Lilley. Several gendarmes on this ridge are passed on one side of the ridge or the other.

The traverse from Mount Hilgard to Mount Gabb is typically done on the southern side of the Mono Divide by following benches (at an altitude of 11,800 feet) from the eastern side of Mount Hilgard to the southern side of Mount Gabb, or vice versa. This is mostly class 2, but some class 3 is encountered along the benches.

Mount Gabb   13,741 ft; 13,711 ft

South Slope and Southwest Ridge. Class 2–3. First ascent June 17, 1917 by H. H. Bliss and A. L. Jordan. Go north from Lake Italy to a band of cliffs south of Mount Gabb. Climb through these via chutes and gullies, then go left to the southwest ridge. Follow the ridge to the summit. It is possible to continue up the south slope to the summit, but this increases the difficulty to class 3; this route is also interspersed with broad, sandy chutes.

Southeast Face. Class 3. First ascent June 17, 1993 by Yorgos Marinakis and Harry Marinakis. There are three ribs on the southeast face of Mount Gabb. This route ascends the left-hand rib. The difficulty increases from easy class 3 at the bottom to more difficult class 3 near the top.

Northeast Ridge. Class 3. Keep to the southern side of this ridge while climbing it from Gabbot Pass.

North Face. Class 4. First ascent August 13, 1953 by Jim Koontz, Ralph Perry, Fred Peters, George Wallerstein, and Al Schmitz. Cross the glacier on the north side of Mount Gabb to a point that is west of the prominent split on the north face. Ascend slabs to the split, then follow the split up and right to a large chockstone. Pass the chockstone via exposed ledges, a 25-foot crack, and a 20-foot chimney, then continue to the top of the west wall of the split. This leads to the northwest ridge. Follow the northwest ridge to the summit.

Glacier Route. Class 2. Head southwest from Upper Mills Creek Lake to the glacier beneath the saddle on Mount Gabb's northwest ridge. Cross the glacier and climb the scree headwall to the saddle. Climb over large blocks along the northwest ridge to the summit.

Northwest Ridge, East Spur. Class 3. From Upper Mills Creek Lake ascend steep, unstable talus to the notch that is right (west) of the prominent gendarme on the east spur of the northwest ridge. Follow the ridge from the notch to the summit.

Peak 12,360ft+   12,320 ft+;
0.5 mi W of Upper Mills Creek Lake

Northeast Couloir. Class 3. First ascent September 8, 1927 by James Wright. Climb over talus from Upper Mills Creek Lake and ascend the snow-filled couloir to the north ridge. Follow the ridge to the summit.

Peak 12,692ft   12,691 ft; 1.8 mi NW of Mount Mills

First ascent August 3, 1864 by William H. Brewer. The east slope is class 2 from the head of the Third Recess.

Peak 12,193ft   12,160 ft+; 0.7 mi S of Frog Lake

West Face. Class 3–4. First ascent July 23, 1953 by Hervey Voge, Jan Collard, and Mary Crothers. Ascend the west ridge and west face from the Second Recess to the top of Peak 12,160ft+ (12,145 ft). Follow the ridge south to the top of Peak 12,193ft (12,160 ft+).

Mono Rock   11,554 ft; 11,555 ft

East Slope. Class 2. First ascent July 18, 1934 by Norman Clyde and friend. Ascend the east slope from Fourth Recess Lake to the saddle south of Mono Rock. Follow the ridge from the saddle to the summit.

East Face. Class 4. First ascent August 17, 1953 by Bill Wallace. Ascend the east face up and right to a small bowl. Climb to the summit from the bowl.

North Face. Class 5. First ascent August 6, 1946 by Lester LaVelle, Paul Hunter, Willard Dean, Fred Foulon, Dan Sharp, Joe Sharp, and Homer Wellman. One difficult pitch is encountered.

WRINKLES

Royce Peak to Merriam Peak. From Merriam Lake, the best route for these two peaks is to climb the southwest ridge of Royce Peak first and then descend to the Royce-Merriam Saddle before climbing Merriam Peak.

Peaks of Little Lakes Valley. Mount Mills, Mount Abbot, Mount Dade, and Bear Creek Spire can be easily climbed in a day from Mosquito Flat during the quota period, eliminating the need for an overnight permit. Little Lakes Valley is a heavily used area, and day outings are preferable to overnight trips in this area.

Gabbot Pass vs. Hilgard Pass. The Mono Divide presents a formidable barrier west of the Sierra crest. Hilgard Pass is a more direct route between Mono Creek and Lake Italy, but Gabbot Pass is much easier, and involves less elevation gain.

Mount Gabb from the northeast. Photo by R. J. Secor.

Mammoth Lakes and the Silver Divide

Many people get their first introduction to the High Sierra at Mammoth Lakes. Mammoth Lakes is a popular resort year-round, featuring one of the largest ski areas in the country. It offers excellent summer fishing as well. But probably few visitors to the Mammoth Lakes area realize that it is located on one of the great edges of North America: the division between the lush Pacific coast and the Great American Desert. Downhill skiers can ski down one run into the Pacific Ocean watershed, and down another into the Great Basin watershed. Typical winter storms move out of the west, and by April, the snowpack at Mammoth Pass, atop the Sierra crest, has an average water content of 42.4 inches. Less than 2 miles to the east, the average April water content drops to 20.0 inches.

This region covers the Sierra crest from Mono Pass (south) to Minaret Summit. Its western limit is Silver Creek and the Middle Fork of the San Joaquin River.

HISTORY

The history of this region follows the pattern of the rest of the High Sierra. James T. Gardiner of the California Geological Survey climbed Red Slate Mountain in 1864. Mountaineers interested in sport climbing visited the region in 1902, with the Hutchinson brothers and Charles Noble climbing Red and White Mountain that year.

By the 1920s this region had become known as a resort, and Convict Lake served the needs of city residents looking for rest and relaxation by providing sport fishing in the mountains. John Mendenhall visited Convict Lake annually with his family during this period, and gradually became interested in the sport of mountaineering, probably by gazing up at the impressive north face of Mount Morrison from the lake. He wondered if

Mount Morrison had ever been climbed, so he wrote to the most experienced Sierra mountaineer of the day, Norman Clyde, to find out. Upon receiving this letter, Clyde hopped into his 1927 Chevrolet, drove to Convict Lake, and made the first ascent of Mount Morrison. As John said to me many years later, "I kept my plans secret from then on." Despite not bagging Mount Morrison it could be said that Mendenhall captured the greatest prize of all, by making the first proper roped climb in the Sierra—on the northeast gully of Laurel Mountain in 1930.

MAPS

USGS. *7.5-minute series:* Mt. Morgan, Mt. Abbot, Graveyard Peak, Sharktooth Peak, Convict Lake, Bloody Mtn., Crystal Crag, Mammoth Mtn. *30 x 60–minute series:* Bishop, Shaver Lake, Benton Range, Yosemite Valley.

USFS. A Guide to the John Muir Wilderness and the Sequoia–Kings Canyon Wilderness (1:63,360).

Tom Harrison Cartography. Mammoth High Country and Mono Divide High Country.

Map Link 15-minute series. Mt. Tom, Mt. Abbot, Mt. Morrison, Devils Postpile, Kaiser Peak.

Wilderness Press 15-minute series. Mt. Abbot, Devils Postpile.

ROADS

Lake Thomas A. Edison Road

This road provides access to the southern part of the Mammoth Region. It is described in Chapter 10, The Mono Recesses.

Mammoth Lakes and the Silver Divide

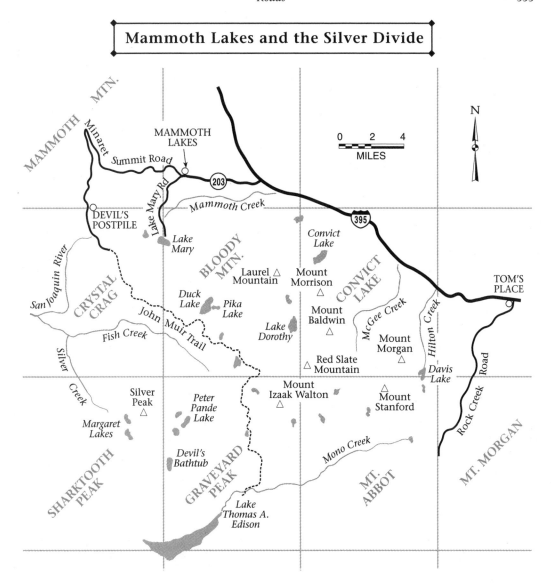

Rock Creek Road

The Rock Creek Road leads to the trailheads for the Hilton Creek Trail and the Mono Pass Trail. It is described in Chapter 10, The Mono Recesses.

Hilton Creek Road

Hilton Creek Road leads to the Hilton Creek Trailhead for the Hilton Creek Trail. Leave Highway 395 at the major interchange approximately 4 miles north of Tom's Place, or about 11 miles south of Highway 203, the road leading to Mammoth Lakes. Go southwest from Highway 395 to Crowley Lake Drive and turn right. Drive through the small community of Hilton Creek (locally known as "Crowley Lake") for 1.8 miles, then turn left onto a dirt road. The road goes past a campground and climbs for 2 miles before arriving at the hikers' trailhead.

The stock trailhead can be reached by turning left off Crowley Lake Drive 1 mile from its junction with the road leading to Highway 395. The trailhead is 0.5 mile from Crowley Lake Drive.

McGee Creek Road

This road provides access to the trailhead for the McGee Creek Trail. (It should not be confused with the creek of the same name, which is located farther south, near Bishop.) Leave Highway 395 about 6.4 miles north of Tom's Place, or about 8.4 miles south of the turnoff for Highway 203 and Mammoth Lakes. Go southwest from Highway 395, cross Crowley Lake Drive, and follow the McGee Creek Road for 4 miles, past a campground, to the trailhead for the McGee Creek Trail.

Convict Lake Road

Convict Lake Road leads to the trailhead for the Convict Canyon Trail. It leaves Highway 395 10.4 miles north of Tom's Place, or 4.4 miles south of its junction with the road leading to Mammoth Lakes, Highway 203. The road goes southwest, and after 2 miles it meets the trailhead for the Convict Canyon Trail. The road continues another 0.7 mile to Convict Lake.

Sherwin Creek Road

Sherwin Creek Road leads to the trailhead for the Laurel Creek Trail. The road begins along Old Mammoth Road in the town of Mammoth Lakes. Go south along Old Mammoth Road from Main Street (Highway 203) for 0.9 mile to where Sherwin Creek Road branches off to the left. There is a fork 1.3 miles later; go left. The road continues east another 1.9 miles, past a campground, and to another road, which branches off to the south. Continue east on the main road another 0.9 mile to another road, which branches off to the south. (This road goes up Laurel Creek.) Sherwin Creek Road goes east and then northeast another 1.5 miles before meeting Highway 395.

Lake Mary Road

Lake Mary Road provides access to the trailheads serving the Duck Pass Trail, the Mammoth Crest Trail, and the Mammoth Pass Trail. The road begins at the three-way junction in Mammoth Lakes where Main Street ends, Minaret Road goes north, and Lake Mary Road goes west. Lake Mary Road goes past Twin Lakes and, after 3.4 miles, it meets the eastern terminus of a road that goes around Lake Mary. This road comes to a junction after 0.2 mile; go left another 0.7 mile, past a campground, to the Duck Pass Trail trailhead. Returning to Lake Mary Road, the road passes the northern shore of Lake Mary for 0.3 mile before coming to another junction; this road goes left and comes to a junction after 0.2 mile. Go right another 0.5 mile to the trailhead for the Mammoth Crest Trail on the northern shore of Lake George. Lake Mary Road continues another 0.9 mile to the Mammoth Pass Trail trailhead on the northern shore of Horseshoe Lake.

Minaret Summit Road

Minaret Summit Road starts at the junction of Main Street and Lake Mary Road in the town of Mammoth Lakes. Minaret Summit Road goes north, and after 1 mile it meets the junction with the Mammoth Scenic Loop, a euphemistic name that makes names like "Freedom Highway," "Friendship Road," and "Peace Road" sound trite (it was actually constructed to serve as a year-round escape route in case of volcanic activity). Minaret Summit Road continues past the Mammoth Mountain Ski Area another 3.9 miles to Minaret Summit, the lowest road that crosses the Sierra crest in the High Sierra. Traffic is restricted beyond this point during the summer; private vehicles may travel the remaining portion of the road only during certain hours. (A shuttle-bus service operates during the restricted hours.) Minaret Summit Road descends the west side of the pass for 2.6 miles to Agnew Meadows. It then turns south and, after another 6.4 miles, meets the junction with the road leading to Devil's Postpile. The right (west) fork travels another 0.4 mile to Devil's Postpile National Monument; the left (south) fork goes another 1.6 miles to Red's Meadow.

CARBON DIOXIDE POISONING

The area surrounding Mammoth Mountain has had carbon dioxide gas (CO_2) venting up through the soil in recent years. This is believed to be due to increased seismic (and perhaps volcanic) activity since the early 1990s. This may be a hazard to health in enclosed spaces, such as restrooms, tents, or perhaps along lakeshores, as heavier-than-air carbon dioxide tends to collect in low, enclosed spaces. Carbon dioxide gas dissipates quickly in the open air, and in most cases, this phenomenon is not hazardous.

But this may be deadly in the winter, as the porous nature of snow captures the gas at dangerous levels. This is not dangerous to someone who is walking or skiing above the snow, but it may be fatal to those who are in a snow cave, igloo, pit, tree well, or even in a tent erected on the surface of the snow. Symptoms of CO_2 poisoning include headache, dizziness, a racing heart rate, and rapid breathing.

This may seem to be a moot point, as camping is prohibited on Mammoth Mountain, summer and winter. But it is possible that there may be other areas with high CO_2 emissions in the Mammoth region that have not yet been discovered.

TRAILS

Mono Pass Trail   15 miles
This trail is described in Chapter 10, The Mono Recesses.

Golden Lake Trail   ¾ mile
The Golden Lake Trail leaves the Mono Pass Trail approximately 2½ miles north of Mono Pass (0 mi; 10,440 ft+). It follows the northern bank of Golden Creek to Golden Lake (¾ mi; 10,994 ft).

Pioneer Basin Trail   2 miles
This trail leaves the Mono Pass Trail a short distance downstream from where the trail to Fourth Recess Lake leaves the Mono Pass Trail (0 mi; 10,040 ft+). The Pioneer Basin Trail goes north, and after many switchbacks it reaches the lowest of the Pioneer Basin Lakes (2 mi; 10,800 ft+). A good use trail continues up into beautiful Pioneer Basin.

Hopkins Creek Trail   3 miles
The Hopkins Creek Trail leaves the Mono Pass Trail ¾ mile downstream from its junction with the trail that ascends the Third Recess (0 mi; 9,260 ft+). The Hopkins Creek Trail goes north, and after many switchbacks it crosses Hopkins Creek. A short side trail leads up to Lower Hopkins Lake from here; the Hopkins Creek Trail continues upstream into the beautiful upper por-

tion of Hopkins Creek (3 mi; 10,400 ft+). A good use trail leads to Upper Hopkins Lake.

Laurel Lake Trail   3 miles
Don't confuse this trail with the Laurel Creek Trail on the east side of the Sierra crest near Mammoth Lakes. The Laurel Lake Trail leaves the Mono Creek Trail 2¼ miles downstream from the Hopkins Creek Trail (0 mi; 8,800 ft+). It ascends with many switchbacks up the west bank of Laurel Creek (not to be confused with the creek of the same name farther north) before crossing the creek and making a gentler climb to Laurel Lake (3 mi; 10,804 ft). A good use trail leads farther upstream to Grinnell Lake.

Further Reading: Steve Roper. *Sierra High Route.* Seattle: The Mountaineers Books, 1997, p. 144.

Devil's Bathtub Trail   4 miles
A quota trail. This trail starts from the end of Lake Thomas A. Edison Road, above Vermilion Campground (0 mi; 7,800 ft+). It follows an abandoned dirt road northeast, then north past Twin Meadows to meet the side trail leading to Graveyard Meadows along Cold Creek (2 mi; 8,360 ft+). The Devil's Bathtub Trail continues north to the outlet of Devil's Bathtub (2 mi; 9,160 ft+).

Goodale Pass Trail   8½ miles
A quota trail. This trail starts from the end of Lake Thomas A. Edison Road, above Vermilion Campground (0 mi; 7,800 ft+). It follows the dirt road of the Devil's Bathtub Trail a short distance, and then turns right, paralleling the northwest shore of Lake Thomas A. Edison. After crossing Cold Creek, it meets the Quail Meadows Trail (1¼ mi; 7,680 ft+). It then goes left and climbs up to Graveyard Meadows (2 mi; 8,840 ft+) where it meets a side trail that leads west to the Devil's Bathtub Trail. The Goodale Pass Trail continues upstream to Upper Graveyard Meadow, where it meets another side trail, which goes west to Graveyard Lakes (2 mi; 9,400 ft+). The Goodale Pass Trail continues up to Goodale Pass (2 mi; 10,997 ft) and descends the north side of the pass to meet the John Muir Trail north of Silver Pass (1¼ mi; 10,320 ft+).

Quail Meadows Trail   4½ miles
This trail leaves the Goodale Pass Trail after 1¼ miles from the trailhead near the western shore of Lake Thomas A. Edison (0 mi; 7,680 ft+). The Quail Meadows Trail goes parallel to the northwest shore of Lake

Thomas A. Edison. It then passes through Quail Meadows along the north bank of Mono Creek before meeting the John Muir Trail north of Mono Creek (4½ mi; 7,880 ft+). Vermilion Valley Resort, located at the southwestern shore of Lake Thomas A. Edison, offers hikers a twice-daily water taxi service across the lake, saving much tedious walking.

John Muir Trail   30¾ miles

A quota trail. After the John Muir Trail crosses Mono Creek on a bridge, it meets the Quail Meadows Trail just east of the meadows (0 mi; 7,880 ft+). The John Muir Trail goes right and ascends the northern bank of Mono Creek before crossing the North Fork and meeting the Mono Pass Trail (1½ mi; 8,320 ft+). The John Muir Trail continues north and, after passing through Pocket Meadow, it crosses the North Fork of Mono Creek. It then meets a side trail leading to Mott Lake (1½ mi; 8,960 ft+). The John Muir Trail goes west and makes a steep ascent before making a gradual climb into the beautiful basin south of Silver Pass. After Silver Pass Lake (3 mi; 10,400 ft+) comes Silver Pass (½ mi; 10,920 ft+), with views of Mount Ritter and Banner Peak to the northwest and Seven Gables to the south. The trail descends the north side of the pass and meets the Goodale Pass Trail (1½ mi; 10,520 ft+). The John Muir Trail goes northeast from this junction and descends into Cascade Valley (bears prowl through this area) to meet the Fish Creek Trail (2¾ mi; 9,080 ft+). The John Muir Trail goes to the right, crosses Fish Creek, and meets the McGee Creek Trail at Tully Hole (1¼ mi; 9,514 ft+). It then makes a steep climb to the north, crosses a small pass (to 10,367 ft+), and crosses the outlet of Lake Virginia (2 mi; 10,338 ft). The trail continues northwest and crosses another small pass (to 10,499 ft+) before dropping down to Purple Lake (1¾ mi; 9,928 ft). Camping and wood fires are prohibited within 300 feet of the outlet of Purple Lake (bears prowl through this area). The trail turns southwest from Purple Lake and traverses around a broad ridge to meet the Duck Pass Trail (2½ mi; 10,170 ft+).

From the Duck Pass Trail junction, the John Muir Trail traverses high above Fish Creek along the rim of its canyon to where it meets the Deer Creek Trail, after crossing Deer Creek (5¼ mi; 9,055 ft+). The John Muir Trail makes a gradual descent from the junction, then slightly ascends to cross a small pass (to 9,186 ft+) to

Upper Crater Meadow to meet two side trails that lead to Mammoth Pass (2¼ mi; 8,924 ft+). The John Muir Trail descends to the northwest to the Fish Creek Trail (3½ mi; 7,611 ft+); Red's Meadow resort is ¼ mile to the north, and the campground (with hot springs!) is ½ mile further. The John Muir Trail continues west to a four-way trail junction (½ mi; 7,415 ft+). One branch of the John Muir Trail goes west and crosses the Middle Fork of the San Joaquin on a bridge. A trail leads south for 1 mile to Rainbow Falls. But the classic route of the John Muir Trail goes north to Devil's Postpile (¾ mi; 7,611 ft+) and continues north to a trail junction (¼ mi; 7,520 ft+). The John Muir Trail goes west on a bridge across the Middle Fork of the San Joaquin River from here, while the Devil's Postpile National Monument Visitor Center is ½ mile to the north.

Mott Lake Trail   2 miles

This trail leaves the John Muir Trail at its upper crossing of the North Fork of Mono Creek (0 mi; 8,960 ft+). At first, the Mott Lake Trail ascends along the south bank of the creek. It then crosses to its north bank before arriving at Mott Lake (2 mi; 10,080 ft+). Those continuing to Bighorn Lake and Rohn Pass should first circle Mott Lake on its southern and eastern shores. The outlet of Bighorn Lake is best approached from the southwest to avoid the cliffs that are due south of the lake; Bighorn Lake is best passed on its east shore.

Hilton Creek Trail   10 miles

A quota trail. Bears prowl through this area. The description for this trail begins along Rock Creek Road, 9.2 miles from Tom's Place (0 mi; 9,840 ft+). The trail goes north from Rock Creek Road and traverses along the western rim of the canyon of Rock Creek to where it meets the stock trail coming up from a lower portion of Rock Creek Road (1¼ mi; 9,960 ft+). The Hilton Creek Trail continues traversing along the bench, turning west and climbing before arriving at a trail junction (2½ mi; 10,080 ft+). A side trail heads southwest from here and leads to the upper Hilton Creek Lakes. The Hilton Creek Trail continues downstream to the eastern shore of Davis Lake (1¼ mi; 9,808 ft). The trail continues down Hilton Creek, at first on the east bank and later on the west, to a fork (4 mi; 8,595 ft+). The hikers' trail goes west and then north to the hikers' trailhead (1 mi; 7,546 ft+). The stock trail continues downstream to the stock trailhead near the community of Hilton Creek (locally known as "Crowley Lake").

McGee Creek Trail   11½ miles

A quota trail. Campfires are prohibited along this entire trail east of McGee Pass. The McGee Creek Trail starts from the end of the McGee Creek Road (0 mi; 8,136 ft+). It ascends the canyon of McGee Creek and crosses the stream twice before coming to a junction (3 mi; 9,449 ft). A trail goes southeast to Steelhead Lake; just beyond the initial junction, another trail goes northwest to an abandoned mine on the southeast slopes of Mount Baldwin. The McGee Creek Trail continues upstream another 2 miles to Big McGee Lake (2 mi; 10,600 ft+). The trail passes north of the lake, climbs up to Little McGee Lake, and climbs farther into the spectacular basin east of McGee Pass. The trail approaches McGee Pass (2 mi; 11,876 ft+) from the north and descends the western side over many grassy benches down to Fish Creek. The trail crosses Fish Creek several times before descending to Tully Hole, where it meets the John Muir Trail (4½ mi; 9,514 ft+).

Fish Creek Trail   21½ miles

A quota trail. The Fish Creek Trail starts near Red's Meadow (0 mi; 7,611 ft+). The trail goes south, crosses the John Muir Trail, passes a fork leading to Rainbow Falls, and descends to Crater Creek. It follows the west bank of Crater Creek a considerable distance downstream before crossing the creek (5 mi; 6,890 ft+). The trail continues south and turns east on the rim of Fish Valley before descending into the valley. The trail crosses Fish Creek on a bridge and then meets a trail that ascends Silver Creek to Margaret Lakes (5 mi; 6,299 ft+). The Fish Creek Trail continues east to meet the Minnow Creek Trail (3 mi; 7,152 ft+). Nearby are the delightful Fish Creek Hot Springs (also known as Iva Belle Hot Springs). The Fish Creek Trail crosses Sharktooth Creek just beyond the hot springs and makes a short, steep climb (to 7,743 ft) before descending to the upper portion of Fish Creek. The trail follows the south bank before crossing over to the north bank and entering Cascade Valley (bears prowl through this area). The Fish Creek Trail meets a side trail leading up Minnow Creek, and soon comes to the junction with the Purple Lake Trail (5 mi; 8,333 ft+). It then continues upstream to meet the John Muir Trail at the head of the valley (3½ mi; 9,080 ft+).

Minnow Creek Trail   8¼ miles

This trail leaves the Fish Creek Trail near Fish Creek Hot Springs (0 mi; 7,152 ft+). It follows Sharktooth Creek and it meets a short side trail that leads to Lost Keys Lakes (1¼ mi; 8,661 ft+). The Minnow Creek Trail makes a slight climb and then gently descends to the junction with Long Canyon Trail (1¾ mi; 9,055 ft+). The Minnow Creek Trail goes southeast, passing Marsh Lake, to meet the junction of a side trail that descends to Cascade Valley (½ mi; 8,989 ft+). The Minnow Creek Trail continues southeast, going around Jackson Meadow to meet a side trail that leads to Olive Lake (2 mi; 9,400 ft+). It then skirts the northern shore of Grassy Lake, passes a junction (¾ mi; 9,560 ft+) with a trail leading to Peter Pande Lake, and meets a short side trail that goes to Wilber May Lake (½ mi; 9,760 ft+). The Minnow Creek Trail turns to the east and, after climbing a small ridge (to 10,440 ft+), rounds the southwestern shore of Lake of the Lone Indian and meets the Goodale Pass Trail immediately west of Papoose Lake (1½ mi; 10,320 ft+).

The Minnow Creek Trail has many side trails branching off from it. The Lost Keys Lakes Trail is 1 mile long, ending at the easternmost of the lakes at 9,514 ft+. The Long Canyon Trail leads 3 miles to Beetle Bug Lake (9,604 ft). The trail leading down to Cascade Valley meets the Fish Creek Trail (1 mi; 8,333 ft+). The Olive Lake Trail ends at Olive Lake (1½ mi; 9,720 ft+). The Peter Pande Lake Trail climbs a ridge (to 10,200 ft+) before descending to the lake (1½ mi; 9,960 ft+) and the trail to Wilber May Lake (½ mi; 9,800 ft+).

Purple Lake Trail   2½ miles

This trail leaves the Fish Creek Trail in Cascade Valley (0 mi; 8,333 ft+) and ascends the northwestern bank of Purple Creek to meet the John Muir Trail north of the outlet of Purple Lake (2½ mi; 9,928 ft+). Camping and wood campfires are prohibited within 300 feet of the outlet of Purple Lake. Bears prowl through this area.

Convict Canyon Trail   7½ miles

A non-quota trail. This trail leads from Convict Lake to Lake Dorothy and Lake Genevieve. From the hikers' parking area north of Convict Lake (0 mi; 7,546 ft+), the trail makes a slight climb and descent to meet the fishing trail that follows the northwestern shore of Convict Lake (½ mi; 7,620 ft+). (Alternatively, one can hike from the end of Convict Lake Road, saving ¼ mile of hiking, but overnight parking is prohibited there.) The Convict Canyon Trail follows the lakeshore and climbs along the western bank of Convict Creek to the remains of a bridge that once crossed the creek (3 mi; 8,989 ft+). The trail continues up the eastern bank of the creek and circles around Mildred Lake. It then makes a brief ascent to meet a side trail that follows the eastern shore of Lake Dorothy and leads to Bighorn Lake (1½ mi; 10,275 ft+). The Convict Canyon Trail crosses the outlet of Lake Dorothy and meets the Laurel Creek Trail (¾ mi; 10,000 ft+). It then passes the southern shore of Lake Genevieve and climbs to Edith Lake before ending along the western shore of Cloverleaf Lake (1 mi; 10,302 ft+).

Bright Dot Lake, a popular fishing spot, is best reached by leaving the Convict Canyon Trail at Mildred Lake. It is easy cross-country hiking for approximately ½ mile to the south to the first stream descending from the east (at UTM 349557). Go east on the south side of this stream and up and over a hill to Bright Dot Lake. A direct ascent or descent between Bright Dot Lake and lower Convict Creek is not recommended.

Laurel Creek Trail 5¾ miles

A non-quota trail. This trail should not be confused with the trail of a similar name that climbs out of Mono Creek. The Laurel Creek Trail is actually an abandoned mining road. The road is in poor shape, however, and it is best traveled on foot. The trail begins along Sherwin Creek Road, 1.5 miles from Highway 395, or 4.1 miles from Old Mammoth (0 mi; 7,289 ft). It ascends the east bank of Laurel Creek for 3¼ miles to a side road that branches off to the southwest to Laurel Lakes (3¼ mi; 9,908 ft+). The Laurel Creek Trail continues southeast over a saddle (to 10,761 ft+) and descends to meet the Convict Canyon Trail at Lake Genevieve.

Duck Pass Trail 7 miles

A quota trail. The Duck Pass Trail leaves the road southeast of Lake Mary (0 mi; 9,055 ft+) and passes by the lakes of upper Mammoth Creek on the way to the summit of Duck Pass (10,797 ft+; Duck Pass is unnamed on most maps). The trail descends the southern side of the pass to Duck Lake (6 mi; 10,482 ft), a beautiful lake with fine views. Bears prowl through this area. The trail crosses the outlet of the lake and descends to

meet the John Muir Trail (1 mi; 10,170 ft+).

Camping and campfires are prohibited within 300 feet of the outlet of Duck Lake.

Deer Lakes Trail 9 miles

A quota trail. The trailhead for this trail is at the end of the road near Lake George (0 mi; 9,055 ft+). The trail makes a steep ascent to the top of the Mammoth Crest (with a side trail that goes by Crystal Lake). It continues southeast along the top of the Mammoth Crest (to 11,286 ft+), which has spectacular views in all directions. The trail eventually turns south off the crest and leads down to Deer Lakes (3½ mi; 10,630 ft+). A rough trail descends Deer Creek to the John Muir Trail (5½ mi; 9,055 ft+).

Mammoth Pass Trail 3½ miles

A non-quota trail. This trail leaves the road near Horseshoe Lake (0 mi; 8,924 ft) and leads to McCloud Lake (½ mi; 9,317 ft+). The trail forks here. The right branch continues west, descending to Red's Meadow (3 mi; 7,611 ft+). The left branch leads 2 miles to the John Muir Trail near Red Cones, and another branch of the left branch meets the John Muir Trail farther south along the upper portion of Crater Creek, 3½ miles from McCloud Lake.

CROSS-COUNTRY ROUTES

"Half-Moon Pass" 11,480 ft+; 11,440 ft+;
0.2 mi E of Golden Lake

Class 3. This is a quick cross-country route across the Sierra crest from Rock Creek to Mono Creek. The route begins along Rock Creek Road near the trailhead for the Davis Lake Trail, due west from Rock Creek Lake. Ascend a broad valley to the sharp notch of Half-Moon Pass. A short class 3 chute is encountered on the west side of the pass. This is followed by a sandy use trail that leads down to Golden Lake. It is best to go around Golden Lake on its northern side.

"Huntington Col" 11,840 ft+; 11,760 ft+;
0.4 mi NW of Mount Huntington

Class 2–3. This is a direct route between Pioneer Basin and Hilton Creek Lakes.

"Stanford Col"   11,560 ft+; 11,600 ft+;

0.7 mi WSW of Mount Stanford

Class 3. This is a direct route between Pioneer Basin and the McGee Creek drainage. The south side of this pass is easy. The north side is steep; however, there is a well-worn use trail winding its way up from Steelhead Lake.

Crocker Col   11,960 ft+; 11,920 ft+;

0.2 mi SE of Mount Crocker

Class 2–3. A narrow chute on the northeast side leads from Pioneer Basin to the Hopkins Creek drainage.

Further Reading: John Moynier. *Backcountry Skiing in the High Sierra.* Evergreen, Colo.: Chockstone Press, 1992, p. 77.

"Hopkins Pass"   11,400 ft+; 11,360 ft+;

0.7 mi E of Red and White Mountain

Class 2. This pass is named on some maps, but not on others. The route leads between Upper Hopkins Lakes and Big McGee Lake. Go east from the outlet of the higher Upper Hopkins Lakes before turning north to ascend over gentle, grassy slopes to the low point of the pass. Go west over the north side of the ridge crest to where a class 2 descent to Big McGee Lake can be made.

Grinnell Col   11,600 ft+; 11,520 ft+;

0.8 mi SE of Red and White Mountain; UTM 367486

Class 2. This pass leads across the long and precipitous southeast ridge of Red and White Mountain. From Upper Hopkins Lakes climb to the higher notch that is above the saddle on the ridge. Continue south and then west to Grinnell Lake.

Further Reading: John Moynier. *Backcountry Skiing in the High Sierra.* Evergreen, Colo.: Chockstone Press, 1992, pp. 77–78.

"Pace Col"   11,600 ft+; 11,600 ft+;

0.4 mi W of Red and White Mountain

Class 2. This pass has also been called "Grinnell Pass" but a plaque on the summit names it in memory of John Pace (1943–1982). It provides a direct route across the Silver Divide between the upper reaches of Laurel Creek and Fish Creek. Hike north past Grinnell Lake and Little Grinnell Lake to the pass. The north side of the pass consists of loose shale, interspersed with patches of snow. Circle around Red and White Lake on its eastern and northern sides.

Further Reading: Steve Roper. *Sierra High Route.* Seattle: The Mountaineers Books, 1997, pp. 155–156.

"Bighorn Pass"   11,240 ft+; 11,200 ft+;

1.1 mi SSW of Red and White Mountain

Class 2. This pass has also been called "Rosy Finch Pass" and "Finch Col," and it is used in combination with Shout of Relief Pass to cross the Silver Divide. It can be approached directly from either Laurel Lake or Grinnell Lake by following a grassy bench southwest to the base of the final slope leading up the eastern side of the pass. Large talus blocks are encountered on the west side of the pass. You can either head directly down to Rosy Finch Lake or head northwest to Shout of Relief Pass.

Further Reading: Steve Roper. *Sierra High Route.* Seattle: The Mountaineers Books, 1997, pp. 144–146, 155.

"Shout of Relief Pass"   11,400 ft+; 11,360 ft+;

1.0 mi SW of Red and White Mountain

Class 2. The southwest side of this pass consists of jumbled terrain with much tedious talus. The northwest side is much more pleasant, the route traversing many meadows and benches.

Further Reading: Steve Roper. *Sierra High Route.* Seattle: The Mountaineers Books, 1997, pp. 146–147, 155.

"Rohn Pass"   11,240 ft+; 11,200 ft+;

0.6 mi NE of Mount Izaak Walton

Class 2. This pass has been named here in memory of Norm Rohn. It crosses the Silver Divide between Tully Lake and Bighorn Lake. The north side of the pass is easy, with the exception of one short, steep section. The south side consists of some stretches of talus. Bighorn Lake is best passed on its eastern shore; the cliffs south of the lake can be avoided by heading southwest before turning southeast down to the stream leading into Mott Lake. And Mott Lake can be circled on its eastern and southern shores.

"Walton Col"   11,720 ft+; 11,680 ft+;

0.2 mi SE of Mount Izaak Walton

Class 2. This is the high pass that is immediately

southeast of Mount Izaak Walton. The lovely basin southwest of the pass is most easily approached from the 10,200-foot level of the John Muir Trail.

Warrior Ridge 11,560 ft+; 11,440 ft+;
0.8 mi W of Mount Izaak Walton

Class 2. This pass crosses the Silver Divide, leading between the basin southwest of Mount Izaak Walton and Warrior Lake. Grassy benches and slabs lead up the southern side of the pass, and slabs and talus lead down northwest and then north to Warrior Lake.

Further Reading: John Moynier. *Backcountry Skiing in the High Sierra.* Evergreen, Colo.: Chockstone Press, 1992, p. 78.

"Corridor Pass" 3580 m+; 11,760 ft+;
1.0 mi E of Red Slate Mountain

Class 2. This pass provides a direct route between McGee Creek and Convict Creek.

The next pass to the west (Pass 3640m+; 11,920 ft+) is dramatically steep, with much loose rock on its northern side.

"Gemini Pass" 3660 m+; 12,080 ft+;
0.7 mi ENE of Cecil Lake

Class 2. This pass leads from Convict Creek to the upper portion of the Fish Creek drainage. Leave the Convict Canyon Trail at Mildred Lake and ascend the gentle valley to the south to where the stream forks. Ascend the right-hand stream southwest to Lake Wit-so-nah-pah (the Piute name for Convict Lake). Continue south over talus and snowfields to the first broad saddle that is west of Red Slate Mountain. Descend the south side of the saddle to the first small lake and continue downstream to Lee Lake. A good use trail leads from Lee Lake down to the McGee Creek Trail along Fish Creek.

"Carter Col" 3800m+; 12,160 ft+;
0.6 mi NE of Cecil Lake; UTM 338532

Class 2. This pass is named here in honor of Tom Carter, one of the pioneers of the Redline ski traverse of the Sierra crest. It has been used during high-level ski tours between Rock Creek and Mammoth Lakes. It is best not to descend the west side of the pass, but rather to make a slightly descending traverse to the northwest in order to reach Bard Pass.

"Bard Pass" 3660 m+; 12,000 ft+;
0.7 mi NNE of Cecil Lake; UTM 333534

Class 2. This pass is used in combination with Carter Col. It has been named here in memory of Allan Bard, another pioneer of the Redline ski traverse. Instead of crossing over the summit of the pass, it is better to make a slightly ascending traverse to the southeast, aiming for the low point of Carter Col.

"Franklin Col" 3580 m+; 11,760 ft+;
0.5 mi SE of Franklin Lake; UTM 315549

Class 2–3. This is another pass that has been used during high-level ski tours. The headwall on the north side of this pass is dramatically steep, at least for skiers. Instead of descending the southern side of the pass, continue climbing to the southeast, and go over the southwest shoulder of Mount Mendenhall (Peak 3737m; 12,277 ft) to approach Bard Pass.

"Pretty Pass" 3620 m+; 11,840 ft+;
1.0 mi SW of Lake Dorothy

Class 2. This pass crosses the Sierra crest between Lake Dorothy and Franklin Lake. Climb into the basin southwest of Lake Dorothy and then to the summit of the pass, just north of Mount Mendenhall (Peak 3737m; 12,277 ft). The west side is a straightforward descent to Franklin Lake and Purple Creek.

"Bloody Pass" 3440m+; 11,200 ft+;
0.5 mi SW of Bloody Mountain

Class 1. This pass has been used by skiers between Cloverleaf Lake and Laurel Lakes.

Further Reading: John Moynier. *Backcountry Skiing in the High Sierra.* Chockstone Press, Evergreen, Colo., 1992, p. 136.

"Pika Pass" 3520 m+; 11,520 ft+;
0.7 mi ENE of Pika Lake; UTM 288578

Class 2. Also used during high-level ski tours between Mammoth Lakes and Rock Creek, this route does not cross the Sierra crest, but instead traverses the west side of the crest by going over the pass northeast of Peak 3632m (11,894 ft). The southeastern side of this pass is really steep!

"Deer Pass" 3420 m+; 11,200 ft+;
0.6 mi SW of Barney Lake; UTM 256585

Class 1. This pass leads between the Duck Pass Trail

and Deer Lakes. Leave the Duck Lake Trail just beneath the southern side of the pass. Go west, up the gentle southern side of the Sierra crest, to the broad saddle northeast of Peak 3560m+ (11,647 ft). Go over the pass and cross the sandy basin beyond to the gap at its western end. A good use trail leads through talus and on to Deer Lakes.

Further Reading: Steve Roper. *Sierra High Route.* Seattle: The Mountaineers Books, 1997, pp. 149–151.

PEAKS

Mount Starr   12,835 ft; 12,870 ft
West Slope. Class 2. First ascent July 16, 1896 by Walter A. Starr and Allen L. Chickering. Climb loose talus east from Mono Pass to the broad, sandy false summit. The true summit is 200 yards to the north.

East Slope. Class 2. From Mosquito Flat along Rock Creek, climb a chute on the northeast side of the peak to the north ridge. Follow the ridge to the summit.

"Pointless Peak"   12,256 ft; 12,252 ft;
1.4 mi SE of Mount Huntington
This peak, which has also been called "Mono Mesa," is easy class 3 from the summit of Half-Moon Pass. The southeast slope is class 1 from Rock Creek Lake; first winter ascent 1980 by John Moynier. The peak is class 2 from Golden Lake; climb the sides of a steep chute on the southwest side of the peak. The east couloirs of Pointless Peak are about 2,500 feet long, and have angles from 25° to 40°. Some technical routes have been done on the north face; the north arête is III, 5.10. The north ridge is class 3 on a traverse from Patricia Peak.

Mount Huntington   12,394 ft; 12,405 ft
Southwest Ridge. Class 2. First ascent July 14, 1934 by David Brower, Norman Clyde, and Hervey Voge. Ascend the ridge from Pioneer Basin.

Northwest Ridge. Class 3. Descended July 14, 1934 by David Brower, Norman Clyde, and Hervey Voge. Traverse the Sierra crest from Mount Stanford.

North Face and Northwest Ridge. Class 2. First ascent August 22, 1987 by Jerry Keating, Dick Agnos, and Elton Fletcher. Ascend the far right-hand (western) side of the north face almost to the crest of the northwest ridge. Traverse beneath the northwest ridge across the top of

several loose chutes on the north face to the summit.

Northeast Ridge. Class 2–3. First ascent June 23, 1973 by Bill Schuler, Bill Sanders, and Ed Treacy. Climb a steep chute on the north side of the northeast ridge and follow the ridge to the summit.

"Patricia Peak"   11,962 ft; 11,962 ft;
1.3 mi NE of Mount Huntington
The northwest ridge is class 3 from Hilton Creek Lakes. There are also many one- and two-pitch climbs on the pinnacles southeast of the south summit, which have been called the "Patricia Spires."

E-Ticket. I, 5.10b. First ascent 1989 by Richard Leversee, Todd Vogel, and Pat Kent. This route climbs the south side of the large, rectangular spire on the left side of the bowl south of Patricia Peak. Follow the obvious crack system for two pitches.

Templo del Sol. II, 5.12. First ascent 1989 by Pat Kent, Todd Vogel, and Richard Leversee. This route climbs the formation that, halfway up, resembles a temple with vertical pillars on each side. Climb the obvious crack/corner system to the left side of a ledge, then go up a thin finger crack on the wall above the ledge. This four-pitch route requires a double set of protection, from tiny to 3½-inch. Two rappels lead down to the bottom.

Diamond Star Tower. I, 5.10. First ascent 1989 by Todd Vogel, Pat Kent, and Richard Leversee. This route climbs the south side of the beautiful tower on the right side of the bowl southeast of Patricia Peak.

"Hilton Peak"   12,508 ft; 12,522 ft;
0.9 mi E of Mount Stanford
First ascent June 23, 1973 by Barbara Lilley and Andy Smatko. The southwest ridge is class 2 to easy class 3.

Mount Stanford   12,838 ft; 12,851 ft
First ascent 1907–09 by George R. Davis, C. F. Urquhart, R. B. Marshall, and L. F. Biggs, during the survey of the 30-minute Mount Goddard quadrangle. This peak is class 2 from Pioneer Basin via the west ridge or the gullies on its southern side. A traverse of the Sierra crest from Mount Huntington is class 3.

The east slope is class 2; from Lake 10,353 ft (10,320 ft+) of the Hilton Creek Lakes, ascend a stream that goes west-northwest towards the saddle that is south of Stanford Lake. The low point of the saddle is best bypassed; instead, head for the far western edge of the saddle (UTM 420502), climbing it via a chute. Go north and ascend the final east slope over a false summit to the true summit of Mount Stanford.

The north-northeast ridge is class 3 in places, and is commonly used during traverses to Mount Morgan.

Mount Morgan   3963 m; 13,005 ft

First ascent July 9, 1934 by David Brower and Norman Clyde, via the class 3 ridge from Mount Stanford. First winter ascent December 1976 by Cuno Ranschau, Ed Omberg, Mary Omberg, and Sam Roberts from McGee Creek. The southeast slope from Davis Lake is class 2. This is commonly used as a descent route following a traverse of Mount Stanford and Mount Morgan. Care must be taken to ensure that the correct chute is selected. Some chutes drain into cliffs near the bottom, and a party could find itself stranded.

Further Reading: John Moynier. *Backcountry Skiing in the High Sierra.* Evergreen, Colo.: Chockstone Press, 1992, p. 175; John Moynier and Claude Fiddler. *Sierra Classics.* Evergreen, Colo.: Chockstone Press, 1993, pp. 222–223.

Mount Hopkins   12,304 ft; 12,302 ft

First ascent July 16, 1934 by David Brower, Norman Clyde, and Hervey Voge. This is a class 1 sand climb from the east. The peak is class 2 from Hopkins Creek.

Peak 12,404ft   12,408 ft;
0.8 mi NNW of Mount Hopkins

First ascent July 5, 1950 by T. H. Hasheim, Elly Hinreiner, and Jean Campbell. The traverse from Mount Hopkins is class 2, as are the western and southwestern slopes. The traverse from Mount Crocker is class 2–3. There is a class 3 chute on the northeast side of the mountain.

Mount Crocker   12,458 ft; 12,457 ft

First ascent August 29, 1929 by Nazario Sparrea, a Basque shepherd. The class 1 south slope leads to the class 3 summit rocks. The south slope can be reached from Pioneer Basin by crossing the saddle between Mount Crocker and Peak 12,404ft (12,408 ft). There are some loose class 2–3 chutes on the northwest face, and the last part of the northeast ridge, after an approach over sand, is class 3.

Red and White Mountain   12,816 ft; 12,850 ft

Southwest Face. Class 2. Descended July 18, 1902 by James S. Hutchinson, Lincoln Hutchinson, and Charles A. Noble. Climb the large chute rising above Little Grinnell Lake. There is quite a bit of loose rock in this chute.

West Ridge. Class 3. First ascent July 18, 1902 by James S. Hutchinson, Lincoln Hutchinson, and Charles A. Noble. Ascend talus from the summit of Grinnell Pass to the knife edge ridge that leads to a false summit. Traverse around the south (right) side of the false summit, then continue on to the true summit. This is an exposed route with much loose rock.

North Face. III, AI1 or WI2. First ascent July 17, 1991 by Tim Pomykata and Catherine Laben. The north side of Red and White Mountain features a rare sight in the High Sierra: a permanent, 900-foot, 40° snow/ice face.

Northeast Ridge. Class 3. First ascent July 3, 1928 by Norman Clyde. This is probably the best route on Red and White Mountain because it doesn't have as much loose rock as the other routes that are commonly used. Head southwest from Little McGee Lake and ascend the northeast slope of Peak 12,360ft+ (12,320 ft+; 0.5 mile north of Red and White Mountain). Descend to the saddle to the south and follow the ridge to the summit of Red and White Mountain, bypassing a false summit on its western side. Keep to the southeast side of the ridge just below the summit. *Variation:* Descended July 13, 1985 by Norm Rohn and Lloyd Brown. Climb from Red and White Lake into the cirque north of the peak. Skirt the northeast side of the snowfield, climbing to the first small saddle northeast of the true summit of Red and White Mountain. Follow the northeast ridge to the top.

Further Reading: John Moynier and Claude Fiddler. *Sierra Classics.* Evergreen, Colo.: Chockstone Press, 1993, pp. 224–225.

Southeast Face. Class 2–3. Climb into the cirque southeast of the peak from Big McGee Lake. Ascend the left-hand (southwest) side of the face via a chute filled with loose rocks. It is best to keep to the rocks on the side of the chute. Go right (northeast) a short distance from the top of the chute to the summit. There is a great deal of loose rock on this route, and it is not suitable for large parties.

Peak 12,238ft   12,238 ft;
0.7 mi SW of Red and White Mountain

North Slope. Class 2. First ascent August 14, 1952 by G. A. Daum, G. F. Hurley, and J. M. Schnitzler. This is an easy climb from either Grinnell Pass or Red and White Lake.

Southwest Face. Class 5. First ascent August 1972 by Tom Flynn and Ken Cardwell. Ascend a shallow chute, which ends atop the northwest ridge at a point about 50 feet from the summit.

Mount Izaak Walton   12,077 ft; 12,099 ft

Southwest Slope. Class 2. First ascent July 5, 1971 by Andy Smatko, Bill Schuler, and Ed Treacy. Ascend talus and scree up this slope to the summit. The slope can be approached from Walton Col, the small saddle southeast of the peak. Another approach is from the 10,200-foot level of the John Muir Trail, far to the west.

Northeast Ridge. Class 3. Descended July 5, 1971 by Andy Smatko, Bill Schuler, and Ed Treacy. This is a good climb along the ridge rising from the saddle northeast of the peak.

East Face. Class 3. First ascent June 13, 1985 by Lloyd Brown, Norm Rohn, and R. J. Secor. Ascend the left side of the east face to the southeast ridge; follow the ridge to the summit. There is quite a bit of loose rock on the east face.

Peak 12,221ft   12,221 ft; 0.7 mi E of Silver Pass

The southwest and southeast sides consist of class 2 scree and boulders.

"Old Izaak Walton"   11,880 ft+; 11,840 ft+;
0.9 mi NE of Silver Pass

This peak was referred to as "Mount Izaak Walton" in old guidebooks. First ascent July 20, 1938 by Jim Harkins and Norman Clyde. The last 50 feet of the northwest ridge is class 4. The south side is class 2, except for the last 100 feet to the summit, where it is class 4.

"Piscator Peak"   11,343 ft; 11,280 ft+;
1.4 mi N of Silver Pass

North Buttress. II, 5.8. First ascent August 15, 1988 by Galen Rowell and Kevin Worral. Ascend the buttress over excellent knobs and solid plates to the summit.

North Dihedral. II, 5.8. First ascent August 15, 1988 by Dick Duane and Sebastian Letemendia. This route climbs the large dihedral that is right of the north buttress. This route eventually leaves the dihedral and joins the north buttress.

Peak 11,424ft   11,428 ft; 0.3 mi W of Silver Pass

The middle summit is the high point. The three summits were traversed on August 17, 1937 by Owen Williams.

Double Barrel Right. II, 5.9. First ascent August 16, 1988 by Dick Duane and Galen Rowell. This 600-foot route is on the right-center side of the east face.

Double Barrel Left. II, 5.8. First ascent August 16, 1988 by Sebastian Letemendia and Kevin Worral. Climb the left-center side of the east face.

Graveyard Peak   11,520 ft+; 11,520 ft+

First ascent September 8, 1935 by William Stewart and David Parish. The northeast ridge is easy class 3. Bench mark 11,494 ft is not the high point.

Silver Peak   11,878 ft; 11,878 ft

The west and south slopes are class 2.

This peak is frequently climbed from Devil's Bathtub. Head north from the lake to the cirque at the head of the valley above the lake. Continue north and cross Pass 11,240ft+ (11,200 ft+; UTM 225475), which is southwest of Peak 11,520ft+ (11,476 ft). Continue down to the tarn northwest of the saddle and climb onto the long, class 2 southeast ridge. Follow the ridge to the summit.

The southeast ridge was also approached from Anne Lake on October 5, 1996 by Rick Beatty and R. J. Secor. Go west from the lake, crossing the northeast ridge of Peak 11,520ft+ (11,476 ft) at the 10,800-foot contour. Remain at or above the 10,800-foot contour on the north side of the southeast ridge until reaching the first saddle southeast of the peak. Follow the ridge to the summit.

Sharktooth Peak   11,640 ft+; 11,639 ft
This peak is class 2 from Margaret Lakes.

Red Slate Mountain   4000 m+; 13,163 ft

First ascent 1864 by James T. Gardiner. First winter ascent January 23, 1972 by Doug Mantle and Dave Gladstone. This peak is a big pile of rubble, and is class 1 or 2 from McGee Pass, Fish Creek, or Gemini Pass. There is a short class 3 pitch along the northwest ridge.

On the positive side, there is a swell view from the summit. The couloir on the north side provides about 1,000 feet of 40° snow and ice climbing.

Further Reading: John Moynier and Claude Fiddler. *Sierra Classics*. Evergreen, Colo.: Chockstone Press, 1993, pp. 226–227.

Peak 3797m   12,400 ft+;
0.9 mi SE of Red Slate Mountain

First ascent August 29, 1952 by A. J. Reyman. This peak is composed of loose slate, and is class 3 from the northwest.

Peak 3776m   12,320 ft+;
1.0 mi E of Red Slate Mountain

First ascent July 17, 1934 by David Brower and Hervey Voge. Class 2 from Corridor Pass.

Mount Baldwin   3845 m; 12,614 ft

First ascent July 2, 1928 by Norman Clyde. The northwest slope is class 2 from Bright Dot Lake. The upper west slope of the peak is remarkably smooth. The north ridge is class 3.

East Face and South Ridge. Class 4. First ascent May 1972 by Gary Valle, Tom Oetzell, and Bill McIntosh. Leave McGee Creek just south of Horsetail Falls and climb into the cirque southeast of the peak. Contour west to the last of three prominent chutes. Climb this steep chute to its head and then follow a shattered ridge to the base of a steep wall. The wall, which has some class 4 moves, leads to Mount Baldwin's south ridge. Follow the ridge to the summit.

"The White Fang"   3735 m; 12,240 ft+;
0.6 mi N of Mount Baldwin

First ascent April 1968 by Galen Rowell, Charles Raymond, and Pat Callis, via the class 3 northwest chute.

White Trash. IV, 5.10X. First ascent 1994 by Alan Swanson, Steve Gerberding, Carla Zezuela, and Denise Brown. The first-ascent party described the rock of this route as being "ultra loose, semi-dolomitic marble." It climbs the northeast face, with nine pitches over loose rock and, with the exception of three belay bolts, poor protection. Helmets are recommended.

Mount Aggie   3525 m; 11,561 ft

First ascent September 1, 1952 by A. J. Reyman. Class 2 via the southwest ridge.

Mount Morrison   3742 m; 12,268 ft

This is the spectacular peak that is seen south of Highway 395 near the Mammoth Lakes airport. The rock is extremely loose, and caution must be exercised on any of its routes. The north side of this peak has earned the nickname, "The Eiger of the Sierra."

East Slope. Class 2. First ascent 1928 by John D. Mendenhall. Go south from near the campground at Convict Lake and climb up into the hanging valley that is east of Peak 3321 m (10,858 ft). Continue up the valley to a small tarn, then turn right (west) and ascend a bowl-shaped valley. This valley eventually turns into a chute. It may be easier to climb the right rib of the chute. Follow the chute or its rib to the summit. *Variation:* Another approach uses the hanging valley that is north of Mount Morrison from the inlet side of Convict Lake. This is more scenic, but much more tiring than the eastern hanging valley.

Northeast Wall and Buttress. IV, 5.7. First ascent September 7, 1946 by Charles Wilts and Harry Sutherland. First winter ascent January 22, 1968 by Reggie Donatelli, Alvin McLane, and Brian Bartlett, who wrote in the summit register, "Never again." Ascend the hanging valley north of Mount Morrison to the toe of the north buttress. Begin by climbing the northeast face just left of the north buttress via two prominent chutes. Go up and slightly right over high angle rock for almost 1,000 feet to the crest of the buttress, meeting it at a point where its angle declines abruptly. Follow the crest of the buttress for some distance, passing an outside corner on its left. Climb a prominent red chimney on the right side of the buttress. (This chimney has a 5.8 overhanging chockstone near its top.) Rappel 50 feet down the other side of the chimney to a class 2 talus chute, which leads to the summit.

Don-Julie. IV, 5.10. First ascent September 1995 by Jim Howle and Paul Teare. This route ascends the central pillar on the north face. Start by climbing from the left side of a band of red rock. Traverse to the right for a long pitch to a right-facing open book. Ascend the book for four pitches to a ledge, using excellent face holds that are to the right of the inside corner of the dihedral. Continue to the top over the upper pillar. The rock on this route has been reported as being more solid than that found on the other routes on the north side of Mount Morrison.

North Buttress. IV, 5.7, A3. First ascent July 5, 1960 by Jim Wilson, Ron Hayes, and Allen Steck. First winter ascent 1995 by Brian Biega and Paul Teare. Start by climbing the northeast wall, then make a 200-foot traverse up and to the right to the base of a crack system on the crest of the north buttress. Ascend directly up the buttress for 500 feet (5.7) to the base of a 60-foot headwall. Climb the wall (5.7, A3) and continue up the crest of the buttress. Pass an outside corner on its left; a prominent red chimney with an overhanging chockstone follows. Rappel from the top of the chockstone down the other side to a class 2 talus slope, which leads to the summit.

North Face Direct. IV, 5.10+. First ascent July 1987 by Dean Hobbs and Gary Slate. From the very bottom of the north buttress, scramble up and right for 200 feet to an area of yellow rock. A 5.10 hand crack zigzags up and to the right to a ramp. The second pitch follows the ramp before run out 5.10 face moves lead to the right and ends on a flake. Next, climb up and left over cracks to a scree-covered ledge at the base of a wide chimney. Climb to the left of the chimney and traverse left beyond an outside corner to an arête. Climb the crest of the exposed arête (5.8) to a sloping ledge. A pair of parallel cracks lead to a pillar. Then comes a shallow 5.9 groove that ends at the base of the Crackless Corner dihedral. Difficult (5.10) run out face climbing then leads up and to the right past a loose block to a small ledge. After the ledge, go up and left past a big ledge to a pair of loose pillars. Climb up the crest of the arête and follow the crest up for four pitches of easier climbing (up to 5.5) to a notch. A steep, right-facing corner (5.10) leads from the notch to the base of a red gully with ledges. This gully ends at the prominent notch atop the north buttress. A steep 5.8 crack leads up from the notch; this is followed by class 3 to the summit.

Further Reading: John Moynier and Claude Fiddler. *Sierra Classics.* Evergreen, Colo.: Chockstone Press, 1993, pp. 228–230.

North Face. IV, 5.8. First ascent May 28, 1967 by Tom Higgins and Charlie Raymond. Begin by climbing a squat, black rock about 200 feet to the right of the toe of the north buttress. This first pitch is tricky and difficult; the route generally goes straight up, but climbs to the right where the black rock turns gray. Traverse down and left (5.8) past a clean, sharp dihedral to a broken area. Continue up broken rock to the base of a large, white rock (shaped like the state of California), which is visible from the hanging valley below. A friction traverse left leads to an exposed corner, and the corner leads to

the crest of the north buttress. Continue up the crest of the buttress to a gold-colored chute. This chute leads to a steep headwall, then a thin ridge, which leads to the summit. After the first four pitches, the climbing is never more difficult than 5.6.

Northwest Couloir. First ascent 1931 by John D. Mendenhall. This route is also called the "Y Couloir" and the "Death Couloir" because it is only safe when it is full (from the very bottom to the very top) of snow/ice. In May 1996, John Dittli and Andy Selters climbed about 200 feet of thin ice (WI3–4) at the foot of the couloir, then climbed moderate 30° to 40° slopes above the foot of the couloir (with a few short, steep steps), finishing via the left branch of the Y.

Further Reading: John Moynier and Claude Fiddler. *Sierra Classics.* Evergreen, Colo.: Chockstone Press, 1993, pp. 219–220.

Northwest Ridge. Class 3. First ascent June 22, 1928 by Norman Clyde. Leave the Convict Canyon Trail at the southwestern shore of Convict Lake and climb a prominent talus slope toward a saddle with some clumps of trees. Just below this saddle, traverse left (east) past a couple of notches and ascend a class 3 rib to the crest of the northwest ridge. Continue up the ridge to the summit.

South Summit from the West. Class 2. First ascent 1928 by John D. Mendenhall. The actual high point of Mount Morrison is the south summit (3765 m; 12,320 ft+). Hike up the Convict Canyon Trail past the bridge and climb a long talus slope to the summit.

South Summit from Mount Morrison. Class 3–4. First ascent May 21, 1966 by Dick Beach, Mike McNicholas, and John Thornton. Follow the very crest of the arête between the two summits.

South Summit from the East. Class 2. First ascent September 9, 1930 by James Van Patten and John D. Mendenhall. Climb to the eastern hanging valley south of Convict Lake, then to the eastern base of the south peak. A steep, loose chute leads to the summit. It may be better to ascend the rocks south of this chute.

"Torre de Miedra" 3129 m; 10,040 ft;
0.7 mi NNW of Mount Morrison

This small peak is low along the northwest ridge of Mount Morrison.

Northeast Buttress. II, 5.4. First ascent November 7, 1992 by John Climaco and Chris Breemer. Most of this seven-pitch route is class 4, over loose rock. The fourth and fifth pitches traverse an exposed narrow arête, the highlight of the climb.

Laurel Mountain   3600 m+; 11,812 ft

North Ridge. Class 1. First ascent September 25, 1926 by Norman Clyde. This ridge can be approached from either Laurel Creek or Convict Lake.

Northeast Trough. Class 3. First ascent 1925 by John D. Mendenhall. This trough is to the right of the cliffs on the east face of Laurel Mountain. The bottom of the trough can be reached easily from the Convict Canyon Trail. This is a nice climb, starting with solid rock slabs that gradually become looser as you get higher.

Northeast Gully. Class 4. First ascent September 7, 1930 by John D. Mendenhall and James M. Van Patten. This historic climb marked the first time that a proper (i.e., belayed) roped climb occurred in the High Sierra. This steep gully is halfway between the northeast trough and the arête that splits the cliffs on the east face of the peak. Ascend the trough to the upper part of the arête, turn right, and head directly for the summit. *Variation:* Class 4. First ascent July 4, 1990 by Chris Keith and Pete Lowery. This variation is achieved by continuing straight up a huge gray slab instead of turning right.

Bloody Mountain   3826 m; 12,544 ft

First ascent July 3, 1928 by Norman Clyde. The northeast ridge is class 2, as are the south and southwest slopes. A class 2 gully on the east side of the mountain was climbed October 6, 1996 by Barbara Cohen, Dave Sholle, and Mary Motheral. To climb the gully, leave the Laurel Creek Trail north of Lake Genevieve and follow the obvious gully heading northwest onto the crest of the northeast ridge. Follow the ridge to the summit. A snow/ice couloir on the north side of Bloody Mountain provides 1,500 feet of climbing, up to an angle of 40°.

Further Reading: John Moynier. *Backcountry Skiing in the High Sierra.* Evergreen, Colo.: Chockstone Press, 1992, p. 177.

Peak 3770m   12,320 ft+; 0.7 mi NE of Cecil Lake

First ascent July 7, 1971 by Bill Schuler, Andy Smatko, and Ed Treacy. The south ridge is class 2.

"Mount Mendenhall"   3737 m; 12,277 ft;
1.0 mi SW of Lake Dorothy

This peak has been named here after the late John Mendenhall. It has also been called "Pretty Peak." First ascent July 17, 1934 by David Brower, via the class 2 north ridge.

"Virginia Pass Crag"   3403 m; 11,147 ft;
0.5 mi NW of Lake Virginia

"Virginia Pass" is crossed by the John Muir Trail between Lake Virginia and Purple Lake. This peak is southwest of this pass.

North-Northwest Chute. This steep chute was first climbed August 16, 1965 by Bob Syndor.

Left Crack. I, 5.10a. First ascent August 14, 1988 by Galen Rowell, Dick Duane, Sebastian Letemendia, and Kevin Worral. This is a 200-foot, overhanging hand crack on the face that faces the pass.

Peak 3762m   12,354 ft; 1.1 mi NE of Lake Virginia

First ascent 1963 by A. J. Reyman, via the class 2 north ridge.

Peak 3632m   11,894; 0.5 mi E of Pika Lake

The north-northeast ridge (class 3) was first climbed September 5, 1966 by Bob Herlihy, Bill Schuler, and Andy Smatko. This party descended via the steep southwest chute.

Peak 3580m+   11,760 ft+;
1.6 mi SW of Bloody Mountain

The east face, which is class 3–4, was first climbed September 4, 1966 by Andy Smatko, Ellen Siegal, Bill Schuler, and Bob Herlihy.

Peak 3681m   12,052 ft; 1.7 mi W of Bloody Mountain

First ascent August 18, 1924 by E. S. Wallace, E. E. Wix, and Bill Dye. This peak is class 2 from the west. The steep chute at the southern end of the east face is class 3.

Crystal Crag   3163 m; 10,364 ft

There is a class 3 route along the west face. Go to the base of the west face from the outlet of Crystal Lake. Climb diagonally to the right and up the west face to within 60 feet of the top. Go to the right and up for about 20 feet to the top of an exposed rib. Follow the rib to the summit.

Further Reading: Alan Bartlett and Errett Allen. *Rock Climbs of the Sierra East Side.* Evergreen, Colo.: Chockstone Press, 1985, p. 118.

Mount Morrison and Torre de Miedra from the northwest. Photo by R. J. Secor.

Mammoth Mountain   3362 m; 11,053 ft

This is a famous ski and mountain bike area; the easiest route to the top is via Gondola No. 2.

WRINKLES

Fish Creek Trail vs. the John Muir Trail. The John Muir Trail leaves the Fish Creek drainage north of Silver Pass. It then traverses high above Fish Creek and passes along the heavily used campsites at Lake Virginia, Purple Lake, and Duck Lake. An often overlooked alternative is to instead take the Fish Creek Trail down through Cascade Valley, Fish Creek Hot Springs, and Fish Valley, eventually reaching Devil's Postpile. Both trails lead to the same place, but the Fish Creek option is much more pleasant, and less visited.

Morgan-Stanford Traverse. Mount Stanford and Mount Morgan can easily be climbed in a day from Davis Lake; this has also been done in a long day from Rock Creek Lake. Mount Stanford is usually climbed first, followed by a traverse along its long north ridge (class 3 in places) to the summit of Mount Morgan. A descent of the east slopes of Mount Morgan must be carefully selected to ensure that the party does not find itself stranded on some cliffs above Davis Lake.

Pace Col vs. Bighorn Pass and Shout of Relief Pass. It is hard to cross the Silver Divide in this area. The most direct route is Pace Col, but it has some loose rock on its northern side. On the other hand, Bighorn Pass and Shout of Relief Pass are more solid, but have some huge fields of talus that must be overcome.

Further Reading: Steve Roper. *Sierra High Route.* Seattle: The Mountaineers Books, 1997, pp. 155–156.

Red and White–Izaak Walton Traverse. These two peaks have been done from the headwaters of Fish Creek. The best route descends the northeast ridge of Red and White Mountain down to the northern shore of Red and White Lake. It then crosses the Silver Divide at Rohn Pass and climbs Mount Izaak Walton via the class 3 northeast arête.

Chapter 12

The Minarets and June Lake

The Minarets are a striking sight from Mammoth Mountain. Most prominent is Clyde Minaret, but those with sharp eyes can make out the thin needle to its left, Michael Minaret. Banner Peak and Mount Ritter dominate the skyline, but this row of peaks is not on the Sierra crest. This subrange is known as the Ritter Range, and while it is scenic, it is also well known among climbers for its loose rock, and the danger of rockfall is high.

This chapter covers the Sierra crest from Minaret Summit to Tioga Pass. Its western limit is formed by the North Fork of the San Joaquin River and the Lyell Fork of the Tuolumne River. The western boundary has been adjusted in such a way that Rodgers Peak and Mount Lyell are covered in Chapter 13, The Clark and Cathedral Ranges.

HISTORY

Mount Ritter is perhaps the most prominent peak in the High Sierra, and can even be seen from certain summits in the southern portion of the range. Clarence King attempted to climb it in 1866, and John Muir succeeded in climbing it in 1872. After guiding a party of artists into Yosemite's wilderness, he set out for a week with his blanket, biscuits, and tea, and climbed the peak from the saddle between it and Banner Peak.

The first recorded climbing in The Minarets was by Charles Michael, the assistant postmaster of Yosemite, and his wife Enid, a seasonal Yosemite National Park naturalist. In September 1923, the couple hiked from Tuolumne Meadows to a camp at Ediza Lake. They crossed North Notch, made their way along the west base of The Minarets, and started up the chimney which they believed led to the high point of The Minarets.

They passed the two lower chockstones easily, but were halted briefly by the third huge boulder. Enid remained behind while Charles climbed past the "ladder with the lower rungs missing." He continued solo climbing to the Portal and surmounted the ledges leading to the top of what is now known as Michael Minaret. A few years later Norman Clyde climbed the highest of The Minarets, now known as Clyde Minaret, but Charles Michael was satisfied with his minaret. He later wrote, "Whether my peak was the highest or not does not matter to me so much, for I can recommend it as a grand and thrilling climb."

The Minarets were the scene of much climbing activity in August 1933, when Walter A. Starr, Jr., was reported overdue from a trip to the Ritter Range. A large search party composed of some of California's finest climbers spent a week in the area, climbing peaks and checking summit registers, continually looking for clues from the missing man. The search was called off on August 19, but Clyde remained, climbing Leonard Minaret and searching the shores of Cecile Lake that day. On August 21 he climbed Clyde Minaret, looking for signs of a fallen climber in the bergschrund along its north glacier. Two days later he searched the cliffs above Amphitheater Lake with binoculars, and continued the search from the summit of Kehrlein Minaret. On August 25 he put all of the clues together, and climbed Michael Minaret via Clyde's Ledge. During his descent a fly droned by, and then another. He moved north, away from the Portal, and turned to face the northwestern side of Michael Minaret. And then he saw the earthly remains of Walter A. Starr, Jr. A few days later, Clyde and Jules Eichorn interred the body on the ledge where it had come to rest, while Starr's father, Walter A. Starr, Sr., watched from below.

MAPS

USGS. *7.5-minute series:* Timber Knob, Cattle Mtn., Mammoth Mtn., Mt. Ritter, Koip Peak, Vogelsang Peak, Tioga Pass, Mount Dana. *National park maps:* Yosemite National Park and Vicinity (1:125,000). *30 x 60–minute series:* Bishop, Shaver Lake, Benton Range, Yosemite Valley.

USFS. A Guide to the Ansel Adams Wilderness (1:63,360).

Tom Harrison Cartography. Mammoth High Country.

Map Link 15-minute series. Devils Postpile, Mono Craters, Tuolumne Meadows.

Wilderness Press 15-minute series. Devils Postpile, Tuolumne Meadows.

ROADS

Minaret Summit Road

Minaret Summit Road leads from the town of Mammoth Lakes to the trailheads near Devil's Postpile National Monument. It is described in Chapter 11, Mammoth Lakes and the Silver Divide.

Minarets Road

Minarets Road can be used to approach the western trailhead for the Mammoth Trail. It is described in Chapter 13, The Clark and Cathedral Ranges.

Beasore Road

Beasore Road serves as another approach to the western trailhead for the Mammoth Trail. It is described in Chapter 13, The Clark and Cathedral Ranges.

June Lake Loop   (Highway 158)

This loop leaves Highway 395 approximately 15 miles north of the junction of Highways 395 and 203. The road goes west from Highway 395, passes through the town of June Lake and by June Mountain ski area, then loops around to the north to the Rush Creek Trailhead near the western shore of Silver Lake. The road continues north, passes the western shore of Grant Lake, and rejoins Highway 395 approximately 5 miles south of Lee Vining.

Parker Creek Road

Parker Creek Road leads to the Parker Lake Trailhead. It leaves the June Lake Loop 1.4 miles from its northern junction of Highway 395, north of Grant Lake. The road goes 0.5 mile to a four-way junction. Drive straight through the junction and, at 1.4 miles, take the left fork, then drive another 0.6 mile to the Parker Lake Trailhead.

Sawmill Canyon Road

Sawmill Canyon Road leads to the eastern trailhead for the Mono Pass Trail. From the four-way junction along Parker Creek Road, go north 0.5 mile to a junction. Take the right fork another 0.3 mile to another junction. Go left for another 2.1 miles to the trailhead, high above Walker Lake and Bloody Canyon.

Horse Meadow Road

Horse Meadow Road leads to Upper Horse Meadow and the trailhead for the Gibbs Lake Trail. The road starts by leaving Highway 395 approximately 1.5 miles south of Lee Vining. Go west to a junction after 0.3 mile. Go straight (or left) 0.7 mile to a four-way junction. Go straight through the junction to Lower Horse Meadow. This is the limit for most passenger cars; four-wheel drive vehicles can continue up the road another 1.4 miles to the trailhead.

Tioga Road   (Highway 120)

Tioga Road leads from Lee Vining, up and over Tioga Pass, and on to Tuolumne Meadows after approximately 20 miles. The trailhead for the Glacier Canyon Trail is at a turnout along the road near the inlet of Tioga Lake. The western trailhead for the Mono Pass Trail is at Dana Meadows. The John Muir Trail runs the length of Tuolumne Meadows, but most hikes up Lyell Canyon start from the hikers' parking area along the side road leading to the Tuolumne Meadows Lodge.

TRAILS

The Mammoth Trail   16½ miles

A quota trail. This historic trail was used to supply the town of Mammoth Lakes during its first heyday as a mining town. Leave the John Muir Trail ½ mile beyond the Devil's Postpile National Monument Visitor Center (0 mi; 7,520 ft+). The trail heads southwest, climbs (to 7,920 ft+), descends, and fords King Creek (2 mi; 7,605 ft). The trail then ascends the southern side of Snow Canyon to meet the Beck Lakes Trail below Summit Meadow, which is no longer a meadow, and which is not at the summit (2 mi; 8,700 ft+). The trail then goes west, climbs over a small ridge (to 9,240 ft+), and descends to Granite Stairway. It continues its descent to Cargyle Meadow (to 7,874 ft+), and then makes a short climb (to 8,005 ft+) before descending to Corral Meadow (5¾ mi; 7,940 ft). The North Fork Trail goes west from Corral Meadow, while the Mammoth Trail descends to the southwest to Snake Meadow (1½ mi; 7,037 ft). (A side trail goes north from here for 2 miles to meet the North Fork Trail at Earthquake Meadow.) The Mammoth Trail continues to descend to the North Fork of the San Joaquin River (2 mi; 5,924 ft). The trail crosses the river on a bridge at Sheep Crossing, then climbs the western wall of the canyon to the western trailhead (3¼ mi; 7,480 ft+), which is 1.2 miles east of Granite Creek Campground along a good dirt road.

North Fork Trail   11½ miles

This trail leads to the headwaters of the North Fork of the San Joaquin River. Start from either Snake Meadow (0 mi; 7,037 ft+) or Corral Meadow (0 mi; 7,940 ft+) along the Mammoth Trail—the two trails join at Earthquake Meadow (2 mi; 8,136 ft+). The North Fork Trail continues north to cross Iron Creek (3 mi; 7,602 ft+). It continues north, crosses Dike Creek, and comes to Hemlock Crossing (2 mi; 7,546 ft+). (In reality, there are *two* crossings of the North Fork of the San Joaquin River at Hemlock Crossing, but it is possible to traverse the east side of the stream to avoid crossing the river unnecessarily.) The trail then ascends the east bank of Slide Creek before crossing it, and continues northward up the east bank of the North Fork of the San Joaquin River. The trail eventually disappears after passing through a long meadow and crossing the outlet stream that drains the Ritter Lakes (4½ mi; 9,711 ft+). Twin Island Lakes are an easy cross-country hike to the west; North Glacier Pass, a harder hike, is to the northeast.

An alternate route (used by stock) to Hemlock Crossing leaves the Isberg Pass Trail 2½ miles from Granite Creek Campground (0 mi; 8,160 ft+). The right fork from this junction leads northeast, passing a stock driveway and a side trail leading down Cora Creek, and comes to another fork (½ mi; 8,80 ft+). Take the right fork northeast, cross Cora Creek and Chetwood Creek,

and then make a long climb (to 8,792 ft+) to the north before turning northeast and descending to meet the main North Fork Trail at Hemlock Crossing (8½ mi; 7,546 ft+).

Beck Lakes Trail   6 miles

A quota trail. This trail can be hiked as a loop trip that starts from Devil's Postpile via the John Muir Trail or the Mammoth Trail. The entire length of this loop is 11½ miles. Follow the Mammoth Trail across King Creek to the trail junction at Summit Meadow (0 mi; 9,020 ft). The Beck Lakes Trail goes north and then west to meet the side trail that leads to Fern Lake and Anona Lake (½ mi; 8,661 ft+). The Beck Lakes Trail goes north to the junction with the side trails to Holcomb Lake and Ashley Lake (1¾ mi; 8,989 ft+) and continues northeast to the junction with the side trail that leads to Beck Lakes (¼ mi; 9,055 ft+). (Beck Lakes are 1½ miles from this junction.) The main Beck Lakes Trail continues east from this junction over soft, dusty trail to meet the John Muir Trail (3½ mi; 8,080 ft+), 1¼ miles from Devil's Postpile National Monument.

John Muir Trail   31 miles

A quota trail. From the Devil's Postpile National Monument Visitor Center, a trail leads south and meets the John Muir Trail just before it crosses the Middle Fork of the San Joaquin River on a bridge (0 mi; 7,520 ft+). The John Muir Trail goes northwest beyond the bridge and comes to a four-way junction with the Mammoth Trail and the Pacific Crest Trail (½ mi; 7,600 ft+). It then continues to the junction with the Beck Lakes Trail (¾ mi; 8,080 ft+), crosses Minaret Creek, and meets the Minaret Lake Trail on the northern side of Johnston Meadow (¾ mi; 8,080 ft+). The John Muir Trail goes north from this junction, climbs to the top of a high plateau, passes Trinity Lakes, and meets a side trail leading to Emily Lake (3 mi; 9,240 ft+). The main trail continues north to Gladys Lake (¾ mi; 9,560 ft+), and then meets Rosalie Lake (¾ mi; 9,280 ft+). The trail makes a short ascent beyond Rosalie Lake and then descends to the upper end of Shadow Lake, where the trail meets the lower section of the Shadow Lake Trail (1½ mi; 8,737 ft). Bears prowl through this area. (Camping and campfires are prohibited at Shadow Lake. Camping and wood campfires are also prohibited south of the Shadow Lake Trail/John Muir Trail and north of Shadow Creek, from Shadow Lake to where the Shadow Lake Trail crosses

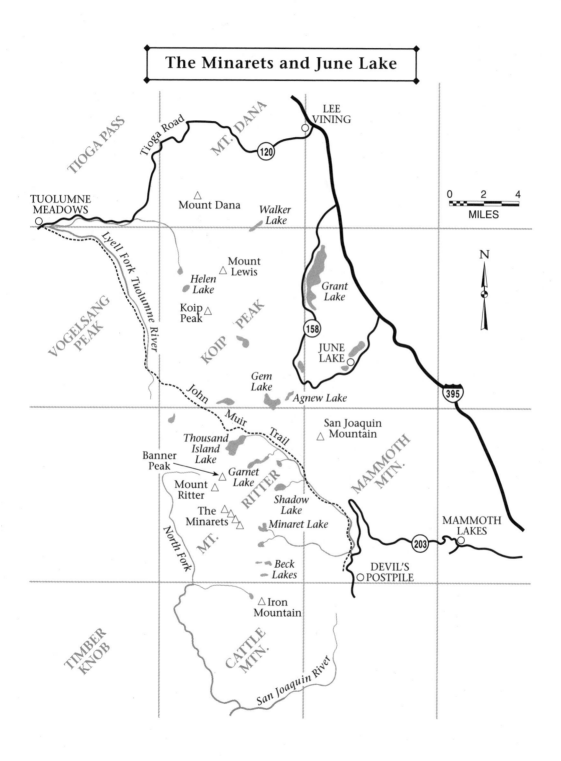

The Minarets and June Lake

TIOGA PASS

Tioga Road

MT. DANA

LEE VINING

120

TUOLUMNE MEADOWS

△ Mount Dana

Walker Lake

Lyell Fork Tuolumne River

Mount △ Lewis

Helen Lake

Koip △ Peak

KOIP PEAK

Grant Lake

158

JUNE LAKE

VOGELSANG PEAK

Gem Lake

Agnew Lake

John

Muir

Trail

San Joaquin △ Mountain

395

Thousand Island Lake

Banner Peak

△ *Garnet Lake*

Mount △ Ritter

The △△ Minarets △△

MT. RITTER

Shadow Lake

Minaret Lake

MAMMOTH MTN.

MAMMOTH LAKES

203

North Fork

MT.

Beck Lakes

DEVIL'S POSTPILE

△ Iron Mountain

TIMBER KNOB

CATTLE MTN.

San Joaquin River

0 2 4
MILES

N

Shadow Creek, i.e., the oulet of Ediza Lake.) The John Muir Trail and the Shadow Lake Trail are the same trail as it ascends Shadow Creek to the next junction (½ mi; 8,989 ft+). The John Muir Trail turns north from this junction and makes a long, gentle climb (to 10,105 ft+) before descending to the outlet of Garnet Lake, meeting the Garnet Lake Trail (3 mi; 9,678 ft). (Camping and campfires are prohibited within ¼ mile of the outlet of Garnet Lake.) The trail follows the northern shore of Garnet Lake, climbs over a small pass (to 10,105 ft+) and descends to Ruby Lake (¾ mi; 9,911 ft). The trail continues to cross the outlet of Thousand Island Lake and meets the Pacific Crest Trail (¾ mi; 9,777 ft+). (Camping and campfires are prohibited within ¼ mile of the outlet of Thousand Island Lake. Bears prowl through this area.) The trail continues northwest to the summit of Island Pass (2 mi; 10,170 ft+). It then descends to the northwest to meet first a side trail to Davis Lakes (¾ mi; 9,645 ft+) and then the Rush Creek Trail (¼ mi; 9,580 ft+). Bears are active in the entire Rush Creek drainage.

The John Muir Trail goes northwest from its junction with the Rush Creek Trail to a side trail leading to Marie Lakes (1 mi; 10,039 ft+). It then continues on to the summit of Donohue Pass (2 mi; 11,040 ft+). The trail descends the northwest side of the pass and continues down the beautiful, long, flat canyon of the Lyell Fork of the Tuolumne River to meet the Evelyn Lake Trail (7 mi; 8,901 ft). Bears prowl through this area. The John Muir Trail follows the Lyell Fork downstream to the junction with the Tuolumne Pass Trail (4½ mi; 8,720 ft+). The John Muir Trail continues west to another trail junction (½ mi: 8,640 ft+). The John Muir Trail goes left to the Tuolumne Meadows Campground. The Pacific Crest Trail turns right, crosses the Lyell Fork and Dana Fork, and leads to the road serving the Tuolumne Meadows Lodge and the parking lot for hikers.

Pacific Crest Trail　　15¼ miles

The Pacific Crest Trail leaves the John Muir Trail ½ mile beyond the Devil's Postpile National Monument Visitor Center (0 mi; 7,600 ft+). It goes north and then descends, passing beneath Minaret Falls, to Upper Soda Springs Campground (2¼ mi; 7,680 ft+). It follows the east bank of the Middle Fork of the San Joaquin River to a trail junction (2¼ mi; 8,000 ft+). The left fork leads to the River Trail; the Pacific Crest Trail goes right and, after some switchbacks, meets the River Trail near

Agnew Meadows (½ mi; 8,320 ft+). The Pacific Crest Trail turns right (east) and passes through Agnew Meadows, at first on trail and finally by road (1 mi; 8,320 ft+).

From Agnew Meadows, the Pacific Crest Trail (also known as the "High Trail" from this point) is a quota trail. It makes a few switchbacks from the road and then climbs high above the eastern slope of the Middle Fork (with outstanding views of the Ritter Range) to where it meets the Agnew Pass Trail (5¼ mi; 9,680 ft+). The Pacific Crest Trail continues northwest from the junction to meet another side trail leading to Agnew Pass (¾ mi; 9,520 ft+). It then goes west to meet the upper terminus of the River Trail (¾ mi; 9,600 ft+) and continues west to meet the John Muir Trail at Thousand Island Lake (1 mi; 9,833 ft). Bears prowl through this area.

Minaret Lake Trail　　5 miles

A quota trail. The Minaret Lake Trail leaves the John Muir Trail at Johnston Meadow (0 mi; 8,080 ft+) and follows the northern bank of Minaret Creek. After the trail switchbacks up a bare granite slope, it meets a side trail that leads north to an abandoned mine south of Volcanic Pass (3¼ mi; 9,055 ft+). The Minaret Lake Trail continues up Minaret Creek and circles Minaret Lake on its northern shore before disappearing in the talus above the lake (2¼ mi; 9,908 ft+). Wood campfires are prohibited at Minaret Lake.

River Trail　　5¼ miles

A quota trail. This trail ascends the east bank of the Middle Fork of the San Joaquin River from Agnew Meadows, meeting the Pacific Crest Trail between Agnew Pass and Thousand Island Lake. Follow the Pacific Crest Trail downhill toward the river for 1 mile from Agnew Meadows (0 mi; 8,320 ft+). The River Trail heads northwest, downhill, to meet a side trail that leads back downstream to the Pacific Crest Trail (½ mi; 8,000 ft+). It continues upstream, past Olaine Lake, to the junction with the Shadow Lake Trail (¾ mi; 8,080 ft). The River Trail continues upstream to a junction with the Agnew Pass Trail (2¾ mi; 8,924 ft+), meets the Garnet Lake Trail (¼ mi; 9,055 ft+), and then meets the Pacific Crest Trail (1 mi; 9,580 ft+).

Shadow Lake Trail　　7 miles

A quota trail. Bears prowl through this area. The Shadow Lake Trail leaves the River Trail 2¼ miles from

Agnew Meadows (0 mi; 8,080 ft+). It crosses the Middle Fork on a bridge and makes a steep ascent near the falls of Shadow Creek. The trail emerges through a rocky gap with a spectacular view of Mount Ritter and Banner Peak. The trail passes the northern shore of Shadow Lake, where camping and campfires are prohibited. It meets the John Muir Trail near the upper end of Shadow Lake (1½ mi; 8,737 ft).

The Shadow Lake Trail and the John Muir Trail go up Shadow Creek to where the upper section of the Shadow Lake Trail branches off to the left (½ mi; 8,989 ft). (Camping and wood campfires are prohibited south of the Shadow Lake Trail/John Muir Trail and north of Shadow Creek from Shadow Lake to where the Shadow Lake Trail crosses Shadow Creek, i.e., the outlet of Lake Ediza.) The Shadow Lake Trail goes upstream (camping and wood campfires are prohibited north of the creek in this area) to a difficult ford across Shadow Creek (2 mi; 9,252 ft+). (A rough use trail has appeared that circles Lake Ediza on its northern shore.) After fording Shadow Creek, the trail circles Lake Ediza on its eastern and southern shores, then climbs to Iceberg and Cecile Lakes (3 mi; 10,239 ft). Wood campfires are prohibited at Lake Ediza, and camping is prohibited along Lake Ediza's eastern and southern shores.

Garnet Lake Trail   1 mile

The Garnet Lake Trail leaves the River Trail approximately 5¼ miles from Agnew Meadows (0 mi; 9,055 ft+). It makes a steep ascent of the southern bank of the outlet stream of Garnet Lake and meets the John Muir Trail at the lake (1 mi; 9,678 ft). Camping and campfires are prohibited along the eastern side of Garnet Lake.

Rush Creek Trail   9¼ miles

A quota trail. Bears prowl through this area. This trail starts from the northern end of Silver Lake, along the June Lake Loop, also known as Highway 158 (0 mi; 7,240 ft+). The trail goes south, up and across the cliff above Silver Lake, to the junction with the Agnew Pass Trail just below Agnew Lake (2¼ mi; 8,680 ft+). The Rush Creek Trail ascends from the north side of Agnew Lake and contours around the north shore of Gem Lake to the junction with the Parker Pass Trail at the northwest corner of Gem Lake (2½ mi; 9,110 ft). The Rush Creek Trail turns south, climbs over a small saddle (to 9,240 ft+), and meets the side trail leading to Clark Lakes

(¾ mi; 9,160 ft+). The main trail remains on the north bank of Rush Creek for 1¼ miles to meet a side trail that leads south, across the creek, to Weber Lake (1¼ mi; 9,320 ft+). The Rush Creek Trail continues upstream, goes around the northern shore of Waugh Lake, and arrives at the junction with the John Muir Trail (2½ mi; 9,580 ft+).

Clark Lakes Trail   2¾ miles

The Clark Lakes Trail leaves the Rush Creek Trail above Gem Lake (0 mi; 9,160 ft+). Bears prowl through this area. The trail crosses Rush Creek on a bridge and ascends to the southwest to Clark Lakes (1¾ mi; 9,840 ft+). The Agnew Pass Trail is a short distance to the east; the Clark Lakes Trail goes south before turning southwest and crossing the Sierra crest west of Agnew Pass (to 10,170 ft+). The trail continues west to meet the Pacific Crest Trail (1 mi; 9,646 ft+).

Agnew Pass Trail   4½ miles

This trail leaves the Rush Creek Trail below Agnew Lake (0 mi; 8,680 ft+) and crosses Rush Creek on a bridge. Bears prowl through this area. The trail zigzags up a steep slope to Spooky Meadow, a scenic spot surrounded by red and black volcanic cliffs. The trail continues southwest to Clark Lakes (2¾ mi; 9,908 ft+). The Clark Lakes Trail is a short distance to the west. The Agnew Pass Trail goes south, down (to 9,777 ft+), and then slightly up and over Agnew Pass (to 9,842 ft+) to picturesque Summit Lake (½ mi; 9,777 ft+). A side trail heads southeast from here to join the Pacific Crest Trail (or High Trail). The Agnew Pass Trail descends to where it crosses the Pacific Crest Trail (¼ mi; 9,449 ft+) and continues downhill to the River Trail (1 mi; 8,989 ft+).

Parker Pass Trail   10¾ miles

The Parker Pass Trail leaves the Rush Creek Trail at the northwestern end of Gem Lake (0 mi; 9,110 ft). It climbs to the northwest over Gem Pass (to 10,477 ft), then heads down to Alger Lakes (3½ mi; 10,607 ft). Bears prowl through this area. The trail continues northwest from Alger Lakes, switchbacks up to the summit of Koip Peak Pass (to 12,240 ft+), traverses across the north side of Parker Peak, and descends to the small basin to the north (to 10,840 ft+). The trail then climbs to Parker Pass (to 11,080 ft+) before descending to the Mono Pass Trail (7 mi; 10,603 ft). This trail junction is unsigned, overgrown with grass, and difficult to spot from the Mono Pass Trail.

Parker Lake Trail   1¾ miles

This trail leads from the trailhead at the end of Parker Creek Road (0 mi; 7,760 ft+) to Parker Lake (1¾; 8,318 ft). It remains on the southeastern bank of the creek.

Mono Pass Trail   9 miles

A quota trail. The trailhead for this trail is at Dana Meadows, along Tioga Pass Road east of Tuolumne Meadows. The trail goes southwest across some lovely meadows to the junction with a side trail leading to Spillway Lake (2¾ mi; 9,959 ft). The Mono Pass Trail begins a slight climb, meets the obscure and unsigned junction with the Parker Pass Trail (1 mi; 10,603 ft), and gains the summit of Mono Pass (north) (½ mi; 10,604 ft). The trail descends the east side of the pass, goes past Sardine Lakes, and enters Bloody Canyon. The trail forks just above Walker Lake (4½ mi; 7,980 ft); take the right fork and make a steep climb to the trailhead at the end of Sawmill Canyon Road (1½ mi; 7,678 ft).

Gibbs Lake Trail   4 miles

The Gibbs Lake Trail leads from the end of the Horse Meadow Road (0 mi; 7,927 ft) to Gibbs Lake (4 mi; 9,530 ft). The upper portion of the Horse Meadow Road requires a four-wheel-drive vehicle. Ordinary passenger cars can go as far as Lower Horse Meadow (7,400 ft); this adds about 1½ miles of hiking.

Glacier Canyon Trail   2½ miles

The approach for this trail starts from a turnout west of Tioga Lake along Tioga Pass Road (0 mi; 9,769 ft). A good use trail leads down, across the inlet of Tioga Lake (to 9,638 ft), and up the south bank of the stream draining Glacier Canyon. Continue up the canyon to Dana Lake (2½ mi; 11,128 ft). There is an impressive view of Mount Dana and its glacier from the lake.

CROSS-COUNTRY ROUTES

"Nancy Pass"   3100 m+; 10,160 ft+;
0.4 mi N of Superior Lake

Class 2. This pass has a plaque on the summit nam-

ing it in memory of Nancy Scanlon (1966–1974). It leads between King Creek and Minaret Creek. Go north from Superior Lake to the low saddle east of Peak 3345m (10,640 ft+). Loose talus on the north side of the pass leads down to the Minaret Creek drainage.

Further Reading: Steve Roper. *Sierra High Route.* Seattle: The Mountaineers Books, 1997, pp. 164–165, 178.

"Deadhorse Pass"   2960 m+; 9,760 ft+;
0.5 mi E of Deadhorse Lake

Class 1. This pass is usually used in combination with Nancy Pass to travel between Beck Lakes and Minaret Lake. Make a gradual descending traverse to the northwest from the summit of Nancy Pass to the base of the small saddle west of Peak 3004m (9,933 ft). Climb to the top of the pass and hike north across some beautiful meadows to Minaret Lake.

Further Reading: Steve Roper. *Sierra High Route.* Seattle: The Mountaineers Books, 1997, p. 165.

"Beck Lakes Pass"   3280 m+; 10,800 ft+;
0.5 mi NW of Upper Beck Lake

Class 2. Talus and seasonal snow slopes lead from Beck Lakes to the summit of this pass. It is best to traverse north about 1 mile from the pass before descending the north fork of Iron Creek.

"McDonald Pass"   3240 m+; 10,560 ft+;
0.5 mi NE of Shellenberger Lake

Class 2. This pass leads between the upper north fork of Iron Creek and the upper portion of Dike Creek. It has been named here in honor of Rob Roy and Doug McDonald, who missed out on the first ascent of Pridham Minaret by a matter of days.

"South Notch"   3440 m+; 11,280 ft+;
0.5 mi SW of Cecile Lake; UTM 086696

Class 2; ice axe required. This pass is between Ken Minaret and Kehrlein Minaret. It is commonly used to approach the hard-to-get-to west side of The Minarets, and for climbs of Michael Minaret and Adams Minaret from Minaret Lake. Ascend snow and talus above the southern shore of Cecile Lake to the prominent pass to the left (southeast) of the east face of Ken Minaret. From the top of the pass, traverse into Minaret Amphitheater and climb over the notch between Michael Minaret and

Adams Minaret. Descend the class 3 chute on the west side of the notch to the base of Michael Minaret. Another route is much longer but easier: Traverse around the southern and western sides of Adams Minaret to the base of Michael Minaret. Care must be taken when crossing the west spur of Adams Minaret to ensure that the easiest route is selected.

"North Notch" 3480 m+; 11,520 ft+;
0.6 mi SW of Iceberg Lake; UTM 077708

Class 3. This pass is used to approach the western side of The Minarets from Lake Ediza and Iceberg Lake. Climb onto the ridge that is northwest of Iceberg Lake and follow it to the chute that leads to the low point between Jensen Minaret and Dyer Minaret. There is a curving ledge that leads from the north into the chute. One small chockstone is encountered in the chute before the notch is reached. The west side of North Notch is composed of steep talus (as is the western side of The Minarets). Steep snow and ice may exist on North Notch until late in the season, and an ice axe may be needed.

"The Gap" 3380 m+; 11,120 ft+;
0.7 mi W of Iceberg Lake; UTM 075711

Class 2; ice axe required. This pass is between Waller Minaret and Leonard Minaret. Climb onto the small glacier north of the pass and cross it to the summit of the pass. The south side of the pass consists of steep talus.

Ritter Pass 3380 m+; 11,120 ft+;
1.2 mi SSE of Mount Ritter; UTM 068714

Class 2. This is the easiest route across The Minarets. Head southwest from Lake Ediza and climb the small cliff to the base of the pass. The correct pass is to the right (northwest); a gentle snowfield leads to its summit. Easy, rocky slopes are found on the southwest side of the pass.

"Volcanic Pass" 3220 m+; 10,560 ft+;
0.9 mi SE of Lake Ediza

Class 2. This pass leads between Minaret Creek and Shadow Creek. Leave the Minaret Lake Trail at the large meadow bench beneath Minaret Lake and ascend the side trail that leads north to the abandoned Minaret Mine. Continue hiking cross-country from the mine to the lowest pass atop Volcanic Ridge. Loose rock on the north side of the pass leads down to Cabin Lake; follow the outlet stream to the Shadow Creek Trail.

Minaret Lake to Lake Ediza

Class 2–3. This may be the most popular cross-country route in the High Sierra. It traverses interesting terrain, and has outstanding close-up views of The Minarets. A good use trail has formed over most of this route.

Circle around Minaret Lake on its northern shore and climb up along the north bank of the stream that enters the lake from the west. The stream makes a dogleg turn to the southwest; leave the stream at this point and ascend a steep, narrow slot (class 2–3) to the eastern shore of Cecile Lake. Circle around Cecile Lake on its east and north shores to its outlet. Descend diagonally to the northeast, aiming for the far shore of Iceberg Lake; a semipermanent snowfield is usually encountered along this section, and an ice axe may be needed. Follow the east bank of the outlet stream of Iceberg Lake down to Lake Ediza. Wood campfires are prohibited all along this route, and camping is prohibited along the southern and eastern shores of Lake Ediza.

Further Reading: Steve Roper. *Sierra High Route.* Seattle: The Mountaineers Books, 1997, pp. 166–167, 178.

"Whitebark Pass" 3200 m+; 10,480 ft+;
1.0 mi E of Banner Peak

Class 2. This pass leads between Nydiver Lakes and Garnet Lake. The south side of the pass is easy, but the north side consists of steep, loose scree and talus, with seasonal snowfields. The easiest route on the north side generally goes northeast from the summit of the pass, bypassing snowfields.

Further Reading: Steve Roper. *Sierra High Route.* Seattle: The Mountaineers Books, 1997, p. 167.

"Ritter-Banner Saddle" 3660 m+; 12,000 ft+;
0.3 mi NNE of Mount Ritter

Class 3; ice axe required. From Lake Ediza, climb to the base of the cliff that is east of the saddle. Climb the cliff, keeping to the right of the black watermarks by zigzagging up class 3 ledges. Ascend snow to the low point of the saddle, then descend the glacier on the northwest side of the saddle to Lake Catherine.

"Garnet Pass"   3080 m+; 10,080 ft+;

0.9 mi NE of Banner Peak

Class 1. This is an easy cross-country route between Thousand Island Lake and Garnet Lake.

North Glacier Pass   3400 m+; 10,080 ft+;

0.9 mi NE of Banner Peak

Class 2. This pass leads from Thousand Island Lake to Lake Catherine. Head southwest from Thousand Island Lake to the low saddle between Banner Peak and Mount Davis. The final approach to the top of the pass is best made from the northwest. Lake Catherine is a short distance southwest of the pass. Circle Lake Catherine on its north and west shores, then descend to the North Fork of the San Joaquin River by keeping on the north bank of the stream that drains Ritter Lakes.

"Clinch Pass"   3500 m+; 11,520 ft+;

0.8 mi NW of Mount Davis

Class 2. This pass, named in honor of Nick Clinch, provides access between upper Rush Creek and the North Fork of the San Joaquin River. It is best to climb to the pass directly from Rodgers Lakes. The south side of the pass consists of steep talus.

"Lost Lakes Pass"   11,440 ft+; 11,360 ft+;

0.8 mi W of Blacktop Peak

Class 1. This pass provides access from Rush Creek to the unnamed lakes at the head of Kuna Creek. Gentle slopes lead from the vicinity of Waugh Lake to the basin that contains Lost Lakes. Continue north in the basin to the summit of the pass, keeping to the east of the small dome on top of the pass. Sand and granite benches lead down the north side of the pass to the lakes that are west of Koip Crest.

"Kuna Pass"   11,812 ft; 11,960 ft+;

1.5 mi NW of Kuna Peak

Class 2. This pass is also known as "Kuna Crest Saddle." It leads from the Parker Pass Trail over Kuna Crest to the numerous small lakes in the upper reaches of Kuna Creek. Leave the Parker Pass Trail at the point where a good use trail leads to Spillway Lake. From the southern shore of Spillway Lake, follow its inlet stream uphill to the eastern shore of Helen Lake. Head southwest from the lake toward the low saddle atop Kuna Crest. Talus and sand are encountered on the north side

of the saddle. Snowfields can be avoided by keeping to the right. Easier terrain on the southwest side of the pass eventually leads south around a small ridge to the lakes in the cirque at the head of Kuna Creek.

PEAKS

Iron Mountain   3318 m; 11,149 ft

South Slope. Class 1. A trail leads north from Corral Meadow (on the Mammoth Trail) to Iron Lake. Climb onto the ridge south of the lake and follow it to the summit.

East Slope. Class 2. First ascent July 17, 1988 by Vi Grasso, Delores Holladay, and Barbara Reber. Climb benches above Anona Lake to the prominent gap between two knobs on top of the face. Pass through the knobs and follow the southern side of the southeast ridge to the summit.

Northeast Ridge. Class 3. First ascent August 6, 1997 by R. J. Secor. Climb the sharp ridge that is left (southeast) of the northeast couloir.

Northeast Couloir. Class 2; ice axe required. First ascent August 2, 1935 by Jules Eichorn. Pass Ashley Lake on its west shore and climb the couloir that gradually steepens near its top. Much of the snow can be avoided by keeping to the rocks on its right side. It is class 1 from the top of the couloir to the summit.

"The Watchtower"   3420 m+; 11,200 ft+;

0.5 mi SW of Deadhorse Lake; UTM 091683

This peak has also been called "Crown Prince Spire." The east face (II, 5.5) was climbed in August 1974 by Rupert Kammerlander and John Schaffert. The north face (II, 5.6) was first climbed July 16, 1978 by Kim Grandfield and Amadeo Tagliapietra.

"Starr Minaret"   3506 m; 11,512 ft;

0.4 mi W of Deadhorse Lake

Northwest Slope. Class 2. First ascent July 14, 1937 by Walter A. Starr, Ansel Adams, and Rondal Partridge. This slope can be reached from South Notch.

Sleeping Beauty Chimney. III, 5.9. First ascent August 1974 by Rupert Kammerlander and John Schaffert. Ascend the 700-foot chimney on the south face.

East Face. Class 5. First ascent September 1960 by Chuck Wilts and Ray Van Aken. Climb to the cirque between Starr and Kehrlein minarets from Deadhorse

Mount Ritter, Banner Peak, and the Minarets

Garnet
Pass

North
Glacier
Pass

*Lake
Catherine*

Garnet
*Garnet
Lake*

John Muir
Trail

N

Whitebark
Pass

Banner
Peak

0   0.5

MILE

*Ritter
Lakes*

Mount
Ritter

Ritter-Banner
Saddle

*Nydiver
Lakes*

Shadow Creek

*Ediza
Lake*

*Cabin
Lake*

Volcanic
Pass

Ritter
Pass

Waller
Minaret

The
Gap

*Iceberg
Lake*

Volcanic
Ridge

The Minarets
1. Leonard
2. Turner
3. Jensen
4. Dyer
5. Dawson
6. Bedayan
7. Rice
8. Eichorn
9. Michael
10. Adams
11. Clyde
12. Ken
13. Kehrlein
14. Pridham
15. Riegelhuth

1

2

North
Notch

3

4
5
6
7

The
Minarets

8
9

11

*Cecile
Lake*

*Minaret
Lake*

12

10

South
Notch

13

14

15

McDonald
Pass

Starr
Minaret

*Deadhorse
Lake*

Dike Creek

Beck
Lakes
Pass

The
Watchtower

*Shellenbarger
Lake*

Beck Lakes

Lake. Ascend the east face, which is mostly class 3 with a few class 4 pitches. The summit pitch is class 5. The northeast couloir is class 3 from Deadhorse Lake.

"Riegelhuth Minaret"   3260 m+; 10,560 ft+;
0.2 mi S of Minaret Lake; UTM 097694

West Face. Class 4. First ascent July 13, 1938 by Jack Riegelhuth, Charlotte Mauk, Josephine Allen, and Bill Leovey. Climb to the saddle between Riegelhuth and Pridham Minarets from Minaret Lake, and ascend a class 4 trough up the west face to the summit.

North Prow. III, 5.7. First ascent August 15, 1980 by Adam Paul and Scott Martin. This prow drops down to Minaret Lake from the summit. The first pitch (5.7) is followed by 200 to 300 feet of class 3–4 climbing. The crux pitch steepens considerably from here, leading over poor-quality rock (5.7) to the base of the large dihedrals atop the prow. Bypass these dihedrals to their right and then climb up for two pitches over extremely loose rock (5.6). Approximately 200 feet of class 3–4 climbing then leads to the summit.

Northeast Face. Class 4. First ascent August 6, 1955 by David Tonkin and Lito Tejada-Flores. Climb toward a prominent gully that leads up and to the left. Follow this gully to a notch on the east ridge, then follow the ridge to the summit. This is a ten-pitch climb. *Variation:* Leave the gully about 200 feet below the east ridge and climb a 5.5 wall directly to the summit.

East Face. I, 5.6. First ascent August 1973 by Gilles Corcos and Steve Roper. Wander up the broad east face, following the line of least resistance.

"Pridham Minaret"   3340 m+; 10,960 ft+;
0.2 mi N of Deadhorse Lake; UTM 094695

East Ridge. Class 2. First ascent July 4, 1938 by May Pridham and Mary Van Velsen. Follow the ridge from the saddle between Riegelhuth and Pridham Minarets.

East Face. Class 3–4. First ascent August 1982 by Alan Swanson. Climb this face from the notch between Pridham and Riegelhuth Minarets.

"Kehrlein Minaret"   3540 m+; 11,440 ft+;
0.4 mi SSW of Cecile Lake; UTM 087696

A party led by Oliver Kehrlein made the second ascent of this minaret, and it has been named after him to avoid confusion. The west summit is the high point.

West Ridge. Class 4. First ascent August 23, 1933 by Norman Clyde. Climb the southern side of the west ridge before crossing to the north. Traverse across a slab leading up onto the northwest face. Climb this face and work left, staying on the north side of the west ridge to the summit.

North Face. Class 4. First ascent August 1941 by Fred Hudson and R. Olson. Climb over broken ledges on the north face to the summit.

East Ridge. Class 5, A0. First ascent September 3, 1961 by Chuck Wilts and Ray Van Aken. This climb starts from the notch between Kehrlein and Pridham Minarets. This notch can be reached by climbing over Pridham Minaret or directly from the south; either way is class 2. This long ridge is class 2, 3, 4, 5, with some rappels. Generally, the route is class 4–5 on the faces of the many steps on the ridge, and some rappels are needed to descend the west side of towers along the ridge. Descend the northern side of the east summit and traverse across the north face below the small spire between the east and west summits. Climb to the notch between the spire and the higher, west summit by means of a difficult class 5 pitch.

"South Notch Minaret"

This small spire is just north of South Notch. The northwest face is class 5, and was first climbed in 1959 by Ray Van Aken and Ernest Bauer.

"Ken Minaret"   3620 m+; 11,760 ft+;
0.5 mi SW of Cecile Lake; UTM 084699

The northwest peak is the high point.

Northeast Face. Class 4–5. First ascent September 5, 1938 by Kenneth Davis and Kenneth Adam. Ascend the left branch of the couloir between Ken and Clyde Minarets for a few hundred feet. Climb onto the face that is left of the couloir and to the right of the crest of the large rib that descends from Ken Minaret's summit. Approach the summit rocks from the north and climb a short class 4–5 crack to reach the summit.

Southeast Ridge. Class 5. First ascent September 1958 by Chuck Wilts, Ellen Wilts, and Ray Van Aken. Climb the west side of the ridge rising from South Notch, aiming for the notch just north of a prominent tower. Bypass the notch, and continue climbing the west side of the ridge for several leads to the top of the wall above the notch. Turn this first step on its east side (class 5). Continue following the crest of the ridge to the tower beneath the next step, which is a big one. Rappel from the tower into another notch, and traverse the east side, and then climb (class 5) to the top of this big step. Continue up the ridge to the summit.

Southwest Face. Class 3–4. Descended September 5, 1938 by Kenneth Davis and Kenneth Adam. The summit rocks are difficult.

"Adams Minaret" 3640 m+; 12,000 ft+; UTM 079699

First ascent July 15, 1937 by Ansel Adams and Rondal C. Partridge. This peak is class 3 from the notch between it and Michael Minaret.

"Clyde Minaret" 3738 m; 12,281 ft; UTM 083702

Central Chute. I, 5.2. First ascent September 24, 1984 by Dale Van Dalsem, Elden Hughes, and J. C. Eckert. Climb to an area of red rock in the cirque above Cecile Lake. Move up and right over the red rock to a wide ledge that runs across the face of Clyde Minaret. On the face above this ledge there are two ribs that separate three chutes. Climb the central chute; this consists of class 3 followed by one technical pitch (5.2), a class 4 pitch, and class 3 to the summit.

Starr's Route. Class 4. First ascent August 8, 1932 by Walter A. Starr, Jr. This route climbs the right-hand chute on the northeast face of Clyde Minaret. Climb onto the ledge that runs across the northeast face of Clyde Minaret from the area of red rock to the east of the peak. Ascend the right-hand chute from the ledge, keeping to the left of a prominent gendarme. Climb above the level of the gendarme to the shallow rib and chute that lead to the crest of the ridge connecting Clyde Minaret with Eichorn Minaret. Follow the ridge left (southeast) to the summit of Clyde Minaret. A short class 4 move is encountered along this ridge.

Rock Route. Class 4. First ascent July 26, 1929 by Glen Dawson, John Nixon, and William Horsfall. This is the easiest route on Clyde Minaret, and is preferred by many over the other routes on the northeast face. Follow the ledge across the northeast face of Clyde Minaret to its western end, where it drops down to the glacier. Just before this drop-off, the ledge crosses a steep chute that goes up toward the summit. Climb this chute, keeping to the right of a prominent gendarme, and follow the face and rib to the crest of the ridge above. Follow the ridge left (southeast), then climb

down a 10-foot class 4 move along the ridge before reaching the summit. *Variation:* The ledge that runs across the northeast face of Clyde Minaret can be reached from the base of the face. Climb up and left to gain the ledge about 300 feet to the left (southeast) of the chute for the Rock Route. *Variation:* The ledge described in the previous variation can also be reached from the glacier to the north of Clyde Minaret. Climb the far left side of the glacier and ascend the moat to the ledge. *Variation:* The chute of the Rock Route crosses the ledge, and it is possible to climb the chute directly from its very bottom. However, the lower portion of the chute is actually a steep, difficult (5.5) chimney, and it is better to approach the chute from the ledge.

Rock Route Descent. Follow the ridge toward Eichorn Minaret from the summit of Clyde Minaret, and make a 10-foot class 4 move along the ridge. Climb to the crest of the ridge, then descend the north side, aiming for the chute that is left of a prominent gendarme and right of a shallow rib, as seen looking downward. This chute leads to a ledge that runs across the northeast face of Clyde Minaret. The ledge ends in an area of red rock, which is descended to where it is possible to make a descending traverse to the right to the base of the east face and southeast face of Clyde Minaret.

Glacier Route. Class 4. First ascent June 27, 1928 by Norman Clyde. Climb to the highest left-hand edge of the glacier north of Clyde Minaret. Cross the bergschrund and make a left-diagonal ascent across some shallow ribs and chutes to the ridge between Eichorn and Clyde Minarets. Follow the ridge toward Clyde Minaret. A short class 4 move is encountered just before the summit.

Traverse from Eichorn Minaret. Class 4. First ascent July 31, 1931 by Jules Eichorn, Walter Brem, and Glen Dawson. Descend approximately 50 feet southwest from the summit of Eichorn Minaret to a ledge that runs across the southern side of the ridge leading to Clyde Minaret. Follow the ledge and ridge to the summit of Clyde Minaret. Most of this traverse is class 3.

Southwest Face. Class 4. First ascent unknown; first winter ascent January 2, 1948 by Bill Long, Jim Wilson, and Allen Steck. Go east from the north end of Amphitheater Lake to a point that is near the notch between Clyde and Ken Minarets. Ledges lead left (northwest) to a gully that goes up to the top of the ridge between Clyde and Eichorn Minarets. Follow the ridge to the summit

of Clyde Minaret. *Variation:* Class 4. First ascent July 22, 1973 by Doug DeWolf and Frank Meyers. Ascend an easy chute from near the notch between Clyde and Ken Minarets. Traverse to the right at the point where this chute suddenly steepens into the next chute. This next chute drops out onto the southeast face of Clyde Minaret. Ascend this chute to the ridge between Clyde and Eichorn Minarets, then follow the ridge to the summit of Clyde Minaret.

Clyde-Ken Couloir. Class 4–5. Descended August 16, 1933 by Jules Eichorn, Glen Dawson, and Richard Jones. Ascend the right branch of this couloir from the east, passing a huge chockstone on its right side. Continue up the couloir to the Clyde-Ken Notch, then follow ledges on the southwest side of Clyde Minaret to a chute that leads up to the ridge between Eichorn and Clyde Minarets. Follow the ridge to the summit of Clyde Minaret.

Clyde-Ken Couloir Descent Route. This is commonly used as a descent route following climbs of the southeast face of Clyde Minaret. Follow the ridge from Clyde Minaret toward Eichorn Minaret to the second gully that leads down to the south; this gully is close to the low point of the ridge between Clyde and Eichorn Minarets. Descend the gully to some ledges that lead southeast to the Clyde-Ken Notch. Descend the east side of the couloir to the chockstone. A short rappel from the right side (looking down) of the chockstone leads to the base of the southeast face. If there is much snow present in the couloir, and if it is late in the day, you may need either an ice axe and crampons or bivouac gear.

Southeast Edge. IV, 5.9. First ascent June 28, 1986 by Joel Richnik and Mike Carville. This route follows the right side of the far left-hand outside corner of the southeast face. Climb a series of shallow corners followed by an off-width crack. Continue up a face on ledges, and move slightly right and then left to the bottom of a right-facing open book. From the top of the book, go up and follow the right side of the ridge to the summit.

Southeast Face. IV, 5.8. First ascent June 22, 1963 by John Evans, Dick Long, Allen Steck, and Chuck Wilts. First winter ascent February 1980 by Galen Rowell and Kim Schmitz. This route is justifiably popular. Ascend the Clyde-Ken Couloir until approximately level with the toe of the rib in the Clyde-Ken Couloir. Make an almost horizontal 125-foot traverse (5.6) to the right to an obscure ledge that is barely visible on the right skyline from the correct start of this, the first, pitch. Climb up and slightly right for four pitches (nothing harder than 5.7) from this ledge, aiming for a large ledge that is left of the bottom of a shallow, left-facing dihedral. Climb straight up a crack for approximately 25 feet and then make a slightly descending traverse to the right with hidden holds that leads to the bottom of the dihedral. Ascend the dihedral (5.8) to a small belay alcove. Climb up and slightly right from the alcove, passing a prominent white scar on its left side. Then climb up and slightly left, mantling over blocks (5.8) to a large ledge at the bottom of the most prominent dihedral on the face. Ascend 90 feet in the dihedral to a belay ledge. An improbable traverse left for 50 feet is followed by 100 feet of 5.6 straight up (with some loose blocks) to a ledge. Another 150-foot pitch of 5.7 leads to the top of the face. Traverse left over class 4 rock to the southeast edge, then follow the right side of the southeast edge to the summit. *Variation:* A direct start of this route begins from the area of red rock directly beneath the southeast face. Hike up to the highest point of the talus, then climb a thin crack (5.9+) in a prominent right-facing open book for two pitches. These pitches lead to the prominent ledge at the end of the normal route of the southeast face. Traverse left across the ledge to meet the normal route. *Variation:* The improbable traverse can be avoided by continuing up the dihedral for one pitch (5.8) over some big, loose blocks.

Further Reading: Steve Roper and Allen Steck. *Fifty Classic Climbs of North America.* San Francisco: Sierra Club Books, 1979, pp. 288–293; *Summit.* January–February 1971, pp. 11–13; *Summit.* March–April 1987, p. 19; John Moynier and Claude Fiddler. *Sierra Classics.* Evergreen, Colo.: Chockstone Press, 1993, pp. 238–241.

East Ridge. III, 5.7. First ascent June 15, 1970 by Marek Glogoczowski and Bill Katra. This route apparently follows the crest of the ridge formed by the junction of the southeast face and northeast face.

"Michael Minaret" 3736 m; 12,240 ft+; UTM 078701

Michael's Chute. Class 4–5. First ascent September 6, 1923 by Charles Michael. This is the further right of

Clyde Minaret from the north. Photo by R. J. Secor.

Michael Minaret from the west. Photo by R. J. Secor.

the two chutes that lead up the west side of Michael Minaret to the notch just north of the minaret. The third chockstone in this chute is passed by climbing the wall to its right; start climbing about 30 feet below the chockstone and climb the wall to a ledge. Traverse left on the ledge back into the chute, then follow the chute to the notch, the Portal. Climb underneath the boulder that forms the Portal, traverse left (southeast), and zigzag up over ledges. The final approach to the summit follows a ledge on the west side of the summit spire. *Variation: The Ladder With the Lower Rungs Missing.* Class 5. This small variation climbs the wall immediately right of the third chockstone in Michael's Chute. Strenuous climbing leads up the wall and back into the chute above the chockstone.

Further Reading: *Sierra Club Bulletin.* 1924, pp. 28–33.

Eichorn's Chute. Class 4. First ascent August 16, 1933 by Jules Eichorn, Glen Dawson, and Richard Jones. This is the first chute north of Michael's Chute. Traverse right from the top of the chute over into Michael's Chute, under two small spires, and to the Portal. Continue to the top of Michael Minaret as described under Michael's Chute.

Further Reading: John Moynier and Claude Fiddler. *Sierra Classics.* Evergreen, Colo.: Chockstone Press, 1993, pp. 235, 242–243.

Starr's Chute. Class 4. First ascent August 3, 1933 by Walter A. Starr, Jr.; this was Starr's last climb. First winter ascent December 29, 1963 by Dick Long, Jim Wilson, George Bloom, and George Marks. This is the easiest route up Michael Minaret, but Starr's Chute is full of loose rock, and this route demands intelligent risk management. Ascend the second chute north of Michael's Chute; this chute leads up the south side of Eichorn Minaret. Follow its right branch at a point about 300 feet beneath the ridge crest, at an elevation of 12,060 feet or 3675 meters. Traverse right near the top of the chute to the head of Eichorn's Chute. Continue traversing to the right, under two small spires, over into Michael's Chute, and climb to the Portal.

Amphitheater Chute. I, 5.4. First ascent August 31, 1958 by Mike Sherrick and Wally Tinsley. This is the prominent chute that leads to the notch between Michael and Eichorn Minarets from Amphitheater Lake. The chute leads up from the north end of the lake, and the right side of the chute is followed to the top. The crux of this route is at the first chockstone; a poorly protected move goes around its right side. Higher, a second chockstone is passed by traversing out about 50 feet to the right. From the top of the notch, work down and west to the Portal, and continue to the summit via the description for Michael's Chute.

South Face. III, 5.7, A1. First ascent August 13, 1962 by John Dorsey, George Steck, and Allen Steck. This route starts from the notch between Adams and Michael Minarets. Ascend an obvious chimney system for three pitches, followed by two pitches up and right toward a small notch in the southeast ridge. Two class 4 pitches then lead to the summit. The first-ascent party used only one aid placement.

Clyde's Ledge. Class 4. First ascent August 25, 1933 by Norman Clyde. Ascend the west face of Michael Minaret to a sloping ledge that leads left (north) into Michael's Chute, above the level of the third chockstone in that chute. Continue up Michael's Chute to the Portal, and on to the summit as in the description for Michael's Chute.

"Eichorn Minaret" 3120 m+; 12,255 ft;
UTM 079703
First ascent July 31, 1931 by Jules Eichorn, Glen Dawson, and Walter Brem. Eichorn Minaret is class 4 from Clyde Minaret. Follow the ridge from Clyde Mina-

ret to where it is possible to descend the southern side of the ridge to a ledge that leads to a point about 50 feet southeast of Eichorn Minaret. A short class 4 pitch leads to the summit.

Eichorn Minaret can also be climbed via Starr's Chute and from the Portal on Michael Minaret. Pass through the Portal, then climb to the notch between Michael and Eichorn Minarets. Eichorn Minaret is class 3, with one short class 4 pitch from the notch.

The northeast face is class 4, but with one class 5 pitch—climbing the face left of the snow chimney. This was first climbed in 1956 by Roy Gorin, Joe Stone, Huey Stone, Dick Kahlstrom, and Allison Tolin.

"Rice Minaret" 3720 m+; 12,160 ft+;
UTM 079704
Starr's Chute. Class 4. First ascent August 11, 1936 by William Rice and Torcom Bedayan. Ascend Starr's Chute on Michael Minaret, but take the left branch instead of the right. Rice Minaret is north from the top of the left branch of the chute.

Traverse from Bedayan Minaret. Class 3. First ascent August 11, 1936 by William Rice and Torcom Bedayan. This traverse is made on the west side of Rice Minaret.

Eichorn-Rice Couloir. Class 5. First ascent September 1965 by Rich Gnagy and Barbara Lilley. Climb this couloir from the east. The hardest climbing is in the upper portion of the couloir, just below the notch. Climb the first chute left from the notch to a small wall, which is climbed on its right side. This is followed by an open book, which leads to the summit ridge.

"Bedayan Minaret" 3680 m+; 12,080 ft+;
UTM 079705
Northwest Chute. Class 4. First ascent August 25, 1950 by L. Bruce Meyer and Hervey Voge. This chute leads to the notch north of Bedayan Minaret. Enter the chute from its right (south) side on a ledge, and climb the chute until you are approximately 300 feet below its top. Traverse to the right into the next chute to the south, and climb the minaret via its south face.

East Couloir. This is the couloir that leads to the Bedayan-Dawson notch. This couloir is full of dangerous, loose blocks!

Northeast Face. Class 5. First ascent July 6, 1963 by Rich Gnagy and Barbara Lilley. This route starts from the high point of the glacier, left of the couloir between

Bedayan and Dawson Minarets. Climb up and slightly left over a series of ledges. A short traverse left and up leads to a sloping ledge, which is followed left to a watercourse. Ascend the right side of the watercourse for two pitches to a steep, seasonal snowfield. Above the snowfield, 300 feet of class 3 and 4 lead to the summit ridge, which is followed west to the summit.

Traverse from Rice Minaret. Class 3. First ascent August 11, 1936 by Torcom Bedayan and William Rice. Most of this traverse is done on the west side of the ridge.

"Dawson Minaret"   3540 m+; 11,920 ft+; UTM 078706

From North Notch. Class 4. First ascent August 16, 1933 by Glen Dawson, Jules Eichorn, and Richard Jones. Traverse around Dyer Minaret on its west side from North Notch. Enter the next chute to the south. Climb directly toward the summit of Dawson Minaret over a broken face, working gradually to the right to a ledge on the ridge. Traverse around to the south side of the minaret, then climb an open chimney to the summit.

The Minarets from the east, September 2, 1965. Photo by Austin Post, No. F655-189, USGS Ice and Climate Project, GeoData Center, University of Alaska, Fairbanks.

The south face of Dawson Minaret can also be reached from the west by climbing the chute directly under this broken face; bypass the chockstone in the chute on its left side.

Bedayan-Dawson Chute. Class 4. Climb to the Bedayan-Dawson notch from the west. A chockstone in this chute is bypassed on its left side. An open chimney on the face of Dawson Minaret leads to the summit.

"Dyer Minaret" 3550 m+; 11,680 ft+; UTM 077707

Northwest Face. I, 5.6. First ascent 1948 by John Dyer and William Horsfall. Climb to a small notch on the west side of this minaret from North Notch. One pitch up the northwest face leads to the summit.

East Face. I, 5.7. First ascent August 1962 by John Dorsey and Allen Steck. Traverse south from North Notch to the base of the east ridge. One pitch from a large sloping ledge leads to a belay ledge on the east face. One more pitch up the east face leads to the summit.

"North Notch Minaret"

This tiny pinnacle is just northeast of Dyer Minaret. It is class 5 from the notch between it and Dyer Minaret. First ascent 1937 by David Brower and Morgan Harris.

"Jensen Minaret" 3540 m+; 11,760 ft+; UTM 077708

From North Notch. Class 4. First ascent June 1937 by Carl Jensen and Howard Gates. There is much loose rock on this route.

Northeast Face. I, 5.4. First ascent July 27, 1943 by Chuck Wilts, Dan Bannerman, and Spencer Austin. Traverse beneath the east side of Jensen Minaret from North Notch. There are two chimneys on the northeast face. Climb the right-hand chimney to a small notch between two small spires on the ridge between Jensen and Turner Minarets. Follow the ridge to the top.

"Turner Minaret" 3547 m; 11,600 ft+; UTM 076709

Traverse from Jensen Minaret. Class 3. First ascent July 14, 1938 by Ed Turner and party.

East Face. I, 5.8. First ascent August 28, 1995 by Dave Harden and Don Palmer. This route starts by ascending a smooth, gray slab on the right side of the east face of Turner Minaret. Begin by climbing a right-facing corner for two pitches to a small notch near the summit. Next, traverse up and right across a steep face to a lower angle corner system that leads to the summit ridge. Follow the ridge south to the summit.

East Side. II, 5.4. First ascent September 1972 by Rupert Kammerlander. This route actually starts on Leonard Minaret. Ascend a crack system that is left of a prominent chimney on the lower portion of Leonard Minaret's east face. Continue up and left to a large, curving open book, which leads to the notch that is to the right of Turner Minaret. This notch is marked by a large block; pass the block on its right side and climb up to the notch. Traverse out onto the west face of Turner Minaret from the notch, and climb a 5.4 pitch to the summit ridge.

"Leonard Minaret" 3520 m+; 11,600 ft+; UTM 078711

Southeast Rock Chimney. Class 4. First ascent August 4, 1932 by Richard Leonard and Herbert Blanks. There is a prominent chimney, which may be filled with snow, on the southeast side of Leonard Minaret. Climb the less prominent chimney that is to the left of the snow chimney. Climb to a wide ramp that leads to the right. Climb up and left from this ledge to the summit ridge.

South Face. Class 4. First ascent September 3, 1964 by Don Wilson and Bob Weyman. This route is to the left (west) of the southeast rock chimney.

West Ridge. Class 4. First ascent August 19, 1933 by Norman Clyde. Follow the ridge from The Gap (between Waller and Leonard Minarets; see the section on cross-country routes earlier in this chapter).

"Waller Minaret" 3557 m; 11,711 ft; UTM 073703

West Side. I, 5.4. Climb the right-hand chute on the west side of the minaret; this chute ends at a point about 300 feet north of the summit. Follow the ridge south to the summit. An impasse on this ridge is turned on its right (west) side via a 20-foot, steep crack (5.4). *Variation:* First ascent September 4, 1993 by Bob Sumner. Instead of going to the right at the impasse, move up and left onto a small, exposed, sloping ledge. This is followed by 10 feet of stemming (5.2) that lead to a large, sloping slab.

West Ridge. I, 5.2. First ascent September 4, 1993 by Bob Sumner. Begin by climbing a chute that leads up

The Minarets from the northeast. Photo by R. J. Secor.

the north side of the west ridge. Take the left branch of this chute, and go past a flat, slabby area of white rock to where further progress is stopped by cliffs. Move to the right and climb a 15-foot jumbled crack (5.2) that leads to a notch on the crest of the west ridge. Stay on the class 4 south side of the west ridge until you meet the north ridge of Waller Minaret, at a point immediately beneath the impasse.

Eichorn Route. II, 5.4. First ascent August 1934 by Ted Waller and Jules Eichorn. First winter ascent December 29, 1963 by Dick Long, Jim Wilson, Dave Beck, and George Bloom. Climb onto the southeast ridge of Waller Minaret from The Gap, and follow a ledge that goes out onto the east face. Follow this ledge for one pitch, and then climb the face, aiming for the arête that rises above the vertical wall of The Gap. Follow the arête north for about 150 feet to a large tower. Climb this by going directly up its center. Scramble over the top of this tower and descend 20 feet down its west side. Traverse around the top of a steep couloir and rib on its west face, then climb another tower to the summit ridge.

East Face. III, 5.5. First ascent July 1961 by Dick Long and Bob Hill. This route begins directly beneath the summit, and seven or eight pitches lead to the ridge just south of the summit. A direct variation of this route (III, 5.8) was climbed in August 1971 by Craig Mackay and Rupert Kammerlander.

Volcanic Ridge 3501 m; 11,501 ft;
0.4 mi E of Iceberg Lake

First ascent August 13, 1933 by Craig Barbash and Howard Gates. There is an outstanding view from the summit. Go north from Minaret Lake and ascend a long, grassy slope to the saddle that is west of the summit. The north ridge from Lake Ediza is class 2, as is the long ridge from Volcanic Pass.

Peak 3734m   12,344 ft; 0.9 mi SSW of Mount Ritter

This is the craggy peak that is on the long southwest ridge of Mount Ritter. The first-ascent party named this peak "Neglected Peak," because it was probably one of the last major summits in the High Sierra to be climbed.

South Ridge. I, 5.7. First ascent 1964 by Mike Loughman and Steve Arnon. Follow the south ridge from Slide Creek to the top of a gendarme that overlooks a prominent, deep notch. Make a short, difficult (5.7) descent into a wide chimney on the west side of the gendarme and gain the notch. A steep pitch (5.2) out of the notch leads to the left onto the broken face that is west of the south ridge. Class 4 rock then leads to the top. The deep notch has also been reached directly from Dike Creek.

Southwest Ridge. IV, 5.9. First ascent 1984 by Claude Fiddler and Vern Clevenger. Follow the long ridge from the North Fork of the San Joaquin River to the summit. The first-ascent party continued over the Ritter Pinnacles and on to the summit of Mount Ritter. The 5.7 north face was climbed in July 1990 by Vern Clevenger and John Moynier.

"Ritter Pinnacles"   3780 m+; 12,320 ft+; 0.5 mi SSE of Mount Ritter

The highest of these pinnacles is class 3 from the southeast glacier of Mount Ritter, and was first climbed August 4, 1936 by Richard M. Jones and William Rice.

Mount Ritter   4006 m; 13,157 ft

Southeast Glacier. Class 3. Descended October 1872 by John Muir. Go west from Lake Ediza to the cliff beneath the snout of the glacier that is southeast of Mount Ritter. Start by climbing slabs to the left of a gully before

Mount Ritter from the southeast. Photo by R. J. Secor.

crossing the head of the gully to reach the left (south) end of a vegetation-covered ledge. This ledge leads diagonally right across the cliff; a few small waterfalls fall upon it from above. The ledge eventually splits. Go up a steep, narrow, grassy ledge before switchbacking up onto another ledge, which leads to the top of the cliff. Skirt the north side of the glacier, and climb a chute that leads to the broad talus slope beneath the summit. *Clyde Variation:* Class 3. First ascent June 28, 1928 by Norman Clyde. The cliff beneath the glacier can be passed on its far southern (left) side. Climb toward the lowest pinnacles to the south and pass through the gap above them onto the glacier. Ascend the southern side of the glacier, keeping to the left of an ice ridge, to where a crevasse bars further progress. Cross to the north side of the glacier, over the ice ridge, to the chute that leads to the talus slope and the summit. Ice axes and crampons are almost always needed on this variation.

Further Reading: John Moynier. *Backcountry Skiing in the High Sierra.* Evergreen, Colo.: Chockstone Press, 1992, p. 178.

East Face. Class 4–5. First ascent September 1961 by Nick Clinch and Tom Hornbein. This route is on the far left side of the east face. Ascend a ledge that diagonals right from the north side of the southeast glacier. This ledge leads to the left side of a prominent scar. Continue up the face to the summit.

Northeast Buttress. Class 4. First ascent August 7, 1941 by Art Argiewicz and Lorin Trubschenk. This is the prominent buttress that rises 2,000 feet above the east cirque between Mount Ritter and Banner Peak. Climb toward the Ritter-Banner Saddle from the east to the top of the cliff that is beneath the saddle. Traverse left from the top of the cliff and climb onto the crest of the buttress. Follow the buttress to the summit.

North Face. Class 3. First ascent October 1872 by John Muir. Climb to the top of the Ritter-Banner Saddle from either the east or the west. Ascend the right-hand (west) chute on the north face; it may be necessary to enter this chute from the left via a broad ledge that starts from the base of the left-hand chute on the north face of Mount Ritter. From the top of the right chute, traverse left to a wide ledge that leads up and left to an arête. Follow the arête to the summit. *Starr Variation:* Class 3. First ascent July 3, 1932 by Walter A. Starr, Jr. Traverse right from the top of the right chute over a ridge, then drop down onto and cross the ledges on the northwest

side of Mount Ritter. Ascend the ledges to the summit. *Variation:* Class 3. First ascent July 20, 1986 by Igor Mamedalin, Jim Farkas, Marty Washburn, Tom Scott, Lisa Freundlich, Steve Crooks, Bruce Parker, Suzanne Thomas, and Jim Floyd. The left chute on the north face may be preferable if there is a lack of snow.

Further Reading: John Muir. *The Mountains of California.* New York: The Century Co., 1917, pp. 52–73; John Moynier and Claude Fiddler. *Sierra Classics.* Evergreen, Colo.: Chockstone Press, 1993, pp. 246–247.

West Slope. Class 2. First ascent August 20, 1892 by Theodore S. Solomons. First winter ascent February 1952 by George Bloom, Bob Swift, and Floyd Burnette. Go south from Lake Catherine to the outlet of the southernmost lake of the Ritter Lakes. Follow the eastern shore of this lake toward the south, past the first talus fan and around a low buttress, to the second talus fan. Ascend this fan (a real slog) to the upper bowl. Traverse right to a chute; be sure to enter the chute about halfway up, and not from its bottom. This chute leads to another talus fan, which leads to another chute. Climb this chute until about you are 50 to 75 feet below its top. Traverse left and up to the top of the ridge, which is followed to the summit of Mount Ritter. The top of this upper chute is difficult to find during descent.

Southwest Ridge. VI, 5.9. First ascent July 1984 by Vern Clevenger and Claude Fiddler. This route begins in the canyon of the North Fork of the San Joaquin River. It traverses Peak 3734m (12,344 ft) and the Ritter Pinnacles before ending atop Mount Ritter.

Further Reading: John Moynier and Claude Fiddler. *Sierra Classics.* Evergreen, Colo.: Chockstone Press, 1993, pp. 244–245.

Banner Peak   3943 m; 12,945 ft

From Ritter-Banner Saddle. Class 2. First ascent August 26, 1883 by Willard Johnson and John Miller. First winter ascent March 1, 1939 by Chester Errett, Bob Brinton, and Lloyd Warner. This route is class 2 from Lake Catherine; a class 3 section is encountered when approaching the saddle from the east. Banner Peak is a talus slog from the saddle.

Southeast Face. Class 5. First ascent July 6, 1946 by Charles Wilts and Harry Sutherland. This route, which ascends the middle of the southeast face, is most readily seen from the vicinity of Lake Ediza. Most of the route

Mount Ritter and Banner Peak from the southeast, August 24, 1972. Photo by Austin Post, No. 72R2-88, USGS Ice and Climate Project, GeoData Center, University of Alaska, Fairbanks.

is class 4; however, two class 5 pitches are encountered. Start by climbing the first couloir to the right of a deep chimney. Ascend easy rock at first, then cross left into another couloir, which branches up from the deep chimney. Ascend diagonally right over almost vertical rock to a large ledge, which usually has a small snow patch. Traverse right about 200 feet from this ledge, then continue straight up to the summit ridge, aiming for a point about 300 feet from the summit. *Variation:* Class 5. First ascent August 17, 1989 by Chris Keith and Pete Lowery. Climb the couloir that branches up from the deep chimney. Climb another chimney to the left of the vertical rock. This second chimney leads to the ridge south of the summit.

East Corner. Class 4. First ascent August 3, 1931 by Jules Eichorn and Robert Underhill. This route starts from the saddle between Banner Peak and Peak 3497m (11,440 ft+; 0.4 mi E of Banner Peak). Ascend a chute (loose rock!) on the left side of the ridge rising from the saddle. It is eventually possible to climb onto the ridge crest and continue up the ridge or buttress until you are stopped by an overhang. Climb up and right for about 80 feet over smooth rock, then follow some broad, steep chutes to the summit.

Further Reading: John Moynier and Claude Fiddler. *Sierra Classics.* Evergreen, Colo.: Chockstone Press, 1993, pp. 248–249.

East Face. III, 5.6. First ascent August 1961 by Allen Steck and Floyd Burnette. Cross the glacier that is northeast of Banner Peak to its highest point. (This high point is in a couloir to the right of a prominent buttress that almost touches the east corner.) Climb the wall about 40 feet to the right of this couloir. Two pitches of 5.6 over steep, blocky rock lead to easier climbing. Climb up and slightly right for three class 4 pitches, and continue climbing an obvious route to the summit ridge, about 200 feet north of the summit. *Variation:* 5.7. Traverse to the right around an arête after the three class 4 pitches. Climb the arête and the wall above to the summit ridge.

East Face, Right Side. III, 5.8. First ascent August 10, 1975 by Kim Grandfield and Arne Myrabo. This route climbs a rib that ascends diagonally from right to left across and up the east face of Banner Peak. Start climbing about 200 feet to the right of the East Face route on the left side of the left-facing open books. Climb about 200 feet to the crest of a rib. Continue up the rib for ten pitches of class 4 and 5 until you are about 200 feet below the summit ridge. Traverse up and left for two easy pitches to some white watermarks on overhanging rock. A short, difficult pitch straight up leads to the summit

West Slope of Mount Ritter. Photo by R. J. Secor.

MOUNT RITTER

Point 3489m

Ritter Lake 3377m

Ritter Lake 3311m

Banner Peak from the southeast. Photo by R. J. Secor.

ridge. Follow the ridge south to the summit.

Northeast Buttress. III, 5.6. First ascent August 28, 1973 by David Harden and Kevin Sutter. This climb starts from the shoulder that is north of the glacier northeast of Banner Peak. Climb onto the shoulder from the north via two class 4 pitches. Two 5.6 pitches lead up a prominent chute to the left from the shoulder. Approximately 200 feet of scrambling leads to a talus-filled notch on the buttress itself. Three very enjoyable pitches lead from here to the summit ridge.

North Buttress. III, 5.7. First ascent 1984 by Vern Clevenger and Claude Fiddler. This buttress is to the right of the northeast buttress. The climb starts from the summit of the small peak to the north of Banner Peak. Follow the crest of the buttress upward, passing the towers on the crest on their left (east) sides to the notch behind the tallest tower. From the notch, climb a steep ramp on the eastern side of the buttress to the shallow summit ridge.

Further Reading: John Moynier and Claude Fiddler. *Sierra Classics*. Evergreen, Colo.: Chockstone Press, 1993, pp. 250–251.

Northwest Shoulder. Class 4. First ascent August 1950 by Sarah Haynes and Jim Koontz. Ascend the north side of the ridge from North Glacier Pass. The last part of this climb ascends the crest of the northwest ridge.

Banner Peak and Mount Ritter from the northwest, September 2, 1965. Photo by Austin Post, No. F655-188, USGS Ice and Climate Project, GeoData Center, University of Alaska, Fairbanks.

"Annie's Spire"   3600 m+;
0.8 mi SE of Mount Davis; UTM 053753

First ascent July 12, 1966 by Ann Gibson, Dave Rossum, and Richard Clough. This pinnacle is on the eastern side of the southwest ridge of Mount Davis. Ascend a snow couloir to the right (north) of the spire from Thousand Island Lake. Climb a 60-foot class 3 crack on the west side of the pinnacle to a ledge. One pitch up a jam crack (5.4) leads straight up to a large ledge on the southwest arête. Climb the arête (5.3) to the summit.

Mount Davis   3750 m; 12,311 ft
Southeast Slope. Class 2. First ascent August 28, 1891 by Milton F. Davis. Keep to the southwest side of the ridge while climbing the peak from North Glacier Pass.

West Chute. Class 2. Descended September 17, 1994 by Dave Dykeman, Matthias Selke, Barbara Cohen, Erik Siering, Nancy Gordon, Al Conrad, and R. J. Secor. There is a headwall on the southwest side of the summit of Mount Davis, with two chutes to the right (south) of the headwall. Climb the northernmost chute to the southeast slope and then on to the summit.

North Buttress. Class 4. First ascent August 20, 1950 by Jim Koontz and Sarah Haynes. This buttress is between the two glaciers on the north side of Mount Davis. Start by climbing the west side of the buttress at first, and later move onto the crest of the buttress to reach the summit.

Northeast Buttress. Class 4. First ascent August 20, 1950 by Hervey Voge and Virginia Romain. This buttress is east of the north buttress, and leads to a lower summit that is southeast of the true summit of Mount Davis. Ascend the east side of the northeast buttress and climb a chute to the crest of the buttress. Climb the crest of the buttress to the lower peak, and walk up the easy southeast slope to the true summit.

Peak 3597m   11,627 ft; 0.7 mi NW of Mount Davis
Northwest Arête. Class 4. First ascent September 1975 by Bill Schuler, Andy Smatko, and Tom Ross. Climb the ridge rising from Clinch Pass. Two class 4 pitches along the top of this ridge lead to the summit.

Two Teats   3460 m+; 11,387 ft
The summit knocks, I mean rocks, are exposed class 3. A four-wheel-drive road followed by a use trail leads to the top from Minaret Summit.

San Joaquin Mountain   3535 m; 11,600 ft
Class 1 from the northwest or southeast. There is an outstanding view of The Minarets, Mount Ritter, and Banner Peak from the summit.

Carson Peak   3325 m; 10,909 ft
The south slope is class 1. There is a good ski tour off the summit to the north.
Further Reading: *Summit.* November–December 1987, pp. 8–11; John Moynier. *Backcountry Skiing in the High Sierra.* Evergreen, Colo.: Chockstone Press, 1992, p. 179.

The left rib on the north face is rated III, 5.9, A1, and was first climbed June 11, 1974 by Pete Kilbourne and Loring Young. Start on the left side of the rib and continue up its center.

The left side of the central rib is rated class 4+, and was climbed by Pete Lowery and Chris Keith on October 17, 1987. Climb about 1,000 feet of class 3 rock until you are level with the bottom of a major chimney on the rib. Climb the chimney past chockstones to its top. Traverse left across many chutes until it is possible to climb straight up to the summit.

The central rib has been rated IV, 5.8, and was first climbed September 6, 1974 by Pete Kilbourne, Vern Clevenger, and Bill Dougherty.

Saint's Way. IV, 5.9. First ascent April 1992 by Dean

Rosenau and Doug Nidever. Climb snowfields from the base of the northeast face to the Y-shaped couloir. Follow the left branch of the couloir and climb the upper, narrow chute that splits the headwall above. The top of the chute ends on a knife edge ridge. Follow the crest of the ridge to the summit.

Donohue Peak   12,023 ft; 12,023 ft
First ascent 1895 by Sergeant Donohue, U.S. Cavalry, on horseback. The northwest slope is class 1. The southwest ridge from Donohue Pass is class 2–3.

Peak 12,245ft   12,223 ft;
0.6 mi ENE of Donohue Peak
The southeast ridge is class 2.

Koip Crest   12,651 ft; 12,668 ft
This is a ridge of pinnacles that extends south from Koip Peak and then southeast from Blacktop Peak. The nine pinnacles between Koip Peak and Peak 12,651 ft (12,668 ft) are class 4, and were traversed August 9, 1939 by George Templeton and Milton Hildebrand. Peak 12,651 ft (12,668 ft) is class 2 from Blacktop Peak. The southeast arête is class 3; the southwest chimney is class 5, and was first climbed August 1950 by Richard M. Leonard and Jim Koontz.

Not much is known about the six pinnacles that are southeast of Peak 12,651 ft (12,668 ft). The buttress on the "third from the left" pinnacle (as seen from northern Lost Lake) was first climbed July 1973 by Art Buck and Allen Fletcher; this six-pitch climb has a II, 5.6 rating.

Koip Crest Traverse. V, 5.8. First ascent 1986 by Claude Fiddler and Ric Cashner. This long traverse starts at Kuna Crest and ends at Peak 11,600ft+ (11,601 ft).

Blacktop Peak   12,720 ft+; 12,710 ft+
The southeast slope is class 2, as is the traverse from Peak 12,651ft (12,688 ft).

Mount Wood   12,657 ft; 12,637 ft
Class 1 from Parker Peak. The east slope is class 2.
Further Reading: Hans Joachim Burhenne. *Sierra Spring Ski-Touring.* San Francisco: Mountain Press, 1971, pp. 80–81; John Moynier. *Backcountry Skiing in the High Sierra.* Evergreen, Colo.: Chockstone Press, 1992, p. 180.

Parker Peak   12,851 ft; 12,861 ft
First ascent 1914 by Norman Clyde, his *first* first ascent. Class 1 from Koip Peak Pass.

Koip Peak   12,962 ft; 12,979 ft
First ascent 1912 by Chester Versteeg. Class 1 from Koip Peak Pass.

Kuna Peak   13,002 ft; 12,960 ft+
First ascent 1919 by Walter L. Huber. The northwest side is class 3, and the traverse from Koip Peak is class 2; the step along this ridge is passed on its right side via a ledge.

Kuna Crest   12,202 ft; 12,207 ft
First ascent 1919 by Walter L. Huber. Class 3 from either the east or the west.

Mammoth Peak   12,016 ft; 12,117 ft
First ascent 1902 by Walter L. Huber. The slabs on the north side of the peak are class 2–3. The west slope is class 2.

Mount Lewis   12,342 ft; 12,296 ft
Class 1 from either Mono Pass or Parker Pass.
East Face. IV, 5.10. First ascent 1980 by Claude Fiddler and Jim Keating. Not recommended due to loose rock.

"Bloody Canyon Crags"
These crags are less than 1 mile from Walker Lake. There is a II, 5.6 route on the easternmost pinnacle. Climb the face to the right of a black open book, and then the book itself for eight pitches to the top of the pinnacle. This was first climbed October 1972 by Art Buck and Allen Fletcher.

Mount Gibbs   12,773 ft; 12,764 ft
First ascent August 31, 1864 by William Brewer and F. L. Olmstead, on horseback. The north, west, and south slopes are class 1.
Further Reading: John Moynier. *Backcountry Skiing in the High Sierra.* Evergreen, Colo.: Chockstone Press, 1992, p. 181.

Mount Dana   13,057 ft; 13,053 ft
First ascent June 28, 1864 by Charles Hoffman and William Brewer. The northwest, west, and south slopes

are class 1. A good use trail starts from the entrance station at Tioga Pass.
Further Reading: Hans Joachim Burhenne. *Sierra Spring Ski-Touring.* San Francisco: Mountain Press, 1971, pp. 78–79; John Moynier. *Backcountry Skiing in the High Sierra.* Evergreen, Colo.: Chockstone Press, 1992, pp. 182–183.

North Rib. III, 5.6. First ascent May 1982 by Harry Marinakis and Yorgos Marinakis. This is the far right-hand rib on the northeast face of Mount Dana. Approach the base of this rib from Dana Glacier, and follow the crest of the rib for twelve pitches or so. Most of this route is class 3 and 4, with a few class 5 moves. The crux is a 30-foot headwall about eight or nine pitches up the rib. The first-ascent party was forced off the rib near its top by some snow cornices. They traversed left and up across a bowl to the northwest slopes of the peak.

Northeast Face. Class 3. First ascent 1949 by Frank Meyers and party. Start climbing this loose face from midway between Dana Lake and the glacier. Follow the northwest ridge to the summit.

Dana Glacier. Class 4. Cross the glacier and ascend the ten-pitch, 40° snow/ice couloir to the southeast ridge. Follow the ridge to the summit. As an alternative, it is possible to climb the loose class 3 rocks on the side of the couloir.
Further Reading: John Moynier and Claude Fiddler. *Sierra Classics.* Evergreen, Colo.: Chockstone Press, 1993, pp. 278–279.

Dana Plateau   12,466 ft; 12,400 ft+
Third Pillar, Regular Route. III, 5.10a. First ascent July 1969 by Phil Bircheff and Bill Bonebrake. The northeastern face of the Dana Plateau is a striking sight from Tioga Road above Lee Vining. This route ascends the prominent pillar on this face, located at UTM 060983. Approach the Dana Plateau from Glacier Canyon and descend the class 3–4 ridge north of the pillar; the top of this ridge is at UTM 059986. Instead of descending all the way to the base of the pillar, leave the ridge where it is possible to traverse south, cross a gully, and climb onto the highest ledge leading out onto the prow of the pillar; this ledge is below and left of a right-facing obtuse open book. The real climbing starts with crack and face climbing leading to a ramp that ends on a large ledge with a small tree and a boulder. Instead of climbing the steep cracks above the ledge, climb up and left (5.9) to a

right-facing, shallow open book. The book widens, becomes left-facing (5.9), and leads to a good ledge. Continue up parallel 5.7 cracks and climb a class 4 chimney behind a flake (or layback the left side of the flake: 5.8). Difficult face climbing (5.10a) up and then left leads to a ledge with a small tree. Go up and right from the ledge to the higher of two ledges. The last pitch, the crux, jams a 5.10a right-facing crack; it is followed by hard face climbing to a ledge immediately below the top. A 5.9+ mantle lands on the summit.

Further Reading: Don Reid and Chris Falkenstein. *Tuolumne Meadows Rock Climbs.* Denver: Chockstone Press, 1986, p. 47; John Moynier and Claude Fiddler. *Sierra Classics.* Evergreen, Colo.: Chockstone Press, 1993, pp. 280–283.

The One That Almost Got Away. IV, 5.10c, A2+. First ascent September 4, 1990 by Miguel Carmona and Alois Smrz. This route ascends the seemingly blank headwall to the right of the Regular Route. (The poor, almost useless bolts noted below were placed by an unknown party on an earlier attempt.) Start by climbing a ramp that leads up and right from the open book at the base of the Regular Route. Strenuous (5.10b/c) climbing leading to the end of the ramp is followed by a horizontal traverse to the left, past a fixed pin, to a belay stance. Easy class 5 climbing goes up and right through an area of broken rock (crossing Lenticular Limbo) to a left-facing open book. Climb the book (5.7) to a large ledge with belay bolts at the base of the headwall. A2 nailing up the knifeblade crack in the middle of the headwall (with one bolt and one drilled hole) leads to a two-bolt belay. The next pitch continues up the middle crack with 5.10 climbing to where the crack forks; aid climbing up the right crack leads past three fixed pins to the shoulder of the Pillar. Walk across the cruddy ledge to the upper headwall, and climb the sharp, steep flake system (5.9) above the right end of the ledge. This is followed by A1 climbing up a narrow and shallow crack on a short pillar that leads to a large, flat ledge. Go to the left end of the ledge (awkward move), then climb the left side of a short pillar (5.9) to its top. A 40-foot A1 crack leads up to a tiny ledge. Move to the right side of this ledge, and follow a vertical finger crack in a corner (5.9) to the top of the Pillar. At least eight short knifeblades and short, thin horizontal pitons are needed, in addition to the usual regalia that decorates the aid climbing expert.

Lenticular Limbo. III, 5.10c. This route starts by ascending a left-facing open book that is to the right of the initial ramp of The One That Almost Got Away. Traverse left from the top of the open book (5.10c) and climb a pair of parallel cracks through the area of broken rock, crossing the route of The One That Almost Got Away. Face climb left (5.10a) from the middle of the easy section to a right-facing open book. Climb the book (more 5.10) and go up and slightly left to the flake on the Regular Route. Surmount the right side of the flake, keeping to the right of the Regular Route and climbing (more 5.10) to the higher of two ledges on the Regular Route. Follow the Regular Route to the summit.

Further Reading: Don Reid and Chris Falkenstein. *Tuolumne Meadows Rock Climbs.* Denver: Chockstone Press, 1986, p. 47.

A 5.7 buttress to the right of the Third Pillar was climbed July 1971 by Phil Bircheff and Gary Ogg.

WRINKLES

River Trail vs. High Trail. Those hiking from Agnew Meadows to Thousand Island Lake have the choice of these two trails. The River Trail is more direct, with less elevation gain, but the High Trail has outstanding views along almost its entire length.

How to cross The Minarets. North Notch is a climbers' route across The Minarets. The Gap is easier, but less direct, but may be preferred if North Notch is full of snow. Ritter Pass is a preferable route for hikers.

The Kuna Connection. Skiers traveling from Mammoth to Yosemite typically cross Donohue Pass and ski down Lyell Canyon, if 300 feet of loss over a distance of 9 miles can be considered "down." In late spring, with sticky snow, Lyell Canyon may be a long, hot, flat slog. An alternate route is to cross Lost Lakes Pass, traverse high across the headwaters of Kuna Creek, cross Kuna Pass down to Helen Lake, then descend the Parker Pass drainage, meeting Tioga Road near Dana Meadows.

Further Reading: John Moynier. *Backcountry Skiing in the High Sierra.* Evergreen, Colo.: Chockstone Press, 1992, pp. 48–49, 88.

Koip, Gibbs, and Dana Traverse. These three peaks have been climbed in a long day from Dana Meadows along Tioga Road.

Chapter 13

The Clark and Cathedral Ranges

These two subranges are west of the Sierra crest, in one of the most scenic regions of the Sierra Nevada: the southern part of Yosemite National Park. Most of the Clark Range is composed of colorful metamorphic rock. The exception is Mount Clark itself, which is composed of the firm granite that the High Sierra is known for throughout the world. The granite of the Cathedral Range has been eroded by glaciers into some surreal shapes. This, combined with its vast forests, meadows, and its position atop the divide between the Merced and Tuolumne Rivers, gives it a commanding presence.

This region is bounded on the north by Tioga Road, on the west by an imaginary line running from Snow Creek to Glacier Point to Chiquito Pass, and on the east by the North Fork of the San Joaquin River and the Lyell Fork of the Tuolumne River.

HISTORY

The first mountaineering in this region was done in November 1864, when Clarence King and Richard Cotter attempted Mount Clark, then known as the Obelisk. An early winter storm struck them at their camp between Mount Clark and Gray Peak, and their retreat through 1½ feet of new snow has become an epic tale. Two years later King and James Gardiner attempted the peak again, during the month of July. King's tale of their ascent of the southeast ridge was even more thrilling than that of the winter retreat two years before. This adventure was followed by John Muir's more modest account of his solo climb of Cathedral Peak in 1869. Mount Lyell was climbed in 1871, and the spires of the Cathedral Range were climbed by rock climbers after the 1930s. But, of course, all these tales of first ascents are moot when you consider that a Native American bow (as in bow and arrow) was found high on Parsons Peak by geologist Francois Matthes before 1920.

MAPS

USGS. *7.5-minute series:* Cattle Mtn., Timber Knob, Sing Peak, Mariposa Grove, Half Dome, Merced Peak, Mt. Lyell, Mt. Ritter, Vogelsang Peak, Tenaya Lake, Yosemite Falls. *National park maps:* Yosemite National Park and Vicinity (1:125,000). *30 x 60–minute series:* Yosemite Valley.

USFS. A Guide to the Ansel Adams Wilderness (1:63,360).

Tom Harrison Cartography. Yosemite High Country, Mammoth High Country.

Map Link 15-minute series. Devils Postpile, Merced Peak, Yosemite, Tuolumne Meadows, Hetch Hetchy Reservoir.

Wilderness Press 15-minute series. Devils Postpile, Merced Peak, Yosemite, Tuolumne Meadows, Hetch Hetchy Reservoir.

ROADS

Minarets Road

This is the direct route to Clover Meadow and the Granite Creek Trailhead. It consists of approximately 50 miles of curving, paved road. The road leaves the town of North Fork and traverses high above the San Joaquin River, passing many side roads and campgrounds, before meeting Beasore Road near Miller Meadow.

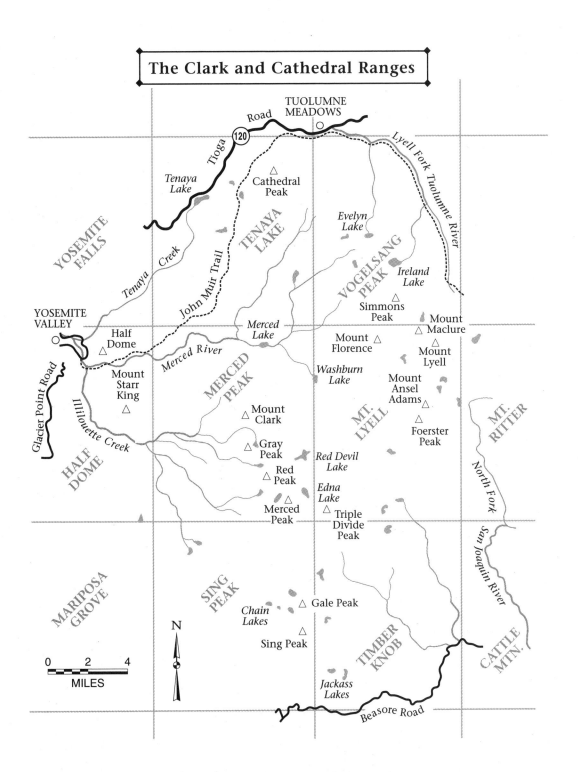

The Clark and Cathedral Ranges

TUOLUMNE MEADOWS

Tioga Road

120

Tenaya Lake

Cathedral Peak

Evelyn Lake

Lyell Fork Tuolumne River

YOSEMITE FALLS

Tenaya Creek

John Muir Trail

TENAYA LAKE

VOGELSANG PEAK

Ireland Lake

Simmons Peak

Mount Maclure

YOSEMITE VALLEY

Half Dome

Merced Lake

Mount Florence

Mount Lyell

Glacier Point Road

Merced River

MERCED PEAK

Washburn Lake

Mount Ansel Adams

MT. RITTER

Mount Starr King

Illilouette Creek

Mount Clark

MT. LYELL

Foerster Peak

HALF DOME

Gray Peak

Red Devil Lake

North Fork

Red Peak

Edna Lake

Merced Peak

Triple Divide Peak

San Joaquin River

MARIPOSA GROVE

SING PEAK

Gale Peak

Chain Lakes

Sing Peak

TIMBER KNOB

CATTLE MTN.

N

0   2   4
MILES

Jackass Lakes

Beasore Road

Beasore Road

Beasore Road, which starts from near Bass Lake, provides access to Chiquito Pass, Jackass Lakes, Norris Lake, and Fernandez Pass Trailheads. It passes Clover Meadow on the way to the Cora Lakes and Granite Creek Trailheads. Beasore Road goes north from its junction with County Road 222, just north of the town of Bass Lake. After 14.2 miles, it comes to a major fork; go left toward Clover Meadow. At 20.3 miles it meets the road that goes left 2.4 miles to the Chiquito Pass Trailhead. Beasore Road continues east, passing many side roads before meeting the Jackass Lakes Trailhead at 26.9 miles. A road goes left (north) at 27.6 miles; it leads 1.9 miles (rough road) to the Norris Lake Trailhead. Beasore Road continues east to a side road at 27.7 miles that goes left (north) another 2.4 miles to the Fernandez Pass Trailhead. The Beasore Road continues east, passes a junction (go straight or left) at 29.7 miles, and meets the Minarets Highway 0.2 mile later.

Go left (north) from this junction another 1.7 miles to Clover Meadow. The road continues north another 1.5 miles to the Cora Lakes Trailhead, then turns right (east) and goes 1.2 miles to the Granite Creek Trailhead.

Glacier Point Road

The Glacier Point Road leads from Chinquapin to Glacier Point. Leave Highway 41 approximately 12 miles north of Wawona, or 9 miles south of Yosemite Valley. The road goes east, past Badger Pass Ski Area and Bridalveil Creek Campground, and meets the trailhead for the Mono Meadow Trail 10.6 miles from Chinquapin. The road continues another 5.2 miles to Glacier Point.

Yosemite Valley

There are two trailheads within the scope of this book that are in The Valley: the John Muir Trail and the Snow Creek Trail. The John Muir Trail starts at Happy Isles at the far southeast corner of The Valley. You can only drive private vehicles as far as Upper Pines Campground; shuttle bus service is available to the trailhead.

The traditional starting point of the John Muir Trail was from the LeConte Memorial Lodge of the Sierra Club when it was located at Curry Village. The lodge has been moved ½ mile further to the west of Curry Village. Starting a hike along the John Muir Trail from Curry Village adds 1 mile to the hike. A start from LeConte Memorial Lodge adds 1½ miles.

The Snow Creek Trail ends (or begins) at Mirror Lake, at the far northeast end of The Valley. Private vehicles can only go as far as the stables near North Pines Campground. Either take the shuttle bus or walk the ¼ mile to the start of the bicycle path that leads to Mirror Lake, which is approximately 1 mile uphill from the bus stop.

Tioga Road

The trailhead for the Forsyth Trail is located near the campground on the western shore of Tenaya Lake.

The John Muir Trail follows the roads around Tuolumne Meadows for more than 3 miles, so this could be considered the biggest trailhead in the High Sierra. To help narrow things down somewhat, the eastern trailhead for the John Muir Trail is located near the hikers' parking area along the road leading to the Tuolumne Meadows Lodge; take the Pacific Crest Trail ½ mile south from the parking area and cross the Lyell Fork of the Tuolumne River on a bridge to meet the John Muir Trail. The central trailhead is in Tuolumne Meadows Campground, between the stock camp and site B49 (south of the hikers' camp). The Elizabeth Lake Trail leads ¼ mile south to the John Muir Trail. The western trailhead is the Cathedral Lakes Trailhead, just west of Budd Creek along Tioga Road. There is a parking area here; this is also where the John Muir Trail (or Sunrise Trail) leads to Cathedral Lakes and Cathedral Pass.

TRAILS

Isberg Pass Trail   23 miles

A quota trail. This trail leads from Granite Creek over Isberg Pass into Yosemite National Park to the Vogelsang Pass Trail, along Lewis Creek. The trail goes north from Granite Creek Campground (0 mi; 6,960 ft+) and passes through The Niche west of Green Mountain to a trail junction (2½ mi; 8,360 ft+). The right fork leads to Cora Creek and the North Fork of the San Joaquin River. The Isberg Pass Trail goes left from the fork, passes Cora Lakes (no camping or campfires along the north and east shores of the central lake), and meets a side trail (2¼ mi; 8,80 ft+). The side trail goes east to Detachment Meadow; the Isberg Pass Trail continues northwest to meet the trail that comes down from Joe Crane Lake (2½ mi; 8,840 ft+). The Isberg Pass Trail goes north to Sadler Lake (1½ mi; 9,362 ft), where camping and campfires are prohibited along its eastern and northern shores. The trail climbs to the west to the top of Isberg Pass (2 mi; 10,480 ft+). The trail descends the west side of the pass to meet the Post Peak Pass Trail (½ mi; 10,280 ft+). The Isberg Pass Trail goes west from the junction, turns north, and gradually descends for another 1¼ miles to meet a side trail that leads to the Red Peak Trail (1¼ mi; 9,880 ft+) along Triple Peak Fork of the Merced River. The Isberg Pass Trail goes north from the junction, travels along benches high above Triple Peak Fork (to 10,000 ft+), and then makes a steep descent to the Lyell Fork (4½ mi; 9,080 ft+). Bears prowl through this area. The trail crosses the stream and climbs northwest to another bench (to 9,840 ft+) above the Merced River before descending to Lewis Creek to meet the Vogelsang Pass Trail (6 mi; 8,680 ft+).

Fernandez Pass Trail   13¼ miles

A quota trail. The lower portion of this trail has also been called the "Clover Meadow Trail." The trail goes west from the Fernandez Pass Trailhead (0 mi; 7,520 ft+), passes a fork to the Norris Lake Trailhead (¼ mi; 7,560 ft+), passes another fork to the Norris Lake Trailhead (1 mi; 8,200 ft+), and passes a third fork that leads west to Vanderburgh Lake (½ mi; 8,240 ft+). The Fernandez Pass Trail descends to the north, turns northwest and west to meet a side trail to Lillian Lake (3 mi; 8,600 ft+; camping prohibited), then continues north to meet the Post Peak Pass Trail (1½ mi; 8,960 ft+). The Fernandez Pass Trail turns west from this junction, climbs to the top of Fernandez Pass (2¼ mi; 10,200 ft+), then descends to the west to meet the Moraine Meadows Trail (3½ mi; 8,680 ft+). The Fernandez Pass Trail continues west to the Merced Pass Trail (1¼ mi; 8,785 ft).

Post Peak Pass Trail   6¼ miles

This trail starts along the Fernandez Pass Trail 2¼ miles east of Fernandez Pass (0 mi; 8,960 ft+). The trail makes a gentle climb to the northeast before turning north, passing Porphyry Lake, and climbing to the top of the Post Peak Pass (5¼ mi; 10,760 ft+). The trail goes north along the ridge crest before descending to the west to meet the Isberg Pass Trail (1 mi; 10,280 ft+), ½ mile west of Isberg Pass.

Chiquito Pass Trail   7 miles

A quota trail. To reach the trailhead for this trail, leave Beasore Road 20.3 miles from Bass Lake and take the side road that goes left (northwest) from this junc-

tion 2.4 miles to the roadhead (0 mi; 7,235 ft). The trail ascends the Chiquito Creek drainage to Chiquito Lake (2¼ mi; 7,960 ft+), then continues to a fork atop Chiquito Pass (¾ mi; 8,040 ft+). One fork goes north to the Moraine Meadows Trail below Chain Lakes (3 mi; 8,640 ft+). The other fork goes left (west) from the junction fording the South Fork of the Merced River (1 mi; 7,440 ft+). The trail climbs and descends to meet the Moraine Meadows Trail (3 mi; 8,280 ft+).

Moraine Meadows
and Chain Lakes Trail   7¼ miles

This trail leaves the Fernandez Pass Trail at Moraine Meadows (0 mi; 8,680 ft+). The trail goes south to a junction (1¾ mi; 8,480 ft+). The Chain Lakes Trail goes to the left to meet a branch of the Chiquito Pass Trail (¼ mi; 8,640 ft+), continuing upstream to the beautiful Chain Lakes (1½ mi; 9,291 ft). Bears prowl through this area.

The Moraine Meadow Trail goes west from the Chain Lakes Trail junction, crosses Givens Creek, then meets another branch of the Chiquito Pass Trail (2¾ mi; 8,080 ft+). The trail then makes a gentle climb to meet the Merced Pass Trail (1 mi; 8,307 ft).

Buena Vista Trail   14 miles

A quota trail. The Buena Vista Trail starts along the Panorama Trail, 1½ miles from Glacier Point (0 mi; 6,400 ft+). It descends to Illilouette Creek and follows its west bank to the junction with the Mono Meadow Trail and the Merced Pass Trail (2¼ mi; 6,360 ft+). Bears prowl through this area. The Buena Vista Trail continues to follow the southwest bank of Illilouette Creek and gently climbs before turning southwest into the Buena Vista Creek drainage. The trail eventually crosses Buena Vista Creek and meets the Chilnualna Creek Trail (8¾ mi; 8,960 ft+). (The Chilnualna Creek Trail leads west to some beautiful lakes, and eventually to Wawona.) The Buena Vista Trail goes east from the junction and crosses a pass (9,280 ft+) northeast of Buena Vista Peak; excellent views, as the name says. The trail goes downhill to the south to meet the Merced Pass Trail (3 mi; 8,720 ft+).

Merced Pass Trail   18½ miles

This trail starts along the Mono Meadow Trail, just north of its crossing of Illilouette Creek (0 mi; 6,400 ft+). The Merced Pass Trail goes east to the eastern branch of the Mono Meadow Trail (1½ mi; 7,000 ft+) and continues east, across the Clark Fork of Illilouette Creek, before turning southeast to the junction with the Red Peak Pass Trail (7¾ mi; 8,920 ft+). It then crosses Merced Pass (9,280 ft+) and continues south to meet the Fernandez Pass Trail (2¾ mi; 8,785 ft). The Merced Pass Trail makes a gentle climb to the southwest (to 9,000 ft), passes a side trail leading to Givens Lake, and descends to meet the western end of the Moraine Meadow Trail (4½ mi; 8,307 ft). The Merced Pass Trail continues southwest from this junction and makes a steep climb to the Buena Vista Trail (2 mi; 8,720 ft+).

Red Peak Pass Trail   21½ miles

The Red Peak Pass Trail connects the higher reaches of Illilouette Creek with the upper portion of the Merced River. The trail starts by leaving the Merced Pass Trail north of Merced Pass (0 mi; 8,920 ft+), then climbs to the northeast to Lower Ottoway Lake (2½ mi; 9,653 ft). Bears prowl through this area. The trail makes a steep ascent from the lake to the top of Red Peak Pass (2½ mi; 11,120 ft+), and descends the north side of the pass before turning east to the Triple Peak Fork of the Merced River (7 mi; 9,080 ft+). (A side trail leads south from here and climbs the east wall of the canyon for 1¼ miles to meet the Isberg Pass Trail.) The Red Peak Pass Trail goes downstream from this junction to beautiful Washburn Lake (7 mi; 7,605 ft). Bears prowl through this area. The trail continues down the Merced River to meet the Vogelsang Pass Trail (2½ mi; 7,240 ft+) near the Merced Lake Ranger Station.

Mono Meadow Trail   6½ miles

A quota trail. This trail starts along Glacier Point Road, approximately 10½ miles from Highway 41 (0 mi; 7,240 ft+). The trail descends to the northeast, passes Mono Meadow, and continues down to Illilouette Creek, where it meets the Buena Vista Trail (2¾ mi; 6,360 ft+). The Mono Meadow Trail crosses the creek, goes past the Merced Pass Trail, and continues north to meet the eastern branch of the Mono Meadow Trail (3 mi; 6,800 ft+). The Mono Meadow Trail goes north to the Panorama Trail (½ mi; 6,600 ft+).

The eastern branch of the Mono Meadow Trail leaves the main trail ½ mile from the Panorama Trail (0 mi; 6,600 ft+). It traverses southeast beneath Mount Starr King to meet the Merced Pass Trail (2½ mi; 7,000 ft+), 1½ miles from Illilouette Creek.

Panorama Trail   3½ miles

A quota trail. The Panorama Trail starts from Glacier Point (0 mi; 7,200 ft+). It descends the east side of the point, meeting the start of the Buena Vista Trail (1½ mi; 6,400 ft+). It goes left (downstream), crosses Illilouette Creek on a bridge, and climbs and then follows the edge of Panorama Cliff to the junction with the Mono Meadow Trail (2½ mi; 6,800 ft+). The Panorama Trail continues east and descends to meet the John Muir Trail (also known as the Sunrise Trail) near Nevada Fall (1 mi; 6,000 ft+).

John Muir Trail   24½ miles

A quota trail. The lower part of this trail is also called the "Nevada Fall Trail," while the upper part is also called the "Sunrise Trail." It starts at Happy Isles (0 mi; 4,035 ft) and ascends the east bank of the Merced River before crossing the river on a bridge. Just beyond the bridge it meets the Mist Trail (1 mi; 4,600 ft+). The John Muir Trail turns south and climbs from this junction. It then passes a side trail leading down to the Mist Trail (¾ mi; 5,480 ft+) and meets the Panorama Trail (1¼ mi; 6,000 ft+). The John Muir Trail continues east from this junction and passes above Nevada Fall (a truly spectacular sight) to the upper terminus of the Mist Trail (½ mi; 5,960 ft+). The trail continues upstream into Little Yosemite Valley to the junction with the Merced Lake Trail (1½ mi; 6,080 ft+). Bears prowl through this area. The John Muir Trail turns to the north from the junction and meets the trail leading to the top of Half Dome (1½ mi; 7,000 ft+) and the Clouds Rest Trail (½ mi; 7,200 ft+). The John Muir Trail continues east along Sunrise Creek to a junction with the Merced Lake High Trail (2 mi; 7,880 ft+). The John Muir Trail goes north from the junction to the Forsyth Trail (¼ mi; 8,200 ft+) and then climbs to the northeast to Sunrise High Sierra Camp and the Sunrise Lakes Trail (5 mi; 9,280 ft+). The John Muir Trail continues north, passing a junction with the Echo Creek Trail (1 mi; 9,320 ft+), through Long Meadow, over Cathedral Pass (1 mi; 9680 ft+), and down past Cathedral Lakes to a side trail that leads to the westernmost Cathedral Lakes (2 mi; 9,360 ft+). Bears prowl through this area. The John Muir Trail goes north before turning northeast, passing the Budd Lake Trail (2½ mi; 9,000 ft+), and meets Tioga Road just west of Budd Creek at the Cathedral Lakes Trailhead (½ mi; 8,560 ft+).

Just before meeting Tioga Road, however, the John Muir Trail proceeds east along the south side of the road, past the Tuolumne Meadows Visitor Center to a trail junction (1 mi; 8,600 ft+). (The old John Muir Trail goes north from here for ½ mile, across Tioga Road to Soda Springs where it meets the current route of the Pacific Crest Trail.) But the current route of the John Muir Trail continues east to the junction with the Elizabeth Lake Trail (1 mi; 8,720 ft+), with Tuolumne Meadows Campground ¼ mile to the north. From this junction, the John Muir Trail continues east to meet the Pacific Crest Trail (1¼ mi; 8,640 ft+). The Pacific Crest Trail leads north for ½ mile to the hikers' parking area along the road leading to the Tuolumne Meadows Lodge.

The Mist Trail   1½ miles

The Mist Trail leaves the John Muir Trail 1 mile above Happy Isles (0 mi; 4,600 ft+). It ascends the southern side of the Merced River canyon, passing close to Vernal Fall, to a branch trail that leads back up to the John Muir Trail (½ mi; 5,200 ft+). The Mist Trail then crosses the river on a bridge and ascends the north side of the canyon (which has awesome views of Nevada Fall) to meet the John Muir Trail above Nevada Fall (1 mi; 5,960 ft+).

Half Dome Trail   2 miles

The Half Dome Trail leaves the John Muir Trail 6½ miles from Happy Isles (0 mi; 7,000 ft+). It heads northwest before turning southwest and climbing the east face of Half Dome via a system of cables and ladders. (These cables are usually in place from June until the end of October.) So many hikers have followed this route to the summit of Half Dome that the 46° rock slope between the cables has become polished, and in places it is disagreeably slippery. There is an outstanding view from the summit (2 mi; 8,836 ft).

Clouds Rest Trail   5½ miles

This trail leaves the John Muir Trail ½ mile east of the junction with the Half Dome Trail (0 mi; 7,200 ft+). The Clouds Rest Trail goes north, and after many switchbacks it leads to the summit of Clouds Rest, an outstanding viewpoint (3¾ mi; 9,926 ft). The trail goes over the summit of Clouds Rest and heads northeast to meet the Forsyth Trail (1¾ mi; 9,080 ft+).

Merced Lake Trail   9 miles

A quota trail. The Merced Lake Trail leaves the John Muir Trail in Little Yosemite Valley and ascends along the north bank of the Merced River (0 mi; 6,080 ft+). The upper portion of Little Yosemite Valley has some impressive domes, cliffs, and cascades. The trail crosses to the south bank of the river on a bridge above Lost Valley and eventually crosses the river again on another bridge before meeting the Echo Creek Trail in Echo Valley (6½ mi; 7,000 ft+). The trail crosses Echo Creek on a bridge, continues upstream along the north bank of the river to Merced Lake, skirts the north shore of the lake, and arrives at the Merced Lake High Sierra Camp (1¾ mi; 7,200 ft+). The trail continues upstream to the junction with the Vogelsang Pass Trail and the Red Peak Pass Trail; the Merced Lake Ranger Station is nearby (¾ mi; 7,080 ft+). Bears are active throughout this area.

Merced Lake High Trail   4 miles

This alternate route to Merced Lake leaves the John Muir Trail at its junction with the Forsyth Trail (0 mi; 7,880 ft+). It descends to the east to meet the Echo Creek Trail (4 mi; 7,480 ft+).

Echo Creek Trail   8½ miles

This trail leaves the John Muir Trail 1 mile north of the Sunrise High Sierra Camp (0 mi; 9,320 ft+). It goes east and makes a slight climb (to 9,480 ft+) before descending the Cathedral Fork of Echo Creek. It crosses Echo Creek twice on two bridges and meets the Merced Lake High Trail (7 mi; 7,480 ft+). It continues down the Echo Creek drainage to meet the Merced Lake Trail in Echo Valley (1½ mi; 7,000 ft+). Bears prowl through this area.

Budd Lake Trail   2½ miles

The Budd Lake Trail leaves the John Muir Trail approximately ½ mile from Tioga Road near Budd Creek (0 mi; 9,000 ft+). It ascends the west bank of the creek to Budd Lake (2½ mi; 9,975 ft). Camping and wood campfires are prohibited at Budd Lake.

Elizabeth Lake Trail   2¼ miles

A quota trail. The Elizabeth Lake Trail starts from Tuolumne Meadows Campground (0 mi; 8,680 ft+). It soon crosses the John Muir Trail (¼ mi; 8,720 ft+) and ascends the east bank of Unicorn Creek to lovely Elizabeth Lake (2 mi; 9,487 ft).

Tuolumne Pass Trail   11¾ miles

A quota trail. This trail leaves the John Muir Trail ¾ of a mile from its junction with the Pacific Crest Trail (0

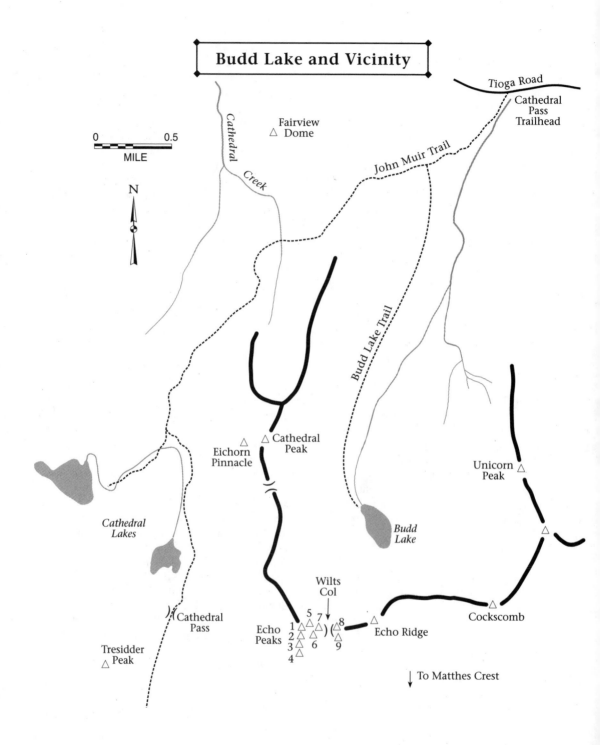

Budd Lake and Vicinity

Tioga Road

Cathedral Pass Trailhead

Fairview Dome △

Cathedral Creek

John Muir Trail

0   0.5
MILE

N

Budd Lake Trail

Eichorn Pinnacle △   △ Cathedral Peak

Unicorn Peak △

Cathedral Lakes

Budd Lake

Wilts Col

Echo Peaks   5   7   8   △   Echo Ridge
1 △ △   △
2 △   △ 6   9 △
3 △
4

Cathedral Pass

Cockscomb △

Tresidder △ Peak

↓ To Matthes Crest

mi; 8,720 ft+). It ascends the west bank of Rafferty Creek to Tuolumne Pass, where it meets the Vogelsang Pass Trail (5 mi; 9,992 ft). The Tuolumne Pass Trail continues to a junction with a side trail that leads to Boothe Lake (¼ mi; 9,920 ft+). The trail goes downstream to another junction, first meeting the Evelyn Lake Trail (2¾ mi; 9,360 ft+) and shortly thereafter a side trail to Emeric Lake. The Tuolumne Pass Trail goes southwest and south to meet a side trail leading to Babcock Lake (2 mi; 8,880 ft+). It continues to descend the Fletcher Creek drainage, crosses Lewis Creek on a bridge, and meets the Vogelsang Pass Trail (1¾ mi; 8,160 ft+). Bears are active throughout this area.

Vogelsang Pass Trail   7½ miles

This trail starts upstream from Merced Lake, where the Red Peak Pass Trail and the Merced Lake Trail meet, near the Merced Lake Ranger Station (0 mi; 7,280 ft+). The Vogelsang Pass Trail ascends the canyon of Lewis Creek to meet the Tuolumne Pass Trail (1 mi; 8,160 ft+). It continues upstream to a junction with the Isberg Pass Trail (1 mi; 8,680 ft+), past a side trail leading to Bernice Lake (3 mi; 9,800 ft+), to the summit of Vogelsang Pass and an outstanding view (1¼ mi; 10,480 ft+). The trail descends the north side of the pass and crosses the outlet of Vogelsang Lake before meeting the Evelyn Lake Trail and the Vogelsang High Sierra Camp (1¼ miles; 10,120 ft+). The Vogelsang Pass Trail crosses the Evelyn Lake Trail and continues to meet the Tuolumne Pass Trail atop Tuolumne Pass (1 mi; 9,992 ft). Bears are active all along this trail.

Evelyn Lake Trail   6¼ miles

The Evelyn Lake Trail leaves the John Muir Trail approximately 5 miles from Tuolumne Meadows in Lyell Canyon. It ascends the west bank of Ireland Creek for 2¾ miles to a junction (2¾ mi; 10,400 ft+), where a trail leads 3 miles south to Ireland Lake. The Evelyn Lake Trail goes west from the junction to where it crosses the outlet of Evelyn Lake (2 mi; 10,320 ft+). The trail continues southwest, passing the north shore of Fletcher Lake to the Vogelsang High Sierra Camp and the Vogelsang Pass Trail (1½ mi; 10,120 ft+). Bears are active all along this trail.

Forsyth Trail   7 miles

A quota trail. This trail leaves the campground on the western shore of Tenaya Lake (0 mi; 8,120 ft+) and climbs to the south to meet the Sunrise Lakes Trail and Sunrise High Sierra Camp (2½ mi; 9,200 ft+). It then descends to meet the northern terminus of the Clouds Rest Trail (1½ mi; 9,080 ft+). The Forsyth Trail turns east from this junction and descends to meet the John Muir Trail along Sunrise Creek (3 mi; 8,200 ft+).

Sunrise Lakes Trail   2½ miles

This trail leaves the John Muir Trail near Sunrise High Sierra Camp (0 mi; 9,280 ft+), climbs north of Sunrise Mountain (to 9,760 ft+), passes the three Sunrise Lakes, and meets the Forsyth Trail (2½ mi; 9,200 ft+).

Snow Creek Trail   9 miles

A quota trail. This trail has also been called the May Lake Trail. This route is frequently used by skiers during ski tours from Tuolumne Meadows to Yosemite Valley. It is described here from top to bottom.

The trail descends from May Lake and crosses Tioga Road approximately 3½ miles west from Tenaya Lake (0 mi; 8,533 ft); this can be identified in winter or spring as the crest of the first ridge beyond Olmsted Point, dividing Snow Creek from Tenaya Creek. The trail goes southwest, more or less along the crest of the ridge, and descends to a trail junction (2¼ mi; 7,680 ft+). (A trail leads east from here 6 miles to Tenaya Lake.) The Snow Creek Trail continues downhill, crosses Snow Creek on a bridge (at UTM 764835), and meets the North Dome Trail (1½ mi; 6,720 ft+). (This area typically is little more than bare ground by late March to April.) Bears prowl through this area. The trail continues southwest to the rim of Tenaya Canyon and switchbacks down to Mirror Lake (4 mi; 4,080 ft+). Continue down the bicycle path (a paved road, in reality) to the shuttle-bus route near North Pines Campground in Yosemite Valley.

Further Reading: John Moynier. *Backcountry Skiing in the High Sierra.* Evergreen, Colo.: Chockstone Press, 1992, p. 88.

CROSS-COUNTRY ROUTES

Cross-country travel is relatively easy in the Clark and Cathedral Ranges, and there are many more routes than those listed below. The Clark Range can be approached from the west via the Merced Pass Trail along Illilouette Creek by hiking through the vast forests; skill with a compass, an accurate map (see Wrinkles, at the end of this chapter), and perhaps an altimeter and a Global Positioning System receiver may be needed to ensure that you are in the correct drainage.

"Merced Peak Ridge"   11,080 ft+; 11,040 ft+;
0.3 mi S of Merced Peak

Class 1. This pass, with Three-D Divide and Walton Ridge, has been used by cross-country skiers. It may be tempting to descend to the north from the saddle between Merced Peak and Triple Divide Peak to Edna Lake and the Red Peak Pass Trail. But Edna Lake is in a hanging valley.

Further Reading: John Moynier. *Backcountry Skiing in the High Sierra.* Evergreen, Colo.: Chockstone Press, 1992, p. 83.

"Three-D Divide"   10,760 ft+; 10,800 ft+;
0.5 mi S of Triple Divide Peak; UTM 909666

Class 1. This pass leads between the upper part of the South Fork of the Merced River and Post Creek.

Further Reading: John Moynier. *Backcountry Skiing in the High Sierra.* Evergreen, Colo.: Chockstone Press, 1992, p. 83.

"Walton Ridge"   10,880 ft+; 10,800 ft+;
0.5 mi ESE of Triple Divide Peak; UTM 916672

Class 2. This steep pass is best approached from the north, making the cross above, and northwest from, the low point of the pass.

Further Reading: John Moynier. *Backcountry Skiing in the High Sierra.* Evergreen, Colo.: Chockstone Press, 1992, p. 83.

"Blue Lake Pass"   11,240 ft+; 11,200 ft+;
0.3 mi S of Foerster Peak

Class 2. This pass leads between the drainages of the North Fork of the San Joaquin River and the Merced River. Steep talus is encountered on the west side of the pass, and there are grassy benches on the east.

Further Reading: Steve Roper. *Sierra High Route.* Seattle: The Mountaineers Books, 1997, pp. 172–173.

"Foerster Ridge"   11,240 ft+; 11,200 ft+;
0.4 mi N of Foerster Peak

Class 2. Climb into the hanging valley between Foerster Peak and Mount Ansel Adams from the Lyell Fork of the Merced River. Head south out of the hanging valley before turning right and crossing the north ridge of Foerster Peak.

Further Reading: John Moynier. *Backcountry Skiing in the High Sierra.* Evergreen, Colo.: Chockstone Press, 1992, p. 81.

"Old Bones Pass"   11,560 ft+; 11,520 ft+;
0.5 mi SW of Electra Peak

Class 2. This pass is named here in honor of the Old Bones Climbing Club. It leads between the North Fork of the San Joaquin River and the Lyell Fork of the Merced River. Instead of making a direct descent of the north side of the pass, it is better to continue north to Lake 10,999ft (10,960 ft+) before turning west and descending the beautiful Lyell Fork.

Further Reading: Steve Roper. *Sierra High Route.* Seattle: The Mountaineers Books, 1997, p. 179.

"Sluggo Pass"   11,520 ft+; 11,440 ft+;
1.5 mi SW of Mount Lyell

Class 2 from either the northwest or southeast. This pass was formerly known as "Ingraham Pass," but it has been renamed here in honor of Tracy Sulkin. It has been used during ascents of Rodgers Peak, Electra Peak, Mount Ansel Adams, and Foerster Peak from the upper portion of Hutchings Creek.

"Rodgers Pass"   12,200 ft+;
0.4 mi NNW of Rodgers Peak

Class 2. This pass leads from Marie Lakes to the headwaters of the Lyell Fork of the Merced River. Circle upper Marie Lake on its northern shore.

"Lyell Col"   12,440 ft+; 12,480 ft+;
0.3 mi SE of Mount Lyell; UTM 003789

Class 3. From the north side of upper Marie Lake, climb onto the permanent snowfield southeast of Mount Lyell. The best crossing is at the far, northwest side of the pass, just below where the southeast ridge of Mount Lyell becomes steep.

Further Reading: John Moynier. *Backcountry Skiing in the High Sierra.* Evergreen, Colo.: Chockstone Press, 1992, p. 81.

"Lyell-Maclure Col"   12,400 ft+; 12,400 ft+;
0.3 mi NW of Mount Lyell

Class 3–4. This provides a direct route between Lyell

Canyon and Hutchings Creek. Cross the Lyell Glacier to the low point between Mount Lyell and Mount Maclure. A steep, loose chute (class 3, with a 10-foot section of class 4) on the southwest side of the pass leads down to the upper portion of Hutchings Creek.

"Russell Pass" 12,240 ft+; 12,160 ft+;
0.5 mi NW of Mount Maclure; UTM 984800

Class 2. This pass, named here in memory of Bill T. Russell, leads between the Lyell Fork of the Tuolumne River and Hutchings Creek; it is an easier route than Lyell-Maclure Col. Ascend Maclure Creek from the John Muir Trail. Slabs lead to the highest lake along this creek; talus and the low-angle Maclure Glacier are encountered on the way to the top of the pass. Descend talus on the southwest side of the pass to the highest lake in the Hutchings Creek drainage.

Further Reading: *Summit.* Summer 1994, p. 85.

Florence Creek

Class 2. Leave the Lewis Creek Trail and climb the east side of Florence Creek to the small lakes above. Big, but stable, talus leads to Florence Lake. Pass Florence Lake on its southern shore and continue upstream over talus and slabs to Lake 10,541 ft (10,480 ft+).

"Hell Hole" 12,160 ft+; 12,160 ft+;
0.6 mi SSE of Simmons Peak; UTM 983806

Class 2. This pass crosses the Cathedral Range between Bernice Lake and Maclure Lake. The eastern side is especially precipitous, and it is best to keep to the north to avoid the steepest cliffs.

Further Reading: *Sierra Club Bulletin.* 1938, pp. 41–42.

"Wilts Col" 10,760 ft+; 10,720 ft+;
0.6 mi SW of Budd Lake; UTM 888899

Class 2–3. This pass has been named here in memory of Charles Wilts. It provides direct access between Budd Lake and Matthes Crest. From Budd Lake, climb the broad scree gully between Echo Peaks No. 7 and No. 8. The south side of the pass consists of slabs that lead to the northern base of Matthes Crest.

Tenaya Canyon

Class 3–4. This adventurous cross-country route should only be attempted by experienced mountaineers. Many tourists are rescued from this canyon each year,

and Yosemite park rangers refer to it as the "Bermuda Triangle of Yosemite." It is best to descend the canyon in late summer or early autumn, when Tenaya Creek has a low water level. The intricate routefinding around hundreds of obstacles (water- and glacier-polished ledges, boulders, and brush) demands at least 2 days of hiking. A 150-foot rope is needed, as well as at least a dozen rappel slings.

From Tenaya Lake Campground, follow the Forsyth Trail for ½ mile, where the trail starts to make a short climb. Leave the trail here, and cross Tenaya Creek as soon as is practical. Remain on the west side of the stream, descending rock slabs to the hanging valley above Pywiack Cascade. Cross the stream well above the falls, then climb onto the dome-shaped ridge to the south. Descend the other side of the "dome," down the shallowest slabs, where some bushwhacking is required. Then traverse down and to the right, descending more slick granite slabs and passing above brush, to the pool at the base of Pywiack Cascade and the head of Lost Valley. Go down the rocky streambed to another waterfall (also with a pool at its bottom), passing it on its eastern (left) side. Continue down Lost Valley, passing through the shady forest and crossing the gentle stream to its right bank to the abyss of the Inner Gorge.

During high water, it is necessary to bushwhack high (250 feet or more) above Tenaya Creek on its northwest side. During low water, however, a more interesting, more technical, and less brushy route can be taken. Seek out a system of narrow, exposed ledges on the right (northwest) side of the creek. (One of the ledges, known as "Initial Ledge," was marked by S. L. Foster, who made annual trips through the canyon from 1909 to 1937. Please don't add your own initials, names, or other marks to this historic landmark!) Down climb or rappel (from a two-bolt anchor) these ledges, and descend through brush to the creek. Down climb (or rappel) through a split rock, then climb about 60 feet above the northwest bank of Tenaya Creek to a scree-covered ledge. (Those who miss this ledge will have to rappel down a huge chockstone that divides the flow of Tenaya Creek.) Continue down the northwest side of the Inner Gorge, passing waterfalls with some short, steep steps, and then climb a short, rocky gully with a narrow keyhole exit. Return to the stream. Two rappels, separated by some steep down climbing, lead to the mouth of the Inner Gorge. Keep to the west side of Tenaya Creek, passing through forests and more dense brush to the bridge over the creek above Mirror Lake. Then follow the trail down to Yosemite Valley.

Further Reading: *Summit.* Spring 1990, pp. 40–43; *Sierra Club Bulletin.* 1900, pp. 230–235; *Sierra Club Bulletin.* 1914, pp. 126–135.

Other Routes

Grayling Lake is surrounded by cliffs on three sides, and it is best approached directly from Red Creek.

An old cavalry trail was established in the late 1800s from the vicinity of Nevada Fall to Starr King Meadow; some blazes can still be seen along this route.

Another army trail went up the Gray Peak Fork. Portions of this trail can still be seen. The Merced River has been crossed at UTM 892783. The trail led to Adair Lake and the route of the trail crossed the Clark Range at the first saddle north of Gray Peak.

PEAKS

Madera Peak   10,509 ft; 10,509 ft
First ascent August 1931 by Mrs. Hermina Daulton, Mr. Garthwaite, Mrs. Garthwaite, and their seven-year-old son, Jed. The southwest slope is class 2.

Red Top   9,973 ft; 9,977 ft
First ascent prior to 1919 by William Frederick Bade. Class 2 via the west slope.

Sing Peak   10,520 ft+; 10,552 ft
The south slope is class 2.

Gale Peak   10,680 ft+; 10,693 ft
First ascent 1920 by Lawrence Fley, Freeman Jones, and Thomas Jones. The northwest and northeast ridges are class 2.

Triple Divide Peak   11,611 ft; 11,607 ft
First ascent 1920 by Norman Clyde. The northwest ridge is class 2, as is the southeast slope.

Merced Peak   11,726 ft; 11,726 ft
First ascent was before 1870 by the California Geological Survey.
Northeast Ridge. Class 2. Leave the Red Peak Pass

Trail near Upper Ottoway Lake, and climb to the saddle between Merced Peak and Ottoway Peak. Ascend the east side of the northeast ridge, taking care to avoid some loose talus blocks.

North Face. III, 5.7. First ascent July 1971 by Ken Boche and Mary Bomba. A ramp ascends up and right across the north face. Loose 5.7 climbing leads to the bottom of the ramp. Climb the poorly protected diagonal ramp to where a short, moderate section at the top of the ramp leads to easier climbing and the summit.

West Arête. Class 3. Descended August 1949 by Alfred R. Dole, Stewart Kimball, Elizabeth Kimball, and Richard Leonard. It is necessary to traverse across the southern side of this ridge in many places.

Ottoway Peak   11,480 ft+; 11,440 ft+
First ascent September 16, 1934 by Ansel Adams. Class 2 from Red Peak Pass, and from the saddle between Ottoway Peak and Merced Peak.

Red Peak   11,699 ft; 11,669 ft
First ascent was before 1870 by the California Geological Survey. The south slope is class 2; traverse west from Red Peak Pass across the south slope to a point beyond the gendarmes west of the trail. Follow the loose south slope to the summit. The northwest slope from Red Peak Fork is also class 2.

Gray Peak   11,573 ft; 11,574 ft
First ascent 1920 by Ansel Adams and Francis Holman. The west peak is the high point. The north and south slopes are both class 2. The ridge running west from the summit consists of easy class 3 blocks; this ridge can be reached easily from either Red Peak or Mount Clark.

Mount Clark   11,522 ft; 11,522 ft
Southeast Arête. Class 4. First ascent July 12, 1866 by Clarence King and James T. Gardiner. First winter ascent February 21, 1937 by Ken Adam, Ken Davis, Hervey Voge, and David Brower. The base of this arête can be reached from either the Merced Pass Trail along Illilouette Creek (easier), or from the Red Peak Pass Trail along the Merced River (harder). Follow the ridge that connects Mount Clark with Gray Peak to the base of the cliffs on the arête leading to Mount Clark. Pass through a small gap at 11,000 ft on the arête and ascend

MOUNT CLARK

Southeast
Arête

gap

Southwest
Face

Mount Clark from the south. Photo by R. J. Secor.

diagonally high on the east side of the arête to just below the summit rocks. An exposed move on the south side of the summit rocks leads to the top.

Northeast Face. Class 4. First ascent July 4, 1916 by Francis Farquhar. The start of this route can be reached from the base of the southeast arête by traversing low across the east face of Mount Clark. Climb the right side of the northeast face via a series of broad, sandy ledges. Pass through a notch on the north ridge of the peak, and traverse south across the west side of the north ridge until you are just beneath the summit. An exposed pitch up a crack and chimney leads to the summit. *Variation:* Class 4. First ascent August 12, 1995 by Dave Jurasevich, Al Benson, Paul Stricklin, Carol Snyder, Mark Adrian, Ken Olson, and Bill Stevens. Climb the center of the northeast face via ledges to a ledge with a large boulder, about 100 feet directly beneath the summit. Climb a class 4 face for 80 feet to the north ridge, and then follow the ridge to the top.

North Face. III, 5.6. First ascent September 1958 by Henry Kendall, Herb Swedlund, Hobey DeStaebler, and Tom Frost. Cross the small glacier on the northern side of the peak, and start climbing the face to the left of a point directly below the summit. Climb to a ledge that runs across the face. Two class 4 pitches go straight up from the far end of the ledge to a pair of chimneys. Climb the right-hand chimney (5.6). This is followed by a 5.4 pitch, which ends on the crest of the northwest ridge. *Variation:* The left-hand chimney has been rated as 5.8.

Northwest Arête. Class 4. First ascent October 1934 by Neil Ruge and Douglas Olds. First winter ascent February 14, 1993 by Les Wilson, Gus Benner, and Steve

MOUNT CLARK

(route continues behind peak)

Southeast
Arête

gap

Northeast
Face

Mount Clark from the northeast. Photo by R. J. Secor.

White. This arête is a striking sight. Approach the arête from the chute to its right (southwest). Slabs and ledges lead up and left onto the crest. Follow the crest until just below the summit, where a ledge leads to the right. Then climb a class 4 pitch up a crack and a chimney to the top.

Further Reading: John Moynier and Claude Fiddler. *Sierra Classics.* Evergreen, Colo.: Chockstone Press, 1993, pp. 260–261.

Southwest Face. IV, 5.8, A2. First ascent August 19, 1970 by Ken Boche and Joe McKeown. Begin by climbing left of the chimney system on this face. Climb about 200 feet to some loose blocks, and traverse to the right into the chimney. Continue up the chimney, where a short aid crack leads up and left. Traverse right, back into the chimney, to a hanging belay. Continue up the chimney to a ledge with a bolt. A 30-foot pendulum to the left leads to a small dihedral. Mixed climbing in this dihedral leads to its top and a ramp. Follow the ramp up and right, across the chimney, to a ridge. Free and aid climb-

ing on the right side of this ridge lead to the southeast arête. Follow the arête to the summit.

Peak 10,480ft+   10,400 ft+;
1.0 mi NE of Mount Clark

First ascent June 30, 1990 by Greg Foerstal, Sigrid Hutto, Rick Beatty, and R. J. Secor. The north peak is the high point. Climb slabs and benches up from the east shore of Obelisk Lake to the class 3 south ridge. Follow the ridge to the class 4 summit rocks.

Mount Starr King   9,092 ft; 9,092 ft

Southeast Saddle. I, 5.0. First ascent August 23, 1877 by George Anderson, James Hutchings, and J. B. Lembert. First winter ascent March 9, 1937 by David Brower and Joseph Specht. Climb to the first saddle southeast of this beautiful dome rising above Illilouette Creek. Friction climbing leads up and left from a slab to a small right-facing open book. Traverse to the right under a flake and up to a big ledge. The second pitch is class 4, and goes up and left from the belay ledge to some slabs. Scramble up to the summit. Two ropes are recommended to rappel this route.

Northeast Side. I, 5.2. First ascent August 1876 by George Bayley and E. S. Schuyler. Climb to the highest trees on the shoulder on the northeast side of the dome. Climb class 3 rock slabs to where the angle steepens appreciably. Traverse diagonally up and right across a 43° face for 40 feet to a small ledge. Climb up and right from the ledge, following a 2-inch-wide, munge-filled crack to easier ground above.

Further Reading: Mark and Shirley Spencer. *Southern Yosemite Rock Climbs.* Oakhurst, Calif: Condor Designs, 1988, pp. 10–17.

Half Dome   8,836 ft; 8,842 ft

The cable route (see the Trails section, earlier in this chapter) was first climbed in October 1875 by George

Anderson. He climbed barefoot, and drilled holes for some big iron spikes for protection. The cables were placed in 1919. The face on either side of the cables is class 5, and was first climbed 1931 by Warren Loose, Eldon Dryer, and Judd Boynton.

The base of the cables can also be reached via an interesting cross-country route from Mirror Lake. The cliffs above Mirror Lake go class 3 at either end. Climb the brush-covered slabs above the left end of the cliffs. Ascend talus to the trail and cables on the east face of Half Dome.

Further Reading: George Meyers and Don Reid. *Yosemite Rock Climbs.* Denver: Chockstone Press, 1987, pp. 262–275.

"Sugarloaf Dome"   7,683 ft; 7,480 ft+;
0.7 mi WNW of Bunnell Point

This dome is located at the head of Little Yosemite Valley.

Mount Clark from the west. Photo by R. J. Secor.

MOUNT CLARK

Northwest
Arête

Southwest
Face

Mount Starr King from the northwest. Photo by R. J. Secor.

South Face. III, 5.9. First ascent 1960 by Tom Frost and Yvon Chouinard. Climb to a brushy ledge halfway up the south face. Continue straight up from the ledge for several pitches. The crux is a friction traverse that goes up and right for several pitches above the brushy ledge.

South and Southwest Faces. Class 5 and A. First ascent November 6, 1951 by John Salathé and Cliff Hopson. This first ascent of this route involved much direct aid. Go up and left from the brushy ledge on the south face of the dome.

Bunnell Point   8,193 ft; 8,193 ft

Northwest Face. IV, 5.9. First ascent June 1983 by Alan Bartlett and Robb Dellinger. There are two dikes just to the right of center on the northwest face. These dikes slant up and left and meet about halfway up the face. This route follows the right dike and slants up and left for fourteen pitches. There are fifteen bolts on this climb, but beware of some off-route bolts that lead to the right at about mid-height.

Further Reading: Mark and Shirley Spencer. *Southern Yosemite Rock Climbs.* Oakhurst, Calif.: Condor Designs, 1988, p. 18.

The Golden Bear. V, 5.10b. First ascent July 1989 by Bart O'Brien and Mike Jauregui. This route follows the left-hand dike that goes up and left from the center of the northwest face. Follow the dike up and over a roof for two pitches to a belay stance on the higher of two ledges. The third and fourth pitches are the crux. Follow bolts to the left into a right-facing open book, then climb the book to a belay at a flake. Climb dikes over the book past two bolts to another belay. This is followed by several more dike pitches up and left to a ledge that is east of an open book with a small pine. Face climbing then leads over a small, prominent white scar to a series of small, right-facing inside corners, which become left-facing higher up. Continue climbing up these corners to the lonely summit pine.

Post Peak   11,009 ft; 11,009 ft
First ascent 1922 by Ansel Adams and Francis Holman. Class 1 from Post Peak Pass.

Sadler Peak   10,567 ft; 10,567 ft
Class 1 from the south.

Isberg Peak   10,996 ft; 10,996 ft
First ascent April 20, 1924 by Ansel Adams and Francis Holman. Class 1 from the west.

Long Mountain   11,502 ft; 11,502 ft
First ascent August 1922 by Ansel Adams and Francis Holman. Class 2 from the south.

Foerster Peak   12,057 ft; 12,058 ft
First ascent 1914 by Norman Clyde. The south slope is class 2. A chute on the southwest side of the peak is also class 2; it was climbed August 20, 1973 by Mary Sue Miller, Neko Colevins, Kes Teter, Bill Schuler, and Andy Smatko. The west side of the north ridge is class 2–3, and was climbed July 1954 by George Whitmore.

Mount Ansel Adams   11,760 ft+; 11,760 ft+
This the impressive peak at the head of the Lyell Fork of the Merced River. First ascent July 11, 1934 by Glen Dawson, Jack Riegelhuth, and Neil Ruge. Ascend the Lyell Fork of the Merced River and climb a chute that leads to the notch between Mount Ansel Adams and the sharp peak to the northeast. Climb onto the class 3 south face from the notch and up to the summit.

Electra Peak   12,442 ft; 12,442 ft
First ascent 1914 by Norman Clyde. The north ridge is class 2, and the southeast slope is class 1.

Peak 12,573ft   12,560 ft+;
0.7 mi S of Rodgers Peak
First ascent July 10, 1924 by Ansel Adams, Cedric Wright, and Willard Grinnell. The east and northwest slopes are class 2.

Rodgers Peak   12,978 ft; 12,978 ft
First ascent August 5, 1897 by Robert M. Price. First winter ascent March 26, 1958 by Max Allen and Bart Hooley. This peak is class 3 from the west. The north face is class 2 and is ascended by means of a ramp that rises from right to left. The northeast ridge is class 2–3; climb to the middle portion of the east ridge from either the north or south, and follow the ridge to the summit.

Mount Lyell   13,114 ft; 13,114 ft
This is the highest peak in Yosemite National Park. Its glacier is the second largest in the High Sierra. This peak is frequently climbed, and there is a grand view from the summit.

Lyell Glacier. Class 2–3. First ascent August 29, 1871 by John B. Tilestone. First winter ascent March 2, 1936 by David Brower, Lewis Clark, Boynton Kaiser, Einar Nilsson, and Bestor Robinson. Leave the John Muir Trail just west of where it crosses the headwaters of the Lyell Fork of the Tuolumne River, below Donohue Pass, at 10,520 ft+ (UTM 011817). Ascend talus and benches to the western part of the Lyell Glacier. Cross the glacier, aiming for the notch between Mount Lyell and Mount Maclure. Climb toward the summit of Mount Lyell along ledges, above the snow but below a rock face, to a chute that leads up to the summit ridge. This route is open to many variations, due to changing snow levels each year on the glacier.

Lyell-Maclure Col. Class 3–4. Descended July 11, 1934 by Ted Waller, Marjory Bridge, Ray Brothers, John Cahill, Leland Curtis, Louise Hildebrand, Helen LeConte, May Pridham, and Helen Simpson. There are two steep, narrow chutes that lead to the notch between Mount Lyell and Mount Maclure from the Hutching Creek drainage. Climb the left-hand chute to the notch; there is a 10-foot class 4 move at the bottom of this otherwise class 3 chute. The top of this chute is about 50 feet above and east of the low point between Mount Lyell and Mount Maclure. Keep to the north side of the ridge before climbing a chute that leads to the crest of the summit ridge.

West Face. Class 5. First ascent August 24, 1963 by Les Wilson, Dennis Schmitt, Tim Gerson, and Peter Haan. The wide west face of Mount Lyell features a vertical prow. Climb two class 4 pitches directly below the prow, in a loose chimney. Go up and then left over better rock to a ledge at the bottom of a broken section on

Mount Lyell and Mount Maclure from the north. Photo by R. J. Secor.

the face. Two class 4 pitches lead straight up over cluttered ledges to where the face steepens against the prow. Climb a shallow open book to the left (class 4), and traverse left around a bulge almost to the prominent diving board that is visible from below. Class 5 climbing then leads up and around an overhang to a ledge above the bulge. Another pitch of easier class 5 goes straight up the face and leads to some fractured blocks.

A short class 4 pitch up and right leads to a ridge that is just northwest of the top of the prow. Follow the ridge to the summit.

Southwest Ridge. Class 4. First ascent July 19, 1955 by George Whitmore. Climb to the saddle between Peak 12,767ft (12,720 ft+) and Mount Lyell. Follow the southwest ridge from the saddle to where the ridge merges with the south face. Several hundred feet of class 3 and class 4 climbing lead to the northwest ridge at a point about 100 feet from the summit.

South Face. Class 4. First ascent July 12, 1934 by Glen Dawson, Tony Chorlton, Milton Hildebrand, Elizabeth Mason, David Parish, Thomas Saunders, and George Shochat. Ascend a talus chute on the south face that leads directly to the summit. The upper part of this chute consists of loose class 4 climbing.

East Arête. Class 3. Cross the Lyell Glacier, aiming for the first col to the east of the summit of Mount Lyell. Follow the east arête to the summit.

Further Reading: John Moynier and Claude Fiddler. *Sierra Classics.* Evergreen, Colo.: Chockstone Press, 1993, pp. 254–255.

East Arête from Marie Lakes. Class 4. First ascent July 3, 1977 by Sonny Lawrence, Diane Rosentreter, and Ian Clarke. Climb onto the crest of the east arête from Marie Lakes, and follow the south side of the arête until progress is stopped by some gendarmes. Pass these on the north side of the ridge and continue to the col that is east of the summit of Mount Lyell. Follow the east arête to the summit.

Mount Maclure   12,880 ft+; 12,960 ft+
Southeast Ridge. Class 3. First ascent 1883 by Willard D. Johnson. Climb talus and ledges to the summit from the Lyell-Maclure Col.

South Face. Class 3. First ascent July 11, 1934 by Ted Waller, Marjory Bridge, Ray Brothers, John Cahill, Leland Curtis, Louise Hildebrand, Helen LeConte, May Pridham, and Helen Simpson. Climb the left side of a prominent chute on the south face. Traverse east to the southeast ridge and follow the ridge to the summit.

Northwest Ridge. Class 4. First ascent by Allen Steck and George Steck. Climb to the V-shaped pass northwest of Mount Maclure and follow the ridge to the summit.

North Ridge. Class 4. Slabs lead from the head of Maclure Creek to the bottom of the ridge. Follow the crest of the ridge to the summit.

Mount Maclure and Mount Lyell from the southwest. Photo by R. J. Secor.

Mount Lyell and Vicinity

Further Reading: John Moynier and Claude Fiddler. *Sierra Classics.* Evergreen, Colo.: Chockstone Press, 1993, pp. 256–257.

Mount Florence   12,561 ft; 12,561 ft

First ascent August 1897 by Theodore S. Solomons and F. W. Reed. The south and west slopes are class 2. The east slope consists of loose class 3; it is better to traverse around to the southern side of the mountain from high on Hutchings Creek and climb the south slope rather than the east slope.

From Florence Creek. Class 2. First ascent September 18, 1992 by Bob Wright and Anne Wright. Climb to the prominent saddle that is south of Lake 10,541ft (10,480 ft+) and follow the west ridge to the summit.

Simmons Peak   12,497 ft; 12,503 ft

First ascent by a Sierra Club party in 1931. The southwest slope is class 2.

East Arête. III, 5.8. First ascent August 1982 by Evelyn Lees and Alan Bartlett. Climb the crest of this striking arête for five pitches to a horizontal section of class 3 and class 4. One more pitch along this ridge includes some 5.8 moves on the face to the left of the prow of the arête.

Amelia Earhart Peak   11,974 ft; 11,982 ft

The northeast ridge is class 2. The west face has a class 4 couloir. Climb the couloir to where it meets a steep wall, then traverse left to the northeast ridge; this was first climbed July 1973 by Allen Steck and Lee Steck.

Parsons Peak   12,147 ft; 12,080 ft+

First ascent by Marion Randall Parsons before 1931. Class 2 from Ireland Lake or the Bernice Lake area. The class 3 north ridge was first climbed August 4, 1982 by Chris Keith.

Vogelsang Peak   11,493 ft; 11,516 ft

First ascent 1923 by François Matthes. Class 2 via the northeast slope. Leave the Vogelsang Pass Trail about ¼ mile south of the outlet of Vogelsang Lake. Ascend a faint gully that leads up to the north ridge of the peak, and follow the ridge south to the summit. The ridge from Vogelsang Pass is also class 2.

Nightingale Arête. II, 5.9. First ascent July 1981 by Gary Colliver and Alan Bartlett. This arête leads to the lower, west summit of Vogelsang Peak (11,120 ft+; 11,120 ft+). Climb slanting cracks (easy class 5) on the left side of the lower buttress. Some 5.7 sections lead to the class 2–3 horizontal ridge that leads to the upper arête. Follow the arête to the summit; a 5.9 pitch in an obvious corner halfway up the upper arête is the crux.

West Face. IV, 5.10, A2. First ascent August 1981 by Evelyn Lees and Alan Bartlett. There are two right-slanting chimneys on the west face. Climb the most obvious crack to the right of these chimneys. Traverses to the right on the fourth and fifth pitches lead to more cracks. The sixth pitch starts with a long traverse left, followed by 30 feet of aid up to an overhanging corner and easier climbing. The first-ascent party used one point of aid on the second pitch, and one point of aid on the fifth pitch. There is much loose rock on this route.

Fletcher Peak   11,410 ft; 11,408 ft

Southwest Slope. Class 2. Climb this slope from the outlet of Vogelsang Lake. Brush, scree, and talus are encountered before reaching the summit.

Northwest Couloir. Class 4. First ascent August 1959 by Ronald Smith and Bob Happle. Ascend the right side of this couloir to avoid the ice. Higher up, traverse back and forth to a large crack. Climb the crack and go left to a small clump of trees, and ascend the southwest slope to the summit.

Modesto Surfer. II, 5.9. First ascent September 1989 by Tom Downey, Todd Handy, Tim Kluender, and Johno Alexander. This route is on the northwest face; it follows a prominent, right-facing open book on the right side of the face. Class 3 scrambling across slabs beneath the face leads to the start of the route. Climb the left crack (5.9) to the bottom of the book. Continue up the book, but move left and face climb (5.7) around a slab. This is followed by a 5.9 chimney and crack to a belay ledge. One more pitch in the open book (5.6) leads up and right to easier climbing.

Drop Your Bungy. II, 5.10b. First ascent August 1990 by Todd Handy and Richard Villa. This route ascends the triangular face that is left of the open book that marks Modesto Surfer. The route starts next to a small, triangular block on the left side of the face. A long 5.7 crack leads up and left, along the left side of the triangular block to the right-ascending crack or ledge system in the middle of the face. A 5.10a move is followed by a pair of 5.9 cracks that barely touch each other. These lead to a right-ascending crack. This crack, a poorly protected 5.10a traverse, is followed by 5.10c face climbing past two bolts to a stance in a crack that is left of Modesto Surfer. Continue up the crack (5.7) to the top. *Variation:* Face climb (5.10a) horizontally left from the top of the second pitch to the Arrowhead route.

Moldy Sole. II, 5.10b. First ascent August 1990 by Richard Villa, Todd Handy, and Tom Downey. This route starts from the top of the first pitch of Drop Your Bungy. Some 5.10b crack climbing is followed by a 5.9 crack. Follow this crack up and right to the right-ascending crack of Drop Your Bungy.

Arrowhead. Class 5. This route follows the left side of the prominent triangular face on the northwest side of Fletcher Peak.

Peak 11,357ft   11,282 ft;
1.0 mi SW of Rafferty Peak

Southeast Slope. Class 2. First ascent 1931 by Julie Mortimer, Alice Carter, and Eleanor Bartlett.

Crowley Buttress. II, 5.8. First ascent July 1968 by Chuck Pratt and Doug Robinson. The far right side of

FLETCHER PEAK

Northwest
Couloir

Arrowhead

Modesto
Surfer

Drop Your
Bungy

Vogelsang
High Sierra Camp

Fletcher Peak from the northwest. Photo by R. J. Secor.

the north face, as seen from Nelson Lake, features many buttresses and ribs. This route ascends the northern-most buttress on this side of the peak. A single crack or chimney descends the buttress from a point just right of the lower, western summit of Peak 11,357ft (11,282 ft). Begin climbing this chimney (5.7), which is surpris-ingly deep. Climb out of the top of the chimney on the third pitch and into the dihedral above. Easier climbing in this dihedral leads to the crux, a bulge on the last pitch. This is an enjoyable, direct route.

Northwest Corner. II, 5.9. First ascent September 22, 1974 by Fred Beckey and Pete Metcalf. This three-pitch

climb is to the right of Crowley Buttress.

Eagle Eyes. IV, 5.9. First ascent July 1973 by Mark Gaylor, Ken Boche, and Chris Vandiver. This route climbs the west face. Climb a chimney on the right side of the face. After 100 feet leave the chimney on its left side and climb a 100-foot 5.9 jam crack. Continue up and left for 600 feet of 5.7–5.9 climbing to the lower, western summit of Peak 11,357ft (11,282 ft).

Rafferty Peak   11,110 ft; 11,120 ft+
First ascent by Edward W. Harnden. Class 2 from the east.

Johnson Peak   11,064 ft; 11,070 ft

First ascent 1933 by H. B. Blanks. Class 2 from Elizabeth Lake.

"Sunrise Wall"

This east-facing wall rises above the left bank of Echo Creek between the Cockscomb and Peak 10,160ft+ (10,160 ft+). (The wall is approximately at UTM 900885.) It is most easily approached from Elizabeth Lake. A good use trail leads over the pass southwest of the lake and into the Echo Creek drainage.

Pamplona. II, 5.9. First ascent July 1984 by Alan Bartlett, Steve Gerberding, and Dimitri Barton. This route starts in a large left-facing dihedral on the right side of the Sunrise Wall. Two pitches lead to a ledge atop the dihedral. Unprotected face climbing to the right of the ledge leads to a crack. Follow the crack to the top.

Blood Test. II, 5.9. First ascent July 1984 by Alan Bartlett, Steve Gerberding, and Dimitri Barton. This route is a short distance to the left of Pamplona. Climb the right-hand of two parallel cracks. The first pitch ends by traversing left into the left-hand crack to a belay. Climb this crack and then traverse left on a long ledge system to the next crack on the wall.

Dihedral Route. III, 5.8, A3. First ascent October 13, 1974 by Fred Beckey, Reed Cundiff, and Karl Kaiyala. This route climbs the obvious right-facing dihedral of the Sunrise Wall. The first three pitches go free, but the fourth pitch uses aid with some bottoming cracks.

Matthes Crest   10,918 ft; 10,880 ft+

This is an impressive, knife edge fin. The high point, the north peak, was first climbed July 26, 1931 by Jules Eichorn, Glen Dawson, and Walter Brem. As camping

View from the summit of Matthes Crest, looking south. Photo by R. J. Secor.

Mount Clark

foresummit

South Tooth

class 3 route

is now prohibited at Budd Lake, approach Matthes Crest from Cathedral Pass along the John Muir Trail. Scramble to the base of the west side of the north peak. One 5.3 pitch up steep cracks on the left side of the face leads to the summit.

Traverse, South to North. II, 5.6. First ascent June 1947 by Charles Wilts and Ellen Wilts (on a north-to-south traverse). This is a classic climb. The climb starts from a group of trees at the extreme southern end of Matthes Crest. Three easy class 5 pitches up the southwest side end atop the intimidating but easy (mostly class 3 with a few class 4 moves) crest, which is followed almost to the foresummit. A class 3 route descends the east side of the foresummit to the base of the north peak. Drop down to the west side of the north peak and climb steep cracks to the summit. Two long rappels down the west face of the north peak lead to the bottom.

Further Reading: John Moynier and Claude Fiddler. *Sierra Classics.* Evergreen, Colo.: Chockstone Press, 1993, pp. 274–275; *Rock & Ice.* No. 68 (July–August 1995), p. 158.

East Face. Class 5. First ascent July 1954 by Donald Harmon and Robert Dohrmann. Climb the east face of the north peak. Slabs lead up to a short chimney just below the summit block.

South Tooth, West Face. II, 5.9. First ascent July 1973 by Roger Gocking, Mike Warburton, and Ken Dekleva. This peak is east of Echo Lake, at UTM 887880. Climb the west face to the summit.

South Tooth, East Face. III, 5.8. First ascent July 1973 by Roger Gocking, Mike Warburton, and Ken Dekleva. Climb the east face to the summit.

Columbia Finger   10,360 ft+; 10,320 ft+

North Ridge. Class 3. First ascent July 22, 1921 by William Staniels, Donald Tripp, and B. H. Bochmer. Climb the north ridge to the summit rocks. Ascend the west side of the summit rocks to the top.

Digital Manipulation. II, 5.11b. First ascent September 1988 by Bob Palais and Galen Rowell. Ascend cracks on the northeast face. The crux, on the second pitch, is a long, rounded, fist-joint layback with tiny footholds.

Southeast Face. II, 5.4, A1. First ascent September 13, 1970 by Richard Hechtel and Jan Mostowski. Go approximately 150 feet to the right of the south buttress to an open book. Ascend the open book, which leads to the right after 140 feet, for two pitches to a small ledge.

Overcome the overhang above the small ledge to a series of small ledges. Follow the highest ledge to its far right side. Climb a small open book and chimney up to the south ridge.

Tresidder Peak   10,600 ft+; 10,560 ft+

The south summit is the high point, and the south arête is class 4. The north arête, also class 4, was first climbed July 4, 1966 by Bruce Kinnison, Alan Zetterberg, and Pierre Zetterberg.

The Keyhole. II, 5.8. First ascent June 1994 by Peter Moakley and Matt Pinelli. This route ascends the far, right-hand side of the west face of Tresidder Peak. The first, long (165 feet) and run out pitch goes up easy slabs, using friction and chickenheads, to a large flake located beneath a small roof. The next pitch, the crux, follows a prominent dihedral to another roof, which is passed on its left side; this long pitch ends at a small tree, which offers a convenient belay stance and anchor. Continue up cracks and slabs to a belay stance about 100 feet beneath the north arête. The fourth pitch climbs steep cracks to the north arête, which is followed (class 4) to the summit.

Echo Peaks
11,160 ft+; 11,040 ft+

There are nine summits in this massif, which is located east of Cathedral Pass.

"Echo Peak No. 1"   11,120 ft+; UTM 886899

East Face. Class 3. First ascent August 4, 1936 by Owen L. Williams. Ascend the center of the east face to the notch between Peaks No. 1 and No. 2. Follow the east side of the ridge north to the summit.

West Face. Class 4. Climb the west face to the notch between Peaks No. 1 and No. 2, then follow the ridge north to the summit.

Direct West Face. I, 5.8. First ascent July 1972 by Ron Cagle and Jerry Anderson. Climb the west face directly to the summit of Echo Peak No. 1.

North Arête. Class 5. First ascent June 1967 by Bruce Kinnison and Ken Gobalet.

"Echo Peak No. 2"   11,080 ft+; UTM 886898

East Face. Class 3. Climb the east face to the notch between Peaks No. 1 and No. 2, then follow the ridge south to the summit.

ECHO PEAKS

No. 3

No. 4

No. 2

No. 1

No. 6

No. 5

No. 7

Cathedral Peak

No. 9

No. 8

Wits Col

Echo Peaks from the south. Photo by R. J. Secor.

"Echo Peak No. 3"   11,160 ft+; 11,040 ft+; UTM 886897

This is the highest of the Echo Peaks, and was first climbed July 7, 1931 by Norman Clyde and Carl Sharsmith.

East Face. Class 4. Climb the gully on the east face leading to the notch between Peaks No. 2 and No. 3. Follow the ridge south to the summit.

West Face. Class 3. Ascend the west face to the notch between Peaks No. 2 and No. 3, then follow the ridge south to the summit.

"Echo Peak No. 4"   11,040 ft+; UTM 885896

First ascent August 6, 1936 by Owen L. Williams and Ethyl Mae Hill.

Traverse from Echo Peak No. 3. Class 4. Descend the east side of the ridge between Peaks No. 3 and No. 4 to a point 30 feet below the notch between the two peaks. Ascend the northeast face from here to the summit of Peak No. 4.

Northeast Face. Class 4. There is a prominent row of shrubs at the base of the northeast face. Start climbing from the left of these shrubs directly up the face to the summit.

"Echo Peak No. 5"   11,120 ft+; UTM 887899

The north ridge is class 3.

"Echo Peak No. 6"   11,000 ft+; UTM 887898

Ascend the vague northeast ridge; class 3.

"Echo Peak No. 7"   11,040 ft+; UTM 888899
The northeast ridge is class 3.

"Echo Peak No. 8"   11,080 ft+; UTM 889899
The north face is class 3.

"Echo Peak No. 9"   11,040 ft+; UTM 889898
This is the most attractive, and most difficult, of the Echo Peaks.

Southwest Side. I, 5.7. First ascent 1945 by Charles Wilts and Spencer Austin. Traverse across the west side of Peak No. 9 from the col between Peaks No. 7 and No. 8. Class 3 ramps and ledges lead upward to the wall on the southwest side of Peak No. 9. Climb straight up the wall for 120 feet before traversing left on knobs to a belay ledge. One short pitch in a corner leads to an arête. Follow the arête to the summit.

Northeast Corner. I, 5.9. First ascent June 1981 by Gary Colliver, Alan Roberts, and Alan Bartlett. This climb starts from the notch between Peaks No. 8 and No. 9. Follow a discontinuous corner system up and right for two pitches. The crux is on the second pitch.

"Echo Ridge"   11,168 ft; 11,120 ft+;
0.5 mi S of Budd Lake
West Ridge. Class 2. Climb to the saddle between Echo Peaks and Echo Ridge from Budd Lake, then follow the ridge to the summit.

North Face and East Ridge. Class 4. First ascent 1949 by Joe Firey, Peter Hoessly, Ron Hahn, and Ed Robbins. There is a lot of loose rock on this route. Climb to the base of the left-hand chimney at the bottom of the north face. Climb the chimney to the broad east ridge, then follow the ridge to the summit.

Cockscomb   11,065 ft; 11,040 ft+
First ascent 1914 by Lipman and Chamberlin.
West Face. Class 4. First ascent 1931 by Glen Dawson and Jules Eichorn. Traverse up and right across the west face from the northwest corner of the peak. Climb to a large, flat ledge and traverse south to a wide notch. The summit is the knife edge east of this notch. *Variation:* Climb a prominent crack above the large, flat ledge to a fingertip traverse that leads to the notch.

East Face. I, 5.6. First ascent October 1983 by David

Harden. This one-pitch route follows an obvious corner system that rises above the highest trees.

East Face of South Tower. I, 5.10a. First ascent September 1987 by Rick Cashner and Alan Swanson. Begin by climbing a knobby 5.10a crack to a pedestal. The second pitch follows a wide, curved crack to the summit bulge. Overcome the bulge by means of a thin crack (5.9).

Unicorn Peak   10,823 ft; 10,880 ft+
There are three summits for this peak; the north peak is the high point. First ascent 1911 by Francis Farquhar and James Rennie, via the northeast face. The regular route is class 3–4, and ascends slabs and talus to the notch between the north and middle summits. A short class 4 move along an arête leads to the summit. Other routes have been done on the north and northwest faces.

The direct north face has been rated II, 5.8, A3. It was climbed September 1965 by Alex Bertulis and Half Zantop.

Cathedral Peak   10,911 ft; 10,940 ft+
West Face. Class 4. First ascent September 1869 by John Muir. Leave the John Muir Trail along the northwest side of the peak and ascend slabs and talus up the west face to a point between the summit of Cathedral Peak and its west peak, Eichorn Pinnacle. Climb a series of ledges to the southern side of the summit block. A 15-foot class 4 crack leads to the summit. *Variation:* The summit rocks can also be reached from Budd Creek. Leave Budd Creek at the 9,500-foot level and climb a brushy talus slope to a small notch on the ridge north of the summit. Descend the west side of this notch a short way before turning south and climbing to a point between Eichorn Pinnacle and the summit of Cathedral Peak.

North Face. I, 5.5. First ascent July 1961 by Wally Reed and Cathy Warne. This climb begins about 100 feet below the east side of the notch on the north ridge of Cathedral Peak. Traverse south and climb an 8-foot-wide, chimneylike depression with an overhang near its top. Continue up to the notch left of the summit block. A 5.8 variation is left of the depression.

Northeast Face. Class 5. First ascent July 1953 by Frank Tarver and Gordon Petrequin. This climb begins

Cockscomb from the northeast. Photo by F. E. Matthes, No. 460a, USGS Photographic Library, Denver, CO.

approximately 300 feet to the right of the toe of the southeast buttress. Climb up and left to a shallow ridge. Follow the ridge to the summit.

Southeast Buttress. III, 5.6. First ascent 1945 by Charles Wilts and Spencer Austin. A short approach, combined with excellent climbing on a beautiful peak in one of the most scenic locations in the world, makes this a classic climb. The climb starts about 200 feet to the right of the toe of the southeast buttress at a prominent bush. Climb up and right over left-facing (but downward-sloping) flakes to a ledge. Go directly up the middle of the buttress to a large ledge beneath a chimney. Start the next pitch either by climbing the chimney (5.6), a knobby face to its left, or a crack to its right (5.7). After starting this pitch, continue straight up to a belay stance above a small horn. The next pitch involves some ledges and tricky cracks before it ends on a big ledge 80 feet beneath the summit. Climb a prominent crack to the summit bolt.

Further Reading: Don Reid and Chris Falkenstein. *Tuolumne Meadows Rock Climbs.* Denver: Chockstone Press, 1986, p. 60; Allan Bard. *Southeast Buttress of Cathedral Peak.* Bishop, Calif: Shooting Star Guides, 1991 (a route card); John Moynier and Claude Fiddler. *Sierra Classics.* Evergreen, Colo.: Chockstone Press, 1993, pp. 266–268.

South Face. I, 5.6. First ascent July 1962 by Wally Reed and Don Harmon. This route ends at the broad saddle between Eichorn Pinnacle and the summit of Cathedral Peak. The right side of the face features a crack

Eichorn Pinnacle and Cathedral Peak from the south. Photo by R. J. Secor.

Eichorn Pinnacle from the north. Photo by R. J. Secor.

that leads straight up to another crack, which leads just right of the summit ridge. Climb these cracks, or the faces on their sides, to the top.

"Eichorn Pinnacle"

This is the spectacular west summit of Cathedral Peak.

North Face. I, 5.4. First ascent July 24, 1931 by Glen Dawson and Jules Eichorn. From the saddle between Eichorn Pinnacle and Cathedral Peak, climb down and to the right over cracks and ledges on the north side of the pinnacle. This leads to a chimney on the north side. Climb the chimney to a ledge just below the west side of the summit. A single 165-foot rope suffices for the rappel.

A Celebrity's Holiday. III, 5.10. First ascent June 1984 by Bruce Brossman and Alan Bartlett. This route climbs the long crack system on the left side of the west face of Eichorn Pinnacle. (This crack system does not reach the ground.) Four pitches of poorly protected climbing lead to the upper pitches of the West Pillar route.

West Pillar. III, 5.9. First ascent July 1972 by Gary Colliver and Mike Cohen. Climb a 6-inch-wide jam crack (5.9) for two pitches to a ledge. Traverse down and right, across an edge, to another crack that leads up a flared left-facing open book (5.8). From the top of the book, a short traverse to the right leads to a hidden 2-inch crack (5.8) that leads up and slightly left for two pitches. Easy climbing (class 4) leads up over towers to wicked 5.9 stemming between two flakes. Easy class 5 climbing then leads up the west side of the pinnacle to the summit. *Direct Variation:* III, 5.10b. First ascent 1979 by Alan Bartlett and Don Reid. From the ledge atop the second pitch of the West Pillar route, continue straight up a pair of parallel cracks (5.9) followed by a difficult (5.10b) left-facing inside corner. A 5.5 pitch then leads to the class 4 towers.

Further Reading: John Moynier and Claude Fiddler. *Sierra Classics.* Evergreen, Colo.: Chockstone Press, 1993, pp. 270–272; John Moynier. "Sierra Six Pack." *Rock & Ice.* No. 73 (May–June 1996), pp. 66–75.

The Erratic Route. III, 5.10a. First ascent September 1991 by Rick Cashner and Alan Swanson. Begin by climbing a ramp up grainy rock (5.8) to the base of a low-angle, right-trending corner. The short second pitch follows the corner to the base of a steep, left-facing dihedral (5.4). Sustained 5.10a climbing up the dihedral leads to an exit to the right above a large, loose flake. This is followed by a nice pitch up a thin crack (5.8) to a ledge beneath a knife edge ridge. Climb onto the crest of the ridge (5.6) and follow it to the base of a wide crack and flake. The last pitch climbs the wide crack (5.9) and continues along the ridge, bypassing gendarmes, to the summit.

Southwest Buttress. II, 5.8. First ascent June 1966 by Wally Reed and Gary Colliver. Scramble up some ledges and slabs on the south side of Eichorn Pinnacle. Ascend and then traverse to the left into a prominent crack. Continue up the crack for three pitches, and then move left off the buttress to a wide chimney. Climb the chimney before moving left to a slanting ledge. Climb steep jam cracks to the summit.

Direct South Face. III, 5.7, A2. First ascent July 1972 by Jim Mitchell and Larry Corona. Climb a chimney on the left side of the south face. The chimney is followed by a 5.7 crack and some aid climbing to a ledge. Traverse left from the ledge to the shoulder west of the summit. A chimney then leads to the top.

WRINKLES

The John Muir Trail vs. The Mist Trail. The Mist Trail is shorter but steeper than the John Muir Trail between Happy Isles and Nevada Fall. The Mist Trail also passes close to Nevada and Vernal Falls (there are breathtaking views of the falls), but expose the trail (and hikers) to spray, which can be (depending on the volume) re-freshing to drenching. Rainbows are an added feature. Those headed downhill may prefer the shorter, steeper, and sometimes slippery Mist Trail, but hikers climbing out of Yosemite Valley may prefer the longer, but more gently graded, John Muir Trail. Also, most of the John Muir Trail is shaded by Panorama Cliff, giving relief on a hot day.

Tuolumne Pass Trail vs. Vogelsang Pass Trail. You can hike either of these two trails between Merced Lake and Vogelsang High Sierra Camp. The Tuolumne Pass Trail is shorter, but it does not have the outstanding views of the Vogelsang Pass Trail.

Clouds Rest from Tenaya Lake. Hiking to the summit of Clouds Rest is justifiably popular, due to the outstanding view from the summit. This involves more than 21 miles round trip and almost 6,000 feet of gain from Happy Isles via Little Yosemite Valley; few accomplish this in a day. A frequently overlooked alternative is a day hike from Tenaya Lake: 11½ miles round trip with a total of 2,560 feet of gain. An approach from Tenaya Lake also eliminates the chore of driving in Yosemite Valley and decreases use in Little Yosemite Valley, one of the most heavily used wilderness campsites in Yosemite National Park.

Errors on the USGS Merced Peak 15-minute map. An approach to Mount Clark from the west involves cross-country travel through a beautiful, but dense, forest. Rigorous use of the map, compass, and perhaps an altimeter and a Global Positioning System receiver may be needed to ensure that you arrive at Mount Clark, and not one of the cirques surrounding Gray Peak. Unfortunately, some editions of the USGS Merced Peak 15-minute quadrangle are in error regarding the terrain west of Mount Clark. For example, Red Creek does not flow into the Clark Fork of Illilouette Creek at UTM 807732; it instead flows south of Point 7,200 ft+ (7,232 ft; UTM 798730). And there is another fork of the Clark Fork of Illilouette Creek that does not appear on some editions of the USGS Merced Peak 15-minute map; this fork flows from the west side of Mount Clark to meet the Clark Fork of Illilouette Creek at UTM 828737. These errors also appear on the USGS Yosemite National Park and Vicinity (1:125,000) map and on the Map Link Merced Peak 15-minute map (which is a reprint of the USGS Map). The Wilderness Press Merced Peak map is correct, however, as is the new USGS Merced Peak 7.5-minute map.

Eichorn Pinnacle
Eichorn Pinnacle and Cathedral Peak from the southwest. Photo by R. J. Secor.

Tuolumne Meadows in winter. Yosemite National Park has kindly provided a hut at Tuolumne Meadows for winter visitors to use. It is located in the summer campsite reservation office at the entrance to Tuolumne Meadows Campground, less than 0.1 mile southwest of the bridge across the Tuolumne River along Tioga Road (UTM 929944). It sleeps ten on a first-come, first-served basis (sorry, no reservations!). Please don't abuse this privilege, and leave it cleaner than you found it. If it is full, don't camp directly next to the hut, but move on to disperse the impact. Also, there are public telephones outside the hut. A skier once answered the phone in early March and asked the caller if she knew where the phone was located. "Somewhere in Yosemite, I believe," she replied, and added: "My daughter tells me that it is lovely this time of year."

Chapter 14

Northern Yosemite

The northern portion of Yosemite National Park is the last wilderness of the High Sierra. Much of it is at lower elevations than other portions of the park, and its deep canyons, dense with old-growth forests, still hold historical artifacts from Native Americans, shepherds, and the cavalry. Because it is not as awesome as other regions of the range, it is less visited—so solitude is a part of the wilderness experience of northern Yosemite.

The southern limit of this region is Tioga Road. It is marked on the west by a line drawn from Mount Hoffman, Pate Valley, Wilmer Lake, and Dorothy Lake Pass. The northern boundary is Buckeye Creek.

HISTORY

There was no National Park Service when Yosemite National Park was created in 1890. The U.S. Cavalry took charge of administering the park, and their priority was to oust the shepherds and their flocks. The cavalry was at a serious disadvantage, however, because the shepherds had been in the Yosemite backcountry for decades, and had an intimate knowledge of the passes, meadows, and trails. The cavalry established patrols to the boundaries of the new park, and worked out their own system of trails, marked by the "T" (for "trail") blazes in northern Yosemite, and the pointed "Obelisk" blazes in the southern portion of the park. The cavalry named places, began to draw maps, and worked out a system to pursue and capture the herders.

In 1894 First Lieutenant N. F. McClure of the Fifth Cavalry led an expedition to scout for shepherds. His party of twelve mounted soldiers left Wawona and headed for Tuolumne Meadows. He arrested four herders and their pack train near Mount Conness, and had them escorted back to Wawona. He continued his patrol, and at Virginia Canyon he came across two large flocks of sheep. He wrote, "The herders fled up into the rocks, and we were unable to capture them; so I had one or two shots fired to frighten them. I do not think they have stopped running yet." He sent patrols up and down Return Creek, and found thousands of sheep apparently abandoned by the herders.

But there were no penalties for grazing in the national park; all that the cavalry could do was to confiscate the stock, herd, supplies, and camping equipment, and order the shepherds out of the park. Seizing thousands of sheep was almost impossible, so Lieutenant Benson of the U.S. Cavalry worked out a plan to scatter the flocks beyond the park boundary on one side of the park, and the herders and their dogs on the other side, several days of travel from each other. In 1898, 189,550 sheep, 350 horses, and 1,000 head of cattle were expelled from the park, and 27 firearms were confiscated.

The ever-resourceful shepherds countered this by hiring spies. A cavalry patrol could not leave Wawona without word being sent far ahead of their approach. Signal fires were lit during the night, and warning notices were nailed to trees along the trails. But the cavalry prevailed in the end, with the help of law and public opinion, and the era of the shepherds in the High Sierra came to an end in the early twentieth century.

MAPS

USGS. *7.5-minute series:* Mount Dana, Tioga Pass, Falls Ridge, Tenaya Lake, Yosemite Falls, Ten Lakes,

Tiltill Mountain, Piute Mountain, Matterhorn Peak, Dunderberg Peak, Twin Lakes, Buckeye Ridge, Tower Peak. *National park maps:* Yosemite National Park and Vicinity (1:125,000). *30 x 60–minute series:* Bridgeport, Yosemite Valley.

USFS. A Guide to the Hoover Wilderness (1:63,360).

Tom Harrison Cartography. Yosemite High Country, Mammoth High Country.

Map Link 15-minute series. Tuolumne Meadows, Hetch Hetchy Reservoir, Matterhorn Peak, Tower Peak.

Wilderness Press 15-minute series. Tuolumne Meadows, Hetch Hetchy Reservoir.

ROADS

Tioga Road

Tioga Road serves as the southern boundary of the region discussed in this chapter. A side road leaves Tioga Road 9.8 miles from Lee Vining and goes north for 2.5 miles to Saddlebag Lake.

The Gaylor Lakes Trail starts from Tioga Road 3.4 miles west of Tioga Pass.

A side road leads north off Tioga Road 6.9 miles west of Tioga Pass. This road leads to the trailhead serving the Dog Lake Trail and the Pacific Crest Trail near Soda Springs.

The trailhead for the McGee Lake Trail is near the north shore of Tenaya Lake, 15.3 miles west of Tioga Pass along Tioga Road.

The trailhead for the May Lake Trail is located at Snow Flat. Leave Tioga Road either 19.4 miles west of Tioga Pass, or 26.6 miles east of Crane Flat, and drive north on the side road 1.9 miles to the trailhead.

Lundy Lake Road

Lundy Lake Road goes west from the junction of Highways 395 and 167, approximately 7.2 miles north of Lee Vining on Highway 395. The road ascends Lundy Canyon for 6.3 miles to the trailhead of the Lundy Pass Trail.

Virginia Lakes Road

Virginia Lakes Road goes west from the top of Conway Summit along Highway 395, approximately 13 miles north of Lee Vining, or 13.3 miles south of Bridgeport. The road goes for 6 miles to Virginia Lakes and the trailhead for the Summit Lake Trail.

Green Creek Road

Green Creek Road leaves Highway 395 approximately 5 miles south of Bridgeport. The road heads south from the highway and goes for 0.9 mile to a fork. Take the left fork for 1.7 miles to another fork. Go left another 0.8 mile to a junction. Turn right, then continue up the road another 5.8 miles to its end and the trailhead for the Green Lake Trail.

Twin Lakes Road

Twin Lakes Road heads south from the western edge of Bridgeport. It leads 13.4 miles to Twin Lakes and Mono Village. The trailheads for the Peeler Lake Trail, Rock Island Pass Trail, and the Horse Creek Trail are in the private campground at Mono Village. The hiker parking area is on private land at Mono Village; a parking fee is charged.

Buckeye Creek Road

Buckeye Creek Road starts along Twin Lakes Road at 7.1 miles from Bridgeport. The road goes north for 2.8 miles to a junction. Go left another 1.3 miles to the trailhead for the Buckeye Pass Trail. As of this writing, this trailhead is on private land and is subject to the control of the owner.

TRAILS

May Lake Trail 4¼ miles

A quota trail. The May Lake Trail starts from Snow Flat, along the old Tioga Road (0 mi; 8,846 ft). The trail goes north to May Lake and the May Lake High Sierra Camp (1 mi; 9,329 ft). It then heads east and then north to meet the Ten Lakes Trail (3 ¼ mi; 8,720 ft+).

Ten Lakes Trail 20¼ miles

A quota trail. The Ten Lakes Trail leaves Tioga Road at the northern shore of Tenaya Lake (0 mi; 8,160 ft+). The trail ascends Murphy Creek to meet the McGee Lake Trail (2½ mi; 8,680 ft+). The Ten Lakes Trail turns southwest from the junction to meet the May Lake Trail

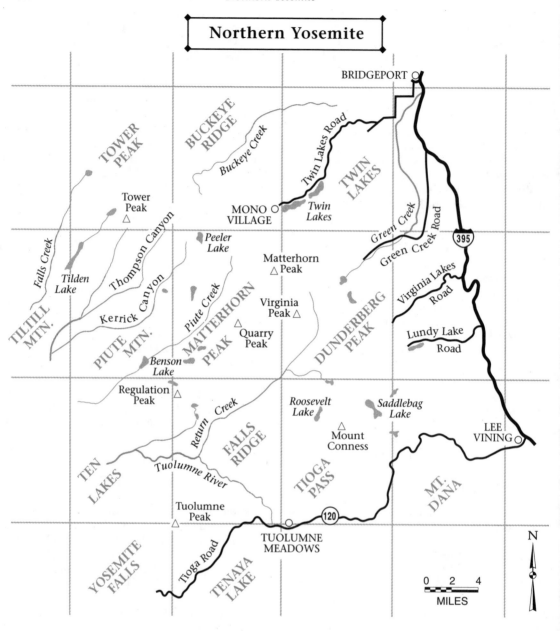

Northern Yosemite

(¾ mi; 8,720 ft+). The Ten Lakes Trail then climbs to the north, and turns west and then southwest around Tuolumne Peak. The trail descends the South Fork of Cathedral Creek before making a steep climb out of this canyon and continuing on to the westernmost of the Ten Lakes (10¾ mi; 8,947 ft). Bears prowl through this area. The trail climbs out of the Ten Lakes basin on its western side, crosses Ten Lakes Pass (1 mi; 9,640 ft+), and descends Yosemite Creek to meet Tioga Road (5¼ mi; 7,480 ft+).

McGee Lake Trail   4¾ miles

This trail leaves the Pacific Crest Trail near Glen Aulin (0 mi; 7,880 ft+) and heads southwest to McGee Lake (¾ mi; 8,107 ft). The trail continues southwest from the lake, crosses Cathedral Creek, and meets the Ten Lakes Trail (4 mi; 8,680 ft+).

Tuolumne Canyon Trail   14 miles

Tuolumne Canyon Trail starts at Glen Aulin (0 mi, 7,880 ft+), which is reached via the Pacific Crest Trail from Tuolumne Meadows. Bears prowl through this area. The trail follows the north bank of the Tuolumne River down the canyon, and passes Waterwheel Falls (3 mi; 6,800 ft+), a sight to behold. The trail continues downstream and crosses Return Creek on a bridge. It continues to descend the canyon and it comes to Muir Gorge (6 mi; 5,440 ft+), where the river roars through a deep chasm. The trail bypasses Muir Gorge by climbing (to 5,920 ft+) and then by crossing Register Creek. The trail continues downstream to Pate Valley, where it meets the Rodgers Canyon Trail (5 mi; 4,360 ft+). Bears prowl through this area.

The lower portion of the Tuolumne Canyon Trail may be flooded during high water, and stream crossings may be extraordinarily difficult if not impossible. On the other hand, the Tuolumne River is an awesome sight during high water.

Rodgers Canyon Trail   12 miles

The Rodgers Canyon Trail goes north from Pate Valley (0 mi; 4,360 ft+) and makes a steep climb to meet the Pleasant Valley Trail (5 mi; 7,760 ft+). It goes southeast from the junction and makes a slight climb before making a gentle descent (to 7,840 ft+) to Rodgers Canyon. The trail continues upstream and meets the Rodgers Lake Trail (5 mi; 8,780 ft+). The Rodgers Canyon Trail climbs north from this junction (to 9,520 ft+), passing Murdock Lake to meet the Pacific Crest Trail (2 mi; 9,360 ft+).

Rodgers Lake Trail   3 miles

This trail leaves the Pacific Crest Trail (0 mi; 9,440 ft+) southwest of Smedberg Lake. After crossing a small saddle (to 9,800 ft+), it descends and circles around the west shore of Rodgers Lake. The trail continues descend-ing, crosses the outlet of Neall Lake (a side trail leads to this lake), and leads to the Rodgers Canyon Trail (3 mi; 9,360 ft+). Bears prowl through this area.

Pleasant Valley Trail   5 miles

The Pleasant Valley Trail leaves the Rodgers Canyon Trail 5 miles from Pate Valley (0 mi; 7,760 ft+). The trail goes north from the junction, traversing at first, then making a steep descent into Pleasant Valley (2 mi; 6,840 ft+). It then meets a side trail that leads north to Irwin Bright Lake. The Pleasant Valley Trail wanders through the valley before climbing out of the western side of the valley to meet the Bear Valley Trail (3 mi; 8,040 ft+).

Bear Valley Trail   7 miles

This trail leaves the Pacific Crest Trail in the lower portion of Kerrick Canyon (0 mi; 7,960 ft+) and makes a steep ascent to the south to the lake at Bear Valley (2 mi; 9,154 ft). The trail crosses the outlet of the lake and goes downstream to a small lake, where it turns south-east and makes a short, steep climb to a saddle (to 9,480 ft+). It then descends to meet the Pleasant Valley Trail (5 mi; 8,040 ft+). The Rancheria Trail goes southwest from this junction and leads to Hetch Hetchy Reservoir.

Pacific Crest Trail   51½ miles

A quota trail. This section of the Pacific Crest Trail starts from Tioga Road near Lembert Dome (0 mi; 8,584 ft). The trail follows a dirt road to Soda Springs and some stables (¾ mi; 8,575 ft). It then leaves the road and becomes a real trail and meets the Young Lakes Trail (½ mi; 8,640 ft+). The Pacific Crest Trail takes the left fork and descends the upper part of Tuolumne Canyon, pass-ing some impressive waterfalls to meet the McGee Lake Trail (3½ mi; 7,880 ft+). Bears prowl through this area. It then descends to the Tuolumne River, crosses it on a bridge, and meets the Tuolumne Canyon Trail at Glen Aulin. The Pacific Crest Trail heads northeast from this junction and ascends Cold Canyon to meet the McCabe Lakes Trail (7 mi; 9,120 ft+). The Pacific Crest Trail goes north, crossing McCabe Creek and descending into Virginia Canyon. It then crosses Return Creek and meets the Summit Lake Trail (1¼ mi; 8,520 ft+).

The Pacific Crest Trail turns southwest from the junc-tion and descends Virginia Canyon before turning northwest and climbing through a small pass (9,760 ft+); it then arrives at Miller Lake (3½ mi; 9,446 ft). Bears prowl through this area. The trail goes north from the lake and descends into Matterhorn Canyon to meet the Burro Pass Trail (2¼ mi; 8,480 ft+). The trail turns southwest from this junction, crosses Matterhorn Creek, and descends the canyon. It then turns northwest and ascends the Wilson Creek drainage to climb to the summit of Benson Pass (4½ mi; 10,080 ft+). It then descends the west side of the pass and circles around Volunteer Peak, passing Smedberg Lake (9,219 ft) and meeting the Rodgers Lake Trail (3 mi; 9,480 ft+). The Pacific Crest Trail goes west from this junction to meet the Rodgers Canyon Trail (½ mi; 9,360 ft+), then goes north and descends to cross Piute Creek (3 mi; 7,600 ft+). (A ½-mile side trail goes west from here to beautiful Benson Lake, the Riviera of northern Yosemite.) The Pacific Crest Trail then makes a steep climb to the north over Seavey Pass (9,120 ft+) to meet the Buckeye Pass Trail in Kerrick Canyon (3½ mi; 8,880 ft+). It then descends Kerrick Canyon to meet the Bear Valley Trail (3¼ mi; 7,960 ft+). As the name indicates, bears are active throughout this area.

After crossing Rancheria Creek, the Pacific Crest Trail makes a steep climb to the north, crosses a pass (8,880 ft+), and then makes a steep descent to another major stream crossing in Stubblefield Canyon (2 mi; 7,720 ft+). The trail continues west, crosses Macomb Ridge (8,920 ft+), and meets the Tilden Lake Trail (2½ mi; 8,360 ft+). Bears prowl through this area. A trail leads south down Tilden Canyon from this junction; the Pacific Crest Trail continues west and descends to Wilmer Lake (spelled "Wilma" on some maps) (1¾ mi; 7,960 ft+) and meets the Jack Main Canyon Trail, which goes south and leads to Hetch Hetchy Reservoir. The Pacific Crest Trail ascends Jack Main Canyon to meet the Tilden Lake Trail (1½ mi; 8,120 ft+). The Pacific Crest Trail continues north up Jack Main Canyon to the Bond Pass Trail junction (6¾ mi; 9,360 ft+), turns northeast, passes Dorothy Lake, and reaches the summit of Dorothy Lake Pass (1½ mi; 9,520 ft+). The trail descends the east side of the pass and gradually moves north. It descends Cascade Creek and comes to a junction (2 mi; 9,000 ft+). The Pacific Crest Trail goes west from this junction, continuing on to Cinko Lake and eventually the Canadian border. A side trail leads northeast from this junction to meet the Kirkwood Pass Trail below Upper Piute Meadows before descending to the West Walker River.

McCabe Lakes Trail   2 miles

This trail leaves the Pacific Crest Trail 7 miles north of Glen Aulin (0 mi; 9,120 ft+). The trail goes east from the junction before turning south and arriving at the lower McCabe Lake (2 mi; 9,820 ft+).

Young Lakes Trail   5¼ miles

A quota trail. The Young Lakes Trail leaves the Pacific Crest Trail ½ mile from Soda Springs in Tuolumne Meadows (0 mi; 8,600 ft). It goes to the right from the junction, crosses Delaney Creek, and makes a gradual ascent to the northeast to meet the Dog Lake Trail (4 mi; 9,720 ft+). The Young Lakes Trail goes around Ragged Peak ending at the lowest of the Young Lakes (1¼ mi; 9,883 ft). Bears prowl through this area.

Dog Lake Trail   4½ miles

A quota trail. This trail starts from the parking area west of Lembert Dome in Tuolumne Meadows (0 mi; 8,584 ft). It goes north and climbs around to the north side of Lembert Dome to meet another trail that comes from the eastern side of Lembert Dome (1 mi; 9,040 ft+). The Dog Lake Trail goes north from the junction, passes Dog Lake (½ mi; 9,160 ft+), and continues north to the junction with the Young Lakes Trail (3 mi; 9,720 ft+).

Gaylor Lakes Trail   2¼ miles

A quota trail. The Gaylor Lakes Trail goes north from Tioga Road, about 3½ miles west of Tioga Pass (0 mi; 9,240 ft+). It then goes north to the lowest of the Gaylor Lakes (2¼ mi; 10,049 ft). Cross-country travel is easy to the other lakes in the basin above.

Another trail leads from Tioga Pass to the Gaylor Lakes. This trail goes west from the Tioga Pass Entrance Station (0 mi; 9,943 ft) and crosses a saddle (to 10,520 ft+) before descending to the southeastern lake (1 mi; 10,334 ft+). It continues north, past the northeast lake, to the ruins of the Great Sierra Mine (1 mi; 10,760 ft+).

Lundy Pass Trail   6¾ miles

A non-quota trail. This trail starts from the southern shore of Saddlebag Lake (0 mi; 10,066 ft). (A good trail goes around Saddlebag Lake on its western shore, and a road circles the lake on its eastern shore.) The trail goes north over Lundy Pass (10,280 ft+) and makes a steep descent into Lundy Canyon (6¾ mi; 8,200 ft+). Campfires are prohibited between Lake Helen and Hummingbird Lake.

Summit Lake Trail   9½ miles

A quota trail. The Summit Lake Trail starts from the end of Virginia Lakes Road (0 mi; 9,880 ft+). It passes the upper lakes in this basin and crosses a small saddle (11,120 ft+) to meet the Green Lake Trail (4¼ mi; 10,080 ft+). The trail continues around Summit Lake to the small pass on its western shore, which is atop the Sierra crest (1 mi; 10,183 ft). It then descends into Virginia Canyon to meet the Pacific Crest Trail (4¼ mi; 9,360 ft+).

Green Lake Trail   6¼ miles

A quota trail. The Green Lake Trail starts from the end of Green Creek Road (0 mi; 8,040 ft+) and climbs southwest to Green Lake (2 mi; 8,945 ft). The Green Lake Trail goes south and climbs for 1½ miles to East Lake (1½ mi; 9,458 ft). The trail continues south to Gilman Lake (1 mi; 9,486 ft), passes Hoover Lakes, and meets the Summit Lake Trail (1¾ mi; 10,80 ft+).

A trail leads northwest from Green Lake to West Lake after 1½ miles, and a good use trail continues from West Lake up Par Value Lakes.

Tamarack Lake Trail   4½ miles

A quota trail. This trail starts from Twin Lakes Campground (0 mi; 7,280 ft+), which is along Twin Lakes Road. It switchbacks up the steep slope to the south of the campground and ascends Tamarack Creek to Tamarack Lake (4½ mi; 9,630 ft).

Horse Creek Trail   5 miles

A quota trail. The Horse Creek Trail switchbacks up the steep slope south of Mono Village (0 mi; 7,092 ft) to the hanging valley portion of Horse Creek (2 mi; 8,200 ft+). A good use trail continues up Horse Creek from here. The Horse Creek Trail goes east, gradually descending to the lower of the Twin Lakes (3 mi; 7,080 ft+).

Barney Lake Trail   6¾ miles

A quota trail. The Barney Lake Trail goes west from Mono Village (0 mi; 7,092 ft) and ascends Robinson Creek to Barney Lake (4 mi; 8,258 ft+). (Some maps may show a trail crossing a pass to the west and descending to the South Fork of Buckeye Creek; this trail has been abandoned for a long time.) The trail passes the western shore of Barney Lake and continues upstream to meet the Peeler Lake Trail and the Rock Island Pass Trail (2¾ mi; 9,160 ft+).

Peeler Lake Trail   2¼ miles

The Peeler Lake Trail climbs to the west from the junction of the Barney Lake Trail and the Rock Island Pass Trail (0 mi; 9,160 ft+). It passes through some enormous boulders before circling around the northern shore of Peeler Lake (1½ mi; 9,489 ft). Peeler Lake has two outlets during high water; one outlet feeds the Pacific Ocean, and the other drains into the Great Basin. The trail continues west to the Buckeye Pass Trail (¾ mi; 9,360 ft+).

Rock Island Pass Trail   3¼ miles

This trail leaves the Buckeye Pass Trail near the southern end of Kerrick Meadow (0 mi; 9,280 ft+). The trail climbs to the southeast (to 9,520 ft+) before turning east and finally northeast to cross Rock Island Pass (2 mi; 10,160 ft+). It then descends the northeast side of the pass to meet the Burro Pass Trail above Crown Lake (1¼ mi; 9,680 ft+). The trail continues downhill to Crown Lake (¾ mi; 9,440 ft+), then continues to meet the Peeler Lake Trail and the Barney Lake Trail (1½ mi; 9,160 ft+).

Burro Pass Trail   10 miles

This trail leaves the Rock Island Pass Trail ¾ mile above Crown Lake (0 mi; 9,680 ft+). The trail makes a steep ascent to Mule Pass (1½ mi; 10,440 ft+), descends Slide Canyon (to 9,360 ft+), and then continues east to the top of Burro Pass (3 mi; 10,640 ft+). It then descends Matterhorn Canyon to meet the Pacific Crest Trail (5½ mi; 8,480 ft+).

Kirkwood Pass Trail   15¾ miles

A quota trail. The Kirkwood Pass Trail starts from the end of Buckeye Creek Road (0 mi; 9,200 ft+). It ascends Buckeye Creek, fording the creek near the start of muddy Big Meadow before meeting the Buckeye Pass Trail (9¼ mi; 8,411 ft). The trail continues west and makes a steep climb to the summit of Kirkwood Pass (2½ mi; 9,920 ft+). (This pass is unnamed on most maps.) It descends the west side of the pass, passing Upper Piute Meadows, to meet the Tower Lake Trail (4 mi; 8,240 ft+). The trail continues downstream to meet the side trail (1¼ mi; 8,080 ft+) that leads southwest to the Pacific Crest Trail. A trail continues north from here down the West Walker River to Leavitt Meadows (10½ mi; 7,200 ft+).

Buckeye Pass and Kerrick Canyon Trail

11 miles

This trail leaves the Kirkwood Pass Trail (0 mi; 8,411 ft) and ascends the South Fork of Buckeye Creek to the summit of Buckeye Pass (4 mi; 9,572 ft). The trail descends the south side of the pass to meet the Peeler Lake Trail (¾ mi; 9,360 ft+). The Kerrick Canyon Trail heads south through Kerrick Meadow to meet the Rock Island Pass Trail (1½ mi; 9,280 ft+). The Kerrick Canyon Trail continues its descent, passing many meadows and forests, to meet the Pacific Crest Trail at the head of Kerrick Canyon (4¾ mi; 8,880 ft+). Bears prowl through this area.

Tower Lake Trail   3¾ miles

This trail goes south from the northern end of Lower Piute Meadows (0 mi; 8,280 ft+) and ascends Tower Canyon to Tower Lake (3¾ mi; 9,523 ft).

Tilden Lake Trail   4¾ miles

The Tilden Lake Trail leaves the Pacific Crest Trail in Jack Main Canyon (0 mi; 8,120 ft+) and leads to the lower end of Tilden Lake (1¼ mi; 8,880 ft+). A side trail follows the western shore of the lake from here, and the main trail continues along the southern shore of the lake (¾ mi; 8,880 ft+). The trail then goes south, descending Tilden Canyon Creek for 2¾ miles to meet the Pacific Crest Trail (2¾ mi; 8,360 ft+) between Wilmer Lake and Macomb Ridge.

CROSS-COUNTRY ROUTES

"Conness Pass"   11,280 ft+; 11,280 ft+;

1.2 mi ENE of Mount Conness; UTM 981051

Class 2. This route crosses the east ridge of Mount Conness. Head northwest from the Carnegie Institute Experimental Station (located ½ mile southwest of Saddlebag Lake), pass a flat area, and climb onto the crest of the east ridge of the peak. Climb the east ridge of the peak to the 11,280-foot level, where a steep spur ridge drops down to the north and leads to the lowest of the Conness Lakes.

Further Reading: Steve Roper. *Sierra High Route.* Seattle: The Mountaineers Books, 1997, pp. 194–195.

"North Peak Pass"   11,720 ft+; 11,680 ft+;

0.3 mi SW of North Peak

Class 2. This pass crosses the Sierra crest between Conness Lakes and Roosevelt Lake. Tedious sand slopes lead up the southeast side of the pass. Head northwest for ½ mile from the top of the pass before turning southwest to Roosevelt Lake.

"Don't Be A Smart Pass"   11,160 ft+;

11,000 ft+; 0.7 mi NW of North Peak

Class 2. This pass leads between Upper McCabe Lake and Roosevelt Lake. Loose talus, interspersed with patches of snow, leads up the north slope of the pass. The south side is easy.

"McCabe Pass"   11,160 ft+; 11,200 ft+;

1.3 mi N of North Peak; UTM 971081

Class 2. This pass is also known as "Secret Lake Pass." It crosses the Sierra crest south of Shepherd Crest. An abandoned mining road leads from the north end of Saddlebag Lake to Steelhead Lake. A good use trail leads around the west shore of Steelhead Lake to the summit of the pass. The west side of this pass is class 2 down to Upper McCabe Lake.

Further Reading: Steve Roper. *Sierra High Route.* Seattle: The Mountaineers Books, 1997, pp. 203–204.

"Sky Pilot Col"   11,640 ft+; 11,600 ft+;

1.4 mi S of Excelsior Mountain; UTM 972086

Class 2. This pass leads between Steelhead Lake and Shepherd Lake. A good use trail leads from Steelhead Lake up the eastern side of McCabe Pass. The route to Sky Pilot Col goes north from here over talus to a small bowl. Climb out of this bowl on its left (west) side over talus to a scree slope, which leads to the top of Sky Pilot Col, immediately east of Shepherd Crest. Descend loose talus on the north side of the col down and to the northwest, descending to Shepherd Lake.

Further Reading: Steve Roper. *Sierra High Route.* Seattle: The Mountaineers Books, 1997, pp. 197–198, 203.

"Virginia Pass"   10,480 ft+; 10,480 ft+

Class 1. This pass leads from Green Creek to the upper portion of Virginia Canyon. A good use trail leads from Green Lake up Glimes Canyon to the summit of

Virginia Pass. The easiest descent of the west side of the pass is made by contouring northwest to the gentler terrain along Return Creek, on the floor of Virginia Canyon.

"Horse Creek Pass" 10,680 ft+; 10,640 ft+;
0.9 mi NW of Twin Peaks; UTM 921181

Class 2. This provides a direct cross-country route between Twin Lakes and Spiller Creek. Leave the Horse Creek Trail at the point where it switchbacks away from the canyon, then continue up the canyon over a good use trail. The use trail forks above a large talus slope. Take the left fork through the trees parallel to the stream, and continue up the canyon to the talus field just below the pass. Travel down the Spiller Creek drainage is easy.

Further Reading: Steve Roper. *Sierra High Route.* Seattle: The Mountaineers Books, 1997, pp. 201–202.

"Stanton Pass" 11,160 ft+; 11,120 ft+;
0.3 mi NE of Stanton Peak

Class 3. This pass extends from Virginia Canyon to Spiller Creek. It is located between Virginia Peak and Stanton Peak. A ledge system on the east side of the pass is used to approach a notch atop the pass near the northeast ridge of Stanton Peak. Descend the west side of the pass via class 3 ledges and loose gullies for a short distance, then head down and across the west side of Stanton Peak to Spiller Creek. A direct descent of the west side of the pass may result in the hiker becoming stranded on some cliffs.

Further Reading: Steve Roper. *Sierra High Route.* Seattle: The Mountaineers Books, 1997, pp. 200–201.

"Twin Peaks Pass" 11,480 ft+; 11,520 ft+;
0.8 mi S of Twin Peaks

Class 2. This pass, between Twin Peaks and Virginia Peak, leads from Spiller Creek to upper Virginia Canyon. The easiest approach to this pass from the west is to traverse diagonally up and right to the pass from a point in the Spiller Creek drainage, which is west of Twin Peaks; a direct ascent leads to cliffs beneath the pass. The east side of the pass has no hidden obstacles.

"Matterhorn Pass" 11,320 ft+; 11,360 ft+;
0.5 mi S of Matterhorn Peak

Class 3. This pass leads between Spiller Creek and upper Matterhorn Canyon. When crossing the pass

from Spiller Creek, approach the top of the pass from the right (north) on a ledge system. The west side of the pass is class 2.

Avalanche Lake and Glacier Lake

This cross-country route leads to the Sawtooth Ridge from Twin Lakes. Take the Horse Creek Trail from Mono Village and cross Robinson Creek. Leave the trail here, then make a diagonal climb up and to the right to Blacksmith Creek, aiming for a point above the falls at approximately 7,500 feet. This leads to the first hanging valley, where the creek forks. Those bound for Avalanche Lake take the left (east) fork; those headed for Glacier Lake take the right (west). Wood campfires are prohibited north of the Sawtooth Ridge, and the maximum party size allowed is eight persons.

"Polemonium Pass" 11,520 ft+; 11,760 ft+;
0.5 mi NW of Matterhorn Peak; UTM 907192

Class 3; ice axe required. This pass crosses the Sawtooth Ridge between The Dragtooth and The Doodad. The north side of this pass is a wide chute, with 500 feet of 45° snow/ice, and is a worthwhile climb in its own right. The south side of the pass is class 2 scree.

"Col de Doodad" 11,400 ft+; 11,440 ft+;
0.7 mi NW of Matterhorn Peak; UTM 905194

Class 4. This pass crosses the Sawtooth Ridge between the Southeast Tooth and The Doodad. The easiest route on the northeast side of the pass ascends the right (west) gully, which is next to the Southeast Tooth. Ascend this 35° snow/ice gully, passing under an overhanging block, and gain the ridge crest. Go to the right (southwest) for 30 feet to a platform, then go left (southeast) to a chockstone at the top of a short, steep chimney. Descend (or rappel) this short class 4 chimney to the scree slopes that lead down into Slide Canyon. When crossing this pass from southwest to northeast, it will be noticed that the first part of the pass is marked by this short chimney with the overhanging chockstone. *Variation:* Class 4. The route described above is difficult to locate from Slide Canyon, and some parties have climbed easy scree to the most prominent notch between the Southeast Tooth and The Doodad. The 45° couloir to the north of this notch is usually filled with snow; otherwise, it is full of loose rock. Rappel down the snow or rock in the couloir for 100 feet to a ledge. Traverse 10 feet horizontally left to the top of a loose chimney. Rappel 90 feet down the chimney to its right (as you look down) wall. This is followed by a third rappel of 60 feet directly to the snowfield below. It is better to develop your routefinding ability and avoid this variation completely.

"Glacier Col"   11,560 ft+; 11,600 ft+;
0.7 mi S of Avalanche Lake; UTM 900200

Class 2; ice axe needed. This pass crosses the Sawtooth Ridge between Cleaver Peak and Blacksmith Peak. The north side of the pass consists of steep snow/ice; the south side has scree and benches, which lead down to Slide Canyon.

"Cleaver Notch"   10,880 ft+; 10,880 ft+;
0.3 mi SE of Avalanche Lake; UTM 905204

Class 2. This is the obvious notch in The Cleaver. Cross the notch on its southern side, only 30 feet above the benches on its east and west sides.

"Hawk's Head Notch"   11,200ft+; 10,800 ft+;
0.6 mi SE of Glacier Lake; UTM 899203

Class 3–4. This narrow notch is located at the base of the north arête of Blacksmith Peak. It is immediately beneath the Hawk's Nest, an overhanging pinnacle on the arête. A steep chute leads up the west side of the notch.

"Ice Lake Pass"   10,000 ft+; 10,000 ft+;
0.7 mi SSE of Kettle Peak; UTM 874209

Class 2. This route ascends Little Slide Canyon from Robinson Creek, crosses the Sierra crest, and descends into Slide Canyon. Leave the Barney Lake Trail at the mouth of the canyon and cross Robinson Creek at a conveniently located beaver dam. Ascend the east side of the canyon, keeping above the willows and aspens that choke the streambed, and cross to the west bank of the stream near the point where the stream makes a sharp turn to the left. Ascend the west bank to a small meadow just below the falls of the outlet stream of Maltby Lake. Traverse east into the east fork of Little Slide Canyon and ascend a ravine next to a rock dome in the middle of the canyon. Circle Ice Lake on its east side and go above the cliffs that drop into the lake. The best approach to Ice Lake Pass is to descend to its low point from the higher, eastern end of the saddle. Benches and meadows on the southwest side of the pass lead to the Burro Pass Trail.

"Tower Pass"   10,080 ft+; 10,080 ft+;
0.7 mi NW of Tower Peak

Class 2. This pass leads from Tower Lake over the Sierra crest to Mary Lake and downstream to Tilden Lake. Climb to the broad saddle south of Tower Lake and descend the west bank of Tilden Creek to join the trail along the western shore of Tilden Lake.

PEAKS

Mount Hoffman   10,850 ft; 10,850 ft

This is a frequently climbed peak, and there is an outstanding view from the summit (if you ignore the radio repeater installed there).

South Slope. Class 2. First ascent June 24, 1863 by Josiah Whitney, William Brewer, and Charles Hoffman. The south slope can be easily reached from either May Lake or Tioga Road.

Southwest Ridge. Class 3. This ridge can be approached from either Hoffman Creek or from Wegner Lake. Follow the ridge to the summit.

Crimson Corner. III, 5.9. First ascent August 1982 by Terri Counts and Alan Bartlett. This route is on the north face of Mount Hoffman; it is to the right of the Merle Alley Route. Two pitches lead to the base of a large, left-facing, reddish corner. Three more pitches in the corner lead to the top. Generally, keep to the right wall of the corner. The crux is an off-width section on the fourth pitch.

Merle Alley Route. III, 5.7. First ascent July 1957 by Merle Alley and George Sessions. Ascend the snowfield on the north side of Mount Hoffman to the base of a chimney that is 200 feet west of the overhanging summit block. Climb the chimney all the way to the ridge. There are three overhangs in this 500-foot crack-and-chimney system.

North Face. III, 5.7, A2. First ascent August 1969 by George Sessions and Bob Summers. This route directly ascends the north face to the overhanging summit blocks. Begin by climbing cracks on the steep face through overhangs for several pitches to a belay stance about 50 feet below a small, red overhang. Climb to the base of this overhang (5.7), and overcome it with aid.

The next pitch traverses left above the overhanging wall and climbs steep cracks (5.7) to a belay ledge. Three more pitches of easy class 5 over flakes and cracks lead to the summit.

East Face. II, 5.7. First ascent September 1970 by Steve Williams and Richard Doleman. This is the face that rises above May Lake. Climb cracks that are to the right of an obvious left-facing open book. These cracks lead to a ramp, which goes left and up to the top.

Approach Face. II, 5.5. First ascent August 1974 by Vern Clevenger and Virginia Wallblom. This is the obvious face that is to the right of the summit when viewed from Snow Flat. The route is reportedly somewhere on this face.

"Hoffman's Thumb"

This is the impressive spire a few hundred feet southwest of the true summit of Mount Hoffman.

Regular Route. I, 5.6. First ascent October 16, 1932 by Jules Eichorn. Begin by climbing the southwest face of the thumb. Climb to a sloping ledge, which leads out onto the exposed east face. Climb the east face to the summit.

Other class 4 and 5 routes have been done on the northeast and west faces.

"Hoffman Turret" 10,280 ft+; 10,240 ft+; 0.3 mi NW of Mount Hoffman

This pinnacle is at the end of the low northwest ridge of Mount Hoffman.

Northeast Face. I, 5.9. First ascent August 1958 by Jerry Gray, George Ewing, and Les Overstreet. First free ascent August 1982 by Terri Counts and Alan Bartlett. Begin by climbing the right-hand crack of two cracks on the face, then climb to a large, V-shaped opening. Ascend the left side of the V to a hand crack that traverses left to the highest of three steps. Go right, around a buttress, and across a friction slab to a difficult open chimney. Climb the chimney; this is followed by easy scrambling to the summit.

"The Bowmaiden" 10,633 ft; 10,480 ft+; 1.0 mi N of May Lake; UTM 808903

Lucky Sailor's Route. III, 5.10. First ascent July 1981 by Evelyn Lees, Louise Sheperd, and Alan Bartlett. This route rises above the headwaters of the South Fork of Cathedral Creek. It is the most impressive of the north faces between Mount Hoffman and Tuolumne Peak. Begin by climbing cracks leading to the right-hand of two obvious open books on the prow of the buttress on the north side of the peak. Exit right after climbing the book halfway, then climb to a large, tree-covered ledge that runs across the north side of the Bowmaiden. Walk right along the ledge, then climb toward another large, left-facing open book, but climb a smaller open book to its left. From the top of this smaller book, go left and climb a 5.10 overhang, then climb up and left to a crack that divides the summit overhang.

"Tuolumne Peak" 10,845 ft; 10,845 ft

The south side of this peak is class 2 from May Lake; the northeast face from the Ten Lakes Trail is also class 2.

East Face, Right Side. II, 5.6. First ascent July 1968 by Bruce Kinnison and Ken Gobalet. Climb a prominent, left-facing open book on the right side of the east face. Climb up and left from the top of the book to the upper left side of a tree-covered terrace. A long class 4 pitch then leads to the summit.

East Face, Left Side. II, 5.7. First ascent September 10, 1974 by Bruce Kinnison, Ken Gobalet, and George Gray. There is an obvious chimney on the left side of the east face. This route starts approximately 50 feet left of this chimney. Fifty feet of easy class 5 climbing leads into the chimney. Climb the right side of the chimney and belay from chockstones in the chimney itself. Climb up the chimney for another long pitch, then traverse left under a roof. Continue upward by climbing cracks to the summit plateau.

Southwest Face. II, 5.7. First ascent July 1972 by Bruce Kinnison and Bob Ashworth. This route climbs the center of the face and ascends a prominent 250-foot chimney. Climb up and left from the top of the chimney to a class 4 buttress. *Variation:* II, 5.9. First ascent August 1987 by Dan Ward and Dave Harden. Climb a steep, right-facing corner directly above the prominent 250-foot chimney.

Giardiasis. II, 5.10. First ascent June 1981 by Kim Walker and Alan Bartlett. The route begins just left of the center portion of the southwest face. Climb up and left through a dirty, black-stained area. Cleaner rock leads up and then up and right for three more pitches.

"SAR Dome" 8,829 ft; 8,829 ft; 1.5 mi SW of Wildcat Point

West Face. II, 5.10c. First ascent September 1990 by

Alan Swanson and Urmas Franosch. This formation is best approached from California Falls. The four-pitch route climbs the obvious dihedral on the west face. The first pitch is the crux. This is followed by a 5.10a, 5.10b, and finally a 5.10a pitch. Protection to 4 inches is needed.

"Big Red Dome" 9,134 ft; 9,134 ft;
0.3 mi NW of McGee Lake
Seam Sealer. III, 5.9. First ascent 1985 by Alan Swanson, Steve "Lucky" Smith, and Kevin. This route ascends the southeast face. The first pitch frictions up a slick slab (5.9; 3 bolts) followed by a difficult seam that widens (5.9). The remaining pitches wander up the face (5.8, 5.7, and class 4, respectively).

Wildcat Point 9,455 ft; 9,455 ft
Class 2 from Mattie Lake.
Wildcat Buttress. IV, 5.9, A4. First ascent August 1972 by Galen Rowell and Dale Bard. This route climbs the buttress above California Falls. The route starts to the right of a prominent dihedral. The first pitch consists of difficult mixed climbing. This is followed by a short 5.9 crack, easier face climbing, and an awesome, but easy jam crack behind a huge flake. Two sections of aid climbing pass giant ledges. The second section is in an overhanging dihedral with difficult aid placements. Traverse left from the top of the dihedral for 50 feet along a narrow ledge to a shallow corner, which leads to the top.

Cold Mountain 10,301 ft; 10,301 ft
Class 2. First ascent 1929 by Glen Dawson and party.

Peak 8,886ft 8,880 ft+; 0.5 mi NNW of Glen Aulin
Southwest Buttress. III, 5.8. First ascent September 1972 by Joe Kelsey, Galen Rowell, and TM Herbert. Climb the prominent dihedral on the buttress.

Ragged Peak 10,912 ft; 10,912 ft
Southwest Slope. Class 2. First ascent July 6, 1863 by William Brewer and Charles Hoffman. This slope can be approached from the Dog Lake Trail, or from Young Lakes via the saddle east of the summit. The high point is the southernmost of the three summits clustered together.
Northwest Face. Class 5. First ascent August 25, 1939 by Boynton Kaiser and party. Slabs and chimneys lead up this face to the summit.

Northeast Face. I, 5.6. First ascent July 1971 by Jeff Genest and Adrian Rosenthal. This route begins in a V-shaped trough midway up the face.
East Face. Class 5. First ascent August 16, 1953 by Warren Harding, Ray Alcott, and Norah Straley. The route is reportedly somewhere on this face.

Peak 11,255ft 11,255 ft;
1.1 mi ESE of Ragged Peak
First ascent October 15, 1967 by John Simon and Mike Etherton. The summit rocks are class 3 from the southeast.

Gaylor Peak 11,004 ft; 11,004 ft
This fine viewpoint is class 1 from Tioga Pass. There is a good ski tour on Gaylor Peak's northeast slope.
Further Reading: Hans Joachim Burhenne. *Sierra Spring Ski-Touring.* San Francisco: Mountain Press, 1971, p. 71.

Tioga Peak 11,526 ft; 11,513 ft
Class 2 from Gardisky Lake.

Mono Dome 10,622 ft; 10,614 ft
The north slope is class 2.

Lee Vining Peak 11,690 ft; 11,691 ft
The southeast slope is class 2.

Mount Warren 12,327 ft; 12,327 ft
First ascent was before 1868 by a Mr. Wackenreyder. The north and southwest slopes are both class 2.

Peak 12,002ft 12,002 ft;
1.0 mi SE of White Mountain
This peak is locally known as "False White Mountain." First ascent June 24, 1969 by Daniel Zucker. The southeast slope is class 2.

White Mountain 12,057 ft; 12,000 ft+
First ascent 1917 by Walter L. Huber. The south slope is class 2.

Mount Conness 12,590 ft; 12,590 ft
From Young Lakes. Class 2. First ascent September 1, 1866 by Clarence King and James Gardiner. This is a very popular climb, and a use trail has appeared over the years. Go east from Young Lakes to Lake 10,560ft+

(10,560 ft+; 1.3 miles south of Mount Conness). Go north up sand and scree into the valley and onto the plateau southeast of the summit. Climb over blocks to the summit from the plateau.

Southwest Face, Right Corner. IV, 5, A. First ascent July 15, 1959 by John Merriam and Don Harmon. Ascend the huge, deep chimney on the right side of the southwest face. Climb the chimney, and leave it via a more difficult chimney that leads directly up, or via a class 4 gully that goes right. There is an awful lot of loose rock on this route.

Morning Thunder. III, 5.9. First ascent August 1976 by Bob Harrington, Bob Locke, and Rick Wheeler. This route ascends the buttress that is left of the huge, deep chimney on the right side of the southwest face. Face climbing leads onto the crest of the buttress. There are five more pitches before the climb ends with 200 feet of class 4 below the summit.

Further Reading: Don Reid and Chris Falkenstein. *Rock Climbs of Tuolumne Meadows.* Denver: Chockstone Press, 1986, p. 57.

Flakes of Fury. IV, 5.10a. First ascent July 11, 1984 by Eric Perlman and Chris Vandiver. This route ascends the right side of the southwest face of Mount Conness. Begin by climbing a prominent groove with vegetation (5.8). This is followed by a loose 5.10a overhang that leads to rotten flakes and a lichen-infested squeeze chimney. Two 5.9 dihedrals lead to the final crux pitch: a 5.10a layback followed by overhanging flakes. A class 4 ramp then leads to the summit ridge. There is much loose rock on this route.

Rosy Crown Route. IV, 5.9, A2 or 5.10c. First ascent June 1974 by Gary Colliver and Chris Vandiver. First free ascent 1994 by Urmas Franosch and Alan Swanson. This route begins approximately 300 feet to the right of the Harding Route. The first pitch goes free, and the second pitch also goes free until the crack becomes shallow. Some aid moves are needed to pass a roof, followed by free climbing to a loose-appearing flake. Eight more pitches straight up the face lead to the summit.

Harding Route. V, 5.10c or 5.9, A2. First ascent September 1959 by Warren Harding, Glen Denny, and Herb Swedlund. First free ascent July 1, 1976 by Galen Rowell and Chris Vandiver. First winter ascent March 6, 1976 by Mike Graber, Dennis Hennek, and Galen Rowell. This is one of the classic big-wall climbs in the High Sierra. The route begins just left of the center portion of the southwest face; a cairn, erected in memory of Don Goodrich (killed during an early attempt), marks the base of the route. The first pitch (5.9) goes straight up. The second pitch, a long, poorly protected traverse that goes right and up over a small roof to a slot, is the crux. Climb up and left (5.8) to a ledge. Move slightly left and climb 250 feet straight up along a crack that eventually becomes off-width. This section ends on a ledge. Leave the ledge on its right side and climb up and right to a difficult inside corner. After the corner, the next pitch climbs a chimney at first and then goes up and right. A 5.9 crack and then an easy chimney lead to a ramp, which goes up and right to the summit slabs.

Further Reading: *American Alpine Journal.* 1977, pp. 73–78; Don Reid and Chris Falkenstein. *Rock Climbs of Tuolumne Meadows.* Denver: Chockstone Press, 1986, p. 56; John Moynier and Claude Fiddler. *Sierra Classics.* Evergreen, Colo.: Chockstone Press, 1993, pp. 288–290.

West Ridge. II, 5.6. First ascent 1957 by Dick Long and friends. This highly enjoyable route ascends the far right side of the west face, close to the edge of the southwest face. Start by climbing the left side of the small crescent-shaped ramp at the base of the face and continue to the crest of the ridge. Follow the ridge to the summit.

Further Reading: John Moynier and Claude Fiddler. *Sierra Classics.* Evergreen, Colo.: Chockstone Press, 1993, pp. 286–287.

West Face. Class 4. First ascent June 1977 by David Hammerbeck; second ascent June 1988 by Sam Roberts. The west face of Mount Conness has many chutes and shallow ribs. The main problem is selecting the easiest chute for the 1,500 feet of class 3–4 climbing over solid rock. Begin in the middle of the face, moving between the chutes and ribs when encountering difficult sections. Continue up and right aiming for the upper part of the West Ridge route, which is followed for the last 100 feet.

The Golden Road. II, Class 5. First ascent September 1992 by David Hardy and Paul Goldammer. This route starts from the south side of the huge tower on the north ridge and climbs the left side of the west face. Traverse up and across the upper west face to the summit, always remaining under the crest of the north ridge.

North Ridge. II, 5.6. First ascent July 1969 by Barry Hagen and Galen Rowell. Scramble up the ridge from the saddle between North Peak and Mount Conness to the top of the huge tower where the ridge changes direction. Down climb (5.6) or rappel the south side of this

MOUNT CONNESS

West Face

West Ridge
Route

Southwest
Face

Mount Conness from the southwest. Photo by R. J. Secor.

tower into the notch and follow the crest of the ridge for several pitches over beautiful rock to the summit. This is a very nice route, with outstanding views and moderate climbing.

Further Reading: John Moynier and Claude Fiddler. *Sierra Classics.* Evergreen, Colo.: Chockstone Press, 1993, pp. 291–293.

Northeast Face. Class 5. First ascent July 1958 by George Harr, Lynn Grey, and Ray Van Aken. Cross the Conness Glacier to the base of the northeast face, to a point almost directly below the summit. Ascend a gully that goes up and left to a prominent buttress that divides the face. Traverse to the north from the top of the gully and cross the buttress. Many class 4 pitches lead to an overhang, followed by a class 5 traverse to a crack that leads to a recess. More pitches lead up to a notch about 200 feet north of the summit.

Glacier Route. Class 3. Cross the Conness Glacier and ascend rock ribs or gullies to the low point of the east ridge of Mount Conness. Follow the ridge to the plateau southeast of the summit.

Y Couloir. First ascent August 1986 by Dave Haake and Chris Keith. Ascend the left branch of this prominent chute to the crest of the east ridge. The angle of the snow is approximately 45°.

East Ridge. Class 3. The entire east ridge can be followed from the vicinity of Saddlebag Lake. Keep to the southern side of the ridge until the summit plateau is reached.

From Saddlebag Lake. Class 2. This roundabout route seems to be the most popular approach from the east. Cross to the west side of the dam at Saddlebag Lake and make a gradual descent to the southwest, passing the Carnegie Institute Experimental Station (camping and wood campfires are prohibited in this area). Ascend to the lowest saddle between Mount Conness and White Mountain along the Sierra crest. This is Pass 11,400ft+ (11,360 ft+; 1.1 miles south-southeast of Mount Conness; UTM 970029). Head northwest from the pass and climb onto the plateau that is southeast of the summit. Scrambling over blocks leads to the summit.

Traverse. V, 5.7. First ascent 1985 by Claude Fiddler and Nancy Fiddler. This traverse started at North Peak and ended at Peak 12,002ft (12,002 ft).

North Peak 12,242 ft; 12,242 ft

Southwest Slope. Class 2. First ascent June 26, 1937 by Smoke Blanchard, Hubert North, and Gary Leech. This slope rises above the highest of the Conness Lakes and leads to the long, flat southwestern slope of the peak. The right side of this slope is easier to climb because it has more solid footing. The left side is sandy, and it makes a good descent route.

Northeast Chimney. IV, 5.8. First ascent August 1969 by Bob Summers and John Gibbins. This is the long,

Mount Conness from the northeast, September 2, 1965. Photo by Austin Post, No. F655-174, USGS Ice and Climate Project, GeoData Center, University of Alaska, Fairbanks.

steep chimney that is between the middle and left-hand snow/ice couloir on the northeast side of the peak. Remain deep inside this chimney for the first six pitches.

Deliverance. IV, 5.9. First ascent August 1980 by Jack Roberts and Alan Bartlett. This route climbs the narrow face between the middle and right-hand snow couloir on the northeast face of North Peak. Nine pitches over loose rock lead to several hundred feet of scrambling and the summit.

Northeast Couloir. Class 4. There are three couloirs to the left of the summit on the northeast face of North Peak. The left couloir is 600 feet high, and is steeper (50°) and narrower (15 feet across) than the right-hand couloir. The middle couloir ends on rock. The correct couloir is the one farthest right. Cross the bergschrund on its left side, but climb the right side of the couloir for five pitches.

Further Reading: John Moynier and Claude Fiddler. *Sierra Classics.* Evergreen, Colo.: Chockstone Press, 1993, pp. 294–295.

Way Up North. III, 5.10a. First ascent September 1983 by David Harden and Richard Leversee. This four-pitch route is on the left side of the broad northeast face. Climb cracks on an otherwise smooth wall that is to the right of a large, right-facing dihedral.

Northeast Face. III, 5.8. First ascent July 1969 by Galen Rowell and Barry Hagen. This route climbs the face to the right of the northeast couloir. The climb starts from a small glacier and heads directly for the summit. The first three pitches are the steepest and most difficult.

Northeast Chute. Class 4+. First ascent October 3, 1987 by Pete Lowery and Chris Keith. This chute is to the right of the summit of North Peak. Climb to the highest point of the glacier that is northeast of North Peak. Follow a chute with loose rock and gravel to the ridge that is to the right of the summit.

Northwest Ridge. II, 5.3. First ascent August 1973 by Kevin Sutter and David Harden. Follow the crest of the ridge to the summit.

Sheep Peak   11,842 ft; 11,840 ft+
First ascent July 1, 1934 by Kenneth May and Howard Twining. Class 2 from Roosevelt Lake; the summit block is class 3.

Shepherd Crest   12,000 ft+; 12,015 ft
First ascent July 13, 1933 by Herbert B. Blanks, Kenneth May, and Elliot Sawyer, via the class 3 avalanche

chute on the south side of the peak. The northeast ridge is class 2, and was climbed July 5, 1941 by W. Ryland Hill and Charles Chesterman.

Further Reading: *Sierra Club Bulletin.* 1933, pp. 68–80; *Sierra Club Bulletin.* 1949, pp. 82–86.

Northwest Face. II, 5.7. First ascent July 1975 by Steve Porcella, Bob Porcella, and Royal Robbins. This route is on perfect rock, with five superb pitches ranging from class 4 to 5.7.

Excelsior Mountain   12,446 ft; 12,446 ft
First ascent June 13, 1931 by Howard Sloan. This peak is class 2 from the pass at the head of Virginia Creek. Leave the trail at the pass, and cross talus to the north ridge of Excelsior Mountain. Follow the ridge to the summit.

Peak 12,126 ft   12,126 ft;
0.7 mi N of Excelsior Mountain
The east slope and south ridge are class 2.

Black Mountain   11,797 ft; 11,760 ft+
First ascent by the United States Geological Survey in 1905. The north slope and south slope are class 2.

Further Reading: Hans Joachim Burhenne. *Sierra Spring Ski-Touring.* San Francisco: Mountain Press, 1971, pp. 74–75.

Dunderberg Peak   12,374 ft; 12,374 ft
First ascent 1878 by Lt. M. M. Macomb and party of the Wheeler Survey. First winter ascent April 10, 1936 by Bob Brinton and Walter Mosauer. The southeast ridge is class 2, as are the south and southeast slopes rising above Virginia Lakes. There is an outstanding view from the summit.

Further Reading: John Moynier. *Backcountry Skiing in the High Sierra.* Evergreen, Colo.: Chockstone Press, 1992, p. 184.

Epidote Peak   10,964 ft; 10,880 ft+
Southeast Slope. Class 2. First ascent 1917 by a Sierra Club party. Climb the prominent red chute rising above Hoover Lake. This chute ends on the ridge left of the summit.

Southeast Face. Class 3. First ascent June 11, 1989 by Robin Ingraham, Jr., and Jim Chapman. This route follows the chute to the right of the prominent chute on the southeast slope. This less prominent chute ascends the face from right to left, and is blocked about 200 feet below the summit. Move left, out of the chute, and climb onto an exposed, knife edge arête. An impasse is turned to the left via a narrow ledge. The summit is a short scramble above.

Page Peaks   10,920 ft+; 10,880 ft+

Class 2 from East Lake. The traverse from Gabbro Peak is class 3.

Gabbro Peak   11,033 ft; 10,960 ft+

Class 2 from either Green Lake or East Lake.

Camiaca Peak   11,739 ft; 11,739 ft

First ascent 1917 by Walter Huber. The south slope is class 2.

"The Pharaoh"   9,560 ft+; 9,600 ft+; 0.6 mi SW of Miller Lake; UTM 867074

This major rock wall is located in the lower part of Matterhorn Canyon, and features a freestanding summit.

Meadowblaster. IV, 5.11b. First ascent 1994 by Alan Swanson and Urmas Franosch. This route ascends the northwest face of the Pharaoh. Nine pitches of sustained, difficult free climbing go up beautiful cracks with

North Peak from the east, September 2, 1965. Photo by Austin Post, No. F655-174, USGS Ice and Climate Project, GeoData Center, University of Alaska, Fairbanks.

views of Tuolumne Meadows—quality rock, sprinkled with knobs.

Hooper Peak   9,575 ft; 9,520 ft+

An ascent of this peak would involve hours of drudgery for rather dubious rewards.

West Peak   10,529 ft; 10,480 ft+

First ascent July 17, 1931 by Kenneth May and Gus Smith. This peak is class 2 from Regulation Peak. The north face was climbed on August 7, 1991 by Fred Camphausen; climb a steep chute by passing underneath a chockstone near its head.

Regulation Peak   10,560 ft+; 10,560 ft+

First ascent 1921 by Ralph Chase. Class 2 from Rodgers Lake, or from Pettit Peak.

Pettit Peak   10,788 ft; 10,788 ft

First ascent August 1, 1934 by Lewis F. Clark and Virginia Greever. Class 2 from Rodgers Lake. It is also class 2 from either Regulation Peak, West Peak, or Volunteer Peak. The best route from Volunteer Peak is to traverse across the west side of Peak 10,640ft+ (10,640 ft+) at approximately the 10,000-foot level.

Volunteer Peak   10,481 ft; 10,479 ft

First ascent 1895 by Lt. Benson and Lt. McBride of the U.S. Cavalry. This is a short class 2 climb from the 9,600-foot level of the Rodgers Lake Trail. The traverse from Pettit Peak is class 2. The best route is at the 10,000-foot level, across the west face of Peak 10,640ft+ (10,640 ft+). And it is better to climb Volunteer Peak first, and then traverse south to Pettit Peak, when these peaks are climbed together.

Piute Mountain   10,541 ft; 10,541 ft

First ascent July 27, 1911 by Francis Farquhar, James Rennie, and Frank Bumstead. This peak is class 2 from Bear Valley. It is also class 2 from Benson Lake; be sure to pass Peak 10,320ft+ (10,368 ft) over its western shoulder.

The northeast ridge is class 2 from Seavey Pass. Leave the Pacific Crest Trail south of Seavey Pass at the 8,600-foot level. Head northwest up a steep, grassy slope to the crest of the northeast ridge of Piute Mountain. Follow the crest of the ridge to where it ends against the east face of the peak. Drop 100 feet to the right and cross a small, flat bowl at the top of the mountain's north chute. Two

chutes leave this bowl and end on the north ridge. The chute on the right is steep and sandy; the chute or ramp on the left is not as steep and has some vegetation in it, along with more secure footing. Follow the ridge to the summit from the top of either chute. The preferred descent for this route is via the big gully that drops down from the summit plateau about ½ mile southeast of the true summit (at UTM 768117).

Price Peak   10,717 ft; 10,716 ft

First ascent July 28, 1945 by A. J. Reyman on a class 2 traverse from Acker Peak. Price Peak is also class 2 from Thompson Canyon.

Slide Mountain   10,458 ft; 10,479 ft

This is the Slide Mountain that is south of the other Slide Mountain in northern Yosemite. This peak is not named on some editions of the Matterhorn Peak 7.5-minute map. It appears to be easy from any direction.

Bath Mountain   10,520 ft+; 10,558 ft

First ascent July 30, 1934 by Glen Dawson and John Cahill, via the easy north ridge.

West Face. IV, 5.10, A1. First ascent September 1974 by Bill Dougherty and Vern Clevenger. This route climbs the long, left-facing open book on the left side of the west face.

South Face. IV, 5.10a. First ascent September 1992 by Ken Kenaga and Patrick Brennan. This route is just left of the southeast buttress. Begin by climbing the left of two dihedrals, and leave this dihedral on the fourth pitch by moving left. This leads to the top of a shoulder, where class 3 climbing leads up and right to the base of an east-facing headwall. Climb the center of the headwall (the first pitch is the crux of the climb) for another three or four pitches to the summit.

Doghead Peak   11,059 ft; 11,102 ft

First ascent 1911 by Harold Bradley. Class 2 from Wilson Creek. There is an outstanding view of Quarry Peak from the summit.

Quarry Peak   11,161 ft; 11,161 ft

First ascent 1905 by George Davis, A. H. Sylvester, and Pearson Chapman of the United States Geological Survey. Class 2 from Wilson Creek.

East Face. IV, 5.10. First ascent August 1977 by Vern Clevenger and Alan Bartlett. This route ascends the smooth left side of the east face of Quarry Peak. It follows a right-leaning, left-facing chimney–and–open book system. The eighth pitch, a shallow, flared slot, is the crux.

Karen's Wall. III, 5.9, A2. First ascent September 11, 1980 by Dwight Kroll. This route ascends the central buttress of the east face. Begin by climbing a right-facing open book (5.8) to the right of the large chimney at the toe of the buttress. Next, traverse to the right to some left-facing books and climb them to their tops. Tension traverse to the right for 20 feet to a right-facing open book. Climb this book about halfway, and follow a large crack (5.9) to some smaller books and a narrow crack that leads to a roof. Move slightly left to a belay stance. A short bit of free climbing leads to two aid bolts, followed by a tension traverse to the right and another left-facing dihedral. Class 3 climbing to the right and slightly down leads to a ramp in a large corner. Climb the corner for two pitches to its end, where a 5.8 crack up and left leads to a short ramp. Traverse to the far left over class 3 rock to another ramp that climbs up and right to some trees, which mark the end of the climb.

East Face, Right Side. III, 5.9. First ascent September 1984 by Fred Beckey and Gary Slate. This route on the northern quarter of the east face can be identified by a dihedral and the reddish tone of the granite to the right of the dihedral. The crux of this eight-pitch route is passing an overhanging block in a dihedral system.

South Peak, East Face. III, 5.10. First ascent 1996 by Fred Beckey, Philip Karl, and Steve Hyde. This eleven-pitch route ascends the east face of Peak 10,360ft (10,400 ft+; 1.2 miles south-southeast of Quarry Peak). The face is broken by numerous ledges.

Grey Butte   11,365 ft; 11,365 ft
This is spelled "Gray Butte" on some maps. First ascent August 1934 by Howard Twining. Class 2 from Virginia Canyon.

Stanton Peak   11,695 ft; 11,695 ft
First ascent May 31, 1934 by Richard G. Johnson, Kenneth May, and Howard Twining. The north ridge is class 2.

Virginia Peak   12,001 ft; 12,001 ft
First ascent July 3, 1934 by Howard Twining and Kenneth May. This peak is easy class 3 from Twin Peaks Pass and from Stanton Pass.

Twin Peaks   12,323 ft; 12,240 ft+
The west peak is the high point. The ridge rising from Twin Peaks Pass is class 3; a better route is to traverse northeast across class 2 talus and scree to the basin between the two peaks, then climb the main summit from there. There are two chutes on the west face of the mountain. The northern chute rises above the upper Horse Creek drainage and is class 3 near its head; it ends at a point about 100 yards north of the summit; class 2 slopes lead to the top from there. The southern chute is loose class 2 and it ends along the south ridge of the peak. Apparently, the easternmost couloir on the north face has been skied.

Further Reading: John Moynier. *Backcountry Skiing in the High Sierra.* Evergreen, Colo.: Chockstone Press, 1992, p. 53.

"Horse Creek Peak"   11,600 ft+; 11,600 ft+;
0.6 mi NW of Twin Peaks
The southwest side of this peak is class 2.

North Buttress. III, 5.4. First ascent July 1972 by Jim Orey and Gene Drake. This route begins by climbing a narrow snow couloir left of the buttress. Ascend it for 200 feet to a headwall. A ramp leads up and right from the headwall onto the buttress. One class 5 pitch on the prow of the buttress is followed by 800 feet of class 4 climbing to the summit.

Whorl Mountain   12,033 ft; 12,029 ft
The middle peak is the high point.

Southeast Chute. Class 3. First ascent July 9, 1933 by Herbert Blanks, Kenneth May, and Eliot Sawyer. First winter ascent March 18, 1966 by Lucien Desaulniers and John Simon. From Horse Creek Pass, go south along a bench that crosses the east side of the peak. This bench ends beneath the east face of the middle peak. Climb up and left to the chute that leads to the saddle between the middle and south peaks of Whorl Mountain. Follow this chute, but leave it 150 feet below the saddle and traverse right (north) across a second chute to the third chute. Ascend the third chute, passing behind and underneath a chockstone. The summit ridge is just above the chockstone, and it is a short, easy climb from there to the top of the middle peak. *Variation:* Class 4. The passage behind and underneath the chockstone may be impassable during heavy snow years. In this case, pass the chockstone on its left side. *Variation:* Class 4. First ascent July 23, 1978 by Harold McFadden, George

Whorl Mountain from the east. Photo by R. J. Secor.

Toby, Fred Camphausen, and party. Climb a small chute that is about 50 feet south of the chockstone to the south ridge of the middle peak. An exposed ledge on the west side of the ridge leads to a narrow slot back across the ridge to the east side of the peak. The middle peak is an easy scramble from there.

Southeast Chute and West Face. Class 3. First ascent July 19, 1980 by R. J. Secor. Ascend the southeast chute from Spiller Creek until you are 150 feet below the saddle between the middle and south peaks of Whorl Mountain. Traverse right (north) past one chute to the second chute. Ascend this chute and cross the south ridge of the middle peak. Traverse north across the west face of the middle peak on a system of ledges to a gully that leads up to the notch just north of the middle peak. Climb this gully to the notch, then follow the ridge south to the summit of the middle peak. *Variation:* Class 3. First ascent June 11, 1996 by Steve Eckert and party. Leave the ledge system on the west face and climb de-composing blocks via a zigzagging class 3 route up and toward the east to a huge slab. Exposed class 3 climbing leads to the upper right corner. This is followed by a slot that leads across the south ridge to the east side of the middle peak. A short scramble then goes north to the summit.

North Peak. First ascent July 17, 1921 by Ralph A. Chase and party. This is class 2 from the saddle to the south.

South Peak. First ascent July 23, 1911 by J. W. Combs, R. W. Messer, and William Goldsborough. The southwest slope is class 2.

Finger Peaks   11,498 ft; 11,440 ft

The middle peak is the high point.

West Face. Class 3 with a class 4 summit block. First ascent July 19, 1931 by Jules Eichorn, Glen Dawson, and Walter Brem. Climb to the saddle between the west peak and the middle peak. Ascend the south side of the west arête to a large notch about halfway up. Traverse north about 200 feet from the notch to the northwest gully and climb the gully to the summit block on the middle peak. The summit block is easy class 4.

The west peak is class 2 from the west.

The east peak is class 2 from the south and southwest. The east ridge is class 3; follow the southern side of the ridge. The north face is class 3–4.

Traverse. II, Class 4. First ascent 1989 by Claude Fiddler.

"Horse Creek Tower"   11,320 ft+;
0.5 mi N of Matterhorn Peak; UTM 912195

This tower is northeast of The Dragtooth, and can be seen from Twin Lakes.

South Face. II, 5.8, A3. First ascent May 16, 1973 by Fred Beckey, Mike McGoey, and Leland Davis. The climb begins from a big ledge. Go up and right from the ledge on bolts to a vertical aid crack. This crack leads to the southeast corner of the spire. This is followed by a tension traverse leading into a dihedral. Free and aid climbing in the dihedral lead to a belay ledge. A short bolt ladder leads to the summit from here.

Northwest Face. II, 5.8. First ascent July 1985 by Alan Swanson and Rich Kropp. This three-pitch route (5.7, 5.8, and ending with 5.4) is marked by the prominent guillotine flake at the top of the second pitch.

North Face. II, 5.7. First ascent May 1975 by Dean Gillman, Don Spittler, and David Babich. This route starts just to the left of center on the north face. Three pitches of assorted cracks and corners lead to the top.

"Petite Capucin"   11,240 ft+; 11,280 ft+;
0.4 mi NE of Matterhorn Peak; UTM 916192

This is the northernmost tower on the ridge that is northeast of Matterhorn Peak.

North Face. II, 5.8. First ascent July 1972 by Gene Drake, Rich Stevenson, and Jim Orey. This route consists of four pitches.

Pillar Route. II, 5.10. First ascent August 1979 by Rick Erker and Harry Marinakis. From the Matterhorn Glacier, climb an easy (5.6) ramp on the north side of the spire to the base of a left-facing dihedral. Instead of climbing the chimney (loose rock!) in the dihedral, climb a wide, prominent crack (5.8) that is to the left of the chimney. This crack leads back into the upper part of the chimney, which leads to a notch between the pillar and

the main spire. Jump (!) across the notch to a small ledge on the main spire. A short scramble then leads to a nice belay ledge. The fourth pitch follows a left-facing arch and open book (5.10) to a good belay ledge just beneath the summit. The last pitch is a short layback along a flake to the summit.

Descent Route. Rappel 60 feet into the notch between Petite Capucin and the spire to its northwest. Walk off to another notch to the southeast.

Matterhorn Peak   12,279 ft; 12,264 ft
This peak, which has an outstanding view from the summit, is poorly named; this is especially evident during an ascent of the snow-free southeast slope in August. In the spring, however, a ski tour from the summit can be one of the finest mountaineering experiences on the continent.

Southwest Side. Class 2. First ascent 1899 by M. R. Dempster, James S. Hutchinson, Lincoln Hutchinson, and Charles A. Noble. Ascend the broad scree gully in the center of the southwest slope. This side of the peak is easily reached from Burro Pass.

Southeast Slope. Class 2. This is an easy climb from Horse Creek Pass.

East Couloir. Class 3. Climb the obvious couloir on the east side of the northeast ridge. This leads to the top of the east ridge, which is followed to the upper part of the southeast slope.

Further Reading: Hans Joachim Burhenne. *Sierra Spring Ski-Touring.* San Francisco: Mountain Press, 1971, pp. 72–73; John Moynier. *Backcountry Skiing in the High Sierra.* Evergreen, Colo.: Chockstone Press, 1992, p. 185.

The Maze. II, 5.6. First ascent 1994 by Daniel Roitman and Sergio Aragon. This route ascends the face that is to the right of the east couloir. The right (northern) side of this face is steep and smooth, while the left (southern) side is relatively broken. The Maze ascends this broken face, and the name of the route comes from the many variations that are possible in this area. The first-ascent party reported some delicate 5.5 moves on the first pitch, which were followed by an interesting 5.6 layback over a large detached flake on the second pitch. The third pitch was easier, but had much loose rock. The last pitch, class 4, ends on the north arête, about 100 feet north of the summit.

North Arête. II, 5.5. First ascent September 1954 by

MATTERHORN PEAK

Double
Dihedral
Route

Petite
Capucin

North
Arête

East
Couloir

Matterhorn Glacier

Jerry Gallwas, Wally Kodis, and Don Wilson. This is the prominent arête that divides the north faces of Matterhorn Peak. The arête begins from a platform partway up the north side of the peak. (This platform is reached by climbing three class 4 pitches on the left side of the face.) Ascend the arête for one pitch and then traverse 75 feet out onto the west face of the arête. Climb a steep crack for two pitches of 5.5 to a large ledge that is to the right of the arête. Traverse left from the large ledge, past the arête, and ascend a chimney with a chockstone. Climb another arête that is left of the main north arête. This is followed by one more pitch to the summit. *Variation:* First ascent July 1956 by James Derby, Peter Lipman, and Thomas Vaughan. The above-mentioned platform can also be reached by climbing the class 4 on the right side of the face. *Variation:* First ascent July 1974 by Rupert Kammerlander and Bruce McCubbrey. The platform can also be reached by climbing the 5.8 face directly above the glacier. *Variation:* First ascent July 1970 by Mike Hane and Frank Uher. The arête can be ascended directly from the large ledge (5.7). *Variation:* Follow the arête for one pitch above the large ledge and then go right to a small notch (5.7). *Variation:* It is also possible to climb the prominent dihedral above the large ledge, and continue to the summit over the Double Dihedral Route (5.8).

Further Reading: Allan Bard. *North Buttress of Matterhorn Peak.* Bishop, Calif.: Shooting Star Guides, 1991 (a route card); John Moynier and Claude Fiddler. *Sierra Classics.* Evergreen, Colo.: Chockstone Press, 1993, pp. 300–301, 305.

Double Dihedral Route. II, 5.8. First ascent July 4, 1965 by Rich Gnagy, Burt Turney, Gen Turney, and Rick Brosch. This route is on the face to the right of the north arête; it ascends the two prominent dihedrals that go up and right. Climb the glacier north of Matterhorn Peak to the base of the right-hand dihedral; the bottom of this dihedral may be filled with snow. A 5.7 pitch up the dihedral leads to a large flake on the left. Descend 20 feet behind the flake to the bottom of the second dihedral. Climb a 5.7 crack in the lower portion of this dihedral for 150 feet to a large ledge that is to the right of the north arête. Climb the upper dihedral to its top. This is followed by a 5.8 move to the left, which leads out onto the exposed face. One long pitch up and left

leads to a good belay ledge. A thin, flaring crack that gradually widens then leads up to the summit ridge. *Variation:* It is possible to traverse left from the large ledge and continue to the summit via the North Arête Route or its variations.

Northwest Face. Class 3. First ascent July 20, 1931 by Walter Brem, Glen Dawson, and Jules Eichorn. Climb a gully, or the face on either side of the gully, from the notch between The Dragtooth and Matterhorn Peak. This notch can be reached from either the Burro Pass area or the glacier north of Matterhorn Peak.

"The Dragtooth"   12,080 ft+; 12,160 ft+; 0.4 mi NW of Matterhorn Peak; UTM 910192

Southwest Slope. Class 2. First ascent July 20, 1931 by Walter Brem, Glen Dawson, and Jules Eichorn. This is a straightforward climb from the basin north of Burro Pass.

Northeast Buttress. Class 4. First ascent 1952 by Joe Firey, Norm Goldstein, Chuck Wharton, and John Ohrenschall. This buttress divides the glaciers between Matterhorn Peak and The Dragtooth. Climb onto the base of the buttress from the glacier that is north of The Dragtooth. Ascend the east side of the buttress before moving onto the very crest of the upper buttress. The climb ends in a short chimney just below the summit.

North Face. Class 4. First ascent July 16, 1941 by J. C. Southard and Hervey Voge. This route ascends the broad face above the glacier north of The Dragtooth. Ascend steep snow on the lower portion of the face to a point about 100 feet to the left of the main chute that descends the north face. Climb ledges leading up and left to a less prominent chute that is 200 feet east of the main chute. Ascend this chute for 200 feet and cross over to the right into the main chute. Ascend the left side of this chute until you are 100 feet beneath the summit ridge. Climb a 75-foot chimney leading up to the ridge to a point about 50 feet northwest of the summit.

North Buttress. III, 5.10. First ascent June 16, 1971 by Reed Cundiff and Jack Miller. First free ascent 1983 by Jay Smith and Paul Crawford. One of the classic climbs in the High Sierra, this route deserves more traffic. The route ascends the prominent buttress that extends farther out onto the glacier than any other part of The Dragtooth. There is a triangular pedestal at the bottom of this buttress. Rope up at a sloping, sandy ledge

Matterhorn Peak from the north. Photo by R. J. Secor.

beneath a wide chimney with two fixed pins on the left side of the pedestal. Climb the chimney (5.7) for 120 feet to a belay with two bolts. Continue straight up for another 100 feet (5.7) and traverse to the right to the base of the prominent dihedral that marks the route. Two pitches (5.9 and 5.10) in the dihedral, with hand, fist, and off-width cracks, lead to a ledge/alcove. A finger crack (5.9) left of and above the alcove leads to scrambling along the summit ridge. Chocks to 5 inches are needed for protection on this route. *Variation:* Traverse up and right from the belay alcove, across blocks to a trough, to exit right to easier climbing.

West Chimney. III, 5.8. First ascent July 1970 by Mary Bomba and Ken Boche. Climb toward Polemonium Pass from the glacier north of The Dragtooth. From a point approximately 100 feet below the northeast side of the pass, climb cracks and chimneys up and left to a large broken area. Continue climbing up and left to a large chimney and climb it to its top. Exit the chimney on its right side (5.8) and climb onto the top of the west ridge. Easy climbing along the southern side of the west ridge leads to the summit.

"The Doodad"   11,680 ft+; 11,600 ft+;
0.5 mi. NW of Matterhorn Peak; UTM 906192

The Doodad is a 25-foot-high cube, overhanging on all sides, perched on a ridge 500 feet above the glacier.

South Side. Class 4. First ascent July 7, 1934 by Kenneth May and Howard Twining. Class 3 climbing starts this climb along an arête on the left (west) side of the

Sawtooth Ridge from the north, August 23, 1972. Photo by Austin Post, No. 72R2-44, USGS Ice and Climate Project, GeoData Center, University of Alaska, Fairbanks.

The North Buttress of The Dragtooth. Photo by R. J. Secor.

THE DOODAD

Polemonium
Pass

Northeast Face

south face. Climb diagonally right, over a short but difficult pitch, to the east ridge. Follow the east ridge around a pinnacle to the main summit. The Doodad itself is 5.2, and is climbed via a crack on its south side.

Northeast Face. Class 5. First ascent July 1956 by James Derby, Peter Lipman, and Thomas Vaughn. Climb the long, left-leaning gully on the northeast face. It is necessary to deviate from one side of the gully to the other to pass chockstones. A hand traverse from the top of the gully leads left to a ledge system beneath the summit block.

"The Three Teeth"   11,680 ft+; 11,600 ft+;
0.8 mi NW of Matterhorn Peak

These three pinnacles are atop the Sawtooth Ridge, between The Sawblade and the Col de Doodad.

Further Reading: *Sierra Club Bulletin.* 1934, pp. 31–33.

The Northwest Tooth is seen to the right when viewed from the north. The deep notch to the left of the Northwest Tooth is the West Notch. Left of the West Notch is the Middle Tooth. The small notch to its left is the East Notch. The Southeast Tooth is left of the East Notch and right of the Col de Doodad.

Traverse, Northwest to Southeast. III, 5.5, A0. First ascent July 2, 1933 by Henry Beers, Bestor Robinson, and Richard M. Leonard. Two 150-foot ropes are needed for the rappels on this route. Climb a series of ledges in a broad depression on the center of the northeast face of the Northwest Tooth. At a point about one-third of the way up the face, traverse diagonally up to the right toward ledges that lead up to the northwest arête. Follow the arête upward to the tunnel underneath the summit block. The tunnel comes out on the southeast side of the summit block. Climb the summit block of the Northwest Tooth on its northwest side.

A long rappel (140 feet) leads down to the West Notch. Climb a loose chimney for 40 feet, then go left and climb another loose chimney to a flat ledge on the right. A 5.5 layback and face climbing lead to the summit of the Middle Tooth.

Descend a short chimney near the northeast side of the summit of the Middle Tooth. After 75 feet, a 100-foot rappel leads down to the gully below; this gully is on the Slide Canyon side of the East Notch. Ascend the gully to the highest ledge on the Southeast Tooth. Traverse right 75 feet along ledges to a narrow, steep chimney. Climb this squeeze chimney to a chockstone, then traverse right a few feet on small holds to a crack. Ascend this crack to the summit of the Southeast Tooth.

And now the fun really begins (I am being sarcastic; I hate to rappel). There is a pinnacle located immediately northwest of the summit of the Southeast Tooth. Rappel 145 feet down the southeast side of this pinnacle to the lowest of two ledges. Go southeast on this ledge for 50 feet and climb down to a block below a small pinnacle. Another 145-foot rappel to an area of broken rock is followed by another short rappel to more broken rock. Head toward the base of the Middle Tooth and rappel 80 feet down to the scree below. This leaves you on the Slide Canyon side of the Sawtooth Ridge, and it is necessary to cross the Col de Doodad to return to the northeast side of the Sawtooth Ridge.

Traverse, Southeast to Northwest. III, 5.6, A0. First ascent July 25, 1934 by Glen Dawson and Jack Riegelhuth. Two 150-foot ropes are needed for the rappels. This traverse starts from the top of the Col de Doodad. Ascend the southeast arête to the base of a tall pinnacle. Pass this pinnacle on the left by crawling through a tunnel on the Slide Canyon side of the Southeast Tooth. More difficult climbing leads back to the southeast arête. Continue up the arête to the top of the Southeast Tooth. *Variation:* You may prefer climbing to the Southeast Tooth from the Slide Canyon base of the Middle Tooth. This would be the reverse of the descent of the Southeast Tooth as described in the Traverse, Northwest to Southeast description, above.

A long rappel leads from the summit of the Southeast Tooth to the East Notch. Descend the Slide Canyon side of the East Notch and climb a large chimney on the southeast side of the Middle Tooth. Ascend cracks and a short chimney to the summit of the Middle Tooth.

Another long rappel leads to the West Notch from the summit of the Middle Tooth. Descend the gully leading down into Slide Canyon from the West Notch. Climb up and right on the southeast face of the Northwest Tooth over steep ledges and cracks for about 100 feet to a 3-foot-wide ledge. Climb thin cracks and narrow ledges (5.6) up a steep face for 75 feet (loose rock)

The Doodad from the north. Photo by R. J. Secor.

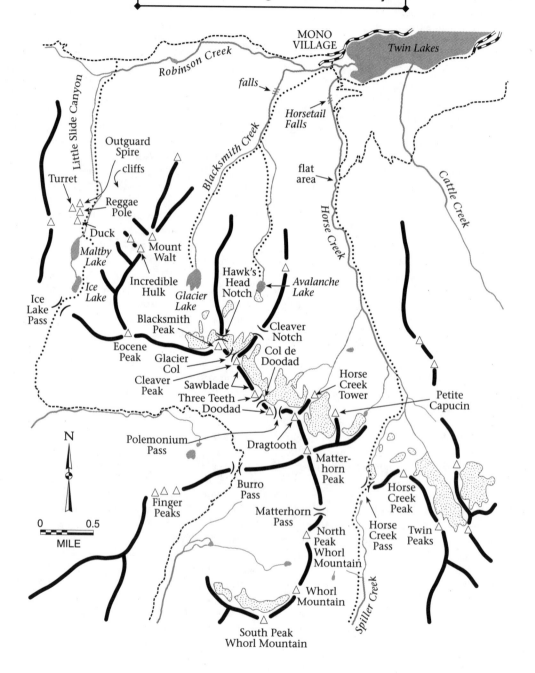

Sawtooth Ridge and Vicinity

MONO VILLAGE

Twin Lakes

Robinson Creek

falls

Horsetail Falls

Little Slide Canyon

Outguard Spire

cliffs

Turret

Reggae Pole

Duck

Maltby Lake

Mount Walt

Incredible Hulk

Ice Lake

Ice Lake Pass

Blacksmith Creek

flat area

Horse Creek

Cattle Creek

Hawk's Head Notch

Avalanche Lake

Glacier Lake

Blacksmith Peak

Eocene Peak

Glacier Col

Cleaver Peak

Cleaver Notch

Col de Doodad

Horse Creek Tower

Petite Capucin

Sawblade

Three Teeth

Doodad

Polemonium Pass

Dragtooth

Matterhorn Peak

N

Finger Peaks

Burro Pass

Matterhorn Pass

Horse Creek Peak

Horse Creek Pass

Twin Peaks

0   0.5
MILE

North Peak Whorl Mountain

Whorl Mountain

Spiller Creek

South Peak Whorl Mountain

Middle Tooth

West Notch

Northwest Tooth

The Three Teeth from the north. Photo by R. J. Secor.

to the southeast side of the summit block of the North-west Tooth.

Descend the tunnel underneath the summit block of the Northwest Tooth to the northwest arête. Descend the arête to where it is possible to descend to the glacier via ledges leading down the northeast face of the North-west Tooth.

Northwest Tooth, Southwest Face. II, 5.6. First ascent July 23, 1941 by David Brower, Bruce Meyer, and Art Argiewicz. Climb the buttress that is left of the scree slope coming down from the West Notch. Go diago-nally left toward a ledge at the top of the lowest chim-ney. A fingertip traverse across the top of the chimney leads to a scree chute above the chimney. Ascend the

scree chute to a point about 30 feet below its top and traverse left on an easy ledge. Swing around a flake that is left of and above this ledge and climb a classic chim-ney to its top. Leave the top of this chimney on its left side, and continue up and right across the southwest face to the 3-foot-wide ledge on the southeast side of the Northwest Tooth. A 75-foot 5.6 pitch over loose rock leads up to the summit block.

Northwest Tooth, West Notch. Class 4–5. First ascent 1949 by Oscar Cook, Joe Firey, Larry Taylor, and Jack Hansen. Ascend the couloir leading to the West Notch from the glacier. From the notch, traverse right on a hand ledge that ends in a chimney. Ascend the chimney to the tunnel underneath the summit block.

Middle Tooth

Southeast Tooth

East Notch

Col de Doodad

The Three Teeth and Col de Doodad from the south. Photo by R. J. Secor.

Middle Tooth, Northeast Face. II, 5.5. First ascent July 2, 1933 by Lewis F. Clark, Richard G. Johnson, Oliver Kehrlein, and Randolph May. Climb the steep snow couloir leading to the West Notch from the glacier. Leave the couloir about 100 feet above a chockstone in this couloir and traverse diagonally left on a ledge. Leave the ledge at a prominent chimney and climb it and more ledges up and right to a loose chimney. This chimney leads to a flat ledge on the right, where a 5.5 layback and face climbing lead to the summit of the Middle Tooth.

Middle Tooth, Southwest Face. III, 5.9, A1. First ascent August 1972 by Mike Heath and Bill Sumner. Climb steep jam cracks to the left of the center portion of the face for 300 feet. Pendulum right across a smooth section to another crack system near the right edge of the face. Three more strenuous and moderately difficult pitches lead to the summit.

Middle Tooth, Southwest Face Direct. III, 5.10. First ascent October 1976 by Jack Roberts and Fred Beckey. This route starts from the gully on the left side of the southwest face. Climb diagonally right to the crack system at the left edge of the prominent orange pillar on the face. Continue up the crack system to the summit. The rock on the lower section of this face is quite friable, but it improves higher up.

Southeast Tooth, Northeast Face. III, 5.7. First ascent

June 1969 by Jim Jones, Fred Beckey, and Galen Rowell. There are four prominent cracks splitting the center of this face. Two are parallel and about 15 feet apart. Start climbing from the base of these two cracks, and climb steep rock for 40 feet to an easy traverse up and right to a belay. Step left into the crack and jam (5.7) up to a small, exposed belay ledge on the right. A long pitch straight up (5.7) leads to a prominent ledge that traverses across most of the northeast face. Go left along this ledge to two cracks, which lead up to the summit. Ascend these cracks over an overhang (5.7) to a ledge just beneath the summit. A strenuous move then leads to the flat summit.

Southeast Tooth, Left Side of Northeast Face. III, 5.10b. First ascent September 1987 by Bruce Runnals and Alan Swanson. This five-pitch route ascends the left side of the face. Begin by climbing a thin crack (5.10b) off a ledge, then move left to a belay stance. The second pitch climbs a perfect dihedral for 120 feet; this pitch is 5.8 and 5.9 followed by a 5.10 crux at its top. Overcome a bulge (5.10) followed by a long, loose left-diagonal flake. Avoid a flared chimney above by traversing right (5.7). The last pitch begins by climbing a classic offset crack to a 5.10 bulge just below the summit. Mantle the bulge and land on top of the summit register.

Descent Routes. The Northwest Tooth has been descended by going down the northwest arête to near the junction with The Sawblade. Four rappels down the south side of the ridge lead to Slide Canyon.

The southeast side of the Northwest Tooth also involves four rappels down the southeast buttress. The last rappel starts from a ledge and is free for over 100 feet.

It is possible to rappel from the West Notch down to the glacier; the last rappel is over 120 feet long.

The south chimney of the East Notch has also been rappelled. This leads down to Slide Canyon.

The Northeast Face route of the Middle Tooth has been rappelled. The last rappel is free. Ugh!

Finally, the north side of the East Notch has been rappelled. One of the intermediate stances involves standing in slings. Ugh! Ugh!

"The Sawblade" 11,760 ft+; 11,600 ft+;
1.0 mi NW of Matterhorn Peak; UTM 901199
Traverse, Southeast to Northwest. Class 4. First ascent July 25, 1934 by David Brower and Hervey Voge. Climb from Slide Canyon to the notch that is northwest of the

pinnacle on the northwest arête of the West Tooth. Traverse the ridge leading northwest. Two 150-foot ropes are needed for the rappels.

The Cleaver

This is the long ridge that runs down and northeast from the summit of Cleaver Peak.

Traverse. III, Class 5. First ascent 1984 by Claude Fiddler and Vern Clevenger.

Goldfinger. I, 5.6, A3. First ascent October 27, 1968 by Fred Beckey and Joe Brown. This is the 125-foot spire atop the Cleaver. It is climbed on its west side.

Further Reading: *Summit.* December 1968, pp. 6–7.

"Cleaver Peak" 11,760 ft+; 11,760 ft+;
1.1 mi NW of Matterhorn Peak; UTM 901200
Northwest Face. Class 3. First ascent July 3, 1933 by Henry Beers and Oliver Kehrlein. Traverse up and left from Glacier Col to a broad depression on the northwest face. Follow the depression to the summit.

Northeast Face. Class 3. First ascent July 27, 1934 by Glen Dawson and Jack Riegelhuth. Ascend a series of ledges and blocks on the northeast face of Cleaver Peak to the crest of the arête of The Cleaver. Follow the arête to the summit of Cleaver Peak.

South Face. Class 5. First ascent August 6, 1950 by M. L. Wade and F. Chisholm. Climb an easy class 4 chute that leads to the notch between Cleaver Peak and The Sawblade. Approximately 150 feet below this notch, a block leans against Cleaver Peak. (A passage underneath this block leads to the notch.) Go left at the lower side of this block, then climb several interesting class 5 pitches on the south face to the summit of Cleaver Peak.

"Blacksmith Peak" 11,760 ft+; 11,680 ft+;
1.3 mi NW of Matterhorn Peak; UTM 898202
Southwest Face. Class 3. First ascent July 3, 1933 by Bestor Robinson and Richard Leonard. Climb the prominent gully on the southwest face, ending among the four summit pinnacles. The northwest pinnacle is the high point, and is rated 5.6. The register is 30 feet below the top of the northwest pinnacle.

The Forge. IV, 5.11. First ascent July 1996 by Mike Davis and Dave Nettle. This route is on the west face of Blacksmith Peak. It starts by climbing the right side of a prominent thin pillar. Climb the pillar, passing a loose flake and going over a 5.10 roof to a ledge. Continue up a thin, right-facing corner (5.10), and then move left across a sloping ledge marking the top of the pillar. Climb a 4-inch 5.8 crack before traversing right and slightly up to a ledge with a flake. Climb a 5.11 crack, passing underneath a roof to a hanging belay underneath and between the left and middle overhanging Three Teeth. Overcome the ceiling and continue up a thin, gritty 5.10 crack, finishing with a 5.9 layback onto a ramp. Follow the ramp up and left to another ledge with a small, right-facing corner. Above the corner, wander up flakes and vertical fins (slightly run out) to one of several belay stances beneath The Slot. The Slot is a square-shaped crack system (5.10), followed by a roof (passed on its right side) ending on a big ledge atop the north arête. Move across the north arête and down into a chimney before climbing up to the summit.

Northwest Face. III, 5.8, A2 or 5.11b. First ascent June 25–26, 1973 by Lito Tejada-Flores and Chris Jones. First free ascent September 1990 by Alan Swanson and Urmas Franosch. Second free ascent July 1992 by Dave Nettle and Jim Howle. This loose route starts by following a thin, left-curving, serrated crack that is above a slab and then goes up and over a bulge (5.10d). The second pitch as-

Cleaver Peak and Blacksmith Peak from the north, August 23, 1972. Photo by Austin Post, No. 72R2-44, USGS Ice and Climate Project, GeoData Center, University of Alaska, Fairbanks.

cends a thin, shallow, flaring crack to a scary roof (5.11b), and ends in a prominent left-facing dihedral. Either climb the dihedral or the loose flakes to its left (both 5.8) to an overhang. Pass the overhang on its rotten right side (poorly protected 5.11b), and continue with laybacks to a belay stance underneath a right-facing inside corner. Continue up the corner for two pitches to a small ledge beneath a prow. Stemming and jamming up the left side of the prow (5.10) leads to the finger, which is passed on its right side (5.8). Follow the class 4 knife edge ridge to the summit.

Further Reading: John Moynier and Claude Fiddler. *Sierra Classics.* Evergreen, Colo.: Chockstone Press, 1993, pp. 302–304.

Northwest Face, Left Side. II, 5.8. First ascent June 25, 1973 by Doug Robinson and Keith Bell. This route starts left of the central, steep portion of the northwest face. Go up and right over broken rock to the summit.

North Arête. II, 5.9+. First ascent August 16, 1973 by Tom Frost and Doug Robinson. This route starts from a ledge in the chute leading up the western side of Hawk's Head Notch. Go up and right over class 4 to the base of a chimney. Climb the chimney, passing a chockstone (5.9) to the big chockstone at its top. Easy class 5 leads to a steep, left-facing crack (5.9). Easy class 5 continues along the crest of the arête, passing The Finger along the way, to the summit.

Further Reading: *Rock & Ice.* No. 73 (May–June 1996), pp. 66–75.

Northeast Gully. II, 5.6. First ascent September 8, 1936 by Bestor Robinson and Carl Jensen. Climb a steep, sloping ledge from the base of the north arête. This ledge leads left and rises above the glacier north of Cleaver Peak. After 200 feet this ledge dead-ends against a face. Climb up and right for about 20 feet (5.5) on small holds to the northeast gully. Ascend the gully to the summit. This is usually used as the descent route after climbs of the Northwest Face.

South Face. II, 5.8. First ascent August 1976 by Willie Sare and Paul Willis. Climb a large, left-facing dihedral for three pitches to its head. Then angle up and left for one pitch to the summit area.

Orangesmith. III, 5.8. First ascent September 1996 by Fred Beckey and Steve Must. This ten-pitch route is on the ridge north of Blacksmith Peak. It starts by climbing a prominent orange wall below Glacier Lake, then a prominent arête to the top of the ridge.

"Eocene Peak" 11,569 ft; 11,851 ft;
1.3 mi SE of Kettle Peak

First ascent July 16, 1932 by Herbert B. Blanks and Richard M. Leonard. The southwest slope is class 2.

"The Incredible Hulk" 11,480 ft+; 11,520 ft+;
0.9 mi ESE of Kettle Peak; UTM 886216

This peak was thought to be unclimbed for many years, while a register on the summit named it "Middle Peak of Outpost Peak" and recorded an ascent on September 6, 1936 by Bestor Robinson, Florence Robinson, Carl Jensen, and Don Woods. The current name, which has been in use for twenty years, refers to the large, west-facing mass on the ridge north of Eocene Peak. All of the routes on the west face end atop the ridge northwest of the true summit, Point 11,280ft+ (11,120 ft+; UTM 885218).

Mountaineer's Route. Class 4–5. First ascent May 23, 1971 by Bob Grow and Joe Kiskis. Ascend Little Slide Canyon to where the stream forks. Follow the east branch to the base of the Hulk. Climb the right couloir (snow-filled in early season; loose rock later in the summer) for several hundred feet. A steep chute on the left wall of this couloir leads to a high notch. Three pitches of roped climbing lead from the notch to the summit.

West Face, Right Side. IV, 5.10a. First ascent August 1992 by Julie Brugger and Andrew de Klerk. Climb cracks and corners up an obvious cracked break on the right side of the wall for ten pitches.

The Red Dihedral. IV, 5.10. First ascent June 1975 by Dale Bard, Mike Farrell, and Bob Locke. This route is also known as "Ygdrasil." It is on the center of the broad west face of the Incredible Hulk. The climb begins to the right of the large triangle at the base of the west face. Class 3 leads to some ledges (some 5.7 moves) and up to a 5.9 chimney. A 5.9 crack then leads up and slightly right to the left-facing Red Dihedral. Climb the dihedral, passing the roof on top on its right side (5.10). Two left-facing inside corners separated by some face climbing then lead to a 5.9 crack in the middle of an otherwise smooth face. The next pitch leads to a notch beneath a shattered pillar. Go up and left from the pillar to a blocky chimney that leads to the crest of the ridge. Turn right and follow the ridge to the top of Point 11,280ft+.

Further Reading: John Moynier and Claude Fiddler. *Sierra Classics.* Evergreen, Colo.: Chockstone Press, 1993, pp. 306–307, 309.

The Donaldson Route. V, 5.8, A3. First ascent 1970 by Greg Donaldson, Joe Kiskis, and Bob Grow. Start by climbing the blocky right side of the large triangular slab at the base of the west face (5.8). The second pitch climbs a small left-facing inside corner (5.10 or A3), followed by a crack that leads up to some terraced ledges. Leave the terrace on its left side and climb a 5.8 crack before traversing up and right over flakes (5.11 or A3, fixed piton) to the bottom of a chimney. Climb the chimney (5.10 or A3) and leave it on its upper right side to the Large Ledge that slopes up and right in the middle of the wall. Go to the far right-hand end of the ledge and climb straight up for 70 feet to some overhangs, then traverse right to a hanging belay beneath a chimney. Climb the chimney, which features some good ledges, and leave it to the right. Some nailing leads to a hanging flake in an open book beneath some ceilings. Climb the flake and the book, then traverse to the right to a ledge high in the middle of the face. A very thin crack leads up and right for one pitch. Continue traversing up and right to the buttress on the right side of the wall. Climb to a notch on the buttress, then continue up the buttress, enjoying progressively easier climbing, to the top of the face. Ten rappels down the west face lead back to the base of the climb.

Astro-Hulk. IV, 5.11+. First ascent September 25, 1996 by Dave Nettle and Mike Davis. This route follows the prominent corner system above the Large Ledge on the west face. Follow a class 4 ramp right and up to a belay stance about 150 feet above the Large Ledge. Go up and left into the bottom of the left-facing inside corner, and climb it to where the crack in the corner disappears. Traverse horizontally left (5.11) to another left-facing corner and follow it up, past a two-bolt belay stance and over the Sea Serpent, a long flake in the corner. Some wild stemming moves lead out of the corner to the right (5.11) and past a couple of fixed pins to right-facing Enduro Corner (5.11), ending at Recliner Ledge. Leave the ledge on its right side and climb a left-facing corner to the summit ridge.

Macedonian Route. V, 5.9, A4. First ascent July 1976 by Rick Wheeler and Dave Bircheff. Climb the Donaldson Route to the large, right-sloping ledge in the middle of the face. Climb the left-facing inside corner above the middle of the ledge. Continue straight up the face to the top. This route includes one pitch of excellent free climbing, followed by five pitches of difficult aid

climbing. Seven rappels down the south side of the west face lead to the bottom.

Positive Vibrations. V, 5.10, A2 or 5.11. First ascent August 1981 by Bob Harrington and Alan Bartlett. First free ascent August 1986 by Dale Bard and Bobbie Bensman. Climb the Donaldson Route to the large, right-sloping ledge in the middle of the face. Go to the left end of this ledge and climb a wide crack up and left (5.9) across an outside corner and then slightly down to a ledge. A thin crack (5.9, stemming) leads up to a roof, but go left back across the outside corner to a sustained 5.10 crack on the right-hand face to a ledge with a bolt. (The thin cracks directly above the bolt are off-route.) Go up and slightly left over thin cracks (5.11), cross the outside corner to a pedestal, and climb a shallow, 5.8 wide crack back to the edge of the corner. Move to the left 20 feet and climb a straight 5.10 crack to a flake underneath a roof. Cross over the flake to a pair of cracks leading to a small ledge atop a pedestal. Drop down to the left before climbing a 5.9 inside corner leading to the crest of the north ridge. Down climb 20 feet in a crack, then move right another 20 feet across a loose dike, passing the first crack to the second crack, a 5.10 crack on the steep face. Easy climbing then leads up and right to the shattered pillar at the top of the Red Dihedral Route. Go up and left from the pillar to a blocky chimney (5.8) followed by a 5.8 move up a left-facing inside corner to a ledge. Follow the ledge to the right to a dirty 5.5 chimney that leads to the crest of the ridge. Turn right and follow the ridge to Point 11,280ft+, a long way from the true summit.

Further Reading: John Moynier and Claude Fiddler. *Sierra Classics.* Evergreen, Colo.: Chockstone Press, 1993, pp. 308–309.

Polish Route. V, 5.10. First ascent August 1976 by Rick Wheeler and Bob Harrington. This route starts about 100 feet to the left of the triangle at the base of the west face. Climb a difficult crack (5.10) in a left-facing corner. Higher up, the route remains to the left of the large left-facing dihedral above and consists of fist jams and off-width climbing with hanging belays. The climb ends on a large, flat ledge. Traverse along this ledge to the east. This leads to rappels and to the chute on the north side of the Incredible Hulk.

Further Reading: John Moynier and Claude Fiddler. *Sierra Classics.* Evergreen, Colo.: Chockstone Press, 1993, p. 309.

The Incredible Hulk. Photo by R. J. Secor.

Northwest Couloir. Class 4. First ascent October 1978 by Dick Benoit, Bill Peppin, John McCartney, and Alvin R. McLane. This 2,000-foot snow/ice climb ascends the chute that is north of the west face of the Incredible Hulk.

A route (III, 5.7, A1) has been done on the east side of Little Slide Canyon, near its entrance. Climb the obvious gully on the three-toothed cliff. First ascent 1973 by Darien Hopkins, Roger Gocking, Dave Warburton, and Mike Warburton.

"Mount Walt"   11,480 ft+; 11,581 ft;
0.6 mi NW of Glacier Lake; UTM 888218

First ascent September 6, 1936 by Bestor Robinson, Florence Robinson, Carl Jensen, and Don Woods. The northeast slope is class 2 from the middle portion of Blacksmith Creek; this has been done as a ski tour.

This peak has been unofficially named in memory of Walter W. Herbert.

Further Reading: Hans Joachim Burhenne. *Sierra Spring Ski-Touring.* San Francisco: Mountain Press, 1971, pp. 68–69.

"Outguard Spire"   10,280 ft+; UTM 876224

This is the northernmost spire on the west side of Little Slide Canyon.

Southeast Corner. II, 5.8. First ascent September 5, 1968 by John York, Joe Kiskis, and Robert Grow. Ascend a narrow talus gully on the west side of the spire to the southeast corner. Climb a rotten chimney for about 80 feet to a short jam crack (5.8) protected by some large chocks. Easier climbing goes up and right to a good ledge, followed by more easy climbing to a notch behind a small pinnacle. Traverse left and get behind a flake, where steep face climbing leads for 70 feet directly up the southeast corner to a ledge. A short pitch up the exposed summit ridge leads to the top, a tiny summit.

Descent Route. Down climb 50 feet along the south ridge to two bolts. A long rappel (i.e., two ropes) ends on a ledge, followed by another long rappel to a notch. Descend the class 3–4 east side of the notch.

Southeast Arête. III, 5.10c. First ascent August 1992 by Andrew de Klerk and Julie Brugger. Climb cracks a few feet to the right of the southeast corner for six pitches.

East Face Direct. III, 5.10. First ascent August 31, 1991 by Dave Nettle and Suzanne Jensen. Walk to the right to the end of a ledge near the left side of the east face. Climb a pair of right-facing books to a ledge system

leading to the right. From the far end of the ledge system climb a 5.10 crack, past an old fixed nut, to a 5.8 book leading up to a roof. Traverse to the right under the book to a small ledge. Climb 20 feet up an arch leading to the right and then go up and left across a thin seam (5.10; only protection is a size 1½ Friend) and climb a 5.10 finger crack to the right of a crackless corner. A mantle then leads to a 5.8 inside corner, and then up and left to another corner. Stem up the corner with a thin crack, then go up and left past Eagles Nest Ledge and continue up loose Fawlty Towers (5.7) to a sandy scree ledge. Climb the corner above the ledge, passing a loose flake, to a rocky alcove. A class 4 pitch is followed by 20 feet of easy class 5 to the summit.

East Face. III, 5.10, A2. First ascent July 1973 by Mike Warburton and Roger Gocking. Climb a corner on the right side of the east face to a small overhang. Go up and right along a ramp to a belay ledge on the corner between the east and north faces. Traverse right across the north face to a scary chimney behind a flake, then climb to a ledge above. Go to the far right side of the ledge and layback to a sloping ledge on the west corner of the spire. A short stretch of aid climbing leads to a hanging belay to the left of a prominent crack. A jam crack then leads to the summit.

"The Turret"   10,320 ft+; UTM 876224

This is the highest of the four pinnacles on the west side of Little Slide Canyon. It is climbed from the notch on its west side. Class 3–4 climbing leads to a short 5.8 section. First ascent 1970 by Joe Kiskis. First free ascent July 1972 by Margaret Quick and Bob Grow. Descend by rappelling to the notch, then climb around Reggae Pole (class 3), and descend the couloir on the south side of Reggae Pole.

East Face. III, 5.9. First ascent July 1994 by Bruce Bindner and Patrick Brennan. This route ascends a double-crack system on the right side of the east face. The first pitch ends on a ledge beneath the cracks. Overcome a roof and climb the cracks (5.9+). The second pitch up the cracks ends on a ledge. Next, go up a 5.9 groove and then move up and left over some ledges. Climb behind a tower (5.7) and then step across to some blocks in a right-facing corner. Climb the blocks and the corner past a roof to a gritty, off-width crack (5.8), ending on some sloping ledges. Continue up the right-facing corner, but keep left of a chimney with some chockstones. Then move to the right to the north side of the Turret on some ledges.

Climb the chimney between the pillars on top of the Turret. One 5.9 move past a bolt leads to the summit.

"Reggae Pole"   10,280 ft+; UTM 876223

South Face. III, 5.10. First ascent July 1970 by Greg Donaldson and Joe Kiskis. First free ascent 1993 by Dave Nettle and partner. Ascend the chute on the south side of this spire and scramble to the highest ledge at the junction of the east and south faces. Climb the loose, dirty left crack in the corner (5.8) above the ledge to a stance. Continue up the dirty crack and make a 5.10 move to the right crack and follow it (5.9) to Big Sandy Ledge. Go up a thin 5.9 crack from the right side of the ledge to a stance beneath a wide chimney. Climb the chimney (5.9) to some ledges in the notch between a pillar and Reggae Pole. Climb out of the notch via 5.9 cracks next to the arête, followed by a 5.10 move of a small left-facing corner to a sloping alcove. A wide 5.9 crack leads up to the false summit. Continue on to the true summit with a short 5.6 pitch to the top.

South Face, Right Side. IV, 5.7, A3. First ascent August 1973 by Mike Warburton and Roger Gocking. Traverse to the right from the bottom of the dihedral on the south face. This leads to a crack system that is followed to a small ledge. Overcome a roof via nailing, and belay in slings. Go left and use more aid to another hanging belay. Bypass a large, rotten flake to its right to yet another hanging belay. More nailing leads up to a ledge, at last. Climb straight up for a short distance, where a hand traverse goes left to a chimney system, which leads to the summit. Descend via two long rappels (i.e., two ropes) to the chute on the south side of Reggae Pole.

East Face. III, 5.11. First ascent September 1, 1996 by Bruce Bindner and Pat Brennan. There are some spectacular dihedrals on the east face of Reggae Pole. Start by climbing the huge, right-facing dihedral on the right side of the east face. After several pitches (up to 5.10R face and 5.10+ off-width), move left into a crack that splits a 40-foot rotten headwall to a ledge. The slightly overhanging corner above (5.11) ends at the summit after two more wild pitches. Double ropes and lots of runners are essential, with protection ranging from tiny to 12 inches.

"The Duck"

First ascent July 1970 by Greg Donaldson and Joe Kiskis. This formation is just south of Reggae Pole. This is easily climbed via a class 4 route.

East Face. III, 5.10c. First ascent July 1994 by Bruce Bindner and Pat Brennan. Start by ascending a right-facing dihedral with a large crack. Then climb the left-facing dihedrals to the left of the prow.

Kettle Peak   11,000 ft+; 11,010 ft

First ascent August 1948 by Bill Dunmire and Bob Swift. Class 2 from Ice Lake Pass.

Suicide Ridge   11,047 ft; 11,089 ft

First ascent May 31, 1934 by Glen Dawson and John Cahill. Class 2 from Rock Island Lake.

Slide Mountain   11,084 ft; 11,040 ft+

This peak is north of the other Slide Mountain in this region of the High Sierra. Class 2 from the Burro Pass Trail.

"The Juggernaut"   11,040 ft+; 11,040 ft+; 0.7 mi E of Rock Island Pass

There is a steep cliff on the north side of this modest peak.

Arches Route. III, 5.9, A2. First ascent September 15, 1973 by Jack Roberts, Fred Beckey, and Dave Black. This route follows the obvious crack system near the center of the prow on the north side of the peak, just right of two huge, overhanging arches. The climb consists of five long hard pitches, with some aid climbing on the second pitch.

Dihedral Route. III, 5.10. First ascent 1974 by Bill Dougherty, Vern Clevenger, Mike Farrell, and Galen Rowell. This route ascends the long, left-facing dihedral that is to the left of Arches Route. The first pitch goes up a chimney that narrows down to a slot and, finally, a 5.10 layback. Higher in the dihedral, you have a choice between an intimidating 5.8 traverse on the outside of the dihedral, or a frightening 5.10 overhang in the dihedral. The last pitch consists of moderate climbing up a broken, open headwall immediately to the right of the overhangs at the top of the dihedral.

Crown Point   11,346 ft; 11,346 ft

First ascent 1905 by George Davis, A. H. Sylvester, and Pearson Chapman of the United States Geological Survey. This peak is class 2 from Snow Lake.

Peeler Pillar. II, 5.6. First ascent September 1971 by Larry Johnson, Geert Dijkhuis, and Greg Donaldson. The route starts about 100 feet to the right of the north buttress, between an overhanging chimney and a sandy gully. About 200 feet of easy class 5, leading to a large ledge, is followed by a short class 3 section. Climb a white face above this easy section. This face is left of a large open book, and is lined with cracks. Four pitches of 5.5–5.6 lead to the summit. *Variation:* II, 5.8. First ascent August 1989 by Dan Ward and David Harden. Climb cracks to the left of the overhanging chimney for two pitches to the white ledge.

Cirque Mountain   10,713 ft; 10,714 ft
First ascent August 16, 1948 by A. J. Reyman. The northwest slope is class 1.

Eagle Peak   11,847 ft; 11,845 ft
First ascent September 1905 by George Davis, A. H. Sylvester, and Pearson Chapman of the United States Geological Survey. This peak is class 2 from either Buckeye Creek or Robinson Creek.

Victoria Peak   11,706 ft; 11,732 ft
First ascent September 8, 1946 by A. J. Reyman. Class 2 from either the north or south.

Hunewill Peak   11,713 ft; 11,680 ft+
First ascent August 1946 by Ken Crowley, R. Dickey, Jr., Ken Hargreaves, and H. Watty. Class 2 from Barney Lake.

Center Mountain   11,271 ft; 11,273 ft
First ascent 1905 by the United States Geological Survey. The south slope is class 1.

Grouse Mountain   10,734 ft; 10,775 ft
First ascent August 3, 1949 by A. J. Reyman, via the class 1 northwest couloir and west ridge. The east face is class 3, and was first climbed August 1953 by LeRoy Johnson, Fred Schaub, and Ken Hondsinger.

Ehrnbeck Peak   11,240 ft; 11,240 ft
First ascent July 27, 1945 by A. J. Reyman, via the class 2 south ridge. The northeast ridge is class 3.

Hawksbeak Peak   11,341 ft; 11,120 ft+
West Face. III, 5.10-. First ascent September 1989 by Alan Swanson and John Nye. This route consists of ten pitches. Most of this route is 5.7–5.8. The crux, on the

sixth pitch, is a thin, 5.9 crack followed by a 5.10a off-width crack.

Wells Peak   11,109 ft; 11,118 ft
First ascent July 27, 1945 by A. J. Reyman. The north ridge is class 2.

Acker Peak   10,988 ft; 11,015 ft
First ascent July 27, 1945 by A. J. Reyman. The east slope is class 2.

Snow Peak   10,945 ft; 10,950 ft
First ascent 1938 by John Dyer. The south slope is class 2.

Craig Peak   11,087 ft; 11,090 ft
First ascent 1938 by John Dyer. Class 2 from either the north or south. A traverse from Tower Peak is class 3.

Tower Peak   11,755 ft; 11,755 ft
This is the prominent peak that rises above the headwaters of the West Walker River. The first ascent may have been made by Native Americans; arrowhead fragments were found just beneath the summit in 1941. The west summit is the high point.

Northwest Chute. Class 3. First ascent 1870 by Charles Hoffman, William Goodyear, and Alfred Craven. From Tower Pass, traverse up across to the west side of the north ridge to a staircase chute that leads to the summit. There is about 100 feet of easy class 3 near the summit. An alternate approach starts from the meadows marking the headwaters of the West Walker River. Class 2 boulders and grassy slopes lead west to the cirque and snowfield (ice axe required) northeast of Tower Peak. Climb the class 3 north ridge to where it steepens, and traverse to the right into the northwest chute.

Further Reading: John Moynier and Claude Fiddler. *Sierra Classics.* Evergreen, Colo.: Chockstone Press, 1993, pp. 312–313.

West Face. Class 4. First ascent July 15, 1941 by Raffi Bedayan and Barbara Norris. Some belaying is required on the face that rises above Mary Lake.

Southeast Chute. Class 3. Descended July 1941 by David Brower, Dorothy Markwad, Pat Goldsworthy, Ted Grubb, and Bruce Meyer. This chute rises above the head of Stubblefield Canyon.

Northeast Face. III, 5.9. First ascent September 1989

by John Nye and Alan Swanson. This four-pitch route ascends a long, shallow dihedral next to the pillar on the northeast face. The first two pitches are 5.9, and feature stemming and laybacks. The last two pitches are 5.7 and class 4. Protection up to 4 inches is needed.

Saurian Crest   11,040 ft+; 11,095 ft

First ascent September 7, 1938 by John Dyer. Long talus slopes from all sides lead to the class 3 summit rocks.

Keyes Peak   10,618 ft; 10,670 ft

First ascent September 1, 1942 by A. J. Reyman. The south ridge is class 2.

Forsyth Peak   11,177 ft; 11,180 ft

First ascent July 10, 1937 by Rene Kast, Don Hersey, Paul Hersey, Al Teakle, Harry Tenney, Jr., Arthur Evans, and Leon Casou. The south and west slopes are class 2. The north ridge is class 3, and was first climbed August 23, 1953 by LeRoy Johnson, Fred Schaub, and Ken Hondsinger.

WRINKLES

Horse Creek vs. Green Lake. The most obvious approach to the upper part of Spiller Creek is from Twin Lakes via Horse Creek. An often overlooked alternative is an approach from Green Lake and over Virginia Pass. This alternate route has less elevation gain and features a good use trail over Virginia Pass. Spiller Creek can be reached by crossing Twin Peaks Pass or Stanton Pass.

Sawtooth Ridge in a day. Sawtooth Ridge is an exception to the general rule that solitude can be found in northern Yosemite. There is a strict quota in effect in this area, and the best option for many climbers is to climb the peaks in a day from Twin Lakes. But this is realistic only for competent climbers who are in excellent physical condition.

Glossary

The following are rough definitions for some of the technical climbing terms found in this book.

Aid. Direct aid climbing, i.e., climbing a pitch by hanging from equipment that has been placed in or on the rock.

Alcove. A belay ledge that is surrounded on all sides by vertical rock.

Arête. A steep, narrow ridge.

Bergschrund or **'schrund**. A crevasse in a glacier or snowfield, formed when the movement of snow or ice diverges away from the fixed mountainside.

Black ice. Very old ice that has been mixed with scree and gravel. This is usually found deep in couloirs in late autumn during drought years.

Bolts. Small metal spikes that are hammered into holes that have been drilled into rock.

Bongs. Extra-wide pitons, now virtually nonexistent; they have been replaced by large chocks.

Buttress. A very steep arête on the face of a mountain. the terms **nose**, **pedestal**, and **pillar** are synonymous with buttress.

Ceiling. See **Roof**.

Chickenheads. See **Horns**.

Chimney. Either a steep, narrow chute with parallel walls, or a wide crack into which the climber can fit.

Chocks. Rock protection that is wedged into cracks by hand. **Nuts** is a synonym.

Chockstones. Rocks that are wedged into cracks, either by nature or by a desperate leader who doesn't have any other protection left.

Chute. This is usually steeper than a gully, and may be subject to rockfall.

Cirque. A deep recess in a mountain; it resembles an amphitheater with steep walls.

Col. A steep, high pass.

Corn snow. Unconsolidated granular snow that has gone through a short freeze-and-thaw process. This type of snow is prevalent throughout the High Sierra in April and May.

Couloir. A steep chute, which may have snow or ice.

Crack. The separation of two rock faces, ranging in size from the width of a chimney to microscopically narrow.

Crest. The very top of a ridge or arête.

Crux. The most difficult move or pitch on a route.

Dihedral. See **Open book**.

Dike. Rock of a different color that has intruded into another rock.

Face. One of the sides of a mountain, a **slope** being more gentle (less steep) than a face.

Firn. Consolidated granular snow left over from the previous year. Closer to ice than snow in density, it may require the use of crampons.

Flakes. Long, narrow horns, or a huge rock slab leaning against a cliff. The sides of such a slab may form dihedrals.

Flared. A crack or chimney whose sides are not parallel, but instead form two converging planes of rock.

Free. Free climbing, i.e., doing a climb or pitch without resorting to aid.

Gully. This usually refers to a wide, shallow ravine on a mountainside.

Headwall. Where the face of a mountain steepens dramatically.

Horns. Spikes of rock that are used for protection or holds. **Chickenheads** is a synonym.

Jamming. Locking a hand and/or foot in a crack.

Lead. See **Pitch**.

Mixed climbing. Either a combination of free and aid climbing, or a combination of rock, snow, and ice climbing.

Moat. The gap between snow or ice and a rock wall.

Move. See **Pitch.**

Munge. Dirt and vegetation that fills a crack.

Nailing. An ancient term used to describe direct-aid climbing with pitons.

Névé. Consolidated granular snow. This is common on glaciers and snowfields during the height of the summer.

Nose. See **Buttress.**

Notch. A small col.

Nuts. See **Chocks.**

Off-width. A crack or chimney too wide to climb but too narrow to climb into.

Open book. The junction of two planes of rock; in other words, an inside corner. The corner can be either acute or obtuse, and can face right or left. **Dihedral** is a synonym.

Outside corner. See **Rib.**

Overhang. A section of rock that exceeds the vertical.

Pass. The lowest or easiest crossing of a ridge.

Pillar. See **Buttress.**

Pitch or **lead.** A section of a climb between belays. A very short pitch is a **move.**

Pitons. Metal spikes that are hammered into cracks.

Ramp. An ascending ledge.

Rappel. Sliding down a doubled rope. A **long rappel** requires two ropes.

Rib. A short, small buttress. An **outside corner** is even smaller.

Ridge. A high divide extending out from a peak.

Rime. Ice formed by freezing rain.

Roof. An overhang that forms a horizontal plane. **Ceiling** is a synonym.

Runners. Loops of nylon webbing that are threaded or looped around chockstones, flakes, horns, or chickenheads for protection.

Saddle. A high pass that is not as steep as a col.

Scree. Small rocks that slide under the climber's feet.

Sierra crest. The divide that runs along the very top of the High Sierra, separating the Great Basin from the Pacific Ocean watersheds.

Slope. See **Face.**

Summit. The high point of a peak or the top of a pass.

Talus. Large blocks of rock.

Tarn. A small lake.

Toe. The bottom of a buttress.

Tyrolean Traverse. Climbing along a rope that has been anchored on two separate horizontal points.

Verglas. Thin water ice on rock.

Water ice. Solid ice that contains few air bubbles. This is typically found in the couloirs of the High Sierra in autumn.

Wilderness Permits

Following are the addresses and telephone numbers of the ranger stations that issue wilderness permits for the areas described in this book. Contact these ranger stations for the most up-to-date information about quotas and advance reservations.

CHAPTER 2. THE WHITNEY REGION

For east-side entry into the Golden Trout Wilderness and John Muir Wilderness: Inyo National Forest, Mount Whitney Ranger District, P.O. Box 8, Lone Pine, CA 93545; tel: 760-876-6200.

In addition to a wilderness permit, a special stamp on the permit is required by those entering the Mount Whitney Zone (including day hikers). The Mount Whitney Zone is jointly managed by the Inyo National Forest and Sequoia National Park. The zone quota is in effect from May 22 to October 15. The zone boundary on the east is immediately above the Lone Pine Lake Trail junction along the Mount Whitney Trail. The southern boundary is from Arc Pass along the Sierra crest to Discovery Pinnacle and along the ridge of Mount Hitchcock. The western boundary is at the outlet of Timberline Lake along the John Muir Trail. The northern boundary follows the ridge from Mount Young to Mount Hale and on to Mount Russell, follows the Sierra crest south, continues over the top of Mount Whitney to Pinnacle Ridge, and follows Pinnacle Ridge to Thor Peak.

CHAPTER 3. THE KAWEAHS AND THE GREAT WESTERN DIVIDE

For west-side entry into the Sequoia–Kings Canyon Wilderness: Sequoia and Kings Canyon National Parks, Wilderness Reservations Office, Three Rivers, CA 93271-9700; tel: 559-565-3708; fax: 559-565-3797.

For southern entry via the Golden Trout Wilderness: Sequoia National Forest, Tule River Ranger District,

32588 Highway 190, Springville, CA 93265; tel: 559-539-2607.

CHAPTER 4. THE KINGS-KERN DIVIDE

For east-side entry into the John Muir Wilderness: Inyo National Forest, Mount Whitney Ranger District, P.O. Box 8, Lone Pine, CA 93545; tel: 760-876-6200.

For west-side entry into the Sequoia–Kings Canyon Wilderness: Sequoia and Kings Canyon National Parks, Wilderness Reservations Office, Three Rivers, CA 93271-9700; tel: 559-565-3708; fax: 559-565-3797.

CHAPTER 5. THE HIGH PASSES

For east-side entry to the John Muir Wilderness: Inyo National Forest, Mount Whitney Ranger District, P.O. Box 8, Lone Pine, CA 93545; tel: 760-876-6200.

For west-side entry to the Sequoia–Kings Canyon Wilderness: Sequoia and Kings Canyon National Parks, Wilderness Reservations Office, Three Rivers, CA 93271-9700; tel: 559-565-3708; fax: 559-565-3797.

CHAPTER 6. MONARCH DIVIDE AND THE CIRQUE CREST

For entry to the Sequoia–Kings Canyon Wilderness: Sequoia and Kings Canyon National Parks, Wilderness Reservations Office, Three Rivers, CA 93271-9700; tel: 559-565-3708; fax: 559-565-3797.

For entry to the Monarch Wilderness: Sequoia National Forest, Hume Lake Ranger District, 36273 E. Kings Canyon Road, Dunlap, CA 93621; tel: 559-338-2251. (At time of writing, a wilderness permit was not required to visit the Sequoia National Forest section of the Monarch Wilderness. Those who plan to enter the Sequoia–Kings Canyon Wilderness from the Monarch Wilderness must obtain a wilderness permit from Sequoia and Kings Canyon National Parks.)

CHAPTER 7. KETTLE RIDGE AND THE LECONTE DIVIDE

For west-side entry to the John Muir Wilderness, Monarch Wilderness, and Sequoia–Kings Canyon Wilderness: Sierra National Forest, Pineridge Ranger District, P.O. Box 559, Prather, CA 93651; 559-855-5360.

CHAPTER 8. THE PALISADES

For east-side entry to the John Muir Wilderness via Taboose Pass: Inyo National Forest, Mount Whitney Ranger District, P.O. Box 8, Lone Pine, CA 93545; tel: 760-876-6200.

For east-side entry to the John Muir Wilderness from the Red Lake Trail to the Bishop Pass Trail: Inyo National Forest, White Mountain Ranger District, 798 N. Main St., Bishop, CA 93514; tel: 760-938-1136.

CHAPTER 9. THE EVOLUTION REGION

For east-side entry to the John Muir Wilderness: Inyo National Forest, White Mountain Ranger District, 798 N. Main St., Bishop, CA 93514; tel: 760-873-2500.

For west-side entry to the John Muir Wilderness and Sequoia-Kings Canyon Wilderness: Sierra National Forest, Pineridge Ranger District, P.O. Box 559, Prather, CA 93651; tel: 559-855-5360.

CHAPTER 10. THE MONO RECESSES

For east-side entry to the John Muir Wilderness: Inyo National Forest, White Mountain Ranger District, 798 N. Main St., Bishop, CA 93514; tel: 760-873-2500.

For west-side entry to the John Muir Wilderness: Sierra National Forest, Pineridge Ranger District, P.O. Box 559, Prather, CA 93651; tel: 559-855-5360.

CHAPTER 11. MAMMOTH LAKES AND THE SILVER DIVIDE

For east-side entry to the John Muir Wilderness from Rock Creek to McGee Creek: Inyo National Forest, White Mountain Ranger District, 798 N. Main St., Bishop, CA 93514; tel: 760-873-2500. For east-side entry to the John Muir Wilderness from Devil's Postpile to Convict Lake: Inyo National Forest, Mammoth Ranger District, P.O. Box 148, Mammoth Lakes, CA 93546; tel: 760-924-5500.

For west-side entry to the John Muir Wilderness: Sierra National Forest, Pineridge Ranger District, P.O. Box 559, Prather, CA 93651; tel: 559-855-5360.

CHAPTER 12. THE MINARETS AND JUNE LAKE

For east-side entry to the Ansel Adams Wilderness from Red's Meadow to Agnew Meadow: Inyo National Forest, Mammoth Ranger District, P.O. Box 148, Mammoth Lakes, CA 93546; tel: 760-924-5500.

For east-side entry to the Ansel Adams Wilderness from Silver Lake to Tioga Pass: Inyo National Forest, Mono Lake Ranger District, P.O. Box 429, Lee Vining, CA 93541; tel: 760-647-3000.

For west-side entry to the Ansel Adams Wilderness: Sierra National Forest, Minarets Ranger District, P.O. Box 10, North Fork, CA 93643; tel: 559-877-2218.

For entry to Yosemite Wilderness: Yosemite National Park, Wilderness Office, P.O. Box 577, Yosemite, CA 95389; tel: 209-372-0740.

CHAPTER 13. THE CLARK AND CATHEDRAL RANGES

For west-side entry to the Ansel Adams Wilderness: Sierra National Forest, Minarets Ranger District, P.O. Box 10, North Fork, CA 93643; tel: 209-877-2218.

For entry to the Yosemite Wilderness: Yosemite National Park, Wilderness Office, P.O. Box 577, Yosemite, CA 95389; tel: 209-372-0740.

CHAPTER 14. NORTHERN YOSEMITE

For east-side entry to the Hoover Wilderness from Saddlebag Lake to Lundy Lake: Inyo National Forest, Mono Lake Ranger District, P.O. Box 429, Lee Vining, CA 93541; tel: 760-647-3000.

For east-side entry to the Hoover Wilderness from Virginia Lakes to Buckeye Creek: Toiyabe National Forest, Bridgeport Ranger District, P.O. Box 595, Bridgeport, CA 93517; tel: 760-932-7070.

For entry to the Yosemite Wilderness: Yosemite National Park, Wilderness Office, P.O. Box 577, Yosemite, CA 95389; tel: 209-372-0740.

Index

About the Author

R. J. Secor has been hiking and skiing since he learned to walk. An enthusiastic peak-bagger, he has attained coveted List Completion status *twice* in the Sierra Peaks Section of the Sierra Club with more than 600 mountain ascents in the High Sierra, climbing as many as 60 peaks in a single year. He has also done extensive climbing in Baja California, Arizona, Nevada, Utah, Idaho, Washington, Oregon, Wyoming, Montana, British Columbia, Alberta, and Alaska. Other mountain adventures have taken him as far afield as the Himalaya in Tibet and Nepal, the Karakoram in Pakistan, the Andes in Argentina, and the volcanoes of Mexico.

This second edition of *The High Sierra: Peaks, Passes, and Trails* is a compilation of more than thirty years-worth of copious notes and exchanges with other Sierra hikers, climbers, and skiers. His other books are *Mexico's Volcanoes: A Climbing Guide* (2nd ed., 1993), *Aconcagua: A Climbing Guide* (1994), and *Denali Climbing Guide* (1998). He is a member of the Sierra Club, the American Alpine Club, the Southern California Mountaineers Association, and the California Mountaineering Club.

THE MOUNTAINEERS, founded in 1906, is a nonprofit outdoor activity and conservation club, whose mission is "to explore, study, preserve, and enjoy the natural beauty of the outdoors. . . ." Based in Seattle, Washington, the club is now the third-largest such organization in the United States, with 15,000 members and five branches throughout Washington State.

The Mountaineers sponsors both classes and year-round outdoor activities in the Pacific Northwest, which include hiking, mountain climbing, ski-touring, snowshoeing, bicycling, camping, kayaking and canoeing, nature study, sailing, and adventure travel. The club's conservation division supports environmental causes through educational activities, sponsoring legislation, and presenting informational programs. All club activities are led by skilled, experienced volunteers, who are dedicated to promoting safe and responsible enjoyment and preservation of the outdoors.

If you would like to participate in these organized outdoor activities or the club's programs, consider a membership in The Mountaineers. For information and an application, write or call The Mountaineers, Club Headquarters, 300 Third Avenue West, Seattle, Washington 98119; 206-284-6310.

The Mountaineers Books, an active, nonprofit publishing program of the club, produces guidebooks, instructional texts, historical works, natural history guides, and works on environmental conservation. All books produced by The Mountaineers are aimed at fulfilling the club's mission.

Send or call for our catalog of more than 300 outdoor titles:

The Mountaineers Books
1001 SW Klickitat Way, Suite 201
Seattle, WA 98134
1-800-553-4453
e-mail: mbooks@mountaineers.org
website: www.mountaineersbooks.org

Other titles you may enjoy from The Mountaineers:

SIERRA HIGH ROUTE: Traversing Timberline Country, 2nd Edition, *Steve Roper*

A guide to a spectacular 195-mile route in the beautiful sub-alpine region of California's High Sierra, from Kings Canyon National Park to northern Yosemite National Park, with overviews of geographical and historical points of interest, maps, difficulty ratings, advice on safety, and more.

MOUNTAINEERING: The Freedom of the Hills, 6th Edition, *The Mountaineers*

The completely revised and expanded edition of the best-selling mountaineering book of all time — required reading for all climbers.

CLIMBING CALIFORNIA'S FOURTEENERS: 183 Routes to the Fifteen Highest Peaks, *Stephen F. Porcella & Cameron M. Burns*

The only guide to multiple routes on each of California's 14,000-foot peaks. Features climbing histories, historical commentary, and spectacular photos, plus route descriptions, from simple trail hikes to scrambles over rough terrain to steep rope climbs up vertical rock.

CLIMBING IN NORTH AMERICA, *Chris Jones*

A reissue of the complete history of North American mountaineering, from the early nineteenth century through the 1970's. Brings to life the climbers and their routes, peaks, and adventures with a storytelling style and historic black and white photos.

75 HIKES IN™ CALIFORNIA'S LASSEN PARK & MOUNT SHASTA REGIONS, *John R. Soares*

A comprehensive guide to popular hiking destinations in the Northern California Cascades. Includes day hikes and extended backpacks, recommendations on gear, safety, and etiquette, plus information on local history and camping options.

100 HIKES IN™ CALIFORNIA'S CENTRAL SIERRA & COAST RANGE, *Vicky Spring & Tom Kirkendall*; and **100 HIKES IN™ NORTHERN CALIFORNIA**, *John R. Soares & Marc J. Soares*

Part of the fully-detailed, best-selling hiking guides.